KU-769-890

THE EDEN MEMOIRS

FACING THE DICTATORS

Companion with this volume

FULL CIRCLE

THE RT. HON. THE EARL OF AVON
K.G., P.C., M.C.

THE EDEN MEMOIRS

FACING THE DICTATORS

CASSELL · LONDON

CASSELL & COMPANY LTD
35 Red Lion Square · London WC1
and at
MELBOURNE · SYDNEY · TORONTO · CAPE TOWN
JOHANNESBURG · AUCKLAND

First published 1962

Made and printed in Great Britain
by William Clowes and Sons Ltd, London and Beccles
F.562

FOREWORD

I had intended that this volume should cover the period from my earliest experience as a Minister in 1931 until the victory of the Labour Party at the General Election of 1945. I found that this was not possible if I was to give a full account of the events, personalities and negotiations of the nineteen-thirties.

From the autumn of 1931 until my resignation, owing to disagreements with Mr. Chamberlain and my colleagues in February 1938, I was, without a break, a Minister at the Foreign Office. For a greater part of the time I had to conduct negotiations which brought me into direct contact with the personalities then shaping world policy. So it happened that I was the first British Minister to hold discussions with Hitler and Stalin. I also had meetings with Mussolini and more frequent exchanges with the statesmen of France, Poland, Turkey and the Little Entente, amongst others. When I read over the many documents of the period which I had either written, received or commented upon, it seemed to me that here was a record which should be set down in some detail.

The chief sources of my material have been the telegrams and despatches recording my missions and conversations, together with the minutes written, either on Foreign Office papers, or to my colleagues, to the Foreign Secretary when I was a junior Minister, to the Prime Minister and other Ministers when I was Foreign Secretary. Another source has been despatches and letters to Ambassadors, recording my interviews and, though I never kept a regular diary, occasional notes set down, often with weeks or months between entries. As in *Full Circle*, this is the thought of the time, written at the time about the action of the time. Presuming that my readers would also want to know my present reflections upon past events, I have described these, but always distinguishing them from my contemporary decisions and reasoning.

The pages which follow are concerned with relations between allies, and either joint or single negotiations with the dictatorships whose appetites then threatened peace and later led to war. The negotiations were for the most part a record of failure, but their lessons are important. Principal among them is the distinction which I defined in a speech in the House of Lords last year:

> When Her Majesty's Government are considering whether or not there is a basis of negotiation, I should like to suggest to my noble friend a test which they might apply: it is whether the agreement for which they are working will serve only to relax tension for a while, or whether it is in the true interests of lasting peace. We must not perpetrate an injustice in order to get a little present ease; and the Government have to consider whether their decision gives peace, not just for an hour or a day or two, but in their children's time. That is the difference between appeasement and peace.

I would hope that the experience of the nineteen-thirties could be of some help in dispelling the perplexities of the present day.

AVON

Fyfield Manor,
Pewsey, Wiltshire

March, 1962

ACKNOWLEDGMENTS

I wish to express my thanks to Mr. David Dilks for his help in the preparation of this volume, and to Mrs. B. W. Scott for valuable preliminary work done over a period of years. I am grateful to the Hon. Margaret Lambert for both general and detailed advice on several chapters. I would also like to thank Miss Kidston, my secretary, who typed this volume, and Miss Johnstone, who assisted in the later stages of its production.

These pages have been read by friends who experienced the events which are here described. They made suggestions which have been helpful to me, but since the responsibility for every word is properly mine, I do not give their names in acknowledgment.

The official documents printed in this volume are Crown Copyright, which is legally vested in the Controller of Her Majesty's Stationery Office, and I am obliged for permission to reproduce them.

ACKNOWLEDGMENTS

I wish to express my thanks to Mr. [illegible] for [illegible] the preparation of this volume; and to Mrs. [illegible] for valuable [illegible] over a period of years. [illegible] Lambert [illegible] for [illegible] general and [illegible] [illegible] and like [illegible] [illegible] typed this volume and [illegible] [illegible]

Those many have seen in [illegible] whom [illegible] the events which are described. [illegible] which have been helpful to me [illegible] is [illegible] in [illegible]

The [illegible] documents printed in this volume [illegible] Copyright, which is [illegible] of the Controller of His Majesty's Stationery Office, and I am [illegible] for permission to [illegible]

CONTENTS

BOOK ONE

Apprenticeship

BOOK TWO

Responsibility

APPENDICES

MAPS

BOOK ONE

Apprenticeship

I

WESTMINSTER

December 1923 – October 1931

Early political memories – I am elected to Parliament – Mr. Baldwin and the General Strike – Parliamentary Private Secretary to Sir Austen Chamberlain – My first visit to the League of Nations – M. Briand and Herr Stresemann – Foreign Affairs – The general election – I advocate property-owning democracy – Speech on air defence – The National Government – I become Under-Secretary at the Foreign Office – The Labour movement and its leaders

The counting of the votes in a parliamentary election is my first political memory. This was in 1910 at Bishop Auckland and I was twelve years old. The two principal candidates, Liberal and Unionist, walked white-faced round the tables as the ballot papers mounted up. The Liberal won with a fair majority, the third candidate, who was Labour, being a long way behind. As we stood on the balcony where the results were announced, I heard him declare: 'One day Labour will win.' Incredulous we were, but he was right.

Whatever interest I had in politics in the narrow sense was swept aside at the age of seventeen by the first world war. In the army I shared the soldier's antipathy towards politicians, which was more widespread and sharper than in the second world war. This was partly due to the volunteer character of the enlistment in the first years and to the delay in enforcing national service, while wounded volunteers were mended and returned to the line. There was no conviction that risks and burdens were being equally shared, nor were they. For this the politicians were blamed. The fighting over, I was with my Brigade among the snows of the Ardennes for the long winter of 1918–19 and I took no close interest in the general election at home. Nor did I respond to feelers that I should stand for a constituency in my home county of Durham.

When I was up at Oxford a year later, Persian and painting were more to my taste than University politics. Indeed, while Mr. Beverley Nichols was President of the Union, I was President of the Uffizi and the Asiatic Societies. Nevertheless, I must have had more interest in politics than my official activities disclosed. When the agent for a local Unionist Member of Parliament encouraged me to speak in the Oxfordshire villages, I accepted. Thus I had my baptism in the crude give and take, often tedious, sometimes stimulating, of a public meeting, probably more worthwhile than the rather precious politics of the Union.

I had spent much of my childhood abroad, particularly in France and Germany. As I grew older, I travelled to foreign countries when I could and read about them when I could not. Despite this interest, I became increasingly less enthusiastic about joining the Diplomatic Service, which had been the purpose of my Oriental studies at Oxford. It seemed to me, in my impatience, that responsibility in one of our embassies would be long in coming. I should be for ever handing round teacups in Teheran. Parliament was an alternative approach to foreign affairs. I had read Lord Curzon's book on Persia, and his early career seemed to offer the work and interest that I wanted. Therefore, when an opportunity to contest a seat in County Durham was suggested to me in 1922, I took it, slender though I knew the chances to be. I was defeated at Spennymoor, coming in a poor second out of three. A year later a by-election at Warwick and Leamington gave me an unexpected opportunity to defeat my sister's mother-in-law, the Countess of Warwick, who had taken up the cause of Socialism. I represented this constituency, or rather it remained faithful to me, for more than thirty-three years.

At the age of twenty-six I knew little except war and schooling. War I hated for all I had seen of it among my family and friends, for the death, muck and misery, the pounding shell-fire and the casualty clearing stations. I was ready to support any effort to stop it coming again, but I was no pacifist, not from any motive of doctrine, but because I was convinced that pacifism on our part would not prevent war. In this mood I went to Westminster, earnest but only sketchily informed.

* * * * *

I entered Parliament with the first, short-lived Labour Government of 1923. These months were for me little more than a period of finding my way about and beginning to judge the leading personalities. I had known none of them save Mr. Asquith, who showed me kindness. The Conservative Party was shaken by the defeat which Mr. Baldwin's appeal for a mandate for a wider tariff had provoked, and the party was sore. There was even talk of rival leaders, Joynson-Hicks being one of those named after a fighting speech in opposition, which it was not within Baldwin's range or character to make.

There were few new Conservative Members in the Parliament of 1923. I remember the advice that Baldwin gave us. He spoke of the Labour Members, now for the first time supporting a government of their own party. In those days the overwhelming majority of them were trade unionists, who had spent their working lives in factories or the mines. 'Though', Baldwin said, 'you may have had better educational advantages, do not presume upon that, they know more about unemployment insurance than you. Above all, never be sarcastic at their expense.' As a newly-elected back-bencher, few things then seemed to me less likely than that I should be Stanley Baldwin's Foreign Secretary.

This administration under Mr. Ramsay MacDonald and that of Mr. Baldwin, which followed a year later, were marked by much industrial strife, culminating in the General Strike of 1926. Baldwin's handling of this critical phase was deft and sure. He sensed unerringly, as he was to do later during the abdication of King Edward VIII, the British people's sentiments and led them without hesitation. In the aftermath of the General Strike, he rejected vengeful acts. No British statesman in this century has done so much to kill class hatred. He was able to do this because he neither believed in class distinctions nor felt them. It was his policy to fuse Disraeli's two nations and his success is no mean monument. If in foreign affairs there were faults of omission, on the home front he practised a positive statesmanship which influenced the future. It was his faith in the British people and his conviction that they should be led in no selfish spirit of class advantage, that drew many of the younger men in his party towards him and held their loyalty. We had seen British soldiers fight and die together, we did not see why the nation should not live together and did not think Socialism necessary to make this possible. Baldwin was the antithesis of the hard-faced men who were alleged to have dominated the Conservative Party immediately after the first world war. In character and purpose he expressed what we wanted to achieve in politics at home.

In my first year in the House of Commons, Mr. Asquith was leader of the Liberal Party and I give him pride of place among the parliamentary debaters of that time. His speeches were models of lucidity and brevity, with the English language at its best. In an age when prolixity was already becoming a substitute for conviction, he never wasted a word.

I was a spectator of the events which led to the General Strike, except for one incident in the negotiations, in which I was involved on the fringes. May 5th, the second day of the Strike, was a strenuous and absorbing one at the House of Commons. I wrote in my diary how, following a speech by Lord Hugh Cecil, J. H. Thomas, General Secretary of the National Union of Railwaymen, declared that a formula had been reached and would have been accepted, had not the *Daily Mail* incident occurred. This was the refusal of the printers to print the newspaper because of the opinions it proposed to express. My diary continues:

> Some restiveness among our people in consequence. Slesser [Solicitor-General in first Labour Government] came and saw one or two of us in the lobby and suggested that, even now, if we could get the P.M. to say 'We will negotiate again at once if you call the General Strike off' instead of 'Call off the General Strike first and then I will negotiate', Thomas might be able to get the General Strike recalled. Conferred accordingly with Sidney [Mr. Sidney Herbert—Parliamentary Private Secretary to the Prime Minister], Hugh Cecil and Mond. Cecil maintained there was no distinction, Mond and Sidney that it might prove a trap. Ultimately P.M. made a statement late at night which at least made the government position clear. But an anxious and topsy-turvy day.

The Prime Minister showed a willingness to negotiate, but not until the strike was off. The distinction is now clear enough and Mond and Herbert were right in their judgement, even if no trap was intended. During these years I had a number of conversations with Sir Alfred Mond, the Liberal Member of Parliament for Carmarthen. I greatly admired both the mind he so clearly expressed in his speeches, and the industrial outlook which resulted ultimately in the giant Imperial Chemical Industries, with its large shareholdings owned by those employed in the company.

* * * * *

At this time Sir Austen Chamberlain was Foreign Secretary. One afternoon in July 1926, his Parliamentary Private Secretary, Roger Lumley, mentioned to me that he was going to Australia on a delegation. This would involve his absence from the House of Commons for six months or more and he would therefore have to give up the work. He asked me whether I would care to take it on. Like most younger Members of Parliament, I hardly knew Sir Austen, who was always correct and polite, but seemed an aloof figure to us. I accepted with some reservations.

The drawback in being a Parliamentary Private Secretary was that this slight responsibility, to keep the Minister in touch with Members of Parliament and to channel their comments or complaints to him, was thought to disqualify the Member from speaking in the House, particularly about affairs for which his chief was answerable. Although I had been less than three years in Parliament, I had already taken part in several foreign affairs debates. A recent occasion had been at the suggestion of the Government Chief Whip in a debate on Germany's election to the Council of the League, in March 1926. I went to see Sir William Tyrrell, then Permanent Under-Secretary at the Foreign Office, to be briefed, and spent an hour with him. The debate was opened by Lloyd George, then leading the Liberal Party and with the renown of his wartime leadership still enfolding him. Austen Chamberlain followed, as Foreign Secretary, then Ramsay MacDonald leading the Labour Party, Hugh Cecil with a very brilliant speech, myself and Sir John Simon, a Liberal leader and an unrivalled advocate. This was an ordeal by any standards, however exceptional the opportunity. But having once broken a lance in such company, it must seem dreary to be silenced, perhaps for the remainder of the Parliament. Chamberlain perfectly understood this and in practice occasions offered, or were created, when I could break the Trappist vow. I am now astonished to read how soon I was propelled into the political stratosphere and wonder whether I have been as indulgent to others in later years.

Austen Chamberlain, in appearance and sometimes in speech, could be stiff and forbidding. This had nothing to do with the real man, who was warm-hearted, considerate and generous. He was incapable of a mean action and conscientious to a fault. I had the greatest affection for him and our friendship grew and lasted until his death. Sir Austen's international policies were based on a traditional Foreign Office pattern. They were none the worse for that. A francophile, he was once ridiculed for observing that he loved France as a woman, for her defects as well as for her qualities. But he was wise to found his efforts to pacify Europe on Anglo-French unity. With the help of the confidence thus created, Germany was brought into the Locarno Treaty.

France, Belgium and Germany undertook to respect each other's frontiers and the status of the demilitarized Rhineland. Great Britain and Italy acted as guarantors for this settlement, undertaking to come to the aid of the injured party in case of a flagrant violation of the Treaty. By the same process of thought, he accepted the significance of the Little Entente and was a friend of their statesmen, believing also that, while the Hapsburg Empire could not be revived, Austrian independence must be defended. Had he lived, I have little doubt what his reactions must have been to his half-brother Neville's Central European policies; for him a war over Czechoslovakia could never be 'because of a quarrel in a far-away country between a people of whom we know nothing.'

A few weeks after I had begun to work for him, the Foreign Secretary asked me if I would like to go with him on one of his periodic visits to Geneva, paying my own expenses, for the rules were very strict. A Parliamentary Private Secretary could not pass muster as a necessity. I could not afford it then, but the next year an opportunity came for me to be present at a meeting of the League Council. In those days this body met regularly four times a year and the Foreign Ministers always attended in person, an arrangement which had obvious advantages. The sessions only lasted about a week and during this time there was opportunity for informal discussion between the men who had active responsibility in world affairs. We were then in the aftermath of Locarno and the League of Nations was at the height of its reputation. The failure of the United States to ratify the Treaty of Versailles and accept membership of the League was a continuing weakness in that organization, but when Germany joined in 1926, Russia became the only other great power not included in its ranks. There was a formidable weight of world opinion behind this attempt to create an international order. The terms of the Covenant were variously interpreted, by France and her European allies as upholding the territorial gains of the peace treaties, by Germany and Hungary as affording an opportunity for revision. The experiment might have appeared hazardous, but it aroused brave hopes for me also. It seemed an opportunity to escape from a balance of power, which had failed to keep the peace, to an international authority which might have the collective strength to do so. Even so, I did not travel to Geneva in a haze of confidence. My mood was rather one of watchful interest with a streak of scepticism.

The British Foreign Secretary's journey to Geneva in those days was something of an event and took place at a measured pace. The top-hatted stationmaster and the Foreign Office representatives at Victoria, the harbourmaster at Dover bowing us on to the ship, the *préfet* and the mayor at Calais, then a drive across Paris and dinner at the Embassy, the night train at the Gare de Lyon, where probably M. Briand and some other of Sir Austen's colleagues were also embarking for Geneva. Finally, the arrival at Geneva, about 7.30 in the morning, when the whole staff was paraded to meet their chief at the station, a barbaric and totally unnecessary custom which I was finally able to suppress when I became Foreign Secretary myself some years later.

* * * * *

In 1927, the meetings of Aristide Briand, Gustav Stresemann and Austen Chamberlain were the main events of the Geneva year. Whatever the official performance, it was their private conversations which mattered. At this autumn session, Franco-Italian relations were causing some strain. They formed the topic of the first international meal I attended, when Chamberlain lunched with Briand in a private room at the Hôtel des Bergues, always the French headquarters, where the French Foreign Minister, in his own inimitable fashion, gave us his view of recent developments. He did this so lightly, so wittily, and yet so forcibly, that I was completely convinced he was right. I even felt a little embarrassed when after half an hour of sparkling entertainment, Briand paused and Sir Austen began, in correct but rather portentous French, '*mais ce que j'ai à vous reprocher, mon ami . . .*' and an admonitory Anglo-Saxon finger was wagged to emphasize each point.

We had a further instalment that evening when Briand came to dine with us at our hotel, the Beau Rivage, with its elaborate and fussy frills of a provincial 1890. To second him in his task, Sir Austen had summoned our Ambassador at Rome, Sir Ronald Graham. After dinner, our host asked M. Briand whether he would let the Ambassador expound the Italian point of view as he saw it. Briand courteously, if unenthusiastically, acquiesced, and the Ambassador did so at some length. M. Briand smoked and made no comment, his expression was distant but his mind was alert. Finally, when the Anglo-Saxon exposition was over and Sir Austen had added a few comments to the Ambassador's account of events, a silence fell and all awaited M. Briand's reaction. Eventually he looked up with a slight smile and remarked to the British Foreign Secretary: 'All that the Ambassador says may be quite true; it may be that Italian intentions towards us are as sincere, even as considerate, as you would have us believe. But if that is really so, perhaps you will explain to me, my dear friend, how it was that only last Thursday some Italians thought fit to remove the coat of arms from the French consulate at X and place it in the public lavatory. No one interfered, not even the police, but this no doubt was out of consideration.'

During this session, Stresemann also came to luncheon, when I sat next to him. I recall chiefly his quick, clear brain, forceful character and formidable appetite. Throughout the meal he laughed often and spoke his part in a harsh voice. His bonhomie gave no inkling of the fixed purpose to restore Germany's power. Had he lived, his ambitions might have been dangerous, but he would have disclosed them carefully.

This visit to Geneva was not full enough for me to make up my mind on the League's usefulness or otherwise, and Chamberlain made no attempt to persuade me, he let me form my own conclusions. It was evident that the meetings of the Foreign Ministers were worth while and the machinery of the League worked well, with a small staff under Sir Eric Drummond's discerning leadership as Secretary-General. I was not sure how much more might be possible.

* * * * *

In the summer of 1928 the Foreign Secretary fell seriously ill, partly as a consequence of overwork. A cruise to South America was recommended to promote his cure. While Sir Austen was away from the Foreign Office, an agreement which he had recently made with France came under criticism. The general election was drawing near and both Opposition parties entered the fray. The agreement dealt with matters, such as naval armaments, which concerned other than our two countries and it was argued that consultation should have been more general. The debate, on November 13th, took place on a Liberal amendment, moved by Lloyd George. Baldwin followed, dealing slightly but sufficiently with each of the points of his brief. I had to follow Ramsay MacDonald, the first three speeches having lasted for nearly an hour each. I had little that was new to say and felt at the time that my remarks were disjointed, but the House for some reason was kindly disposed. Perhaps I was helped by a short exchange with MacDonald, who was always courteous to younger Members, and by a firm conviction that my chief had been right.

Good relations with France, their nature and consequences, came to dominate foreign policy until the outbreak of war. Austen Chamberlain believed that the way to keep the peace in Europe was to be on the best possible terms with France and to move with her towards an understanding with our former enemy. Others, including many in the Conservative Party, were impatient with France and wished us to pay less consideration to what I thought were reasonable French fears, and to move towards reconciliation with Germany, with only surface regard for French opinion. This school of thought was to become more influential with the passage of time. I did not agree with it, nor with the assumption that Germany, having been defeated, had been unjustly trampled on, though I considered the allied demands in reparations indefensible. Years later, at Yalta, I joined with Mr. Churchill in resisting like Soviet demands, with limited success.

The result of the 1929 election was not what I had expected. Churchill, as Chancellor of the Exchequer, had taken the duty off tea, which seemed a proposal likely to appeal to the women electors, who had just been enfranchised on the same terms as men. The Conservatives could claim almost five years of competent administration, even though unemployment was only bettered, not mastered. The Liberals were divided, and it seemed sensible to expect endorsement of Mr. Baldwin's leadership, but there was also a certain unimaginative smugness about our campaign with its appeal to 'safety first'. The electorate seldom votes in gratitude for the past, which is probably wise. It did not do so this time. The Labour Party won many seats and returned to office under Mr. Ramsay MacDonald for its first spell as the largest party in the state. I held my own constituency, for the only time on a minority vote.

After our party's defeat, I received a kindly letter from Austen Chamberlain in which he told me that Baldwin had promised him that I would be his Under-Secretary at the Foreign Office, if we won the election. I was surprised and pleased at such a possibility, but saddened that the opportunity had been denied me. It seemed to me then that it would not come again and that my political career was over, so strong did the Labour Party appear in the first flush of victory and so raw was my own experience at thirty-two.

* * * * *

Opposition is the time of opportunity for a young Member of Parliament. Early in the new year, 1930, half a dozen of us agreed to meet at a weekly dinner and work as closely together as possible in the life of that Parliament. Noel Skelton, Oliver Stanley, William Ormsby-Gore, Walter Elliot and W. S. Morrison made up our loose fraternity. We held the same views, our domestic politics being to the left of centre in our own party. With the exception of Skelton, who died young, all the group were future Cabinet Ministers. Oliver Stanley was the most promising of us. Even then a brilliant wit and a most engaging companion, he had a searching mind, perhaps a shade too destructive for leadership. 'Shakes' Morrison, with his shaggy charm, fervent sincerity and the pleasant turn of speech of the Western Highlands, also seemed destined for the highest positions in party politics. When, a decade later, I came to have my differences with Neville Chamberlain, these younger men were generally more sympathetic to my viewpoint than my elders.

The Labour Government soon found itself in trouble at home. The unemployment figures were stubbornly impervious to any of the cures which they could think of, while the fact that there was no majority in Parliament for nationalization was exasperating to Socialists, who sincerely believed that all would be well if only this panacea could be applied. The Conservative Party at Westminster was shrunken and its leaders no longer preoccupied with the burdens of office. As a result, there were more opportunities for the rank and file to know them. Stanley Baldwin was accessible and to members of our small group he was the most sympathetic, sharing our youthful ideas for a progressive Conservatism which would have positive aims, and knowing what we meant by such expressions as 'a property-owning democracy'. I believe that it was Noel Skelton, a thought-provoking young Scotsman and a close friend of mine, who first used this phrase in our talks together during this Parliament. After our defeat, many years later, in the general election of 1945, I was able to revive it and keep it as the central theme of our policy.

My first speech on this subject was at the end of November 1929, when I said to party workers in London:

> . . . the outcome of the general election will not prove an unmixed evil if it affords the Conservative Party an opportunity to set its own house in order, to re-examine its own beliefs, to reaffirm them, and to present to the country the policy by which it hopes to see them realized. . . .
>
> The Conservative objective, therefore, must be to spread the private ownership of property as widely as possible, to enable every worker to become a capitalist. The status of the worker in industry must be raised. This Socialism can never do. In order to achieve this the first task is to assist

productive industry to a greater prosperity than rules today. We must be prepared to assist those who are at work, and there lies, incidentally, the greatest measure of help that we can give to those who are at present unemployed.

I then described three methods by which industry could be helped. First, by providing stability through an active policy for peace at home and abroad. Secondly, by easing existing burdens on industry, to help it to prosper and share its wealth with all engaged in it, including the wage earner. Thirdly, by helping industry to new markets or the greater development of old. This I illustrated from a recent visit I had made to the principal countries of the Empire. I added a fourth point:

There must be a steady and ever-increasing development of schemes of co-partnership in industry. If the Conservative ideal is to be attained, the workers in industry must have an increasing personal share in its progress, with which will then march a greater personal concern for its well-being. There are many schemes of co-partnership of one kind and another in industry today. A careful examination of their mechanism and their results ought to be undertaken, and the Conservative Party should concern itself actively with the extension of the best among them.

The wider we can spread the basis of national well-being, the larger the share of it every worker in the land can enjoy, the more real and direct his incentive to promote the welfare of the industry in which he is engaged, because it is his concern, the more certainly shall we create a Britain where her people may dwell in peace and plenty.

At intervals in these Opposition years, between 1929 and 1931, criticism of Stanley Baldwin was a recurring theme in the party, often vehemently expressed. He was not, by temperament, an Opposition leader, having no combative desire for parliamentary battle for its own sake. We in our small group gave him all the support we could, privately and publicly, being convinced that his leadership would keep our party truly national, both in the sources of its strength and the objectives of its policy.

After a defeat, a political party has often to endure a kneading process to consolidate and toughen it. So it was with the Conservative Party in that period. We sloughed off some of the old husk. It was typical of the times that at a party meeting held to discuss the leadership, one of Stanley Baldwin's critics should complain: 'At every luncheon party you go to you hear criticism of him.' Noel Skelton cried out from the gallery: 'But what do you hear in the back streets?' We might not have known as much about back streets as we thought, but at least we knew it was their confidence we must win and their conditions we intended to improve. We meant to realize the property-owning democracy, though few in our party had much confidence in our faith and the opposition was derisive.

A note I wrote on March 12th, 1931, runs:

> S.B. has got away with it again. He has won back from the edge of the precipice. I was, of course, highly delighted—and not a little incensed at the Bertie Clay [Col. Herbert Spender-Clay] point of view: 'Now he will be able to go after we have won St. George's' [a by-election then in progress]. Why should he? He is the only statesman we possess. Unhappily, we have too few who can recognize one, still fewer who will fight for one.

* * * * *

I spoke occasionally on international affairs, and I used opportunities to meet men in all countries who were in touch with events. There was nothing expressly encouraging in the outlook. The Locarno spirit had begun to fade and no substitute had been found to take its place. One evening in March 1931, Stanley Baldwin spoke to me of some work he wanted me to do. The Prime Minister, Mr. Ramsay MacDonald, had decided to set up a three-party committee to prepare for the Disarmament Conference which would convene early in the following year. This body was to meet in private, as a sub-committee of the Committee of Imperial Defence, and have access to all necessary documents and papers. Our party would be represented by Austen Chamberlain, Sir Samuel Hoare, a former Secretary of State for Air, and myself. The Prime Minister would preside, the Foreign Secretary, Arthur Henderson, and other Ministers attending; the Liberals would be led by Lloyd George. This was an entirely novel experience for me. The committee sat at irregular intervals during the year, usually in the Prime Minister's room at the House of Commons, against a background of mounting economic problems. Mr. Lloyd George was an active investigator at the committee and, as a result of his questions, some useful and informative papers on the international and military aspects of our problems were prepared and circulated to us. This was my first taste of discussion at the Cabinet level and I liked it.

Our three-party committee did not get very far or move very fast, there was so much else to vex harassed Ministers in that second Labour Government, nor did its proceedings determine my views. I strongly favoured an arms agreement, in the national as well as the international interest. The alternative was nervous tension in the world and costly rearmament on our own account, for we were lagging behind. I had long been sceptical about how the Germany of the Weimar Republic might evolve. When in the army, I had been several times in the Rhineland during the period of military occupation soon after the war. Rather more than two years later I travelled in Germany as a visitor and thought I noticed a change of mood, a restlessness which economic distress alone could not explain. This, I feared, might have its consequences for us all.

I first expressed my thoughts publicly on these matters in my maiden speech, in a debate on air defence, as early as 1924. It was not possible, I pointed out then, to provide hastily and at a moment's notice for air defence. I told the first Labour Government that, because London was so vulnerable to attack from the air, they had a responsibility to carry out the programme they had inherited and to safeguard our country, as far as they could, from the greatest peril of modern war. As a speech it was a crude effort and may not have been in tune with the pacifism of the time, but as a warning it was not wide of the mark.

I returned to this theme with more experience a few years later, on June 29th, 1931, when the Labour Party were again in power. I reminded the House of Commons that after the war we had scrapped seven-eighths of our air force, at the time the finest in any part of the world, and I repeated my warning that we were the nation most vulnerable to air attack in Europe. In the last five years we had reduced our air armaments slightly, while others had increased theirs sharply, yet 'it is the air defence of this country that will most concern future generations'. The anxieties in Europe, I went on, were many; it was of the first importance that our influence, as the stabilizing nation of Europe, should be strong. There was a danger now that, if we were too weak, even in a purely military sense, those nations holding guarantees to which we had put our name would become doubtful of their value. I continued:

> The seeds of war psychology still exist in Europe. I even doubt whether during the last two years what is usually called the spirit of the League has grown in strength in Europe. On the contrary, the probability is that it has weakened. I do not wish to be alarmist, but I do not think that anyone who studies the European situation today can be otherwise than anxious about it. It seems to me that we can divide Europe for this purpose into two groups of nations. There is the group which is, if not dominated, at least influenced by fear, and the group which is dominated or influenced by impatience.

ICELAND
BRITISH ISLES
North
Sea
DENMARK
Oslo
Stockh
Copenhage
London
Amsterdam
HOLLAND
Berlin
Atlantic
Ocean
Brussels
BELGIUM
R. Rhine
GERMANY
Paris
SUDETENLAND
CZECHO
Prague
R. Danube
Vienna
AUSTR
FRANCE
Berne
SWITZERLAND
Nyon
Geneva
Stresa
ITALY
PORTUGAL
Madrid
Lisbon
SPAIN
CORSICA
Rome
SARDINIA
BALEARIC IS.
Tangier
GIBRALTAR
SPAN. MOROCCO
Mediterran
ALGERIA
TUNISIA
SICILY
MALTA
EUROPE 1931
0
100
500
1000 MILES

THE SAAR
GERMANY
BELGIUM
LUXEMBOURG
Luxembg
R. Moselle
R. Rhine
Merzig
SAAR
Homburg
Saarbrücken
Zweibrücken
Metz
FRANCE
R. Saar
Nancy
Strasbourg
0 25 50 miles
THE RHINELAND
Demilitarized Zone
Maginot Line
HOLLAND
Wesel
Düsseldorf
Cologne
R. Rhine
BELGIUM
Coblenz
Frankfurt
R. Moselle
Mainz
LUXEMBOURG
GERMANY
Mannheim
SAAR
Metz
R. Saar
Nancy
Strasbourg
R. Rhine
FRANCE
Basle
SWITZERLAND
0 25 50 miles
FINLAND
Helsinki
Tallinn
ESTONIA
Riga
LATVIA
Moscow
LITHUANIA
Kaunas
U. S. S. R.
Warsaw
LAND
KIA
ROUMANIA
Bucharest
R. Danube
Black Sea
BULGARIA
Sofia
Istanbul
TURKEY
GREECE
Athens
CYPRUS
CRETE
n Sea

France's feelings of fear, I said, were very real, as were those of the nations bordering Russia, because Russia had the largest standing army in Europe. At the same time the vanquished were impatient:

> Therefore, there are surely evidences in plenty of sore spots in Europe. One of the unhappy features is that in many countries of Europe, and France is not one of them, the youngest generation is being trained up into military formations, taught and encouraged in military methods of thought and military drill, with consequences which can hardly be happy for the future peace of Europe. . . .
>
> Those who have seen war are the least likely to want to see its repetition. . . . Those who saw the last weeks of the last war had a vision of what the next war might be expected to be. I remember an evening, in the last stages of our advance, when we had stopped for the night at brigade headquarters in some farm house. The night was quiet, and there was no shell-fire, as was usual at the end of the war, but quite suddenly it began literally to rain bombs for anything from ten minutes to a quarter of an hour. I do not know how many bombs fell in that time, but something between thirty and forty, I suppose. It seemed to us to be hundreds. What rests in my mind is not only my own personal terror, which was quite inexpressible, because bombing is more demoralizing in its effects than the worst shell-fire, but the comment made when it was over by somebody who said: 'There now, you have had your first taste of the next war.'
>
> There will be no heroics in a war where the safest place will be the front line, if there is one, and the most dangerous the houses of our civilian population.

* * * * *

Domestic difficulties, aggravated by world events, piled up against the Labour Government. The economy was in serious trouble and by the late summer of 1931 we were in an atmosphere of crisis. The Labour Cabinet could not agree upon the action recommended by its Chancellor of the Exchequer, Mr. Philip Snowden, and would surely have split the party if it had. The Prime Minister went to Buckingham Palace to resign, but, encouraged by King George v, returned to form a government of the three parties, losing all but a splinter of his own in the process. This seemed to me and to the majority of the nation a necessary deed and a brave one, though it left the Labour Party with a furious conviction of betrayal. Liberals and Conservatives rallied to MacDonald in the certainty that the state of the nation left them no choice. The coalition, or National Government, as it preferred to be called, found its path smoothed by the willingness of Baldwin, at the head of the largest party within the grouping, to accept to serve under MacDonald, who had only a handful of followers.

These great events had their repercussion for me, leading to my appointment as Under-Secretary at the Foreign Office. My diary records:

August 27th: Lunched with Austen who told me there was a chance I might go to F.O., that he had spoken strongly to Reading [just appointed Foreign Secretary] and that S.B. had agreed to his doing so. He hoped something would result, but S.B. had given away so much to the Liberals it was impossible to say. He—S.B.—apparently greeted my name with more enthusiasm than any other. The F.O. in a National Govt. with the S. of S. in the Upper House is higher than I hoped for and I do not expect that I shall get it.

August 28th: In due course the summons came. S.B. could not have been kinder. He told me that he wanted me to go to the F.O. where he had intended to send me for a spell himself if our party had been returned, and added that he regarded me as 'a potential Foreign Secretary' in about ten years' time and that was why he wanted me to have the experience as soon as possible. Unhappily there had been a hitch. Ramsay wanted his son to go there. He did not propose to agree. Reading wanted me at F.O. as well as himself. He did not think Ramsay would press the matter, but he did not like to wire 'No' in present delicate state of negotiations on all subjects, but he would see him Monday. He had sent for me because he did not wish me to think during the weekend that I had got nothing. Ramsay's son had been going to the Dominions Office but 'one of them shall be yours'. I thanked him and told him that I had not counted on anything in a coalition, knowing what his difficulties must be. He said he was afraid some of his late colleagues had sore heads, but he could not help that, he was there unhappily for that purpose among others. I told him that I would prefer the F.O. of the two. He said 'Of course you would, of course you would,' and added that he hoped this might still be possible. We had some general conversation in the course of which he showed me the draft of his letter to M.P.s urging constant attendance. Finally he showed me out on the words: 'I hope this may be the beginning of a long and successful but,' with a laugh, 'I won't say prosperous career. That is not in politics.'

By Tuesday, September 1st, all was settled and I went to work at the Foreign Office for the first time as a Minister, the beginning of an association which was to last, with intervals, for nearly twenty-four years. My first day was typical of many at that time. Thomas Dugdale, Baldwin's Parliamentary Private Secretary, called on me unexpectedly at breakfast and we walked down to the Foreign Office together. In my diary I commented:

> I spent my morning reading of China and the Shanghai concession negotiation. More reading all the afternoon. There are many threads to pick up and the task is likely to occupy me fully—until the Government goes out.

In this I was wrong, I was to be out before the Government.

The reading of papers soon presented me with some perplexities. As I was the only Foreign Office Minister in the House of Commons, a senior member of the Government on the Front Bench would often mention to me some telegram, or perhaps some despatch or Cabinet paper, which he had seen and which had not reached me. The cause for this lay in the working of the Foreign Office hierarchy of that day. This was the only government department where the Permanent Under-Secretary, who was an official, ranked higher than the Parliamentary Under-Secretary, who was a Minister, with the result that, though I could expect to see most documents in due course, they went to the Secretary of State from the Permanent Under-Secretary on the way up and I only saw them on the way down. If the matter were urgent and required action by the Permanent Under-Secretary, it might be a still later date before the papers reached me. There have been many changes since those days and the number of Ministers in the Foreign Office is now three times the modest representation Lord Reading and I afforded. Then the Secretary of State seemed hedged about by senior officials and the Parliamentary Under-Secretary had to make his own way. I found nothing to complain of in all this, except the subterfuges to which I was sometimes reduced in conversation with my ministerial seniors about topics on which I was not as well briefed as I thought it right to appear, both for my own authority and for that of the Foreign Office. I was, however, soon made welcome and in the years I worked in that department I never knew anything but the best and most disinterested service.

My significance in those September days of 1931 was due solely to the fact that I was the Foreign Office spokesman in the House of Commons. My opinion on foreign affairs would clearly be of little account in Whitehall, though I found myself on the parliamentary stage sooner than I had bargained for. At the session held after the appointment of the National Government, the first Private Notice Question was addressed to the Foreign Office and had to be replied to by the Parliamentary Under-Secretary. This was not on a matter of controversy, but it meant that I had to be the first Minister in the National Government to reply and that I had to do so in a House crammed to the doors and with packed galleries.

On its formation, the National Government had at once engaged in drastic economic action which failed to keep us on the gold standard, but smoothly cushioned our departure from it. This was interwoven with weeks of palaver about a general election. My diary comments on these exchanges are few, but impatient. As a decision to appeal to the country was delayed, I wrote on September 28th:

> Some of our people talk gaily of going to the country without Ramsay and winning. I don't think that they have at all weighed the situation and I should look upon such a prospect with the utmost dismay. A general election with a National Government appealing would not greatly damage sterling, might indeed strengthen it, but a party dog-fight would have an opposite result.

Two days later I wrote an account of a dinner at Ralph Glyn's to meet Ramsay MacDonald. Duff Cooper, Ormsby-Gore and Herbert Lawrence, who had been Haig's Chief of Staff in the last year of the war and was now a merchant banker, were also there. The Prime Minister spoke of party machines and the effect on foreign opinion of their alignment in an election. Herbert Lawrence had no comment on this, though he had said earlier that he was confident an appeal to the country by a National Government would have an excellent effect on opinion overseas. I told the Prime Minister I was sure foreigners did not think in terms of machines but of victory or defeat and, since an appeal by himself, Stanley Baldwin and a prominent Liberal must succeed, they should not worry. He shook his head. Then the division bell rang and we broke up to vote.

The disintegration of the Labour Government had caused bewilderment and indignation in that party. The majority of the rank and file were resentful of the desertion, as it seemed to them, of men like MacDonald, Snowden and J. H. Thomas. These three, especially Snowden, blamed the party for not accepting the truth when it was bitter. One evening, in October 1931, I was on the Front Bench during a debate when a Labour Member who was speaking referred to what a general election might show. Snowden muttered: 'They will learn a lesson then all right,' at which I commented: 'What do you mean, that not so many of them will come back after the election?' 'Not so many,' said Snowden, 'not fifty of them.' This was brilliant political prophecy, spoken with such venom about men who had recently been his colleagues that I was taken aback. But the Chancellor of the Exchequer had had much to put up with in educating his party in the economic facts of life. In the few dealings I had with Snowden, whether personal or political, then and after he left the Government, I always found him gentle rather than sour, despite the constant pain of a physical disability. He was a man of the finest courage.

The election had to come and it resulted in a sweeping victory for the National Government. Snowden's prophecy was almost literally fulfilled and the Conservative Party was returned far the strongest in the new House of Commons. The overwhelming nature of the victory carried with it certain seeds of danger which Baldwin was quick to note. The decimated ranks of Labour had to be encouraged to act effectively as a parliamentary Opposition, though the odds were tough against them. They did so bravely, sparing the nation the alternative, a pursuit of political ends by industrial action.

Locally, I had a larger majority than I could have dreamed of, over 29,000. The victory brought some changes in the Government which were not good news for me. I had found it easy to work with Lord Reading, who was always a thoughtful and courteous chief. I was therefore grieved when he sent for me and told me that he must give up the Foreign Office. In the words of my diary:

> He was as charming as ever and frankly regretful at having to go. He said he thought that he now had a real grip of the problems and their close relation. None the less he felt he had to relieve the Prime Minister of his obvious difficulty in finding the places by cutting the Gordian knot.

The next day I was walking across Parliament Square with Austen Chamberlain when he asked me if it was true that Reading was not carrying on. I said that unfortunately it was. He asked me if I knew who was to succeed. I said that I did not for sure, but there was a rumour that it was to be John Simon. He stopped in the middle of the Square and looked at me. 'I had not heard that,' he said. 'Had I known it was a possibility I would have tried to go back myself.' But in his heart he must have realized the odds against this. In the make-up of the National Government, the Foreign Office had to fall to the Liberal Party. Compromises of this kind are the weakness of coalitions.

* * * * *

I knew the successive leaders of the Labour Party in those years. Among them MacDonald had the most statesmanship. It is the fashion nowadays to decry him and many of his party have never forgiven him for his formation of the National Government in 1931, though what would have happened if he had not is usually left rather vague. MacDonald had certainly a taste and instinct for foreign affairs. He probably overburdened himself in trying for a while to combine the Foreign Office with No. 10, as Lord Salisbury had been able to do in another kind of world, and later he made a mistake in appointing Simon to a post for which he was miscast by temperament and training. But when listening to MacDonald in Cabinet on international topics, I was conscious at times of the touch of the master. Much has been written of his failings, but there was stature about him and courage.

George Lansbury was more an evangelist than a leader, a kindly man who did not like to think things through. The conclusions were too often unpleasant and therefore it was better to fluff them. Though he could be a surprisingly effective debater at times, I doubt if he would have chosen the position the fates forced on him after the general election in 1931, but he did his best with it. I liked him, for he was tolerant of the failings of the young and inclined to think well of his fellow men. Internationally, this last was a weakness at that period, but personally it was an endearing characteristic.

MacDonald and Lansbury expressed in their character and in their lives the essentially emotional appeal of the Labour Party at that time. If their call was one of uplift, there was both cause and room for it. They, and leaders like J. R. Clynes, Arthur Henderson and John Wheatley, knew the conditions of which they spoke at first hand and they were often bad, in unemployment, housing and health. Socialism could not supply the remedy, but there had to be one, and to the Labour movement will belong much of the credit for stirring the national conscience to compel it.

II

THE FAILURE OF DISARMAMENT

February 1932 – May 1933

The Disarmament Conference assembles – Franco-German differences – British reservations – I go to Geneva – We draft a Convention – Reception of the MacDonald Plan – Our Convention debated – Four Power Pact – A parliamentary debate

In the later months of 1931 events in Germany were displayed against a darkening background. Unemployment, embittered by resentment, was growing in the cities, creating conditions of political unrest. The situation was all the more dangerous since the massed parties each had their own private armies, who fought out political battles in the streets. The Brüning Government were compelled to rule increasingly by presidential decree rather than through parliament. As economic problems multiplied and bewildered him, the ageing President Hindenburg played an uncertain part, while the Nazis pressed turbulently for power.

The long-awaited Disarmament Conference finally assembled at Geneva on February 2nd, 1932. It was born under a dismal star. In numbers it was unwieldy, sixty nations sending delegations. An international preparatory commission had toiled for years to make ready a schedule on which the Conference could work, but the weakness of its plan lay in the failure to propose specific limitations on the forces of any nation except Germany, whose Government soon gave notice that they would accept no such discrimination. Committee on committee sprang up and choked themselves with minutely detailed discussions about the size of aeroplanes or the tonnage of ships. Within a few months of the opening ceremonies, the French and German Governments were exchanging acrimonious notes. The schedule had to be abandoned and the Conference seemed headed for breakdown.

Not being a member of our delegation at the Conference, I

watched these events unhappily, for the discussions were not reaching the core of the problem. At a dinner given by the Rhodes Trust in June, I recalled the nature of our peril:

> While one half of Europe has been dominated by apprehension and the other by impatience, there has been the tendency to pay too much attention to the mechanics of peace and too little to its fundamentals. . . . As I have watched some of these ingenious contrivances which have occupied the minds of international statesmen for too long, while the more sinister spirits of a selfish nationalism and an outworn jingoism were gaining influence in the background, I have been made sad by their futility. As well use a mouse-trap to catch a goblin.

With Nazism gaining strength every month, this diagnosis was true.

I thought His Majesty's Government dilatory. The French Government told Sir John Simon as early as March 12th that German armament already exceeded the limits imposed by the Versailles Treaty. Britain could not deny it, yet it was July 7th before I wrote in my diary of a British plan to reduce the size of armaments as a first step:

> Our proposals were finally announced this afternoon and reasonably well received, though of course shorn of the effect they would have had if announced six months ago. . . . They would not have been announced even now but for strong pressure by S.B.

By the autumn of 1932, Germany was refusing to take further part in the Conference, unless her claim was met for equality of rights with the other powers. Anglo-French talks in London in the early days of October decided that the only way to deal with this situation was to hold informal discussions at Geneva between Britain, France, Germany and Italy, and to hold them soon. The Germans were not eager. The Chancellor, Herr von Papen, retorted: 'The condition of affairs in which we are definitely forbidden the use of arms, which other states are allowed to possess as indispensable weapons of defence, cannot continue.' The opinion of the British Embassy in Berlin was that Germany did not care, for the moment, to submit herself to any outside scrutiny, and would probably push ahead with rearmament. His Majesty's Government had to create a policy which took account of these unpleasant realities, but did not surrender to them.

In November, M. Joseph Paul-Boncour, then French Minister of War, produced a plan for disarmament and mutual security which was ingenious, but hard to execute. Paul-Boncour was a man of erudition, eloquence and vitality, and in later years we worked most closely together. His plan accepted that all countries would not undertake the same obligations, the United States in particular being then unwilling to assume any political commitments overseas. The British Government did not agree with Paul-Boncour. They disliked the distinction between themselves and the United States, on its own account and for its possible influence on the Dominions, who might be embarrassed if asked to accept commitments from which the American Government were specifically excluded. However tolerable such a division of responsibility might have been in practice to all concerned, the British Government did not want to enshrine it in a treaty. They were even more firmly opposed to committing their naval and air forces in advance on the verdict of a simple majority of the League Council, as the plan proposed.

* * * * *

At the end of October I had already had my first share in disarmament affairs. John Simon, Sir Robert Vansittart, Permanent Under-Secretary at the Foreign Office, and I worked during several days on a paper for the Cabinet defining our policy towards Germany's claim for equality of rights. Our task was certainly tangled. The Foreign Secretary was depressed when we had finished and doubtful whether the Cabinet would accept our work. 'Nevertheless,' I noted, 'they must look at it and Simon must make 'em. There's the rub, because this is precisely his weakness.' This was, unfortunately, a true criticism, despite Sir John's remarkable intellectual gifts, or perhaps because of them. I concluded:

> The policy is as good as can be expected in the circumstances and it now only remains for Simon to go for it. Anyway the inkwells at the F.O. are dry and if the Cabinet will not have it, Simon should ask them to send someone else to Geneva. I told him this—but that he must not ask me to go!

I was in fact due at Geneva as a substitute delegate on November 2nd. The Government were then still discussing the proposals we had put to them. So I set out for my first international responsibility 'without a single syllable of instruction or advice'.

This experience was happily brief. The Government having taken the decision we had hoped for on the paper we had prepared, Ramsay MacDonald and Simon came to Geneva four weeks later to make their effort in persuading Germany to take part in the Conference again. Long talks followed. The French Prime Minister, M. Herriot, was resourceful and never rigid. He accepted to grant Germany equality of rights 'in a system which would provide security for all nations'. Von Neurath, the German Foreign Minister, did not respond, showing only reluctance to be drawn into further discussions. At length, he yielded enough to allow the British Prime Minister to announce on December 11th that Germany would rejoin the Conference. The understanding was that the armaments of all states should be limited in the proposed Convention. At the end of 1932 I still had hopes that good might come from the Geneva discussions, MacDonald's efforts having yielded some results.

A dark event was soon to overcloud this advantage. Hitler came to power in the following January. This man, compounded of mystic and megalomaniac, orator and self-hypnotist, faithless and merciless in pursuit of his aims, was to bring upon his own country, upon Europe and more distant lands, suffering, destruction and death. He was to do worse. In the name of racial purity, he inspired a surge of beastliness unparalleled for centuries.

Hitler was a failure, for he transformed the world in the sense in which he least wished. When the struggle was over, Europe lay prostrate and power had passed to Russia in the East and the United States in the West, countries he dreaded or despised. His opportunity came at a climacteric in history and he made terrible use of it. The fall of Empires has only too often created opportunities for ruthless ambition. The virtual elimination of the Turkish Empire in Europe made possible the first world war, as a conflict between Teuton and Slav. The collapse of the Austro-Hungarian Empire made possible the second world war, foreshadowing Hitler's first dreams of conquest in Central Europe. There is evident danger that the disappearance of European Empires in Africa may lead to the third.

* * * * *

Hitler's advent to power stirred the anxieties of a French Government already distressed by the British reply to the Paul-Boncour plan. I understood only too well that our chances were slipping, so did some others. Sir Alexander Cadogan was chief adviser to the United Kingdom delegation at Geneva, and he carried out his thankless task with a rare blend of intelligence, sensibility and patience. He had able assistance, notably from Ashley Clarke, later Her Majesty's Ambassador in Rome. In the early days of 1933 we had some discussion together about the prospects, and it seemed to us that, if the Conference was to have any chance, the proposals so far put to it should be drawn together so that the discussions could follow an ordered pattern. To give practical effect to this, Cadogan and I devoted several days in London to drafting a programme of work. This done, I was in Yorkshire when I received a letter from him explaining the difficulty he was having in persuading the Foreign Secretary to submit our plan to the Cabinet:

> I only write you this plaint to show you that we are drifting to disaster. To navigate difficult seas you must have both a chart and a Captain. I had hoped to get the latter, but you know the difficulties that have arisen there. I thought at least we were going to get a chart, but even that seems doubtful. . . .
>
> This blessed Conference will fail unless it is taken properly in hand. We are the people who ought to do that. The French won't; if the Italians did, the French wouldn't follow; the Germans would wreck everything; the Americans talk very big when there is nothing doing, but old Norman Davis is the direct spiritual descendant of the Duke of Plaza Toro. We are the only people who could make it a success. . . .
>
> If the Conference is not driven along hard, it will fail. . . . The Conference cannot survive many more pauses or adjournments. . . .

I agreed with this. One difficulty was that the Foreign Secretary was nominally leader of the United Kingdom delegation and by temperament he was not suited to drive the Conference. John Simon's brilliant, analytical mind hated to take decisions. As a consequence, he was tempted to dodge them, for which there was always an ingenious reason, while the difficulties in Europe grew. Early in the New Year, I recorded a conversation with Simon, who said that he felt it essential to spend less time at Geneva and suggested that I might take some of that work off his shoulders. I accepted, but I could obtain no clear definition of what my authority would be. He did not want to do the work, yet he could hardly bear anyone else to do it.

I left London on January 17th. On my way I stopped in Paris, where I had a long talk with Lord Tyrrell, our Ambassador. He thought it possible to get agreement with the French on disarmament, but that this would entail delicate negotiations; we should have to stick at it for some weeks. Pierre Cot, for a time my opposite number, was going to Geneva and Tyrrell was very anxious that I should undertake the task. 'I should like it,' I wrote, 'but doubt whether I can obtain authority.' My doubts were justified. On my arrival in Geneva I had several conversations with Simon, who had come out for the League Council's quarterly meeting. Eventually and with much difficulty I induced him to talk of disarmament. I asked to be allowed to open discussions with Cot. He said he would raise the matter in the Cabinet the next day and telephone to me in the evening. He then left by the night train. I did not get permission to hold private Anglo-French talks, but Simon and his colleagues endorsed the programme of work Cadogan and I had drafted and I could now take soundings about this among the other delegates.

Not least among our difficulties was the uncertain political life of those with whom we had to deal. As early as the end of January 1933, I wrote to Simon: 'Governments fall on every hand every day.' Once again our initiative had come too late, for Herriot's Government fell, to be replaced by a ministry under Daladier, ardent for the Paul-Boncour plan. So while most delegations liked our programme, the French had other thoughts than to endorse it. On February 10th, my expectations still high, I wrote to Baldwin:

> The most hopeful sphere is the air, in respect of which Paul-Boncour told me yesterday that he hoped something might be done. This is the only sphere where the French do not tightly link disarmament with security. I do hope that we shall be able to continue to press for total abolition of military and naval aircraft as the only real solution of the problem. . . . I know that you will appreciate how difficult it will be for us, however, to maintain a lead in air disarmament . . . if at every stage we are to make technical reservations which will encumber our own footsteps and cast grave doubts, however unjustified, upon our sincerity.

I had written to Baldwin in the same sense nine months earlier, pointing out that since we were so weak in air power, any international limitations were bound to be to our advantage. Baldwin had tried hard in the summer of 1932 to persuade the Government to offer the total abolition of the military and naval air arm, but the objections of the Air Ministry and, more surprisingly, the Admiralty, proved too strong. Both argued that the total abolition of military and naval aircraft would not be to our national advantage. Now, in February 1933, the same question had to be faced again. These plans may well have been at all times too ideal, but experience was to show how difficult intermediate positions were to fix and hold. As the months passed their chances faded.

Relations between Geneva and London were not always easy. Inevitably matters looked differently at the receiving end of the telephone.

The following extract from my diary of February 9th gives one example:

> Lunched with Dutchman. While I was there John Simon dragged me to telephone box and tried to dictate sentences of my speech *re* air disarmament. I said I had no one to take them down. No pencil, speech already typed. He was not pleased, and turned me on to Charlie [Londonderry, Secretary of State for Air] who was more reasonable, although his own service is at stake. They both wanted to make explicitly a statement about bombing for police purposes. I said right time was Air Committee, if set up. Working Committee would be staggered. Simon unhelpful, but I eventually convinced Charlie far enough for him to ring off. On return to hotel found telephone message from Simon that I 'must' specifically mention police bombing. Decided not to.

I was indignant with the Foreign Secretary for making, as it seemed to me, no attempt to defend our work against the Service Departments. On the contrary, he was out-Heroding Herod. My indignation was increased when I learned that the Prime Minister had said in a reply in the House of Commons on that same afternoon that the Air Committee was the proper place for any reservation. This was not my only experience of the kind.

In these difficult days I often took refuge in contacts with one of my British Empire colleagues, particularly Mr. Stanley Bruce, who represented Australia, then on the Council of the League. Bruce, though not yet fifty, had been Prime Minister of Australia and possessed almost inexhaustible good sense and patience. His counsel was invaluable to me then and later, in even rougher weather.

* * * * *

After another week of discussions, reasoning and pleading, Cadogan and I came to the conclusion that unless we could inject some new life into the Conference, it was doomed. Everyone talked of principles, but no one of facts and figures. Britain was not without blame. I explained our opinion in a letter to Baldwin on February 22nd:

> We are cutting an inglorious figure on the Air Committee . . . the air experts seem quite unaware of the falsity of our position as instigators of the Committee who now find themselves without a plan of their own. . . . At present the Committee is divided into three camps—those who believe that a scheme of supervision and control can be worked out sufficient to justify abolition; those who believe that internationalization will first be necessary;

and those who have expressed no definite opinion. We belong to none of these camps, since we have no scheme, only conditions. . . .

Our own position here is not of course made any easier by the fact that our own air people are convinced that we can produce no scheme to control civil aviation and are therefore purely negative in the discussion. Attempts to secure any helpful contribution are as exhausting and ineffective as beating one's fists into a row of pillows.

After this complaint, I set out our new proposal:

As to disarmament as a whole, I am beginning to believe that the only way in which we could realize progress over the whole field would be for us to produce a convention complete in all its details and lay it on the table and ask that the Conference should accept it. I am much tempted to try to work out such a convention, for even if the Conference then failed we should at least have made the greatest effort in our power to achieve success, and I am not so sure that it would then fail.

This was almost a revolutionary departure, for it implied not only that we should draft a convention, but that we would write into it figures for our country and for every nation represented at the Conference. Security could then be discussed in terms of reality. Armaments are the expression of political ambition or fear. Even though in 1933 weapons were not so lethal as they have since become, this carried with it an inherent danger. A nation with plunder in its heart could still accept the risk of war. Today the certainty of mutual destruction in total war can drive the country which aims to dominate to other methods, which may prove more menacing to the free world, but need not be so evident.

I deliberately made my first approach to Baldwin, thinking that he would be the more sympathetic. Two days later I wrote to Simon:

The Disarmament Conference does not go well and everyone is deeply depressed at the prospect. I am afraid we must reconcile ourselves to the fact that despite our programme of work and all our efforts, we have not really emerged from the doldrums. We do make a little progress here and there, but it is insufficient to realize any gains of any value. We may drag on a few weeks more like this, but before long the time will come when the French will say that they cannot get enough of their Plan to justify major disarmament, or that some other Power or Powers may declare in despair that the matter can be carried no further. . . .

We then come to our own position: is there nothing further that we can or should do? I have been discussing this question in the last twenty-four hours with Drummond, Malkin [legal adviser at the Foreign Office] and Cadogan, and though I had no detailed talk with Henderson [President of the Conference], from the few words I had time to exchange with him this morning I am fairly certain that he shares this pessimism. There seems to me to be only one course left to us which might save the Conference and would at least, whatever the consequences of failure, mark plainly to the world that we have done our utmost to achieve success. When, as I fear is inevitable in the course of the next ten days, it becomes clear that the Conference can make no more progress, if we were in a position to lay before the Conference a complete convention, it is just possible that it would be accepted.

Anyway, in this trend of thought Cadogan and I and Malkin are going to try and do some work upon such a convention this weekend. There is a good deal of material and we think we could draw up something presentable and something which will mean more to disarmament than the French Plan. Of course this project will be kept entirely to ourselves, and if and when we produce a convention we will send it straight home to you on the chance that you should consider the idea worth further thought.

The three of us spent the weekend doing this. We filled in the details of a complete scheme, the representatives of the Service Departments giving us the technical assistance we needed. We were very fortunate in the officers chosen to help us at the Conference; in particular, General Temperley, our senior military adviser, was inexhaustible in his sagacity and experience. Our secretarial help was exiguous. I marvelled then, as I have often had cause to do since, at the devotion which the Foreign Office typing staff always showed. Only too often they were tapping on their machines far into the night.

Our draft was copied in all secrecy at Geneva and I left for home with it on March 2nd, taking Cadogan with me. This was my first venture of the kind and I was full of hope; I was also convinced that the Convention would only have a chance of success if the Prime Minister himself introduced it. As usual, we reached Paris early in the morning and had breakfast at the Embassy. To my relief, Tyrrell approved of the idea of our presenting a draft convention. He was a shrewd judge, both of what was politic and of what the French Government would take.

On arrival at the Foreign Office, I had a preliminary talk with Simon and Vansittart, the former with a heavy cold, and then luncheon with Simon and the Prime Minister. My diary for the day continues:

Explained to them my anxieties about prospects of Disarmament Conference. Prime Minister seemed interested. Simon suggested Cabinet

Committee Monday. I said that I wanted to be back in Geneva by then. Prime Minister said he quite understood that and would like me to talk to Cabinet Committee, as I had talked to him, that evening.

I did so, expounding the whole situation. Eventually the Prime Minister said he thought on the whole perhaps he ought to go out to see what could be done. We would sleep on it.

The Committee met again the next morning when the Prime Minister, who never lacked courage, said that he was willing to go to Geneva to present our Convention. The rest of my day was taken up by other discussions with the Prime Minister and with Stanley Baldwin, who had arrived from Birmingham and backed our proposal.

I returned to Geneva on Sunday, March 5th, leaving Cadogan to fight the remaining battle at home. He wrote on March 7th to say that despite difficulties with the Air Ministry, Lord Londonderry having tried to insist that Britain should be allowed some dirigibles under the Convention, the Government had agreed that the Prime Minister and Foreign Secretary should both attend the Conference and would have discretion to use our plan as they thought fit. On the same day, I received a message telling me to await the Prime Minister's arrival and then go home. I heard later that our delegation were much put out at this instruction. All, sailors, soldiers and airmen asked for a remonstrance to be sent to London, saying that I alone understood the problem. When the rumour reached me, I refused to take any action, though I was a little disappointed at the prospect of not being there for the critical hour. In the event my sentence was commuted.

On March 11th the Prime Minister and Foreign Secretary arrived. I told them that the position had not changed during the last few days, though the atmosphere was now more tense. I still saw no hope, I said, unless we could put on the table a convention complete with figures, as I had advised in London a week before. A condition of this was, however, that the convention should be fair. The attempt might fail, but I knew of no other that could be made. Adjournment spelt failure, a limited convention was no better, for it meant the rearmament of Germany. A convention with serious disarmament which might bind Germany, was, I persisted, the only solution.

The Prime Minister had separate conversations during that morning with Mr. Arthur Henderson, M. Eduard Beneš, the sympathetic and resourceful Czech Foreign Minister, and Baron Aloisi, the Italian representative, which revealed nothing new except that Aloisi wanted a disguised adjournment. For the first time I noted that night: 'I fear that I think Mussolini is playing a double game.' We now know that he was pursuing his own plans, rather than being actively hostile to ours. He was eager for his Four Power Pact. Until he got it, he wanted the Disarmament Conference out of the way and Aloisi's instructions were to see to this. The result was unhelpfulness from an unexpected quarter, the Italian delegation having hitherto always supported us well.*

I had a desultory luncheon with MacDonald and Simon, both of whom were sceptical about the Convention. On their way through Paris the previous day, the French Government had expressed anxiety to them about German rearmament; now at Geneva they had to listen to the arguments and counter-arguments of Nadolny, the German delegate, and Beneš. Paul-Boncour was increasingly uneasy, because it seemed to him that Italy was now acting with Germany. The Prime Minister, however, was less troubled about Mussolini's motives, and on the 14th, on my return from a secret meeting of the Council in the afternoon, I found him deep in talk with Simon and Aloisi, who was urging a meeting with the Duce in Rome. My diary that evening records:

Prime Minister highly delighted at idea of Rome visit and abandoning all idea of Convention. After Aloisi had gone the Prime Minister and I had a talk alone. I told him I thought it would cause a most unfortunate impression if he left Geneva after a week with nothing even attempted. It would look like running away. Moreover, Mussolini would want to talk about revision of Treaties. Whether wise or unwise, French would be scared stiff at this at such a time. Nothing could result for some time at least, and the Conference would probably die meanwhile. Eventually he agreed and admitted the Conference must have some meat.

He presented the Convention on March 16th in a speech which was criticized for rambling and ranting, but which did the job.

* * * * *

We had been faced with conflicting difficulties in drafting the Convention. Our chief hope was that when the various delegations saw the balance-sheet as a whole and in detail, they would be willing to make concessions at one point in order to gain advantages at another. The document proposed a solution of the central problem, to reconcile

* Baron Aloisi : *Journal*; Plon, 1957.

German demands for equality with the French call for security. The Draft Convention, from then onwards known to the world as the MacDonald Plan, allowed France 200,000 troops for home service and a further 200,000 for her overseas commitments. Germany was eventually to have 200,000 troops in Europe. The Convention would operate over a period of five years, during which a system of international control would be tested and a permanent disarmament commission set up to study unsolved difficulties. Bombing from the air was to be outlawed. Limitations on naval power were proposed, as were qualitative reductions in armaments; for example, the Convention allowed no tanks above sixteen tons in weight. We would all, including, I hoped, the United States, join a consultative pact, under which members would take counsel together if a breach of the peace were threatened.

The reception of the plan was favourable. After debate and without too many reservations, the Conference accepted the British draft as a basis for its future work. It then adjourned for one month, which was too long. I thought, and observers like General Temperley agreed with me, that there was more than an even chance that the Convention would be accepted, but only if the advantage now gained were pressed.

Meanwhile, MacDonald was in Rome. He had agreed with Aloisi at Geneva that a four-power meeting would be valuable, Mussolini having suggested this in a recent speech at Turin. The Duce had drafted an agreement which was to be signed by France, Germany, Great Britain and Italy. In this way, he said, the danger of a split in Western Europe would be averted. The proposed Treaty prohibited any changes in the Treaty of Versailles without the consent of all four signatories. Mussolini's argument was that, unless the situation were taken in hand, Germany would claim revision of the Treaty and would rearm, with or without permission. In this analysis he was perfectly right, but negotiations for the pact took the attention of the principal governments away from Geneva and our Draft Convention at the moment when we most needed their intelligent concentration. The Four Power Pact was discussed and signed in Rome by Italy, France, Germany and Britain in June 1934. It infuriated Poland, the Little Entente and a number of smaller powers, and unhappily had neither substance nor good consequence. Hitler never paid it any heed and a few months later made a breach in the military clauses of the Treaty of Versailles, without even a reference to his fellow signatories.

On his return home, MacDonald commended our Draft Convention and the Italian plan in a diffuse speech to the House of Commons on March 23rd. Churchill used the occasion to renew his attack on the Prime Minister, who, he said, had dominated foreign policy in the past four years and had brought us nearer to war than ever before. He called the Disarmament Conference 'a solemn and prolonged farce'. While we had been in Opposition in the years 1929–31, Churchill had parted from his colleagues over their attitude to India. They were prepared to endorse the recommendation of the Round Table Conference held in 1930, at which they had been represented by Hoare. Churchill was not, and continued his opposition to the India Bill in the following Parliament.

I had arrived back from Geneva, but the decision that I should reply was only taken half-way through the debate, and this was my first speech of any importance from the Front Bench. I thought the attack on MacDonald unfair, for the troubles in Europe were certainly not of his making. I dismissed as 'a fantastic absurdity' Churchill's allegation that MacDonald was personally responsible for the deterioration of international relations. In fact, I felt admiration for the courage MacDonald had shown in coming to Geneva to present the Convention. I went on to defend the method of diplomacy by personal contact, which Churchill and I were later to practise together, and MacDonald's journey to Rome, which, I argued, would help to bring France and Germany together. Churchill interjected at this point that 'the removal of the grievances of the vanquished should precede the disarmament of the victors.' The weakness of this argument, as we were soon to find out, was that the vanquished nourished their grievances and had decided to rearm, whether the victors liked it or not. Churchill, who had at one point told me that he could not be in the House to hear me, ended by staying and afterwards generously complimented me on my speech. We had a conversation which was the forerunner of many more while I held office and he was still, unhappily for us, but perhaps happily for him, outside the Government.

Our first meeting had been many years earlier. During one winter vacation from Oxford, my mother and I had gone over to Wynyard, the Londonderrys' house a few miles from my home at Windlestone. The occasion was a political rally in Sunderland, where the chief speaker was their guest and cousin, Winston Churchill, who asked me whether I was going into politics. I remember vividly the crowded hall, and especially a sentence in Churchill's speech referring to Soviet ambitions: 'The ghost of the Russian bear comes padding across the immense field of snow.'

* * * * *

In a minute to Simon on March 27th, I emphasized that His Majesty's Government must know their own mind and capitalize the advantage they had gained from the friendly reception accorded to the Draft Convention. I urged consultations with the French to see if we could meet them on security and pointed to the weakness of our position in upholding our right to bomb 'for police purposes in outlying regions'. Despite some discussion with Simon, no progress was recorded.

The Conference resumed at the end of April and began to discuss our Draft Convention. I saw Henderson and agreed with him that our line should be 'steady pegging ahead and no committees'. I next saw Nadolny, with whom I argued about Germany's refusal to include her military police in the figures allotted to her. The Nazis wanted amendments to our chapter in the Convention on the size of armies. These would have prolonged the period of training and swollen the total of their trained troops. The Conference would not agree and I was asked to make this plain to the German delegate, which proved an unpleasant business, with Nadolny banging the table and being generally truculent.

Writing to Baldwin on May 1st, I said:

> I only wish we had more to show in the way of results. The Germans are exasperating and progress is very slow. One feels it is rather like a 1917 campaign in Flanders; we can only make such progress as we may in the mud between the pill-boxes and leave the strong points to be attacked at the last—and as in Flanders, the pill-boxes are occupied by Germans. . . .

Later in the letter I referred to the difficulty in getting decisions from a large international assembly:

> This job is like trying to force a bill through an international House of Commons with no whips and no government majority. . . .

The account of events the next day shows that my pessimism was well founded:

> I asked Soragna [second Italian delegate] and Wilson [second United States delegate] to come and see me in the morning. I told them frankly that I thought that the Germans were taking up an indefensible attitude, that I could take no further step to bring about agreement and that I must

now report my failure and its attendant circumstances to the General Commission tomorrow. Both agreed with me. Soragna offered to make representation with Aloisi to the Germans. I said I should be grateful but would do no more myself. Lunch with Italians. Nadolny rather sore. I gave him no balm.

Soragna was consistently helpful and, after more than a week, Nadolny appeared to understand that we were in earnest. He departed to Berlin for fresh instructions. With the spur of a remonstrance from London, the Nazi Government eventually yielded and included the military police in the total allotted to them.

* * * * *

On May 15th I spent the morning at a meeting of the Council of the League, wrestling with the affairs of Bolivia and Paraguay. These countries, after six months of fighting, had now formally declared war. In the afternoon, Vansittart rang me up from London and said that Simon wanted me to come home. I protested; because of the work which had to be done at Geneva, I should have less than twenty-four hours in England and the journeys were exacting. It seemed, however, that the Foreign Secretary wanted to see me before making up his mind about his own plans, and so I set out on the usual all-night journey to Paris, flying from there. Simon appeared to be unwell when I saw him before luncheon and he told me that a sea cruise had been suggested to re-establish his health.

We had further discussions in the afternoon with the Prime Minister, who had just returned from Washington, and Stanley Baldwin. These two, particularly the Prime Minister, were clearly a little impatient of Simon's illness. When we were alone I advised him to go for his cruise soon. He eventually agreed. The next day I spent a heavy and hurried morning at the Foreign Office, during which I learned that the Foreign Secretary had again changed his mind about the cruise. He would not go, but would hang on somehow. I thought that if Simon were as ill as he seemed, he would be wiser to go for his cruise then, for as long as was necessary, fearing that, if matters continued as they were, we would in effect have no Foreign Secretary, only the appearance of one, which would be worse than none. I flew off from London in the afternoon, reaching Geneva after four hours and ten minutes of flight, which was fast travel for those days. The last portion was across the Jura, looking their best in the soft light of an evening in early summer.

While in Washington, Ramsay MacDonald had persuaded Mr. Roosevelt that our efforts deserved public encouragement. On May 16th, the President issued a message approving the Draft Convention and even suggesting that the United States might, in a case of aggression, be willing to abandon strict neutrality. I was glad of this, for every sign of American interest in Europe was good for peace. President Roosevelt's announcement was pleasanter hearing than the orders which I now received from London. I had once more to defend Britain's decision to reserve the right to undertake 'police bombing' in outlying areas, despite my pleas that our reservation was indefensible. I was instructed to do this at Geneva on May 27th and in the House of Commons on July 5th. My speech on the latter occasion was held by the Air Ministry to be insufficiently firm and a tart exchange of letters followed between the Secretary of State for Air and myself, of which the Prime Minister had to be informed. However, I survived.

The first reading of our Draft Convention was concluded at Geneva in an unsatisfactory scramble. Despite anything that I had been able to do, too many major points had been left unresolved. This was in part because another international event was now distracting attention. A World Economic Conference had been summoned to meet in London to attempt in the economic sphere what we were singularly failing to achieve in disarmament. It proved a total loss; a principal casualty being Mr. Cordell Hull's initiative, torpedoed from home. An adjournment to attend this unproductive occasion was a welcome diversion for some at Geneva and inescapable for all. In the interval, Mr. Henderson was charged with preparing a draft for a second reading and set himself dauntlessly to the task, but the Conference was slipping again, through no fault of his.

Henderson was dedicated to his work and this devotion probably shortened his life. With the advantage of a disinterested sincerity, which was accepted and admired, he had some serious disadvantages too. The greater part of the speeches at the Conference, and much of the informal discussion, was conducted in French, which language he did not understand, and listening to translations can be a tedious and unsatisfactory business. Perhaps partly as a result of this, when Henderson lashed out on occasion, which the Conference richly deserved, his presidential rod was as likely to fall on the innocent as the guilty. The French showed a certain mistrust of his methods, while after Henderson's deep differences with MacDonald within the Labour Party, his relations with the Prime Minister at Geneva, though correct, were never again to be cordial. Personally I always found him a completely loyal President of the Conference and I valued the friendship he showed to me, though half his age and a member of another party.

* * * * *

While the Conference toiled to devise some effective scheme of disarmament, in the Far East a militant Japan had taken up arms to push its aggressive plans. On September 18th, 1931, the first stages of this dangerous game were played out in Manchuria. Later the conflict spread to Shanghai, on the pretext of an anti-Japanese boycott, which was centred there and was the most effective Chinese weapon of defence.

China brought the Japanese action in Manchuria before the League three days afterwards, invoking Article 11 of the Covenant. Four months later, China also invoked Articles 10 and 15. The United States and Soviet Russia were the two powers most intimately concerned with these developments in the Far East and their absence from the League complicated and restricted action. The responsibility in the Pacific area among League members was therefore almost entirely a British one. During February the Council of the League devoted four public meetings to a consideration of the Sino-Japanese dispute, without effective decision. I had myself no direct part in these happenings, except for occasionally representing His Majesty's Government on the Committee of Twelve, which deliberated in private from time to time as the grim events unrolled.

On March 27th, 1933, although no action had been taken against her, Japan withdrew from the League of Nations, having driven her war-planes and weapons through the Covenant. The 'Manchurian precedent' had fateful implications. The long road to war upon which Japan embarked, with the bombers in Manchuria and the rain of fire over Chapei, led to the wider conflagration of 1937 in China and ultimately to Admiral Nagumo's special naval task force, whose six aircraft-carriers struck Pearl Harbour, blasting the United States into the second world war and determining its outcome.

III

HITLER WITHDRAWS

June – December 1933

French fears over German arms – My talks with MM. Daladier and Paul-Boncour – Proposals for a two-stage Convention – Germany withdraws from the Disarmament Conference – Herr Hitler increases his demands – I become Lord Privy Seal

Mr. Norman Davis, the United States delegate, told me at the end of May 1933, that he was extremely disturbed by the trend of French policy at the Disarmament Conference, and it was he who was primarily responsible for organizing the talks held in Paris on June 8th between himself, MM. Daladier and Paul-Boncour, Lord Londonderry and myself. They had one consequence which should have helped us. The French wanted effective supervision and sanctions against the offender before they disarmed, while Davis refused to consider any system of supervision unless linked with a detailed programme of disarmament. I wrote to Henderson:

> It eventually emerged from a long discussion that the French might ask for a trial period—say the first three years of the period of the Convention—during which they would undertake to construct no material of the types forbidden in our Draft Convention. What the French really want, I think, is a look round—through the spectacles of supervision—before actually destroying anything.

In the existing world conditions it was increasingly hard to argue against this caution. The proposal for a Convention of two periods first appeared at these talks. Despite the further complications it introduced, I thought it realistic and that we should use it. Eventually the Germans accepted the two periods, but by then the French Government which had sponsored them was no more and their successors were preoccupied with other troubles. Fatalities of this kind constantly dogged the Conference. Wise decisions were too often taken after they ceased to be useful.

The Paris discussions were a fair reflection of national states of mind. France, nearest to Germany, feared most and would yield least in the face of mounting danger. This tenacity would have been more admirable if accompanied by efforts to set her own house in order and to prepare to meet the perils which her statesmen rehearsed. Britain, a stage removed from danger and with the Channel still creating a certain isolation, was patronizing rather than understanding of French fears. Slow to make preparations herself, she was anxious for compromises which would eliminate the need to do so. The United States, most remote and, in consequence, purist in her attitude, wanted the highest degree of disarmament while contributing the least to security by any undertaking on her part.

I agreed with the French view, that it would be futile for the Conference to meet again until private conversations had made some progress with the main difficulties. The next day I returned to London and reported to my colleagues accordingly. I asked that we should persuade the Heads of Governments, then in London for the World Economic Conference, to consult together about disarmament. I added a condition:

> But—and it is a large 'but'—the possibility of conversations is dependent on our being able to modify our own attitude somewhat—principally in regard to supervision. I understand our present position is that we can make no further concessions in this direction. I think we should be literally alone in this; I can think of no other delegation at Geneva that would make any difficulty about making the provisions for supervision more stringent. We may have the best of reasons for our attitude, but we must realize that we should appear as single-handed obstructors.

I urged that the Government should reconsider their attitude towards questions where their view was at variance with that of most other members of the Conference, for example in the matter of 'police bombing'. This was a claim to be allowed to use bombing in 'outlying regions' to restore order. Such areas as the frontiers of the Aden Protectorate were given as examples for the exception. The provision had proved indefensible in international debate and raised such unanswerable questions as 'outlying from where' and 'what parts of the world are to have the privilege of being bombed by the British'. Exceptional cases make bad law. My argument with my colleagues was that it was impossible to demand consideration for special conditions when drawing up an international convention which was to govern the world's armaments. We should also, I thought, try to meet the wishes of other powers in questions where our draft seemed unduly to favour Great Britain. I warned my colleagues that, if no negotiation could be set going within the next fortnight, the search for the victim would begin. I did not want my country to be cast for that part, 'a fate which, in the circumstances of this Conference, can neither be evaded without concessions nor endured without ignominy.'

Nothing was going right. The early collapse of the Economic Conference deprived us of anything more than a fleeting opportunity for discussions on disarmament by Prime Ministers. Moreover, the Government decided that until acute differences between France and Germany were removed, the Draft Convention could not be modified. This was a mistake, for the action I had proposed would have increased our authority, and the modifications had to be made later anyway, with less effect.

After some discussion with other powers, it was agreed that Mr. Henderson should visit the European capitals for private conversations and that I should accompany him to Paris. This was a game quest by Henderson. On July 11th, he and I held talks with French Ministers, and he then went on to Rome, Berlin and Prague. At the end of the tour, Henderson had to report that he saw little hope of agreement on the two principal points. Incontestably there was no progress to show on a two-stage Convention, which was the French demand, or on the disposal of heavy armament, which was the German demand. M. René Massigli had told me privately that if talks were reopened, the French Government might be willing to go further than they had done in their memorandum. This was encouraging and I considered how to create another opening.

Massigli was Sir Alexander Cadogan's opposite number and the leading French adviser on disarmament questions. Quick, tenacious and fertile in expedients, he was already an experienced diplomat and had the confidence of the British representatives with whom he had to deal. Our personal friendship began in these difficult months and was to continue through nearly thirty years of work together.

* * * * *

In view of the information now reaching London about Germany's military preparations, France's distrust of the Nazi Government seemed to me justified. It was openly admitted to our Air Attaché in Berlin on

July 10th that Germany was manufacturing military aircraft, carrying out work on fortifications and intensifying military training. Lord Tyrrell told me that, because Hitler's assumption of office had increased French fears, the demand for a trial period and for supervision was a pre-condition for any agreement on their part. This view I commended to my colleagues in a memorandum in the middle of August.

It was, however, the French who made the next move, by asking for further conversations with the British Government alone. I was in France for a few days' holiday and broke it for a visit to Paris on September 18th. My talks with Daladier and Paul-Boncour showed that the French position had not been substantially modified. It hardly could be. In a conversation at luncheon, Daladier told me that there were three courses open to France. The first was a preventive war, which he ruled out, since no democratic country could indulge in one. The second was to say that, in the light of recent events in Germany, France could not continue to offer co-operation in the work of the Disarmament Conference, and would go ahead with the construction of armaments to maintain the lead she now enjoyed. This was to condemn Europe to a race in armaments which he was extremely reluctant to do. He preferred the third course, which was to seek, in conjunction with us and, if possible, with Italy, some common accord which might save the Conference, though he had little doubt of Germany's determination to rearm.

I thought Daladier's conclusion right, and that we must do all we could to give it effect. Together we agreed to extend our discussions at once to include the United States, and to bring in senior British Ministers. I flew back to London and returned to Paris with Simon, while Baldwin, from Aix, and Norman Davis joined us. The French Government held to the position that Germany, during the trial period, should not be allowed to possess samples of those weapons denied to her by the Versailles Treaty. If Germany observed the conditions in the trial period, she would be allowed the same weapons as France in the second period. In any event, some guarantee of the execution of the Convention must be given. Daladier would not be content with anything less than a promise to apply sanctions to any power found to be violating the Convention. Norman Davis criticized the French Government for this new demand. Neither Simon nor Baldwin could commit Britain in advance to meet it, though we decided to support the French in their idea of a trial period. We agreed to set up a permanent commission to inspect each state from time to time, and to consult if any breach of the Convention were reported.

So our Paris meetings were only of limited usefulness. Perhaps a more forthcoming attitude on our part towards further engagements in Europe would have allayed French fears, and I argued in this sense with my colleagues in London. But this was not the whole problem. Most Frenchmen believed that in the last resort we should be with them; their main anxiety was Hitler's policy, for German rearmament was now throwing a deepening shadow across Europe.

* * * * *

During September the Nazi Government strengthened their demands. On the 15th, von Neurath declared that Germany could make no further concessions and that, if the armed powers continued to evade their obligation to disarm, Germany 'would have the right and duty to provide for the equality and security of her own people according to her own judgement and without hesitation or false scruple.' Sir John Simon and I saw von Neurath at Geneva on September 23rd. Our arguments did not have the slightest effect on unwelcome events which were making sad havoc of the hopes for our Draft Convention. We made one more attempt to meet French needs and German demands, but it was still-born. Before even the Cabinet approved it, the German Chargé d'Affaires in London called on Sir John Simon on October 6th and announced that von Neurath would not return to Geneva for the moment. Nadolny, he said, would address the Conference and tell them that Germany could not accept any trial period at all and must insist on equality from the start. Signor Suvich, in an understatement, called this 'a remarkable step backward'. The next day I travelled with Henderson to Geneva and recorded:

> He [Henderson] is anxious to conclude a convention even if the Germans won't play their part. The danger of this is that we should expose the differences between friends on minor issues, to German satisfaction.

At Geneva, Paul-Boncour told me he was convinced that Germany did not want a convention, the only hope for the peace of Europe was Anglo-French accord. I thought that he was probably right on the first count and certainly right on the second. A talk with Nadolny did not modify my views, for he refused to make any substantial concessions, saying that Germany could never agree to a convention divided into two periods. Nadolny was hostile to von Neurath and ambitious to succeed him, critical of the Nazis, but clumsy in his methods. My notes call it 'the usual hammer and tongs interview'.

The Government condemned the German position and so did most world opinion. Simon told the German Ambassador in London on October 10th that his country's refusal to accept the two periods meant that other nations would have no sense of security, without which there could be no disarmament. It would, he said, aggravate international suspicion and European tension. When Simon reached Geneva, Nadolny informed him that his observations to the German Ambassador were entirely unacceptable to his Government and that he was leaving Geneva for consultations in Berlin.

On October 14th the Conference met. Most politicians suffer from nerves in some form before making a speech, they are usually bores if they do not. Simon, however, went to greater extremes of agony than any public figure I have ever known. This made life hard for those who tried to serve him. My diary of October 14th reads:

> At his suggestion I saw French and Italians and Davis. A few unimportant amendments were suggested [by the French and Italians] to Simon's speech. J.S. first said 'no' emphatically to both, then agreed to Italian amendments but not to French. I could not move him, but had to go to Bureau ahead to seek to appease Paul-Boncour who was much annoyed. When J.S. at length arrived, forty-five minutes late, Davis persuaded him to be reasonable, but he then made P.-B. purple with rage by going to sit ostentatiously on opposite side of room to whisper to German (God knows what about!) and holding up business for this. Henderson looked annoyed and I am not surprised.

When eventually delivered, Simon's speech, while leaving Germany every possible opportunity to revise her attitude, stated plainly that His Majesty's Government considered that no agreement could be reached on the basis of a convention which provided for immediate rearmament. This speech was supported by Davis, Aloisi, Paul-Boncour, Beneš, Politis of Greece and others.

At three o'clock that afternoon, Arthur Henderson received a telegram from von Neurath stating that Germany must withdraw from the Conference, since it was clearly not going to achieve its sole object, general disarmament. On the same night Hitler declared in a broadcast that Germany would also leave the League. The hopes for progress with our Convention or for disarmament at Geneva were dead, the dangers for Europe were very much alive. My diary that evening refers to the Nazi departure:

> The Conference was becoming a sham so that it is perhaps just as well now. All the same I should not like Simon's conscience about the earlier part of last year when Brüning was still in power. We missed the bus then, and could never overtake it.

This was a sweeping and youthful judgement. It is, however, possible that if we had shown more initiative in the earlier months of the Conference, we might have been able to forestall events with our Disarmament Convention, instead of pursuing them. The prestige which the agreement might have brought would have helped the Brüning Government in their struggle with rival and undemocratic forces at home. Even so, the French demand for security would still have had to be met, for even then the German Government were insistent upon equality of rights and their policy of arming for power would not have been affected. We now know, for instance, that research for the dread rockets had begun as early as 1930, unhampered by any budgetary limitations, and without Nazi inspiration.

* * * * *

The withdrawal of Germany from the Disarmament Conference left the British Government with several disagreeable alternatives. In law at least, they could use force against German rearmament; or they could give up any idea of a disarmament convention and let events take their course; or, finally, they could make further efforts for a disarmament convention and try to persuade Germany to return to the Conference at a price. This last, combined with some rearmament at home, was the policy chosen. With varying degrees of conviction, most friendly powers agreed with it.

Nevertheless, concern at Germany's clandestine rearmament was growing sharper in London. By November 1933 we knew that Hitler was starting to build military aircraft in quantity and that para-military organizations were being equipped and trained. In a few years Nazi Germany would be an armed menace. The British Ambassador at Berlin, Sir Eric Phipps, reporting on Hitler's speech of October 14th, said that while he believed that the Chancellor wanted peace for the moment, the future was quite another matter. He was an abnormal man whose past gave no guarantee of his reliability. The Annual Report of the British Chiefs of Staff, presented that autumn, suggested that the object of Germany's rearmament was to make it possible for her to secure a revision of frontiers in the East, a political assessment not necessarily endorsed by the Foreign Office and certainly not shared by me. It was never my belief that Nazi ambitions were only Eastern. The Chiefs of Staff had no doubt that German rearmament would continue whether a disarmament convention were signed or not, and that Great Britain might very easily be called upon to implement her Locarno obligations within the next few years. Therefore, a steady increase in the defence estimates would be necessary.

The dangers to the unity of the Versailles powers latent in this state of affairs soon showed themselves. Early in November a bitter quarrel broke out in the League between France and Italy. The Foreign Secretary was alarmed and suggested that he and I should both go out at once. We did so. Exchanges with the delegations allayed the storm; they also convinced us that nothing more could be done for the moment at Geneva.

Hitler played his hand skilfully in these weeks, declaring that the League was merely an instrument designed to keep the defeated powers in permanent subjection, but protesting his friendly feelings towards France. Meanwhile, he increased the pressure on the diplomatic front. The British and French Ambassadors were told of new German demands for an air force. The Foreign Office calculated that Germany was asking for about seven hundred machines, which would give her an air strength 30 per cent. greater than that of the British Metropolitan Air Force. Hitler also asked for 300,000 troops instead of the 200,000 proposed in our Draft Convention. On October 24th, Hitler openly told Sir Eric Phipps that he sought 'a certain expansion in Eastern Europe', a threat which was also calculated to reassure those who believed, wrongly in my opinion, that Hitler's ambitions could be tolerated if diverted that way. He asked for some submarines and demanded that the victors should not increase their armaments during the period of the proposed agreement.

This was alarming and menacing. The last condition might bear hardly on the United Kingdom in its existing state of weakness and was unacceptable. The Americans and the Italians had been told much the same, yet the rather surprising consensus of opinion among the Ambassadors was that Hitler intended these mounting demands as the opening of a serious negotiation. His Majesty's Government, though they did not like these moves, were sluggish in their reactions. I was disturbed by the slow motion in stating our position in Berlin. On

December 5th I urged the Foreign Secretary not to delay longer, fearing that Nazi demands must increase, unless we quickly made our opinion known. Six weeks had passed since Hitler's interview with Phipps and there had been no definite reply from us. I wrote to Simon:

> All of this means that every hour we postpone sending the telegram to Berlin we increase the risk. Once the telegram has been despatched we have at least occupied the ground. The use we put it to can be considered later.

But the Foreign Secretary preferred to move tentatively. The Government were still prepared to negotiate, believing that a convention which controlled the extent and speed of German rearmament would be better than nothing at all. This reasoning had force, but delay could only make matters worse. Hitler now had control of a lever and we were past the point when any disarmament could be asked of France or any other ally. The evasions of the Treaty of Versailles and the troubled politics of the Weimar Republic had combined to produce in Germany a variety of illicit fighting formations and private armies across the country. This alliance of national pride and popular regimentation had been embodied in the Freikorps. Out of the 'Sports Section', founded under the supervision of Major Röhm, grew the Nazi political army which became the Sturm Abteilung. The Schutzstaffeln, over which Himmler came to have command, grew more slowly but on its own distinctive lines. After January 1931, Röhm gave new impetus to the S.A., which intensified its military training and increased its numbers from 250,000 to 400,000. By April 1932, Himmler's S.S. had grown to not less than 30,000. These, even in German calculations, were part of the military resources available in the last resort to the state.

Sir Eric Phipps saw the Chancellor on December 8th and questioned him about the training and functions of the para-military organizations. Hitler said that the S.S. and S.A. might be compared with the Salvation Army, at which the Ambassador laughed openly. The German Government repeated in a note of December 12th that the S.S. and S.A. were in no sense military organizations; they were an inseparable feature of the political system of the Nazi state and their 'sole mission was to organize the political masses against the Communist peril'.

Diplomatic exchanges continued over the next few weeks. The

argument on the British side was mainly to refute or question Hitler's statements and demands, while asking for information on any point where hope of progress remained. On December 20th London sent a sharp remonstrance, stating that despite the German Government's protestations, Germany was the only power which was unwilling to resume the discussion of disarmament in January. Hitler was told that his demand for 300,000 troops would produce the most disturbing effects on European opinion. An unhappy consequence of these exchanges with the Nazi Government was that, although the British Government kept their French allies informed, they did not always have their agreement in advance. For such behaviour there was the excuse that the French Government were themselves committed to the Disarmament Conference, not because Nazi Germany would accept any result it might reach, or from confidence that it would reach one, but because this seemed to them the only way to preserve the legal position and a common front within the League against an absent Germany.

Opinion in France was hardening, and with it the conviction that Germany's rearmament should be denounced publicly, under Article 213 of the Versailles Treaty. His Majesty's Government did not like this action, but they could not stand in the wings refusing to join in French protests, while Nazi demands grew larger as well as louder. The position was complicated by clever moves from Hitler, who made offers of non-aggression pacts to his neighbours, although Austria was not among them. Some action must be taken which would at least expose realities, even if there were slight hope that it would have more encouraging consequences. The Government concluded that Britain should probe the views of France, Germany and Italy separately. There would then be just a chance that we might find some common denominator, on the basis of which the powers could be brought together.

On December 9th I wrote:

> No French Government could be expected to agree to negotiate with Germany on the basis of rearmament for the latter. The only course, and I have felt this strongly for a fortnight, is for us to do that work of unmasking the German batteries. Tell the French what we are doing, but not ask them to participate. The weaker the French Government the less it can do so. If, on the other hand, we tackle Hitler skilfully as Phipps can be trusted to do, we shall discover whether the German demands are in truth exorbitant, as I anticipate, or reasonable. If the former, the sooner British public opinion

wakes up to the fact the better. If the latter we shall then have something definite upon which to work.

While I brooded over these thoughts, a sullen and suspicious Europe saw in the New Year of 1934.

* * * * *

One evening just before Christmas, the Prime Minister sent for me and explained that it was essential to have a Foreign Office representative in the Lords, who would be an Under-Secretary. He was determined not to have two Foreign Ministers in the Cabinet. Previous experience had proved to him that this would not work. After careful consideration, here was the offer: he would like me to accept the office of Lord Privy Seal without a seat in the Cabinet, my work to continue as at present. The appointment was to be announced on January 1st, if I agreed. Baldwin and Simon concurred, he said.

I thanked the Prime Minister and told him that I would like a few hours in which to think it over and consult Stanley Baldwin. I went to see Baldwin after dinner and we had a long talk. He was pleased with the solution and confessed that they had had much trouble in arriving at it. He himself had suggested a K.C.B. for me. He thought that Sir Anthony would sound well. I replied that, if the idea was Geneva status, I was quite happy as I was, for nobody troubled about status there. Baldwin volunteered that he was uncertain about the Privy Councillorship. I should not have had it in the normal way, since he and the Prime Minister had decided it should be given in strict seniority. But while there were precedents for a Lord Privy Seal not being in the Cabinet, there was none for the holder not being a Privy Councillor. I did not in fact become a Privy Councillor, the most cherished of parliamentary honours, until six months later. Baldwin concluded our conversation by saying that he was very glad, because if I got no further in this Government it would give me strong claims in the next. I was grateful, but noted my concern about the 'little scheme' at the time, that, 'although it brings the appearance of more authority, it actually gives none. I shall not even be a member of the Cabinet Committee that decides the policy I shall be expected to carry out.' I hardly expected then to be so soon in Berlin under the portentous title of *Lordsiegelbewahrer*.

I went to Sandringham to receive my seals of office, and was a guest for the weekend. During my visit Sir Stafford Cripps delivered himself of an attack, not on King George v, but on what he called Buckingham Palace influence. The King was not unnaturally indignant, deeming that this excuse only made it worse. I was summoned for an audience on Sunday after church: 'What does he mean by saying that Buckingham Palace is not me? Who else is there I should like to know? Does he mean the footmen?'

IV

HITLER STATES HIS TERMS

December 1933 – February 1934

Italian views on limited German rearmament – The British Memorandum – A European tour proposed for me – The Stavisky affair and its repercussions – My talks with MM. Doumergue and Barthou on Germany – My first meeting with Herr Hitler – His offer – Luncheon at the British Embassy – I visit President von Hindenburg – My impressions of Nazi Berlin

In December 1933, His Majesty's Government had begun to think of another negotiation with Germany. Rumours of this made French Ministers uneasy. Sir John Simon first tried to mollify them through the embassies, then he visited Paris on December 22nd to see what could be done by direct contact. A full day's talks brought some reassurance, but the French feared that any discussions with the German Government would result in more concessions. In this they were probably right, but they were less ready to face the consequences of no negotiation. When, on January 1st, the French made their reply to Germany, it was still positive enough to keep open the discussions between them, however stubborn the disagreement.

Simon broke a holiday in the Mediterranean to see Mussolini in Rome on January 3rd. In the Duce's opinion, the choice was between no agreement, when not only would world opinion be profoundly disturbed, but Germany would rearm at pleasure, and a practicable agreement which would have to concede some rearmament to Germany. He did not think the demand for an army of 300,000 likely to be whittled down, but he insisted that in the Convention, Germany would be content with defensive armaments proportionate to the army allowed to her. Mussolini was against a period of probation for Germany, he was sure she would never accept it. The Italians had put their proposals into a document, which provided for the return of Germany to the League. The Duce was emphatic that German and Italian policy did not follow a common line and gave their differences over Austria as an example. Hitler was backing the local Nazis, while Mussolini upheld Dollfuss in power.

The German replies to the British and French notes, made known on January 19th, showed no sign of concession. They complained that the heavily armed powers would not disarm as they had promised to do at Versailles. The only convention which Germany could accept in these circumstances was one which allowed her to rearm to the level of others. In these conditions, His Majesty's Government produced their Memorandum of January 29th.

It was an admitted compromise. While denying that Britain had ever departed from the principles of the Draft Convention, reluctant recognition was given to the inevitability of some German rearmament. The intention was still partial disarmament by the armed powers, aimed at providing equality of rights at a level lower than that proposed by Hitler. The Memorandum kept the number of German troops down to 200,000, instead of the 300,000 asked for by Hitler, but Germany was to be allowed tanks of up to six tons. It advocated the abolition of military and naval aircraft and the supervision of civil aviation, and called for a thorough inquiry into the whole question of air power. This policy would be prejudiced if 'any party not hitherto entitled to possess military aircraft should claim such possession pending the results of an inquiry'. But the Memorandum admitted that Germany and other disarmed states could not be asked to postpone their claim indefinitely, and proposed that these states should be entitled to aircraft, if agreement on total abolition had not been achieved by the end of two years. They would be entitled to parity by the end of the ten years which the Memorandum now proposed as the duration of the Convention. This parity would still have meant a marked German inferiority in relation to her neighbours, many of whom were in alliance.

The true nature of our difficulties was underlined by a message from our Ambassador in Berlin at the end of January. He wrote that the Weimar Republic had been replaced by a regime whose radically different methods might at some future date precipitate an international conflict, 'for Nazi Germany believes neither in the League nor in negotiation'. German foreign policy had four aims: fusion with Austria, rectification of the eastern frontiers, an outlet for German energy towards the south and east, and the recovery of some colonial foothold overseas. If his neighbours would allow him, Hitler would become strong by the simplest and most direct methods. The mere fact that he was making himself unpopular abroad would not deter him. If he found that he was arousing no real opposition, the pace of his advance would increase. On the other hand, if he were vigorously opposed, he was unlikely at this stage to risk a break. The Ambassador thought Germany still sufficiently conscious of her weakness and isolation to be halted by a united front abroad. Once the Saar had returned to the Reich, Hitler's objective would be a rectification of the eastern frontiers and expansion southwards or eastwards. Sir Eric Phipps 'hazarded a guess', however, that it would be a decade, or probably more, before Germany deliberately risked a war.

The House of Commons debated the Government's Memorandum on February 6th. There was little enthusiasm for it, but the House did not divide against it. In the same debate the Foreign Secretary announced that I was to visit Paris, Berlin and Rome, to explain the proposals contained in our Memorandum and to investigate at first hand the attitude of the powers towards our suggestions. Parliament approved. I had no illusions about my task and, winding up the debate, I said that we had reached the point of no return:

> We believe that the general balance of this document is just and therefore it should be maintained and not be departed from. . . . I am convinced that, unless the nations of the world will accept the proposals of this memorandum or something very like it, then there will not be a Disarmament Convention.

* * * * *

The negotiations in Paris must in any event have been difficult, if the common front was to be preserved between France, Italy and ourselves. They were further complicated by the fantastic happenings which first rocked and then destroyed the Chautemps Government in the first weeks of 1934. These became popularly known as the Stavisky Affair.

It all began from the laudable desire of Bayonne to have a pawn-shop. Bordeaux and Toulouse both had municipal pawn-shops, but the citizens of Bayonne had to content themselves with branch establishments maintained in their city by their larger neighbours. Accordingly, the Municipal Council formed the *Crédit Municipal de Bayonne* to carry on the business and, having obtained the formal consent of the Ministry of Labour, was authorized to issue bonds to the value of fifty million francs. Unhappily, the general scheme of this enterprise was drawn up by a M. Serge Alexandre Stavisky, whose financial past had been, to say the least of it, chequered. The plans were approved by the relevant Ministers of the Republic in Paris and the bonds were issued, many of them being taken up by leading insurance companies in France. After a few months, suspicion was aroused, an investigation followed and the counterfoils were found not to tally with the amount of bonds issued. Several million francs were missing. The documents in the case were sent to the Public Prosecutor and the storm burst. After disappearing for a time, Stavisky was apprehended and subsequently died or committed suicide or, as some maintained, was murdered in prison.

Bitter parliamentary debates followed, to the accompaniment of rioting. The Prime Minister, M. Camille Chautemps, promised a full investigation. For a time it seemed as if the storm might blow itself out, but fresh charges were brought, involving some Ministers, including M. Georges Bonnet, the Finance Minister. M. Bonnet's defence seemed weak and when the Minister of Justice, M. Raynaldy, resigned on January 26th as a result of the attacks upon his conduct, the Government's hours were numbered. The extent and ramifications of the scandal havocked the reputation of parliamentary government in France. In an effort to redeem it, M. Chautemps was succeeded by a national administration under M. Gaston Doumergue, a former President of the Republic, who, though aged, was much respected. Perhaps the strangest aspect of the whole affair was that a man of Stavisky's record should have been asked to take part in so responsible a task and should have been at liberty to do so. Arrested as long ago as July 28th, 1926, on a charge of forging a cheque for three million francs, he was remanded for different periods, mostly on the grounds of ill health, so that the case was not finally due to be heard until some days after the pawn-shop scandal broke. The suspicion that Stavisky must have had friends in high places, the mysterious circumstances surrounding his death and the personal abuse which followed in parliamentary debates, caused disgust, bitterness and alarm in France.

This was a blow to my own work. I had now to face the virtual certainty that neither M. Doumergue nor M. Louis Barthou, the new Foreign Minister, would have had time to study the details of the disarmament position, still less to bring an impartial judgement to bear, fully preoccupied as they must be with their country's scandals. Yet this could have been a moment of opportunity. If our mission were to succeed in the only sense in which I wished it to, I must carry the

French with me. I thought my best chance of success, and this was slender, was to get specific proposals from Germany, sufficiently moderate to make them acceptable in a convention. To do that, Germany's appetites had to be restrained and Hitler would have to accept the retention of heavier weapons by the armed powers. Mussolini would support us in extracting this acceptance.

I thought, therefore, that geographically my journey should begin in Paris, continue to Berlin and to Rome, and end in Paris. By this method, I would try first to establish confidence in my purpose among the new French Ministers and then, if I were able to record any progress in Berlin, I hoped to get endorsement in Rome and discuss the result to best advantage on my return to Paris. Before I set out, von Neurath had made the first move by telling Sir Eric Phipps that, in the German Government's view, the key to the whole disarmament question lay in Paris. This was so far from being true, that the outcome would depend upon my extracting concessions from Berlin. By arranging my journey in this order, I should guard, as far as I could, against the exaggeration by Germany of any differences there might be between ourselves and France. The itinerary was agreed to.

★ ★ ★ ★ ★

In my small party was Mr. William Strang, my chief Foreign Office adviser, with whom I was to work on many other missions in the next few years. I found him always diligent, patient and well-informed, a master hand at any draft. Lord Cranborne came with me as Parliamentary Private Secretary, thus beginning a political association which was to last all my public life. The third member of my team was Robert Hankey, who had become my private secretary. He was a perfect choice for the post, cheerful, indefatigable, with many of his father's gifts of organization, an extraordinarily youthful appearance and a retentive mind.

We left London on February 16th. We were given a grand, if distinctly embarrassing, send-off upon our travels, with John Simon, the French, German and Italian Ambassadors and Nevile Butler, representing the Prime Minister, among others at the station. I longed for the train to start. At our Embassy in Paris that evening we laid our plan with Tyrrell and his staff. The next day I had luncheon with the French Ministers. I liked Doumergue, and Marshal Pétain, for me very much the 'hero of Verdun', was also sympathetic. Herriot, with whom I became friends in later years, looked ill and shaken, as well he might, having narrowly escaped a ducking in the Seine by the angry Parisians. My first impressions of Barthou were not favourable. As I got to know him better I revised my views and grew to admire his courage and brilliant mind, even though his love of epigram must have cost France some friends. After luncheon we had three hours of talk. Doumergue was friendly, if prolix, and I felt I could trust him. Barthou made a speech at me, and a spiky one at that, but the talk became smoother at the close.

Doumergue's only definite point concerned Germany's unofficial military organizations. He insisted that the French reserves, when called up for service, did only about a week's training a year, and that their military value was not high. The opening of the Great War had proved that it was only the army under arms which was capable of offering immediate resistance. Reserves needed three months further training before they could fairly meet fully-trained troops. However that might be, the Prime Minister continued, the various constituents of the French army, as it existed, were all known and written down on paper. In other countries this was not so. In Germany, side by side with the Reichswehr, there were pre-military and para-military organizations about 1,200,000 strong. It could not be said that these formations had no military value. Thanks to them, the Germans could put 700,000 to 800,000 men into the field at once. That was why the French insisted upon their clear definition. M. Doumergue added that this was the only statement he wished to make and he trusted that I would remember it when I held conversations in Berlin and Rome. I did.

Barthou spoke of events in Austria, which, he argued, had limited the liberty of manœuvre open to governments when our Memorandum was drafted. The militant arm of the Christian Socialist Party had just suppressed the Social Democrats, with the compliance of Dr. Dollfuss, at the cost of over a thousand lives. This Catholic–Socialist quarrel seemed sure to redound to the advantage of the local Nazis, who had the closest links with their fellows in Germany. Indeed, Nazi propaganda and outrages in Austria were increasing, relations between Dollfuss and Berlin were tense. In these circumstances, the French were apprehensive about the future. They had reason to be; within six months Dollfuss was murdered in an uprising fomented by the Nazis.

In a discussion of our Memorandum, Barthou complained that the probationary period for Germany had been eliminated, except for the air, no doubt because Britain was vulnerable from the air, but the French were deprived of their probationary period for land armies. He stated categorically that, in the view of the French Government, it was better to have a convention which really satisfied no one, but which created reciprocal rights and obligations, than to suffer failure. This was exactly my opinion, but we could not get the result without some help from French Ministers. Barthou observed that as regards naval and air armament, equality of rights had been put off for two years and that these were both spheres of special interest to the United Kingdom, whereas in the matter of land armaments, His Majesty's Government had said: '*Que messieurs les Français désarment les premiers!*' He had spoken with frankness and sincerity, he added, but also in friendship.

I told M. Barthou there had been no such discrimination. The naval conference would open next year, probably before any disarmament convention could come into force. The amount of the proposed reduction in land armaments was not serious for France in the early stages. Moreover, M. Barthou had ignored three important, favourable points. First, the proposal for a ten year, instead of a five year, convention. This would give France superiority in war material for a decade. Secondly, the proposal for air armaments, which meant that even if no further agreement were reached, Germany would not attain parity with other great powers until ten years from the coming into force of the convention. Thirdly, the proposal for consultation in the event of any breach of the convention was an advance on anything His Majesty's Government had offered before. I had no authority, I told the French Ministers, to offer more than His Majesty's Government had done in the Memorandum, but speaking unofficially I added that, if there were conditions in the sphere of security or elsewhere, upon which the French Ministers could accept our Memorandum, let them say what these conditions were. The proposals contained in our Memorandum would not make France inferior to Germany, but would secure the superiority of France in armaments for ten years, a superiority which it might be difficult to preserve if there were no convention.

Barthou admitted that the French Government had been preoccupied with internal problems and had not even been able to hold a Cabinet meeting to decide their attitude to disarmament. During luncheon he had asked me to come back via Paris; he now assured me that they would be ready for me when I did so. This suited my plans. Barthou also asked me to try to bring a precise answer from the German Government, and to assure them that the French Government were sincerely desirous of peace.

This discussion showed that the chief French concern was with the German para-military activities and the retention of their own war material. They also wished for some further undertaking in respect of security. On the first two points I had to try to get a contribution from Berlin, on the last we might be able to do something ourselves. My dominant impression at the end of the meeting was of France's unhappy political condition. I doubted whether the Government could last long and feared the lack of confidence in the parliamentary system now being displayed. In this I was probably too gloomy, as foreign observers of France often are. I was nearer the mark in my scepticism as to whether the French Government would in fact be ready for me on my return.

The French Ministers were, I thought, now convinced that I would commit no follies in Berlin. They had spoken to me, I felt sincerely, of their confidence. I considered that I had fair room to manœuvre, so far as Paris was concerned. There would be no uneasiness at anything within reason which I attempted in Berlin. In return, I promised to tell Barthou of every move I made. This I did, but reckoned without London, as the narrative will show. The French newspapers were favourable to my visit. Even those which doubted whether I could obtain concessions in Berlin and Rome showed sympathy with its purpose and were kind to me personally. On my last evening, I dined with Mr. Ronald Campbell, then our Minister in Paris, and his wife, and we went to a witty and brilliantly acted play by Edouard Bourdet appropriately entitled *Les Temps Difficiles*.

* * * * *

The next day was spent in the train, our journey taking us through the Ruhr, which still showed few signs of life, Essen boasting scarcely a smoking chimney. We arrived in a Berlin already regimented under Nazi rule, with von Neurath's glossy top hat at the station almost the only reminder of a less military former age. The next morning, February 20th, Sir Eric Phipps and I called upon the German Foreign Secretary, whom I had known for some years. Herr von Bülow of the German Foreign Office and General von Blomberg, the Chief of Staff, were with him. Baron von Neurath, long trained in diplomacy, was smooth and agreeable to meet. He had a commanding presence, in contrast to which Hitler appeared insignificant, but later experience was to show how little this meant in terms of authority. He understood his business well, but he had little strength of character and was putty in Hitler's hands. I took up with von Neurath the question of European anxieties about German para-military organizations, and told him I hoped that during my visit the German Government would make proposals on this subject designed to allay our fears. Von Neurath was not entirely unresponsive. General von Blomberg was the most helpful of the three and von Bülow the least so. The Germans were critical of the ten year period for the convention laid down in our Memorandum, as being too long. I defended this, because I thought it necessary if we were to create confidence. I knew also that it would help the French Government with their public opinion. After our talk I lunched with von Neurath, and in the afternoon the Ambassador and I called on Hitler for my first meeting with the German Chancellor.

We were received in a vast room of *palais de danse* proportions, which we approached through many passages lined with guards and the trappings of dictatorship. Hitler had just completed his first year as Chancellor. Smaller and slighter than I had expected from his photographs, his appearance was smart, almost dapper, despite his incongruous uniform. He was restrained and friendly. Though talking at some length when once he got going, he was always quite ready to accept questions or interruptions. I was told that he was quieter than usual. Certainly he listened to what I had to say at each meeting, waiting patiently for the translation. There were neither fidgets nor exclamations. As I spoke he fixed me quietly with his pale, glaucous eyes, which protruded slightly, a feature often associated with an over-active thyroid. Hitler impressed me during these discussions as much more than a demagogue. He knew what he was speaking about and, as the long interviews proceeded, showed himself completely master of his subject. He never once had need to refer either to von Neurath or to any official of the Wilhelmstrasse.

The Chancellor said he was convinced that it would be a happy event if peace could be guaranteed for a number of years by a convention. The German Government were confronted by grave economic and internal problems and all their efforts were directed towards their solution. But Germany in her present defenceless state was like a vacuum, pressed upon by neighbours for whom she would be too easy a prey. The precondition of an international guarantee must be the possibility of self-defence, and this was all that Germany had asked for. Hitler did not say which country was likely to attack Germany, but declared that the value of the British Memorandum was destroyed by its proposals for air armaments. Germany was defenceless in the air.

She had no desire for offensive weapons and was prepared to renounce all military aviation if other nations would do the same. Hitler declared that Germany had no interest in aggression. The war had taught his country that it was easier to destroy than to build up, and this formerly militarist people now saw that peace ought to be the permanent state of mankind.

This was earnestly said. I replied that it was not true that Germany would be defenceless for the first two years of the convention. Great Britain had an obligation towards Germany, no less than towards France, under the Treaty of Locarno. The Chancellor was obdurate. The French, he said, would certainly not disarm. All that Germany wanted was defensive weapons. I remembered that Sir Eric Phipps had reported a few days earlier that the Nazi Government had not been more forthcoming with definite proposals, because any system of supervision would immediately have disclosed the air rearmament already undertaken.

I remarked that there were difficulties in the Memorandum for everyone. There were other important points. It would assist us if the Chancellor could state his position about the S.S. and S.A. and Locarno. Hitler declared that the German Government would 'scrupulously and faithfully observe every treaty into which they had entered of their own free will, including Locarno.' The world must not expect to obtain Germany's signature on all occasions, but Germany's signature, once given, would be honoured. No assurance could have been firmer or more specific, if it could be believed.

The argument was also clear enough. Hitler did not regard the Versailles Treaty as binding, because it had been signed under duress, but I thought at the time that Hitler might be genuine in this distinction and that he could intend to observe treaties 'freely' signed by Germany. This possibility remained in my mind until the occupation of the Rhineland destroyed any further confidence I might have had in Hitler's statements.

We discussed the topic of para-military organizations at some length. Here it appeared that our arguments had an effect. Hitler seemed willing to make concessions. He told me that if a convention were concluded, he would give a guarantee for the future, to the effect that the S.S. and S.A. would have no arms, receive no instruction in the use of arms, take no part in manœuvres and undergo no training by officers of the army. The fulfilment of these assurances would be subject to verification by a system of control.

I thought that this offer was important. It made possible a system of international supervision applicable to Germany. We could thus have guarded against a most menacing danger, that Germany might build up a force behind barriers over which we could not look. In later years I have taken the same view about Soviet Russia, and I still regard the establishment of an effective system of international supervision as the most important contribution which can be made to confidence between nations, and therefore to peace. I felt then that in this offer of Hitler's I had something to take on with me. At this early date in his run of power, Hitler had not gone back on any undertaking that he had himself given. Whatever doubts Phipps and I might have about Nazi intentions, it would at least be a test, and might be of more enduring value, if we could get the acceptance of the German Government to a system of international supervision.

I was less successful about Germany's return to the League. Hitler showed no desire to hasten this event and refused to link the question with disarmament. I had not expected much else in view of his recent withdrawal, for which the Nazis had won popular acclaim in Germany. As against this negative, we did make progress on the topic to which Mussolini and the French had rightly attached importance, the retention of heavy armament by the powers who had won the Great War. Hitler offered to agree that France should keep all her weapons during the first five years of a ten year convention. He was prepared to accept our Memorandum as a basis for discussion. This last phrase, I knew, need not mean anything.

On the other hand, there was no denying the potential value of the offers he had made as a counterpart to his demand in the air, the future of the para-military organizations and the agreement on retention by the allies of their heavy weapons. These were two of the most critical points in dispute. Some of Hitler's other proposals were astute rather than convincing. He said that he would not regard it as an unfriendly act if His Majesty's Government were to increase their guarantees of security to France. This was not much of a favour, though it could be useful later. The most disturbing part of the discussion was on air armament, as I told the Chancellor. We then adjourned until the morrow.

News now reached me of a helpful statement by the United States Government about the Memorandum on which my mission was based. This noted that our proposals did not go as far as the Americans would have wished in disarmament, but accepted that they were 'drafted with a view to meeting the effects of the present situation in Europe, and at the same time to achieve a large modicum of real disarmament.' The United States Government made it clear that they were not in any way participants in European problems. While reserving their position on a few technical points, the statement added: 'The American Government is in sympathy with the principles of the British suggestions, and hopes that a successful resumption of talks on disarmament may thereby be brought about.'

The next morning I spent with my advisers and the Ambassador. The Chancellor came to luncheon at 2 p.m. Von Neurath, Hess, the deputy Führer, and Goebbels, Minister of Propaganda, were with him. This was, I believe, the first occasion on which Hitler had been to a meal in a foreign embassy. I can still recall the scene as Cranborne and I stood watching the German leaders file into the Embassy drawing-room. They made an incongruous pattern. 'Athos, Porthos and Aramis,' murmured Cranborne to me, looking at the Chancellor, von Neurath and Goebbels. Hess was quieter and less conspicuous behind his heavy black brows.

Hitler sat next to me at luncheon. He seemed little interested in food or drink. I wrote at the time:

> We talked freely enough with the help of an interpreter and my limited German. Hitler thawed materially, especially when we discussed the war, which he likes to recall like most Germans. We discussed the various sectors we had each been on. I took the chance to rub in that ex-soldiers should be the last ever to wish for another war. He assented heartily. We also spoke of Bavaria, and he begged me to come and stay with him in his cottage on the Austrian frontier. He warmed up as he described its scenery. It is clear that he does not like Berlin, and the rumour that he thinks of moving his capital to Munich may not lack foundation.

This was the first time I heard the name Berchtesgaden. I also had a talk with Goebbels:

> He seemed principally delighted at the visit of so young a Minister and harped on that theme, as also my war experiences. They are my two chief assets here.

Immediately after luncheon Hitler and I had another long conversation at the Embassy. The Chancellor said that since the meeting of the previous day, he had spoken to General von Blomberg and was now in a position to make more detailed proposals on certain points. If the period of the convention was fixed at ten years, he would be prepared to agree to postpone the destruction of French aggressive weapons until after the fifth year of the convention. In respect of aviation, he must maintain his demand for defensive measures. This demand was made without prejudice to any conclusions which might be reached later by the inquiry proposed in the British Memorandum. He was prepared to fix these measures of defence so that France would be free from any menace. The number of Germany's defensive aircraft must be calculated in some proportion to the combined air forces of her neighbours. He emphasized that Russia must never be forgotten, because if Russia were not a menace today, she would be a very formidable menace tomorrow. At that time, tomorrow seemed a long way off. But, Hitler continued, demands which Germany might justly put forward on a military basis, might not be politically feasible. He proposed, therefore, to ask for 30 per cent. of the combined number of military aircraft possessed by Germany's neighbours. In view of the fact that France might see some danger in this demand, he was also prepared to agree that the numbers possessed by Germany should never exceed 50 per cent. of the numbers possessed by France. I asked the Chancellor what he meant by defensive aircraft. Short-range machines, not bombers, he replied.

Hitler gave some explanation of the offer he had made about the S.A. and S.S. He said that control over their character and activities ought to be quite easy, much easier, for example, than verifying whether or not a factory was manufacturing machine-guns. He added that his own common sense and political instinct would never allow him to sanction the creation of a second army in the state. Never, never! The lesson of history was that it was undesirable to allow such an army to come into being. It was still doubtful whether Mussolini had been wise in creating a Fascist militia. It could be useful at present, but after Mussolini had gone, it might turn out that it had been a mistake. All this was said with clarity and every appearance of conviction. This conversation was also the forerunner of the destruction of Röhm, the head of the S.A., on the Night of the Long Knives a few months later, the first indication of Nazi horror, though many did not interpret it so.

We then had a discussion about the future of the Saar. Hitler maintained that he had offered to negotiate an agreement with the French, more favourable to them than the provisions of the treaty, but that the French had rejected it. I asked whether the suggestion was that France and Germany should come to an agreement over the Saar and that this should be submitted to a plebiscite. Hitler said yes, his proposal was designed to clear the atmosphere. If it came to a vote in 1935, the result would be a defeat for France and he wished to avoid this. Both sides would have to make propaganda in preparation for the plebiscite, and this would tend to provoke excitement. I said I understood that the French Government insisted that the people of the Saar should not be deprived of the right to vote. Hitler replied that as no prior agreement had been reached, the Saar question would now have to be settled in the manner laid down by the Treaty of Versailles.

Hitler complained of the weakness of parliamentary governments. They sought to improve their internal position by taking a strong line in foreign policy, he said. I told him I could not admit that this was a feature of all parliamentary government. Hitler acknowledged that in England, of course, the situation was quite different, because there parliamentary government was a natural growth and founded on national tradition.

After some further discussion, in which I told the Chancellor of President Roosevelt's declaration, I tried out the idea of carrying negotiations a stage further, perhaps by a meeting between the Heads of Governments chiefly concerned. This was because of the difficulty I foresaw in negotiating these matters by diplomatic correspondence. Here was an early suggestion for a summit and, for the definite and limited purpose, not outlandish. The Chancellor was reserved on the topic, but we discussed which states might attend. He emphasized that the proposals just put forward were, in themselves, a compromise and did not represent complete equality of rights, but something very much less. He also suggested that it was not necessary for His Majesty's Government to tell the world what he had said, but that they might use his proposals as material for a new compromise. I replied that the five years' postponement of disarmament would be a big consideration on the one side, as also would be the demand that Germany should have aircraft at once, on the other. Governments must be expected to have serious objections to this. Hitler said that the Germans would get only part of their equality of rights. What they proposed represented the largest possible margin of security for France. They were anxious to put an end to the present state of animosity between the two countries. The Chancellor then offered tentatively to reduce the Green Police from 140,000 to 90,000. These were para-military police whose existence had been an important French complaint. Von Neurath seemed somewhat uneasy at this proposal.

I said that I must think over Hitler's suggestions very carefully. It might be considered that the United Kingdom Memorandum had been torn up and a new memorandum substituted. The Germans contested this and referred to the details they had now added on several points. It was evident that the German Foreign Office, at least, had hopes that by these proposals they could separate us, and probably Italy, from France. Von Neurath put this rather crudely, in reply to some comments of mine on how to handle the situation, by saying that the best course might be to go straight home to London from Rome without stopping in Paris. I refused, adding that the French were to give me their detailed view on our Memorandum on my return journey.

There had been large crowds outside the Embassy during the greater part of the day, especially while Hitler was there. As he left they gave him a vociferous greeting. Clearly, this man had a hold upon their imagination far exceeding that of any of his predecessors. For the first time I had a glimpse of what the fanatical devotion of a German crowd could be. Hess and Goebbels had left after luncheon and I had been amused to notice that Goebbels had watched closely from the window to see what kind of reception Hess was given, before venturing out himself to get his acclaim.

★ ★ ★ ★ ★

I talked over the situation with Phipps and my party after Hitler's departure and we were not dissatisfied with the result. It seemed to us that the Chancellor had attempted to meet our points of criticism. I remembered how, in a conversation at the Foreign Office a few weeks before, the French Ambassador had told us that, to his mind, the matter of the huge reservoir of trained men constituted by the S.A. and S.S. detachments was the chief obstacle to agreement and the chief menace for the future. Hitler's offer on this, and the supervision that went with it, could do something to meet French fears, so would an agreement that they should retain their own heavy armament. A consequence was to restore to France, in effect, the two-stage convention for which she had asked. I was glad to get Germany's acceptance of a ten year period for the convention, for this had been one of the objectives much insisted on by my colleagues before I left London. Even though there might be a sinister explanation for this in the long term, over the next five years it could only be welcome to the French. The next five years seemed to me very important.

We had to handle the position now revealed to best advantage. In a telegram to London that night, in which I gave an account of Hitler's proposals, I told the Foreign Secretary that the Ambassador and I considered that with the concessions about the S.S. and S.A., the Chancellor had taken us far into his confidence. Their publication and the offer about the police might make difficulties for him in Germany. I suggested that they should be kept strictly confidential until my return. I also reported a suggestion of Hitler's, to which I had not attached great importance, that the proposals should not be put forward as coming from the German side, but that we should suggest them as points which experience of my tour indicated would be likely to be accepted by the several powers. I did not think that Hitler really expected us to do this, and my view was confirmed when I reached Rome and found that he had informed the Italian Government fully, except on the matter of the Green Police.

The next morning Phipps and I had a final meeting with von Neurath and von Bülow, when we confirmed Hitler's proposals. No hint was given that we should sponsor any of them. After so many diplomatic sessions, I went for refreshment to the Kaiser-Friedrich Museum, which I much enjoyed, in particular the Botticellis and an ethereally beautiful Raphael, and other good things, for example Dürer and Cranach. I revisited the silver and gold Darius fawn which had come to London recently for the Persian Exhibition.

In the afternoon I called, with Phipps, by invitation upon Hindenburg, as President of the Reich. This was a rare compliment, but an eerie experience. Having inspected a guard of honour, I was ushered into the Field-Marshal's presence and received with military courtesy. After a few somewhat perfunctory exchanges about the work I had to do, we were soon plunged into the past. For some reason or other, the Field-Marshal was convinced that I had served in the cavalry. Perhaps the briefing had gone wrong somewhere and he was mistaking me for my eldest brother, John, who had been killed with the 12th Lancers early in the war. He asked me if I had been in the British cavalry charge at Cambrai in 1917, 'one of the finest episodes of the war'. I said that I had not and explained that I had been a Rifleman, Jäger to the Germans. We had cause to know the Jäger regiments, which, on our sector of the front, had, with perfect discipline and tenacity, covered the retreat of the German army as it began to break in the last weeks of war.

My correction brought a brief glance and inclination of the head in understanding. But we were soon back in the battle on which Hindenburg's mind was set. 'You had a great opportunity at Cambrai,' pursued the Field-Marshal, 'it was a brilliant operation in which you took us by surprise.' He went on to explain that for a time the German front was open and he had expected us to exploit our break-through, but we had not done so. He had always wanted to know why. Unhappily, I could not enlighten him, having no other knowledge than that of a junior officer in another sector of the line. As I left, I reflected on the contrast between this renowned military figure, compounded of Prussian squirearchy and soldierly application, with the newly appointed Chancellor, so frenetic where the other was monolithic, so unpredictable where the other followed his rigid code.

This meeting was also an undreamt of experience for me personally, Hindenburg having been such a dominating figure in my early life. Just seventeen when the 1914 war broke out, the next two years saw the destruction of the world as I knew it. My eldest brother was killed in the first autumn and my father died a few months later. My other elder brother was interned in Germany, while my uncle, the commander of a squadron in the Royal Flying Corps, was shot down and captured. News reached me when I was in the trenches at Ploegsteert Wood that my youngest brother, to whom I was closest in age and affection, had been killed at Jutland at the age of sixteen. When a few weeks later I heard, during the battle of the Somme, that my sister's husband had been seriously wounded nearby, it seemed to me that the worst that could happen had happened. Every single male member of the family, with whom I had spent my life before the war, was dead, wounded or captured.

During this period of destruction, the man who had overshadowed the enemy scene was the man I had met that day, Hindenburg, the victor over the Russians, the prototype of Prussian military power in those early years of the war. Yet I felt no hate, as I must have done had he been a Nazi leader later, only curiosity and a mild respect. He had been true to his tenets and had broken no faith.

* * * * *

In Berlin there was not the same obvious tension as in Paris after Stavisky, but I thought the atmosphere depressing. A year of Nazi rule had had its consequences already in the complete absence of any liberty of thought. No criticism whatever of the Government was tolerated.

When I got home I reported on this and gave my colleagues two examples from my own knowledge. Despite my *laisser passer*, my English and French newspapers had been closely examined by the customs when entering Germany. The officials had lifted up the seats of the carriage to see if there were any more tucked away. My newspapers were very reluctantly left with me, but I was sure that, had I not held an official position, they would have been confiscated. There had also been the instance known to the Embassy of a man who, when having his hair cut, had remarked that according to British newspapers the Welfare Fund was a swindle; he was overheard and sentenced to two and a half years' imprisonment. There seems nothing extravagant in these tales now, when dictatorships are multiplying in so many continents, but in the greater freedom of the early 1930s, they had an ominous ring.

I was also impressed by the amount of talk about the last war, at least at the dinners and luncheons I attended. Everybody liked to exchange recollections upon it, which does not now seem so surprising as the Nazis were young men who had served actively in the war, unlike most senior Ministers at home. As I watched the changing of the guard from my hotel window, I saw the whole population marching in step with the bands. That could be harmless enough and mean no more than the love of Germans for playing at soldiers, or it could be part of something more significant.

At these meetings Hitler had not made the grim impression upon me which I recorded a year later. Perhaps this was because he was cautious and on his guard in his first interview with a Minister of a leading foreign power. Or it may have been in part due to the deep distrust I had for the older school of the German ruling class, of which von Bülow and von Papen were examples. This type was rigid, embittered by defeat, hating the French, and quite likely ourselves as well. I was not yet so sure about the National Socialists. Even then I thought them dangerous so far as Austria was concerned, because of their racial theories, but they had not at that time and for that very reason, any evident ambitions against France. The new men could need time to carry through their internal policy, and had anxieties about their country's economic position. But I was not confident that this would help us. Rearmament and military ambition might be the means to combat unemployment. The Embassy held the opinion in these early days that the Nazi doctrine was not chauvinist; there was much suspicion on my part, but as yet no certainty.

The descriptions I gave of some of those whom I met for the first time in Berlin were not far wide of the mark. Goebbels, I told my colleagues, was clever and unscrupulous and without principle. At my later meeting with him in the following year I had no cause to modify this verdict, only to underline it. Röhm, then very much a leading personality, was a more flamboyant figure, scarred and scented, with a jewelled dagger at his waist. We met for the first time at von Neurath's luncheon. Afterwards we had some talk, when he told me of his fighting experiences the world over, the last instalments of which had been, if I recall correctly, in Bolivia. But he was not just a perverted swashbuckler, he had intelligence of a kind and, a rarity in the modern world, he was a man who boasted of his bravery, yet was brave. But he was hardly of the modern world; a *condottiere* of the Middle Ages might have looked and behaved like that.

* * * * *

In concluding a letter to the Prime Minister on the night of February 22nd, I wrote:

> Our view here is that the Chancellor's proposals were much better than we expected. Phipps is frankly delighted, though of course the air aspect raises a formidable difficulty. But should not we be much better off with such a Convention than with none at all? Maybe that is the true alternative.
>
> We are off to Rome early tomorrow. These three days have been very interesting but extremely tiring and we begin to look for the train as a haven of refuge.

I might have added that it would be a gain to end the existing impossible treaty position and to fix definitely a limit for German armaments. Although Hitler would no doubt have broken these agreements, as he later broke others, we need not have been any the worse off on that account and world opinion might have been much the better off. The reason for this was that the agreements, as they emerged from my talks with Hitler, did not call for any concessions from France, Italy and ourselves, while the armament which they allowed Germany was to be limited, regulated and observed. Even after the Nazis had begun to rule in Germany, an arms agreement which they had voluntarily accepted could have been a document worth negotiating, and its later violation by Hitler would have flashed a clearer warning than breaches of unequal restrictions imposed by the victors.

Before leaving Berlin, I saw André François-Poncet, the French Ambassador, already renowned for his wit and perspicacity, and wrote to Tyrrell, giving each some background to the official telegrams. I added to Tyrrell:

I hope that the French Government will not become too suspicious of me. François-Poncet should be able to reassure them.

V

MUSSOLINI, THE FIRST MEETING

February 1934

London's reaction to my Berlin visit – An audience with the Pope – My first meeting with Signor Mussolini – 'All now depends on France' – A further talk with M. Doumergue and M. Barthou – French difficulties – I receive no answer – Our failure to restrict Herr Hitler

On February 24th I arrived in Rome and found telegrams awaiting me from the Foreign Office. Their contents surprised me. One of them, addressed to Phipps, began: 'Your telegram puts us in a position of great embarrassment.' This referred to the message Phipps and I had sent from Berlin, reporting Hitler's proposals and suggesting that some of them should remain confidential or even be brought forward in Britain's name, and asking for comments, for which there was ample time. In any event, this tactical aspect of the business had little significance in comparison with the substance of the Chancellor's suggestions. When I returned to London, I found that Ashley Clarke, who had worked with Cadogan at Geneva and was fully conversant with the whole disarmament question, had minuted in agreement with the judgement we had formed in Berlin. The telegram to Phipps, therefore, was not the result of official advice at the level where first-hand knowledge could have been obtained.

Phipps dealt firmly with this London reaction, which also seemed misplaced to Sir Eric Drummond, our Ambassador in Rome, as well as to ourselves. He replied direct from Berlin, without consulting me:

> Proposals which the Chancellor suggested our putting forward as a compromise by His Majesty's Government after Mr. Eden's tour only referred to those contained in paragraphs 4 and 5 of my telegram, viz., to conditions proving non-military character of S.A. and S.S., and to a reduction of German police force. Reason for this is clear, for it would naturally place the Chancellor in an awkward position himself to suggest such conditions by Germany.

Phipps added that he had consulted von Neurath, who now said he had no objection to all the proposals, S.A. and S.S., police force reduction and aviation, being communicated confidentially by me to the two Governments as German proposals.

He followed this up with a further message the next day:

Baron von Neurath told me late last night that he had informed Italian Ambassador of *all* the proposals of Chancellor to Mr. Eden. He still hopes, however, that the offer of reduction of Green Police by 50,000 will not be made public. He fears Quai d'Orsay leakage.

I have, therefore, this morning given similar information to French Ambassador, who quite understands internal reasons which make it desirable that Chancellor's offer regarding police should not be published as coming from Herr Hitler himself.

M. François-Poncet realizes so well the habit of leakage in the Quai d'Orsay, that he will only tell his Government that Chancellor indicated to Mr. Eden the possibility of a certain reduction in police forces.

French Ambassador agrees with me in desiring a convention; otherwise hundreds of German military aeroplanes will shortly be flying about openly. We shall then be publicly flouted and receive no compensation in return in the form of control or other counter-concessions offered by Herr Hitler.

This coincided with a message sent by me from Rome to London:

I regret that my report of Herr Hitler's proposals contained in Sir Eric Phipps's telegram should have put you in a position of great embarrassment. I have at no time suggested that his proposals should now be sponsored by ourselves, still less, of course, did I give Herr Hitler any encouragement to think that we could accept them. I was instructed to make inquiries as to the attitude of German Government to our memorandum; Herr Hitler's proposals are their reply.

These proposals are, however, as I feel sure you will appreciate, in two respects more favourable to France than our own memorandum, namely, in respect of the S.A. and S.S., where Herr Hitler offers important assurances and in respect of France's own disarmament, which, while it is completed in ten years, does not in Herr Hitler's proposals begin to take place until after five years. Offer in respect of Green Police may also prove important.

I added that I would communicate Hitler's proposals confidentially to Mussolini, when I saw him, and try to get his view on them as well as on the British Memorandum. I would do the same in Paris, concluding that:

. . . His Majesty's Government in the United Kingdom have not and will not be committed in any way in these conversations. I fully recognize that my task is one of inquiry.

It must be remembered that I was not at this time a member of the Cabinet, nor even a Privy Councillor, so that my authority was slender enough without being undermined, if I were to do my job in the various capitals. These exchanges would have had no importance, except that they showed a lack of confidence in my handling of the tour. If London regarded my efforts in such a temper and this were to seep out, the French would be discouraged from paying any attention to me, or, what mattered more, to the proposals I brought.

The next day, February 25th, my apprehensions were justified by an article published in the *Observer* which, as I said in the draft of a letter to Baldwin, had all the appearance of being inspired. It was headed: 'Berlin Disappoints Mr. Eden: No Possible Basis of Agreement' and described the 'deplorable' impression made in London by the results of my visit, professing to represent the views of 'governmental quarters'. Another note, while reserving judgement on the outcome of my tour, contained the phrase: 'He is not competent either to negotiate or to prepare for negotiation.' If the purpose of the article was, as I supposed, to allay imaginary fears in Paris, it was superfluous, for I had been at pains to keep in touch with the French through François-Poncet and their Ambassador in Rome, and by letters and telegrams to Tyrrell. The Quai d'Orsay was not dismayed by my activities, even if Whitehall was. My postscript to one of these letters to Tyrrell read: 'I like François-Poncet very much, and if Paris will but take his advice I feel sure that France will have every reason to be grateful hereafter.' This was, I think, a just comment. Unhappily his advice was not taken.

What made the indignation expressed in the London telegrams hard to excuse was that 'governmental quarters' were completely without any alternative policy and were unable to face up to the grim reality if no agreement were reached, as events were soon to show. Before I left London, the Prime Minister had told my colleagues that he hoped I would not be sent away with specific instructions, or in the frame of mind as though I had been given such instructions. He felt that I must be given wide discretion to use my own judgement in accordance with the situation as it might develop. This hardly fitted in with the present rebuke.

On the morning of Monday, February 26th, I dressed in evening clothes for an audience with Pope Pius XI. Sir Robert Clive, our Minister to the Vatican, came to fetch me. Though I was to have other audiences in later years, this first experience made a lasting impression. We approached through room after room, each occupied by its posse of guards in beautiful and variegated uniforms, all presenting arms with a modest skill which made the ceremony more picturesque than military. I had half an hour's talk with the Pope in his own room. His Holiness was sympathetic and encouraging. At the time I attached chief importance to that part of his conversation in which he spoke of Germany. He felt it impossible to believe that even if Germany meant war, she would be in a position to wage it for ten or fifteen years, at least. My own estimate, which I put in writing on several occasions about this time, was five years at least. The Pope was gracious enough to dub me *Apôtre de la Paix*.

After the audience, I had a conversation with the Secretary of State, Cardinal Pacelli, the future Pope Pius XII. I remember this for the lucid analysis to which I listened of Europe's problems and perils. Afterwards I found time for a hasty visit to look once again at the Raphael stanzas, the Borgia rooms and the Sistine chapel. The American Ambassador lunched with us. In the afternoon came a good telegram from London after a Cabinet Committee meeting, 'in sharp contrast to the message I found here', as I wrote at the time. But the discouragement had already been given to Paris. I was not surprised when *Le Temps* reproduced some parts of the *Observer*'s peccant article, together with a report from its special correspondent in London, saying that British Ministers, who had counted on the relative success of my mission, now realized their mistake.

* * * * *

At 5 p.m. Drummond, Strang and I left for the Palazzo Venezia. This was my first meeting with Mussolini, who had Suvich and Aloisi with him. He was lively, friendly, vigorous and entertaining. He showed a journalist's inquisitiveness for news. The National Government at home had recently done badly in a by-election; he knew the figures and asked the cause of our failure. Our immediate business completed, his main interest was in Hitler, whom he had never met. He plied me with questions. What was he like? How did he look, talk and act? What were my impressions? I did my best. When I remarked that, while the Nazi leaders insisted they were pacific, they seemed to take pride in talking about their war experiences, he laughed and said: 'Yes, like all Germans.'

A few months later Hitler and Mussolini were to meet in Venice for their first conversations. These, so Suvich told Drummond, lasted four hours, with Mussolini for the most part a patient listener. Hitler was much moved at his reception and tears were continually in his eyes. Mussolini noticed this and remarked to Suvich: 'That is his weakness.' I felt then and later that Mussolini envied Hitler, not the man or his characteristics, but his power over the German people, more malleable, more ready to follow anywhere he led, even to war, than the less predictable Italians. For all their enthusiasm and individual courage, Italians take less kindly to the regimented theme than the disciplined and earnest-minded Germans.

My discussion with Mussolini was crisp and easy. He said that the attitude of the French was most important, because upon this depended the whole question whether or not there was to be a convention. In his view, the convention ought to provide for a limitation of German rearmament, such rearmament to consist of defensive weapons only. If the French were willing to recede somewhat from the attitude they had adopted in the past and agree to disarm during the second five years, no one would be better pleased than himself. In reply to an observation of mine asking for his help in Berlin, Mussolini said that he, too, attached great importance to Germany's return to the League and would do all he could to bring this about, though he doubted whether it should form part of the convention. He thought that if the convention were not drafted in too great detail, Germany might be persuaded to sign. Such signature must, of course, take place at Geneva.

Drummond observed that the postponement of any French disarmament for five years ought certainly to be a matter of great importance to the French Government. Mussolini agreed and said that their whole point was that they should not be asked to disarm immediately. He observed that, of course, the Germans had already rearmed and that no one could prevent them. There was only one way to stop German rearmament and that was war. We then discussed the German air proposals, when I commented on the difficulty of determining how these percentages would work out. Mussolini replied that he had received a memorandum from the German Ambassador. After examining this together and after telephoning in my presence to find out the latest figures for the French air force, Mussolini estimated that the percentages would work out at about 700 aeroplanes for Germany, for he thought the German claim would only take into account the French aeroplanes actually in commission. In this he proved to be right, for the time being.

Mussolini asked me what I had learned in Paris of the French position. He then told me of a recent statement made to him by the French Ambassador that, if the French Government could obtain satisfactory answers on three points, they might after all be able to make some move towards a convention. They wished first to be satisfied about the S.A. and S.S., and Signor Mussolini thought that Hitler's five-point assurances to me ought to meet them. Secondly, they wished to be sure of the Italian attitude towards the control of armaments, as on this point the Italian memorandum had not been clear. Mussolini had told the Ambassador that Italy would accept a system of control. Thirdly, the French wished to be satisfied about the Italian attitude towards the Locarno Treaty. On this Mussolini said he had given the necessary assurances.

We discussed how to handle matters in the immediate future, Mussolini favouring an informal meeting of delegates from the Western powers. I reminded him of the French objections to any four-power meeting and asked him whether I could report to my colleagues that if the United Kingdom Memorandum could be accepted as it stood, the Italian Government would agree, but they had no hope of such an outcome. Failing this, the modifications proposed by Hitler might offer a basis for agreement. If nothing else would serve, it would be best to fall back upon the Italian plan, which was much better than failure. Mussolini replied: 'Yes.' Pressing my point, I emphasized that Hitler's proposals on aviation would, of course, create very great difficulties. Mussolini said that it should be remembered that Germany had four frontiers to defend.

The course of our discussions had proved so satisfactory that I decided to raise with Mussolini the date of my departure from Rome. It seemed to me that the sooner I could get on with my journey, the better my chances in Paris, and I said that, if he had no objection, I would like to leave the next day instead of Wednesday, as previously intended. Mussolini said he understood my reasons perfectly and agreed with my decision. This curtailed visit, which resulted from my initiative, was used later as evidence that, even at our first interview, Mussolini and I had been at odds. There is no truth in the legend. As Aloisi wrote in his diary*:

> Hitler has given way on a number of important points. Now all depends on France. Mussolini is completely in agreement with Eden. . . .

In a final comment, Mussolini added that the French were obtaining a system of control of armaments, the assurances about the S.A. and S.S., and a postponement of French disarmament. Their Ambassador

* op. cit.

had given him the impression that these things went far to meet French fears. Suvich was less optimistic, thinking that the French objected not only to French disarmament, but equally to German rearmament, if this were to begin at once. Mussolini, throughout the conversation, kept repeating how important he thought it was that a settlement should be reached on armaments at the earliest possible moment, otherwise the German demands were certain to increase, a development for which he evidently felt no enthusiasm. I agreed strongly with this judgement and began to search in my mind for some possible further contribution on our part, which might hasten decision. Mussolini by no means despaired of Hitler's last offer making some impression on the French and I so telegraphed to London. But I was not at all confident that he was right. At this moment Mussolini could have been sincere in wishing for an arms agreement which would have reduced tension in Europe, an event which he might have calculated was more likely to help than to hinder the Abyssinian venture, for which we now know he had already laid his plans. He had no reason to want trouble on several fronts.

In an interval during this visit I was taken to the Fascist Museum. I did not find the place congenial and I did not want to be uncivil to my hosts, so that I was glad when the embarrassing ordeal was over. All the same, Fascism as practised in Italy at this time was less dragooning and pervasive than Nazi rule in Germany.

* * * * *

Back in Paris, I met M. Doumergue and M. Barthou on the morning of March 1st. Our discussion was sadly disappointing. It was soon clear that owing to their many domestic preoccupations, the French Government were in no better position to state their view of our Memorandum than when I had passed through Paris twelve days before. The Cabinet had not even considered it. As a result, after I had given them an account of my journey and of what I had learnt during it, they thanked me for what I had done and for the assurances I had gained, but said they were not able to give me any positive answer to work upon.

M. Doumergue explained that, although it was quite true that Germany had declared herself willing to issue rules to govern the activities of her para-military organizations, these rules would merely change the appearance of these formations and would do nothing to limit their numbers. He did not see how the execution of these rules was to be supervised once they were applied. If it were to be proved that they had not been duly fulfilled, there would have to be sanctions. This was essential. There was no provision for anything of this kind in the German proposals. They could not therefore be said to satisfy French preoccupations. He went on to point out that the German attitude towards the League was not very encouraging. It was true that in aviation Germany did not ask for bombing planes until after the air inquiry, but the Germans had a strong civil aviation and their civil planes could easily be transformed into bombers. He thought Hitler's suggestion, that French disarmament should be postponed, lost a great deal of its value once the principle of German rearmament was admitted. The point upon which he must again insist was the one of sanctions. This was the question which stood before all others. Here was an argument which had not been mentioned on my outward journey.

When I inquired what the French Government expected in this connection, M. Barthou remarked that he was not able to give a full reply on behalf of the French Government about sanctions and guarantees. Owing to pressure of work, there had been no opportunity for a meeting of Ministers. The truth seemed to me to be that the Government were still reeling under the impact of the Stavisky scandals and depended upon Doumergue's reputation for their survival. Barthou produced and read extracts from a recent consular report from Germany showing that the S.A. were being increased, and giving an account of the training of the S.A. and S.S. He referred to a joint meeting of several committees of the Senate, which had unanimously resolved that France should return to the Paul-Boncour plan of security of November 1932. This meeting appeared to hold the opinion that unless that plan were accepted, it would not be possible for France to agree to any rearmament of Germany. M. Barthou argued that what he was saying did not amount to a blank refusal of the proposals I had brought, but he felt bound to give a clear statement of a very grave situation. He still wanted, however, the present conversations on disarmament to continue.

I replied that the British Government cared as much as the French did about the return of Germany to the League. I had asked Mussolini to help in this and he had said that he would. The French Ministers could see that Hitler's proposals did at least allow France five years before asking for any disarmament. During these years there would be supervision over the S.A. and S.S. and, generally, over the execution of the obligations of the Convention, which I thought important. If the present situation were what M. Barthou's report showed it to be, there was surely all the more need for a convention embodying such rules and a system of supervision. The abuses to which M. Barthou had referred showed how much they were needed. They were arguments not against, but for, a convention. I made this reply although I understood Barthou's suspicions of German intentions and largely shared them. But we had now reached the point where at no cost to themselves in equipment, not even one gun, the French could get a convention which would tie Germany to definite figures limiting her armaments in a fashion which would give France a superiority she was otherwise unlikely to have. This was the kind of convention Barthou had told me, on my way to Berlin, he thought better than none. So did I.

I therefore spoke to Barthou of my dilemma. My mission had been to get the views of the three Governments on our Memorandum. I knew the German view and the Italian view, but not the French. What was I to report? I wanted to find out if the French Government agreed to the Memorandum as a basis for the Convention, subject to the acceptance by His Majesty's Government of the guarantees of execution set forth in a letter to Mr. Henderson, to which M. Barthou had referred; or if the French Government stood by the resolution of the four Senatorial Committees, which seemed to exclude any rearmament of Germany. I would like, I continued, to be able to report as fully upon the French view as upon the German and Italian. This question was all the more pressing, because I had come to Paris a second time to learn the views of the French Government. I was prepared to stay a day or two longer, if such a statement could be forthcoming, despite the admitted difficulties of the French Government. It would be a pity to have to return with information so incomplete.

M. Doumergue looked embarrassed and perplexed. He said that I could inform His Majesty's Government that the French Government were anxious to pursue conversations. He drew attention to France's falling numbers in manpower during the lean years. With this in mind, the French Government did not think that the proposals for consultation gave adequate protection. Later, M. Doumergue repeated that in our Memorandum the question of Germany's return to the League was not sufficiently accentuated, and that the sanctions provided were more theoretical than real. I said that it would not be enough for me merely to return to London and report that the French Government thought that the sanctions provided in the Memorandum were inadequate. Such a declaration could not be said to advance matters.

Barthou replied that the two points mentioned were not of crucial importance. The essential point was whether the French Government accepted German rearmament. This was a question of security and national psychology. It was a very grave one, upon which only the Government as a whole could reach a decision, in the light of the advice of the Committee of National Defence. When the Committee had reported and the Government had deliberated upon the report, he would be able to give me a reply, but not before. He begged me to give them a few days or even a few weeks. The results I had brought from Berlin and Rome were in no sense negative. After some more remarks by Barthou in this strain, Doumergue said that the right course would be to continue the conversations, taking due account of the naked facts of the situation. Slow and sure was the motto. I said that it seemed to me, on the contrary, that the longer the solution was delayed, the more difficult it would become.

* * * * *

The conversations I held on this journey brought home to me a condition of affairs on which I have often had occasion to reflect since. In Berlin and Rome, the men I met were completely in command of their subject, familiar with its every detail and ready to take decisions. In France, as often in other democracies, the Ministers were overcharged with parliamentary business. On this occasion they were also elderly, had no particular knowledge or training in the subjects they discussed and no sufficient command of them; they would also have had the gravest political difficulty in giving effect to any decision they might have reached. In these days of France's internal crises, the order of priorities was all wrong for the interests of France. The Government had to concentrate on keeping alive, which meant maintaining a parliamentary majority. Leaders of parties and Deputies had to be seen, explanations, official and unofficial, to be given about the Stavisky scandals. By one contrivance or another, enough Deputies had to be got into the Government lobby to ensure survival. While all this was going on, Ministers had no time to consider, much less to take decisions on, issues upon which France's life might depend. They had instead to prevaricate and to pretend, and their visitor, if only out of politeness, had to conform by not observing the bare evidence that his hosts had not done their homework.

This contrast was not exceptional in my experience of international encounters. Through their failure to take decisions at this juncture in their fortunes and in the first year of Hitler's power, the allies lost an opportunity to circumscribe Hitler by an agreement which would have deprived his later actions of some specious pretext, and reinforced allied authority and justification in resisting them. An opening was missed. I do not put it higher than that. But it remains true today that if the Western democracies are to make headway against communist and other like-minded dictatorships, they must find men who have the capacity, courage and experience, and give them the time to know their subjects as the dictators know them. They must also have the organization at their command to enable them to prepare their policies in advance and together. Then they may determine events, instead of confusedly pursuing them.

VI

TENSION AND THE SAAR

March 1934 – January 1935

I report to London on my tour – French and British views on the Disarmament Convention – Rejection by France – Herr von Ribbentrop expounds the German position – American policy on intervention in Europe – M. Barthou's speech at the Disarmament Conference – The British attitude to Germany in the 'thirties – My misgivings on British armaments – Franco-Soviet rapprochement *– Russia joins the League – Mistakes in military reckoning – The Saar and German claims – Arrangements for the plebiscite – M. Barthou succeeded by M. Laval – Dangerous situation develops in the Saar – Mr. Baldwin supports the British action – My difficulties – The lesson of the plebiscite*

When I returned to England on March 1st I found the Government hesitant to take decisions and the outlook murky. No course was apparent which would advance agreement on our Convention, only a virtual certainty that if decisions were not taken soon, any opportunity glimpsed on my tour would be gone. In London there was another pointer to what our Embassy in Berlin was thinking. The Military Attaché had come home suddenly, having been asked by the Ambassador to see the Secretary of State for War, Lord Hailsham, about the messages he and I had sent from Berlin, and to report his impressions. Sir Eric Phipps had taken strongly the view that Herr Hitler's offer was the most we could possibly get from him and that, if maintained, it would represent a concession. The French Ambassador in Berlin, M. François-Poncet, thought much the same, although it was difficult for him, Sir Eric reported, to put any pressure on his own Government. Lord Hailsham rightly informed his colleagues of these opinions. A fortnight later I received a message from Phipps, which confirmed his judgement that Hitler's proposals offered a favourable opportunity for arriving at a convention. He feared, however, that the French would let the chance slip.

I had hoped that if the discussions on my journey went well enough, we might be able to follow them up with a meeting of several powers, but now the reluctance of the French Government to return an answer closed that opportunity for the present. I could see no further opening, except that we should find out more clearly from the French what security proposals they wanted and try to help them to take a decision on our Memorandum. I had suggested to my colleagues before I left on my tour that I should ask the French a question on these lines, but the Foreign Secretary had been against it. He said that care would be needed if any question of this kind were put to the French, in order that it should be quite clear that we did not propose to go any further. I was now sure that we had to do better than that.

My colleagues asked for my impressions of Paris on these two visits. I told them that it was impossible not to be oppressed by the feeling of gloom and tension which persisted. *Coriolanus* was being acted at the Comédie Française, but it had to be taken off because of its effect on the public. I had asked Marshal Pétain whether he thought that the worst of the internal difficulties were over. He replied no, they were only beginning. Public opinion seemed to have been strongly against the shooting by the Gardes Mobiles which had taken place in Paris a month before in connection with the Stavisky affair, though it was probable that failing such action, the crowd would have burnt the Chamber and attempted to drown the deputies. It was consequently hardly surprising that Ministers were reluctant to take any step which even verged on the unpopular.

In comparing the three countries, I told my colleagues that if France was a country which might be going to have a revolution, and Germany was a country in the throes of one, then Italy, which had just got through her revolution, was in the firmest position. Italy was trying to build on an existing monarchical foundation while Germany was erecting an entirely new social structure; this, I said, was one of the differences between Italian Fascism and German Nazism. Though this distinction might seem slender, it had its influence on later events during the war in Italy, when the king played a part in getting rid of Mussolini.

My colleagues wanted to know my opinion of the probable tenor of the French answer. I told them that it might take one of two forms, either that of a manifesto setting out plainly what they could not accept in our document, or, alternatively, an acceptance of our document in principle, provided that we would agree to give more security. If M. Daladier had been in office, I thought the second course would have been more likely, with the present Government, the first was quite probable. This forecast proved correct. In answer to a further question, I told them that I had spoken to our Military Attaché in Berlin, who thought that Herr Hitler's regulations would bring the S.S. and S.A. back to their original political complexion. In his opinion the proposals were definitely worth having. I spoke to my colleagues of the importance of trying to stir up the French to reply. When I was in Berlin, I said, von Neurath had told me he was proposing to reply to the last French note to Germany, which was couched in rather stiff terms. I had asked him to hold up this action until after my return and he had undertaken to do so. If there was much further delay, there was no doubt that Germany would weigh in with an answer and the position would get worse.

I also asked my colleagues to consider whether, if we did press the French to reply, we should express any opinion on Hitler's amendments to our Memorandum. I had had no authority to do so on my tour. Now, perhaps we could tell the French that, in our opinion, it would be better to have a convention with the German modifications than to have none at all. France, I said, might be attracted by the proposal that she would not disarm for five years. I also thought that we ought to re-examine our position on security to try to help the French. There was, however, little response to my suggestions and our moves, when they came, were tentative and slow. It would not be just to ascribe this reluctance merely to British dislike of definite commitments for an uncertain future. There was much genuine anxiety about what was to happen in France, even among experienced Ministers whose sentiments were friendly to that country. Some expected, and all recognized that there might be, dangerous consequences from the internal dissensions which were racking the French nation.

On March 14th I gave the House of Commons an account of my journey, muted by the failure to get an answer from France. Members in all parties were, however, generous and accepted my impressions as the most I could tell. It was symptomatic of the Opposition mood of the time that a Socialist spokesman, Mr. Morgan Jones, should have suggested that our recent and small increases in the Service Estimates had handicapped me in my work. As these were a negligible percentage of what Germany was doing, and Italy and France had either done or would like to have done, I had no difficulty in replying that they had not the least effect on the work I was trying to do, nor were they likely to have, in view of their extremely modest proportions.

I took the opportunity of this debate to speak of our relations with the United States and to thank the American Government for the support they had given to our Draft Convention. This was deliberate, for I wanted to draw the United States back into the main current of European politics, from which she had been withdrawn in 1919 by the Senate's refusal to enter the League of Nations or to ratify President Wilson's guarantee of French frontiers. All through the 1930s I took every opportunity to work closely with the Americans, even attending a conference in Brussels in 1937, to which they attached importance, though I saw little hope from it, because I was convinced that the presence of the United States deliberating in Europe would steady the climate of opinion there and induce caution among the most hotheaded. As for our own position, I reminded the House that the days had long passed when Britain could choose whether to involve herself in Europe or not. If no agreement were reached, our country would have to rearm more speedily than any other, because it had already disarmed so much.

I prepared some notes for Simon. The most effective contribution we could make, I believed, was to help the French by more definite offers on security. I was sure that a tug of war was going on in Paris as to what the French answer should be, and a definite proposal on security might give a prizing foothold to those who were tugging our way. I then summarized what I thought our line of policy for Geneva ought to be:

(i) We stand by Convention as amended by our Memorandum.
(ii) We are prepared to accept Hitler's amendments, or something like them, on condition Germany returns to League.
(iii) If France can accept above we are prepared to help her by accepting guarantees of execution or something analogous.

When, however, the Foreign Secretary, after more than an hour of rambling discussion, at length put these proposals to his colleagues, they were not well received. I wrote at the time that some regarded them as a manœuvre and considered the Conference as already a failure. The majority condemned them and argued, as usual, for a policy of negation. They did not want more commitments, which my third suggestion entailed. I wrote that I was 'somewhat irritated by their attitude and I fear cheeky in consequence.... The timidity is almost terrible.' As I see it now, waiting for the French answer proved too comfortable a rocking-chair for us.

These discussions among colleagues were seldom satisfactory, our committee being mainly composed of senior Ministers with many other duties, who were apt to come and go. The outcome, however, was clear enough. I had to leave for Geneva without anything new in policy to offer on our part. I regretted this all the more when Phipps reported François-Poncet's opinion that Barthou was slowly coming to realize the necessity for a convention. 'Presumably', Phipps added, 'M. Barthou is at last becoming impressed by the advice consistently given by M. François-Poncet and by his conversations in Brussels.' The Belgians had spoken in favour of a convention. François-Poncet's opinion has been clearly expressed in his own writing*:

> A limited and controlled rearmament was of more value than an unlimited, uncontrolled and unrestrained rearmament by Germany, which would result in its turn in a general rearmament and a new arms race, which was precisely what the Geneva Conference was intended to prevent. Even a mediocre convention was preferable to the absence of any convention and of any sanction. To avoid the worst, did not common sense dictate that we should accept the lesser evil?

On April 8th, the last day I spent in London before leaving for Geneva, Norman Davis came to luncheon. His chief concern was for the naval conference. He was clearly anxious to line us up with the United States against Japan, and to do this soon. I wished that he could have been as definite about Europe. My diary records:

> P.M. proposed himself to dinner at 7 p.m. He arrived first and we wandered round my pictures. John Simon joined us later. P.M. showed himself much concerned at European situation. 'The next week may decide the future, for peace or war.' He seemed inclined to thrust responsibility upon Bureau [of Conference], but I doubt advisability of this. I do think, though, that we should not adjourn indefinitely until General Commission meets. J.S. helped by drafting some sentences for my speech. By no means a useless evening. It was clear that P.M. was making up his mind to a further attempt to find security and as a result agreement, as alternative to rule by service departments 'which I will never endure'. He hinted strongly that this would be end of National Government as far as he was concerned. Preaching to the converted to-night.

*André François-Poncet: *Souvenirs d'une Ambassade à Berlin*; Flammarion, 1946.

But the follow-up lagged. As a result, there was nothing I could do at Geneva but repeat the old themes, though in London, Simon did go so far as to make careful inquiries of the French Ambassador, to find out exactly what was meant by guarantees of execution.

* * * * *

Despite the announcement of a sharply swollen German defence budget, the tug of war in Paris continued, and Massigli told me at Geneva that the French were still in doubt about the value of a convention. Our Embassy in Paris confirmed this. On April 17th the final decision came and it brought to an end negotiations which had now been in progress for five months. Special complaint was made that Germany 'without waiting for the results of the negotiations which were in progress, has wished to impose its determination to continue every form of rearmament, within limits of which it claims to be the sole judge.' Our Embassy reported that this decision had been for long in the balance. Barthou's words in handing the reply to Campbell also showed that he had been in the minority and had been unable to get his way with his colleagues. Later information confirmed that Doumergue had been over-persuaded by André Tardieu and Herriot, while Barthou had not felt able to force a ministerial crisis in a period of continuing internal tension. A firm British offer of guarantees of execution might have tipped the scale, I thought, but we did not make it.

The German attitude stiffened, following the French rejection of further negotiations. At this time Herr von Ribbentrop had been appointed Special Commissioner for disarmament negotiations. I knew little about him in those days. He had been present at my first discussions with Hitler, but had taken no part. Nor had he attended my interviews with von Neurath, who had no friendly feelings towards him. In later years our contacts were frequent and unsuccessful. Ribbentrop was essentially a salesman and his ideas of statesmanship and diplomacy began and ended there. His task was to sell Hitler's Germany, but above all Hitler. I never had cause to doubt the sincerity of his conviction or that his methods would be completely ruthless. His tragic weakness, for himself and for his country, was that he could not understand. He had not the intellectual equipment to enable him to learn of other countries, even if he had possessed the character to use the knowledge, once gained. He was without imagination and it was his instinct to run in blinkers. So that the one man who might have undeceived Hitler, toadied him.

On April 28th, Ribbentrop told Sir Eric Phipps that the only way out of the deadlock was for Great Britain to persuade France to change her mind, for it was quite impossible for Germany to reduce her demands in any way. If they were not accepted, he said, Germany would feel free of all limitations. He thought that British public opinion would support this attitude and quoted a leading article in *The Times* of the day before in justification.

When Ribbentrop visited London, Simon and I showed no sympathy with his views. On May 10th we had an interview with him. The Foreign Secretary, having to attend another engagement, asked me to continue the conversation. Left alone with Ribbentrop, I criticized Germany's ambiguous attitude towards her return to the League. He replied evasively that personally he had no doubt that Germany would return. Ribbentrop then changed the subject, saying that he would tell me frankly the Chancellor's mind on foreign affairs, which he thought that he knew very well, since they had often talked these over together. He claimed that he had been the Chancellor's personal guide in knowledge of England and France, of which countries the Chancellor had no first-hand experience. Ribbentrop said that Hitler could see no reason for political differences with England, that he wanted England's friendship, that he had no intention of attacking France, and that he wished for a peaceful settlement even in the more difficult question of Poland's frontier. I replied that none of this altered the fact that opinion in Great Britain had become uneasy about German intentions. The last budget figures had made a bad impression, so had Germany's failure to make any declaration about a return to Geneva. I remarked that Herr von Ribbentrop had mentioned the need for European confidence. I fully agreed, and Germany, more than any other nation, could contribute to this confidence. The interview ended coldly, for Ribbentrop, having repeated what he had come to say, was impervious to the views of others.

* * * * *

In mid-May I went out to Geneva for the quarterly meeting of the Council of the League. The Chaco War between Bolivia and Paraguay was on our agenda. This bloody conflict had now been waged with intermittent violence for over a year. The recent publication of a report by the League Conciliation Commission focused attention on a proposal that members of the League should forbid private traffic in arms with the belligerents. The report made it clear that the war could only continue with the help of imports of arms by both Bolivia and Paraguay. During the Council meeting I learned that it was intended to postpone the whole business until the end of the month. I declined to agree to this and asked for the dispute to be placed on the agenda forty-eight hours later, while I got London's consent to a new move on my part.

This was forthcoming and on May 17th, in a speech to the League Council, I proposed an immediate embargo on arms destined for either of these countries:

> In the opinion of His Majesty's Government in the United Kingdom this is an issue of capital importance in the Commission's report and offers to countries other than the two parties an opportunity to make a positive and decisive contribution to bring hostilities to an end.

I recalled that His Majesty's Government had made a similar proposal as early as February 25th, 1933, which had been accepted by the Council of the League. It had then only remained, I said, to secure the adherence of certain countries whose co-operation was vital to success. I knew that the Government of the United States had not been empowered by Congress to support an embargo, but I thought that we should get nowhere by waiting on each other. Having determined that we should make the move, I had earlier approached M. Barthou, who gave me immediate support and declared roundly at the Council table that the League must show that it possessed the necessary means to enforce its suggestions. The Council agreed unanimously with my proposal.

The response from the United States seemed better than in fact it was. President Roosevelt requested, and was granted, power to ban the export of arms and ammunition. I was delighted both at the character of this reaction and that the British initiative should have met with American support. Later, difficulties in the United States about the fulfilment of existing contracts caused several months of delay, but the League decision was the first effective move in strangling a war which was bleeding two countries to death.

This meeting of the League Council was also remarkable for its firm dealing with Liberia, where atrocities had been committed against the Kru tribes. The Liberian Government denied these reports, but in a speech to the League Council on May 19th, I stated that the British Government did not believe the denials. As a consequence, the Council withdrew its offer of assistance to Liberia, made because a League Commission had reported that Liberia's finances were in an appalling state, there being no accounts, no budget and no money. I said that it was the view of His Majesty's Government that Liberia had so grossly failed to observe her obligations to secure just treatment of the native inhabitants of the territory, that the League would be quite entitled to consider her expulsion. I suggested that the Council should approach the United States Government, as the country most closely connected, historically and economically, with Liberia, to find a remedy for the prevailing state of affairs, which course was approved and adopted.

After a few days' adjournment, which I spent with Ashley Clarke at my sister's villa on Cap Ferrat, we returned to Geneva, where on May 28th John Simon joined me for what proved to be the final meeting of the Disarmament Conference. We learned that Henderson, Davis and Politis, the Greek representative, who was usually well informed by Ministers of the Little Entente, all seemed to think that the French attitude would soften and that France would finally accept some German rearmament, in return for guarantees of security. Any such hopes were rudely dispelled within twenty-four hours.

When the General Commission assembled on the following day, even Arthur Henderson, normally so optimistic, admitted in his opening speech that 'the present situation of the Conference is really critical.' He was followed by Norman Davis, who announced that the United States, although anxious to co-operate in the preservation of peace, 'would not participate in European political negotiations and settlements and would not make any commitment whatever to use its armed forces for the settlement of any dispute anywhere. In other words, the policy of the United States is to keep out of war, but to help in every possible way to discourage and prevent war.' This contradiction in terms was more discouraging than we had expected, even in our pessimistic moments. It could only indulge Berlin.

In his speech the next day, John Simon marshalled the facts with customary lucidity. Two days earlier, I had noted on Simon's arrival: 'He had his first interview with Barthou. The latter at his worst, like our first interview in Paris. Interview in consequence far from successful.' That evening Norman Davis told me that the French had complained to him that they could not trust Simon. I replied that there was no excuse for this mistrust, but, even if it did exist, there was still no justification for Barthou's methods and manners.

I was therefore expecting Barthou to be firm, even caustic, in his statement, but his speech outpaced my worst fears. Appallingly witty at the expense of his allies, at its close, his audience was either convulsed with laughter or suspended in horror, according to mood and sense of responsibility. The pencils of the French secretariat were busy, but too late to overtake the consequences. The speech was a stern warning that France would consider only her own interests, and an emotional attack on Germany and on the British Foreign Secretary, with a thrust or two for Henderson. Barthou referred to Simon's speech of October 14th, in which the Foreign Secretary had opposed immediate German rearmament, and wanted to know why Germany's withdrawal from the Conference and the League should make that position untenable. Barthou drew attention to German budget estimates. Who threatens Germany? not France. Simon he termed '*mon cher collègue et presque ami*' and asked why he had laid so much stress only on the British proposals. What of the Italian Memorandum? '*M. Mussolini, qui n'est certes pas un homme incapable de paternité, a eu, lui aussi, son enfant. Cet enfant est solide et bien constitué....*'

Simon thought the speech a calculated performance and telegraphed home accordingly. He was no doubt right, in the sense that Barthou was voicing his Government's policy, but the barbs with which he armed it were his own. As I wrote that night: 'It will be grand material for our isolationists at home, and almost converted me into one.'

* * * * *

It is not easy at this length of time to reconstruct the mood of the British people at this period. The occupation of the Ruhr by French troops in 1923, against specific British advice, seemed to many an example of the unreasonable rigidity of the victor towards the fallen foe and created a certain sentiment against France. This was fostered by sincerely felt, but not always well-informed, criticism of the Treaty of Versailles. There were those among the military who respected the Germans for their efficiency, thoroughness and other soldierly qualities. It was not unusual to hear the expression: 'I hope they will be on our side next time.' There were industrialists and politicians who compared favourably the effective employment of manpower by Nazi methods with our failures in north-east England or south Wales. The recurrent parliamentary crises in France, often mistaken in England for political ones when they were not, encouraged the attitude of disparagement towards our allies. This also flattered what we like to think is the British tendency to help the weak against the strong, but which may only be an instinct for the balance of power. These influences explain some of the writing in the newspapers of the early 1930s which, if indulgent to Germany, was more often critical of France.

In a broadcast from Geneva the next day, I summed up the conclusion to be drawn from Barthou's speech, that there were no guarantees which would enable France to legalize any immediate German rearmament, without which the German Government would not sign the Convention. Simon left Geneva two days later and I stayed behind to see what could be done to pick up the pieces. The French Socialist leader Léon Blum's deprecating comment was apt; the majority of Paris newspapers, he wrote, tended to regard Geneva as a tennis tournament and to be elated at Barthou's brilliant play which won him the first set. Even my own mood at that moment was that Britain should draw herself back for a little time from Europe, arm in the air and watch events, which events were soon to make any such indulgence impossible.

Belgium was represented at Geneva in those years by a respected and much loved statesman, M. Paul Hymans, who was always troubled when Anglo-French relations went awry. I was not, therefore, surprised when, a few days later, he invited me to luncheon and I learnt that Barthou was to be the only other guest. Courteously but firmly Hymans delivered his message. Anglo-French solidarity was indispensable to Europe. Any deterioration in relations between the two countries must cause anxiety, especially in Belgium. Lately there had been some indications of this tendency; he thought it would be useful to see if we shared his opinion and, if so, whether there was anything to be done. Belgium, which was a small country but a friend to both, was at our disposal to help in any way she could. Barthou showed more patience than usual, then he cut in: 'It's quite simple. Belgium has a wife, France, and a mistress, England. That is why Belgium pays more attention to the mistress than to the wife.' But he took note all the same.

Barthou sent the leaders of other nations besides ourselves flat as ninepins. The position of Poland on the League Council in those days was somewhat equivocal. Admittedly not one of the leading powers, she aspired to a position near them and this sometimes involved some lobbying for membership on committees. Harmless enough, but Barthou was impatient and when Colonel Beck, the Polish Foreign Minister, referred to his country as a great power, he was exasperated. The next day at a luncheon attended by members of the Council, with Beck present, he indulged in an acid assessment which concluded: 'And then there are the great powers'—pause—'and Poland. Poland we all know, because we have been told so, is a great power'—pause—'a very, very great power.' Impossible to describe the tone of obsequious sarcasm in his voice. Some tittered, Beck flushed, France had flipped on the raw a man who was not a friend.

Despite this and other incidents, I came to modify my judgement of Barthou, respect his statesmanship, and understand that he was often right, even if he seasoned all he had to say with bitter aloes. He was a prodigious worker as well as an entertaining talker, extremely vigorous for his seventy-two years. Even Massigli, himself no sluggard, had been heard to bemoan his chief's excessive vitality. Barthou told me that the note of April 17th was written by him in person between 5 and 6.30 a.m. upon that day, and claimed that even on his idlest morning he never stayed in bed after six.

The Aga Khan was the representative of the Government of India at the League of Nations at this time and took a direct and vigorous interest in our proceedings. Urbane, shrewd and friendly, I had many talks with him and on one occasion presided at a lecture which he gave on Persian literature. One day I was lunching with Barthou and found my host impatient on the doorstep. 'You are late,' he said reproachfully. 'I have been waiting for you. Explain to me what is the Aga Khan.' I did my best in a few words. '*Ah, je comprends. Espèce de Pape. A ma droite.*'

Gradually through the following days other opportunities occurred to mend matters. Having overcome my first indignation at Barthou's speech, I needed little persuading and worked at reconciliation between our two countries with the conviction of a fervent believer. A week later, on June 8th, I wrote: 'Late into the night after a dinner with Barthou we secured an agreement.' This was a compromise resolution which enabled Barthou to modify the tone of his previous comments on Anglo-French relations.

* * * * *

Sir George Clerk, who had succeeded Lord Tyrrell as our Ambassador in Paris, reported the view of the Radical newspapers that our country, France and the United States had been brought closer together, largely as a result of British initiative. Even so, I did not want our agreement at Geneva, which only covered the immediate future of the Conference, to raise false hopes. I thought I should take an early opportunity of telling my constituents in Warwickshire of the true position:

> We have in no sense solved the main difficulties of the European situation. These consist in the present relations of the chief powers of Continental Europe. Unless they can be improved there will be no disarmament agreement, no political *détente*, and in consequence no extension of international trade recovery in Europe. . . . That is the problem which besets European statesmanship today, and which such statesmanship has so far signally failed to solve.

It seemed to me that the hope of an arms agreement was now so remote as to count for little in our councils. I became, in consequence, the more concerned about our own defences. The estimates for 1934–5 had been announced in March and showed modest increases in the budgets of all three services. I was far from satisfied that they were enough. As Lord Privy Seal, I was the junior member of a committee which was at this time considering questions of defence, in which we were revealed as lamentably weak. In particular, the rate of air expansion seemed to me too slow. To complete the 1923 programme of air defences by 1939, in the prevailing state of Europe, was sadly below our needs, and I said so. On the day following this discussion, I had luncheon with Walter Runciman, President of the Board of Trade. He confessed to me that he was horrified at the state of our supplies. He wanted British participation in Europe limited to air and sea. This was a view often held by Ministers at this time, their minds being shadowed, I have no doubt, by the terrible casualty lists of the first world war, as well as by the effort needed by us to put an effective army into the field. I knew that the army's needs would probably have to come last, but I never accepted the opinion that the defence of Europe by land could be left to our allies.

At Stoke-on-Trent on July 5th I spoke of my concern about our weakness. There was no nation, I said, which at that time looked on our armaments with suspicion:

> On the contrary, if there is anxiety at all in respect of our armaments, it is rather a doubt lest, having reduced them so far in a world which has been increasing its armaments, we should not be in a position to fulfil the commitments which we have undertaken.

I was therefore pleased at the Government's proposal to add another forty-one squadrons to the strength of the Royal Air Force during the next five years. But this programme, too, fell behind the schedule prepared for it. Upon its announcement, the Labour Party, supported by Opposition Liberals, greeted this very necessary expansion with a vote of censure, regretting that 'His Majesty's Government should enter upon a policy of rearmament neither necessitated by any new commitment nor calculated to add to the security of the nation, but certain to jeopardize the prospects of international disarmament and to encourage a revival of dangerous and wasteful competition in preparation for war.' It would be difficult to find words less appropriate to the situation as it was and as it developed.

Being strongly in favour of an increase in our air power, I defended it publicly, pointing out that there was nothing rigid about the new programme, which was obviously capable of adjustment if international agreement could be reached. The reductions in our air force since the war had not been followed by others, I said, nor had they really helped us to reach international agreement:

> Britain is essentially a stabilizing and not an unsettling influence in world affairs. An undue weakness in her defence, if over-long maintained in a world that is increasing its armaments, would be no aid to peace.

This might have been smug, it was also true.

* * * * *

It was during a discussion with M. Barthou in May that I had first learned that the imminent visit of Mr. Maxim Litvinov, the Soviet Foreign Minister, to Geneva might have an ulterior purpose. If he came, Barthou told me, it would be to discuss a Soviet proposal for a pact of mutual assistance between France and the Soviet Union, and also perhaps to consider Russia's entry into the League. Barthou assured me that, although we might hear a report that the projected pact of mutual assistance was to be European in character, this was not so. The arrangement, if any, would be limited to France and Soviet Russia. If ever anything more ambitious were contemplated, he would tell me.

Litvinov arrived and had his conversations with Barthou, who told me of the progress he was making. The proposed pact between the two countries was still, he said, in its early stages and had nothing to do with the various Geneva suggestions for security. It was rather in the nature of an Eastern Locarno. This may have been the intention, but it was never realized, Poland being unwilling to take part. Barthou went on to explain that the French Government had told the Soviet

Government that they could not be party to such a pact unless Soviet Russia were a member of the League. Consequently, a parallel negotiation had been proceeding on the subject of Soviet membership of that body. Barthou was confident that the Russians wished to take up membership, but they did not want to appear as suppliants. This, he said, perhaps explained why Litvinov had not asked to see me. The Russians had sought to attach conditions to their country's entry into the League. Barthou hoped, however, that he had persuaded Litvinov that these were either superfluous or unacceptable. There remained the difficulty of the permanent seat. Russia would certainly insist upon having one and the Poles would then be sure to make a similar demand.

This new phase of Franco-Soviet relations and Russian enrolment at Geneva were developments of the first importance. The difficulties were gradually overcome and I did what I could to help, for I was convinced that the League of Nations must gain from wider membership, whatever our views about Soviet policy. The League could not survive as a club, it might as a forum. The Soviet Union was admitted at a League Council on September 17th, when I said on behalf of His Majesty's Government that our foreign policy had been based upon the League of Nations ever since the creation of that organization, and that our objective must accordingly be to make 'this common council of the world as truly representative as we can'. We therefore associated ourselves with a step which would make the League more nearly universal by including the Soviet Union within its ranks.

I doubt if there was much enthusiasm in Moscow for joining the League, which action was hardly of a piece with Stalin's extreme caution. Litvinov no doubt favoured membership, which the others accepted as part of the price for the Franco-Soviet Pact. The lead and drive, however, came from France, personified by her Foreign Secretary. During the last days of the Russian negotiation, I was at a luncheon with Barthou, with some other members of the Council as fellow guests. M. Titulescu, the Roumanian Foreign Minister, looking at a handsome wristwatch which Barthou was wearing, remarked: 'Is that new? No doubt Litvinov gave it to you for getting him into the League.' 'No, no,' replied Barthou, 'if ever Litvinov gives me a watch there will be a chain attached.'

Barthou was pursuing the traditional policy of many French statesmen, including Clemenceau, calling in the power of Russia to balance the growing threat from Germany. The fact that Soviet military power was unproved and that he himself was a man of conservative opinions did not deter him. I think that his decision was justified and thought so then, but this policy was not popular with some of my colleagues, particularly the older ones, who were less realistic than M. Barthou. It had the effect of increasing their reservations about France and deepening their desire to come to terms with Germany. They could not be persuaded to see that the more cause they gave the French to doubt British policy, the stronger the pressure on France to look elsewhere for allies, and elsewhere meant Soviet Russia. It was excusable to regard communist Russia as anti-Christ, it was a mistake to defend that attitude with the argument that anyway the Russians were not any good.

The military appraisal given us of the value of the world's fighting forces in these years before the second world war was almost universally at fault. The quality of the French forces and their readiness for action were over-estimated, those of Italy still more so. Fascist rule was said to have transformed the fighting spirit in the peninsula. The truth is that Italian soldiers, especially those from the north, have for centuries proved good infantrymen, if well trained, equipped and led. The dictatorial regime, with its censorship and bluster, was more skilled in concealing deficiencies in these essentials than a democracy would have been. Soviet military power was greatly underrated up to the hour of the German invasion. The Greeks were grossly undervalued, they fought gallantly and well. The Japanese air force was under-estimated, to our heavy cost. One judgement was correct, the Germans were expected to build and man a first-class fighting machine and did so; only its unintelligent direction saved us.

* * * * *

At the end of the first world war, Germany had ceded the coal mines of the Saar to France. An international commission of five members was to govern the territory. After fifteen years, the inhabitants could choose between maintenance of the system established by the Treaty of Versailles, union with France, or union with Germany. The Council of the League of Nations was to arrange the plebiscite 'in such a way as to secure the freedom, secrecy and trustworthiness of the voting.' After the results were known, the League would decide under whose sovereignty the Saar should be placed. So statesmen had devised.

The years passed peacefully in the Saar until the Nazis came to power in Germany. French Governments had hoped that the economic bond between the Saar and France would lead eventually to political union. But Hitler's call to deliver his country from the discrimination imposed by Versailles and his claim to reunite all Germans in a single racial community, had its immediate echo in the territory. As early as August 1933, Hitler coupled one of his frequent pleas for good relations with France with a declaration that there could be no compromise over the reunion of the Saar with Germany. In a broadcast a few weeks later the Chancellor promised, in terms to become familiar in the next few years, that once the problem was solved, the last obstacle to permanent reconciliation between France and Germany would have been removed. To this, the French Government, in the person of M. Paul-Boncour, replied that it was not permissible for France and Germany to settle the matter privately, since it was the duty of all members of the League to see that the provisions of the Versailles Treaty were carried out.

Accordingly, in January 1934, the Council of the League placed on its agenda the preparatory measures to be undertaken for the plebiscite, which, by treaty, was due in the Saar a year later. In the interval Germany had left the League, but this did not affect our responsibility. A Committee of Three, consisting of Baron Aloisi as Chairman, and the representatives of Spain and the Argentine, was appointed to prepare a report for the Council to consider at its May session. The Committee did its work well and suggested a course of action to ensure the conditions that the Treaty required. Aloisi appealed to the French and German Governments, who pledged themselves to abstain from exerting pressure of any kind upon the Saar election, and the Council decided that voting should take place on Sunday, January 13th, 1935.

These arrangements did not prevent the Nazis in the Saar from carrying on a vehement campaign in favour of reunion with Germany. The President of the Governing Commission of the territory was Mr. Geoffrey Knox, a francophile British diplomat of courage. In the earlier part of 1934, he had to protest against Nazi interference by hostile broadcasts and at the illegal detention of Saar inhabitants. This led to a Franco-German negotiation and an exchange of letters on June 2nd, which failed to put an end to Knox's causes for concern. As a result, he was compelled to address a number of communications to the League Council, with evidence that the Deutsche Front was a continuation of the Nazi Party, of whose activities he had complained. The police were unreliable, many of them known to be Nazi sympathizers. The Saar having no armed force of its own, Knox resolved to try to recruit more police abroad, while Barthou told the Council that if an emergency arose, France would not hesitate to send troops into the territory.

Later in the summer the situation became more obscure and on September 21st, after talks with Knox and General Temperley, I wrote to Simon about the problem of policing the Saar during the forthcoming elections:

Knox tells us that he has raised some 300 local *gendarmerie* and he is still hoping to increase this force by recruitment from Luxemburg and Switzerland. Time, however, presses and I fear that this force is never likely to be of very much use. If we take the most optimistic view, we may perhaps hope that it will be able to cope with minor local riots. Certainly it will not be able to do more.

What then is to happen in the event of any kind of *putsch*, either from within or without? For to cope with this would be quite beyond the powers of Knox's *gendarmerie*. Clearly the only effective action in such an event would be the intervention of French troops.

I explained that the French had apparently not made adequate plans for an emergency, so that several days might well elapse between an appeal for troops and their arrival:

We know enough of German methods to be confident that, if they do attempt a *putsch*, two or three days will at least be a dangerous, and might be a fatal, interval . . . the knowledge on the part of the Germans that Knox can call in French troops is the one really effective sanction he has at his disposal. . . . Is it not likely that if the Germans get to learn, as no doubt they will, that the plans of the French General Staff have been well laid and the French troops are available in case of need at short notice, this in itself would give the Germans serious cause for thought were they contemplating a *putsch*?

On November 5th, Simon answered a question from George Lansbury in Parliament, saying that the Government did not anticipate that any disorder serious enough to call for military intervention would take place in connection with the plebiscite.

A fortnight later I had a long talk at Geneva with M. Pierre Laval, who had become Foreign Minister upon the calamitous assassination of M. Barthou and King Alexander. Laval was a native of the Auvergne, whose peasants are noted for their shrewdness and diligence. His early career was entirely to his credit. The father was a butcher in Puy-Guillaume, a village in the Puy-de-Dôme. Laval told me how he used to deliver meat to his father's customers by pony and trap. Often he would spend his time reading, leaving the horse to find its own way. He made good use of his studies, a series of scholarships helping him to a successful and lucrative career at the Bar. Thus, Laval built up a considerable fortune, which he increased by skilful investment. With the understandable pride of the local boy who had succeeded, he bought the ramshackle castle, which he put in order, at Châteldon, near his old home.

Laval's political life began in 1914, when he was elected deputy for Aubervilliers. Starting out as a man of the left, he moved markedly to the right, preserving always his white tie. In practice, he made light of party allegiance and for five years, from 1919–24, enjoyed little political success. Under Briand his fortunes changed. Laval stood avowedly for a policy of conciliation with Germany and was inclined to criticize both the firm policy of his predecessor and the views of Mr. Litvinov. Laval told me that he would take no step in the Saar that was not internationally sanctioned, and if France were asked to send police in an emergency, then he would invite the League Council to ask other countries interested, notably Britain and Italy, to do the same. This was a retreat from Barthou's earlier offer of troops, for police would not have been adequate.

I telegraphed Laval's intentions to the Foreign Office and on November 23rd Knox came to see me at Geneva. He told me he could give no undertaking that it would be possible to get through the next two months in the Saar without serious disturbance. The period after the plebiscite could be even more difficult than the period before it. He needed a police force of 25 officers and 140 men. This seemed to me modest, but Knox informed me that at the moment he had 12 officers and 24 men. I wanted no more persuading about the gravity of the dangers we were running. Knox told me that the only sure way of meeting the situation was by the use of regular soldiers. He had asked the Committee of Three for 2,000 troops, but the request had been turned down on the grounds that no country would supply them. He feared a repetition of the events of July in Austria, when Dr. Dollfuss, the Chancellor, had been murdered at the instigation of the Nazis.

After these two conversations, I was convinced that His Majesty's Government must determine and declare their policy. Furthermore, I expected that when the Council reassembled at the beginning of December, Laval would ask whether Britain would send a contingent of police to co-operate with any French force which might be called for by Knox. We must be ready for this, and I warned London accordingly.

The Foreign Secretary put before his colleagues a number of alternative courses, one of which was that, subject to the approval of the Council and to similar action by Italy, we should supply one half of the 2,000 troops stated by Knox to be necessary. This force was to be despatched immediately. The Government showed little enthusiasm for this action, which they had only been asked to consider. They approved, however, in principle; the choice of backing French intervention, or giving it token support, appearing to them even more dangerous.

I felt strongly that the situation was urgent and could only be met by a lead from the United Kingdom. I therefore prepared a memorandum on November 30th in which I explained that we must expect certain consequences in the following week, the French Government having confirmed what Laval had said to me. The Council of the League would be asked to declare that any police operations which France might have to undertake in the Saar, in response to an appeal from the Governing Commission, should be international in character. If we said yes to this, the implication would be that we were prepared to be parties to a mandate for French troops to enter the Saar, if asked to do so. If we declined, the Governing Commission would have no resources. I suggested that it was better to avoid either course, by ourselves offering a contribution to an international force to police the Saar throughout the whole period of the plebiscite, and I drafted the terms of the announcement which I wished to make. On the assumption that Mr. Knox would assure the Council that an international military force, supplied by powers with no direct interest in the result of the plebiscite, would enable the arrangements to be carried through, my draft announcement concluded that His Majesty's Government expressed their willingness to despatch a force of British troops immediately, at the invitation and with the approval of the Council.

I then returned to London, where I told my colleagues, including Sir John Simon, Lord Hailsham, the Secretary of State for War, and Neville Chamberlain, then Chancellor of the Exchequer, that I was sure the chances of trouble were very great, if matters were allowed to drift or left to an initiative by others. Having failed to convince them sufficiently, I saw Mr. Baldwin on December 3rd to enlist his support, so that the Government might decide their policy at once in the sense I wished. I had to return to Geneva the next day. After some talk between us, Baldwin told me he would help and was as good as his word. In informal discussion held shortly afterwards, Lord Hailsham said that the proposal would be unpopular, the country did not wish to see British troops on the Continent again. At this, Baldwin showed unusual vigour on an international issue, saying: 'I don't agree. On the contrary, I think that the country wants us to display more decision in international affairs and this is an occasion to do so.' Once Baldwin had spoken in this sense, there was no more immediate difficulty. At a meeting of colleagues later on the same day, I was given the authority I had asked for and it was left to my discretion how to handle things at Geneva. Our acceptance was conditional upon agreement by France and Germany.

I flew confidently back to Geneva on December 4th and saw Knox that evening. He confirmed his previous judgement that a British initiative in offering the force would be the most helpful action possible. The next morning I saw Laval and told the French of our proposal. He was greatly relieved and accepted at once. Then, while Stanley Bruce was lunching with me, I received a message from Simon urging me not to be too definite in anything I decided to say to Laval. As I had been definite, it was evident that the League Council would soon be aware of the fact. Even allowing for the difference in climate between London and Geneva, this blow hot blow cold was becoming too much of a pattern. I decided that I must go on with my action and try to enlist the Italians also. This was necessary because the Italian Government had hitherto been making reservations about the creation of an international force. Bruce firmly endorsed my judgement. Time was short, the Council being due to meet that evening. The position was further complicated by messages from London telling me that Ministers were to meet at 3.40 p.m. Geneva time, and that meanwhile the Council should be postponed or adjourned. This was not possible on an issue of such importance in which others were deeply interested, without giving rise to rumour and confusion. These arrangements were made all the more difficult by being intertwined with the threatening crisis which followed the assassination of King Alexander and M. Barthou.

I therefore decided to call on Baron Aloisi and told him of our willingness to make a contribution to an international force. I explained how this exercise depended mainly on Anglo-Italian co-operation. If we were to succeed, we must have Italian military participation, and I had come to ask for it. He looked a little brighter at this. He asked what Italian contribution I had in mind. I said at least a battalion, preferably a brigade. He said he would telephone to Rome at once, would I wait? I said I would. A few minutes later he came back, much elated. He had his reply from Mussolini. The Italians accepted and would contribute a brigade. We agreed to fix matters so that Aloisi should speak at the Council immediately after I had announced our decision. For once I was thankful to be dealing with a dictator capable of taking decisions in a short space of time. Later on this advantage seemed dubious.

I returned to my hotel pleased with the progress we were making. Here I found a further telephone message from London, this time drawing my attention to the view of Ministers that an international force should be representative of at least three powers. British and Italian troops were not enough, there must be a third contingent, preferably Dutch; a fourth contingent, Belgian or Swiss, was also desirable. Four detachments were better than three, but three was the essential minimum. Here was an unexpected difficulty, due, I suppose, to some unnecessary nervousness about taking the lead almost alone. The Council was due to meet in an hour and I could not possibly enlist a third country's help by then, nor could Laval, if I were to tell him of our condition. None of the countries proposed by London was even a member of the Council at the time. Furthermore, I had not mentioned this condition to the Italians, who were unlikely to be enthusiastic about it. The fact that this was essentially an Anglo-Italian operation made, I thought, a special appeal to them. On the other hand, if our offer were accepted, as I was confident it would be, the chances were that at least one other power would help. I decided to go ahead without the third contingent which British Ministers considered essential.

When the Council met in private session, the Italians were late and the President told me that he understood they were speaking to Rome on the telephone. I passed some uneasy minutes waiting in my chair, more anxious than I hope I seemed. I had jumped the gun so far as London was concerned and, if anything went wrong, I knew where the blame would lie. When at length Aloisi arrived, he nodded to me that all was well and I at once asked the President's permission to make my proposal as soon as Laval had spoken. It was unanimously approved. German acceptance was declared the next day, while in France, where any initiative by Britain to send troops as part of an international force had long been despaired of, surprise and relief were expressed on all sides. Sweden and the Netherlands joined with Italy and ourselves in making military contributions. The plebiscite passed off without incident, our troops earning much international praise for their appearance and conduct, which the British people found pleasant reading.

These Saar discussions resulted in one unexpected controversy between Laval and myself. When we were working on some documents late at night, he asked me to agree to a French text. I said I could not, I must see the text in English the next morning. Laval was incensed, declaring that I knew French well enough to make this unnecessary. I said this was not the point, but that it was a sensible precaution to see any important document in one's own language before approving it. Laval continued to complain, inveighing in particular against Clemenceau for having ever agreed that English should be an equivalent language to French in the League of Nations, but I got my way.

* * * * *

French Ministers hoped that the voting would show a large minority in their favour in the Saar, and expressed the view to Sir John Simon, when he was in Paris just before Christmas, that Germany would be easier to deal with after the decision. Remembering Hitler's confidence, I did not share this optimism, but since the French Government did not want to settle out of court, an orderly election was the only alternative. When the voting came in January it gave Germany an overwhelming majority.

As an early attempt at policing by an international authority, the scheme in the Saar was a notable success during the two months of high tension through which it operated. Its purpose was not to repress but to restrain. This it did admirably. No dispute between the various contingents tore at its contrived unity. There were no futile wrangles between the established civil power and the improvised international force. The machinery in the Saar both before and during the plebiscite gave a glimpse of a supra-national salvation to a world which was imprisoning itself all the while more closely within the confines of the national state. The dilemma persists today, in other continents than Europe, complicated by ideological cross-currents and a multiplicity of dictator states pursuing their ambitious and often unscrupulous plans without need to care for world opinion, even if such existed. The experience in the Saar did not detract from the lesson that an international authority cannot discharge its function unless it has a force of its own at its disposal. I have long held this view, but neither I nor others who shared it were able to make it prevail, although later we tried to do so when the United Nations was formed. Even in the service of the United Nations, such a force will only avail if the Security Council is scrupulous never to employ it except to uphold international order. It would be less damaging to the United Nations to be without a force than to misuse it.

VII

ASSASSINATION AT MARSEILLES

October – December 1934

Yugoslav state visit to France – King Alexander and M. Barthou assassinated – What France lost in M. Barthou – Yugoslav-Hungarian tension – The League invoked – Parallels with 1914 – The League Council meets – M. Beneš finds my speech 'trop neutre' *– I am rapporteur – My talks with M. de Kanya and M. Yevtitch – Hungary yields – The value of the League – Consequences of the assassinations*

In the early days of October 1934, King Alexander of Yugoslavia was due to pay a state visit to the French Republic. This was to be much more than a ceremonial occasion. The close relations of France with the Little Entente were part of the pattern of Europe, and King Alexander represented his country in authority as well as in name. Czechoslovakia, Roumania and Yugoslavia, then in alliance to each other and upheld by France, were hostile to the resurgence of German power and the practice of Hungarian intrigue.

The King arrived by sea, landing at Marseilles on October 9th, to the accompaniment of the usual panoply of flags and troops and famous figures. M. Barthou met him at the quayside on behalf of the French Government and together the two statesmen drove through the streets of Marseilles, strangely ill-guarded for so internationally significant an occasion. This was the terrorists' opportunity and Petrys Kaleman was not slow to seize it. Breaking through the Gardes Mobiles, spaced five yards apart, Kaleman advanced to the car and fired several rounds point-blank at King Alexander and Barthou, before being cut down. The King died at once, while in the confusion Barthou was neglected and bled to death. These were the first shots of the second world war.

Barthou's death grieved me personally as well as politically. As I wrote in my diary that night: 'Having learnt that Anglo-French co-operation had to be, he had vigour enough to make such co-operation real.' He was not mean in friendship nor in ambition and, at the close of the League Assembly a few weeks earlier, I could describe Anglo-French relations as better, essentially franker, than I had ever known them. His policy was direct and disinterested, depending on the personal enthusiasm with which he alone could back it. I could see no obvious successor, certainly none of his stature. I bitterly regretted a man who had, I thought, become a friend. To this day I value the copy he gave me of his life of Mirabeau, with an inscription which, from a man of his experience, generously flattered my years.

For France the day was fateful. At no time after this did she have so courageous and forceful a statesman to serve her as Foreign Minister. Intrigue there was and sincere devotion, but, until war engulfed all five years later, never the inspired direction and blunt speech which might have warned Rome, for instance, while there was still time.

That night I could not foretell the consequences of the King's death, but the dangers were clear enough, all the ingredients of the fatal weeks before the first world war were there again. At best the Little Entente would be weakened. If, as seemed only too possible, the Croatian terrorists had the support of Hungary, perhaps of Italy, and the connivance of either of these two countries could be traced, we should have an international situation of the utmost danger.

Serb rule in Croatia had been resented under King Alexander's dictatorship. Croat refugees had fled and settled in Hungary and Italy, where for the last five years a number of them had been responsible for outrages which caused the Yugoslav Government to send a formal note to Hungary in March 1934. The note ended:

> Yugoslav *émigrés* . . . who have chosen Hungary as their refuge and have been received there with special hospitality and consideration by the Hungarian authorities, are carrying on criminal activities against the Yugoslav state without the Royal Hungarian authorities having taken steps to stop them—a state of affairs which is quite intolerable and incompatible with neighbourly relations between states. . . .

Six weeks later the Hungarian Government replied with a denial of the charges. Yugoslav *émigrés* would remain subject to surveillance, they said. In June, it was the turn of the Hungarians to put a complaint to the Council of the League, this time about frequent shooting incidents on the Yugoslav–Hungarian border. M. de Eckhardt, the Hungarian representative, promised in the debate that the Hungarian Government would punish atrocities committed in Yugoslavia by refugees settled in Hungary. As a result there had been a temporary improvement. Now, after the assassinations, all the danger signals were out again.

In Europe, the consequences of King Alexander's death caused consternation. The Yugoslavs were indignant, the Hungarians defensive. Behind Hungary stood Italy, behind Yugoslavia, France. Italy's relations with Yugoslavia had been bad since the quarrel over Trieste and her friendship with Hungary was a useful make-weight. The Little Entente, Czechoslovakia, Roumania and Yugoslavia, was in a ferment. There was at least a suspicion that Mussolini had known what was afoot, and in general terms he had. The danger of war mounted and the League Council had to be summoned. It was soon learnt that the assassin was a Croat refugee who had lived for some years at the Janka Puszta camp in Hungary, about which the Yugoslav Government had already made protest. It also emerged that he had accomplices in Italy. Here was fuel for much fire. Baron Aloisi's diary* shows that he was shocked at Fascist complicity in these terrorist activities when he first learnt of them. He realized what the consequences must be if they were found out and tried to limit them.

The conspirators probably hoped that the death of King Alexander would result in the disintegration of Yugoslavia. If so, they were wrong. The following weeks witnessed unprecedented demonstrations of affection for the King and loyalty to the state. These were not confined to the Serb elements in the population, but were as notable in Zagreb and Ljubljana as in Belgrade.

The funeral was attended by a nation in mourning and a great number of foreign rulers and princes, presidents and prime ministers. The Little Entente powers used the occasion to hold a conference under Titulescu's chairmanship, when the Greek and Turkish Foreign Ministers sat with them. Together they concluded that the crime at Marseilles 'was committed under the influence of forces beyond the frontiers. . . . The Council of the Little Entente holds it to be necessary that all States, without exception, should co-operate in a tranquil and objective spirit to establish the guilty parties.' The Council demanded measures to stop the recurrence of such acts. If they were not taken and carried out in loyalty and good faith, 'new and most serious disputes will follow. . . .'

The Little Entente Ministers were fiercer in a statement on their own

* op. cit.

account. 'The Marseilles murder was directed not only against the life of the late King Alexander and against the union of Yugoslavia, but it was in fact an outrage against the present international order in Europe.' While declaring their solidarity and their intention to continue the restraint which they had shown from the first, they warned that they 'would insist with all possible force that the perpetrators of the crime and their assistants be discovered, also the real organizers of the plot in all its extensive scope, which has as its aim to upset the present state of affairs in Europe'. This demand expressed the exasperated conviction of the Little Entente that more lay behind the murder than the fanaticism of terrorists. A bitter press campaign was loosed against Hungary and Italy. Newspapers published photographs of the alleged murderers and of the Hungarian Prime Minister and Foreign Secretary side by side.

Our own action for the time being was confined to counselling moderation through our Ambassadors. We learnt from our Embassy in Paris that the French inquiry into the outrage was expected to drag on indefinitely, as the Stavisky inquiry had done. I did not like the sound of this. Later reports brought no comfort. Within a month of Barthou's death, Doumergue had retired into private life, M. Pierre-Etienne Flandin had succeeded him as Prime Minister and M. Laval was Foreign Secretary. These were unwelcome changes to us, even then, though the future was veiled and the part each man was to play in the tragic years of his country's history all unknown. Meanwhile, the Little Entente waited for the results of the French inquiry and for the outcome of their own efforts to establish Hungarian complicity. If the French investigation were to show the need for joint action to prevent abuse of the right of asylum, the Little Entente and France would act together, so Beneš told our Minister in Prague. But the French did not hurry.

* * * * *

In the middle of November, I had to go to Geneva for Saar and disarmament affairs. The Foreign Office warned me before I left that the Yugoslav Government must be expected to bring charges of complicity in the assassinations against Hungary and perhaps Italy too, under Article 11 of the Covenant. This action was foreshadowed for an Extraordinary Session of the League Council in December. The dangers ahead were mounting. On November 19th, Signor Grandi, the Italian Ambassador in London, called on Simon to say that Mussolini would feel it necessary to take up the cudgels in defence of

Hungary if the latter were attacked in this manner and there was, as a result, the prospect of very unhappy controversy between Italy and Yugoslavia at Geneva.

On the same day as Grandi saw Simon, Beneš told me in Geneva that he thought it difficult to exaggerate the gravity of the situation. The activities of terrorist organizations formed, he said, part of Hungary's plan for the revision of treaty boundaries. The demands which Beneš put to me, as the minimum necessary to appease Yugoslav opinion, included the expulsion of the murderers' associates from Italy and Hungary and an international convention to deal with terrorists. I did not enter into detailed argument, but Beneš soon saw that I had doubts on the subject, for he made an earnest appeal for British co-operation in the difficult situation in which the Little Entente found itself. I replied by telling him that I felt anxious about the effect of prolonged and acrimonious discussion on Franco-Italian relations. Even though Hungary and not Italy were the target, Italy must be expected to feel much sympathy with the position of Hungary, with whom she had established a close friendship. Beneš did not deny this and said that he wanted to handle the matter as quietly and tactfully as possible, to minimize friction between France and Italy, but he begged me to believe that it was impossible to avoid taking some effective action. Opinion in Yugoslavia was in a ferment and a safety valve must be provided.

On November 21st, it was the turn of M. Yevtitch, the Yugoslav Foreign Minister. He told me that the Yugoslav memorandum would soon be circulated and that everything had been done to make it as moderate as possible. He had been at pains to suppress any charges of Italian complicity with terrorist organizations. Yevtitch, I felt, had to show that some international action had been taken to deal with terrorists on foreign soil, or his position in Belgrade would be untenable, which would make matters worse.

The next day, Laval arrived and told me privately that the real reason he had come to Geneva was to try to calm Yevtitch and the Yugoslav delegation. He was keenly conscious of the dangers. The Yugoslav memorandum published at that moment showed he had cause to be. It was backed by identical notes from the Roumanian and Czech Foreign Ministers to the Secretary-General. The Yugoslavs reinforced their remonstrance with a formidable dossier on the history of recent relations between their country and Hungary, with photographs of terrorists and their Hungarian documents. According to this account, the three criminals chosen to carry out the murder at Marseilles had left Janka Puszta with Hungarian passports.

In retort, the Hungarian representative blamed the prevailing tension on the Yugoslavs and asked that the Council of the League should take the charges into consideration. The Italian Government publicly supported the demand for immediate discussion, following this up by announcing their refusal of a French request to extradite Pavelić and Kwaternik, who were wanted as leaders of the Ustasi organization which plotted the assassinations. Pavelić was to play a grim and brutal role in his native land on behalf of the Berlin–Rome Axis in the second world war. It would have saved much later suffering if he had been extradited then, but he was a useful pawn in Mussolini's game. It was in this highly charged atmosphere that the Council met in Extraordinary Session on December 7th.

To many it seemed that events were developing after the fashion of 1914 and there was an obvious parallel with the murders at Sarajevo. But, though the danger was acute, there were differences also. Beneš once remarked, as our Minister in Prague, Sir Joseph Addison, had reported to us: 'Wars on a large scale are not started by the small powers, but by the interference of great powers.' This was true of 1914, when Germany and Russia lined up behind Austria and Serbia and when the uncertainties of Britain's policy postponed her deterrent intervention beyond the time when it might have been effective. In 1934, the great powers did not want immediate trouble; neither France nor Italy wished to push matters to extremes, while Britain was able to exercise her restraining influence from the start. Above all, Germany was not yet in a position to wage war. Until she could do so, conflict in Europe could only arise by accident rather than by intent. At this time the danger came from the bellicosity of the smaller powers and this was serious enough, sharpened as it was by a sense of injury in Yugoslavia and of some guilt elsewhere.

I had hoped to postpone public debate until January, so that the temperature could have been brought down meanwhile. When in London a few days previously, I had told the French Ambassador, M. Charles Corbin, of my purpose and he had agreed, but, once in Geneva, I was compelled to change my mind. With both sides demanding a discussion, delay would only have increased the dangers. We had some tactical advantages. The first was that we met under the chairmanship of Senhor Vasconcellos, an experienced Portuguese diplomat. The ancient alliance and our personal friendship assured me of his support. Secondly, France and Italy were both alarmed at the growing risk of open conflict. Mussolini told Drummond that he looked largely to His Majesty's Government to exercise a calming influence, but the Italians understood how difficult was the solution, since the Little Entente powers must support Yugoslavia. If they failed to do so and Yevtitch were to fall, Yugoslavia's unity and the Little Entente's authority would be in fragments.

With all this tinder around, the less public discussion we had the better. Much would depend on the appointment of a rapporteur, responsible for handling the dispute on behalf of the Council, and on his ability to make use of remorse and fear to fashion an agreement. I had already been approached by Laval about the possibility of acting in this capacity myself. I did not respond, merely commenting that I had thought the Spanish representative, Señor de Madariaga, a good choice. In the last hours before the Council met, the Yugoslav Government suddenly expelled thousands of Hungarians living within their territories. There was no pretence that these unfortunate people had any connection with the crime. The deed was political and harsh, but an indication of the upsurge of feeling in the country.

* * * * *

We began with a day's general debate on December 7th. The protagonists stated their cases without surprise. Yevtitch had been persuaded not to make any accusations against Italy, nor any direct charge against the Government of Hungary, as distinct from their subordinate authorities. Despite this restraint, the Hungarian, Eckhardt, made a tart reply and in return Beneš was less conciliatory than I had hoped. I held my hand, believing that Britain was the only great power on the Council which might decisively influence the solution of the quarrel. I wrote in my diary that night: 'The question is, when should I intervene and how? All may depend on our choosing the psychological moment.'

That evening, and the next morning, I worked on my speech and then had luncheon with Avenol, the Secretary-General, and my colleagues on the Council. I sat next to Beneš, but did not enter into detailed argument on the dispute, for I did not want to commit myself too early. We spoke instead of Beneš' wartime experiences. He was hardly his usual buoyant self in those tense days, but I liked him very much and on such a theme he was cheerfully entertaining. He delighted to tell of his two separate arrests by British authorities as an Austrian spy. I had also a useful talk with Madariaga, who was helpful, and we concerted our ideas.

The Council session in the afternoon went better from our point of view. Laval and Aloisi supported their protagonists firmly, but not extravagantly. I thought it best, while roundly condemning the assassinations, to take up a reserved and somewhat judicial attitude upon the events leading up to them:

I feel some difficulty in forming any opinion as to the responsibilities for the tragic events which have occurred, while the trial of those charged with being concerned in the assassinations in Marseilles has not yet taken place.

I added that proceedings were still *sub judice* in France where the crime was committed and in these circumstances we must proceed with extreme caution.

This did not please the Little Entente, who had no doubt expected some outright condemnation of Hungary. My speech and the support it received from Madariaga, Beck and the Latin-Americans put them out. Beneš did not conceal his disappointment. I had been '*trop neutre*' he complained. I did not relent or apologize. Titulescu came to me in some embarrassment at the end of the meeting and asked if I would mind if I were not appointed rapporteur that day; Yevtitch would imperil his position if he agreed directly after my speech. I replied that of course I did not mind, the last thing I wanted was to be rapporteur; I should much prefer that they should find somebody else. 'Oh no,' he said, 'we want you and will ask for you on Monday.' 'Monday', I replied, 'must take care of itself.'

We agreed on no rapporteur that day and no undertaking on either side about Monday. I suspected that the real reason for the Little Entente's chagrin was that I had added to my speech some stiffish sentences about the importance of not extending the area of the dispute, aimed at preventing both sides from parading the revisionist issue. Hungarians were always eager to attack the Treaty of Trianon, the charter of the Little Entente powers, and there had been signs the night before that the next debate would bring a violent clash. If this were to happen, it would rule out an immediate settlement of the dispute and I had to lower the temperature. The Yugoslavs, moreover, were not happy at a warning I had added at the end of my speech, that those at the Council table ought not to allow local conditions to deteriorate. This was a reference to the Yugoslav expulsions and I believe that, coupled with some remonstrance from London to Belgrade, it had an effect. At least, the expulsions ceased.

The next day was Sunday and Sir William Malkin, Strang and I decided to spend it away from Geneva. Malkin was the brilliant, modest and wholly likeable legal adviser at the Foreign Office. My secretary, Robin Hankey, came with us. The next Council meeting was fixed for Monday and there seemed little we could do meanwhile. Accordingly, we set off by car for the mountains and spent the morning walking in the Jura foothills north of Geneva. We came back to an inn for luncheon. While waiting for our food, I could not help wondering what was going on at Geneva. I knew that the position was very tricky and I had doubts about being out of touch all day. I suggested that Hankey should ring up our delegation and get news. Malkin spoke up against this. He reminded me that I had left Geneva with a purpose, to keep out of the ferment. Probably my colleagues would be missing me, they had better go on doing so a while longer, then they would be prepared to listen to me when I got back. This was bold advice, but sound, and I took it.

We went for a further walk in the afternoon, then sat down on a hillside and decided that I should only accept to be rapporteur if I were given a free hand. Thus reinforced, I returned to Geneva in the evening, to find the place in a great hubbub. There had been insistent demands for me and nobody knew where I had gone. I learnt that the press reaction to my speech in France, as well as in the Little Entente countries, had been bad, 'Pontius Pilate' being one of the epithets, and not the worst, in a usually friendly Paris press. There was some criticism in the delegations and several requests to see me. Among these I selected Laval and went round to his hotel. I found him reproachful. He implied that I was taking my duties lightly; unless he and I could find a solution, there would be war. Yevtitch had been much disappointed by the speeches in Saturday's debate; he had been in communication with Belgrade and had told Laval that, if the League could not help him, he would have to return home as soon as our discussions were over. Laval added that there would then be a change of government in Belgrade with disastrous consequences. I reflected that if both sides were now frightened, this would be the right moment for us to play our part.

The Little Entente, Laval continued, wanted me to be rapporteur and Beneš had been looking for me all day to discuss terms. I said that I had no wish to be rapporteur, but if I were, it could not be on conditions imposed by one side. It would have to be on terms which would give me complete freedom of action. Laval raised his eyebrows at this and demurred, but I said I was sorry, that was how it was. 'Well, anyway,' he retorted, 'you had better see Beneš. He is coming round to join us at dinner.' Beneš duly arrived, a worried man, and enumerated the conditions he and his colleagues had proposed for the acceptance of a rapporteur. He was not, I think, surprised at my negative response. At any rate, he accepted to put it to his colleagues.

We sat down to dinner, Laval very serious and Beneš, I thought, trying to scare me. Afterwards we examined the draft on which the French and Little Entente had been working all day. I did not like it, for there were irrelevant references against revision of the Treaty of Trianon. Beneš was unhappy when I had to point out that the Covenant was misquoted in a sense favourable to himself. Eventually he and Laval agreed to leave out all references to revision. I took the draft back to our hotel, where Massigli and Basdevant, Malkin's loyal opposite number in the French delegation, drew up with us a much better resolution for the Council, on the lines we had discussed on our walk. I was clear that none other had any chance of acceptance. Late that night I received the invitation from the Little Entente to be rapporteur. The other side, having heard of my refusal of Beneš' conditions, endorsed me. The League Council did not meet until the next afternoon, when the invitation was unanimous. Counting on this support, I had already entered upon my most important and toughest assignment to date.

* * * * *

The two Foreign Ministers with whom I had principally to work presented a sharp and intriguing contrast. Yevtitch, the Yugoslav, was small, wiry and determined, a representative of his people's peasant qualities. M. de Kanya, the Hungarian, was a polished Ballhausplatz diplomatist, smooth and missing no tricks. Behind them stood the French and Italian representatives. My method was to see the principals separately and make what progress I could this way. I would then report back to the major partners, Laval and Aloisi, and use my discussions with them to help resolve the more stubborn difficulties, which were Yugoslavia's demand for retribution and Hungary's denial of all guilt. I had to get results quickly because tempers were up, especially in Yugoslavia. If the proceedings dragged, they would fail.

I discussed the resolution we had prepared on the telephone with Simon on Monday morning and, having agreed that it, or something like it, would serve our purpose, I then saw Aloisi, who was helpful. Together we asked Kanya to come to see us and told him that in our judgement he would be wise to accept our draft. Kanya produced one of his own, which merely invited his Government to inquire into certain matters connected with the plotting of the crime at Marseilles. I declined to discuss this and said I would prefer to hear his view about mine. It was a painful interview and I was sorry for the old man, but I knew that the impartiality of my speech on Saturday had given weight to my counsel and, if agreement was to be reached, I had to use this advantage. Kanya would not accept any reference to Article 10 of the Covenant, which called upon countries to respect each other's territorial integrity. Yevtitch, after some pressure from Laval, was prepared to meet the Hungarians' wishes on this point, provided that there was some admission of their responsibility.

When our discussions were finished, two points were left. I wished to stop the expulsion of Hungarians by Yugoslavia, but Yevtitch would not agree to anything as definite as this in the draft. Finally, we agreed that our formal resolution would only make a veiled reference to expulsions but that my introductory speech would be more explicit. We decided to follow the same procedure to fix Hungarian responsibility for the assassinations, both sides accepting the device of putting into my own mouth expressions about which they could not agree. As the words were mine, they had no responsibility for them, but each could take satisfaction from those phrases which met his needs.

A debate at the League Council that afternoon neither advanced nor retarded matters noticeably. The Council over and my appointment confirmed, I had a further discussion with Kanya, at which Laval and Aloisi were present. Kanya's anxiety was that, if our resolution were passed, there was still nothing to prevent the Yugoslavs bringing up the discussion at any time they saw fit. I explained that this was inevitable, for, so long as there was a rapporteur, the item with which he dealt had to remain on the agenda. But, as a matter of practical politics, he need have no fear that the Council would want to touch it again. In the end he promised to consider this, being convinced, so my colleagues believed, that the rapporteur would hold the scales evenly.

Meanwhile, the evening was advancing. I had invited Laval and Aloisi to dinner at my hotel to have them handy when I wanted them. The meal was frequently interrupted by consultations with one side or the other, or with eager go-betweens. Litvinov had suggested that the Council should meet again late that night. This was wise and helped us to keep the momentum of the negotiation at a sharp pace. Eventually, Kanya undertook to consult the Regent of Hungary, Admiral

Horthy, about the terms of our resolution. While he was communicating with Budapest, we saw Yevtitch once again and confirmed that he could accept my speech and the resolution as amended and agreed.

We repaired to the Council at 10 p.m. and, after some general observations by the Chairman, had to adjourn, for there was no word from Kanya. I still have some notes which were exchanged during these moments. The first was from Aloisi: 'Kanya tells me that it is impossible, or almost, to have the reply by 10 p.m.' 'Then 11 p.m.,' wrote Laval across this, 'we are courageous', and, a little lower, 'otherwise they will all let us down and everything will have to be begun again from the beginning. Thank you.' These notes were passed to me and I agreed that we must sit it out. By 11.30 p.m. the answer had come.

Though my resolution did not directly blame the Hungarian Government, my opening words censured the negligence of their subordinates. The Council asked the Hungarian Government to take at once appropriate, punitive action against any of its authorities whose guilt could be established. They were told to report the result and agreed to do so. A month later their unenthusiastic fulfilment of this instruction was presented in a memorandum, of which the Council took note. The Hungarian Government did, however, then admit that some of its officials had not exercised proper supervision over the Croat refugees and declared that they had taken disciplinary action against them.

* * * * *

This was a dispute of the type which the League of Nations was well qualified to handle. The League had one notable advantage over the United Nations. The regular meetings of its Council were occasions for the Foreign Secretaries to attend. These men knew each other and had the authority to take decisions. There was no cumbrous machinery or swollen staff. In this dispute it was important to find a way to satisfy the demands of the injured parties, without humiliating, beyond the point which they could endure, those who had at least abetted the crime. The method we employed was the same that I used so many years later, after the second world war, to try to isolate the more difficult of the problems, eliminating minor ones which, though not capital, could still be dangerous.

By the end of the year 1934, our authority and the League's stood higher than at any time in the National Government's life. Success had been cumulative, as, like failure, it often is. Without our contribution to the Saar, Britain's leadership in the Yugoslav–Hungarian dispute would not have been so easily accepted. Initiative encourages confidence, as hesitation begets mischief.

In Europe the public reaction to these events was one of relief. Among the participants, Hungary was vocal in self-righteousness, but had learnt a lesson. In Yugoslavia, Yevtitch and moderation were for the moment secure, though continuing in some internal danger. In France and Britain there was pleasure at this success for the League of Nations and satisfaction at the part their countries' representatives were deemed to have played. The Italian press was gratified at the outcome, acclaiming me in my role as rapporteur in this pre-sanctions period, as Aloisi had done at the Council table. Without doubt a nasty corner had been turned, but no more than that. The wounds inflicted at Marseilles were deeper than they seemed. The deaths of King Alexander and Barthou had consequences which continued to be felt until the outbreak of war and beyond. Neither country was to know such decisive leadership again, though in France Blum, in particular, and Delbos did all they could in their late hour. The Little Entente was severely shaken, with its resentment against Hungary and its suspicion of Mussolini both sharpened. The antagonists of another conflict were taking post. There was an unhappy personal equation also. It is inconceivable that Barthou would have been equivocal to the point of horse-trading over the Italo-Abyssinian conflict, or that King Alexander would have compromised with Hitler or, from over-confidence, have allowed his air force to be destroyed on the ground when the attack came.

VIII

HITLER'S APPETITE

October 1934 – March 1935

Scandinavian tour – M. Laval in Rome – A Berlin visit proposed – British Service Estimates – Herr Hitler's weekend decision – My visit to Paris – The Stresa Conference is arranged – Berlin – Herr Hitler after twelve months – We discuss Russia – Germany refuses to return to the League – We discuss armaments – A train journey across Poland

For a few days, just after the assassinations at Marseilles, I had journeyed in Scandinavia. M. Sandler, the Swedish Foreign Minister, was a personal friend who had invited me to pay a visit to his country as a representative of His Majesty's Government. The Danish and Norwegian Governments also sent invitations. My colleagues having approved, Robin Hankey and I sailed on October 11th for a most kindly ten days in Scandinavia, my only regret about our plans being that I had not the time to travel further to Finland. My welcome in Denmark was perhaps the warmer on account of my mother's Danish ancestry. Her grandmother, a Schafflitzky, was of the same family, I believe, as one of the commanders in the Thirty Years War, later settled in Denmark. This lady married a Plowden of the Anglo-Indian family and her daughter became the wife of Sir William Grey, nephew of the Prime Minister and my grandfather. She was a lovely woman, with large, dark, lambent eyes. After Copenhagen I visited the Swedish capital, its architecture and sculpture even surpassing my expectations. I had seen no buildings of their period anywhere which could eclipse its Town Hall and Concert House.

Events in Germany in the last few years had thrown a shadow over German–Swedish relations and, though these were still correct, they were no longer cordial. I felt in the three Scandinavian kingdoms a close affinity with our thought. For all their tenacious neutrality, they were anxious about the sombre world into which we were moving. The assassinations at Marseilles added to the apprehension which was felt by all with a knowledge of European politics, and there are many such in Sweden, Norway and Denmark. Though my visit had no declared political purpose, it was instructive to me and useful all the same, because it gave my hosts a chance to show their feelings without modifying their policies.

Back in London I had an audience of King George V, who was anxious to talk of Scandinavia. In the course of this conversation a passing reference was made to the controversy between Lloyd George and Haig. In this connection the King told me, with some indignation, how his renunciation of alcoholic drink had come about during the war. It seemed that Lloyd George had come to him much troubled about heavy drinking among munition workers, which, he said, was having an influence on output. Could not an example be set by His Majesty? The King was reluctant, asked for more information and said he would consider it. Whereupon Lloyd George went out and told everyone that the King had agreed. 'A scurvy trick', His Majesty thought.

I wrote in my diary for that day:

> I had some conversation with Wigram [Sir Clive Wigram, the King's principal Private Secretary] before and after. Not pleased with municipal elections. His hope was Government would get back, S.B. and older men then carry on for a year or two, then hand over 'to you and Oliver [Stanley] and the younger men. That I know,' he added, 'is what the King wants to see too.'

This is the first reference, of which I have a record, to a suggestion that the younger men should take over. I was to get used to hearing it in the next twenty-one years.

* * * * *

The French Government were anxious that the Yugoslav–Hungarian dispute should not damage relations between France and Italy. Accordingly, Laval visited Rome, as Barthou had intended to do, in January 1935, and there concluded an agreement with Mussolini. This recommended that a pact of non-intervention should be signed by Austria's neighbours, to guarantee that country's independence and as a warning to Hitler. The two powers also declared that no country could be allowed to modify its armament obligations by its own action and agreed to act together if this principle were ignored. The agreement led to secret military clauses with promise of mutual support, the terms of which were not communicated to us, nor did Laval ever do more than hint that their existence must influence his conduct. Finally, Mussolini and Laval compromised on a number of geographical and economic questions in Africa which had for long caused trouble between their two countries.

France ceded territories, mostly desert, adjoining the Italian colonies of Libya and Eritrea and offered the Duce two thousand shares in the Djibouti–Addis Ababa railway. Mussolini gave up claims in Tunis, where there was a considerable Italian population. Laval being ignorant of Africa and mainly concerned with the appearance of the agreement, it is not surprising that its interpretation was soon to give rise to worse consequences. This related to the negotiation concerning Abyssinia which was accompanied by verbal exchanges between Laval and Mussolini alone. These two masters of chicanery were to go on arguing about them in a secret correspondence after Laval's fall from power. The truth of what was said will never be known. My own opinion, having heard and read their explanations, is that Laval was sufficiently equivocal to give Mussolini the chance to exploit his attitude. Certainly the Duce got the worst of the bargain, on paper, and the best in licence.

On January 13th, the Saar voted to return to Germany and did so a few weeks later. In the second half of that month, Sir Eric Phipps reported from Berlin, warning us of the increasing difficulty of treating with Germany:

> In the matter of disarmament there are indications that German requirements are likely to be assessed at an ever-increasing figure

and it was not likely to be easy

> to lure the German Government back to Geneva. For the purpose of gaining advantages for Germany the sacrifice might be made, but the general opinion appears to be that Geneva promises rebuffs rather than solid advantages and that, besides, Germany has already by her own efforts obtained what she requires. As a Serbian patriarch is said to have remarked to the Archbishop of Canterbury: 'For years we prayed for deliverance from the Turks. But at last we took up arms and did it ourselves.' By means of the expansion of German strength, it is believed, more friends will be made than by lobbying

behind the scenes at Geneva. . . . I feel it my duty to warn you that the result of the Saar plebiscite has been to render Herr Hitler more independent and the omens less propitious for the success of any negotiations with this country. In all the circumstances it must be greatly regretted that the French Government did not show more foresight and liquidate the Saar question by negotiation with Herr Hitler out of court, as he publicly suggested, and in accordance with the advice of their Ambassador in Berlin.

I minuted:

A most important despatch, and a gloomy one. Germany is now well on the way to rearmament, she is no longer afraid of a 'preventive war' against her and in a few years—four I am told is the popular figure in Berlin—she will be strong enough to ask, in a tone which will not brook refusal, for her desiderata. I have for long past feared that the last chance of an agreement with Germany was on the basis of Hitler's February offer. The French however did not look at it, nor did we endeavour to make them do so—but all that is spilt milk.

* * * * *

At the end of the month, Flandin and Laval came on to London at Simon's invitation and some easily conducted talks were held in Downing Street during the next few days. MacDonald, Baldwin, Simon and I represented the British Government. This was the first occasion on which I had been a negotiator for my country at an international conference in London, though very much the junior of the team. We were glad of the appearance of better relations between France and Italy and, together with the French Ministers, we decided, despite the bleak outlook, to make another attempt at negotiation with Germany. In a communiqué issued on February 3rd, our two countries proposed discussions to include armaments, pacts of mutual assistance in Eastern Europe and Germany's return to the League. We also advocated, for the first time, an air pact. In an attempt to counter any sudden attack from the skies, the nations were to pledge the assistance of their air forces to the victim of unprovoked aggression by air.

The French were fertile in suggestion and met a German demand by accepting that the armaments clauses of the Treaty of Versailles should eventually disappear. All this would have been unexceptionable as policy, if it had been accompanied by the vigorous expansion of the one argument Hitler understood, military preparedness. France, however, was relying too much upon the equipment she had already and was not able to make a sufficient contribution of quality to match the Germans in aircraft. Our own effort was getting under way in a laboured fashion and under shrill Opposition criticism. We had made a late start and were still far from understanding, much less accepting, the contribution required of us on land as well as by sea and air, if Hitler's intentions were to be influenced.

At this stage the Swedish Government, with whom I had kept in close relations since my visit to Stockholm, gave us a helping hand, and unofficial advice from the King of Sweden in Berlin probably influenced the German Government to draft a reply which was more accommodating than usual. The Germans accepted that there should be negotiations such as we and the French had suggested, inviting the British Government, as a partner in the London discussions and a guarantor of Locarno, to a direct exchange of views.

Simon was favourable to a visit to Berlin and, having made sure that the scope of the discussions would include all the items we and the French had raised, he accepted. France with confidence and Italy with more reluctance endorsed the decision, Simon making a visit to Paris to ensure that we were all in line. Meanwhile, the Russians, through Mr. Ivan Maisky, their active and ingenious Ambassador in London, had shown some desire for a British visit; so had the Poles, the Czechs and others. These invitations called for decisions. On February 28th I had a luncheon party at home which included Signor Dino Grandi, the Italian Ambassador, and to this Vansittart took me in his car. I wrote in my diary that night:

> He was melancholy at the Foreign Secretary's continuous indecision. Last Monday John Simon was decided that he and I should go together to Berlin, Warsaw and Moscow. Now all was apparently in the melting pot again. Simon had gone off without leaving any indication of his mind, the Russians had not been answered at all, poor old Maisky with his invitation burning a hole in his pocket no doubt.

As we were still no nearer making replies two days later, I sent Simon a minute suggesting that a meeting with the Prime Minister and Baldwin was indispensable, to agree who was to go to Berlin, Moscow and any other capitals. The meeting of the four of us and Vansittart duly took place on March 4th and it was decided that Simon and I should both go to Berlin, while I alone should go on to Moscow, Warsaw and Prague. The Prime Minister was very much against the joint visit to Berlin, for political reasons. I assume he thought it wrong that two Ministers should go to the German capital and one to Moscow. On the face of it, there was something in this, but the Russians made no difficulty. To me the odd part of the business was that Simon showed no wish to go further than Berlin; I thought that much the more intriguing part of the visit lay beyond. No British Minister had been to Moscow since the Revolution.

These arrangements were endorsed by our colleagues and announced in the House of Commons and all seemed set fair when, on March 4th, His Majesty's Government issued a White Paper on defence, signed by the Prime Minister. This explicitly drew attention to German re-armament and stated that, if continued at its present rate, it would aggravate the existing anxieties of Germany's neighbours and 'may consequently produce a situation where peace will be in peril.' The Government therefore proposed to modernize the equipment of the Army and Navy and to expedite the increases in strength of the Royal Air Force, already announced. Even now, the Service Estimates rose only by ten million pounds. The Paper also drew attention to the spirit in which the population, and especially the youth of Germany, was being organized, which lent colour to and substantiated 'the general feeling of insecurity which has already been incontestably generated.' I had been all in favour of the Paper and its language, but it was rougher stuff than anything which had been officially written of German behaviour hitherto and it bred a germ. The next morning von Neurath told Phipps that Hitler had a cold and asked that the forthcoming visit by Simon and myself should therefore be postponed.

There were vehement protests in Britain at the increased armaments estimates which the White Paper proposed, and in reply to a letter from a number of Liberals in my constituency, I wrote:

> The present situation is, of course, profoundly disappointing to the Government, as it must be to all who love peace, and it was fully realized that the disagreeable realities set out in the Paper would come as a shock to many high-minded men and women. The British democracy has, however, a right to be told the true position, and the Government would be false to the great responsibilities entrusted to them if they failed to adopt the precautionary steps they are now taking. These steps are regarded as a service to peace by many countries and as a menace by none.

Most surprisingly, as it seems now, the Labour Party and the Opposition Liberals censured the Government, not for too little action to improve our defences, but for too much. To this day I wonder what the policy of the Labour Party would have been on armaments, if it had been in power in 1935. I can hardly believe that it would have left the country defenceless before the growing menace of Hitler. I prefer to think that the Opposition adopted that attitude simply to oppose the Conservatives, as has been done on other occasions.

On March 11th, Mr. Attlee moved a resolution

> . . . that, in the opinion of this House, the policy of His Majesty's Government with respect to defence is completely at variance with the spirit in which the League of Nations was created to establish a collective world peace, gravely jeopardizes the prospect of any Disarmament Convention, and, so far from ensuring national safety, will lead to international competition and the insecurity thereby engendered and will ultimately lead to war.

In the course of his speech Attlee said:

> We believe in a League system in which the whole world should be ranged against an aggressor. If it is shown that someone is proposing to break the peace, let us bring the whole world opinion against her. . . . We do not think that you can deal with national armaments by piling up national armaments in other countries.

These remarks did not match the realities of the situation. We were not living in a world where either Locarno or collective security could be guaranteed by pen and speech alone. The Government had to work through a League system which was incomplete, neither the United States, Germany nor Japan being members. World opinion was not enough to deter military aggressors, either then or now. The more truculent nations were in the lead in rearmament and further neglect of our own defences would have cost us our national survival. I had expressed my convictions about this four days earlier in a speech at Swindon:

> We must continue, we will continue, to work by every means in our power to increase the authority of the League, but this cannot absolve us from the duty of recognizing that all countries do not share this aim. You may be a member of the fire brigade yourself, but would you be wise to rely upon it exclusively in an emergency if some of the members had already given notice that they would not come to play their part when sent for? Surely, then, there would be an obligation upon you, while responding whenever the alarm-bell rang, to ensure at the same time that the fire-escape was working in your own house.

On the day of the debate I wrote to Baldwin:

> During the weekend I have been thinking over the quotation which you told me that you were thinking of using to-day from *The Knights*. If I have found the right one it runs as follows:

'*Agoracritus:* If one of two orators proposed to equip a fleet for war, and the other suggested the use of the same sum for paying out to the citizens, 'twas the latter who always carried the day.'

I have just one anxiety about the use of this quotation which I think it right to put to you. Is there not a danger that it might be twisted by the Opposition to imply that in your view a democracy, if it is to remain virile, must be equipping itself for war? They might even try to find in this some substantiation of their war-mongering talk.

This was not good advice and I should have encouraged Baldwin to use his quotation. However loud the immediate howling, it might have saved some tears later and this is the statesman's duty; but he must not expect to be thanked for discharging it or that democracy will know of the pain he has saved them. The popular course is almost always to coast along, but it can be deadly.

Sir Austen Chamberlain was blunt:

If war breaks out, if we become involved in a struggle, and if the Honourable Member for Limehouse [Mr. Attlee] and his friends be sitting on the government bench while London is bombed, do you think he will hold the language he held today? . . . If he does, he will be one of the first victims of the war, for he will be strung up by an angry, and justifiably angry, populace to the nearest lamp-post.

The White Paper had critics upon other grounds. Lord Lothian, for instance, wrote a letter to *The Times* which appeared on March 11th:

The statement in the White Paper that German rearmament may 'produce a situation where peace will be in peril', and generally making Germany the scapegoat, touched Herr Hitler and Germany on their most sensitive complex. It is a reaffirmation of the attitude of the Versailles Diktat, which regards Germany (with her allies) as the sole author of the War, the sole cause of European unrest, and therefore not entitled either to equality or to the same kind of treatment as other European or Asiatic Powers—an attitude, too, which it is only possible to take to a disarmed Great Power.

His was unfortunately by no means an isolated opinion.

* * * * *

Meantime, Hitler's own indignation at the White Paper, expressed through his cold, appeared to have abated and our journey was fixed for March 25th, when an announcement much graver than our modest White Paper was made from Berlin. Already on March 9th Göring had made public the existence of the Luftwaffe, Germany's military air force. On Saturday, March 16th, the Nazi Government decreed the adoption of compulsory military service, in defiance of the terms of the Treaty of Versailles, and the organization of a large army on a peacetime basis of thirty-six divisions. This was one of the early Hitler weekend decisions of policy, soon to become ominously familiar. The pretexts were Russian armaments and the recent increase in French military service from one year to two, which was the only way by which France could maintain her existing figures in the lean years of her manpower. In a speech the next day, General von Blomberg argued that Europe had become too small to be the battlefield of a second world war, but this did not assuage opinion all over the Continent, which was now deeply disturbed.

The Cabinet met on Monday, March 18th, and decided to lodge at once a formal protest in stiff terms against Hitler's action, but destroyed the effect of this by inquiring in its final paragraph whether the German Government still wished our visit to take place with the scope and purposes previously agreed. The Nazis, of course, said that they did; for Hitler this was an easy way out. The main argument for persisting with the Berlin visit was that, if things were as bad as they seemed, Simon and I might as well get the answer direct from Hitler, and I could then continue on my tour with the knowledge of it. The wiser course would have been to say that Hitler's unilateral breach of a treaty, on the eve of Simon's visit, deprived it of any usefulness and it was therefore postponed, but that I would continue with my journey to the other capitals as arranged. In other words, we ought to have returned the diplomatic cold. However, opinion inside the Cabinet, as well as outside it, would certainly not have favoured anything so like the encirclement of Germany, salutary as it would have been for Hitler. On the other hand, however popular and plausible the pretexts for continuing with the Berlin visit, it was certainly wrong to do so without agreeing our action in advance with our French and Italian allies and concerting our reply. This neglect was the more inexcusable because the French Ambassador had called twice in the last days at the Foreign Office, to stress the importance of consultation on armaments. The second time he delivered a written warning:

> The decision of the German Government, the state of mind which it publicly reveals, constitute a new fact. In these circumstances the French Government would be glad to know whether the projected visit of Sir John Simon to Berlin still offers in the eyes of the British Government the same justification or the same usefulness.

As a result of our failure, the three Governments delivered at intervals notes of protest in Berlin which were different in tone. This evident lack of solidarity brought comfort to Hitler.

Sir Robert Vansittart, while remaining of the opinion that we should not cancel our visit to Berlin, minuted that to proceed without even the appearance of consultation was to run a very grievous and certain danger and had made my task more difficult. It certainly had. Faced with indignant protests from Paris and Rome, the Government decided that, though not a member of the Cabinet, I was to be offered as a visitor to Paris. There I was to see Laval and meet Suvich, Mussolini's Under-Secretary at the Foreign Office, to explain what we were doing. From Paris I was to join Simon in Holland and travel with him to Berlin. I asked Vansittart to see Mr. Maisky in my absence and try to allay Soviet suspicions, for Lord Chilston, our Ambassador in Moscow, had told us that there was anxiety in Russia lest we should come to a separate agreement with Germany. This Vansittart did.

In these days there came to me an unexpected but agreeable offer, which had nothing to do with politics. The Prime Minister was completing his seven-year period as a Trustee of the National Gallery and asked me if I would like to take his place. I was delighted and there followed two spells of seven years which I much enjoyed, particularly when Sassoon was our chairman and Kenneth Clark our director. Austen Chamberlain once told me that his father had reproached him, when he was young in politics, with being too completely absorbed in his work. 'You must have something else to think about or you won't sleep, and then you will get ill,' was Joseph Chamberlain's advice, 'find a hobby.' Austen's interest in rock gardening was the result and he would sometimes escape from League of Nations meetings at Geneva for an hour or two in pursuit of some alpine plant. Until I could afford a country home and garden of my own, pictures provided the escape for me.

* * * * *

At the Cabinet meeting which I was invited to attend shortly before I left for my journey, Baldwin passed a note across to me while our colleagues were giving their views. This suggested in a humorous, if insular, fashion my outfit for Moscow:

2 dozen whisky
2 ,, siphons soda water
Case of dry champagne

1 dozen bottled Bass
Tinned sardines
,, corned beef
,, vegetables

Lamb's wool combinations
Concertina boots
Astrakhan cap
Ski-ing suit
Fur coat

My mission to Paris was most unenviable. The French and Italian press were indignant at our lonely action and on March 20th the French Government addressed an official protest to Geneva against Germany's violation of a treaty by introducing conscription. At their request, the Chairman of the Council summoned an Extraordinary Session to meet in April to hear the French complaint. I flew to Paris with William Strang and Robin Hankey on Friday, March 22nd. Lord Cranborne joined me there. My diary records:

> We had a really filthy crossing by special aircraft, being blown out of our course to Rouen and badly shaken up. Our radio went wrong for a while and Le Bourget did some anxious waiting in consequence.

That evening I dined with Sir George Clerk and the Embassy staff and worked in preparation for the next day. I wrote that night: 'French are watchful, sad at us and, beneath outward calm, profoundly disturbed.' Laval had made a conciliatory speech in the Chamber the same evening, in which he said:

> Germany, by her gesture, has only slowed down the hour of peace, from which we do not want to exclude anyone. The policy which France pursues with her friends is not a policy of aggression. It is not directed against any other country. The world knows that. I want to repeat it from the tribune of the French Chamber.

The Ambassador, Strang and I called on Laval the next morning. Most of the discussion took place between Laval and myself alone. There were few of the reproaches which I felt we deserved, Laval having clearly been much relieved by the decision to hold the meeting of Ministers in Paris. He told me that he had been through anxious days between our reply to the German Government and that decision. His task, he added, would have been considerably easier if we had been able to give him earlier knowledge of our projected note to Berlin.

Later, Laval and I met together with Suvich. I gave three definite assurances about our visit to Berlin. Its purpose was purely exploratory, the scope of our conversations would be the scope of the London communiqué of February 3rd, and we would report fully and faithfully to the French and Italian Governments upon the outcome of the visits to Berlin and other capitals. There would be a meeting of the three Governments to do this, with Mussolini as host, when I had completed my journey.

After some battling and a heavy luncheon, we agreed a respectable text. Appearances at least were restored. Suvich's language gave no indication that Italy's attitude towards Germany was softening. Mussolini, he said, insisted that agreement must be reached as to the limits to be placed upon concessions to Germany and the agreement must then be upheld. If Germany were to be allowed to continue to violate one engagement after another, in a very short time she would try to absorb Austria and that would mean war. In Signor Mussolini's opinion, it was essential that the French, Italian and British Governments should 'take steps immediately to stop the rot'. That was why the Italian Government attached such importance to the meeting in northern Italy taking place at the earliest possible moment.

Our statement declared in reference to the journey which Simon and I were making to Berlin:

> It was decided that after this visit and the other British visits to Moscow, Warsaw and Prague, all of which were undertaken with the good wishes of the other two governments, the British, French and Italian Foreign Ministers would meet at Stresa on April 11th. M. Pierre Laval, Mr. Eden and Signor Suvich noted with satisfaction the complete unity of purpose of their governments.

At luncheon Laval remarked that Baldwin had told him in London that I was to be Secretary of State. Why, he wanted to know, was I not already? I wondered if Baldwin had really said anything of the kind; it was not like him.

* * * * *

I left Paris by air on Sunday morning, March 24th, flying over Béthune and Ypres, of many memories. Off Zeebrugge my aeroplane met Simon's coming from England and we flew on in company to Amsterdam where we had luncheon. Later we refuelled at Hanover, where I was surprised to find a large, passive crowd at the airport. This was repeated at Berlin and in the streets of the capital as we drove to the Adlon Hotel. We had been met by von Neurath and a warlike guard of the S.S., whose commander drew a long and flashing sabre and delivered a message from the Führer to the Foreign Secretary, who looked unhappily down his nose.

That night Simon and I dined at the Embassy and prepared for the meetings of the following day. Opinions were divided; Newton, the Counsellor, was most optimistic and told Cranborne he thought that the German Government really did want an agreement and would stretch a point to get one. He even believed that they might come down below the thirty-six divisions which they had claimed as their minimum. The Ambassador did not share this hopefulness. He thought that a wonderful chance had been lost the year before and would not come again. The Naval Attaché, on the other hand, suggested that matters had not been improved by my visit to Paris and our subsequent communiqué, which stressed the unanimity of Britain, France and Italy. Germany wanted a separate agreement, he said. No doubt she did and then Europe would have been at her feet. Unhappily, there were those who, at a later date than this, continued to believe that Hitler should be satisfied on this count, without understanding the reckoning.

The meetings were held over two days, March 25th and 26th, at the Chancellor's palace, with morning and afternoon sessions each day and an official dinner at night. Simon, Phipps and I represented His Majesty's Government, with Strang and Ralph Wigram of the Foreign Office in attendance. Hitler, von Neurath and Ribbentrop represented the Germans, with von Neurath's private secretary in attendance and Schmidt interpreting ably. Hitler was definitely more authoritative and less anxious to please than a year before. Another twelve months of a dictator's power and growing military force to back it had had its consequence. At this second interview I was most unfavourably impressed by Hitler's personality. Unlike Stalin as I was to know him, or Mussolini, he appeared negative to me, certainly not compelling; he was also rather shifty. Stalin and Mussolini were, in their separate ways, men whose personality would be felt in any company. Hitler was essentially the man who would pass in the crowd. Though the interview was well conducted by the Chancellor, without hesitation and without notes, as befitted the man who knew where he wanted to go, I was becoming familiar with this kind of expertise. We sat grouped round a low table. Hitler enjoyed displaying diagrams to illustrate his mounting needs.

This made an occasional break in the talks while we went to a desk to study one or other of them.

Simon opened by giving his account of how we came to be in Berlin. He said we had gladly accepted the original invitation, adding that there had been difficulties in undertaking the present visit as a result of the new developments of the preceding ten days. He did not, however, go into the nature of these difficulties, against which we had protested, but said we had come in spite of them. Describing the views of the Government and people of Britain, Simon said that they wanted to preserve general peace and earnestly wished that Germany would work with all countries for that object. They thought that the future would take one of two forms, general co-operation or a division into two camps, 'isolation on the one side and combination, which might look like encirclement, on the other'. He went on to explain how people in Britain had been very greatly disturbed by a series of acts on the part of Germany. The result was that public opinion at home was doubtful, and trying anxiously to estimate what was the real course of German policy.

Hitler's reply was a skilful piece of special pleading, which was none the less threatening in its undertones. He argued that the first and only great aim of his policy was to revive and make happy a people stricken by immeasurable disaster. His political acts during the last two years had been willed and approved by the German people, just as all his future acts would be. Then came the assurances. He maintained that the object of German policy in its new political conception was not a menace to anyone. Germany was surrounded by national states which were either as densely populated as herself or inhabited by intensely nationalistic peoples. To say that Germany intended to 'tear away territory' from others was to disregard the difficulties of the economic situation from which Germany was at present suffering. Annexation of territory, he said, would merely add to the political and economic difficulties with which he was faced. This was an argument Hitler was to continue to use even after it was belied by his own deeds. It was a clever cover plan and calculated to evoke a response from the spokesmen of parliamentary governments deeply troubled by large scale unemployment. The assurance was never more than a useful formula to Hitler. I have never known a dictator influenced to more modest courses by economic difficulties, which are as often a spur as a curb.

In reply to Simon's observations on uneasiness in England, Hitler said: 'If England had been as unlucky as Germany since 1914, every

Englishman would have acted as I have done.' The decision to withdraw from the League had been approved by 94 per cent. of the German nation. He was convinced that, in similar circumstances, Great Britain would have done the same and, in fact, would never have joined the League at all. Germany did not threaten Austria, but he could not forget that the regime in Austria was in contradiction to the great majority of the people over which it maintained power. Many difficulties resulted from this. Germany could not co-operate with a Government which, both at home and abroad, insulted the German Government and the German ideal. The same was true, he added, of Lithuania; a reference to Germans living in Memel. Hitler said that he had been accused of violating the Treaty of Versailles. He himself would never have signed the Treaty. He would rather have died, he added, fixing Simon with his jellied eyes. On an earlier occasion, Hitler continued, Germany had had to violate a treaty. In 1806 Napoleon had imposed a treaty on Germany, but on the evening of Waterloo, Wellington had not protested when the Prussian army arrived, although that army could only have done so in violation of a treaty. This must have been the nearest to humour Hitler ever approached; I thought it a good thrust, delivered without a flicker of a smile.

When we came to the detailed agenda, Simon put the case for an Eastern Pact of mutual assistance comprising the governments of Eastern Europe, on the model of Locarno. But it was soon clear that Hitler would have none of it and preferred individual non-aggression pacts, which were soon to be recognized as the sinister first move in destroying the victim. Then followed two firm assurances, both volunteered and both to be broken. Hitler told us that war between Germany and Czechoslovakia could be excluded, because there was an arbitration agreement, and assured us that Germany would never declare war on Russia. He denounced Moscow's policies and said that the Russian desire for an Eastern Pact was in order to have a freer hand in the Far East.

At this point I argued with Hitler about Russia's alleged external ambitions. The country, I said, which had most to do at home, which had great territories to develop, was Russia. I did not think that a nation could win a war by the air weapon alone, or that Russia would be a military menace for many years. Hitler agreed about the limitation of the air arm, certainly against Russia. No doubt he forgot this judgement when he tried to subdue Britain by just these methods in 1940 and 1941. He was nearer the mark in forecasting Soviet Russia's formidable military power in ten years' time. Here perhaps was the germ of the Nazi attack on the Soviets in 1941. There was at that later date some military opinion, even outside Germany, which believed that Hitler would be strategically wise to deal with Russia before her power was further developed, on the assumption that a clash between the two powers was one day inevitable. Hitler, as he now told us, based his assessment of Russia's growing strength on his military advisers, who, as he truly said, 'at least know their business'. Perhaps behind this observation lay the experience of Reichswehr officers during the period of collaboration with the Soviet army after the Treaty of Rapallo* in 1922. They were well-qualified to appraise the Russian military machine, for they had helped to develop it.

In the afternoon, we came to speak of Austria again. Hitler continued his argument that if a free vote were possible, the population of Austria would vote for closer relations, if not complete union, with Germany. Three years later he was to deny to the Austrian Chancellor the right to this very appeal. On this occasion Hitler assured us once more, as one who knew Austria, that he had no desire to increase the economic difficulties of his own country by the annexation of another whose economic difficulties were greater still. The Chancellor declined to take the lead in giving Austria a guarantee of non-interference. Since Germany contemplated no aggression, the Austrian question was not a problem at all. He would be glad if Austria could disappear from the chessboard of European politics. Hitler was fertile in excuses, but it was clear that we should make no more progress with the Central European Pact than with the Eastern one.

Worse, however, was to come. When we discussed Germany's return to the League of Nations, Hitler referred to the 'great disillusionment, owing to the coupling of the Covenant with the Treaty of Versailles. . . . If I had been Chancellor in 1914 there would have been no war, and certainly not a war with England; and if I had been Chancellor, the war, had it taken place, would not necessarily have been lost. The Treaty of Versailles imposed upon the German nation an inferiority which they have never recognized.' I contested Hitler's argument about the victors and the vanquished. It was true that the Covenant was born of the Treaty of Versailles, but technically the two could be divorced. In the minds of the British Government, I said,

* A treaty signed in 1922 between Germany and Russia re-establishing diplomatic relations between the two countries, which resulted in a number of close German-Russian contacts, for a time.

Germany was the complete equal of the other powers in the League itself and on the Council. Germany had entered the League after the Locarno Treaty. One service which that Treaty had rendered was to bring to an end the conception of victors and vanquished. Germany took her place at the Council as one of its permanent members, I concluded, and there were many nations at Geneva who had fought on opposing sides in the war.

Simon asked whether the separation of the Covenant from the Treaty of Versailles would help to bring Germany back to the League. Hitler agreed with me that the problem was partly one of the technical separation of the Covenant and the Treaty. But what remained over and beyond that was the actual fact of Germany's position of inferiority on all those points which she had not rectified for herself. He gave one illustration of the German position of inferiority: Germany would still not be thought fit to administer a colony, while Japan, who had left the League, could administer a former German one. From this there soon followed a claim for the return of the former German colonies. 'Perhaps they have little economic value for the British Empire. Probably they cause financial loss to the British Empire and would cause financial loss to Germany too. But it is the moral and legal aspect of the question, the whole position which Germany occupies in the world is affected by it.' Then came for the first time an offer to stand by Britain in future years if she would agree to these concessions. 'It might be that even the British Empire will one day be glad to have Germany's help and Germany's forces at her disposal,' Hitler said. 'If we can find such a solution and give satisfaction to Germany's most urgent and elementary demands, this will lead Germany back to co-operation and friendly relations with Great Britain.'

In reply, Simon attempted a tepid correction. He told Hitler that the British Government wished to have the closest association with Germany, but without prejudice to their relations with France. They did not want to substitute one friend for another, because they wanted to be loyal friends to all. On the subject of Germany's former colonies, Simon said he would take note of what Hitler had said and would report on it, but he pointed out that, as regards mandated territories, they were not at Britain's sole disposal. Hitler had produced a diagram showing a large part of the world as British colonial territory. Simon told the Chancellor that this area included not only colonies but the great Dominions. These, in their relationship to Britain, did not compare in any way with the colonies of other powers.

Evidently, Hitler might have been tempted to return to the League but only to become a mandatory power, while flouting its rules. There was as yet no clear understanding that the struggle then developing was one between collective security and regional pacts. Those who became allies in the second world war believed that peace must be upheld collectively by the powers who wished to see international order defended. Unhappily, we were not yet agreed as to the methods of doing so, nor upon what military contribution, if any, each should make. The result was that collective security had no magnet powerful enough for Germany's neighbours when Hitler offered each of them pacts, seemingly innocuous, but whose true design was to pick off his enemies one by one.

So ended seven hours of talk in a day of mounting demands. If Hitler were conceded even a tenth part of them, I reflected, he would have had a triumph, while no concession of any value was offered in exchange. The future looked ominous. I wrote in my diary that night:

> Results bad . . . whole tone and temper very different to a year ago, rearmed and rearming with the old Prussian spirit very much in evidence. Russia is now the bogey.

* * * * *

Despite these overcharged discussions, we were made welcome, in part no doubt because of the isolation Germany felt from her other neighbours. The Nazis would not abate their demands one jot, but they would have liked to be friends with us, if they could have got their own way. This, strangely enough, was not only as a passport to their own power. We were, I suppose, regarded as Nordic, but there was also something akin to respect for the British Empire which then still existed and commanded authority, if not decisive military power, in the world. This may seem surprising, but there was a streak of it in the twisted Nazi complex, which admired the dominance of the many by the few. I give one example within my experience. A film, *Lives of a Bengal Lancer*, which was then being shown in Berlin and romantically depicted fighting and adventure on the North-West Frontier of India, created an astonishing impression. Everyone, from Hitler downwards, mentioned it with enthusiasm.

On the first night of our visit there was a state dinner at the Reich President's House, which Lord Cranborne well described as 'a tremendous affair in a huge square rococo room with painted ceilings and damask walls, and hordes of flunkeys with powdered hair in splendid liveries.' I sat next to Frau Hess, who had the Führer on her right, while Frau Goebbels was on my left with Göring beside her, he too in a splendid livery of his own devising. My chief recollection of the evening is a comment I made that we were near the anniversary of March 21st, 1918, the last great German offensive of the first world war. Hitler picked this up at once and we were soon discussing the fronts and the forces engaged. It emerged that we must have been opposite each other round about La Fère on the river Oise, which had formed the left flank of the German attack. I told the Führer that the Germans had been ten to one. Together we drew a map on the back of a dinner card, which I still possess, signed by both of us, Hitler marking in some places and I others. The corporal on the German side had as clear a recollection of place names and dispositions as the young staff officer, as I had then just become, on the British. François-Poncet observed all this. After dinner he came up to me and said: 'It is true you were opposite Hitler?' I replied it seemed so. *'Et vous l'avez manqué? Vous devriez être fusillé.'*

★ ★ ★ ★ ★

On the following morning we took up the question of armaments. Simon remarked that His Majesty's Government had recently been engaged in separate discussions with other powers in preparation for the modification of the existing naval treaties; they were due for revision that year. He invited the German Government to take part in similar informal discussions. Hitler accepted. Simon then referred to a proposal which had recently been made to Phipps by the Chancellor that Germany should have a fleet equal in tonnage to 35 per cent. of the British. Hitler had apparently thought that this would give him a navy equal to that of France. The Foreign Secretary pointed out that the French navy was in fact more than half the size of the British. He added that the figure of 35 per cent. appeared to the British Government to be so large as to make general agreement almost impossible. Hitler, however, declared that he did not see any heavenly or earthly authority which could force Germany to recognize the superiority of the French or Italian fleets. This was tough talking, but Simon, in view of the forthcoming discussions in London, preferred not to probe the naval question further.

At this point we had a taste of a Hitler technique which was later to be more freely indulged. The Chancellor read out a telegram purporting to announce a verdict which had just been given in a trial at Kovno against German Nazis from Memel. They had been tried for treason. Hitler asked furiously what Britain would do if the Treaty of Versailles had torn away part of her territory and placed it under a country like Lithuania and if Englishmen, merely because they were Englishmen, were tortured and put in prison. For a while the storm raged; von Neurath looked embarrassed, Ribbentrop coldly approving. Simon and I made no comment and it died away.

We then discussed military armaments, arguing against Hitler's recent announcement of thirty-six divisions. We made no headway. I said that if these thirty-six divisions implied, as had been suggested to our Ambassador, 500,000 men, that was a figure to which other Western European powers could never attain. It would make parity impossible and give Germany superiority. The British Government could not accept this figure as a basis for discussion. Hitler in reply produced a diagram showing the strength of his neighbours and demonstrating the possible combinations against him. France had forty-four divisions, Poland had thirty-four, Russia had a hundred and one. Hitler added, as another pretext for so large an armed force, that Germany had undertaken at Locarno to respect the demilitarized zone in the Rhineland. He was soon to make this argument invalid. To round off his demands the Chancellor said that he wanted the necessary equipment for his thirty-six divisions. If the intention of our journey was to discover Hitler's full purpose, we were certainly near our objective.

At one time the discussion became almost ridiculous. We were criticizing para-military formations. Hitler pooh-poohed their significance in Germany. He added that in foreign countries there were para-military organizations receiving training with rifles, even at Eton. I laughed, but Hitler did not, and pointed out that I had been an officer in the first war, yet I was very young. Where had I received my training? Clearly at Eton. I denied this and said our Officers' Training Corps were not taken so seriously. For many boys they were the occasion for smoking on field days. It was not until the war had broken out that we began to train seriously. We were standing looking at the diagram while we argued. I appealed to von Neurath for support; he was silent. The Führer shook his head, completely unconvinced. For him English public schools were para-military organizations with military instruction as their first duty and he thought this an excellent plan and praised them for it. The Germans should do the same. My protests were disregarded as patriotic deception.

Air armaments came last in our discussions and presented the grimmest picture, revealing how far matters had deteriorated since my visit the year before. Hitler now claimed parity with the French air force. If Britain brought her air force up to French strength, he announced, then it would be that parity which Germany would demand. If we persuaded France to come down to our level, then Germany would accept that parity. On cross-examination by Simon, it became clear that the parity he demanded was with the French air force in Metropolitan France, plus that in North Africa. Finally, Simon put last, as he had often told me a cross-examiner should, the question that to us mattered most: what was the present strength of the German air force? After a moment's hesitation, Hitler replied that Germany had reached parity with Great Britain. There was no triumph in his tone, but there was grim foreboding in my heart.

The final session remained, at which we discussed an air pact, which Hitler would only accept if there were no limitation on the size of the air forces. We were pledged to our allies not to agree to one except as part of a general settlement and of this there was no sign. That evening I summed up in my diary that the total results of the visit were very disappointing. In a comment on Hitler's obsession with Russia, I wrote that I was strongly against letting Germany expand eastwards: 'Apart from its dishonesty, it would be our turn next.'

We dined again with Hitler that night, but on a smaller scale, in a room in the Reich President's House. The occasion was informal and much pleasanter, the decoration and lighting restrained. I was told that this was Hitler's own dining-room. It was certainly in better taste than anything else we had seen in Berlin. Hitler was an easy host, moving about among his guests and making sure that all wants were satisfied. The company was much the same as the night before, except that I had on my right Princess Philip of Hesse, who was pretty and well-dressed and seemed rather out of place in these surroundings. Tragically, she was sent nine years later to a concentration camp, where she died. I had to leave before the end of the evening to catch my train to Moscow, though nobody mentioned this leprous journey except von Blomberg, who was then Germany's leading military figure and War Minister. I had known and liked him from my earlier visit and we had some talk after dinner. He asked me to convey his greetings to Marshal Voroshilov, who was a friend. I thought at the time that, however untouchable the Russians might seem to Hitler, the German General Staff appeared to have no such inhibitions. I judged them wiser, little suspecting that, just over four years later, Ribbentrop would himself be in Moscow making the second world war inevitable.

* * * * *

The whole of the next day, March 27th, was spent in the train, while the Polish landscape, flat, dreary and poor, crept by. I had a talk with Maisky, but I was tired, and so rested and read a book called *Russia's Iron Age*. This leisure gave me the chance to reflect on the last two days in Berlin. Though I was not a member of the Cabinet and had not been asked for an opinion, I felt I had a responsibility to give it. Accordingly, I drafted the following telegram which I sent home when I got to Moscow:

During the thirty-six hours train journey there has been opportunity to think over results of our Berlin conversations and I venture to submit a few personal reflections for what they may be worth.

The essential question seems to be does a basis now exist for a general European settlement? A year ago I believe there was such a basis, but it is exceedingly difficult to maintain that it exists now. An important purpose of our visit to Berlin was to learn whether German Government was willing to take her place at Geneva. We now know she will not do so except at a price which includes return of her colonies and probably other unspecified conditions as well. It would seem in principle that, quite apart from merits of this demand, it is highly undesirable to establish a precedent that a bribe should be offered to any nation in any circumstances to induce it to take its proper place as a good European at Geneva. Moreover, since Germany in leaving the League acted without justification in the view of His Majesty's Government and of most other Governments, will it not merely encourage her in her blackmail to offer a price for her return?

Apart altogether from question of Germany's return to the League is there elsewhere any basis of agreement? Germany's demands on land and at sea, in respect of neither of which is there any sign of abatement, seem to make an agreement impossible, while her attitude to Eastern Pact and Danubian Pact makes any security agreement extremely doubtful, to say the least.

If, as it would seem from this analysis, there is in fact no basis for a general settlement, what should be the policy of His Majesty's Government? It should be borne in mind that in view of Germany's demand in respect of colonies our position is no longer merely that of an honest broker. We have now become a principal. In such conditions it remains to be considered whether there may not be only one course of action open to us: to join with those powers who are members of the League of Nations in re-affirming our faith in that institution and our determination to uphold the principles of the Covenant. It may be that the spectacle of the Great Powers of the

League re-affirming their intention to collaborate more closely than ever, is not only the sole means of bringing home to Germany that the inevitable effect of persisting in her present policy will be to consolidate against her all those nations which believe in collective system, but will also tend to give confidence to those less powerful nations which through fear of Germany's growing strength might otherwise be drawn into her orbit.

Sir Robert Vansittart minuted on this telegram: 'These views seem very sound', but the Cabinet did not think so. At any rate they took a different course.

IX

STALIN

March – April 1935

My arrival in Moscow – I talk to Mr. Litvinov – My first impression of Mr. Stalin – Russian distrust of Germany – The ballet and sightseeing – Drafting a communiqué – Reflections on my Russian visit

That evening, as the light was failing, the train slowed down and we passed a barbed wire entanglement. Maisky bowed slightly and said: 'Let me welcome you to Russia.' At the frontier we had to change trains because of the broader gauge railway. On the track the Soviet guards stood tall and motionless in their long cloaks, flashes of ochre against the white snow background, and around us the stillness of Russia that can be felt. The train was very luxurious, my own quarters such as I had never seen before, and all rolling comfortably across the Russian countryside. It was not a cheerful reflection that this must have been part of the old Imperial train, the cypher and crown were still on the cutlery. Immediately we were summoned to a large dining-room with chairs and a table running down the centre. Refreshments were laid out, caviar, vodka and fruit, and wine from the Caucasus.

The next morning, March 28th, as we approached Moscow, precautions which seemed to me extravagant were taken. From the windows we could see troops lining the permanent way on either side of the train quite a while before we reached our destination. On arrival we found the station freely decorated with Red flags and Union Jacks. I thought that the Union Jacks were not quite right, but did not like to look too closely. They were obviously home-made and the makers could not have had much practice. Anyway, it is a difficult flag to reproduce and it was the intention that mattered. Litvinov and members of the Soviet Foreign Office, our Ambassador, Lord

Chilston, and his staff, were all waiting on the platform with the attendant cameras, which seemed continually active throughout our visit, and more Red Guards. Ordinary passengers appeared to have been entirely excluded. Though the welcome on the platform was cordial, it did not extend beyond our official group. For one of those unfathomable Russian reasons, no announcement whatever of the visit had been made in advance, except the bare fact without a date, quite a while before. During this time our Ambassador was reporting elaborate and painstaking preparations, but no publicity. Maybe our hosts thought that I might not come and did not want to be at risk, or that the outcome of the Berlin meeting might be such that they would not want to receive me.

The dismal two-mile drive from the station to the Embassy left a lasting impression upon me. Large, drab crowds, unsmiling, poorly dressed and ill-fed by our standards, went disinterestedly on their way. The weather, the streets, the people, all seemed grey, sad and unending. I was surprised when the Ambassador told me that conditions were better than they had been even a year or two before. They must indeed have been pitiful.

Our party stayed in the British Embassy, in the ugly grandeur of a former sugar merchant's house, but with a splendid view of the Kremlin across the Moscow river. Elegant in its lovely soft rose colour, there are few more beautiful sights in the world. We got down to work at once, in a first conversation of two hours with Mr. Litvinov that afternoon at the Soviet Foreign Office. Mr. Maisky was with him, while Lord Chilston and Mr. Strang came with me. I gave Litvinov an account of our Berlin meetings which was rather fuller than that which Simon had given to the French and other Western Ambassadors in Berlin. When I was speaking of Hitler's attitude to the League of Nations, Litvinov asked me whether one of the conditions of the return of Germany to Geneva concerned the demilitarized zone in the Rhineland. He no doubt thought Hitler wanted to reoccupy it. I replied, no, the zone had only been mentioned once and that in connection with Locarno, by which the Chancellor declared that he was prepared to abide. When we discussed armaments I told Litvinov of the extent of the German demands and that the thirty-six divisions would now reach a total of 550,000 men of all arms. The conversation continued:

EDEN: In defence of this figure, Hitler produced a map showing the forces of Germany's neighbours. The French had thirty-four divisions within easy call and the Czechoslovakians seventeen divisions. The Soviet Union a hundred and one divisions.

I pointed out to the Chancellor that the Soviet Government had plenty of work to do at home and plenty of territory to administer, and was unlikely to embark upon a policy of conquest. The Chancellor, however, took quite a different view and regarded the Soviet Union as a serious menace from the point of view both of world revolution and military aggression. In view of this, he said, Germany must be strong.

LITVINOV: Did the Chancellor speak about expansion in the east?

EDEN: I pointed out to the Chancellor that Herr Rosenberg's* plans were a cause of apprehension and asked why he allowed these plans. At this both the Chancellor and von Neurath merely laughed. My impression is that Rosenberg is not much in favour at present.

After some further talk on naval and air armaments, the conversation resumed:

LITVINOV: What are your conclusions from the conversations?

EDEN: The point really is what ought to be done next, and this is no doubt being considered in London now. I have not been in touch with the Government and I do not know their views. For my part, I think that those governments which believe in the collective system will have to hold to it even more strongly than before. This question will no doubt be considered at Stresa as it is now being considered between you and me. What do you think?

LITVINOV: What were the grounds for the Chancellor's fear of the Soviet Union?

EDEN: He apparently fears both the military strength of the Soviet Union and her intentions to promote world revolution. The Chancellor regards Germany as a barrier against this double danger. He asked what we thought the Soviet army should amount to. In reply we drew attention to the table in our Draft Convention, where the Soviet Union is given 500,000 men as compared with 200,000 for France, Italy and Germany.

LITVINOV: Was there any talk of Japan?

EDEN: The Far East was not mentioned. When I was in Berlin in 1934 it was France that the Chancellor had in mind. Now it is the Soviet Union.

Litvinov then gave an account of the development of relations between Germany and the Soviet Union.

* Head of the Nazi Party's Foreign Office and editor of the Nazi newspaper, the *Völkischer Beobachter*. He was a notorious exponent of German expansion eastwards.

Litvinov: For many years relations were excellent. After the Treaty of Rapallo, which was not an alliance and contained no secret clauses, relations with both the Government and the Reichswehr were good. These relations continued until just before Hitler came to power, when Herr von Papen proposed to the French Government a secret agreement aimed at the Soviet Union. This was followed by the Hugenberg memorandum* at the London Economic Conference and the programme of aggression in *Mein Kampf*. The original German plan was to attack France and then to attack in the East. Since then German plans have changed. The plan now apparently is to leave France alone, but to attack in the east only. Von Neurath has assured the Soviet Government that nothing has changed in the attitude of Germany towards the Soviet Union and that what Hitler and Rosenberg may have said is of purely historic interest. The Soviet Government are not satisfied with this explanation. If Hitler's and Rosenberg's books continue to be a basis of education in Germany, this can only mean that Germany takes these plans seriously. Words are not enough. The Soviet Government wants deeds.

To test these German expressions of goodwill I proposed to Germany early in 1934 the conclusion of a Baltic Pact which would include a reciprocal guarantee by Germany and the Soviet Union of the integrity of the Baltic States. This pact was to be open to access by other powers. Although the German Ambassador of the day, Herr Nadolny, was in favour of this pact, the German Government refused it without giving any substantial reason.

I remembered that Nadolny had been recalled soon after this and had not, so far as I knew, been re-employed. Chilston then asked what Poland's attitude had been in this matter.

Litvinov: I made a somewhat similar proposal to Poland, namely, a joint declaration of common interest in the maintenance of the independence of the Baltic States. Beck accepted the idea of such a declaration, but, immediately after the conclusion of the Polish-German agreement, the Polish Ambassador here informed me that his Government could not enter into such a declaration.

Germany's refusal of the Baltic Pact has increased apprehensions in the Soviet Union and in France also.

Litvinov then gave an account of his discussions with France, explaining that the pact of mutual guarantee with that country would have to take a different form, since the French Government were unwilling to give any guarantee to the Baltic States.

* An intransigent document submitted to the World Economic Conference by Hugenberg, then Reich Minister for Economics and for Food and Agriculture. This asked for colonies and *Lebensraum*, which evoked Russian protests.

LITVINOV: I do not regard mutual assistance as a real guarantee of defence, but rather as a deterrent; as a last resort the Soviet Union has to rely upon her own forces. But if Germany knew that she would find ranged against her a coalition composed of a number of states she might hesitate to risk her fate.

After criticism of Polish policy as having been similar to the German, Litvinov admitted that there had recently been some slight improvement.

LITVINOV: If Hitler is now saying that he is not interested in the west and has his eye only upon expansion in the east, this can only be because he thinks his policy acceptable to Great Britain and other powers. He is building on the assumption of continued antagonism between Britain and the Soviet Union. I do not think that Hitler is sincere in disclaiming interest in the west, but even if he is, he obviously considers that hatred of the Soviet Union in the world at large is so great as to excuse any adventure on his part.

Hitler, however, is not the only man in Germany. The Reichswehr is much less hostile to the Eastern Pact and is always ready to make a bargain with the Soviet Union. I have evidence of this from secret sources. The plan of the Reichswehr is always to dispose of France first, rather than to waste valuable time and energy on Russia. What is absolutely certain is that Germany intends to attack somewhere. Hitler's assurances are not to be believed, not even when he says that he has resigned Alsace-Lorraine. Germany is bent first upon revenge, then upon domination.

We then spoke of the Far East, about which Litvinov was more confident, before coming back to the general scene.

LITVINOV: The Soviet Government are concerned not merely with their own frontiers, but for peace in Europe. They have enough work to do at home to keep them busy for half a century and it will take them decades to catch up with the rest of the world in technical developments and the standard of life. We do not want to be disturbed, and we believe that a war in Europe, even if we are not directly involved, will eventually drag us in. For this reason we strongly support the idea of collective security and approve of the Central European Pact as well as the Eastern Pact.

EDEN: It is difficult to draw any hopeful conclusion from Germany's reply about the Eastern Pact.

LITVINOV: Germany is still trying to separate the other powers one from another. There is perhaps, however, some chance of persuading Poland to join the pact. This is where British policy might play a big part, because Poland now attaches great importance to what is said in London, particularly since she has quarrelled with France. It might be worth while trying to detach Poland from her present line and draw her towards the Eastern Pact.

The alternative is a pact without Germany and Poland, but this would lose 50 per cent. of its value.

In general, however, much will depend upon the attitude of Britain. What do you think?

EDEN: Speaking personally I think that, in view of Germany's attitude, the collective system will become more important than ever, and our faith in it should be reaffirmed in some way with others who form part of it. I do not think that Germany will be happy in isolation. If it is clear to Germany that the alternatives are either to come into a collective system or for the world to be ranged against her, she will not be able to stand out very long. In 1934 I thought that there was a basis for a general settlement with Germany and that the French were unwise to refuse the German offer. Now I find it very difficult to see what basis there is. Apart from Germany's attitude towards the League of Nations, I cannot see any prospect for an arms and security agreement.

LITVINOV: I wonder whether His Majesty's Government could possibly do more for security than is contained in the Covenant and Locarno. Is there any possibility of a British guarantee for the Baltic States?

EDEN: In my view there is not.

LITVINOV: Do you think that the integrity of the Baltic States is a British interest?

EDEN: It would be extremely short-sighted of anyone to think it better to have a war in the east to avoid war in the west. The interest of His Majesty's Government in the Baltic States is not like their interest in Belgium and the Low Countries, though they are, of course, interested from the point of view of general security in Europe.

After some discussion about obligations under Article 16 of the Covenant, Litvinov concluded by commenting that I should have difficulty in finding out anything from Pilsudski or Beck. His reason for being anxious to include both Germany and Poland in the pact was that he was afraid Germany might lead Poland into adventures. Chilston wondered whether any Polish attack on Russia was credible. Litvinov thought Poland might attempt this if she had a promise of assistance from Germany and some expectation of neutrality from other great powers. I said I could not conceive that Poland would attack the Soviet Union. I understood it to be Litvinov's view that Germany's first attack might be on the Baltic States and not upon the Soviet Union. He assented.

In the evening Litvinov and his wife gave us a dinner at the Spiridonovka, another large, former merchant's house used for these purposes. Except for Stalin, every important commissar was there and high officials who, our Ambassador informed me, were rarely present at entertainments where there were foreigners. Voroshilov, then People's Commissar for Defence, was among them. I was to see more of him in the war years. Stalin's close companion and friend, he was always pleasant and relaxed and a little gayer as the evening wore on. I gave him von Blomberg's message and we had some talk of German intentions. Kaganovich was there too. He was to remain a power in the land until well into Khrushchev's reign. Ordjonikidze was another of the commissars present; he was soon to be hoist with his own purge.

Litvinov made a speech in English. It was ominous about the world situation, 'never since the world war have there been such misgivings about the fate of peace as now', but friendly to Britain. He believed my visit to Moscow to be not merely the beginning of co-operation between our two countries, but a pledge that it would continue. He ended with a generous personal tribute and raised his glass to drink the health of His Majesty the King of England, the first such toast in Russia since the Revolution.

I replied to Litvinov in a short speech proposing 'the happiness and prosperity of the peoples of this great country' and asking those present to drink 'to the President of the Central Executive Committee, and Mr. Litvinov, to your very good health'. I noticed that the next day the texts of our speeches were published in the Soviet press, without the toasts. The dinner was followed by a reception for the Diplomatic Corps and a dance. Ballerinas and journalists and officers of all three services made up our numbers. Karl Radek, then the editor of *Izvestia*, was amongst the journalists and we had some talk together. I found him lively and intelligent, though re-telling much of the official patter of his Party in his comments on Europe. I little thought that within two years he would have been eliminated.

It was 1.30 in the morning before supper was over and we were able to go to bed. In spite of the dancing and the apparent gaiety, there was a sense of strain, due, I think, to recent events in Moscow of which everyone in the room was conscious. Kirov, a most powerful commissar, an intimate of Stalin's and Secretary of the Party's Central Committee, had been murdered. In apparent retaliation hundreds, if not thousands, of victims had been arrested and condemned or deported. It had been a drastic purge. Kirov had been shot by the husband of a woman he had loved, but the probability is that this was only cover for a deeper political motive. Years later during the war, Stalin referred in conversation to one of these purges. He explained, not in any sense in extenuation of his deeds, for this was not Stalin's habit, that drastic action was indispensable to deal with pro-German elements in the army and the administration. In the process he appears to have dealt with thousands of others as well.

* * * * *

I continued my conversations with Litvinov the next day. We discussed what could be done to make a stronger collective system. Litvinov asked me what the attitude of Great Britain would be, supposing the German Government were to continue to refuse to take part in any security pact and other parties went on alone to conclude such security agreements as they could. I said my personal impression was that there was not likely to be any objection to such a course, provided that the security arrangements were open to accession by other states and were under the auspices of the League. He seemed to like this reply, so I asked him whether he had any such plan. He said that he was not quite sure, the Soviet Government might perhaps want to do this. He was pessimistic about the power of the League, unless buttressed by outside regional agreements, and he shared my opinion that the German attitude towards numbers in the armed forces and heavy war materials gave little hope for any arms agreement.

Litvinov then observed that the real point of difference between His Majesty's Government and the Soviet Government was that the former did not believe in the aggressiveness of German policy. I said I thought it would be fairer to say that His Majesty's Government were not so convinced of it as the Soviet Government. It seemed to me significant that Sir John Simon, in a statement in Parliament on the previous day about our discussions in Berlin, had referred to 'the considerable divergencies of opinion' they had revealed. Litvinov repeated his apprehension that the air pact would be concluded with Germany whether that country came into a European settlement or not. I said that this was definitely not so.

We had some more discussion on the respective positions of our countries, which was useful in clearing suspicion and in showing how few points of friction remained between us. Near the end of our talks, Litvinov gave his summing up. 'The Soviet public', he said, 'sees the situation thus. On the one hand, there is Germany with obviously aggressive designs. On the other hand, there are a number of states trying to check Germany. Great Britain, by failing to support these attempts, appears to be going to the aid of Germany. The Soviet public cannot be expected to understand the play of internal politics and public opinion which influences British policy.' I replied that this was a misreading of British psychology. 'The British public is not anti-German at present,' I said, 'but it would be opposed to any country which showed the intention of breaking the peace. A great many people in England think that French rigidity has helped Hitler's rise. People in England are neither pro-French nor anti-German. If they were finally convinced that Germany intended to break the peace, they would align themselves accordingly.'

That afternoon, before going to see Stalin, we had a short spell of sightseeing in the Kremlin. We were shown a glowing collection of vestments, jewels, silver, embroidered dresses and Persian rugs. The world since the Middle Ages had poured its gifts at the feet of the Czars of all the Russias and here they were, carefully kept and presented, for us to see: the silver which Queen Elizabeth had sent to Ivan the Terrible, the wedding dress of Catherine the Great and priceless mediæval jewels. It was an Aladdin's cave glittering with history.

* * * * *

My interview with Stalin nearly foundered on an unexpected obstacle. Before leaving London I had been assured, and so had the Cabinet, that I was to meet him. On arrival this was confirmed, but with the added condition that Stalin would see me alone, the Ambassador could not accompany me. The argument in support of this ruling was that Stalin was General Secretary of the Communist Party, not a member of the Government, so that there was something more than protocol in his refusal to see an ambassador. On the other hand I was determined to take Chilston with me. He spoke Russian and I did not. Moreover, I knew that there were colleagues at home who were against the visit and against me, too, for that matter, and I wanted his authoritative witness to my words.

As we were not to take an interpreter of our own and Mr. Litvinov himself was going to be the sole translator, I thought it indispensable to have someone with me who could check what was being said by the Russians and, at least as important, how far the Russians understood the replies I gave. I had no doubt of Litvinov's good faith, but he was not a trained interpreter. Anyone with experience of international conferences will know what risks there are in amateur translations, however brilliantly executed. The Soviet reluctance may also have been due to Stalin's dislike of international discussion in a crowd. In this he was undoubtedly right, and the addition of Chilston meant that Maisky must be there too. For some days the argument continued, until I began to fear that the interview for which I had travelled so many thousands of miles might not take place. Then the Russians relented and we were invited to Molotov's room in the Kremlin. He was then President of the Council of Commissars.

This meeting, the first occasion when Stalin received a political representative from the West, was the central experience of my tour. As we entered I saw standing there a short, thick-set man with hair *en brosse*. He was in a grey tunic, with rather baggy dark trousers and calf-length black boots. I never saw Stalin in anything but a variant of this uniform. He always appeared well laundered and neatly dressed.

Stalin impressed me from the first and my opinion of his abilities has not wavered. His personality made itself felt without effort or exaggeration. He had natural good manners, perhaps a Georgian inheritance. Though I knew the man to be without mercy, I respected the quality of his mind and even felt a sympathy which I have never been able entirely to analyse. Perhaps this was because of Stalin's pragmatic approach. It was easy to forget that I was talking to a Party man, certainly no one could have been less doctrinaire. I cannot believe that Stalin ever had any affinity with Marx, he never spoke of him as if he did. During our several meetings in the war, sometimes with Churchill but as often alone, I always found the encounter stimulating, grey and stern though the agenda often had to be. I have never known a man handle himself better in conference. Well-informed at all points that were of concern to him, Stalin was prudent but not slow. Seldom raising his voice, a good listener, prone to doodling, he was the quietest dictator I have ever known, with the exception of Dr. Salazar. Yet the strength was there, unmistakably.

The conversation began with an exchange of facts and assurances about the policies of our respective Governments. In the course of this I told Stalin that the Soviet Government, we believed, intended to conduct their relations with us in the spirit of collaboration and non-interference which was inherent in our common membership of the League of Nations. We were confident that Russia recognized that the continued integrity, tranquillity and prosperity of British territories were an advantage to peace. Mr. Molotov replied that I had accurately defined the attitude of the Soviet Government towards His Majesty's

Government. The Soviet Government had no desire to interfere in any way in the internal affairs of the British Empire. Stalin confirmed this.

After this rather formal opening, I wondered whether any discussion of more serious import was to follow because, as is the custom with the Russians, no hint of any kind had been given me in advance about what was to take place. This was in Stalin's hands. I was thinking of leaving when Stalin launched into an exposition of the European scene as he saw it. This discussion lasted more than an hour. He began with a question: 'Do you consider the present European situation as alarming as, or more alarming than, the situation in 1913?'

EDEN: I would use the word 'anxious' rather than 'alarming'. The existence of the League of Nations, of which every European power but Germany is a member, is an advantage of importance which we lacked before the war.

STALIN: I agree on the value of the League, but I think the international situation is nevertheless fundamentally worse. In 1913 there was only one potential aggressor, Germany. Today there are two, Germany and Japan.

Future events were soon to justify these words.

Dealing first with Japan, Stalin said that while it was true that it would probably take Japan some little time to digest Manchuria, he was confident that she would not rest content with that conquest. It was Japan's policy either to overthrow or to dominate the Government of Nanking and the opening moves of that game were already being made. I said that, while I was conscious of the anxieties of the Far Eastern situation, it seemed to me that the wise statesmanship of the Soviet Government in settling the difficulty of the Chinese Eastern Railway had brought about, for the moment at least, a considerable *détente* in Russo-Japanese relations. Stalin agreed that this was so, but added that this achievement alone was not enough to ensure peace in the Far East.

Stalin went on to speak at some length of Germany. The Germans were a great and capable people with exceptional powers of organization and great industrial strength. Moreover they were smarting from a sense of injury inflicted upon them by the terms of the Treaty of Versailles. We must expect that they would be actuated by motives of revenge. Stalin was perhaps more understanding of the German point of view than Litvinov, in the sense that he was less scrupulous and had no prejudice against Nazis as such, which Litvinov no doubt felt for their treatment of the Jews. Stalin agreed when I remarked that the sympathy created for Germany by some of the actions of other governments since the war had been, until recently, an important element in world opinion in dealing with Germany. I added that Germany was now losing that sympathy by her own acts. Stalin said that German diplomacy was generally clumsy, but maintained that the only way to meet the present situation was by some scheme of pacts. Germany must be made to realize that if she attacked any other nation she would have Europe against her. As an illustration he said: 'We are six of us in this room; if Maisky chooses to go for any one of us, then we must all fall on Maisky.' He chuckled at the idea, Maisky grinned somewhat nervously. Stalin continued that only by this means would peace be preserved. The League as it was today was not strong enough for the purpose. It had suffered too many humiliations; even Paraguay had been able to flout it with impunity, he added with some exaggeration.

Then Stalin walked across to a map of the world hanging on the wall and remarked in friendly tones upon the power and influence of so small an island as Britain. Much must depend, he said, upon the part which His Majesty's Government were willing to play in a collective system in present conditions. It would be fatal to let events drift, since there was no time to lose if a check were to be placed on a potential aggressor. That should be in our power now, when actual war was probably some little time distant. At the last moment a check might fail.

Complaining of the duplicity of German policy Stalin then revealed to me details of a curious transaction. Some time ago, he said, the German Government had approached the Soviet Government and almost begged them to place orders in Germany, for which they had promised the Soviet Government a long term credit of 200,000,000 marks. In order to test Germany, the Soviet Government deliberately included in their list of orders some important contracts for war material. To their astonishment the German Government accepted those orders, 'and now,' added Stalin, 'Herr Hitler says he is frightened of us.' The Germans were also pretending that the Soviet Government had asked them to give them these credits, whereas in fact it was Germany who had made the first approaches. But I wondered whether the Russians had really been so astonished. There had been many similar orders before, as I was soon to learn when I was shown the Junkers aircraft factory near Moscow.

Stalin also referred to some story, of which I have no recorded details, but which he said was spread by the Germans, to the effect that General Tukhachevski, Vice-Commissar for War, had made contact with General Göring and had pressed upon the latter some anti-French scheme. This was a strange report, for at this time Tukhachevski had published an article so violently anti-German that it had drawn a diplomatic protest from Berlin. Two years later Tukhachevski, by then a Soviet Marshal, was shot for treasonable conspiracy with the Nazis. The mazes of the Kremlin are impenetrable.

I was then asked by Stalin why Herr Hitler would not take part in any pacts of mutual assistance. I replied that Hitler had expressed reluctance to enter into a pact which would compel him to fight in a quarrel between two other parties, in which he was not directly concerned. In the event of his having a difference with a neighbour, he was prepared to deal with that himself and did not wish to be helped. Stalin remarked drily that rather than help to keep the peace, Hitler might prefer to make a profit out of the differences of others.

At one stage of the conversation, Stalin referred to the latent danger of hesitant policies pursued by certain countries at a period of international tension. I thereupon explained to him that it was important to distinguish in these matters between a country such as ourselves, with an active and impressionable public opinion which closely followed events, and some other countries. It might be that at times we seemed vacillating or hesitant, but I asked him to believe that what appeared to him as weakness on our part did not conceal sinister designs at the expense of others. Stalin must not forget that His Majesty's Government had world-wide interests to consider before they could come to any decision of policy. Our concerns were not only European. Stalin said: 'I agree, Great Britain will have to think many times before she comes to a decision on such issues.'

At the end of these discussions, I telegraphed home the following conclusions:

> Stalin showed in the course of this conversation a remarkable knowledge and understanding of international affairs. In the latter respect his sympathies seemed broader than those of Litvinov though his conclusions were no less firm.
>
> Stalin spoke throughout in measured tones so quiet that at times Litvinov himself could not catch what he said. He displayed no emotion whatever except for an occasional chuckle or flash of wit.

Impression left upon us was of a man of strong oriental traits of character with unshakeable assurance and control, whose courtesy in no way hid from us an implacable ruthlessness.

* * * * *

That night we were invited to the Opera House to see a production of the ballet *Swan Lake*. Madame Simeonova, the wife of Mr. Karakhan, the Soviet Ambassador in Turkey, danced the principal part. We occupied the former Imperial Box. On our arrival I noticed that the whole of the foyer of the theatre was barred to the general public and the box was surrounded by armed plain clothes officials of the N.K.V.D. The ballet astonished me by its old-fashioned décor. As Madame Alexandra Kollontai, the wise Soviet Ambassador to Sweden, remarked later to Lord Cranborne, 'We are such a very conservative people.' The dancing, however, was superb. I had never seen anything to approach it.

There was clapping when we arrived in the box. Shortly afterwards the director of the theatre appeared on the stage and announced, somewhat superfluously, that we were in the audience and called for applause. More clapping resulted. The orchestra then did its part by playing *God save the King* followed by the *Internationale*. Throughout the playing of both anthems the whole audience stood, and after them the clapping was renewed. This was certainly the first occasion since the Revolution when a Russian orchestra played the British national anthem. I later found that even this courtesy did not palliate the sentiments of King George v who, though he understood clearly the value of contacts with Moscow as a deterrent to war, had the most affectionate recollections of his cousin the Czar. It did not seem to him good that 'my anthem' should be played in company with the *Internationale*.

As there was no other indication of popular interest or enthusiasm during the visit, I was intrigued to know how far this isolated demonstration was organized in advance. The audiences in Moscow theatres normally consist of a high proportion of Party members and, as Lord Chilston put it, 'others whose docility can be relied upon to withstand any strain.' On the other hand, Chilston thought that there was evidence that the audience had not been specially picked for the occasion, and we drew some encouragement from the fact that there was clapping before the official announcer played his part. It was also true, the Ambassador told us, that the inhabitants of Moscow were pathetically grateful for any relief from the drabness of their normal existence as it was in those days. The people of Russia are also, it must in fairness be added, remarkably polite, even towards those whom they have been taught to regard as their natural enemies. As hosts the Russians cannot be surpassed in the consideration which they show. No trouble is too great to meet their visitors' wishes, within the limits which the communist system imposes.

The next morning I was given a special treat. I had heard of the famous collections of French Impressionist paintings which had belonged before the Revolution to Shchukin, a prosperous Moscow merchant, and to Morosov, of a well-known family of collectors. I also knew that in those days the pictures were not publicly shown. I was most eager to see them and the request was reluctantly granted. The collection was admirably housed and hung. Every important Impressionist and Post-Impressionist French painter was represented and the examples were splendid, surpassing even my expectations. I recall particularly some glorious paintings by Degas and Gauguin. The pictures have since been widely shown and admired, but when I saw them they aroused no enthusiasm whatever among our hosts, who referred to them in derisory terms as 'bourgeois art', an unexpected description for some lovely early paintings by Picasso.

After this relaxation, we drove out of Moscow for luncheon with Litvinov, it being the day of rest. We were taken for about twenty miles through pleasant open country over good roads until we came to the villa standing in its woods, with a garden and even some ducks. Mr. Litvinov and his niece met us outside the gates and suggested that we should have a walk before luncheon. This we did, on the snowy, slippery surface of the road. The walk proved to be quite a long one and it was a quarter to three before we got back to the villa. Most of the English guests were beginning to wonder what had happened to their luncheon, but there was no need. The *dacha* was simply furnished but in excellent taste and the luncheon almost a banquet, even by the standards of our hospitable hosts, with the caviar and sucking pig, as ever, in the forefront of the meal and plum pudding to satisfy what British appetites survived to its end. The centre-piece, however, both physically and politically, was the butter, decorated with roses and bearing an inscription 'Peace is Indivisible'. I agreed with the sentiment, but even if I had not, I could hardly have argued against it after that welcome. The talk covered the same topics as the official discussions, though in a more relaxed atmosphere. Our hosts did not conceal their fear of German intentions, if Hitler's ambitions were not checked.

This late luncheon over, Cranborne and I were driven back to Moscow for a visit to the House of the Red Army, a surprising building consisting of rooms for the study of armaments of all kinds and a museum of the Revolution, which included photographs of the shooting of Czarist officers. I was naturally unenthusiastic. At the conclusion of our hastily conducted tour through miles of corridors, we reached the dining-room where wines were laid out and the inevitable toasts proposed. The cameras were busy and both Cranborne and I had our doubts about the enthusiasm of our constituents for these pictures of us drinking to the health of the Red Army. But that health turned out to be quite important, even decisive, for victory in the second world war.

That evening our Ambassador and Lady Chilston gave a dinner to which most of the commissars came. The wife of one of them was on my right, and after a discussion of Russia and its new ways, the following dialogue took place between us: 'It must be hard for a man to live in England.' 'Why?' 'Because the women are so ugly.' I replied indignantly: 'I can assure you that they are no such thing.' 'Oh, yes, you have to say that, but we know that they are.' Exasperated, I looked across at Lady Chilston who was definitely a decorative ambassadress. 'How can you say that? Look at Lady Chilston.' 'Yes, Lady Chilston is all right, but we know that is part of your propaganda.'

On the last day of the visit I spent quite a strenuous morning with Litvinov, Maisky and others, inspecting the Moscow underground railway which had just been finished. The Soviet authorities were very proud of it and, as far as I could judge, rightly so. The decoration was simple but splendid, each station being built in its own coloured marble from the Urals. What I could not judge, of course, was how good an underground it was, for the trains were not yet functioning for the public. As we made a short run over part of the system, trundling slowly from one station to the other, the Russian chief engineer explained the plans to me, concluding with the question: 'Have you ever been in a train like this before?'

My next visit was more important, to an aeroplane works at Fili on the outskirts of the city. This factory had been built by the Junkers Company in 1922 during the harmony which followed Rapallo and,

I was told, now employed fifteen thousand workers. They did not look either well fed or well cared for. I was shown one of the large bombers, giant by the standards of those days, of which the Soviet Government claimed to be constructing about two hundred a year. It was clear that the Soviet authorities wished me to be impressed by this evidence of their ability to support any international assurances they might give. I certainly was, for, with Europe facing ominous anxieties, signs of growing Soviet military power could be a helpful restraint upon Hitler's ambitions.

* * * * *

That afternoon was set aside for rest, but it did not work out that way. Early in the visit I hoped that I had shown forethought by handing Litvinov a draft for our communiqué. This had seemed to please him and we had discussed it the night before during the reception after our Ambassador's dinner. Now, however, in the concluding hours of our stay, the Russians proposed a number of amendments and additions of substance to the text which we had previously agreed upon, thereby showing that my forethought had not been as intelligent as I had supposed. The pretext was that the changes had been made by Stalin himself, which did not make it easier to persuade the Russians to modify them. They wanted me to urge the signature of an Eastern Pact, irrespective of the other proposals which the British and French Governments had mentioned in their declaration of February 3rd. I could not agree. The argument continued through the intervals of the ballet which we saw later that evening, right up to the moment of our departure by train that night. Almost at the last gasp we agreed to declare that it was more than ever necessary to build up a system of collective security in Europe as contemplated in the Anglo-French communiqué of February 3rd.

The statement continued:

It was emphasized in the conversations by MM. Stalin, Molotov and Litvinov that the organization of security in Eastern Europe and the proposed Pact of Mutual Assistance do not aim at the isolation or encirclement of any State, but at the creation of equal security for all participants, and that the participation in the pact of Germany and Poland would therefore be welcomed as affording the best solution of the problem.

The Representatives of the two Governments were happy to note, as the result of a full and frank exchange of views, that there is at present no conflict of interest between the two Governments on any of the main issues of international policy and that this fact provides a firm foundation for the development of fruitful collaboration between them in the cause of peace. They are confident that both countries, recognizing that the integrity and prosperity of each is to the advantage of the other, will govern their mutual relations in that spirit of collaboration and loyalty to obligations assumed by them which is inherent in their common membership of the League of Nations.

In the light of these considerations, Mr. Eden and MM. Stalin, Molotov and Litvinov were confirmed in the opinion that the friendly co-operation of the two countries in the general work for the collective organization of peace and security is of primary importance for the furtherance of international efforts to this end.

The ballet, where we arrived an hour late, was a modern one entitled *The Three Fat Men*. These characters occupied the centre of the stage, wrapped around in voluminous clothes. 'Who are those fat men, shovelling in the food and fussed over by flunkeys? They look like Michelin tyre advertisements,' I said to Litvinov. After an embarrassed pause I got the answer: 'They represent three capitalists.' I laughed, but he went on doggedly, 'Personally I dislike politics mixed up with my ballet. I love the ballet for the relaxation which it gives me.' This time the décor was less conventional and the dancing, as always, marvellous. Unfortunately, I was not able to stay long enough to see the final overthrow of the capitalists by the proletariat, for I had to leave to catch my train to Warsaw. I was made anxious by the sudden illness of our Ambassador in the middle of the ballet. He had to be taken home. No head of a mission and his wife could have risen more splendidly to the occasion than he and Lady Chilston had done during this most exacting visit. I was sorry that he could not be with us to the end, to the last stretch of red carpet, statuesque soldiers, blazing arc lights and clicking cameras.

The long drawn-out argument over the communiqué had one uncalculated consequence. Mr. Strang and I were so busy in our discussions with the Russians that we had no time to send a telegram to London explaining what we had done and why. It was not until we had pulled out of the station and were immured in our train for the long journey to Warsaw that we realized that we had kept London in the dark and that Whitehall was not likely to be particularly pleased by our failure.

As Litvinov stood at our carriage door, once more the Imperial coach, he held my hand in his for an instant while the train prepared to start and said in tones loud enough to be overheard: 'I wish you success. Your success will be our success—now.'

* * * * *

There was time enough to reflect next morning as we rolled across the limitless Russian plain. On the whole I was content. Obviously my visit had effected no revolutionary change in Russian policy, nor had I expected it to. It had, I hoped, destroyed some Soviet suspicion of British policy. I had been astonished at the depths of this, not so much in Stalin's mind, or Litvinov's, but often revealed in casual comment and conversation. An almost Machiavellian subtlety was attributed to us in encouraging Hitler to satisfy his appetites in the east at Russia's expense. To me, the passage in our joint statement, that there was at present no conflict of interest between the two Governments on any of the main issues of international policy, mattered most. When joined to the reference to our friendly co-operation in organizing peace, it expressed what I believed should be the true nature of relations between our two countries at that time. I thought that we ought to try to bring this influence to bear with good effect in Europe, where dangers were every day more threatening.

I also wondered what the reaction of my colleagues was likely to be; unenthusiastic I felt sure. Something would depend on the extent to which they might have been influenced by Simon's report on Berlin. The graver they judged the German danger, the more acceptable our work in Moscow might seem to them. Two points of view were, however, strongly held in the Cabinet and between them they might militate against any effective pursuit of the openings the Moscow visit had created. Some, religious in their views, regarded communism as anti-Christ. Others were brave enough to consider supping with the devil, but doubted whether he had much fare to offer. There was an almost universal opinion in Britain that the military power of the Soviets was in disarray and of poor quality. When Stalin executed the leadership of the Soviet armed forces in 1937, critics combined to see in this the ruin of any military efficiency the Russians might have possessed. These exaggerated estimates were damaging to Anglo-Russian relations up to the moment when German troops crossed the Soviet frontier.

Litvinov was himself a victim of this failure of our two countries to realize their opportunities. I liked Litvinov, intelligent, shrewd and with a theme of foreign policy in which he believed sincerely. He knew

Western Europe as one who had lived there and his outlook was more sophisticated than that of other Soviet leaders of the time. He spoke English so fast that he was difficult to understand and once provoked Barthou to exclaim to me: '*Qu'est-ce qu'il parle? C'est l'anglais, ça? C'est incroyable.*' I wish that we could have helped Litvinov more, for he realized that Hitler's ambitions must be contained and that our two countries had to take a major part in doing so. Stalin had to be rid of him before he could come to terms with Hitler. Litvinov was a communist and a loyal Russian, of course, but he was also a good European. I found him fair and reliable as an international colleague.

Darkness fell over the plain as it was soon to fall over Europe.

X

BECK AND BENEŠ

April 1935

Success of my visit to Russia – Colonel Beck's views on Russia and Germany – Marshal Pilsudski in old age – Summing up Colonel Beck's policies – A day in Prague – M. Beneš and the Eastern Pact – My perilous flight home – I strain my heart – A memorandum to the Cabinet – The Stresa Conference – The League endorses Stresa – Germany's air strength – Divergence between the Foreign Office and Air Ministry – Herr Hitler's false claims – My speech at Fulham on air parity

When, after about twelve hours of travel, we reached the Polish frontier and changed trains once again, I felt a sense of relief so strong that it took me aback. It was not just relief from tension now that an important mission was over, it was a sense of freedom, an air no communist state can give the visitor to breathe. For the rest of the day we travelled through the Polish countryside, which seemed gayer and less impoverished than on our outward journey, and reached Warsaw late at night, to be greeted, rather to my surprise, by a number of people in top hats, with Colonel Beck at their head. We drove to our hotel, where we stayed in very comfortable quarters as the guests of the Polish Government. In 1934, this Government had made non-aggression pacts with Moscow and with Berlin. These moves were essentially the personal policy of Marshal Pilsudski and Colonel Beck and they were proud of it. I knew that they were not likely to take kindly to any arrangement of mutual assistance in Eastern Europe unless their two great neighbours were parties to it. They preferred to keep both at arm's length, a policy which had obvious attractions, but was of doubtful validity in a world now so much more dangerous.

A telegram arrived from our Moscow Embassy that evening telling me that leading articles in *Pravda* and *Izvestia* had expressed 'great satisfaction at the outcome of the Moscow visit', thus completing one of those sharp changes of direction which the communist press never finds embarrassing. *Pravda* declared that our conversations demonstrated the full agreement of 'the two greatest powers in the world' on the need to continue efforts to shape a system of collective European security, in the interests of peace. The article also accepted the Anglo-French communiqué issued in London on February 3rd as providing the basis for this work. *Izvestia* wrote on similar lines that 'the initiation of a serious *rapprochement* is an accomplished fact.' This was as good as I could hope for. There was already a useful contrast between these sentiments and Simon's negative comment in the House of Commons about Berlin. It would be salutary for Hitler to note improved relations between London and Moscow.

I began my talks with the Polish Foreign Minister the next morning, April 2nd. After I had given him an indication of our conversations in Berlin and Moscow, Colonel Beck put his first question: whether I thought that the divergence of view between Berlin and Moscow was rigid, or whether there was any sign of elasticity. This question was repeated more than once during our conversations. I told him that I thought I should first speak of the joint communiqué we had issued in Moscow, in which we mentioned the Eastern Pact. I had received the impression, I continued, that both Mr. Stalin and Mr. Litvinov were perturbed by German intentions. I doubted whether Russia was in a position to take an offensive. Colonel Beck was not to be reassured. He said there were many factors to be taken into account in reaching a judgement on that point, and that it was difficult to arrive at a definite opinion. It was important to know whether there was any chance of an agreement on the Pact, and whether the Soviet Government stood firmly upon its original form. His own impression was that the views of Berlin and Moscow were in absolute opposition. This was said with some cheerfulness. My opinion, I replied, was that the Soviet Government were anxious to negotiate a security arrangement for eastern Europe and wished it to contain provisions for mutual assistance. They thought that events in Germany, of which they were deeply suspicious, made it necessary for the great powers to strengthen the collective peace system.

I told the Foreign Minister that while I was in Moscow, Mr. Litvinov had thrown out the suggestion of a general European pact of mutual assistance, but I was not certain that His Majesty's Government would agree. Unless something were done, Mr. Litvinov had said, Russia must increase her armaments. If it were impossible for Germany and Poland to enter the Eastern Pact, it might, in his judgement, be necessary to go ahead without them. After giving Beck a further account of Russian opinion and of what I had seen, including the factory which was building military aircraft, I added that I had told Litvinov that some of Russia's neighbours would not wish to be helped by Russian military forces. To this Litvinov had replied that it might be possible to arrange that military assistance should be forthcoming only at the request of the country attacked. I had the impression, I told the Foreign Minister, that the Soviet Government were convinced that Germany would attack somewhere.

Beck then resorted to a justification of the policy of non-aggression pacts he had been pursuing, maintaining that it had improved his country's relations with both its neighbours. Poland now had no troublesome frontier, he said, but two comfortable ones. If Poland bound herself to Germany alone, or the Soviet Union alone, she would immediately have one bad frontier again. I said that in England there was understanding of Poland's geographical difficulties and sympathy for her, but if France and Russia should agree to a pact of mutual assistance, I wondered what the position of the Polish Government would be. Beck said that he could have no objection to the pact. As there was no indication that he was in any way favourable to it, I was obliged to say that I was trying to find some element in the Polish view which was not common to the German view.

Colonel Beck made no reply to this, but repeated that Poland was glad to have brought about appeasement with her neighbours. I asked him whether the Polish Government shared the anxiety of the Soviet Government about German intentions. Beck replied that the Soviet Union had no common frontier with Germany. He could not understand why the Soviet Government should be so anxious. In a further discussion of existing relations with his two neighbours, Beck commented that it was the incidents of international daily life which really mattered, not the great, possibly less immediate, dangers. If the daily difficulties were smoothed over, a normal atmosphere would be created and the new generation would grow up with a better outlook. Colonel Beck said at this time: 'For several years Poland has been accused of having unduly bad relations with Germany and of endangering Europe. Now we have created better conditions and put that right and we are accused of betraying Europe!' This seemed to me too easy a doctrine and I expressed the opinion that the Baltic States would be very glad if an Eastern Pact could be concluded. Beck replied that he thought their chief preoccupation was how not to become the objects of a diplomatic game. He doubted whether they were enthusiastic about the Eastern Pact, they approached it with many reservations. Beck contended that they had not, in fact, much fear about their own danger from direct attack. I thought this too unquestioning a faith.

When we spoke of armaments, I asked Beck whether he saw in the recent German demands any possibility of concluding a limitation agreement. He admitted that it was extremely difficult to see how to proceed. What I had told him about the German demands had much impressed him. He had not thought that they would have asked for so much. The Foreign Minister came back to his conclusion that the animosity between Berlin and Moscow was very great and was characteristic of the present period. They were both governments which based their actions on doctrine, or vast popular movements. They differed in this from other countries. I told Beck that the growth of armaments was continuing. The rearmament of Germany was formidable and was causing anxiety in Britain. Beck concluded our meeting by saying that he had told Litvinov that he did not think there was any danger to Russia from Germany unless Poland participated, and that Poland had not the slightest intention of doing so. There were two factors, Beck said, in the Soviet position, namely Germany and Japan. There appeared to be an improvement recently in Soviet–Japanese relations. It seemed to him that the Japanese knew how to deal with the Russians. They provoked them up to the very limits of prudence, but they knew exactly when to stop. He wished he could find the formula.

This conversation disturbed me. The Poles would not join the Eastern Pact, even with the condition Litvinov had suggested, that Russian help should depend on invitation, but Beck could not suggest anything else. His whole aim was not to be embroiled, yet his country was bound to be, if war broke out in Eastern Europe. It seemed to me also that Beck was over-confident of his country's position. It might be that a policy such as he was following with so much adroitness would be possible for a strong power with two neighbours of approximately equal strength, or for an island power. I doubted whether Poland had the resources to carry it through. Of her two great neighbours, one, Russia, was not expansionist at that time, the other, Germany, showed unmistakable signs of being so. As a cold calculation in power politics, it did not seem to me wise for a power of moderate strength to incline towards the expansionist neighbour, or even to appear to do so. The Poles could block any peaceful proposal, I was not so sure that they could check any warlike one in their part of Europe. But, as I telegraphed to London that evening, Polish policy 'was based upon good relations with her two great neighbours and she would not therefore enter into any arrangement which was liable to endanger those relations with either. My impression is that while the present regime lasts in Poland there is no likelihood of any material modification of this attitude.'

Our conversations were interrupted by a luncheon with the President at the Belvedere Palace. This took place with much ceremony. After the guests had assembled, Beck and I followed President Moscicki into the room, heralded at our entrance by a loud fanfare blown by four trumpeters with long silver trumpets. The addition of two cavalrymen in grey uniform with drawn swords at each door added to the glamour of the occasion, if also a little to its unreality. The Zemek Palace, which we were shown after luncheon, was very splendid and principally remarkable for some fine paintings, with views of Warsaw, by Belotto, Canaletto's nephew. Unhappily they were hung too close together for good effect.

* * * * *

After my interview with Beck in the morning, I had comforted myself that I was to see Pilsudski late that afternoon and that his was the authority which took the vital decisions. The Marshal was universally revered, and deservedly so, for his brilliant military service in the liberation of Poland after the Russian revolution. His opinions, or what were thought to be his opinions, for he now rarely emerged in public, were accepted with the utmost loyalty and respect. My interview took place in circumstances very different from those I had expected. I went into the room with Beck, who was almost too anxious to please Pilsudski and make the meeting a success. The Marshal's mind was failing but his authority was undiminished. Nobody had warned me how ill he was, for I suppose that nobody knew who might have told me; it was a closely kept secret. The Marshal had clearly had one, if not a series of, strokes. I found it difficult to make contact with this enshrined and almost inarticulate figure. We spoke in French. At one time while we talked of Europe, Pilsudski kept reiterating what sounded like 'jamaïque' and then, more rarely, the name Lloyd George. I was completely mystified and so, quite evidently, was Beck. It was not until some minutes afterwards that I understood. Pilsudski had had little love for Mr. Lloyd George, with whom he had clashed at many conference meetings. At one of these, when Lloyd George had been expressing his views on Polish policy and frontiers, Pilsudski had retorted that Britain had nothing to do with Eastern Europe and should keep out of it. She should mind her own business, which was with other parts of the world, like Jamaica. I suppose that obscurely in the recesses of the Marshal's mind I was figuring once again as the man who interfered. At least, with all Polish charm and good manners, the project for an Eastern Pact was coldly bowed out.

I telegraphed to London that night:

> The main political theme, so far as it could be disentangled, was that he had his pact with Germany and Russia, that the latter country's policy was always very difficult to fathom, that other nations often misunderstood it, Mr. Lloyd George in particular being a crowning example of English errors in judgement. As an instance of British errors he referred to Mr. Lloyd George's support of Denikin. The Marshal had always known that Denikin never had a chance, but Mr. Lloyd George had sadly miscalculated the situation. . . .

This judgement was harsh on Lloyd George, who was never, as I have understood, an enthusiast for intervention in Russia.

I told the Marshal that, for our part, we wished for nothing better than to leave Europe to her own troubles, but our experience was that these troubles had an unhappy knack of involving our own country. Pilsudski did not dissent, but he was not to be drawn into a discussion of current international politics. 'So far as he seems to visualize his own country's position in the present conditions,' my telegram continued, 'it is as one which clings to its pacts with each of its great neighbours and refuses resolutely to move from its position or to face any events which might compel it to revise the attitude which it has taken up.' I felt every sympathy with the Poles. I thought I understood their fear of their eastern neighbour, which in this company was stronger than the fear of Germany. But I came away from my encounter with the venerable Marshal more than ever concerned for the future.

The atmosphere of the Polish capital was extraordinary, lovely houses, beautifully dressed men and women, books, pictures, Persian carpets, everything that could give grace to diplomatic occasions which are usually so stiff and artificial. Yet all the time I could not escape the feeling of impermanence, of another Duchess of Richmond's ball. It made me uneasy, and sad too, for I liked these people. That night Colonel Beck entertained us to dinner in the beautiful house of Count Raczynski, then the much liked Polish Ambassador in London. Nothing emerged of political importance, though Cranborne told me later that Beck had said to him, with great emphasis, that he was 'not a bit afraid of German rearmament, there was plenty of time.' My conversation with the Foreign Minister the next morning marked no progress and we left Warsaw late in the afternoon, after the publication of a communiqué which said little and meant it. I asked Beck what his Government's attitude would be if, within the framework of an Eastern non-aggression pact, some of the parties concluded separate arrangements for mutual assistance. He replied that Poland would have no serious objection, provided that her obligations towards her two neighbours and the League of Nations were not infringed. I thought that this might help.

In the years which followed, I grew to know Colonel Beck better and to note his gifts and failings. He was always personally friendly. I was told that on his first arrival at Geneva, he did not take kindly to his colleagues on the Council and expressed relief when he found that I at least had once been a soldier. At any rate he sought me out, in part on that account, and I was surprised to be invited to dinner at our very first meeting. Beck's manner was tortuous and slightly sinister and it sometimes required much patience to grasp his meaning. He disliked the French, which was a misfortune for his country, though it may be that he excused this sentiment to himself by a conviction that French military power was overrated. In the earlier years, his judgement was often at fault and his prejudices misled him. He had not the necessary experience or weight and was in all things the Marshal's adjutant. This resulted in capital mistakes, too much confidence in the Nazi word, too much indulgence in antipathy to the Czechs, who had to face the same dangers as his own country. After Pilsudski's death, which followed within a few weeks of my visit, General Smigly-Rydz, the Marshal's successor as Inspector-General, saw the German danger more clearly, but failed to impose any restraint on practices which weakened Poland's relations with those who should have been her natural allies, particularly France. When the testing time came, bringing with it the failure of Beck's calculations and policies, the Foreign Minister's courage did not falter, nor did that of his heroic country which we could not save, either at the outbreak of the war or at its close. Poland had left it too late and so had Britain, but Poland still pays.

It can be argued that no decision taken by Poland in 1935 would have prevented Hitler and Ribbentrop from doing a deal four years later with the Soviet leaders to destroy Poland and the Baltic States. I am not so sure. There were many threads in Russian policy at that time, the failure of the West to stop the Italians in Abyssinia, the growth of German military power in Europe, the mistrust of the West on account of Munich and fear lest the Western powers should try to divert Nazi appetites towards the east. Supporters of the Polish policy of this period can also contend that experience of Russian occupation ten years later justified the earlier refusal of the entry of Russian forces on Polish soil on any pretext. Even so I believe that the Polish leaders would have been wiser to throw in their lot whole-heartedly with the Western powers, at a price which would have included the acceptance of an Eastern Locarno on the terms Litvinov offered. Such a decision could have had a number of consequences. The policy which Litvinov upheld, of collective security and joint resistance to Hitler's demands, would have been strengthened. Had the Eastern Pact come into being it would also have influenced German policy towards Czechoslovakia, not in its intention but in its execution. It might even have averted Munich and the surrender to German demands there, in which Poland selfishly shared, aggravating her own danger and isolation.

In the last hour or so, I had my only chance to see something of the city of Warsaw. A kindly Under-Secretary, Count Szembek, with a love for beautiful buildings and their contents, but a less discerning view of politics, took me round. While we were looking at the Lazienki Palace, a little eighteenth-century summer residence of the Kings of Poland, we had some intermittent political discussion. Count Szembek suggested that Hitler had put Jews and liberals everywhere against him, and these were now exaggerating Germany's strength. I told him that I did not agree, there was also the evidence of our own eyes. Unfortunately, either because I became so absorbed in what I was being shown or because my host had got the time of the train wrong, we were six minutes late at the station, delaying the Prague express. A flurry of handshakes and a friendly farewell from hundreds of the citizens saw us off. I reflected sadly how little I could do for the future of these gay, brave people.

* * * * *

From Warsaw I travelled overnight by train to Prague, where I spent a pleasant day in the sympathetic company of Beneš and Masaryk and was lavishly entertained with Pilsener beer and Prague ham. Jan Masaryk was the son of the liberal statesman and patriarchal founder of the Czechoslovak state. A lovable personality himself, Jan revered his father and was in these years loyally working to fulfil responsibilities which his tastes would never have chosen. We remained close friends until he was murdered in 1948.

Prague was a beautiful capital. It was also an easy-going, international city with more political toleration than most and where the newspapers of almost any nation could be bought without an eyebrow being raised. Beneš was eager and dexterous, perhaps a little too dexterous. His active mind was forever scheming new plans and projects; they were so numerous that they could not all be good. But I liked to listen to this man, the sincerity of whose love for his country shone through all his stratagems. I gave him an account of my talks in Berlin, Moscow and Warsaw and he approved our course.

Beneš developed his case in favour of a Central European Pact and an Eastern Pact. He had also some forthright views about Germany, Russia and Poland. According to Beneš, German opposition to the Eastern Pact was not based on fear of Russia but arose out of the Polish question. Both Germany and Poland had good reasons for the recent agreements into which they had entered with each other. There was uncertainty in Poland and dispute about the Marshal's policy. The Germans could now advance a case which would gain a sympathetic hearing in Western Europe. They could represent themselves as a check on Bolshevism. It would be disastrous to leave Russia in isolation. If this were to happen, Moscow would make an agreement with Berlin at the expense of the West. This was a view, Beneš added, with which Mussolini had expressed agreement. I asked him why the Poles so gaily ignored the German menace. Beneš offered this explanation. Poland considered herself a great power. She looked upon her help to Western Europe as indispensable. Had not a Polish diplomat at Geneva in 1925 declared that the war of 1914 came about because Poland did not exist? Poland resented the emergence of Russia as a European power, for this thrust her into the background.

Beneš maintained that Litvinov was right in saying that there were two tendencies in Germany, those favoured respectively by Hitler and by the Reichswehr. The former was temporary, he thought, the latter permanent. The Reichswehr were the people who initiated the policy of Rapallo and still wished to have the possibility of manœuvre with Russia. Beneš seemed to me surprisingly confident about his relations with Germany. He said that he had had no real conflict with Germany in sixteen years. He did not want one and was convinced he would not have one. If a conflict arose, it would be out of some other European dispute. In the event of major European trouble, Czechoslovakia must either be completely out of it, like Switzerland, or in the thick of it. Czechoslovak policy must always be a Western policy. This I understood, but not his confidence. He seemed so sure that if left to face Germany alone, he could still make terms.

In a reference to the smaller ex-enemy powers, Austria, Hungary and Bulgaria, Beneš said that if they followed the German example and repudiated the disarmament clauses of the Versailles Treaty, Czechoslovakia would break off relations and appeal to the League. Roumania would mobilize. The Little Entente wished to regulate the affairs of these three countries at Geneva by way of a general disarmament convention. I asked Beneš how he thought this was possible, in view of Germany's present demands. I did not get any clear reply, though Beneš said euphemistically that he thought peace could be saved. It was his opinion that, if Germany and the other ex-enemy powers knew that the three Western powers were agreed on a general line and that the Little Entente was with them, the *Anschluss* with Austria would not come to pass. It should be possible to hold the position until there was a change of regime in Germany. If the soldiers came into power there, the immediate danger would fade, although the more remote danger might be increased. An ebullient optimism was part of Beneš' character, it was probably indispensable to any Czech in such times.

We lunched together at the Czernin Palace, now agreeably redecorated as the Czech Foreign Office, and afterwards looked down from the windows over the city and the river. After luncheon, Beneš drove me to the airport and we had some further talk on the way. I told him of the anxieties our interview in Berlin had left on my mind, which were, I thought, shared by the Russians. He nodded. I also gave Beneš the view of our Military Attaché in Berlin, that it would be five to eight years before Germany was ready. To my surprise he agreed, professing calm, 'if only we hold firm.' Germany, he was sure, could attempt no tricks just yet and in five years many things could happen, mortality played its part.

Beneš was right in his conviction that his country's future must lie with the West. The Czechoslovakia of Thomas Masaryk and Beneš was a true democracy. Thirteen years later, forceful Soviet guile and, it must be sadly admitted, Western weakness and delay, brought another result in the hour of victory. The Czech people were given no chance to have their say. As I think back over that journey from the Russian borders through Poland to Prague, it is a sad reproach that those countries, with Hungary and Roumania, continue to suffer a tyranny sustained by foreign power. While this endures the conscience of mankind ought not to rest.

* * * * *

As we neared the airport I glanced uneasily at the sky. It was blowing hard and there were heavy, dark clouds scudding across. The trees were bending and twisting unhappily before what looked uncommonly like a gale, but to travel by train meant a break in our journey in Berlin, which I did not want. I was not ready for a further meeting with Hitler, nor did I wish to appear to dodge one. An aeroplane was available which was to open a new regular service to London and the Cabinet wanted me home for consultation. I decided to divide our forces. My Private Secretary, Robin Hankey, and I would fly home; Cranborne and Strang would go by train, for them Berlin would present no embarrassment. I did not know that Beneš had arranged a special train to take me through to Ostend without stopping in Berlin. He did not tell me, thinking that the Legation would have done so but that I had determined to fly. The message was never given to us, which was careless and had some consequences.

We reached Leipzig without misadventure, but soon after we had taken off from there, we ran into very rough weather. My experience of flying dates back to a course on R.E.8s in the first world war. I have flown around and about the world ever since, but I have never had a flight like this. We learnt afterwards that we were the only aircraft in the air in that part of Europe that day. We flew into a snowstorm somewhere near the Black Mountains and were hurled about with a seismic violence. For the first and last time in my life I was airsick and quite exhausted by the buffeting. I hardly cared when the pilot told us that the weather was too bad to go on and we must come down at Cologne. We had just touched down when a German officer marched up, saluted smartly and said: 'The Führer's compliments. He greatly regrets your bad flight and offers you his private aircraft for the rest of the journey, if it can be of any assistance to you.' I thought this offer an impressive example of German courtesy and efficiency, but there was no further flying for me that day. I felt very feeble and exhausted, a sensation entirely new to me. A German doctor was sent for and announced my pulse was 45; my heart, he kept repeating, '*sehr schlecht*'. I was put to bed at the Dom Hotel, which I had first known sixteen years before as a young officer in the Rhineland. This was an exasperating, not to say humiliating, end to my European odyssey.

I summoned another doctor in the morning, in the hope of getting permission to go home. He, too, was gloomy about the heart, refused to sanction air travel and did not want me to move at all, but eventually agreed that I should journey by train and boat to Dover. I learnt without surprise that a Dutch aircraft, attempting the flight from Prague to Cologne that day, had crashed in bad weather, all its occupants being killed. In the event, we arrived an hour or two after Cranborne and Strang, the tortoise beating the hare. My wife and John Simon met me at Victoria and Vansittart came to see me when I reached home. Conditions, I wrote in my diary next day, were clearly bad in the office, with much friction and everyone very anxious about the coming meeting with Mussolini at Stresa.

My doctor in London gave a reasonably encouraging report, but would not commit himself until the cardiogram had been taken the next day. King George v was kind enough to telephone and was firm that I should see his heart specialist, Sir Maurice Cassidy. This examination took place and, to my dismay, I was told that I must have a complete rest for six weeks, the heart having been strained, thus putting paid to my journey to the Stresa Conference. I saw John Simon and explained the position to him, before we broke the news to the Prime Minister. Mr. MacDonald took the unusual course of issuing a highly charged statement from Downing Street: 'The Prime Minister is distressed beyond measure, both on personal and public grounds, to hear of Mr. Eden's illness.'

Later he came round to see me and said that in the circumstances he would go to Stresa himself. I was glad to hear this and told him so, for though his own health had not been good, I felt that his sense of values in foreign affairs might be indispensable at the conference. John Simon would certainly try his hardest, but he once complained to me that he never knew what people were thinking. In fact, his antennæ were weak. MacDonald, at this stage of his life, had to rely much upon his own, for his eyesight was failing sadly. At the Stresa meeting experience and sensitivity could count a lot, for it was necessary to probe intentions as well as devise what must be done.

The Cabinet was to meet on April 8th and I handed in the notes from which I had intended to speak. These began by explaining that I had reported fully from each capital and had now only a few words to add on the general situation. I wrote that I saw no reason to modify the views I had set out in my telegram from Moscow, following on my reflections in the train from Berlin.* I annexed a copy of this telegram to my report, which continued:

> The essential at the present time is that we should pursue a straight and steady course in support of the League of Nations and of the collective peace system. It may be that we can do, and should do, something more to strengthen peace, but this is not so important as that we should make clear to any potential breaker of the peace that he can count on our active opposition.
>
> I found a certain suspicion of British foreign policy, varying in intensity, in each of the capitals I visited. It was of course worst in Moscow. It was due to uncertainty as to our policy and to anxiety lest our desire to be the honest broker would lead us to yield to Germany's ever-growing demands, even at the expense of our friends.

While I was in Warsaw, *The Times* published a leading article entitled 'The British Role'. It reasoned that Germany had been somewhat hastily condemned, because of her refusal to enter the proposed Eastern Pact, and emphasized Hitler's readiness to conclude non-aggression treaties with all his neighbours except Lithuania. The article welcomed the end of 'the Versailles habit of mind' which had kept British statesmen in too narrow a groove. 'The role of Great Britain', it said, 'is once more to be a mediating and above all an educative force.' Far too much stress had been laid, the article continued, on the negative side of the Führer's statements on the subject of armaments. These were described as 'constructive proposals'. Unfortunately, *The Times* was widely regarded in Europe as the organ of the British Government. My memorandum continued:

> *The Times* bears a heavy measure of responsibility for this. Its leader of the 4th April was a calamity. In every capital I visited I made it clear that we could *not* regard Germany's demand for 550,000 effectives as a basis for negotiation, nor her naval demands either. Clearly they cannot be, for the former would give Germany military advantage over France and Italy, and the latter, naval advantage by reason of the newer tonnage. Anyway, what does Germany want with a navy of that size? She has neither colonies nor a seaboard comparable with that of France and Italy.

**See* Chapter VIII, pages 142–3.

But *The Times* regards these as 'constructive proposals', and Europe regards *The Times* as the organ of His Majesty's Government. Sir E. Phipps' telegrams show how much harm that leader of the 4th April has done in Berlin. I can undertake that it will have done as much, or more, harm in Moscow, Warsaw and Prague, to say nothing of Paris and Rome. It is of little use for members of the Government to make long journeys if a part of the confidence they have striven to create is thus to be destroyed. If we are to pursue an effective foreign policy in Europe, it is essential that it should be made clear that *The Times*, with its defeatist leaders, does not represent His Majesty's Government. If this is not done, all our efforts will be in vain. I suggest a question and answer in the House as the best method of doing this.

As to the policy of His Majesty's Government, I have said that we must be stalwart in support of the League and the collective peace system. Opportunity could perhaps be taken of Stresa to reaffirm our attachment to the Covenant and our determination to carry out the obligations of Locarno.

There remain the problems of Central and Eastern Europe. As to the former, we should ask the French and Italian Governments to speed up in conjunction with the Austrian and Hungarian Governments and the Governments of the Little Entente the draft of the Danubian Pact, so that it may be presented to Germany as she herself has asked. As to the latter, there is much to be done about the Eastern Pact. Attention should be drawn to the difference now apparent in the attitude of the Polish and German Governments to this pact. Colonel Beck admitted to me that, given certain conditions which should not be difficult of fulfilment (see my record of conversation with Colonel Beck for the exact terms of his reply), he was prepared to agree to a superstructure of pacts of mutual assistance erected upon a general non-aggression pact to which Poland herself would be party. Germany has refused this most unreasonably. At Stresa we should, I think, make it clear that we consider this idea of a superstructure of mutual assistance above a general non-aggression pact as worth pursuing by the interested powers, and indicate that if they were prepared to do this, we should be ready to bless their endeavours as we did the original proposal for an Eastern Pact last summer. If Germany then still persists in her refusal, the world will be the better able to judge Germany's motives.

The greatest care should be taken to avoid any suggestion that Germany's proposed non-aggression pacts are enough, since they are less in fact than the obligations all members of the League undertook towards each other and less also than the obligations which we have undertaken under Locarno.

The above proposals may give some useful work for Stresa, but they will not finally solve the European problem, since Germany will refuse to play her part at present in any collective peace system. It is possible that the effect of seeing His Majesty's Government standing loyally, not against Germany, but in favour of the League and of peace, may have more important consequences in modifying Germany's attitude than we can at present foresee. Germany does not like isolation, nor is she so strong internally as to make her willing to endure it. There were indications that even the Moscow visit and the reply of the Secretary of State for Foreign Affairs to a question in the House of Commons admitting 'a wide divergence of view' were having their effect, until the *Times* leader of the 4th April brought Germany fresh cheer and confidence in England's funk.

It may be, however, that His Majesty's Government will consider a reaffirmation of the loyalty to its existing obligation as insufficient to ensure peace. There may be, I hope there will be, a determination to examine whether anything further can be done. If this is contemplated at all, I believe that the most fruitful line of study would be that of a European pact of mutual assistance which would be open to all nations. This might be something in the nature of the protocol of 1924, but limited to Europe. It must not be thought that I am advocating such a proposal off-hand. I do no more than suggest that from experiences gained in these European capitals, if any further contribution is contemplated by His Majesty's Government, it is on these lines that it might well be made. My own conviction is that it is likely that, if we are firm enough in support of our present commitments, nothing further may be necessary, but this is difficult of estimate until after the Stresa meeting.

To sum up, I am not myself alarmist about the present European situation, but anxious because the attitude taken up by His Majesty's Government in the next few months may decide the future for years to come. I do not believe a decision for us is so very difficult. We should show ourselves firm in defence of collective peace. If we refuse to be scared or weakened by Germany's growing demands, if we resist the temptation to accept everything Germany asks for as a basis for discussion between us, if for a moment we can cease to be an honest broker and become the honest facer of truths, then I am confident that there is no call to view the future with alarm. If, on the other hand, we appear to the outside world to be weak and vacillating, if we allow *The Times* to continue to preach defeatism and to continue to be regarded as the organ of His Majesty's Government, then we shall encourage Germany's demands, and, no less serious, encourage the weaker powers to take refuge with her in the belief that the collective peace system can never be effective because England will never play her part in its support.

I was distressed to be away from this Cabinet because, although I was not a member, my journey would have given me a chance to express my opinions more freely than I could do in notes. I knew that there were divergent points of view in the Cabinet, some members being most reluctant to agree to any alignment with France and Italy and anxious to continue 'the role of the honest broker'. They would not admit that Hitler would only be willing to talk business if the nations who were opposed to Germany's repeated acts of defiance could join in firm resistance.

* * * * *

I was much troubled about another part of the world, with which my journey had nothing to do. The situation between Italy and Abyssinia looked increasingly menacing and I felt sure that the mounting dangers there must be faced and discussed at Stresa. The fact that I was not able to go to Stresa had at least this advantage, both the French and British Prime Ministers, as well as their Foreign Ministers, would attend. Such an encounter should give an exceptional opportunity for a direct approach to Mussolini, who appeared to be intensifying his preparations against Abyssinia, but had as yet taken no decisive step. I spoke separately to the Prime Minister and to John Simon about this when they came to see me in bed. Both agreed that Mussolini must be confronted on the subject. The Foreign Secretary, being familiar with the many negotiations which had already taken place at Geneva, told me that he was taking an Abyssinian expert with him for the purpose, Mr. Thompson, who knew every detail of the business.

Then came the let-down. The subject was not raised at all, even though Mussolini commented at one stage that the League had been effective in Europe, instancing the Saar, but ineffective in Asia and South America. The opening was passed by, though Drummond had urged, at least upon Vansittart, that the subject should be raised. This failure was the more extraordinary since, on British insistence, time was found at Stresa for a discussion on Memel, where admittedly we had responsibilities, but where the danger to the unity of the three countries was not comparable. Moreover, the Abyssinian representative was by then known to be waiting to state his case at the League Council at the first opportunity. Here was a most unhappy lapse for which the Foreign Secretary, knowing the dangers better, was more responsible than the Prime Minister.

Admittedly, it is always difficult to intrude matters into an international conference at such a level and this applied particularly to Stresa, where there was much coming and going by motorboat and the opportunities for informal discussion do not appear to have been good. It has also been argued that if the topic had been raised, Mussolini would have given some assurances which would not have been kept, as his spokesman did at the League Council a few weeks later. I do not think that this is so, for at the time of Stresa, Mussolini had not committed himself publicly to a venture in Abyssinia. It is also true that the Italians had had a number of warnings before Stresa from Vansittart, myself and others, but there still remains some substance in the complaint that Mussolini should have been confronted on this occasion, when the leading statesmen of the three nations were in council together for four days.

Stresa suffered from one other shortcoming. The Cabinet had agreed before the Ministers left London that they did not wish to discuss the Rhineland by itself, but only to reaffirm the Locarno agreements as a whole. This was a mistake, which should have been the more obvious when the French Ministers tabled a formidable paper about conditions in the demilitarized zone, containing reports from sources which they claimed were absolutely sure and revealing activities which should have caused alarm. The intensive training of Rhenish paramilitary formations, the creation of a huge military camp a few kilometres from Cologne, where barracks and rifle ranges were being constructed, the evacuation of four barracks in Cologne in which poor families had been living since the Armistice, were all cited.

The French paper gave figures and descriptions of the scale of these and other developments, including the construction of fortifications west of Coblenz and the doubling of military aviation flights within the last month. It was reported, for instance, that night flying of military aircraft in formations of ten was taking place over the demilitarized zone. The French added that the pace of the military reoccupation of the Rhineland was being accelerated and that there was a danger that very soon we should find ourselves faced with an accomplished fact. One of the chief foreign policy correspondents of the *Kölnische Zeitung* had admitted that this state of affairs might induce Germany to denounce the Locarno agreement at the first opportunity. The report concluded that the spirit of the population of the zone had changed in a marked manner and, from being peaceful, had become arrogant.

It seems strange that a document of this disturbing character should not have been discussed and that the Conference should have been content with the reaffirmation of Locarno in general terms. The Stresa meeting was only satisfactory in so far as it appeared to align the foreign policies of the three countries, who agreed on the terms of a resolution to be moved at the League Council the following week.

Diplomacy has to determine which difficulties will resolve themselves and which will spread their rot when shoved under the rug. If the leaders of the three countries had fairly faced the real difficulties which confronted them, whether Germany could be stopped if she reoccupied the demilitarized zone in her own country and what Mussolini's real ambitions were in Africa, Stresa might have influenced history. As it was, the Conference only marked it with a bourne.

Sir John Simon and M. Laval went straight from Stresa to Geneva, where the Council overwhelmingly endorsed their resolution, only Denmark abstaining. The terms strongly condemned the German military law of March 16th, because it conflicted with the principle that no power can liberate itself from treaty engagements without the consent of the other parties to the treaty. This is the principle which of recent years has been more honoured in the breach than in the observance. The Western powers have frequently condoned such conduct, sometimes even salting their appeasement with a loan. They have thereby incurred a direct responsibility for the steady deterioration of international relations. In the 'thirties leadership had not the same reckoning to read as we have before our eyes today, which makes our present failure the more incomprehensible. It should be an accepted rule of conduct for the free nations that they will not be parties to a loan, whether on their own account or international, to a nation which acts in defiance of this principle.

At Geneva it was agreed that action must be taken against any state which should in future 'endanger peace by unilateral repudiation of its international obligations.' Preparatory steps were approved to determine the methods to be used to do this and to make the Covenant more effective.

There was, however, an embarrassing moment. Litvinov referred to the end of the resolution, which proposed measures against the violation of international treaties. From the wording, he said, it would seem that these were to be limited to the violation of treaties in Europe. It might be deduced that violations outside Europe were quite justified and could always pass unpunished. He would like some explanation or interpretation of the resolution. Simon answered him by saying that the reference to Europe was natural, since the series of meetings and events which had brought them to this point were concerned with Europe. The resolution did not involve new and increased obligations by members of the League, which obligations extended alike to all its members. After some further discussion Litvinov expressed his agreement, but there must have been many present whose minds were on Africa and Abyssinia, though Litvinov was probably more concerned with the Far East.

* * * * *

One result of the discussion which Simon and I had held with Hitler in March was to stir up afresh a long-standing controversy between the Air Ministry and the Foreign Office, each of which had its own sources of information about German air strength. Since 1933, reports had been coming in about Hitler's growing and illegal power in the air. The Air Ministry at this early period saw no immediate cause for alarm, while the Foreign Office believed that Nazi Germany was fast approaching our own strength.

An example of this divergence came in June 1934, when the Air Ministry sent to the Foreign Office a note about the commands and units into which they believed that the German air force was to be organized within the next fifteen months. The Foreign Office comments on this paper, particularly those of Mr. Leeper, who was an early prophet of the Nazi menace, showed a conviction that the Air Ministry was under-estimating Germany's potential strength. I minuted: 'I share the prevalent scepticism of Air Ministry estimates.' This disagreement between the two departments was the cause of much argument in the Cabinet and before ministerial committees. For the moment, the Government accepted the Air Ministry's estimate of existing German strength.

Earlier that year, the Government considered plans to remedy the worst deficiencies in Britain's armaments. At that time, even the Conservative Government's 1923 programme of air defences was not complete, and I protested that now the hopes of disarmament had faded we must make a greater effort. Nor was I satisfied that the modest scheme of expansion announced in July 1934 fulfilled our needs. However, Baldwin told the House of Commons on November 28th that in twelve months' time the Royal Air Force in Europe would have a margin of superiority over Germany alone of 'nearly 50 per cent.' He also said that he could make no forecast for the more distant future or look 'more than two years ahead.' This statement was, unfortunately, widely taken to mean that we should still have a margin of safety in November 1936, which was certainly not assured. A consequence of this apparent comfort was that the urgency of the issue became blurred in the public mind.

When the Foreign Secretary and I heard from Hitler himself that he had reached parity with Great Britain, he showed us a diagram putting British air strength at 2,100 machines, including reserves. Simon at once questioned this estimate, saying that Britain's first-line strength, as distinct from total strength, was only 690 aircraft. While I continued my journey to Moscow, Warsaw and Prague, this disturbing claim was examined in London.

The growth of Nazi Germany's air power had been studied most carefully in the Foreign Office by Mr. Creswell, who had practical knowledge of aviation, by Mr. Ralph Wigram, head of the Central Department, and by Sir Robert Vansittart. I frequently discussed this matter with them and wholly endorsed their opinion of the alarming speed and scope of German expansion. I found on my return to England that the Air Council had already challenged Hitler's claim to possess 2,100 aircraft. They thought that he was either exaggerating or speaking without knowledge. But the Air Council admitted that, when the machines of the British Fleet Air Arm and of the auxiliary units were excluded from calculation, we had, stationed at home, only 453 first-line aircraft in regular units. They were also worried about the thorough preparations which had been made in Germany to organize the aircraft industry for mass production, which meant that in the event of war, Hitler would be better-equipped than his opponents to expand rapidly and to make good his losses.

While I was still in bed at my house in London, Simon and Vansittart came to talk over this situation, among others, and I strongly encouraged the dispatch of a warning to the Prime Minister on the lines advised by the Foreign Office. On April 10th, Simon addressed a letter to MacDonald, asking that the whole question of German air strength should be urgently investigated by the Committee of Imperial Defence. He wrote:

> A high official of the German Air Ministry yesterday informed our Air Attaché in Berlin that the precise meaning of the Chancellor's statement to me in Berlin that Germany had 'attained air parity with Great Britain' was that Germany's first-line strength had now reached that of the British front-line strength including machines stationed abroad and in the naval air arm (some 900 machines in all). The regular Royal Air Force squadrons stationed in this country amount to only one half of this figure (453 machines) and even though we have in addition a further force of some 130 machines in the auxiliary squadrons . . . the German superiority over all first-line machines stationed in United Kingdom aerodromes under Air Ministry control now seems to be some 30 per cent. I can see no likely motive for the German Air

Ministry deliberately to exaggerate to our Air Attaché the figure of their present air armaments.

Simon then pointed out the discrepancy between Foreign Office and Air Ministry estimates of German strength:

I understand that the Air Ministry now believes there to be 1,375 machines of military type in Germany; and our secret reports give a total of 3,000 machines of every type now in existence. In fact, therefore, the front line has already considerable reserves.

Still more disturbing than the *numbers* of first-line military aeroplanes in Germany is the information we have from secret sources as to the *speed at which these aeroplanes are being manufactured*. The same German Air Ministry official recently told Group Captain Don that Germany was aiming at a factory output sufficient to double her first-line strength in two months; and we have very good reason to believe that the present rate of production of aeroplanes is at least 200 per month and very probably more. The number of men employed in the German aircraft industry doubled between the autumn of 1933 and the autumn of 1934, and has increased by a further 83 per cent. since last October. I very much doubt if our own factory production can equal these figures; and I understand that the true measure of a country's strength in the air is just this factor of the relative power of output and rapid expansion of production....

...one may have considerable doubts whether once left behind by Germany in the air we shall ever be able to attain a level of parity with her again.

The conclusion which might have to be drawn from the above figures, if they are correct, is that this country is seriously open to the threat of sudden attack by a Continental Power in a degree to which it has not been exposed for hundreds of years.

Even if exaggerated, this was a warning of the gravest possible kind.

On the same day that Simon sent this letter to the Prime Minister, the Secretary of State for Air, Lord Londonderry, circulated to his colleagues a memorandum based upon an appreciation of the situation by the Chief of the Air Staff, Sir Edward Ellington. This memorandum recalled that, in June 1934, the Air Staff had estimated that by October 1935 Germany would possess approximately 500 first-line aircraft and that her ultimate intention was to create an air force at least three, and possibly four, times that size. On this forecast, the ministerial committee had made recommendations for the increase of the R.A.F. In the autumn of 1934, the Air Staff had produced a revised estimate of German intentions. This showed that a second stage had been 'designed' in Germany, with the object of attaining a first-line strength of about

1,300 aircraft by October 1936 and an eventual expansion to 1,500–1,600 aircraft.

Lord Londonderry continued: 'There is no ground for alarm at the existing situation. Whatever first-line strength Germany may claim, we remain today substantially stronger *if all relevant factors are taken into account*. But the future, as opposed to the present, must cause grave concern.' The conclusion was that the action authorized up till that time was in danger of proving inadequate to fulfil the pledge Baldwin had given, that Britain's air strength should not be inferior to any country within striking distance of its shores. The memorandum said that the Air Staff could not, in the absence of more definite evidence, believe that Germany already possessed a first-line strength such as Hitler claimed to Simon and myself in Berlin, organized in squadrons and at operational aerodromes. They had to admit, however, that there was no reason why she should not shortly have that number of squadrons. They thought that, though the German expansion programme aimed at reaching a strength of 1,512 first-line aircraft by April 1937, it would take another two years to produce an air force 'so fully organized, equipped and trained that it will be adequately prepared for war.' The Air Staff therefore recommended a programme which would give Britain a total of about 1,500 first-line aircraft, on the written assumption, included in their own tables, that the German air force would still be at the strength of April 1937 in April 1939 and, indeed, in April 1940. Later in their paper, the Air Staff discussed the state of readiness of war reserves and material on which the Government had been working, and held to their previous opinion that 'Germany will not be ready for, and is not intending to go to, war before 1942'. The Foreign Office vigorously dissented from this conclusion, which, as Sir Robert Vansittart rightly maintained, was shared by no one else in Europe.

All our discussions at the time were bedevilled by the difficulty in arriving at an accurate standard of comparison between one set of figures and another. The British Air Ministry used the term 'first-line aircraft' to mean machines fully organized into squadrons, with adequate reserves of aircraft, men and supplies. The Führer's claim was certainly false, for we now know that, in March 1935, his total number of operational aeroplanes, as the Air Ministry stated in their memorandum of April 1935, was probably rather over one thousand, whereas Great Britain's was more than twice as great. I do not believe that the Chancellor was in error about the facts. More probably he was lying to impress us. If so, that was a miscalculation, because the result was to strengthen those at home who wanted to speed the expansion of our air force. Indeed, the British Government accepted that Hitler had already reached parity.

Hitler later affirmed to the Austrian Foreign Minister, Herr Guido Schmidt, that only his claim of air parity compelled Britain to conclude the Anglo-German Naval Agreement. He was wrong in this. The British Government, and particularly the Admiralty, negotiated the agreement, however mistakenly, on its own merits, because they wished to limit Hitler's naval power to a third of their own. This pragmatism showed an extravagant faith in Hitler's word, but the British pursuit of the Naval Agreement would not have been slackened whatever air figures Hitler had revealed. There is another possible explanation for Hitler's false claim. He was no doubt already determined to enter the Rhineland and it could have suited him to have us believe that the striking power of the Luftwaffe was greater than it was. However that may be, the Führer lost no time in making his figures truly comparable with ours. By the spring of 1935 he had made all preparations for the rapid development of his air power on a war basis. Britain had taken no similar action at that time and such preparations as she made were being vehemently contested by the Opposition in Parliament.

I still think it was prudent to encourage Simon to send to MacDonald the warning of April 10th, 1935, for although our estimate of Hitler's actual strength was exaggerated, our forecast of his potential power and of his intentions was right. Although the Prime Minister announced on May 2nd that the Royal Air Force was to be further expanded, the whole scale of our effort was insufficient. As Simon's letter had predicted, Germany showed an astonishing capacity for expansion in the air. She rapidly overhauled us and we never again reached parity with her before the war. Financial reservations also played their part, as late as 1938, and even after that. Such judgements and the complacent forecasts of German intentions proved quite erroneous. The gallantry of our young airmen redeemed, but could not excuse, a failure which was not their own.

* * * * *

After a fortnight of enforced leisure at home, the doctors seemed content that I should make plans to get away to the country. The evening before we left, Clive Wigram rang up from Windsor with inquiries from the King who, he said, had been much perturbed by my absence from affairs at this time. On the morning of our departure John Simon came to see me and we talked for an hour. My diary says:

> ... he is clearly confused as to what to do next, which is not surprising. One suggestion frightened me: that he should make clear in the House of Commons that our attitude towards violations of a dictated treaty would be very different to like violations of a negotiated treaty. I did my best to discourage him from that which in Germany's present mood would be a most hazardous invitation to open still wider a greedy maw, and France?! ... I also told J.S. that denunciation of Versailles was being overdone. Little but the territorial clauses remained, and, if we believed in the right of nations to determine their own future, these were by no means unrelievedly bad.... I fear that J.S. is uncertain which way to turn. Vansittart drives him his way, but J.S. is reluctant to travel. Yet he clings to the F.O. It is an unhappy situation for us all.

That afternoon, April 24th, my wife, my son Simon and I motored to St. Margaret's Bay in Kent, where a comfortable little house by the sea had been kindly lent us by John and Violet Astor. There I spent some days rapidly gaining strength, reading, sleeping in the garden in the afternoon and playing cricket with Simon after tea, with enjoyment to us both, but without benefit to his cricket from my poor efforts.

Before returning to full work at the Foreign Office we spent a week-end with Philip Sassoon at Trent Park. My wife and I were many times under his hospitable roof during these years. Philip was a wonderful host and impresario. His gift was to get people together who wanted to see each other and then efface himself. The resulting performance was his pleasure. He once told me that he got all the news worth hearing that way without the trouble of reading what the press had to say. He was a rich man who liked to spend his money making his friends happy around him; there was a touch of the Arabian Nights in the wonder of his entertainments. He was kindly and unselfish, asking nothing for himself, though when he became First Commissioner of Works he proved a most intelligent and imaginative holder of that office. For me there was also the tennis court, with the patient professional, and the swimming pool in which to revel, to say nothing of our host's lovely pictures, furniture and porcelain to discuss and admire. No contrast could have been more complete from workaday London, yet Trent Park was so close that I would sometimes escape from Whitehall for an hour's tennis there even on a weekday. On this occasion Mr. and Mrs. Churchill were among the guests. Mr. Churchill was kind enough to tell my wife of the telegram he had sent to Mrs. Churchill, who had been abroad at the time, about my unhappy flight from Prague: 'Now the only good member of the Government has had a heart attack in an aeroplane.'

During this time I spent many hours over a speech I had to make in Fulham. Little was being said by the Government to indicate the grave dangers from Germany. The note struck too often suggested we were only trying to settle differences between two almost equally troublesome contenders, France and Germany. I did not feel like that and thought that I should say so. I began with a reference to my journey, saying that no one who had made it could doubt the very real difficulties of the present European situation. The Anglo-French agreement of February 3rd was the most important event in recent international history. This should have made it clear, I continued, that any lingering doubts about Germany's equality of status were no longer justified. That agreement had dealt with security and armaments. On neither of these had we been able to record substantial progress in Berlin. Germany had made an offer of a pact of non-aggression with countries in Eastern Europe, but she had declined to resume her membership of the League. The German Government had emphasized that they wanted an arms convention, but the value of this declaration depended upon a willingness to accept limitations which gave a prospect of general agreement. Our Draft Convention had proposed 200,000 men as the figure for German military forces and those of France and Italy, while Russia was given half a million. I recalled that Germany had frequently praised this document and had regretted 'departures from its principles'. A year ago the principle of parity between the three Western continental powers was nowhere disputed. If Germany now maintained its need for 550,000, clearly parity was unattainable.

I then dealt with the German pretext for the increase, which was eastern Europe and, in particular, Soviet Russia. I said of Russia: 'I have never been in any country which has more clearly cause to be fully occupied with work at home for many years to come.' I added that, since the re-creation of the great Polish state, 'the possibility of an aggression by Russia upon Germany has become a geographical anachronism.' My speech ended:

> The British are not 'anti' any nation in Europe. They are not hostile to any people, nor do they regard any as antipathetic to them. The British people have never been good haters. Their inclination has always been to

forgive and forget at once. Sometimes indeed this readiness has even seemed a little incomprehensible to those who have been our comrades in arms, but it is an essential element in the British character. As in the past, so today. We are not 'anti' any nation, but we should be, we must be 'anti' any who might seek by force to break the peace. We shall always be found arrayed on the side of the collective system against any government or people who seek by a return to power politics to break up the peace which by that system we are seeking to create.... Inevitably ... our public opinion will ... be most influenced not so much by declarations however sincerely or indeed fervently made, as by the constructive contribution that any given government is willing to make to secure the common good.

This speech received wide publicity and brought a sharp reaction from Germany, where it was dubbed unjust. In retrospect, it seems to me to have been a fair analysis.

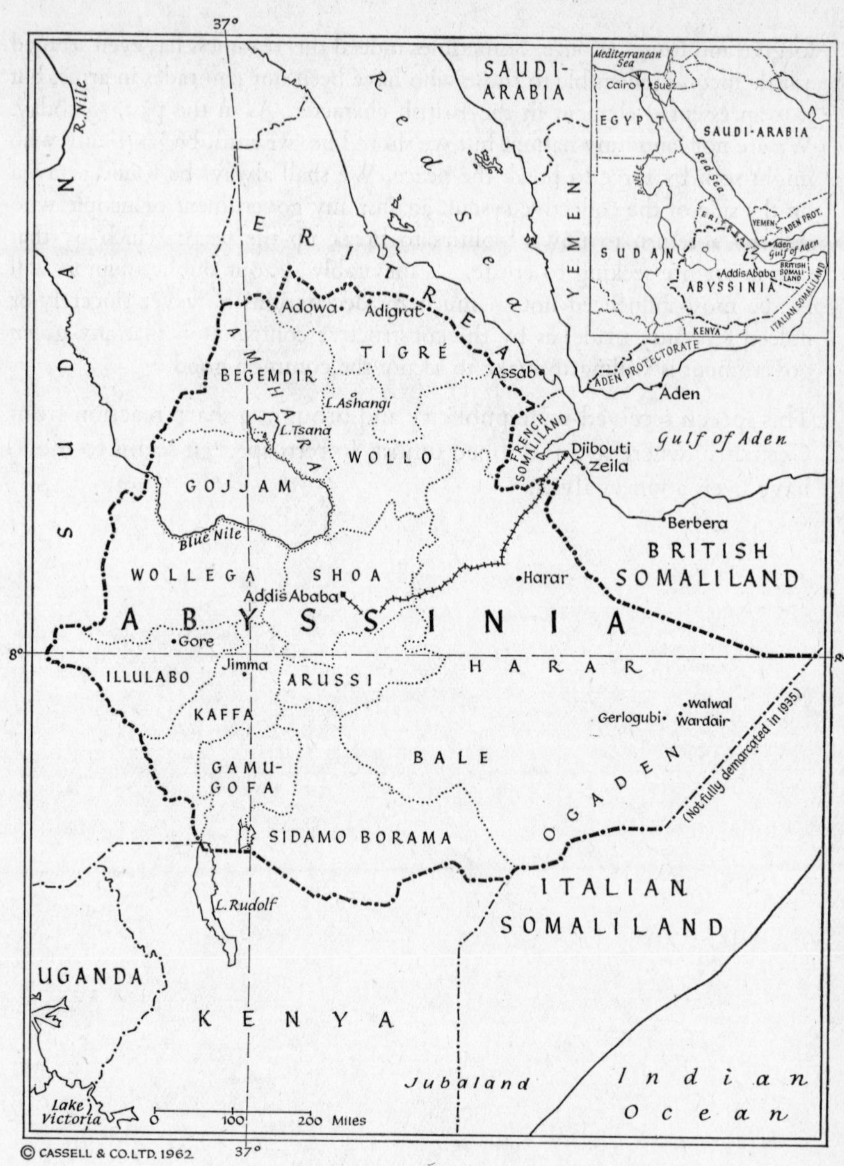
37°
R. Nile
SUDAN
SAUDI-ARABIA
Red Sea
ERITREA
YEMEN
Mediterranean Sea
Cairo
Suez
EGYPT
SAUDI-ARABIA
Nile
Red Sea
ERITREA
YEMEN
ADEN PROT.
Aden
Gulf of Aden
SUDAN
Addis Ababa
BRITISH SOMALILAND
ABYSSINIA
ITALIAN SOMALILAND
KENYA
ADEN PROTECTORATE
Aden
Gulf of Aden
Adowa
Adigrat
TIGRÉ
AMHARA
BEGEMDIR
Assab
L. Ashangi
L. Tsana
WOLLO
FRENCH SOMALILAND
Djibouti
Zeila
GOJJAM
Blue Nile
Berbera
BRITISH SOMALILAND
WOLLEGA
SHOA
Addis Ababa
Harar
ABYSSINIA
8°
Gore
Jimma
ILLULABO
ARUSSI
HARAR
KAFFA
Walwal
Gerlogubi
Wardair
BALE
(Not fully demarcated in 1935)
GAMU-GOFA
OGADEN
SIDAMO BORAMA
ITALIAN SOMALILAND
L. Rudolf
UGANDA
KENYA
Jubaland
Indian Ocean
Lake Victoria
0
100
200 Miles
37°

XI

ABYSSINIA PRELUDE

November 1934 – May 1935

Trouble on the Abyssinian border – Appeal to the League – Signor Mussolini's intentions – An oblique warning by Sir John Simon – The shaping of British policy – I prepare for Geneva – Baron Aloisi on Abyssinia – M. Laval arrives at Geneva – Sir Eric Drummond's interview with Signor Mussolini – An Anglo-French resolution on Abyssinia – Signor Mussolini gives way – Danzig – I am attacked by Fascist press

For a long time Italy had had uneasy relations with Abyssinia, who was neighbour to her colonies of Eritrea and Somalia. The frontiers were ill-defined or not defined at all, which made armed clashes easy. This instability did not prevent Italy and France from sponsoring the admission of Abyssinia to the League of Nations in 1923, despite the hesitant reserve of Britain. Five years afterwards, in another peaceful interlude, Mussolini and the Emperor Haile Selassie signed a Treaty of Friendship and Arbitration. I remember a later occasion, during a Council session at Geneva, when an Abyssinian delegation had brought a gift which included some splendid ivory. The speeches in reply were eloquent, especially that of the French representative, M. Paul-Boncour. He spoke of the Three Wise Men who had come out of Abyssinia with a star to guide them, to worship at Bethlehem, and ended bravely '*suivons l'étoile*'.

Unhappily, the Treaty of 1928, which undertook to develop and promote trade, did not bring the results which Mussolini may have hoped for. From 1932 onwards the Italian press began to speak of Abyssinia in increasingly hostile terms. By the autumn of 1934 the situation had deteriorated so badly that even a public exchange of declarations in Rome, proclaiming that neither Government had any aggressive designs on the other, did little to mend matters. Mussolini was surreptitiously setting the stage for his aggression, but neither we, nor the world, nor the Italian people knew it.

At the end of November an Anglo-Ethiopian Boundary Commission, of which Colonel Clifford was the British leader, was making a survey of grazing grounds in the Ogaden, an arid province in the south-east of Abyssinia, where tribes from British Somaliland had long-established rights for their herds. This was an area where the boundary between Abyssinia and Italian Somalia had never been demarcated. Italy had been in effective control of part of this territory for some time, but Abyssinia had never admitted foreign ownership. When Colonel Clifford arrived with the Abyssinian Commissioner and an escort of six hundred Abyssinians at Walwal oasis on November 23rd, he found it occupied by Italian troops. Clifford and his colleagues of the Commission prudently decided to withdraw, but the Abyssinian and Italian contingents remained. Sir Sidney Barton, our experienced Minister in Addis Ababa, reported three days later that the Emperor Haile Selassie had received a message from the chief Abyssinian member of the Boundary Commission, to say that the Italians had installed themselves at one kilometre from Walwal; there they had hoisted the Italian flag. Five Italian officers were in the neighbourhood with a numerous garrison equipped with war material and wireless telegraph. The message concluded: 'We have just received a letter coming from Italian troops who are at Walwal, written in Arabic, in which they say to us: "Why have you come here? We ask you to quit the place in two hours." If there is eventually an aggression we shall have to retaliate.'

Not surprisingly, the Emperor was apprehensive and applied to Sir Sidney for advice. He in turn asked the Foreign Office, who replied that the Commissioner in British Somaliland was being asked to establish immediate contact with Clifford and that the Emperor could not be advised until his report was received. Up to this time there was no reason to suppose that these events would develop into an important international crisis. When the Counsellor at the Italian Embassy in London, Signor Vitetti, called at the Foreign Office on December 3rd, he was told that our interest in Walwal and Wardair related to the ancient grazing and watering rights enjoyed by the nomadic tribes of British Somaliland. While we could not in any circumstances disregard these rights, the matter was certainly not one which should be allowed to do any harm to Anglo-Italian relations. At the same time the British Government suggested to the Emperor that the most satisfactory way to end the present uncertainty on the Italian frontier would be to go ahead as soon as possible with agreed demarcation on the ground. But when, on the following evening, Drummond told Suvich of the advice we had given, he received the impression that the Italian Government 'did not much relish the proposal'.

Within twenty-four hours fighting had broken out. How it originated will probably never be known. All that is certain is that Italian military power, which included aircraft, was markedly superior to that of the Abyssinians, who retreated leaving a hundred and ten men dead and many wounded.

A few days later, during the December session of the League Council in 1934, when both the Saar and Hungary's dispute with Yugoslavia seemed in a fair way to settlement, Massigli of the French delegation rang me up at my hotel in the afternoon and asked me to come urgently to the League building. He said that he would explain when I arrived, but it was important. I went down and to my surprise found him closeted with the Abyssinian delegate. Massigli invited him to repeat to me what he had just told him about an incident between Italians and Abyssinians on the border of their territories. I listened while Massigli looked on gloomily. At the end, he drew me aside and said: 'It smells bad to me, like Manchuria.' I was inclined to agree with him and suggested that he should ask his chief to come down, which he did. Laval listened to the Ethiopian's account, in the course of which the delegate mentioned his country's capital, Addis Ababa. This appeared to be a new name to M. Laval who was highly delighted with it and kept repeating: '*A-bé-ba. Que c'est chic, ça. A-bé-ba.*' However, he agreed that we should see Aloisi, and thus began the first of interminable negotiations. For the moment we could do no more than alert London to our misgivings.

* * * * *

Meanwhile Simon, from the Foreign Office, rightly decided that our Boundary Commission should not risk becoming involved in the territorial dispute, so Colonel Clifford was told to withdraw to British territory, inviting his Ethiopian colleague to go with him. Our Minister was also told that while Simon agreed to the Emperor doing all he could to reach agreement by direct negotiation, it seemed probable that the co-operation of the League would be needed in the end. We would do anything we could to help. Drummond, in telling

Suvich this, said he hoped that in any event the Italian Government intended to settle this question amicably. Suvich replied that they did; Italy had sent two notes, requesting that an indemnity should be granted and honour paid to the Italian flag. This, he contended, was customary in such cases.

When the terms were delivered to the Emperor they turned out to be tougher than that and included:

Governor of Harar Province to proceed in person to Walwal to offer ceremonial apology;

Payment of 200,000 dollars indemnity;

Arrest, dismissal and punishment of those guilty, after they shall have honoured the remains of their victims in accordance with Somali custom. . . .

The Foreign Office now being increasingly doubtful whether any result were possible by direct negotiation, told Barton so, while the December days passed in conciliatory efforts on our part in Rome and Addis Ababa. These did not get far, though the Italian Chargé d'Affaires came round to see the Foreign Office and repeated that his Government were most anxious to avoid trouble and to settle the whole business. They did not want war with Abyssinia, but felt it right to regard the Walwal incident and the demarcation of the boundary as two separate questions, the former to be disposed of before the latter could be tackled. This all seemed plausible enough, even though it involved delay. The Emperor, meanwhile, had made a conciliatory move on his side by offering to deposit 200,000 dollars with the League of Nations, pending the fixing of responsibility for what had happened.

Then came another clash of arms with casualties, at Gerlogubi, where events were as much in dispute as at Walwal. All that was clear was that Gerlogubi was thirty-five miles west of Walwal, and therefore thirty-five miles further into Abyssinia, as Simon pointed out to Drummond, following up this information with a demand on New Year's Day 1935 that the Ambassador should postpone his interview with Mussolini no longer. He was instructed to make effective use of the full information on the Abyssinian attitude which we had sent him. In the event, it was another fortnight before Drummond succeeded in having the meeting.

No real progress being recorded, the Abyssinians decided to put their dispute with Italy upon the League Council's agenda for its January meeting. When the Council met, their representative, while reserving his right to take action if necessary during the next few days, held back the formal request for its inclusion on the agenda. In an attempt to promote a solution at Geneva, Simon came out for the first day or two, when he and I saw both the Italian and Abyssinian representatives. The Foreign Secretary was particularly impressed by what he called, in a telegram to Rome, 'the very conciliatory and constructive attitude' of the Abyssinian. On the Italian side there was a strong wish to prevent intervention by the Council. Simon therefore telegraphed to Barton, suggesting that the Emperor should take the initiative by a note to the Italian Government in which he would first express in general terms his regret that lives should have been lost in an encounter between their forces. Secondly, Simon suggested an undertaking to pay into a bank in neutral territory, other than Geneva, 200,000 dollars, on the understanding that an Italo-Ethiopian boundary commission would distribute this sum for the relief of sufferers from the Walwal incident, or for any special expenditure caused by it.

Simon felt that such a note might be accepted by Mussolini as a settlement of the incident, if accompanied by an assurance that, until the frontier was defined, the Abyssinian forces would avoid contact with the Italians, on the understanding that they did not attempt to advance. He repeated his telegram to Rome, asking Drummond to see the Duce and do his best to persuade him to agree to this way out. The Ambassador was also to point out that unless some results could be shown, the dispute would be placed on the agenda of the existing session.

Unhappily this ingenious proposal met with no response in Rome. When Drummond at length saw Mussolini on January 14th, he was told that three of the original four points demanded by the Italian Government must stand, only the punishment of the guilty could be dropped. Also the money must be paid into a bank in Eritrea, in other words, into Italian possession. Drummond replied that these conditions could hardly be accepted by the Emperor, who, after all, had stated that he was ready to submit the whole question to an impartial tribunal. It seemed to him, therefore, that the matter would have to go before the League. Mussolini shrugged his shoulders and said that if it did, the consequences might be very serious. To Drummond's plea that to meet the present Italian request might endanger the Emperor's position, Mussolini replied that he did not much mind whether this Emperor or another ruled in Ethiopia; the indisputable thing was that whoever governed should be strong. The rest of the interview was in the same tenor. Drummond concluded that the situation was not only serious, but was becoming threatening.

On Simon's early departure from Geneva, Laval, Aloisi and I got into a huddle, as we had done many times before, but we made little headway. By the 16th, I was telephoning to London that the Italians should be told we could do no more, and that proceedings at Geneva should take their course.

I had a number of reasons for advocating this. First, the news of Mussolini's rough rebuff to Drummond at their interview. Secondly, as I told London, it was not much use putting pressure on Aloisi at Geneva, for he had little or no power to influence the decisions taken in Rome. My third reason was the increasing Italian suspicion of our motives. Aloisi had complained to me of the arrival of consignments of arms, apparently supplied by British firms, which had passed through Aden. In one particular instance, he announced, cases marked 'Machinery', but known to contain weapons, had been carried in a vessel which normally would have proceeded direct to Berbera. Owing to action taken at Aden, her course had been altered to include a call at Djibouti, so that these cases could be landed at a French port for delivery to the Abyssinian Government. The implication was that British authorities at Aden had intervened. I asked London to inquire about this. If the Italians were so convinced of our ill-will, our good offices could not be of much value, for the time being at least.

In this same mood I telephoned the next day that the Abyssinian delegate felt he could no longer delay his request to the Council to consider his country's appeal urgently, under Article 11 of the Covenant. I did not think that we could advise him to postpone action. This forecast brought fresh efforts by the Foreign Office in Rome and at Addis Ababa and further informal meetings at Geneva. For two days these continued, Laval and I working together in our interviews with Aloisi and the Abyssinian. Eventually, we were able to make some impression upon Aloisi. If he would not have the procedure under the League Covenant, we told him, he must accept that under his country's own treaty with Abyssinia. By many telephone calls to Rome and numerous discussions, the last of them in the Secretary-General's room, a letter was drafted for each party to write to the Council. Italy and Abyssinia declared 'their readiness to pursue the settlement of the incident in conformity with the spirit of the Treaty of Amity of 1928 between Italy and Abyssinia and with Article 5 of the said Treaty'. That article bound both parties to follow methods of conciliation or arbitration in differences between them, while the Italian letter to the Council itself referred to direct negotiations as being in accordance with the spirit of the Covenant and with the traditions of the League.

If words meant anything, this was clear enough. Mussolini was no doubt influenced to offer this apparent concession by reluctance to face a public discussion. One other piece of information may have helped a solution. The packing cases said to have contained arms turned out to hold furniture from Messrs. Waring & Gillow, supplied for the new palace at Addis Ababa and diverted to be in time for the visit of the Crown Prince of Sweden.

Despite the last-minute reprieve, I was not sanguine and telephoned a message to London that the suggested procedure 'if accepted by both sides will meet the immediate difficulty of today's Council meeting. But, of course, the larger problems of settlement would still remain and the responsibility of the two parties, more particularly of the larger party, to avoid fresh incident would be very heavy.' The result was acclaimed by press and public in many lands, but all we had gained was time.

* * * * *

My forebodings were soon justified. A month after the exchange of letters at Geneva, Barton was telegraphing that the Italian Minister at Addis Ababa continued to declare he had no instructions. Meanwhile Italian military preparations gathered pace. Our Military Attaché in Rome reported shipments of aircraft to East Africa, and Drummond reported on February 11th an admission by Suvich that two divisions, a total of thirty thousand men, had been mobilized, as a warning to the Abyssinians that Italy 'would defend herself if the need arose and not yield to pressure.' Drummond thought it seemed probable that, while the Italians had at present no aggressive intentions, they were genuinely afraid of overwhelming Abyssinian attack. Extravagant rumours of every kind were prevalent, but public opinion was, he thought, very far from favouring a policy of adventure, both on financial and on general grounds.

I did not share this confidence. In view of Laval's recent meeting with Mussolini, much depended on the French and I found no encouragement there. On February 19th, M. Corbin called at the Foreign Office to say that his Government, after further examination of the Italo-Abyssinian situation, had decided that there was no need for them to intervene with advice, or propose their good offices in Rome or Addis Ababa. From conversations which the Comte de Chambrun, the

French Ambassador in Rome, had had with Signor Suvich, it was apparent, M. Corbin said, that direct negotiations between the Italian and Abyssinian Governments for the purpose of establishing a neutral zone were proceeding satisfactorily. This statement was so far from the evident facts that I found it most disturbing. So did Sir Sidney Barton, who handled his exacting responsibility with remarkable coolness and sagacity throughout the crisis. He now telegraphed a message from Addis Ababa, two sentences of which seemed to me to contain the heart of the matter:

> There is only one real issue and that is independence of Ethiopia.... Personally I can think of only one course likely to prevent perpetration of what may be widely regarded as an international crime and that would be for England and France to tell Italy that she cannot have Ethiopia.

I thought that our information from Rome confirmed Barton's judgement. Suvich made it clear to Drummond on February 23rd that the Italian Government had no intention of entering upon negotiation until a neutral zone had been established in the Ogaden. Here was a new demand which had no place in the agreement we had made at Geneva the month before. As I had been largely responsible for this, I felt that I must set down my opinion on the action we should now take. I did so in a memorandum to the Foreign Secretary on February 26th, which has its significance in view of after events. I wrote that Drummond's telegram raised in an acute form our responsibility as a member of the League, and more particularly of the Council, in respect of recent developments in the Italo-Abyssinian dispute. In our telegram, I contended, we had asked the Ambassador to try to secure assurances from the Italian Government that they would take action without further delay to give substance to their Geneva promises. His reply showed that the Italian Government were not prepared to do this.

I continued:

> The understanding of the Council in adopting its resolution a month ago was that there would be no resort to arms, but that both parties would adopt methods of conciliation, in the first instance, by direct negotiation. It was only as a result of the terms of the letters addressed by the two parties that the Council felt justified in postponing the discussion of the Abyssinian request until the next session.
>
> Now Signor Suvich in his reply has told Sir Eric Drummond that instructions had been given to the Italian Minister at Addis Ababa not to begin the negotiations foreshadowed at Geneva until a neutral zone had been established. There is nothing about a neutral zone in the letters of either party to

the Council, nor in the terms of the Council resolution itself. In the circumstances I suggest that we should instruct Sir Eric Drummond to approach the Italian Government once again and to draw their attention to the Council resolution and to its direct reference to Article 5 of the Treaty of Amity between Italy and Abyssinia and to ask them how, if direct negotiations are not yet to be entered into, the Italian Government propose to give effect to the terms of this resolution. Sir Eric Drummond might also repeat that in our view it is most important that such negotiations should be begun without further delay, adding that if the good offices of our Minister at Addis Ababa can avail to further their course he will be instructed to offer his co-operation.

The Council resolution goes on to note that both parties have pledged themselves 'to take all expedient measures and to give all useful instructions for the avoidance of fresh incidents.' It is difficult to reconcile the recent movements of Italian troops to East Africa with the terms of this undertaking. I suggest that Sir Eric Drummond should, therefore, also be given instructions to remind the Italian Government of this passage in the resolution accepted by the Council and to recall the responsibility which all members of the Council share to ensure that that resolution is carried out.

I went on to advise that the French Government should be informed and asked to make similar representations on their own account, since their responsibility as a member of the Council was equal to our own. M. Laval's obligation and mine were especially direct, since it was as a result of negotiations which we pursued together that the two parties agreed to address these letters to the Council. I admitted that it might be thought that the terms of such a communication were strong, but argued that we could and should say no less if we were to fulfil our duty as members of the Council. I wrote:

Personally, I have for some time past been anxious at the drift of events in Ethiopia. It is hard to believe that Italian ambitions are limited to a few wells. It would seem now that Italy aims at no less than the absorption of Ethiopia morsel by morsel. In this connection it is perhaps not without interest to note that Sir Miles Lampson fears that, were our ships absent during trouble in Egypt, Italian ships would arrive on the scene. Wholly apart, therefore, from our League responsibilities I venture to think that it must be a matter of serious concern to us that Italy should seek to secure such a dominating position in this part of Africa. What we may expect is set out in Sir Sidney Barton's telegram, which foreshadows an objection by Italy to nomad tribes, including our own, having a right of access to the wells. . . .

The impression that is left on my mind by all this is that unless some hint, and a pretty strong hint, is given to the Italians that we should not view with indifference the dismemberment of Ethiopia, then this dismemberment will take place. . . . It is surely at least possible that a clear indication from ourselves and from France, as members of the Council, might effectively discourage Italy from the more ambitious of her plans. In any event, whether we succeed or no I believe that representations on the above lines to the Italian Government are called for. . . .

On the same day, Sir Robert Vansittart, Mr. Ronald Campbell, who was head of the Egyptian Department, and I drafted telegrams to Rome and Paris in the sense of my paper. These were despatched, with Simon's approval, that night. Drummond's reply was not encouraging. He told us he had drafted a memorandum 'of a thoroughly friendly character' embodying the main points of our telegram. He continued:

On my arrival at the Ministry of Foreign Affairs, I found the head of Government reading the memorandum, and when he came to the passage emphasizing that negotiations should progress more rapidly, he stated with the utmost emphasis that until a *modus vivendi* was reached between the two countries, he would continue to send troops up to half a million if necessary. I managed to interrupt this outburst to say that much depended on what kind of *modus vivendi* he had in mind, but His Excellency was not to be drawn on this point.

Drummond observed that the remarks of the British Government were not animated by any desire to criticize Italian action. Mussolini replied that he quite understood our position, which he believed was inspired by interest in the League of Nations rather than in Abyssinia. If, however, the League took action contrary to Italian interests, he would know what conclusions to draw.

I was not happy about this interview, which I thought too apologetically presented by our Ambassador. Firmness at this early stage could have saved many reproaches later. I also thought that Mussolini's comments about our attitude to the League should have had some reply. It was indispensable that he should understand that, since the policies of both our countries in Europe were founded on support of the League, we, at least, could not pursue a divergent policy in Africa. To attempt to do so would be to wreck the League and with it the basis of our joint enterprise in Europe.

My memorandum was also taken by Sir Robert Vansittart as his text when the Italian Ambassador called upon him to express his doubts about Simon's projected visit to Berlin. Grandi complained that this could injure the harmony of relations between Britain, France and Italy. Vansittart reassured him that 'at best the visit might be useful and at worst it would be wise'. He went on to warn Grandi 'lest proceedings considerably more dangerous than a visit of exploration to Berlin' might disturb Anglo-Italian harmony. He then spoke of Italy's dispute with Abyssinia, pointing out that so long as Italy had not fulfilled her undertaking, she was herself hopelessly in the wrong and thereby also involved her sponsor, His Majesty's Government. It had been freely said and generally believed that the terms of the last German note were an attempt at driving a wedge between the three powers. Surely the Italian Government themselves would, by a failure to fulfil their obligations, be offering the occasion for such a wedge at the very moment when it was most inopportune. Grandi told Vansittart that he did not believe Mussolini to have come to any irrevocable decision over Abyssinia. If Grandi was right, this was hopeful, almost a hint.

* * * * *

Towards the end of the month, Simon was in Paris, where he learned that the telegram sent as a result of my memorandum had produced some effect. Laval said that he was prepared to make representations to the Italian Government and declared that he had already warned the Italian Ambassador that, unless Mussolini were prepared to arbitrate, he would be faced with a new appeal by the Abyssinians at Geneva.

The new appeal was not long delayed. The Emperor could hardly be expected to gaze with unconcern at the Italian build-up of forces. Accordingly, on March 17th, M. Tecle-Hawariate, Abyssinian Minister in Paris and representative at the League of Nations, presented a request to the Secretary-General that the Council should intervene. He accompanied this with an embracing offer 'to accept any arbitral award immediately and unreservedly, and to act in accordance with the counsels and decisions of the League of Nations'. For the moment, however, these moves were overshadowed for me by events in Europe, notably by the German announcement of conscription, our visit to Berlin and my journey to European capitals. Such information as we had about Abyssinia was superficially more reassuring. On the eve of the Stresa Conference, the Italian Government announced that they were prepared to make the necessary arrangements for arbitration, as urged by the Council and as provided for in Article 5 of the Treaty of 1928. This was a well-timed tactical move.

When Simon and Laval came from Stresa to Geneva for the Council meeting, the Abyssinian delegate made an attempt to bring his country's dispute with Italy before the Council, but failed. The Council had decided a year before that the provisional agenda of an extraordinary session should contain only those items for which it had been called. There was also a proviso that at the outset, when the agenda was adopted, the Secretary-General should communicate to the Council a list of other most urgent questions. M. Tecle-Hawariate explained his country's motives in asking for immediate discussion. The Italian Government, he pointed out, were sending an unceasing stream of troops and war materials to Africa and were steadily carrying out works on the frontier between Italian territory and Abyssinia, which could only be regarded as preparations for an impending military operation. The Italian Government had confirmed their acceptance of arbitration, but they had not appointed the arbitrators called for under the Treaty. The Abyssinian Government had done so and were ready to give their names. They asked that an early date be fixed by which the Italian Government would do the same.

This request cannot have been easy to refuse. Sir John Simon suggested that it would be very unfortunate if, when the Council met for its ordinary session in May, the situation were exactly the same as it was that day, with no conciliators appointed and no terms of reference settled. He looked for an assurance from both parties that this action would be taken before the main session. Baron Aloisi's diary* shows that he regarded even this limited intervention as underhand. It would certainly have been more useful if addressed to Mussolini at Stresa a few days before. Aloisi replied in general terms that the Italian Government would do its utmost to see that the procedure of conciliation and arbitration was opened as rapidly as possible. With this vague assurance of good intent as against mounting military activities, the Council left the business for four weeks, while the tension and the commitment grew.

* * * * *

Early in May, Mussolini sent a message through his Ambassador appealing to His Majesty's Government, in Simon's description, to adopt and manifest the most friendly and helpful attitude towards Italy's proceedings in Abyssinia. Grandi spoke of the situation there as a cancer which had to be cut out. He conveyed, in veiled though un-

* op. cit.

mistakable terms, so Simon reported, that Mussolini was 'contemplating a forward policy of the most serious dimensions.' The Ambassador did not justify Mussolini's proposed proceedings, but he was emphatic in asserting that his country could take no other course. In reply to a question as to what it was that his Government really wanted, he admitted that new territory was involved and talked about uniting the two Italian colonies in that region.

Simon told the Ambassador that it was always the object of British policy to be helpful and friendly to Italy and we had given many proofs of this, but he expressed the gravest anxiety about the effect of Italy's contemplated action upon British public opinion. The Government did not control that opinion; it was the free expression of the judgement of the British people and it would be no service to Italy to attempt the impossible task of trying to restrain it. Simon said that he had already been questioned many times in the House of Commons about Italy's policy towards Abyssinia and had found difficulty in answering, without appearing to reflect on the long drawn-out failure to carry out the conciliation procedure which Italy, as well as Abyssinia, said she was ready to apply. The Ambassador must see that the gravest criticism would be expressed, if a great power like Italy were engaged in aggressive action against a state like Abyssinia. Nothing could be more distasteful to His Majesty's Government than that British opinion should be critical of Italian policy, but, Simon said, this depended upon the policy which Italy pursued, not upon His Majesty's Government.

Simon also referred to the possible effect of such a policy upon the European situation. The Stresa meeting had demonstrated the solidarity of purpose of Italy, France and Britain. If Italy became involved in prolonged military operations in Africa, might not this, Simon asked, weaken the steadying effect upon Germany which Stresa had produced. It was our duty as friends to call attention to considerations which so greatly disturbed us. Finally, Simon asked Grandi to consider how parliamentary questions which were bound to be put in connection with these developments, were to be answered by His Majesty's Government. Grandi then referred to the understanding recently arrived at between Italy and France on the latter's special interests in Abyssinia and inquired whether we were not prepared to follow a similar course for our own special interests there. Italy wished to conduct her relations with Abyssinia in a way which would not trench on British interests at all. Simon replied that he had already heard of Italy's inquiries on this head and these would be considered, but our main concern over Italo-Abyssinian developments was more fundamental.

* * * * *

While I was still convalescing and spending a weekend at Trent, my Foreign Office box arrived with Simon's account of this conversation. I had no confidence that the Foreign Secretary's rather oblique warning would produce a change of heart in Rome. Once again we were resting our case on the effect of Italian action on British opinion. No firm indication was given of how His Majesty's Government would have to react against an Italian aggression in Abyssinia, not from choice but because we were pledged under the Covenant, upon which our alignment with France and Italy and peace in Europe were based. I wanted to preserve the Stresa front, but with the best will in the world, I did not see how this could be done if Italy launched herself upon the conquest of Abyssinia. Grandi was the most astute and experienced of ambassadors and probably realized the dangers to his country of the Abyssinian adventure, but the only conclusion he could draw from his exchange with the Foreign Secretary was that we were troubled and uncertain in our course. I wrote of Simon's interview in my diary that night: 'Even from his own account nothing like stiff enough. Italy's request was a diplomatically phrased demand for a free hand in Abyssinia. This should have been strenuously resisted, emphasis laid on our support of the League, etc. It is useless to ask Musso how he thinks that Simon can answer questions on the subject in the House.'

I returned to duty at the Foreign Office a few days later, when my conclusions were soon confirmed by a speech from Mussolini to the Senate, on May 14th, in which he said:

> ... one rumour which has been spread in certain foreign states must be formally and immediately denied—the rumour, that is, of an Anglo-French diplomatic *démarche* at Rome ... the truth is that no *démarche* has taken place up to now ... we will send all soldiers that we think necessary.

Mussolini's denial was true, but he should have been in no position to make it.

This speech was grim reading a few days ahead of the date when I would have to go to Geneva for the League Council. A collision there seemed inevitable. I wrote some of my anxieties in a letter to Drummond which concluded: 'I am the more preoccupied over the whole outlook because I have always believed that there was no reason why

Anglo-Italian relations should not be excellent.' I told him that Britain's belief in the League was now so deeply felt that any conflict between Italy and the League over Abyssinia must clearly have the worst possible effect on the relations of our two countries. 'All this, of course, you know only too well, and it is certainly going to make our task at Geneva next week difficult if the Italian representatives are not authorized to play a really active part in bringing about an agreed settlement.'

These developments had not passed unnoticed within the Government and on my return from convalescence several of my colleagues spoke to me of their concern. A memorandum on the situation had been called for urgently from the Foreign Secretary. This showed clearly that Italy had, from the start, pursued a policy of diplomatic dalliance while building up her military strength. Simon had no doubt that, if matters continued as they were, Italy would launch a large-scale offensive when the rainy season was over in Abyssinia, at the end of September or beginning of October. Evidently in such a situation Abyssinia would press the League Council to consider the dispute at once. This memorandum, though admirable in its analysis, contained no recommendation as to the action which His Majesty's Government should take.

I was summoned during the meeting of my colleagues which considered this paper on May 15th. Mussolini had announced that morning the names of the Italian members of the Conciliation Commission, as Simon had asked him to do at the League a month before. It was, therefore, probable that the Italian representative would argue that the League could not act, since the conciliation procedure was being carried out. Although there were some suggestions that we should not come to grips with an unpleasant reality just yet, the Government finally refused to agree to a procedure which would result in no action being taken to prevent hostilities before the Council held its next meeting in September. Apart from this guidance, I was given wide discretion on the handling of the crisis at Geneva. I was authorized to discuss the question with the representatives of other powers there, especially from the point of view of dangers to the League. The Cabinet also decided to summon Drummond to London immediately, which would at least show Mussolini that they were taking the business seriously, if belatedly.

Sir Eric arrived in time to attend a second meeting two days later. It was agreed that he should see Mussolini at the first opportunity.

Meanwhile, Mr. Ingram, the First Secretary at our Embassy in Rome, was asked to give Signor Suvich a warning which was firmer in language than anything that had been used to Mussolini hitherto. In particular, he was to be reminded how strongly the United Kingdom felt about the peaceful solution of international disputes through the League. We considered that the Council of the League could not neglect the dispute between the present meeting and the September one and asked that instructions should be given to the Italian representatives at Geneva to discuss the best method of securing a solution, under the League's auspices. I had a hand in drafting the terms of the message myself, but I was doubtful whether it would be effective. The hour was now so late, and I left for Geneva with reluctance and foreboding.

* * * * *

On arrival at Geneva for the Council meeting on May 19th, I made a first contact with Massigli. We shared anxieties, but could neither of us devise a solution. My next task was to see the Abyssinian representative and this took quite a while, for M. Tecle-Hawariate, whom I much respected, was accompanied by a learned French legal adviser, M. Jèze, who talked well and liked to hear himself. In effect, however, the message was clear enough. The Abyssinians would make no difficulties about the details of arbitration, or its speed, if the Italians would enter into a pact of non-aggression with them before the Council, which pact would remain in force until a final settlement was reached. The only arrangement which they could accept would be one engaging the authority of the League on their behalf; assurances by the Fascist Government they considered worthless.

That night, Baron Aloisi dined with me alone, when we had two hours' conversation. My guest was something more than an accomplished Italian diplomat. If he was smooth there was fibre in him too and he was loyal to his Duce. The trend of our talk was of ever-deepening gloom. Aloisi began by saying he was afraid that the Abyssinian question would prove more difficult of solution than the Saar. More than a colony was at stake for Italy, there was the whole prestige of the regime. A man like Signor Mussolini could not be expected to spend six hundred million lire in order to change his mind at the request of the League of Nations. He recalled the earlier history of that part of Africa. There had been a tragedy of military defeat at Adowa, which must be washed out in blood. Abyssinian conduct towards Italy had been a constant source of aggravation. Pin-pricking had never ceased. Now at last there was a chance of dealing with this and Italy could not be expected to forgo it. Aloisi said Italy had never based her whole policy upon the League, she had always been more realist. It was perhaps unfortunate, he added, that the matter had not been raised at Stresa. He fully understood the importance of trying to save the face of the League. Signor Mussolini, he felt sure, shared this opinion and was prepared to do all he could in conjunction with us, but only provided that this did not affect in substance the final outcome.

I replied that this must depend upon what was the substance for which Italy sought. Baron Aloisi had seen the recent message to Rome and I emphasized to him that this represented the view of the Cabinet and was only a modest expression of anxieties which were deeply felt. He and I had done so much work together that he would expect me to speak frankly. If the Italian Government were really engaged in a policy of military aggression in Abyssinia, I viewed the future with the utmost concern. In our judgement Italy was indispensable to peace in Europe at the present time. It was hard for us to believe that Signor Mussolini did not understand this all-important fact as clearly as we and the French Government did. There was nothing I would deplore more than that Aloisi and I should, as the outcome of this dispute, witness a steady deterioration in Anglo-Italian relations, all the result of the attitude we would be obliged to take up. At the present moment I did not see how that could be avoided.

When we came to discuss the immediate mechanics of the problem, Aloisi argued that conciliation must be confined to the Walwal incident. I asked him how he thought the Council was to maintain touch, since clearly we could not just adjourn until September. Had Aloisi thought of a committee of the Council or of a rapporteur? He did not like either, but eventually undertook to think over this suggestion as well as our conversation and to meet Massigli and myself the next day. I telegraphed to London late that night, adding that Aloisi seemed finally to grasp how serious matters were. He had repeated many times his anxiety to find a way through. I was sure that he would send to Rome a depressing account of what had passed between us. My summing up was that at best we were faced with many weeks of a very tough negotiation. I supplemented this with a personal letter to John Simon:

Our talk was extremely depressing and I fear that the Italians, or Signor Mussolini at least, have not yet fully appreciated the issues which they are raising by their Abyssinian adventure. I received fresh confirmation that Drummond is right in believing this to be purely a 'Mussolini policy'. Aloisi himself gave me an instance of the difficulty he was in when trying to negotiate here. Before leaving Rome he had apparently induced a reluctant Mussolini to agree not to persist *à outrance* in his refusal to agree to Abyssinia's being represented by other than natives of that country on the Conciliation Commission. On arrival here Aloisi told me that he found a telegram that he was not to give way on this matter, nor to depart from his instructions in any way.

Aloisi was emphatic that we should achieve nothing by bludgeoning Mussolini. Such methods would, he maintained, only exasperate the Duce and might make him take hasty action. The procedure from which Aloisi apparently hoped most was that we should be able in some way to divert Signor Mussolini from his present policy and encourage him to take the lead himself in modifying it. If we could persuade Mussolini that it was in his own interest to modify his policy and if we could at the same time give him the prestige which might be gleaned from having initiated such modification himself, then in some such method lay our best chance of success. All this, I am afraid, is rather obscure, but then so was Aloisi—and worried too.

In the back of his mind I am sure that Aloisi has the Manchurian precedent. At one moment he said that we had swallowed *la couleuvre* of Manchuria; why was Abyssinia creating such difficulties? In addition to this there is of course Italy's sense of resentment that she lacks the colonies and mandated territories that others possess and her feeling that now she has an opportunity, perhaps the last, to seize the territory, the possession of which would place her definitely among the Great Powers with important colonial possessions.

I really believe that I was able last night to make Aloisi understand the seriousness with which we view the situation. I was told by someone who met him afterwards that Aloisi had come away extremely depressed from our interview. Our talk was, however, absolutely friendly and I shall, of course, do my utmost to maintain this basis for our relations. At the moment it is hard indeed to see any daylight in this dark business.

The following day, I met with Massigli and Aloisi, as arranged. Aloisi declared that he had faithfully reported all that I had said to him the night before and that our Ambassador was seeing Mussolini that day. The next twenty-four hours would therefore bring some guidance. Meanwhile, he made one or two suggestions to help the Council keep in touch with the dispute. Massigli and I thought these useful and said so, but we also told Aloisi of the alternatives which confronted us. Either we must work out a procedure which would enable the Council to remain in close contact and do its work of removing the threat of war, or inevitably we should have a debate at the Council table that week about the merits of the dispute, which would be prolonged and acrimonious.

Aloisi emphasized what he called the irrevocable nature of the Italian Government's decisions on Abyssinia and asked whether Drummond had made this clear to us. Massigli and I both argued against this description of the Italian attitude. We maintained that no government's decision on a matter of this kind could be regarded as irrevocable and reminded him of the position in which our two countries would be placed, if his Government persisted in the manner he described. To this Aloisi repeated that we must understand that the prestige of the whole regime was at stake.

Laval arrived the next morning and I had a short talk with him before the Council. He, like all of us in Geneva, was becoming steadily more perturbed. Mussolini seemed to be mad, said Laval, and assured me most earnestly that at no time during the Rome conversations did France give Italy any encouragement whatever to military action in Abyssinia. On the contrary, when discussing the economic arrangements which had been embodied in the Rome agreement, Laval had himself said, half in jest, '*Vous avez les mains fortes*', and had gone on to warn Signor Mussolini to be careful that his efforts in Abyssinia were confined to economic objectives. Laval, I told London, appeared fully alive to the impossible position in which our two Governments would be placed as members of the League if Mussolini persisted in his Abyssinian venture. We agreed to keep in continuous consultation and to act together. I was quite sure that the only hope of putting effective pressure on Mussolini lay in strong Anglo-French unity and I made this the dominant purpose of my negotiation in the days which followed.

* * * * *

As if the skies were not dark enough at Geneva that morning, a great thunder cloud came rolling up from Rome. Drummond reported on his much anticipated interview with Mussolini, which, to use his own words, 'could not have been of a more disquieting nature'. Mussolini thought that since Italy had now nominated her two members of the Conciliation Commission, the League Council would only take note of the constitution of the Commission and wish it all success. Firmer language from Drummond soon brought the Duce's intentions into the open. The Ambassador said that if Mussolini forced Britain to choose between her old friendship for Italy and her support for the League, she might well choose the latter. Mussolini replied that the situation between Italy and Abyssinia was intolerable and that an end must be made to it. He had not carried through all these preparations, he said, and spent all this money simply to obtain a settlement of the Walwal incident. If, in order 'to clarify the situation and to obtain security, it was necessary for him to resort to arms, in short to go to war, he would do so and he would send sufficient men to obtain his objective.' That was his will.

Drummond pointed out the extreme seriousness of this statement and its implications as regards the League, relations between Great Britain and Italy, and security. To destroy the League would be to destroy the whole existing political system, including Locarno. Mussolini's retort showed how grave was our failure to take him personally to task over Abyssinia weeks or months before. Collective security, he said, should be confined to Europe as emphasized at Stresa. If the League seemed to support Abyssinia against Italy, he would have no choice but to leave it, never to return.

As soon as I saw Drummond's account of his conversation, I telegraphed to London, with special reference to Mussolini's statement that if it was necessary for him 'to resort to arms, in short to go to war' in Abyssinia, he would do so. This, I pointed out, was a declaration to us that if he could not obtain his objects by other means, he would take action in breach of the Covenant of the League, the Kellogg Pact and the tripartite Treaty of 1906, to all of which both we and Italy were parties, not to speak of the Italo-Abyssinian Treaty of 1928:

> It seems to me impossible for us to allow this statement to go unchallenged and I suggest that as a first step Mussolini should be reminded of these treaties and of obligations which we share under them. It should be made clear to him that if he should decide to engage upon a policy which from his own showing would run counter to obligations he has assumed under these treaties, then he cannot expect us to condone much less to support him in doing so either at Geneva or elsewhere. It seems essential to make this clear at once, in order that there may be no doubt as to our own attitude and to avoid the charge being made at any future time that we had been accessories before the fact. If you approve I would use similar language officially to Baron Aloisi here tomorrow.

I went on to explain to London that with the declaration of intentions which Mussolini had now given us, we should have to be more careful than ever not to be parties to a procedure which merely postponed the issue, without prospect of intervention by the Council or a modification in the Italian attitude. Nor must we put pressure on the Abyssinians, whose consent would be necessary, to accept any such arrangement.

Early that evening I saw Laval again. As a result, we agreed that it was of no use to wait further upon events; we must take the initiative together and put forward a resolution such as the Council might reasonably be expected to accept, then we should see what Mussolini would do. The French delegation undertook to produce a draft, and after dinner we met again with a text before us. This was based on the Emperor's request that the arbitration procedure should deal with all the incidents which had taken place since November 23rd, 1934, and should not be restricted to the Walwal incident alone, as Mussolini had demanded. We also called attention in the resolution to the obligations of both Governments under the 1928 Treaty to arbitrate and not to fight. If no decision had been reached by arbitration within a time limit, the Council would meet to examine the situation. I telegraphed:

> It is my impression that if this text were accepted by the Italians it would constitute a reasonable proposal to put before the Council, but it is a minimum.

Drummond was not happy about the remonstrance to Aloisi which I had proposed in my telegram to London. Such action, the Ambassador said, would without doubt lead to a serious explosion on Mussolini's part and to anger directed against His Majesty's Government. He greatly feared that a communication in the terms I proposed would cause the Duce to refuse any concessions at Geneva and prejudice altogether the remaining chances, however small, of an agreed solution at the Council meeting. He suggested that it might be wiser to await the results of the Council meeting before finally deciding on the policy we should adopt.

However, a few hours before I received this message, Baron Aloisi called to give me the version he had received from Rome of Sir Eric Drummond's conversation with Signor Mussolini. His report did not differ in any point of substance from the Ambassador's record. I determined to use this opening to make the comments I had referred to London. When, therefore, Aloisi reached the stage in his recital at which Signor Mussolini spoke of the possibility of having to take armed action in Abyssinia, I reminded Aloisi that if such an eventuality arose, as I most sincerely hoped it would not, then the Italian Government would be acting in disregard of the terms of three treaties to which we and they were both parties. In such circumstances, they could not expect us to condone, much less to support, such action. Aloisi said he very clearly understood our position, which caused him grave anxiety. This was one of the reasons why he hoped that a solution could yet be found which would avoid such an eventuality. My action did not provoke an explosion, but played its part in the events which followed.

Laval and I, having agreed the terms of the resolution we would lay before the Council, asked Aloisi to come to see us and pressed him to submit this text to Mussolini. He finally consented and promised to put to the Duce, as forcefully as he was able, the argument we had used, but warned us gloomily that it was ten to one that Mussolini would not accept. Both Laval and I made it clear that we could go no further towards securing a settlement than this text allowed. During these conversations, I found the French much preoccupied for the safety of their own nationals in French Somaliland and in Abyssinia. Laval appeared increasingly anxious as the conversation developed and as the cynicism of Mussolini's view became more evident. I told London of the French preparations to reinforce their troops in French Somaliland. Massigli for his part warned Laval of the uneasy reaction already noticeable in the opinion of the Little Entente and of the Balkan Entente.

On the following morning, May 23rd, the Italian delegation produced a counter-proposal. I regarded it as unacceptable, since no assurances were offered that force would not be used. The Italian draft also debarred incidents other than Walwal from the conciliation procedure and explicitly excluded the Council from association with the course of the dispute. During a series of meetings with Laval and Aloisi, I insisted that arbitration must cover all the incidents, be concluded by a given date and be accompanied by an undertaking by both parties not to go to war. Laval agreed; all now depended on Mussolini.

I soon had cause to be glad that I had spoken strongly to Baron Aloisi. After midnight Massigli rang us up to say that the Italian delegation had received a reply from Rome, accepting the greater part of the French draft, but finding it impossible to agree to the declaration not to use force. Although this was a notable improvement, I thought it essential, especially in view of Mussolini's bellicose declarations to Drummond, that the Italian Government should reaffirm its obligation under the 1928 Treaty not to settle differences by force of arms. I telephoned to the Foreign Office asking that Simon should give Grandi no encouragement to suppose that our resolution on this question of principle would weaken. Simon agreed and summoned the Ambassador, to whom he said firmly that my handling of the dispute at Geneva had the full support of His Majesty's Government, who were convinced that my view as to the minimum necessary to secure an agreed resolution at the League Council was correct. Simon emphasized, most helpfully, that the Council could not be expected to forgo a reference to the 1928 Treaty, which bound both sides to settle their differences peaceably. Grandi said he would do his best, asking only that Drummond should be given similar instructions at his end.

Perhaps Mussolini was impressed by the closeness of Anglo-French accord and the strength of feeling against him in both countries over the dispute, or maybe he thought it best to accept for the present, meaning to break these new engagements also when the time came. Whatever the motive, he gave way. The Abyssinian delegation declared, entirely on their own initiative, their acceptance of what had now become two draft resolutions. We sat late into the night. At length all was ready, text and speeches, under Litvinov's orderly chairmanship. The unanimous vote was taken by the Council at two-thirty in the morning. Nothing had seemed less likely forty-eight hours before.

The Italian delegation had come to Geneva under orders to persuade the Council to postpone the issue and content itself with taking note of the appointments to the Conciliation Committee. They had been compelled to acknowledge the right of the Council to keep in touch with arbitration and to intervene if necessary. Mussolini had also to accept a time schedule within which to complete the phases of conciliation and arbitration specified in the Treaty. Should delays occur, he would have to satisfy the Council that their cause could not be laid at his door. Finally, attention had once more been drawn to the obligations assumed by both parties under their Treaty of 1928 not to resort to force. This was, on paper, as good as we had a right to ask and better than the world had expected.

Although the Prime Minister sent generous and enthusiastic congratulations and the press of many countries acclaimed our Geneva resolutions as the prelude to a solution of the Abyssinian dispute, I was not so confident. To Sir Eric Drummond, who wrote warmly in congratulation, I replied: 'It was indeed good of you to write so kindly, though, in fact, I do not myself feel that we have achieved so much. There are, I fear, greater troubles ahead.' To Sir Miles Lampson, our High Commissioner in Egypt, I commented that 'we have done little more than make it harder for Mussolini, in the eyes of the world at least, to proceed to extreme measures against Abyssinia.'

* * * * *

This session of the Council was by far the most exacting I had yet been through. Public interest was intense and a newspaper comment that I was carrying my political life in my hands was probably no exaggeration, though it was not what mattered most. I was rapporteur on six subjects, of which the gravest was the situation which had developed at Danzig. The League's High Commissioner for the free city was Mr. Sean Lester, an Irishman with gentle manners but a firm will. Despite his protests, the Senate in Danzig had changed the electoral law, put opposition leaders in prison, suppressed hostile newspapers and then held an election. The chairman of the Senate, Herr Greiser, had made a speech supporting this action in terms derogatory to the High Commissioner. The Council sustained the authority of its High Commissioner and Herr Greiser was obliged to express his regrets, pleading that no offence had been intended.

The legal opinions at issue were then, at my suggestion, referred to a small committee of jurists. Herr Greiser gave assurances that the Senate of the free city would act as the Council required, should the committee find that the constitution of the free city had been violated, as I had no doubt it would. Arguments and meetings about Danzig ran parallel with the Italo-Abyssinian crisis, so did the final stages of the dispute between Hungary and Yugoslavia, which had given us so much trouble six months before. When all was over, my colleagues on the Council expressed more gratitude than I had earned, Litvinov, who was in the chair, and Aloisi, being particularly outspoken.

In the House of Commons, when the time came to give my opinion, I credited two men, Laval and Aloisi, with the survival of the League's authority. The temporary firmness of the first had done most to decide the issue. Aloisi's task had been more unenviable, he had had to persuade Mussolini. Public men in a dictatorship know the path they are choosing. Yet those who stand by their opinions, even when they run counter to their leader's convictions, because they believe them to represent their country's true interests, show a special quality of courage. Aloisi and Grandi both did this on occasion.

The outcome of this session at Geneva brought upon me some personal attacks in the Fascist newspapers. The fact that Count Ciano was the Minister of Propaganda encouraged this activity, his object being to add to his own authority. Confident in the support of Mussolini, his father-in-law, he was eager to show his independence of the wiser counsels of the Italian Foreign Office. These attacks continued, at first intermittently, then with increasing fervour, in the newspapers of both the Italian and German dictatorships until their fall. Naturally they never did me anything but good with the British people.

XII

MUSSOLINI, THE SECOND MEETING

May – June 1935

A talk with Mr. Baldwin – An exchange in Prime Ministers – Sir Samuel Hoare becomes Foreign Secretary – I am Minister for League of Nations Affairs – Sir Samuel Hoare and Abyssinia – The proposed Zeila exchange – I arrive in Rome – My interview with Signor Mussolini – He rejects the Zeila proposal – The second discussion – Signor Mussolini reveals his ambitions – Paris – M. Laval and the Anglo-German Naval Agreement – He suggests a protectorate for Abyssinia – My mistrust of M. Laval

In May 1935, the lobbies of the House of Commons and the newspapers were full of rumours of the impending reconstruction of the Government. It was taken for granted that Baldwin and MacDonald would exchange places, Baldwin becoming Prime Minister in name as well as in practice. The temperaments of the two men had made the National Government possible. Under most leaders the huge Conservative majority would have compelled a Conservative Prime Minister at an earlier date, but Baldwin was content to be the loyal power behind the throne. Now this could last no longer. There was also much canvassing of the Foreign Office and I would have been naïve to pretend I did not know that my name was being urged upon Baldwin, publicly and privately. I resolved to have a talk with him on May 16th, before I left for the League of Nations at Geneva.

I opened what would have been a difficult conversation with any other man by saying that I did not, of course, ask him what his intentions were about the Foreign Office. I should perfectly well understand if he thought me too young to be Foreign Secretary, apart from other considerations. If that were his view, I would be content to work in any other department, or none. There was, I said, just one thing I would ask him not to do, and this was my reason for wanting to see him, I hoped that he would not ask me to go on at the Foreign Office under a new chief. This was not on account of pride, but simply because I would not really be of use in such conditions. I held a certain point of view on foreign affairs, the country knew it, foreigners knew it. I could not, after all these years, usefully play second to a new chief. But I repeated that I would willingly serve anywhere else, or nowhere. Baldwin, friendly as always, said he quite understood and that he was glad I had spoken to him as I had done. He told me that the changes would not take place before I was back from Geneva and that we would have another talk before anything was settled.

On my return to England on May 26th, the new appointments were being more vigorously canvassed than ever. But, though I had a talk with Baldwin about the work I had done at the League, he made no reference to Government changes, nor could I bring the business up again. To other inquirers and well-wishers I merely said that I knew no more than they did, which was true. At noon on June 5th, Sir Maurice Hankey, the Secretary to the Cabinet, rang me up at the Foreign Office and said he understood that it had been decided that I was to have the Foreign Office. He congratulated me and asked if he could come over and have a talk. I replied that I had heard nothing. Hankey said: 'There is no doubt about it; Ramsay has just told me it's settled.' I could only repeat that I had heard nothing about it and Hankey agreed to postpone our talk until I had.

After questions in the House of Commons that afternoon, we voted on business and, as we went past the teller, Baldwin touched me on the shoulder: 'Come to my room please, after this.' Thinking that Hankey was right after all, I followed him through the House and out behind the Speaker's Chair. He was then in the Lord President's room, now used by the Leader of the Opposition. Before the door was closed he said, speaking quickly and with some embarrassment: 'Sam [Hoare] is to go to the Foreign Office and I want you to stay on and help him there.' I reminded him of our earlier talk. He replied that conditions were so difficult now at the Foreign Office and work so heavy that he had decided two men were needed there. I would be in the Cabinet and carry some special title to designate my work, such as Minister for League of Nations Affairs. I said that unfortunately this did not meet the objections which I had previously put to him. It was not selfishness nor a question of personalities. I did not like the plan of two Ministers in the Cabinet, each with a responsibility for foreign affairs. I did not believe that it would work, there would be danger of conflicting advice. To this Baldwin replied that Hoare would advise the Cabinet on foreign affairs generally; my province would be League affairs. I retorted that League affairs were foreign affairs and that it would not be possible to separate them. I asked Baldwin earnestly to let me serve somewhere else, perhaps in a Service department, but he would have none of this. After some further talk, he urged me to go to see Hoare and talk it over. 'Sam is most anxious to have your help.' In spite of our friendship, he doubtless thought me a little unreasonable. 'After all,' he added, 'it isn't everyone who has the chance to be in the Cabinet before he is thirty-eight.' I did not feel that he had understood my predicament.

I climbed the stairs to see Hoare in his India Office room. He appeared very friendly, but I deployed to him at greater length the arguments I had used to Baldwin. I told him that, with the best will in the world, this system was not the right answer. I explained how, in the Foreign Office, work was arranged in pyramidal fashion up to the Secretary of State. The Permanent Under-Secretary ranked second, and that was right. There was room for a Minister such as I had been under Simon, but not for a Cabinet colleague who shared responsibility for decisions. At best it must put a drag on the machine and I begged him not to insist on the proposal. Hoare admitted the force of these arguments and hinted that if I would accept the arrangement for a while, perhaps it need not last for long. What would I like to do? I said that I realized that I had no experience outside the Foreign Office. I thought it might be good for me to get some, perhaps in a Service department. I should like the Admiralty best. Hoare said that might be difficult, but after some further talk, we agreed that my acceptance of the office was only to be on a temporary basis and that we should both say so to Baldwin. On this I left, unhappy.

I was not sure that I had succeeded in explaining my thoughts in full. The international situation was tangled and menacing, decisions would have to be taken quickly. Was I to know of each one of them before the Secretary of State acted? If so, that would mean a fifth wheel to the coach and, perhaps, dangerous delay. If not, I would have no choice but to acquiesce after the event and share responsibility. That was how it worked out, as it was bound to do.

Most of all it was the European scene that troubled me. I did not know what Hoare's views on foreign affairs might be, though he had the reputation for being astute and had piloted the India Bill skilfully through the House. I felt that I knew what was needed in British foreign policy and I could not help realizing that the Foreign Office would have been glad to see me appointed. Now I felt out of the stream. Looking back over the years, I am sure that these appointments were a mistake. They had all the elements of compromise at a time when decision was needed, the kind of compromise to which a Prime Minister is often tempted; it had in it the seeds of future trouble. If Hoare were the right choice, then I ought to have been moved somewhere else. I cannot blame myself for accepting the arrangements. I was relatively very junior and had no taste for blackmailing my colleagues, or even being thought to do so.

Afterwards, I was told that Baldwin had virtually decided to offer me the Foreign Office, the explanation, no doubt, of Hankey's telephone conversation with me. Neville Chamberlain had then pressed Hoare's qualifications, not out of hostility to me, but because he considered that Hoare could now be transferred from the India Office and had a prior claim; my time would come later. Mr. Geoffrey Dawson, editor of *The Times* and a close personal friend of the Prime Minister was, I learnt, another who had spoken up for Hoare, no doubt because he thought Sir Samuel's policies, particularly towards Germany, more in line with his own opinions. Others considered that Hoare should see his reforms through into practice. Baldwin's instinct was sure and steady in domestic affairs, but the uncertainty he felt on international questions encouraged him to accept excuses for not facing unpleasant facts. He therefore decided to choose a man who might, from his reputation, be ingenious enough to find a way through and save Baldwin and the Government from what must otherwise be disagreeable decisions in a dangerous future. The weightiest arguments against this choice were Hoare's health, he was much in need of a holiday when he took over at the Foreign Office, and his lack of experience in international affairs. Nor was he firm in his opinions. Our two appointments were not received with any enthusiasm by the public or the press and were soon heavily battered by Mr. Churchill from below the gangway in the House of Commons. In these new arrangements I found one solace. I was to have an Under-Secretary to help me and Cranborne was chosen.

Sir John Simon now moved to the Home Office. His weakness as Foreign Secretary was that he found it difficult to devise and hold to a policy. His training and his active mind enabled him to see its shortcomings all too clearly, with the result that he was tempted to hedge and trim to meet the objections, until little was left of the original purpose. Too penetrating a discernment and too frail a conviction encouraged confusion where there should have been a fixed intent. Simon could master a brief quicker than any man, but this is only part of the business in foreign affairs. His colleagues used to complain that he was more apt to turn to them for a policy than to champion his own.

* * * * *

Unpleasant developments in the Italo-Abyssinian dispute were not long in making themselves felt. In the last week of May, I found the Foreign Office doubtful whether our opinion had been made sufficiently clear in Rome. I wrote that I agreed. On May 31st, Drummond reported an interview with Suvich, who spoke stiffly. A solution of the kind Italy wanted could be reached within the framework of the League of Nations, Suvich said, if Abyssinia were convinced that she would get no help from Great Britain and France. At any rate, he hoped that the Ambassador understood clearly what Signor Mussolini had said to him. 'I observed', replied Sir Eric, 'that, as I understood the conversation, there were certain things which Italy was determined to obtain. She would prefer to obtain them peaceably, but, if this could not be done, then she would be prepared to use force.'

The Ambassador continued that he would not for the moment argue the point further, but assumed that this summed up Signor Mussolini's conclusions. Suvich said that it did and repeated that he still believed that, with the help of Great Britain and France, from both of whom 'they', presumably the Italian Government, had every right to expect assistance, a solution could be found.

The copy of this despatch, with the department's minutes, only reached me a fortnight later, when I commented my regret that Signor Suvich's concluding words 'appear to have been allowed to pass unchallenged. Signor Suvich had no right to expect assistance from us', I added, 'to assist the Italian Government to tear up treaties.' Sir Samuel Hoare minuted that the account of this interview confirmed his view that 'our representatives in Rome have not yet succeeded in making the Italians face up to the realities of the case.' More information was constantly arriving of Fascist reinforcements for Abyssinia.

On taking over, Hoare began an examination of the Italo-Abyssinian situation. He held a number of discussions, some with Vansittart alone and others at which I made a third. For some years, government departments had been mulling over the possibility of offering Abyssinia access to the sea at the small port of Zeila, in exchange for an improvement in the frontier of British Somaliland, to give greater security to the grazing facilities on which our tribes depended. We now considered using our share of this offer on Italy's behalf, ceding Zeila to Abyssinia in return for territorial concessions to Italy in the south of the country in the Ogaden. This was unattractive country, but as a prestige solution might just get by. I was not enthusiastic about the proposal, still less so when it was suggested that I should be its sponsor in Rome, if the Cabinet agreed.

We decided to ask Drummond's views on the merits of the plan and on my presentation of it. Rather to my surprise, in view of the modesty of the offer and what I understood to be Mussolini's mood, he considered the attempt well worth making, arguing that even if I did not succeed, it would show our willingness to make serious sacrifices to help in a most difficult situation. His personal estimate was that the chances were about fifty-fifty. The Ambassador added that my coming would give the lie to a campaign in which we were being accused of wanting to shirk conversations with the Italian Government. He felt sure that the visit would be welcomed and that the press campaign against me could be ignored. The Cabinet endorsed the venture. Mussolini replied that he would be delighted to see me and agreed to use as cover the discussions on naval armaments and the Air Pact, which I had to hold uncomfortably in Paris two days before.

Whatever slender chance this proposal might have had was reduced by a leakage to the press, presumably as a result of the indiscretion of a colleague. A sufficiently full account of the offer appeared in a Sunday newspaper, which unhappy information greeted me on my arrival in Rome on June 23rd. Drummond and I agreed that the odds against acceptance had now lengthened.

* * * * *

Mussolini had returned to Rome from Riccione to meet me and our first discussion took place next morning. Drummond accompanied me, but after some preliminary and quite useful talk on the agreed topics, he and Aloisi withdrew. So many legends have grown up about the quarrel which Mussolini and I are supposed to have had at this meeting, that I now print the record in full as I made it at the time. We spoke in French. It is interesting to note that the official Italian Foreign Office account substantiates my own.

At the conclusion of this conversation [about the Anglo-German Naval Agreement and Air Pact] Signor Mussolini and I had a conversation on the subject of Abyssinia as we had previously agreed. Signor Suvich was the only other person present, but took little part. I began by telling Signor Mussolini that His Majesty's Government were gravely concerned at the turn events were taking between Italy and Abyssinia. Our reasons were neither egoist nor African, but European. His Majesty's Government were irrevocably committed to the League, upon which their foreign policy was founded. They could not therefore remain indifferent to events which might profoundly affect the League's future. Upon this issue I begged Signor Mussolini to believe there was no real division of opinion in the British public. Men of the right who were not in the Government like Sir A. Chamberlain and Mr. Churchill cared just as much as Labour Opposition in Parliament. Moreover the generation which had fought in the war and also the young generation now growing up in England were firm believers in the League, as they judged that it was only by collective security that peace could be preserved and only through the League that Britain could play her part in Europe. For these reasons, therefore, His Majesty's Government had been anxiously studying this dispute between Italy and Abyssinia to see whether there was any constructive contribution they could make which might assist to find a solution. I then outlined Zeila proposal and made clear to Mussolini that we intend to ask no concession for ourselves in return, save grazing rights for our tribes in territory ceded as a result of agreement with Italy. I told him also His Majesty's Government would be willing to assist Italian Government in obtaining economic concessions in Abyssinia; for instance, I understood that though there were foreign advisers, Italy had none and we would gladly help to remedy this state of things. If Abyssinia were willing to open up any part of the country to foreign settlers, we would wish that Italians should have a fair share.

Signor Mussolini replied that our proposal had certain very grave objections. It would give Abyssinia outlet to the sea which would make her stronger, as it would give her a corridor through which she could import arms. I interjected that if this were the only difficulty some means might be found of meeting it in any final settlement. Signor Mussolini continued that the scheme had still more serious disadvantages. It would not enable Italy's two colonies to be connected and it would result in Abyssinia claiming a victory for herself. Abyssinia would point out that concessions had been made not to Italy, whom she detested, but out of friendship for England. His Majesty's Government would appear as a protector and benefactor of Abyssinia, in exchange for whose gift Abyssinia had consented to make some territorial adjustments with Italy. I replied this was not in the least the position which we desired to create and Signor Mussolini could surely trust us to put the matter in a fairer perspective. Signor Mussolini said he did not doubt our good intentions, nor did he doubt the outcome of this proposal, were any attempt made to put it into force. He regarded it not only as unsatisfactory but as positively dangerous. He could not accept it. I answered that since His Majesty's Government had been at pains to think out this scheme, which involved a concession on their part, in an attempt to secure final settlement and to avoid conflict, I would ask him not to reply to me now. Signor Mussolini rejoined that in any case his point of view would not be modified. He had thought carefully before he had spoken. He understood that the Abyssinians wanted an outlet to the sea. Italy might have been prepared to offer one. She too had open roadsteads, but Abyssinia had not been willing to agree with Italy about this.

Since, however, I had come to Rome, Signor Mussolini continued, and since he appreciated the sincerity of what I had said and the good efforts of His Majesty's Government, he would reciprocate by explaining with complete frankness what were his objectives in Abyssinia. These objectives might, he still hoped, be obtained without war. If Abyssinia came to terms without war, he would be content with surrender of those parts of Abyssinia which had been conquered by Abyssinia in the last fifty years and which were not inhabited by Abyssinians. In saying this Signor Mussolini made a circular gesture which I took to mean that he regarded such territories as existing on all four sides of Abyssinia. The central plateau could, he continued, remain under Abyssinian sovereignty, but only on condition that it was under Italian control. If, however, Abyssinia could not come to terms with Italy upon these lines, then, if Italy had to fight, her demands would be proportionately greater. Signor Mussolini made a sweep of his hand indicating that Italy would then have the whole country. Italy had already sent 150,000 men to Abyssinia. He realized that this number would be insufficient. He was quite prepared to increase it and would do so up to 500,000 men if necessary, but the eternal difficulty of Italy's relations with Abyssinia must at length be finally disposed of. Great Britain must realize how serious was the matter for Italy. Some people thought Italy too poor for a great effort. But despite that poverty, Italy had made great sacrifices in the past and could, and would if need be, do so again. I replied that we were fully conscious of that spirit and that we realized also the courage of the Italian army and the tenacity of purpose of the Italian people and their leader. It was for this very reason we had been at such pains to find a solution which involved some concession of territory on our part. Our offer had not been lightly made. I would not conceal from him how gravely I viewed the future of relations between our two countries if this offer were rejected and no final settlement were reached. If Italy were to take the law into her own hands in Abyssinia and if the consequences were to be fatal to the League, the British people would inevitably and deeply resent it. The gravest injury would be done to good relations between our two countries.

Signor Mussolini replied that I had just made two observations which had greatly pleased him when I referred to the courage and tenacity of his people.

He fully understood the point of view of British public opinion. He had two main preoccupations: 1. potential military task in Abyssinia, and 2. the effect upon the relations with our two countries, and of these two the second was far the more serious. He had, however, carefully weighed them and all their consequences. As for the League of Nations, Signor Mussolini went on, he had no desire to leave the League, though other countries had done so, Germany and Japan, without loss to themselves. If however the League made Italy's position impossible, then he had not closed his eyes to the fact that he might have no choice but to leave it, though he repeated that this was not what he wished to do.

I said to Signor Mussolini that our conversation had profoundly perturbed me as it must do all who cared for the friendship of our two countries. Signor Suvich then remarked that after all the French were also members of the League. I said that I knew M. Laval also was very anxious, because he himself had told me so and had asked me to inform Signor Mussolini.

Signor Mussolini then went on to explain at some length that when M. Laval had been in Rome, it had in his view been clearly understood that Italy was to have a free hand in Abyssinia. I interjected 'economically'. Signor Mussolini replied that that might be so, as far as written document was concerned, but since he had yielded to France the future of 100,000 Italians in Tunis and received in return half a dozen palm trees in one place and a strip of desert which did not even contain a sheep in another, it must be clear that he had understood that France had disinterested herself in Abyssinia. We were the only people who had given him anything; we had given him Jubaland. He was quite clear that the implication, if not the written word, was that Italy was free in Abyssinia so far as France was concerned. I contested this, telling Signor Mussolini that when M. Laval had described in Geneva his interview with Signor Mussolini he had emphasized to me that he had insisted that France had only given a free hand to Italy in economic matters and that he had added to Signor Mussolini '*vous avez les mains fortes. Faites attention*', making it clear to Signor Mussolini that French good will did not apply to other than economic enterprises. At this Signor Mussolini flung himself back in his chair with a gesture of incredulous astonishment.

I returned to the charge several times in the conversation, which lasted about an hour, but I was unable to make any impression on Signor Mussolini's original answer. The tone of the conversation was at all times friendly and Signor Mussolini spoke quietly and even resignedly. There was no attempt at bluster of any kind. Both Ambassador and I had the impression that he looked ill, and he was certainly depressed. Only time when he showed any sprightliness was when describing the worthlessness of the territories ceded by France.

I had a few minutes conversation with Signor Suvich as I was leaving, when he undertook to arrange a further conversation at a luncheon which Signor Mussolini is giving for me today. I have however only very faintest hope of any modification in Signor Mussolini's decision. There was a gloomy fatality about his temper which I fear it may be beyond the power of reasoning to modify.

I have the impression that the Italians do not at present intend to attack until the middle of September.

I had considered the terms of my part in this conversation both in London before leaving and with Drummond in Rome. The opening sentences about the League were as agreed with Hoare and Vansittart. Later, at the luncheon, there was only a brief opportunity for personal conversation between Mussolini and myself. He assented without demur that we should have another meeting the next day, but referred once again to what I had said about the Italian army and spoke of the need for avenging Adowa. I protested against this determination, which seemed so strong with him, and argued that we could none of us re-fight past campaigns and turn these into victories. Certainly the British could not. We would have to start with Bunker's Hill.

The luncheon party was quite a large one, with ladies present. This occasion displayed to me the astonishing contrast between the two Mussolinis. When alone and in serious discussion, the Duce was calm, relaxed and reasonable, at least in my experience. There were no attitudes or airs. But the moment more than two or three were gathered together the man was transformed, jaw thrust out, eyes rolling and popping, figure strutting and attitudinizing. When luncheon was announced, Mussolini made a imperious gesture towards me and marched on. I hung back, English fashion, waiting for the ladies, and the Duce strode in alone.

★ ★ ★ ★ ★

The next day the Ambassador, Lady Drummond and I went to luncheon at Ostia, at the invitation of Count Ciano and his wife. This was an interlude without political significance. At one point during the meal conversation died. In the silence we heard the Italian guests murmuring '*il Duce*, *il Duce*' in a mounting chorus. We looked out to sea, and there was Mussolini dashing over the waves in a speedboat, standing in its stern with his chin thrust out. I thought for a moment that he was going to dive in and join us for luncheon. The Italians in our party seemed deeply impressed.

That evening, June 25th, I had my second conversation with

Mussolini. This time Strang was with me and Suvich with the Duce. The main part of our conversation was once again on the Abyssinian situation. I said that I had reported to London the conversations which we had held on the previous day. I had since had a message in reply, deeply regretting that the British proposal had not been successful. His Majesty's Government, I continued, wished to work with the Italian Government in order to help both parties to settle the Italo-Abyssinian dispute. That was why they had offered a contribution. The difficulty I saw, however, was that it now seemed impossible for us to be of any help. I had understood from Signor Mussolini on the previous day that his object was to annexe all those parts of Abyssinia which did not form part of Abyssinia proper, but which had been conquered by the Abyssinians.

Signor Mussolini confirmed that this was so and, at my request, showed on a map where these regions lay. According to him, Abyssinia proper consisted of the Provinces of Tigré, Amhara, Gojjam and Shoa, stretching from the western part of Eritrea to south of Addis Ababa. The territories which Italy required were those which almost surround this central block of territory, namely, the region bordering on south-eastern Eritrea, the Aussa country, the Province of Harar, the Ogaden, two Sultanates in the south of Abyssinia bordering on Kenya and a strip of territory bordering on the Sudan, reaching up to the extreme south-western point of Eritrea. As regards Abyssinia proper, Italy wanted control. The position of Abyssinia, Signor Mussolini said, would then be similar to that of Iraq, or Egypt, or Morocco.

I remarked that these examples were by no means similar. Iraq was independent and was a member of the League of Nations. Morocco, however, was a French Protectorate. Suvich observed that the Ogaden itself was uninhabitable and useless to Italy. In 1931, Italy could have had the Ogaden from Abyssinia in return for giving Abyssinia access to the sea. I said that I understood that Italy required the Ogaden for the defence of Italian Somaliland. Mussolini agreed. I then observed that this could not be the reason why Italy wanted the territory bordering on Kenya and the Sudan.

Mussolini again agreed and said coolly that these lands were required for colonization and for the sake of their mineral wealth. There was gold round about Jimma. The possession of these territories, he pointed out, would also permit Italy to open railway communication between Italian Somaliland and Eritrea by a line running west of Addis Ababa. This line was foreshadowed in the 1906 agreement. It went west of

Addis Ababa so as not to cut the Djibouti railway. I said that I understood that Mussolini wished to acquire this territory by peaceful means if possible. I believed that the Emperor would not agree to cede it without war. If Italy went to war in order to acquire this territory, she would be acting in contravention of the Covenant and of the 1906 Treaty. Mussolini replied that it was Abyssinia which did not respect the Treaties. Abyssinia had half a million men ready and would certainly attack Italy if there were a European crisis. I said that His Majesty's Government were ready to do all they could with the Emperor at Addis Ababa, if this were the cause of the tension. Mussolini observed that no one would help Italy if Abyssinia attacked her. I replied that, according to my information, it was the Abyssinians who were in fear of an attack.

Mussolini admitted that the Emperor himself was a cautious and educated man, but the Rases* were quite different. War was their national pastime, a kind of necessary amusement. The Abyssinian people would not work and were only of value as soldiers. Great Britain ought to allow Italy to get on with her task. A solution in the Italian sense would be useful to Great Britain also. Remarkable progress had been made in Libya, but it could not be made into a colony. On the other hand, the colonization of Abyssinia would occupy Italy for many a long year. Hundreds of thousands of colonists could be settled on the plateau to the advantage of the native population. There were already Italian doctors and priests there, working for the good of the people with the consent of the Emperor.

I said that it was because His Majesty's Government were so anxious to find a solution of the question without war that they had made their proposal. Mussolini repeated that if he accepted a settlement without war, he would require the territories which had been conquered by Abyssinia. The remaining territory, namely, Abyssinia proper, would have to be controlled so as not to become a focus for renewed hostility. On the other hand, if he had to go to war to achieve his ends, his aim would be to wipe the name of Abyssinia from the map. When the natives were disarmed, they were quiet. So long as they were armed, they would cause trouble. When they took possession of the territory, the Italians would disarm everybody and the colony would be the quietest in North Africa.

I said that I hoped Signor Mussolini was under no delusion as to the

* The Rases were the feudal chieftains of Abyssinia and sometimes acted independently of the Emperor.

attitude of British public opinion. I had noticed suggestions that there would be support in England for a proposal such as Signor Mussolini outlined. This was not so, nor was it the point of view of His Majesty's Government. Public opinion in England took its stand on this question upon the League of Nations. Mussolini replied that the League must not make it necessary for Italy to withdraw from it. If Abyssinia remained in the League and Italy went out, that would be a strange result. I retorted that it was not my business to defend the presence of Abyssinia in the League. The fact was that Abyssinia was a member. Signor Mussolini could be assured that His Majesty's Government would do their very best to promote a settlement; they had already done so. Mussolini said that I must take home with me a clear impression that Italy was determined to settle this question once and for all. The Italian people were never so quiet or so satisfied as at present. It was a lie to say that there were internal difficulties. The regime had immense military, political and moral strength. He realized that the point which worried His Majesty's Government was the question of the League of Nations and the principles of the Covenant. He had taken this into account.

The discussion continued for a while longer over much the same ground, I saying that I believed, from Sir Sidney Barton's information, that the Emperor earnestly desired a peaceful settlement and Mussolini replying that the only way to bring the Abyssinians to a settlement was to let them see with their own eyes the Italian divisions, the Italian aircraft and tanks. He argued that if Italy had had five thousand, or even three thousand, more men at Adowa, the result would have been very different. There were in fact, he said, fourteen thousand against ninety thousand. Two Italian generals out of four were killed as well as 48 per cent. of the staff officers. For his own peace of mind he would rather send one division too many to East Africa than one division too few.

I concluded by saying that I could not conceal from Signor Mussolini that I was profoundly disappointed and that I viewed the future relations which might result between our two countries with grave anxiety. I then thanked him for the patient way in which he had listened to my representations, adding that there was happily still a little time in which to seek a peaceful settlement.

On our return to the Embassy, Drummond, Strang and I could find no comfort in the situation. Mussolini seemed fixed in purpose and impervious to the evident dangers. We agreed that I should so report to my colleagues, who would now have to determine their course between upholding the League and losing an ally, or undermining the foundation of peace in Europe. The series of pacts and agreements which criss-crossed Europe were, almost all of them, related to the League. If it were once shown that these engagements were of no avail when a great power wanted to swallow a smaller one, confidence would be shattered and the temptation to make terms with the biggest bully in the neighbourhood would be irresistible. It might be that Mussolini's success at Corfu twelve years before had given him a contempt for the League's authority.

I felt sympathy with Drummond in his thankless duty. His work for the League, as Secretary-General, had been exceptional, his patient care and guidance had given confidence to those who worked under him and authority to his advice. Now he was in a post where his past services were a liability rather than an asset. A conscientious and sensitive man, he was aware, perhaps too much so, that his association with the League must be expected to prejudice Mussolini against him. This was added to the distress any ambassador must feel at seeing opinion in a formerly friendly country stirred against his nation.

* * * * *

Nine years passed before I was in Rome again in October 1944, this time on my way back to England after a journey with Mr. Churchill to Moscow. When I arrived in Rome, the Italian Ministers, including the Prime Minister, Signor Bonomi, came to dine at our Embassy where Sir Noel Charles was now Ambassador, and we spent a pleasant and useful evening rebuilding Anglo-Italian friendship and confidence.

The next morning, I had an hour to spare before leaving for Field-Marshal Alexander's headquarters near Siena. I was alone and decided to call in at the Pallazzo Venezia. There I found a well, if hastily arranged, display of some of the loveliest pictures from the galleries in Rome. I stood for a few moments watching soldiers and airmen in uniform, both British and American, gazing from one masterpiece to another, some of them old favourites of mine from the Borghese Gallery.

After a while, my thoughts wandered back to the last occasion when I had been in that room, discussing with Mussolini what I felt to be the inescapable consequences of his policy. I looked across at the windows and at the balcony where he had so often stood declaiming to the crowd upon his evanescent triumphs. Now he was alone, a haggard prisoner of the Nazis. A dictator has no friends. The room was almost bare, even the table at which I had sat opposite Mussolini had gone.

As the military boots moved heavily from picture to picture in the improvised gallery, their wearers seemed unconscious that the Duce had ever been.

* * * * *

The following morning I took the train for Paris. My outward journey had been caused by the Anglo-German Naval Agreement which had created a formidable outburst of indignation in the French capital. Under its terms, speedily negotiated in London in May and June 1935, Germany agreed that her navy should not exceed 35 per cent. of British strength. Less satisfactory was the concession to Germany of the right to build submarines up to 60 per cent. of British strength or even, in particular circumstances, up to 100 per cent. of the strength of the whole Empire. But it was not so much the terms of the Agreement that aroused opinion in France and among France's allies. The way it was done was a classical example of the truth of Lord Salisbury's dictum that the methods by which a policy is executed in diplomacy are commonly as important as the policy itself. In these negotiations, London once again made the mistake of acting in isolation. Paris and Rome were inevitably offended and indignant when it was known that the Agreement had been signed without any consultation with them.

Though I had no part in this negotiation, the Government thought it prudent, when the French reaction became known, that I should visit Laval and do what I could to mend relations. Laval's reproaches were sharp. The Agreement, he said, had caused great difficulties for the French Government. Opinion was thoroughly roused and the recent French note was not generally regarded as sufficiently strong. Not only was the Agreement an infringement of the Treaty of Versailles, but it was also contrary to the undertaking contained in our communiqué of February 3rd, that the various parts of the security and armaments problem were to be treated as an indivisible whole. Moreover, at Stresa we had, Laval thought he was right in saying, told the French that we would not accept a German claim of 35 per cent. of the British fleet. The united front of Stresa was clearly broken in pieces. He asked me why other powers should not now deal separately with Germany. France might have, she had not done so and would not do so. It was German policy to deal separately with each subject and with each party. He wished to make peace with Germany, but on the condition that Germany would make peace with everybody else. These were fine arguments, but it was doubtful whether Laval, in view of the dubious bargain I suspected he had made with Mussolini over Abyssinia, was the man to put them.

I replied that it had been the British intention to conduct only preliminary conversations with the German naval experts. The German representative had, however, refused to continue them, unless a definite answer were given as regards the 35 per cent. This offer was one which no government of the United Kingdom could possibly have refused, especially in the light of the experience of the past year and the increase in German claims in respect of land and air armaments. An increase in the German claim for naval armaments, I continued, would be more serious than, for example, an increase in German claims for air armaments. It was bad enough to have to double the air force; it would be still worse to have to double the fleet in these days of budgetary difficulties. I understood that Germany might be trying to drive a wedge between our two countries, but she would not succeed. If we had refused the German offer to meet French criticism, the outcry in Britain might have driven such a wedge. I assured Laval that we would not have accepted the German offer if we had not been convinced that to do so was in the interest of both our countries.

The discussion went on for two sessions. At the end of the first evening, June 21st, I telegraphed in a personal message to London:

> The Anglo-German Naval Agreement is regarded here as having struck a blow at the communiqué of February 3rd. Nothing that we can say will modify that judgement. None the less Monsieur Laval is himself not unduly disposed to cry over spilt milk. He is, however, determined to preserve what is left in the can of February 3rd.

Laval eventually admitted reasonably that it was more the form and method of which he had to complain. At intervals during two days we discussed the armaments and security problems of our two countries, including the possibility of an air pact. Laval was firm that we could not proceed by bits and pieces any further and I was sure that we must not give Anglo-French confidence another sharp jolt. In this sense I telegraphed to London some suggestions for the future guidance of our affairs and undertook to discuss the Cabinet's reply with Laval on my way back through Paris. This was as good as we could do. The French reacted helpfully, putting out a statement that, as a result of my visit, the cracked crockery of Franco-British co-operation would be entirely mended.

I did not tell Laval the terms of the proposal I was to put in Rome, thinking it better to handle that first with Mussolini direct. It seemed more prudent to tell him only that I proposed to speak to Mussolini about Abyssinia and would report to him fully on my way home. When, on the return journey, I prepared to speak of Abyssinia, Laval took the war into my camp, complaining that Britain had very nearly played a trick on France by offering to cede Zeila to Abyssinia. If this had happened, France would probably have had to declare Djibouti a free port. The Djibouti railway was perhaps the only one in the world which paid a dividend; it provided for nine-tenths of the expenditure of French Somaliland.

Alexis Léger was then Secretary-General to the French Foreign Office. Born on a rocky islet which I saw one afternoon off the coast of Guadeloupe, Léger had quiet charm and gentle manners. I found him sympathetic, but he had not the strength of character of his predecessor, Philippe Berthelot. It was not in him to impose his judgements on men like Laval and Flandin, even if it had been proper for him to do so. Léger now added the comment that to give Abyssinia access to the sea would have been contrary to the Treaty of 1906. I answered that if we had been able to obtain agreement between Italy and Abyssinia at this price, thereby saving the League and ourselves from a grave crisis, it would certainly have been worth while.

I then told Laval what Mussolini had said to me of his territorial demands in Abyssinia, and my reply that the Emperor would never consent to surrender this territory by peaceful means. Laval asked me whether Mussolini had thought of the possibility of a protectorate over the whole of Abyssinia. I replied coldly that I had not put such a question. Unperturbed, Laval said the advantage of this to the Emperor would be that he would thereby maintain the integrity of his territory as a whole, at the expense of some relaxation of control. He might in this way obtain a guarantee of his throne against the Rases. Italy would offer her friendship to Abyssinia, together with integral sovereignty for the Emperor, under a protectorate. This solution might appeal to the Emperor, whose position would then be similar to that of the Sultan of Morocco, who was Sultan over the whole of Morocco. I interjected that I thought he had little to say in the government of the country. Léger replied that the Sultan was the spiritual sovereign and that he enjoyed every regard and respect when he came to Paris. I could not see Haile Selassie in such a part, nor his subjects accepting it if he were.

Laval and Léger continued their arguments, Laval saying that this was the solution which he could support, though, of course, he had not mentioned it to either party. 'I now for the first time know the full extent of the Italian demands,' he added. I think it unlikely that Laval had been so reticent and certain that Mussolini had told him his demands. Laval then suggested that if the Emperor thought that our two countries looked not unfavourably upon some such arrangement between himself and Mussolini, he might acquiesce. Léger commented that Italy would have to take the initiative; Mussolini probably would not agree to our taking it. What he clearly wanted was to dismember Abyssinia. I replied that the Emperor would prefer to fight and that if he did not fight he would probably be deposed by the Rases. One of these had already sent a telegram to the Emperor: 'What are you waiting for? Are we women?'

The French then returned to their complaint that we had not consulted them about Zeila before approaching the Italian Government. Léger added that if the Italians had accepted the suggestion it would have disturbed Franco-Italian relations, while Laval wondered out loud how it would be possible to start the idea of an Italian protectorate over Abyssinia. I thereupon told Laval all that Mussolini had said to me about the conversation they had had together in Rome ending with the Duce's contention that, apart from the document, it had been clearly understood that Italy would have a free hand in Abyssinia.

Laval replied by giving me his explanation to the Foreign Affairs Committee of the Senate on the previous day and mentioned the three concessions the French had made in Somaliland, of land, shares in the Djibouti railway and a free hand economically. I reminded him of the warning he had told me that he had given Mussolini about his strong hands. Laval made no comment on this, but said that French policy was to refrain from doing anything which would disturb existing Franco-Italian relations or make them less intimate. France would do everything to promote a settlement by arbitration and conciliation. If these attempts did not succeed, Mussolini would go on with his projects with all the risks that they implied. I said there were risks for my country and for France too, as members of the League. I told him Mussolini's comments on these topics, and added my belief that the Duce had given the French Ambassador in Rome a similar account of his requirements. I thought that His Majesty's Government had done all they could for the present, it was now the French Government's turn. If Mussolini could be convinced that the French Government were greatly disturbed, perhaps he might state his minimum terms.

This brought a repetition of Laval's suggestion that Abyssinian integrity should be maintained under Italian suzerainty. I asked whether this meant Italian troops in Addis Ababa and Laval said yes, just as there were French troops at Rabat. The Emperor, I believed, would fight rather than agree to this. I told Laval so, adding that I myself saw no way out, but that it might help if he could tell Mussolini of his own anxieties. I once again asked him to do so, though with decreasing confidence about how strongly Laval would speak, or what the effect of his words would be in Rome.

Laval's firm convictions, expressed when we had been together in Geneva the month before, seemed to me to have evaporated, and this phase of our discussions left me deeply uneasy. It is true that he would have been willing to settle at the League for less than we got in the form of undertakings from Mussolini, but he had firmly supported me in our persistence to get better terms. As a result of this day's conversation, I suspected that more had passed between the Duce and himself than Laval would admit. I am sure now that he was playing both the British and Italian Governments along, hoping against probability that some solution could be contrived. Laval was a man who during his parliamentary life had shown much dexterity in handling his fellow members. For him the essential was to get Deputies into the same lobby, even, if need be, by telling them different things. In parliament these tactics might win a vote, in foreign affairs they could destroy an alliance.

* * * * *

This discussion was followed by one equally as long and as difficult on the question of further arms agreements with Germany. Here the shadow of the Anglo-German Naval Agreement still hung heavily over us. The contrast was between the British pragmatic approach and the French more legalistic one. I had sympathy with the French argument. At this time Great Britain wanted an air pact, so did Germany. We feared that with the growth of German strength, the desire for the air pact would grow less; the French feared that the conclusion of a pact would make negotiation with Germany on land armaments, which they thought concerned them most, more difficult. In this they were right. On the other hand, there was also force in our contention that an air pact including Germany, if it were of any value at all, would benefit France as well as ourselves. The French were on the firmest ground when they argued that the piecemeal approach which now attracted us was not consistent with our joint policy declared on February 3rd. Why had His Majesty's Government changed their minds so soon? Laval asked me. He also reproached us with being too much impressed by Germany. Great Britain had shown weakness after weakness, he complained, and the result would be that Germany would have superiority everywhere. This reproach was hardly consistent with his earlier argument that, for financial reasons, Germany could not go on rearming much longer. But that did not trouble Laval. He had a genuine grievance and could hardly be blamed for exploiting it.

That night I telegraphed a warning to London. I was convinced that we could not persuade the French of the usefulness of an air pact unless we reinforced it with practical arrangements between the parties, which would strengthen its effective working and give them confidence. Laval's position, I told London, was undoubtedly very difficult. Unless we could help him, either in this way or by upholding his stand on land armaments, further progress was not possible. About naval armaments I concluded: 'The French complain that they have not been allowed to submit their own perfectly legitimate programme until they can be told of the pace at which Germany is breaking the Treaty of Versailles.' This was putting them at the end of the queue, with contumely.

I returned home with an increased presentiment about the Italo-Abyssinian dispute, and with the conviction that we must clear our minds and align our policies with France on this and the arms pacts, if our alliance was to have either substance or meaning any more. In the event, Britain gained nothing from the naval agreement, which Hitler broke at his convenience.

XIII

THE ANGLO-FRENCH DILEMMA

June – August 1935

The Peace Ballot – The Government consider my memorandum – Vain pressure on Signor Mussolini – The Maffey Report – Sir Robert Vansittart – Dangers of not speaking plainly to France and Italy – I see Laval in Paris – The League Council – Doubts about the Mediterranean Fleet – The Three-power Meeting – Signor Mussolini rejects the proposals – Abyssinia appeals to Britain for arms – My anxiety about our defences against Italian action

I arrived back in London on June 27th. My warning to Mussolini and to Laval, that the Emperor Haile Selassie would fight rather than accept the conditions proposed for him in Rome, was soon confirmed. Sidney Barton, who knew of my conversations, telegraphed that he could conceive of no offer which the Emperor could make to prevent Mussolini from proceeding to extremes, so long as his objectives remained as now revealed. Barton suggested that we should immediately convene a conference between British, French, Italian and Abyssinian representatives, believing this to be the only method by which we could make use of the Emperor's known desire for peace. The Minister then sounded a new note; His Majesty's Government ought to consider whether any active measures were called for on their part, to prevent present Italian policy being put into effect.

I made my report to the House of Commons on July 1st, giving details of our offer to Mussolini, because I thought Parliament entitled to them, although Suvich had been against my doing so. I did not, however, tell of Mussolini's demands, in the hope that he might yet have to moderate them. There was no enthusiasm for our offer and no strong criticism either, most Members probably accepting the view, expressed by *The Times* the next day, that the proposal would have been justified if it had succeeded.

The next three months was a period of diplomatic effort to avert war on the one hand, and of time-wasting until bombs and guns were in position on the other. The strength of British feeling in favour of the League was exemplified by the results of the Peace Ballot, which were announced at the end of June. This Ballot, organized by the League of Nations Union under Lord Cecil, consisted of questions to which 'yes' or 'no' answers were to be given. The questions, however, were too complex to admit of simple answers. For instance, question 5 asked:

> Do you consider that, if a nation insists on attacking another, the other nations should combine to compel it to stop by
> (a) Economic and non-military measures?
> (b) If necessary, military measures?

Ten million people answered part (a) in the affirmative, while only 635,000 said 'no'. The answers to part (b) were considerably different. 6,784,000 men and women voted for military sanctions and 2,351,000 against.

These declarations took on a closer significance in view of Mussolini's now thinly veiled intentions. The separation of economic and military sanctions implied that the former could be applied against an aggressor without any risk of provoking war. This was not so. I doubt also whether it was sufficiently realized by the balloters that the brunt of applying military sanctions would fall upon Great Britain. None the less, the eleven and a half million who answered the questionnaire did not merely record a pacifist vote. Some of them at least were prepared to use force in a righteous cause.

On July 2nd the Foreign Secretary instructed Sir George Clerk to approach Laval immediately to find out whether he intended to take definite action of any kind. The reply came two days later and was quite cynical. Laval, who was now Prime Minister as well as Foreign Minister, had been so busy with plans for budget economies that he had not given close thought to the Italo-Abyssinian problem. He added that he was not prepared to do anything that would entail Italy's departure from the League, or impair the existing harmony between Italy and France. When I heard of this, I thought it a pity that Laval had not been pressed to explain how he proposed to reconcile this tolerance of the invasion of Abyssinia with his obligations under the Covenant, on which his country's foreign policy rested: 'If M. Laval can perform such a conjuring trick,' I wrote, 'we should be very glad to be let into the secret.' Clerk reported that it was unlikely that Laval would support any policy of pressure upon Mussolini, though he had said that he would give his mind to trying to find a way out. Such faint hopes as Laval may have had of a successful issue were based, Sir George concluded, like those of Mr. Micawber, on something turning up.

The account of my conversations in Rome had been circulated to my colleagues and on July 3rd the Government considered the whole Italo-Abyssinian dispute at length. My visit to Mussolini was judged to have had the advantage of removing all doubt about his intentions, which was only too true. There was no dispute that the action the Duce contemplated would involve a breach of the Treaty of 1906, of Article 10 of the Covenant and of the Kellogg Pact. An invasion of Abyssinia would therefore compel members of the League to fulfil their commitments or accept the collapse of the only organization through which collective security might be made to work. To my mind the danger could also be expressed in other terms. If our obligations in the Abyssinian crisis were evaded, all the pacts and engagements on which the post-war system in Europe had been built would be in jeopardy. Such a consequence must dismay those who were trying to uphold international order and be an invitation to trouble-makers. Here was the heart of the matter. The violation of agreements is habit-forming and brings war nearer, a lesson which is being repeated to us in these days.

The Government concluded that everything depended on the attitude of France. This conclusion was excusable, France's fate being as much at stake as our own, but negative, unless the pressure upon Laval were firm and persistent. At this point his latest views had not reached us, Clerk's telegram arriving only the morning after our discussion, to show a further shift to neutralism in Laval's temper.

Meanwhile, early in the month, I took the opportunity in my constituency to deal with what I called some of the unfounded criticism directed against the efforts which the Government had made:

> The fact that this offer to cede the strip of British Somaliland territory was made at all is surely a most significant testimony to the concern with which we view the future should no settlement be arrived at.
>
> It is complained that we took risks in making such an offer. I plead guilty. Of course we took risks. There are always risks in any positive action taken by a government situated as is our own in a dispute of this most anxious character. But the gravest risk of all would surely have been to sit idly by and allow conditions to deteriorate and events to take their course in a

dispute between two nations who are both members of the League and both neighbours of ours in Africa. It is not possible to maintain for one moment that such a dispute is no concern of ours.

Our offer failed of its purpose—that I deeply regret—but I do not regret that the offer was made. On the contrary I am confident that some of our critics today, when they come to appreciate the seriousness to themselves of this dispute, the importance of which they are ready to dismiss so cavalierly today, will modify their present ill-considered judgement. That patriotism is in the end the truest that can take the longest view.

Some of this language was closely reminiscent of that which I used in another dispute twenty-one years later.

On July 5th the Foreign Secretary gave Signor Grandi a stiff warning. He told him that His Majesty's Government deduced from Mussolini's attitude that there was no further opportunity for negotiation, that the Duce had made up his mind to dismember or obliterate Abyssinia and that our attempt to help with a peaceful settlement had been summarily rejected. This being so, it did not seem possible to avert a great calamity. Grandi in reply asked, as Barton had done a few days earlier, whether it might not be possible to hold a meeting of the signatories of the 1906 Treaty.

This suggestion was passed on to Clerk in Paris, who was told to broach the subject with Laval. During their conversation at the Quai d'Orsay, Laval was called to the telephone. When he returned he told the Ambassador that it was Mussolini who had been on the line. Laval had sounded him about the prospects of a meeting of the signatories of the Treaty. The Duce had replied: 'Such a meeting is useless and might be dangerous unless it is known what can be discussed.' Though it was clear enough what could be discussed, Laval was not prepared to persist.

Since the conciliation procedure laid down in the resolutions of May 25th had now broken down, the Council was pledged to meet on July 25th. The British Government accepted that unless negotiations could be got going quickly with some chance of success, a grim choice would confront us at Geneva. By displaying this stark future, Hoare tried to put pressure on France and Italy, but, Laval not being effectively lined up with us, these efforts were sporadic and without consequence, while the July days sped by.

I thought it important that the Government should endorse the views I had expressed to Mussolini, otherwise he would think my warning purely personal and be encouraged to ignore it. Though the Cabinet did so promptly, no despatch was sent for nearly four weeks. This delay was due to the pursuit of Mussolini's assent to a three-power meeting. Hoare and Vansittart thought that he would not be tempted to such a meeting if formally presented with a despatch endorsing what I had told him. I was less impressed by this argument than by the dangers of allowing Mussolini to think that we were not in earnest. On July 9th, two days before the House of Commons was to debate foreign affairs, I wrote in a Foreign Office minute:

> I am concerned at the prospect of further delay and would prefer to register His Majesty's Government's, as opposed to my, reaction to Signor Mussolini's demands at once, not on account of Thursday's debate but for the following more important reasons.
>
> 1. Some time has already elapsed since I returned from Rome and it is high time His Majesty's Government were on record.
>
> 2. If the date of Sir E. Drummond's note is long subsequent to my interview, the House may well notice the fact and ask, 'Why so much delay?'
>
> 3. We told the Cabinet on my return that we would send such a despatch at once, and the need for it was emphasized by several of our colleagues.
>
> 4. Some incident may occur which may make our note hopelessly out of date, or a mere empty gesture, and we must be on record before that happens.
>
> 5. I do not believe that this note will harden Mussolini's heart. I told him I would report at once to my Government, and he must therefore be expecting some communication of this kind. Until this note is delivered His Majesty's Government are accessories before the fact.

In another minute I noted that I expected no results from the meeting of the three powers. In the event, this conference was not held until after the Council meeting, which meant that Mussolini had gained more than six weeks.

Drummond believed the Italian Government to be convinced that we had some other reason than support of the League for opposing their plans. Even the most well-disposed in that country were suggesting that we disliked especially the prospect of having Italy as a neighbour to the Sudan. A committee under Sir John Maffey had been set up by the British Government to inquire into our interests in Abyssinia. This was a fact-finding body of experts, which issued a confidential report in June. It was not their business to formulate policy. The report showed, however, that our interests were neither mysterious nor far-reaching, Lake Tsana, the waters of the Blue Nile and certain grazing rights for tribes under our protection in Somaliland, being the most important.

It might have been thought that the Fascist Government, having purloined, by whatever means, a copy of this document, would have been reassured that our attitude was not selfish. It is also possible that, having read a report not meant for him, the Duce failed to understand that its purpose was not to declare policy and therefore assumed that British warnings were not to be taken seriously, but were merely meant for purposes of propaganda at home. Dictators habitually deceive their own public opinion and naturally take it for granted that others will do the same. Although he did not know at the time that Mussolini had seen the report, our Ambassador wanted His Majesty's Government to reaffirm in public that we had no ulterior motives beyond peace and the maintenance of League principles. This I did, with the more conviction because the statement was the plain truth, though Mussolini was certainly beginning to make me wonder what kind of neighbour he would be to Egypt and the Sudan.

At this period our Ambassador in Washington, Sir Ronald Lindsay, reminded us of the suggestion of the United States Government, the only one they had made so far, that we should keep them closely informed of developments. I commented that we ought to do this and that it was important, even though Lindsay admitted that the attitude of the United States Government was, and would continue to be, dictated by their internal politics. These influences were strongly averse, the Ambassador said, to anything even remotely likely to involve the United States in complications.

* * * * *

The international politics of this time would not be intelligible without some reference to the part played by Sir Robert Vansittart, Permanent Under-Secretary at the Foreign Office. After a period as principal Private Secretary to the Prime Minister, Sir Robert returned to the Foreign Office as its official head in 1930. He was a man of brilliant gifts with a capacity for friendship and a keen, active mind, sometimes obscured by tortured language. Vansittart held decided views on international affairs and his instinct was usually right, but his sense of the political methods that could be used was sometimes at fault. For instance, he clearly saw the growing military power and political ambition of Nazi Germany as the principal danger. To meet this he was determined to keep the rest of Europe in line against Germany, and would pay almost any price to do so. He did not discern that to appease Mussolini beyond a certain point in Abyssinia must break up the alignment which Italy was intended to strengthen. Even about Germany, where he was abundantly right, he expressed himself with such repetitive fervour that all except those who agreed with him were liable to discount his views as too extreme. As a result he sometimes injured the very causes he wanted to promote.

In my long service at the Foreign Office as a junior Minister and as Secretary of State I have known many heads of the department and appointed some of them. I have never known one to compare with Sir Robert as a relentless, not to say ruthless, worker for the views he held strongly himself. The truth is that Vansittart was seldom an official giving cool and disinterested advice based on study and experience. He was himself a sincere, almost fanatical, crusader, and much more a Secretary of State in mentality than a permanent official. When Sir Samuel Hoare went to the Foreign Office, Vansittart was soon not only impressing his opinion upon him, but endeavouring to align the Foreign Secretary. In the main Hoare accepted the advice tendered by the stronger personality, but sometimes Vansittart showed so much persistence that Hoare's patience began to wear thin and he would answer tersely.

* * * * *

There were many counsels in these days. On July 15th Drummond was advocating some form of Italian protectorate over Abyssinia, lest worse befall. His Majesty's Government could not accept this. I was asked by the Prime Minister and a small committee of Ministers to state my views for my Cabinet colleagues and, although these were never printed, they were known to all of them and discussed. I wrote:

> The most important question which I shall be asked at Geneva, and upon the answer to which it is essential that I should be given guidance before I leave for Geneva, is the following:
>
> If the worst comes to the worst and one of the parties resorts to war in disregard of its obligations under the Covenant, what should be the attitude of His Majesty's Government? The answer to this question may have to be given in two stages, the first private in negotiation, the second public at the Council table. It is with the first stage of the reply—the reply in private—that I am primarily concerned, for that reply is vital for the purpose of negotiation at Geneva. I suggest that I should be empowered to reply in negotiation that if such a situation should arise, and if the case were clear beyond dispute, His Majesty's Government would be prepared to fulfil their obligations under the Covenant, if others would do the same. If I cannot give some such reply as I have indicated, the Cabinet will appreciate that I

shall be placed in an almost impossible position at Geneva. I shall certainly be asked this question by M. Laval and by others, e.g. M. Litvinov as President of the Council and perhaps by the Spanish delegate as representing the neutral group, and by the representatives of one or two of the smaller powers. If I cannot answer the question in definite terms, the impression will at once be created that Great Britain is not sincere in her support of the League and any opportunity that might still remain of bringing about peace by the use of the League's moral authority will be destroyed. Moreover, we may be quite sure that an indefinite attitude at this juncture by Great Britain would soon become public knowledge with disastrous results in domestic as well as foreign politics.

If on the other hand I am able to give a firm reply to this question in private to M. Laval and others, this more than anything else will bring M. Laval face to face with the realities of the situation and will make him realize that if his Government is not to be placed in the almost intolerable position at Geneva of ignoring the obligations of the Covenant, then he must really exert himself to bring pressure upon Signor Mussolini.

The situation of the Council next week may easily develop upon lines similar to the Council of last May. It was fear of a public session then which largely contributed to induce the Italian Government to reconsider its attitude. It may well be that fear of public criticism on this occasion will have precisely the same effect upon the French Government, in which case we may hope for far more loyal and energetic co-operation from the French in seeking to achieve a settlement of the dispute than we have had recently. Then if such collaboration is once assured, 1906 conversations at Geneva or elsewhere might be pushed forward with the best chance of success, faint though that may be.

(*Perhaps for later use*)

If I am empowered to give the answer I have suggested in negotiation, I do not think it likely that matters will reach a stage in public, in the near future at all events, when His Majesty's Government have to state their attitude to the Covenant. This eventuality becomes the more remote the more firm we are able to be in private. Should it arise, however, I would ask for authority to make a statement upon the lines suggested, modified as I may find necessary to meet the time and circumstances, and to avoid so far as possible any undue division between us and the French.

We had reached a climacteric in the 'thirties; the time had come to take a stand. Mussolini had probably convinced himself that he could win his war in Africa and yet uphold the *status quo* and the fabric of peace in Europe. In this he was wrong. At that time, it would have been possible to uphold international order in Europe, but not while abusing it in Africa. No man could play these two parts, not even the

Duce. The chief blame was his, but not only his. An unmistakable warning to Mussolini that we understood the choice which we had now to make, between the League with the peace of Europe on the one hand and his friendship on the other, that we knew what our decision must be and were determined to give effect to it, might have halted Mussolini even then, more especially if given privately. Admittedly there was the risk of a leakage, about which my colleagues expressed their fears, and that Mussolini would in consequence be much exasperated. That was a risk which I thought had to be run, nor was it so dangerous. A report that if forced to it, we meant business, could have done no great harm. Unhappily my colleagues did not accept my recommendation.

There was also a wish to avoid crude questioning between the French Government and ourselves about the willingness of either of us to carry out our obligations under the Covenant. The Foreign Secretary shared this reluctance and expressed it steadily during this period. As a result plain-speaking between France and Britain to determine their course of action, should Mussolini attack the Emperor, was delayed, with mischievous consequences. I did not think that we need be so queasy, for this was the opposite course to the one I had advocated in my paper. On the other hand, even so early in the dispute, there were those in the Cabinet who declared that we should be on our guard against proposals for a settlement which were not fair to Abyssinia. There were others who feared that if the French joined with us in sanctions, this might lead to conflict between us and Italy and that wars were easier to start than to stop. The pervading strength of this sentiment should not be forgotten nor roundly condemned. Many felt sincerely that any course was to be preferred to one which might end in war with Mussolini. But this masked the greater danger, that failure to take action early, even at the risk of conflict, would result in a much stronger threat later. Against this the free nations would have to fight a war in more terrible conditions or submit. So it proved. Whenever the nations fail to insist on respect for international engagements, they lay up trouble for themselves later on. This bilking is the modern equivalent of Ethelred the Unready's attempt to buy off the invaders of his land. It can have no more success.

We were powerful in those days, both in resources and influence. Though our military equipment was in poor shape, it was adequate for the immediate task. As for the latent dangers, these would grow greater or less according to how we conducted ourselves in the present one.

Appeasement is more likely to breed doubting friends than daunt would-be enemies. I date our Abyssinian failure from these weeks, its consequences stretched far into the future. A year afterwards, on the afternoon when sanctions having failed, I advocated their repeal, an official, not of the Foreign Office, exclaimed fervently in my hearing: 'Thank heaven for that, now there will not be a war with Mussolini.' I replied with equal fervour and some bitterness: 'No, but there will be a much worse war later on.'

* * * * *

On July 30th I left for Paris to see Laval before going on to Geneva. The best ammunition I had was a speech made in the foreign affairs debate on July 11th by Sir Austen Chamberlain, which met with no contradiction from any part of the House. Sir Austen said:

> We are coming very near to what may be a test case for the League as to whether it does mean collective security; whether it does mean anything for any one or nothing for any one. It is not to be supposed that the League can be flouted under the eyes of Europe, that League methods can be repudiated, a policy of force and conflict engaged in, and that the League can pass all that by, because it happens to occur in Africa and not in Europe, without thereby destroying the value of collective security not for Africa only but for Europe. . . . In the last resort we have to take our decision at the Council table at Geneva. We have to take the risk of saying, 'We are prepared to fulfil our obligations under the Covenant if others will do the same.'

I was sorry that the Government would not authorize me to say as much, for there were indications that whatever Laval's twists and turns, French opinion was beginning to harden in support of the Covenant and loyalty to the League. The Little Entente was also pressing Laval to be more resolute.

In an attempt to agree our policy with the French Government, the Foreign Office drafted a memorandum for Clerk to hand to Laval. This gave a lucid analysis of the effect which a failure to grip the Italo-Abyssinian dispute would have upon the influence of the League. The purpose of such a war would not, it declared, be in doubt outside Italy. It would be held by all ordinary persons to be plainly a war of aggression by a strong member of the League upon a weaker, for the purpose of annexation. If the League acquiesced, it would fall into universal and everlasting contempt. Were it divided against itself, it would in the future be not an organ of peace, but a theatre for the interplay of national policies. If the League were formally but ineffectually to condemn the action, Italy would join the number of scoffing dissenters.

This document reached Laval on the morning of my arrival in Paris. Unerringly he immediately fastened upon its weakness, remarking that he agreed with its principles, but had sought in vain for any practical suggestion for solving the difficulty. This was because the despatch did not contain an indication of our readiness to fulfil our obligations under the Covenant, and my request to be authorized to do so myself had not been approved by my colleagues. The delay caused by not having discussed sanctions beforehand with Laval increased the confusion and hesitation, once the decision had been taken to give effect to the Covenant. This was the kind of uncertainty in which Laval revelled. He could only be kept to a narrow path if there were no gutters in which to drag his feet.

As a result, our talks retraversed old ground, Laval saying grimly that he had very little hope of stopping a war. Léger, however, maintained cheerfully that Mussolini, who a month ago had regarded war as inevitable, now regarded it as possible and in another month would think it out of the question. I had respect for Léger's judgement, but I was sceptical of this opinion to the extent of telephoning a warning to London that Léger might only be optimistic because he was trying to persuade me to dally.

Laval professed not to understand Mussolini's shock tactics. I asked him whether the Duce knew how gravely the French Government were troubled by the present situation and quoted reports that the French Ambassador had cried '*Evviva Italia!*' to demonstrators outside his Embassy. Laval insisted that Mussolini clearly understood the French attitude, but I had my doubts how this had been expressed to him. Chambrun was not one to speak roundly to the Duce. Laval and I agreed to see Aloisi separately at Geneva and then to meet, compare notes and decide our action.

Later that evening Senhor Monteiro, the Portuguese Foreign Minister, asked to see me. Having already been with Laval, he came to warn me of the effect this dispute could have in Africa. He thought it inevitable that, if war broke out, nationalism would come to the surface all over that continent. I commented to London that Monteiro seemed to know what he was talking about; his warning was in much the same terms as one we had received from Barton a few weeks before. This was the first meeting of what was to develop into a lifelong friendship. Monteiro later became Portuguese Ambassador in London. During the war his confidence in our victory never faltered and he played a courageous part in securing a most valuable agreement between our two countries for the use of the Azores against enemy submarines. His fervour may well have cost him his post, but his country's loyalty to an ancient alliance saved us many ships and lives.

The League Council meeting proved repetitive of what had happened in May, with the added danger that we were two months nearer the critical hour. When I saw Aloisi I learnt that, according to his instructions, all the Council need do was to interpret its decision of last May and set the four conciliators to work again. There was no need even to appoint an arbitrator. I replied that this position was not tenable. The Council could not be expected to adjourn discussion of the dispute, unless it could be assured of progress with negotiations for a peaceful settlement. When Aloisi said that my chief object was to satisfy Labour opinion at home, I assured him that it was not only the Labour Party that cared about the League's reputation, as Sir Austen Chamberlain's speech showed. If Italy went to war in defiance of her engagements under the Covenant, I went on, her friends in England would be both few and unimportant.

Aloisi kept telephoning to Rome, while Laval and I argued with him about the League's part in further discussions. We explained that we were ready for a three-power meeting under the 1906 Treaty, but it must be authorized by the Council. When I reported this, Hoare sent me a personal telegram that he too attached great importance to the three-power meeting being under the auspices of the League. In the last resort, however, failure to reach agreement on this point should not, he said, be allowed to prejudice the chances of three-power discussions taking place. He stated that this was in accordance with the Cabinet conclusions of the previous week. This was not my recollection of what the Foreign Secretary had himself said to his colleagues. I saw no likelihood that the League Council or the Abyssinians would accept this weakening of their position, which would, in effect, have taken the dispute out of their hands. But fortunately I did not have to argue the matter further with Hoare, since Laval and I got our way, Signor Mussolini yielding to the extent of accepting that the three-power meeting should take place under the League's authority. The French representatives at the Council were once again working markedly in line with us, Léger in particular being helpful. Mussolini made his modest retreat either on this account, or from a wish to postpone the more serious divergence until a later date.

It was further agreed that in any event the Council should meet on September 4th to consider the whole dispute. I promised that I would then report the outcome of the three-power meeting. The members of the Council showed no signs during this session of weakening in their attitude of resistance to Mussolini's demands. Avenol, the Secretary-General, told me that almost every delegate had instructions to follow the British lead. Litvinov, who was in the chair, suggested to me privately that the Council as a body should declare that it was prepared to carry out its obligations under the Covenant. I reported this to London because, my paper not having been accepted, I had no authority for anything so formal yet. There is no doubt that such a declaration at this juncture would have had far-reaching influence, not least in the United States. By itself it would not have been decisive in Rome.

Before returning home I broadcast on the situation, making no attempt to minimize its dangers:

> You can well imagine, if you have followed the military preparations of Italy, that we have had in our minds graver preoccupations than an isolated frontier incident. We have, in fact, been meeting under the shadow of a thunder cloud which, if it were to burst, would have consequences which no one can foresee.

I added that we had named a date by which either negotiations must succeed, or the Council would have to discharge the obligations placed upon it under the Covenant.

By the time I reached London, Parliament was in recess, the Prime Minister had departed to Worcestershire and the Cabinet could not be convened without difficulty. But it was essential to hold a meeting of Ministers who had the authority to determine our policy for the forthcoming Paris conversations. Baldwin therefore returned to London and on August 6th I reported to him and to Hoare at 10 Downing Street. We talked for two hours. It was agreed that I should represent His Majesty's Government in Paris and that Vansittart would go with me. We decided that the best method to follow was first to hold conversations with the French alone. I was to maintain close relations with Laval and try in these preliminary discussions to draw up a programme with him which would force the Italians to face realities. Either Mussolini must moderate his demands, or be prepared to see the League carry out the procedure of the Covenant. This was tougher language, but I was still instructed to proceed on the basis that we and the French both realized our obligations, rather than attempt to discuss how to give effect to them.

We also decided on some preparatory military action. The Chiefs of Staff were asked to examine the position, should Mussolini single us out for attack in the Mediterranean, and advise what steps ought to be taken at once to get ready for this. Meanwhile, Hoare and I made it clear that we had no objection to immediate action to improve the anti-aircraft defences of Malta, even if the movement of guns and searchlights became public. The Prime Minister was to be in France, at Aix, where I could keep in touch with him from Paris, so that the Cabinet might be summoned on my return if need be.

* * * * *

After a few days' holiday in Yorkshire, I set off for Paris and the three-power meeting. Before leaving London, I read in the Foreign Office the correspondence which had passed between Sir Ernle Chatfield, the First Sea Lord at the Admiralty, Sir Robert Vansittart and the Foreign Secretary. Chatfield spoke of the unreadiness of the Services and of the consequent need to move cautiously in Paris. It was felt that Great Britain was so weak in the Mediterranean that the fleet could not deal with the Italians until reinforcements had been sent out. Vansittart and Hoare agreed that this factor must govern our actions in Paris. Vansittart wrote: 'We shall have to be exceedingly cautious in Paris.' I minuted: 'but we must be *clear*, no use going otherwise.' I was disturbed at what appeared to me to be the uncertainties of our policies, comparatively firm language at a ministerial meeting with the Prime Minister and now limiting clauses. I wrote to one of my Cabinet colleagues, William Ormsby-Gore, First Commissioner of Works, who had been consistently sympathetic and helpful:

> I am simply dreading these conversations more than anything I have ever undertaken—vague instructions from home and a thieves' kitchen in Paris. . . . I have scarcely any hope of good results. My chief fear is lest we should be led into taking part in some attempt to make the Abyssinians accept an unjust and unworthy settlement. This would rob us of our good name. . . .

Vansittart and I impressed on Laval at our first meeting, on August 14th, that we must either reach a peaceful settlement, acceptable to both parties under the Covenant, or be prepared to meet the Council of the League and face the problem of applying its procedure. Laval did not like these alternatives. We tried once more to explain to him that the discredit or destruction of the League would have a disastrous effect on the future of France and of Europe and that this was the real issue. The League was a rallying point of British public opinion; if it were destroyed, the results for British participation in European affairs might be crippling.

There was now little hope of a settlement and on Aloisi's arrival, our talks followed the familiar pattern. It was soon evident that only a miracle would save the conversations, or indeed prevent war, and there was no miracle. Aloisi made the astonishing statement that Italy had never reckoned upon the opposition of Britain in this matter. He admitted that I had frequently explained to him that the League was the foundation of British foreign policy and said he believed me to be sincere, but he was none the less unconvinced by my explanation. I doubted whether Aloisi himself really held these opinions. 'The truth', I wrote in a message home, 'is probably that since Mussolini's own policy is by nature opportunist and agnostic, he finds it quite impossible to believe in the British faith in a new system of international order.'

Aloisi was now being Mussolini's echo, saying openly that he had instructions to be uncompromising. The Duce's demands were still as he had outlined them to me in Rome; economic concessions in Abyssinia would be of no use unless reinforced by Italian military garrisons. Vansittart and I replied that, on this basis, no agreement was possible. This was the gist of our opening talks.

At the first formal meeting we went over the ground once more. In an attempt to give the discussion an impetus, Laval suggested that some of Italy's demands might be satisfied by economic concessions, the appointment of Italian technical advisers and rights of settlement in certain parts of Abyssinia. Aloisi rejected this immediately. Laval then telephoned, in the presence of Vansittart and myself, to the French Chargé d'Affaires in Rome, telling him to see Mussolini and make it clear that he could go no further in his efforts to find a basis for agreement. If the proposals were turned down, he said, he would then be compelled to range himself on the side of his English friends. The talks had deadlocked on their first day.

I sent a long telegram to Hoare summing up the situation. Laval and Léger had been fertile, but also firm, in their efforts. Their attitude had been loyal and, I said, we had cause to believe that if all reasonable compromise failed, they would stand to a firm line at Geneva, even if it led to economic sanctions. This was strengthened by an assurance which Léger had whispered to Vansittart. I added that, so far, the Italians continued intractable; they might merely be playing for time. I asked Hoare to circulate my telegram to the Chiefs of Staff so that they could consider precautionary measures of defence.

No meeting took place on August 17th, because Aloisi was without instructions. It appeared that Mussolini cared so little about the conversations that he had left Rome and could not be contacted. Laval told me that he had tried unsuccessfully to reach the Duce by telephone. He was convinced that Mussolini had deliberately avoided speaking to him.

It was no surprise when Laval and Léger told me the next morning that Mussolini had flatly rejected the French suggestions as being 'unacceptable in all respects'. This could only mean that the Duce had now set his face against all compromise, for the proposals would have met all Italy's demands, except those which would destroy Abyssinia's separate national existence. Aloisi said that he could suggest no alternative basis for our discussions. I telegraphed to Hoare: 'We are now therefore in presence of the breakdown which we have always foreseen.'

Laval and I had a gloomy, final conversation before I left Paris. Laval said he had long reflected whether there was anything further we could have done to avoid this outcome. He feared there was not; Mussolini had made no step towards us. He seemed determined to go ahead, without even seeking to improve his position in world opinion. Laval continued that he knew I would understand the extreme difficulty of his position. He had made a treaty with Italy; its collapse would leave him without allies in Europe, for he could not rely upon Russia. I interjected that Locarno still existed. Laval said he valued this, but traditional British policy always made it difficult for us to state our position in advance. This was just what Locarno did. Laval continued that I had heard Aloisi's remarks at the close of our conversation the day before, Mussolini had sent him an assurance of his loyalty and support. I would, of course, understand what that was intended to convey, Mussolini would keep his troops upon the Brenner. But to maintain this large army in being, Laval added, was an extremely heavy strain on Italy. One could sympathize with his predicament, but Laval's policy was not wise. To find excuses for Mussolini he would pay a price in prevarication which would cost his country dear.

We then considered the position in Geneva for the next month. Laval had not yet examined its consequences, for he was not by nature a man who faced unpleasant dilemmas in advance, but he assumed that some form of condemnation of Italy's act would be inevitable. Beyond that he would not look. He spoke of the fever pitch of enthusiasm to which Mussolini had raised his country. If he were thwarted, it was impossible to foresee what folly he might commit. It was not out of the question, even, that he would allow Malta to be bombed. I agreed about the difficulties of the situation. It seemed as though Italy were determined to ignore her obligations and flout a body of which she herself was a member. If so, there would be consequences. I told Laval that one likely and immediate result of our failure to reach agreement in Paris would be an increased demand that we should raise the virtual embargo on the export of arms to Italy and Abyssinia, which we had imposed while negotiations were in progress. I did not know what His Majesty's Government's attitude would be, but if they decided to raise the embargo, then I supposed it would be raised for both Italy and Abyssinia. To do this would be to favour Abyssinia, which had very few arms and less means of obtaining them.

Laval showed that he did not propose to vary the existing French procedure to enforce the embargo, but he expressed no concern at our following the course which I had indicated as possible. I had long favoured this action, believing that with our obligations under the Treaty of 1930 to ensure a supply of arms to Abyssinia, it was indefensible to maintain an embargo on both countries, which in effect penalized Abyssinia. At the end of our conversation we talked again of the now inevitable meeting at Geneva. Laval spoke with an earnestness which had every appearance of sincerity, assuring me that he had no intention of turning his back upon the League, or upon the policy which we were pursuing. At the same time, he felt sure that I understood his own difficulties and begged me to take account of them in any advice I might give to my colleagues.

It was these difficulties that had brought a man of Laval's character to power. France had been split wide open when the politicians of the right had compelled a national coalition in February 1934. Organizations on the right, known as the *Ligues*, thereafter increased their membership. There were those among them who felt an affinity with Fascism in Italy, but less sympathy with a League of Nations championed by the left. The fact that the Government in Britain was Conservative did not really help. The attitude of most of the press was characteristically revealed when Aloisi and I left Paris at the end of August; Sir George Clerk wrote that there were mild compliments to Great Britain for her evident intention of fulfilling her League obligations and warmer ones to Italy for having so recently become France's best friend. A divided France had now to face a major international crisis, while in the background the *Ligues* and the *Front Commun* watched and waited. The *Front Commun* was an alliance of French parties of the left, including the Communists. It was born in the riots of the Stavisky affair and was the prelude to the *Front Populaire* Government of 1936.

* * * * *

After the failure of our meetings I received the Abyssinian Minister, who made an appeal on behalf of the Emperor to His Majesty's Government to reconsider their attitude towards the arms embargo. It was surely evident to everyone now, he said, that Italy intended to attack Abyssinia and to attack her soon. All Abyssinia asked of the world was the right to self-defence. Even that was being denied her by withholding arms. He implored me to ask His Majesty's Government to allow Abyssinia to supply herself with at least a few arms for her national defence. I was thoroughly sympathetic to this appeal, but had to content myself with referring it to London, where I argued in its support on my return. Finally, the arbitrator, whom both sides had accepted, asked to see me. He was M. Politis, an ingenious Greek advocate, well versed in international affairs, but he had no progress to report.

Before I left Paris I sent one more personal and secret message to Hoare. This concerned the preparation of our own defences against possible action by Mussolini; I had been troubled because it was slow. I told Hoare that the attitude of the French representatives was indecisive and embarrassed; now that we had reached the point where almost all the resources of negotiation had been exhausted. There was, I felt, little justification, and perhaps considerable danger, in deferring our own precautionary measures any longer. Either Ministers should, on their own initiative, authorize the minimum steps that were indispensable on a realistic view of the situation or, if they could not do that, a Cabinet ought to be held earlier than the end of the month. My anxiety was the greater because even the despatch of the anti-aircraft guns and searchlights to Malta, which I thought had been authorized at our meeting with the Prime Minister a fortnight before, did not seem to have begun. Hoare replied promptly that he agreed, and asked me to telephone to the Prime Minister at Aix and fix a very early meeting of the Cabinet. This I did and we arranged to come together within three days.

XIV

THE BRITISH ENIGMA

August – September 1935

Mr. Lloyd George on Abyssinia – The Cabinet meet – M. Laval prevaricates – The League Council meeting – Italy walks out – Sir Samuel Hoare's resolute speech – The Fleet arrives at Gibraltar – M. Herriot – The Committee of Five – The British Government hesitate – The Emperor Haile Selassie asks for observers – Abyssinia mobilizes

While Sir Robert Vansittart went to Aix-les-Bains to give Mr. Baldwin an account of our failure, I returned to London. Much interest and excitement had been aroused by the knowledge that Ministers were coming back from their holidays to attend a Cabinet. In preparation, I summed up my impressions of our abortive Paris meeting and retailed them to those of my colleagues already available. I still felt uneasy about Anglo-French relations. As so often, Laval, after indefatigable gyrations, had ended up with us. I knew that the Italian Embassy in Paris had put every kind of pressure on him to come down on their side and had spoken freely of the British Empire's military decline. Abyssinia, they said, was to be the first of their African conquests; they would then seize control of the Mediterranean from the British and in general renew the glories of the Roman Empire. Laval had to some extent resisted this wooing.

On August 20th, Hoare told me that, in his judgement, there would be a wave of public opinion against the Government, if it repudiated its obligations under Article 16, and he so reported to the Cabinet. He also told them that powerful countries which were not members of the League, the United States, Germany, Japan and Brazil, might be willing to take part in certain economic sanctions; they might, for instance, refuse to accept imports from Italy. I was not so confident, but we both held the opinion that Mussolini would go to war by the end of September.

The Foreign Secretary decided to invite, in turn, a number of the leading figures in Parliament who were not members of the Government to come to see him, so that he might learn their opinions. I was back from Paris in time to be present at some of these interviews and remember most vividly that with Mr. Lloyd George. After some general discussion, Hoare asked Lloyd George what action he thought we should take about the supply of arms to Italy and Abyssinia. Lloyd George replied: 'Revoke the embargo.' He went on to say that we should see that the Abyssinians got arms, this was the key to the whole business. There was no need for us to take an active part in the arrangements. 'Just drop a hint to Vickers,' was his advice, 'they will see to it.' I was the more encouraged by this judgement because it exactly expressed my own, which I had been putting forward repeatedly and unsuccessfully. I felt it indefensible that we should maintain the embargo on weapons of war to Mussolini and to the Emperor, when the Duce had all he needed and the Abyssinians were pitifully short even of small arms. This was an argument which continued for weeks and one on which I wrote minutes and had discussions with Hoare and Vansittart, but I was unable to make my opinion prevail, though Cranborne supported me strongly. I felt badly about this failure, on which many hours and much energy were fruitlessly expended. At the time I considered that the experience was typical of what might be expected with two Cabinet Ministers in the Foreign Office.

On August 22nd, the Cabinet sat for nearly five hours, but its conclusions added very little to previous decisions. There were undercurrents of uneasiness which affected the instructions given me for my next journey to Geneva. It was announced publicly that the British representatives were authorized to reaffirm the statements already made in Parliament about our intention to fulfil our treaty obligations. Privately, we were told to keep in step with the French and follow closely the procedure laid down in the Covenant. But we were also asked, somewhat cryptically, to avoid trying to force nations to go further than they wished, and to be on our guard lest others might not in practice fulfil their commitments. If war broke out and sanctions had to be considered, we were to be careful to keep in touch with Ministers in London.

With a League of limited membership, everything depended on Anglo-French accord. Hoare now began to question Laval more closely about what he would do. When Sir George Clerk saw Laval, he had just returned from the country. The Ambassador inquired whether the peace and quiet of the Auvergne had enabled him to evolve a policy for Geneva. It appeared that they had not. Laval said unhappily that his own position was even more delicate than that of His Majesty's Government, for if France voted for sanctions, the Rome agreements would be torn up and heaven knew what the policy and decisions of France would then be. Nothing could now stop a war. Hitler, he continued, with a woefulness real or assumed, for he was an actor, was sitting quietly in Berlin waiting to take the fullest advantage of the break-up of the Stresa front. Clerk told us that Laval would struggle to the last before committing himself publicly to any action against Mussolini. It was better news that Herriot was trying to stiffen Laval's uncertain mood.

Meanwhile, Mussolini's preparations continued apace. On the evening of August 28th, the Council of Ministers met and heard a statement by the Duce. The Fascist Government gave out that a colonial dispute should not have repercussions on the European situation, 'unless it is desired to run the risk of provoking a new world war, with the object of preventing a great power such as Italy from bringing order into a vast country, now given over to the most atrocious slavery and primitive conditions of life.' Talk of sanctions, the statement added, meant placing oneself on a slope which could only lead to graver complications. All of which was prefaced by an assurance that British Imperial interests were not threatened.

This mixture of carrot and stick neither mended nor influenced matters, for other governments were beginning to take up their positions. Many of them looked to London for leadership. The Spanish Ambassador came to tell me that his Government were anxious for close collaboration with us in the League. The Ministers of the Little Entente took counsel at Bled and issued a statement declaring that they would remain faithful to the League, which they regarded as the one and only instrument for their policy of peace. Both Beneš and Titulescu went out of their way to draw the attention of our Chargé d'Affaires to their words; he was told that the Balkan Entente also held these views. Perhaps most remarkable of all, the Scandinavian Foreign Ministers, despite their strong neutral tradition, let the Foreign Office know that they would follow the British lead.

* * * * *

After spending a few days with Philip Sassoon at Lympne, I returned to the Foreign Office at the end of August. There I learnt that Hoare had taken advantage of the presence in London of Sir Ronald Lindsay, our Ambassador in Washington, to sound him about American reactions. Lindsay replied that so far as the merits of the question were concerned, we should never have a better opportunity to take strong action, for public opinion was almost unanimous against Italy. We must not, however, expect any effective action from the United States. The French Ambassador then asked to see me. M. Corbin spoke of the extreme embarrassment of Laval's position. He referred to the Italian assurance that her expansion in Africa would not harm British Imperial interests. I said that I did not attach any great importance to this, since the gravity of the Abyssinian problem was due not so much to potential reactions in Africa, as to inevitable reactions in Europe.

Reports reached us from our Embassy that Italian propaganda in Paris, where some of the newspapers were known to be subsidized from Rome, had not been without its effect. A French Cabinet Minister had complained that British armed strength had sunk to a dangerously low ebb. He referred also to the possibility of a clash between decadent Britain and virile Italy, to the inadequate defences of Malta, the difficulty of protecting the Suez Canal and the British position in Egypt. Laval was reported to have spoken in the same vein, which I was not surprised to hear, for he was apt to take the short view. I did not believe for one moment that we could be so easily brushed aside and minuted that it was time the French were told that Italian talk of our effeteness and their succession to our position in Africa was dangerous nonsense. We might be weak, I added, but the Italian fleet was still very far from being comparable with ours.

On the evening of September 2nd I was again on my way to Geneva and stopped in Paris for an hour's conversation with Laval and Léger, Vansittart and Clerk being with me. As soon as we began to discuss action, Laval remarked once more that it was important to gain time. I replied that it seemed to me more important that the Council should not give the world the appearance of meeting at Geneva and achieving nothing. Laval admitted that, though British public opinion had not always been so enthusiastic for the League, it certainly was so at this time. Could I be sure that it would be as enthusiastic in the future. There was, Laval continued, one question he might put to me some day, though he did not propose to do so now. He then put it. Could I give him the assurance that Britain would be as firm in upholding the Covenant, to the extent of sanctions in Europe in the future, as she appeared to be today in Abyssinia. He made it clear that he was referring to a comparable example of deliberate military aggression and a violation of the Covenant, and not merely repudiation of treaties.

I replied that I had no objection to giving Laval an answer immediately. If the Covenant were upheld over Abyssinia, the authority of the League would be immensely strengthened and our own moral obligation to assist in supporting and enforcing the Covenant correspondingly increased. If, however, the Covenant were now violated with impunity, the authority of the League would be so impaired that its future influence must be negligible in Europe or anywhere else. Laval said that I had given him the answer he expected, but it did not really meet his question. This may have been true, but the British Government's wariness and the state of our defences made it impossible for me to promise unconditional support of the Covenant for the future, regardless of the outcome of the present dispute. Like it or not, Abyssinia had become a touchstone.

Laval professed a fear lest sanctions might lead to war. 'I am myself a man of peace,' he said, 'and will never willingly embark upon a course which might result in the spread of hostilities from Africa to Europe.' Moreover, he did not think that economic sanctions could work in this instance, but he was prepared to visualize a moral condemnation and the refusal of exports of arms, which might be extended to cover a wide category of supplies necessary for war, such as vital minerals, rubber and oil. Laval was to have second thoughts about oil, but at the time he did not seem unalterably opposed to a refusal to take Italian exports. Yet he said emphatically that he would have nothing to do with anything in the nature of a naval blockade, for he was confident that this policy, given Mussolini's state of mind, must lead to incidents and probably to war. At intervals, Laval returned to the dilemma which faced him. Thinking of Hitler, I remarked that if economic sanctions did not work now against Mussolini, they would never work against any country hereafter.

* * * * *

When the League Council's meeting opened on September 4th, I recounted the history of our abortive Paris conference and gave details of the offer we had made to Mussolini. Laval associated himself with my account, and felt certain that the Italian representative would bring 'a spirit of broad-minded conciliation' to the consideration of any further proposal which might be made to him. Aloisi's speech at once belied these hopes. He dwelt upon Abyssinia's treacherous dealings and barbarous state, which made her unfit for equality with more civilized countries like Italy. As Aloisi spoke, the Italian indictment of Abyssinia, consisting of two volumes of print and a collection of photographs of revolting brutalities, was distributed to members of the Council. They gave grim cause for Italian uneasiness about raids across their frontiers. We too had suffered these, but they were no pretext for the attempted conquest of the whole country.

In my speech, I had given a warning about the possible collapse of the League of Nations. Colonel Beck had never been an enthusiast for the League and he was the last man to be a visionary about the fate of an international authority, yet he asked for a special interview afterwards to tell me that he would view such an eventuality with the greatest alarm. I had never known him speak in this way before. He realized, no doubt, that if the League failed this time, it would be no shield for his country thereafter. Nor was it.

On the evening of the 5th, the Council met to hear M. Jèze reply to the Italian charges. Since Baron Aloisi had now been instructed that Abyssinia could not be treated on a footing of equality with Italy, he immediately withdrew from the Council chamber. A few minutes later his deputy, Signor Rocco, followed. This demonstration seemed to impress my colleagues unfavourably. I found Laval much irritated at the brusqueness of the Italians. He told me that he felt they were dragging him through the mire without showing the smallest concern for his position as Prime Minister of France. 'It is foolish of them,' he complained, 'to behave like this, for some day, perhaps not so far distant, they will have need of us both. Then, if they go on in this way, they will find we are not there to help them.'

After hearing the Abyssinian reply, which asked the League to consider the possibility that in a few days a war of extermination might be waged, the Council decided to set up a Committee of Five to come to grips with the whole problem. Despite Italian protests, Laval and I were both appointed members, together with representatives of Spain, Poland and Turkey. Our chairman, Señor de Madariaga, was authorized to establish immediate contact with both parties. He was an experienced negotiator, but he was soon brought up short by the entirely negative Italian response. Laval now began to twist and turn again and suggested that the Paris proposals should be reshuffled and expanded, so as to make them more acceptable to Mussolini. He also told the Committee that it should satisfy itself that Abyssinia had in fact lived up to its League obligations.

Hoare and Laval met on September 10th, the Foreign Secretary having come out to Geneva for the meeting of the League's fifty members. Now, for the first time, Hoare had to grapple with the problem at first hand. Laval, who had been warned by the Duce that Anglo-Italian conflict would force him to denude the Brenner Pass, tried to persuade the Foreign Secretary that Mussolini had not finally decided on war and that there was room for further discussion, especially if it were to take place outside the League. Hoare repeated what I had previously remarked to Laval, that many people in Britain had been greatly stirred by the present threat to the system of collective security at a time when the German danger was impending. The Abyssinian case was seen as a test of the efficacy of the Covenant which, if abandoned now, would certainly be ineffective against Germany later. Hoare said that he hoped to see some definite result from the work of the Committee of Five. But, he added, any arrangement must preserve the sovereignty of Abyssinia and be accepted by her and by the League. It might help if Laval made it clear to the Duce that Britain was not bluffing and that France and Britain both took the view that the whole future of the League was at stake.

At a further meeting that evening, when I was again present, the discussion followed familiar lines. Laval said that we must not threaten Mussolini with sanctions, which might be regarded as an act of war. He would not agree to prohibit the importation of Italian goods until Mussolini had refused all possible means of conciliation. If Mussolini, thinking himself blockaded, were to bombard Malta or attack the British fleet, the principles of the Covenant might be preserved, but Germany would come in and disturb Europe. This would be too high a price to pay, he said. Hoare replied that he attached importance to prohibiting the entry of Italian exports into other countries. He thought that the League should not take action which would appear to the world ineffective, or as a means of saving face. So the argument continued, Laval failing to perceive the truth that, if Mussolini could be shown that lawlessness did not pay, Hitler would take note.

On his arrival at Geneva, Hoare had shown Cranborne and myself the draft of his speech. We were both considerably surprised by its strength, which surpassed anything that the tone of discussions with our colleagues had revealed up to the time when I left London a fortnight before. While we were pleased and impressed by much of the text, some of it seemed to Cranborne and myself to go too far, not in the context of the present dispute, but in the general affirmation of our intentions, which might exceed our powers and perhaps the obligations of the Covenant. One declaration in particular appeared to commit us to intervene by force in the Far East, where the Sino-Japanese conflict was then raging. I was quite sure that we could not do this, except in conjunction with the United States, and Cranborne and I were agreed that nothing but harm could result from raising false hopes.

Hoare made one or two corrections to meet us, but he was not prepared to consider any major changes, arguing that the speech had been approved by his senior colleagues. Neville Chamberlain in particular had been through the text with him paragraph by paragraph. The Prime Minister had also read and endorsed it. I remained puzzled that Ministers should have supported such firm language, particularly in the light of their refusal to allow me to give warning to Laval earlier of our intention to fulfil the Covenant. I could only suppose that, while Cranborne and I had been at Geneva, they had been brought up against the character of the obstacle which faced them and had decided to make a clean leap over it. Cranborne and I were to have reason to think over this unexpected experience many times during the months to come. Never for an instant was a hint dropped that the speech was intended to bluff Mussolini into surrender. We should both of us at once have expressed the strongest opposition to any such folly. Mussolini was a man to practise bluff, not to be its victim at faltering hands.

Hoare's speech contained three main assurances. He began by reaffirming the British Government's support of the League and the British people's interest in collective security. He pointed out that the fulfilment of the Covenant was a collective obligation, and ended with this statement of the position of His Majesty's Government:

> In conformity with its precise and explicit obligations, the League stands, and my country stands with it, for the collective maintenance of the Covenant in its entirety, and particularly for steady and collective resistance to all acts of unprovoked aggression. . . .
>
> There, then, is the British attitude towards the Covenant. I cannot believe that that attitude will be changed so long as the League remains an effective body and the main bridge between the United Kingdom and the Continent remains intact.

This speech naturally made an immense impression upon the whole Assembly by its unequivocal resolution and sweeping character. The delegations were delighted, with two important exceptions. Aloisi referred to it as '*une bombe glacée*' and Laval was uneasy. A characteristic reaction was that of M. Hymans, of which I heard later. He summed up the judgement of the men of international experience who heard the speech: 'The British have decided to stop Mussolini, even if that means using force.' To this day I consider that this was the only possible interpretation of the speech, if the words meant what they said. The effect of the pledge given was immediate and world-wide.

* * * * *

The day after Sir Samuel Hoare's speech, a large part of the Home Fleet, including the battle-cruisers *Hood* and *Renown*, arrived at Gibraltar. There could have been no more spectacular curtain to his words. Three weeks earlier, the Mediterranean Fleet had sailed from Malta to the Levant. These moves by the strongest naval power in Europe did not pass unnoticed. Added to Hoare's speech, they seemed overwhelming. In matched strength, everyone knew that the British power was stronger than Mussolini's. Many, not least in Nazi Germany, convinced themselves that Britain truly meant business. All was very quiet in Berlin. Göring's comment, when shooting with Prince Janusz Radziwill in Poland early in October, fairly summed up much contemporary opinion: 'I wouldn't like to be in the Duce's skin at this moment.'* The Nazis never credited us with any good intentions in support of the League; they judged our opposition to Mussolini to be due to our African imperial interests, but thought us clever to use the League to protect them.

Meanwhile news from Rome was pessimistic. Sir Eric Drummond telegraphed:

> In their present mood, both Signor Mussolini and the Italian people are capable of committing suicide if this seems the only alternative to climbing down. Rome today is full of rumours of an impending declaration of war on Great Britain. . . .

Hoare had another conversation with Laval on the evening of the 11th, in which he repeated that we could not contemplate support for any proposal which would give Italy military control over Abyssinia. Laval remarked, very characteristically: 'International morals are one

* Comte Jean Szembek : *Journal* ; Plon, 1952.

thing; the interests of a country are another.' He could not see that if international order collapsed, Hitler and Mussolini would be the beneficiaries. After an interview with Beneš, who assured him of the Little Entente's support, Hoare left Geneva for London on September 13th.

During the Assembly I had an opportunity for a talk with M. Herriot, who was a member of the French delegation. Our views coincided completely. Indeed, our positions in our two Governments were alike. We both thought that the League's life depended upon its handling of this crisis, though Herriot's authority and experience were, of course, much greater than mine. He was the most eloquent orator in his own language I have ever heard; it was a delight to listen to him displaying his complete mastery. Herriot was a warm-hearted friend, he was also a loyal ally of Britain and strove repeatedly to keep Laval to the line of Hoare's speech, but he could not always be there, nor be certain to prevail when he was. We were both convinced that having taken so firm a stand before the world, we must see the business through. For the present I was fully occupied with the work of the Committee of Five and with listening to the opinions of foreign delegates retailing to me their governments' attitudes. These did not lack variety, though almost all were prepared to carry out the procedure of the Covenant. The Yugoslav delegate, M. Pouritch, while ready to follow a Franco-British lead, asked what would happen if a country were attacked while carrying out its obligations under the Covenant. My own view, I replied, was that under Article 16, all members had obligations to support each other.

As soon as he got back to England, the Foreign Secretary sent me an encouraging message from which it appeared that his firm speech was going to be backed by action. He said that he and Vansittart agreed that we must now show strength and not allow the Committee of Five or the Council to delay, or make some futile proposal. For the immediate future, Hoare asked me to consider at once how and when we should begin discussions about economic pressure, since Mussolini had burnt his last boat. His own inclination was to bring matters to a head quickly. He considered that the course of events at Geneva had had an invigorating effect upon his colleagues and on sailors, soldiers and airmen. Certainly the atmosphere was now more favourable to decision and steps were being quietly taken to build up our Mediterranean strength.

I was glad of this temper while it lasted, for I was still far from confident about Laval's intentions. In this I was not alone. M. Pouritch told me that he and others, notably the Turkish Foreign Minister, M. Rüştü Aras, were becoming apprehensive about the attitude towards the Committee of Five of some of the French delegation. They regarded the Committee, Pouritch said, as a method of giving the Italians the maximum of satisfaction, even to the extent of legalizing the war. I replied that his estimate might be correct, but this did not mean that their view would prevail. Pouritch added that he had good reason for uneasiness. If the Committee were going to give Italy control over Abyssinia, this would be a very unwelcome precedent which might be repeated in Albania. He was right, for on a later Good Friday Mussolini was to help himself there too.

In a letter to Hoare I wrote:

> I have been somewhat perturbed by Laval's attitude at times on the Committee of Five. Maybe it is only his natural twistiness, but he has tried more than once to give our work an interpretation which it could not in decency bear. Moreover the French press of the Right and Centre is still bad, even very bad. Unfortunately Herriot is still away laid up at Lyons, so that he lacks that element of pressure. Whatever the reasons, I am confident that the lack of straightforwardness in Laval's attitude gives Mussolini an excuse for not admitting to himself the reality of Anglo-French understanding.

Laval professed to have no doubts that Mussolini was determined to shoot his guns off. The idea of some sudden attack on Malta, or on one of the ships of the Mediterranean Fleet, came to be known as the 'mad-dog' act. I was inclined to discount it, but not to trust Laval and continued in my letter:

> My own view is that Laval will act with us as loyally, and in so far as he is compelled to do so.

After considering the reports of experts, the Committee of Five made a very fair offer to Italy. It proposed that the Emperor should be given assistance in the reform of his country under the ægis of the League. European advisers, including Italians, would be appointed by the League Council, with the agreement of the Emperor. The Committee took note that Great Britain and France had offered to make sacrifices of territory on the Somaliland coast, so as to give Abyssinia an outlet to the sea and facilitate an exchange of territory between her and Italy. Britain and France also offered to recognize a special Italian interest in the future economic development of the country, so long as their existing rights were safeguarded. These proposals, which were put forward as a basis for discussion, leaked into the press, where there were suggestions that Mussolini could not accept them. Some thought that this influenced the Duce's prompt rejection of the Committee's suggestions. My own view was and is that he was not at this time prepared to accept anything less than Italian control of Abyssinia.

Shortly before the proposals were published, Rome had been trying to persuade us to weaken our stand. Suvich told Chambrun, on September 18th, that Mussolini would be glad of an assurance that the sanctions which might be contemplated would not be a military or economic menace to the life of Italy. If such an assurance could be given, the Duce would renounce certain military precautions which he had been forced to take. Suvich pointed to the British fleet in the Mediterranean and the three divisions of Italian troops in Libya. He feared that our two countries would be dragged into war unless means were found of easing the tension.

On September 20th this jejune proposal was traded to me by Laval, who went on to say that he had had a long conversation with Aloisi on the same subject. When Aloisi asked what kind of sanctions were visualized by our two countries, Laval had apparently replied that France would adjust her position to that of Great Britain, however much he might try to moderate the British programme of sanctions. Laval now asked me whether we could withdraw some ships from the Mediterranean, if some Italian troops were withdrawn from Libya. In any case, he would like an assurance, for transmission to Mussolini, that we were not considering military sanctions, the closing of the Suez Canal, or the use of a blockade; that our ideas about sanctions, in fact, were limited to the refusal to sell certain products to Italy and refusal to take Italian exports as a whole.

Laval intimated that he would be glad of an early reply to these questions. I undertook to submit the whole conversation to Hoare, but on my own responsibility said at once that it seemed very doubtful to me whether we could withdraw any ships. Laval seemed to have no hope that Mussolini would accept the report of the Committee of Five. The whole tenor of his conversation was based on the assumption that war between Italy and Abyssinia was inevitable. I sent an account of all this to Hoare and followed it up with a telegram containing my ideas. I suggested that we should repeat to Laval that we had no individual quarrel with Italy and no concern except to fulfil our obligations. Laval might assure Mussolini that the reinforcement of the Mediterranean Fleet was dictated solely by the necessity of providing for our security. While we hoped that the question of military sanctions would not arise, we could promise nothing.

The reply which I received from London was unexpected and extraordinary. I was now told that in no circumstances should we take any action on our own account; to that extent it would be more correct to say that we should be adjusting our position to that of France. The telegram continued:

> If M. Laval has made up *his* own mind that he will not go beyond a certain point in League action and intends to make this clear at Geneva, it is for *him* to tell Signor Mussolini what *his* position is; and that would automatically and concurrently eliminate any apprehension on the part of the latter as to *our* intentions.

So ran the argument of my instructions, the italics being in the telegram in the style, but not the spirit, of Queen Victoria.

The genesis of this strange message was presumably resentment at Laval's habit of placing all possible blame upon us when speaking to Mussolini, and fear of the Duce's consequent reaction. But it seemed to me unacceptable, since we should be abandoning our power of decision to Laval, if such advice were followed. On September 22nd I telegraphed back to Hoare:

> I fully agree that it is essential that the French Government and His Majesty's Government should act in complete agreement, but we have undertaken in your speech at the Assembly to fulfil our obligations under the Covenant. It is at least possible that M. Laval only shares this determination to a very limited extent. If, as your telegram suggests, we are to leave it to M. Laval to tell Signor Mussolini how these obligations are to be interpreted, then we may be sure that M. Laval, in his anxiety to escape from the dilemma in which he is placed, will indicate to Signor Mussolini that the action to be taken by France will be of the mildest and, this being so, the attitude of His Majesty's Government will be determined by M. Laval and Signor Mussolini will be free from further anxiety.
>
> In the circumstances of the present dispute and in the light of our knowledge of M. Laval's character, it is clear that effective action by the League is dependent upon a lead from us. This was admirably shown by the effect of your speech. If we are absolutely to surrender the leadership to a France represented by M. Laval and to allow the pace to be dictated by him, no effective action will be taken and Signor Mussolini will be free to prosecute his campaign unhindered. . . .
>
> Furthermore, in the light of recent telegrams from Rome, it seems more

than ever desirable not to carry any further than the present state the process of relieving the Italian Government from anxieties which undoubtedly preoccupy them during the present time. The action which we have already taken by the issue of communiqués should suffice to eliminate the danger of a mad-dog act.

For these reasons I still hold strongly to the line . . . that we cannot give any undertaking for the future which still remains unknown.

My arguments were apparently accepted. At least no further instructions to align my policy with Laval were received.

During these erratic days I took care to keep in touch with the representatives of the Dominions, not only because this was my duty, but because I found these exchanges of opinion most helpful. I told a number of them, on September 17th, of a talk lasting two hours which I had had with Mr. Lester, the High Commissioner at Danzig, who was in an excellent position to gauge German opinion. His view, supported by our Embassy in Berlin, was that if the League succeeded in Abyssinia, Nazi policy would probably follow a moderate course for several years. If, on the other hand, Mussolini showed that the League could be flouted with impunity, then Nazi demands on other countries would come fast and furious.

* * * * *

Despite so many discouraging signs, His Majesty's Government continued to hunt for a compromise. At the stage we had reached this was a course of doubtful wisdom, likely to create uncertainty about the firmness of our attitude. Our Embassy at Rome wanted to see some relaxation of the tension, which was natural enough, viewed from their windows. The error lay in our direction, the Government wanted at one and the same time to obtain the results of Hoare's speech at Geneva and to be reconciled with Mussolini. A friendly personal message from the Foreign Secretary to Signor Mussolini, sent while I was at Geneva, said that we had not considered military sanctions, which was true, but hardly likely to discourage Mussolini. It produced no tangible result beyond a temporary cooling of the Italian newspapers' anti-British ardour. In London, Corbin raised the question which Laval had mentioned to me on September 2nd, what would be the attitude of Great Britain if the Covenant were to be violated in Europe. Léger had also referred to this in conversation with me at the Council. I told him that Hoare's speech seemed to me to give the answer and telegraphed to London in that sense, adding that the French Government had exactly the same duty as ourselves to discharge their obligations under the Covenant; they could hardly press for a future price for the present fulfilment of their word. This judgement was finally endorsed by the Cabinet and the Foreign Secretary's answer to Corbin took the form of an emphatic restatement of his speech.

By September 25th, we had in the Mediterranean five battleships, two battle-cruisers and two aircraft-carriers, whereas Italy had only two battleships, one aircraft-carrier and no battle-cruisers. Our margin of safety in smaller craft was not great and our docking accommodation was limited, so that we needed the use of French ports. Drummond thought that the Duce might regard the refusal to take Italian exports on the part of ourselves and the smaller powers as a *casus belli*, but that he would not do so if the French were also involved. This caused the Foreign Secretary to ask for an assurance from the French Government that we should have their support in the event of any hostile act directed against us before Article 16 had been applied. The French reply was slow but satisfactory. There were so many reports that Laval was once again blowing cold that I took an opportunity at Geneva on September 23rd to ask him point-blank whether his position had changed. He replied that he stood by every word he had said before the Council and in the Assembly. His one desire was to work in close collaboration with us and carry out his obligations.

By the evening of that day the Committee of Five had drawn up a report reviewing its work and recording failure to reach a solution both parties would accept. In view of London's fluctuating mood, and as a follow-up to my telegram to Hoare the day before, I thought this the moment to set down my assessment of the situation at Geneva:

> There is no sign of any weakening in the overwhelming support for the Covenant which was a feature of the debate in the Assembly, nor any sign that members of the League would be unwilling to shoulder their obligations should the situation demand it.

While admitting the uncertainty of the French attitude and Laval's perpetual 'tacking to and fro', I thought that the French Government would be driven in the end to support the League. I concluded:

> I submit that it would be fatal in any way to reduce pressure on Signor Mussolini . . . to relax pressure upon him could only restore his confidence and undo the good work that has been done. Action of Committee of Five

> today in reporting to the Council must increase his anxieties. In the circumstances, there would appear to be no other course open to us but to carry out to the full our obligations under the Covenant.

This message, which I had prepared for the Cabinet, reached the Foreign Office in the small hours of the morning, yet it was unfortunately not available for Cabinet discussion at 11 a.m., nor, apparently, was it sent in during the meeting.

Late that evening, September 24th, I was disturbed to receive the following instruction from the Foreign Secretary:

> I trust that you will not allow any haste on the Council in regard to the discussion of sanctions. The feeling of the Government is that, though the efforts of the Committee of Five have proved unavailing and they have rightly remitted the matter to the Council, the latter should make a further effort to find a solution, and that it might not yet prove hopeless in view of the somewhat altered atmosphere produced at Rome by the combination of pressure and friendly message.

The first sentence of this telegram was in flat contradiction with the firm statements in the message I had received from Hoare on his return to London ten days before. As for the rest, if there were an altered atmosphere, I considered this to be due to the firmness which the League was showing, nor could I perceive what further effort the Council could make to find a solution, even if its members had been willing to do so. As always when we had been decisive, I now felt more confident about the French attitude, while the strengthening of our fleet in the Mediterranean was continuing to produce its powerful effect. Several delegates had told me so. The next day I received a letter from Hoare complaining of the difficulties made by colleagues, telling me that he was very far from well and urging my return. I replied on the same day expressing sympathy with his difficulties:

> In present conditions it is so very easy to criticize any positive course of action, but not so easy to substitute another....
>
> The situation here is difficult, but no more so than usual, and there are even compensating elements. First the Dominions, who, as you will remember, were some of them at least distinctly doubtful in their attitude, are all cordially at one with us. If anything they want the League to be more vigorous than it is. They insist that the pressure must be kept up on Mussolini, and if possible increased.

I quoted as an instance of this a letter from the Aga Khan to me. He declared that he was all for action and for the most extreme measures, since he considered that Italian ownership of Abyssinia would be a serious menace to the vital position of the British Empire in the Near East and to India and Ceylon. I added that the South African representative took much the same line, while Bruce considered that once engaged in this business, we must see it through to the end. I concluded: 'There is indeed no other course that I can see.'

* * * * *

The Council, being in agreement with the conclusions of its Committee of Five, had now to draw up its report in accordance with Article 15 of the Covenant. I did not think that the leading Ministers need do this work themselves and I planned to escape to London for a few days, having now been in Geneva for the best part of a month. Hoare had asked me to come home and I was myself anxious to contact my colleagues, expound my views and try to secure firm agreement on policy against my return. The visit would have to be short, for all our information showed that events were moving swiftly to a climax.

On the evening of September 25th, the Council received a telegram from the Emperor Haile Selassie. This referred to his earlier orders to his troops to withdraw thirty kilometres from the frontiers, so as to avoid incidents which might serve Mussolini as a pretext for aggression. His message went on:

> We remind you of our previous request for the despatch of impartial observers to establish the facts in regard to any aggression or other incident that might occur in order to fix the responsibility therefor. We further ask that the Council should take any other precautions it may think advisable.

There was strong feeling on the Council that the Emperor's plea should not be turned down this time, and the Dominion representatives were unanimously of the same opinion. On my instructions, Robin Hankey telephoned to the Foreign Office giving my judgement that it would be very difficult not to support this request. When London demurred, Strang, from Geneva, backed me up. In the afternoon the reply came that I should not be too cordial towards the proposal and that in any event there should be no British observers. It was considered that our relations with the Fascist Government were already so bad that other countries might find the men. This was one of several examples of London blowing cold in this one week. The Council agreed to appoint a sub-committee of three experts to advise whether the observers would be able in fact to do any useful work in that difficult country. Before any conclusion could be reached, Mussolini took charge.

During the evening of September 28th, the Abyssinian Minister came to tell me that the Emperor could no longer delay the general mobilization of his forces, which he was ordering forthwith. The Emperor's telegram to the Council drew its most serious attention to the increasing gravity of the threat of Italian aggression. The Abyssinian mobilization would not affect his previous orders to his troops to remain thirty kilometres from the frontier, nor his resolution to co-operate closely with the League of Nations in all circumstances. The long, tortured period of diplomacy was now over and we faced the arbitrament of war, upon which we now know that Mussolini had decided in principle in January 1933, when he sent his representative to Addis Ababa to deceive the Abyssinians with fair words.*

* Baron Aloisi: op. cit.

XV

SANCTIONS

September – November 1935

The first bomb drops on Abyssinia – M. Laval wants to compromise – I warn Sir Samuel Hoare – The League on trial – London curbs me again – My views on a general election – M. Laval's sophistry over sanctions – The Committee of Eighteen – President Roosevelt proposes a proclamation of neutrality – We deny arms to Abyssinia

After a day spent in drafting the Council's report, I left the further work in Lord Cranborne's capable hands and flew home. In the event, I had to curtail my visit to London to thirty-six hours, for our information showed the Italian invasion to be imminent. During my stay I found that possible terms of settlement were being examined once again. These involved the cession to Italy of another province of Abyssinia, Bale, as well as Ogaden, in return for an outlet to the sea. Though the change was not capital, this did not seem to me the moment to go beyond the terms we had agreed so recently with the other nations at Geneva. Accordingly, I wrote a minute warning against trying to expand the Committee of Five's proposals in any way:

The tendency of the Council will be to restrict rather than expand anything which was put forward by the Committee of Five.

It has to be remembered that the Committee of Five was engaged upon a task of conciliation. For this reason it could put forward proposals, even though they were somewhat unorthodox, in the hope that they would result in a peaceful settlement, and that the Council as a whole would accept, as part of the price of peace, proposals of a nature which it would not be prepared to champion in other circumstances. During the secret meeting of the Council which followed the failure of the Committee of Five, certain members made it quite clear that they could never themselves have been party to *putting forward or approving in advance* such proposals as the Committee of

Five were willing to champion. Both M. Titulescu and Mr. Litvinov took this attitude and other members of the Council are known to share it. Their argument is that the proposals of the Committee of Five do seriously infringe upon the rights of sovereignty of Abyssinia. They also touch upon the question of minorities. Therefore they are not prepared to agree to putting forward proposals which might constitute a precedent.

At about the hour of my departure from London on October 3rd, Signor Grandi asked to see Sir Robert Vansittart, in the Foreign Secretary's absence. The Ambassador spoke vaguely of a forward move into Abyssinian territory to increase Italian military security. A few moments later, news reached London of an air-raid on Adowa. Sir Sidney Barton sent a telegram from Addis Ababa that the first bomb had been dropped on a house containing hospital stores and flying the Red Cross flag. The invasion had begun.

That evening, Sir George Clerk, Mr. Strang and I went to the Quai d'Orsay. M. Laval said he had reports from his Ambassadors at Rome and at the Vatican. As a result of these, he maintained, as he so often had before, that there was a chance to negotiate with Mussolini. The League, he said, was to give Italy a mandate for the parts of Abyssinia inhabited by other than Amharic races. For Abyssinia proper there was to be League assistance on the lines worked out by the Committee of Five, with Italian participation. Laval asked me whether we could put this forward as an Anglo-French proposal. If I thought it had a reasonable chance of success, he was even prepared to act alone.

I said that I would refer his suggestion to London, but it seemed to me that at this moment, when we had just received reports of Fascist aggression upon Abyssinia, it was scarcely possible to put forward proposals which went further than those previously offered. We should then be rewarding the aggressor. Laval argued that his proposal did not go so far as the Paris offer. I asked whether his solution would give Abyssinia access to the sea. Without it, the Emperor had no inducement to offer concessions. Laval replied that he had not considered this, but that the suggestion might be included. The attractions of the proposal were not increased when we came to examine an Italian map, which showed that the 'colonial portion' consisted of three-quarters of Abyssinia, including Addis Ababa. This interpretation was a little too wide, even for Laval.

I then told the French Prime Minister that there was no change in the policy of His Majesty's Government. They were still determined, persistently, without provocation and without weakening, to fulfil their obligations. In doing so, they assumed that they would be working step by step with the French Government. In my country at the present time there was considerable anxiety about France and the attitude of the French press was extremely disquieting. This was clearly an occasion for Anglo-French collaboration; if it failed now, the consequences for the future might be calamitous.

Laval replied that we must not judge France by its press. For political and other reasons, by which he meant Italian lire, then being poured into the coffers of some French newspapers, it was not a true criterion of French opinion. But it was true that views were much divided in the Cabinet as well as in the nation. He would now seek a mandate for sanctions of an economic character, in spite of the fact that French opinion was not at all unanimous in support of such a step. He then asked for my judgement on the form which economic sanctions should take. I said that His Majesty's Government considered it important that from the outset the sanctions decided upon should be substantial.

A curious interlude now followed, when we discussed whether or not Mussolini would formally declare war on Abyssinia. M. Léger pointed out that the importance of this lay in whether the Italian Government would be entitled to claim belligerent rights. Laval was greatly astonished. He appeared never to have heard of belligerent rights and protested vehemently at the idea that the Duce would in any circumstances dare to stop a French ship. 'I have put up with much from Signor Mussolini,' he exclaimed, 'I would never put up with that.' I did not myself believe that a government which was breaking the Covenant could acquire belligerent rights merely by declaring war against its victim, but I was sure that Laval's reaction was not just play-acting for my benefit. As I said in my report to London, the effect of this part of the discussion was to make Laval realize, as he had never done before, the many problems this conflict must force upon us. But this did not necessarily mean that he would stand with us. Finally, Laval asked me whether his presence at Geneva was indispensable. I replied that this meeting of the Council must be of the first importance. We should have to decide whether or not there had been a violation of the Covenant and, if so, by whom. Laval then agreed that he must be present and undertook to continue our discussion when he arrived.

During my journey onwards to Geneva for the League Council meeting, I reflected on this disturbing meeting in Paris. On arrival, I thought it worthwhile to send a telephone message to Hoare to the effect that we could not, in my opinion, endorse Laval's proposed concessions. At the end of my message I underlined a factor too often forgotten in this dispute:

In any event, no such solution would be likely to be accepted by the Emperor, except as a result of an Italian victory in the field.

London's reactions to my conversation with Laval seemed to be mixed. That evening I received three telegrams from Hoare. In response to my account of the Paris conversation, he agreed that Laval's terms were unacceptable, but revived interest in the suggestions of which I had learnt in London. He wondered whether Laval could now put these ideas to Mussolini. I had not liked this plan before Mussolini attacked, I liked it a great deal less afterwards and now telegraphed to Hoare:

I am frankly very dubious as to the wisdom of approaching M. Laval on this matter at the present time. It is hard to believe that the offer of one additional province to Signor Mussolini, even associated with a promise of a number of benefits, would be likely to secure cessation of hostilities and negotiation of a peaceful settlement with Abyssinia.

Moreover, the whole dispute is now at a most critical stage of its examination by the Council, and the whole world is watching to see how the League will acquit itself of its duty. To set M. Laval on to this new tack at this moment (and we could hardly do so without our action becoming public) would, I fear, arouse suspicion in many quarters as to the integrity of our policy at Geneva. M. Laval would be only too glad of a hint from us, if he thought something might be gained by separate contact between himself and Signor Mussolini. He will jump at any chance to delay the functioning of the League machinery, and if we give him any excuse to do so we may have reason to be sorry for it.

If we had someone less zig-zag than M. Laval to deal with, and if the suggestion were likely to bridge the gap between the two parties, the foregoing objections would not apply so strongly, but I have little hope that the suggestion could possibly provide material for a settlement, and I think it very likely that M. Laval has already offered more than this to Baron Aloisi in his interpretation of the Committee of Five's report.

In the event, these London suggestions were dropped, but Laval returned to the charge about his own.

* * * * *

The League was certainly now on trial before the world and its best hope lay in swift action. When the Council assembled on October 5th,

I told them that since war had broken out, the Council must act with the greatest possible speed. I proposed that we should appoint a committee to consider the facts and report within twenty-four hours whether either of the parties was in breach of the Covenant. This course was adopted and a Committee of Six gathered a few minutes after the end of the Council's meeting. Under the chairmanship of Senhor Monteiro, this Committee rapidly came to grips with the problem. France and Great Britain were both members. Laval happening to be absent from Geneva at this moment, I found Léger most helpful. By the evening of October 6th the report was ready. It included the sentence:

> The adoption by a state of measures of security on its own territory, and within the limits of its international agreements, does not authorize another state to consider itself free from its obligations under the Covenant.

This was the only point at which we ran into difficulties. The implications of the statement, for instance with reference to the Rhineland, were evident. The French delegation drew up five texts, each of which was torn up, before the final version was approved.

The Fascist Government's action was unequivocally condemned:

> The Committee has come to the conclusion that the Italian Government has resorted to war in disregard of its obligations under Article 12 of the Covenant of the League of Nations.

Condemnation in these terms involved Article 16, which stated that 'should any member of the League resort to war in disregard of its obligations under Articles 12, 13 or 15, it shall *ipso facto* be deemed to have committed a war against all other members of the League.' Our determination to ask for firm action was increased by the account of Signor Grandi's latest visit to the Foreign Office. The Ambassador made no attempt to conceal his hope and belief that the Italian troops would press forward into Abyssinia. He contrived to add that it was perhaps his fault that he had not seen earlier the latent imperialism which must lie behind British actions. Vansittart very rightly pointed out in reply that Italy's action had brought all international treaties into disrepute.

By the morning of October 7th Laval was back in Geneva. He asked me to call on him. Léger met me, looking troubled, and said he wanted to have a few words with me before I saw Laval. He took me into his bedroom, which was still in some confusion, with the bed unmade, and told me that Laval was very angry with him for agreeing to our report of the day before, that his position was in jeopardy, but that I could come to his rescue. Would I make it clear to Laval that he had done all he could to restrain me and that I had been much dissatisfied with his attitude? Only this would reassure Laval. The report having been adopted by the Committee of Six and wishing to help Léger, I said that I would.

I did some pretty quick thinking as I was taken down the short passage to Laval's room. The news Léger had told me was grim enough to ensure that my concern would be genuine. I found Laval twiddling the knobs of a wireless set. He told me afterwards that he was trying to get a station in which he had an interest, I think a financial one. Before he had a chance to say anything, I told him that I had a serious complaint to make. We had agreed that, whatever else happened in this troublesome Abyssinian business, our two countries must stand together. Yet at the very first meeting, when I and others had proposed action on which I had thought we were agreed, Léger had at once begun to make difficulties. I said to Laval: 'I know that you have been out of Geneva, but this kind of thing is unacceptable between allies. I have now called upon you to find out where I am.' Laval's brow cleared. He looked relieved and said: 'We will have a talk.' We settled down to a discussion of sanctions, with Laval at his ease and Léger, for the time being at least, secure. At my suggestion, we agreed that our two delegations should seek agreement on this subject at once, before it was formally discussed.

This incident was typical of much that was deplorable during the sanctions period, whether Laval or Flandin was Foreign Minister. These two were wriggling on a hook. They did not really want any effective sanctions against Italy at all, but their Governments were divided and they would not say so. Nor would they whole-heartedly support action by others. The result was exasperated allies and continuing confusion in League ranks. The smaller countries, though tied to French policy by treaties, were disillusioned. In France's neglect of her obligations, they thought they saw the mirror of their own destiny.

Laval lived for the hour, at most for the day. He did not want to look ahead. Future troubles could be cared for by future devices. In this he was no worse than many politicians then and since; it was only in degree that his habits were unmatched.

The Council now met for a private session as notable for its sense of urgency as the deliberations of the Committee of Six had been. Aloisi's request for an adjournment which would allow him to consult his Government was refused. We heard an appeal from Tecle-Hawariate, who reminded us that Abyssinia had no organized army, no arms and no credit. His was a weak and poor country which must rely on the justice of its cause. All members of the Council, except Aloisi, accepted the report of the Committee of Six. Laval raised no protest. The Council had now to determine the sanctions which had to be imposed. But, since the Assembly was due to meet within forty-eight hours, we thought it better to associate all members of the League with this important act of policy.

This gave us a day's breathing space. In lovely weather I motored with Laval to a small inn in the Haute Savoie for luncheon. As we crossed the frontier into France, there was a slight hold-up, during which a French policeman gave Laval so unenthusiastic a salute that the latter glowered back, muttering '*sale communiste*' under his breath.

I had hoped for a frank political talk over our meal. In fact, much time was taken up in good-natured chaff with the innkeeper about the effect of decrees which Laval had recently made as Prime Minister. At intervals the innkeeper's wife uttered voluble protests about the burden of the taxes she had now to pay upon some property near Nice. I was also invited to admire a tame fox, in company with which we were all photographed. When at length we came to serious subjects, Laval repeated that he wished to treat with Mussolini on the lines of the proposals he had made to me five days earlier in Paris. I did not, I said, think his suggestions a possible basis for a settlement; only in return for an outlet to the sea could the Emperor be pressed to make concessions. In any event, I added, the Council would now have to give its assent in advance before conversations were opened with Mussolini. Laval said no more and, for the time being, appeared to drop the idea.

While the League Assembly was in session in Geneva, the Government in London were considering the situation. As a result, I was told that the Board of Trade and the Admiralty were very nervous of refusing to allow Italian shipping to use the ports of members of the League. They thought this policy provocative and impossible to realize, except by force. Any such proposals should be referred to London. It also seemed that uneasiness was now felt about refusing supplies to Italy. The Government wanted to get assurances that all members of the League would stand together if one of them were attacked when applying sanctions. They also hoped that, as a starting-point, we could discuss any League proposals which might be available, rather than work on the basis of a British initiative. Even allowing for the novelty and the risks entailed in trying to constrain a man like Mussolini, I was too often first given my head and then curbed.

The Assembly met on October 9th under the presidency of Beneš. He called upon those delegates who did not wish to accept the conclusions of the Council. There were only two, the representatives of Austria and Hungary, who each explained the special position of his country towards Italy. When the debate ended the next day, fifty states had agreed with the conclusions of the Committee of Six to apply sanctions. On the proposal of the Scandinavian countries, the Assembly set up a committee to co-ordinate action to be taken under Article 16. Each assenting member of the League nominated one delegate. This unwieldy body in its turn appointed a Sub-Committee of Eighteen which was in effect responsible during the coming months for the organization of sanctions. It worked well. The embargo on arms destined for Abyssinia was raised at last and imposed on Mussolini, to whom, however, it mattered little.

* * * * *

I now had to advise on a complicating factor. A general election in Great Britain could not be long delayed. Hoare had considerately written to ask my views about its timing and effects. I replied on October 12th that I had no doubt, so far as domestic politics were concerned, that this was the right moment. It was for the national good that for the next five years, which were bound to be difficult both at home and abroad, there should be a government with a sufficient majority. If the National Government went to the country at that moment, I thought that it would secure such a majority. The foreign front was much more difficult to estimate. The fact that all sections of opinion at home had been behind the Government's policy in recent weeks had been an invaluable asset, which we would lose if an election were held. Unfortunately, I could not answer that a general election in January, in the spring, or in the summer would be any less harmful. Therefore, it was hardly possible to maintain that this should be the overriding consideration in the Prime Minister's decision.

I added that the country might have the impression that we were playing a 'dirty trick' by calling for an election at a time when a virtually united nation was supporting us:

> Previous khaki elections have a nasty record and I had rather our majority was less striking than that the country should feel any resentment at the way in which we gained it.

I ended this part of my letter with a further suggestion. This was that Baldwin might send for the leaders of the various oppositions and say to them: 'It is the unanimous view of the Cabinet that, in the light of the present international situation, some increase in our national defences is essential, if we are to be in a position to play our part in collective security in the future.' After this, he could give them some idea of the extent of the rearmament which the Government intended. It could be explained to the Opposition leaders that it was this imperative need for immediate rearmament that had led us to think it right to appeal to the country for a mandate. We were anxious not to give any grounds for supposing that we were taking advantage of a difficult international situation to forward our own party interests. Therefore, we would like to know what their attitude would be towards such a programme of rearmament. If they would support it, no general election would be necessary now. If, on the other hand, they felt compelled to oppose it, then we should feel obliged to appeal to the country.

It seemed worthwhile to use this opportunity to explain to Hoare the full seriousness of the situation as we saw it from Geneva. I believed that the next few days at the League of Nations were likely to be decisive. We should know whether members would take effective economic action or not. If not, the League would be very sick indeed. It was extremely difficult to foretell the result, but I was not optimistic. I concluded by telling Hoare that Cranborne would be returning to London the next day. He knew my mind and was available for any further consultation.

* * * * *

Laval was still hoping, against all evidence, that some means would be found of negotiating a settlement before sanctions came into force. He would certainly make difficulties for any who attempted to follow a resolute policy. This may have been the cause of the taint of pessimism in my letter to Hoare. To the Committee of Eighteen, I reported the opinion of His Majesty's Government that the most expeditious action to take would be the prohibition of the import of Italian goods. The object of this ban was to deprive Italy of a large part of her power to buy supplies abroad. If all members of the League applied this embargo, 70 per cent. of Italy's export trade would be cut off. We should also consider curtailing supplies of essential materials. Members of the Committee, I suggested, should furnish the Secretariat immediately with a provisional list of those commodities which they thought it most essential to prohibit. In conversation with Massigli and Coulondre of the French delegation, I insisted that a decision about refusing to receive Italian exports must be taken by the end of the week. I so reported to London, where my words apparently fluttered the dovecotes.

Britain had now taken a decision, as one of fifty nations, to try to stop Mussolini. I believed that the sooner we put our plans into action and the more firmly we pressed home our intention, the better. It was too late to haver and hesitate now for fear of offending Mussolini. If we were to pull our punches, we should get the worst of all worlds, since our authority was now engaged in the success of the League's action. To the Government at home, on the other hand, it seemed that I was over-enthusiastic. A telephone message arrived from Hoare saying that we ought not to be the sole active influence and initiator at Geneva. Was it true that we were? I replied at once that we were not bearing the whole burden and called in evidence the unequivocal attitude of almost all Europe and the Dominions. Holland, Belgium, the Little Entente, the Balkan Entente, Scandinavia, the Iberian peninsula and Soviet Russia were all in line. I admitted that the one weakness was the attitude of Laval, who should be pressed for specific assurances of support.

Laval was playing his hand cleverly. Much of the press in France was bitterly hostile to British policy. Laval alternated between lamenting this and making use of it; he never made a sincere attempt to lead French opinion in support of the decisions to which he had pledged himself, or to explain them. On October 15th, Sir George Clerk saw the French Prime Minister on Hoare's instructions, and said that in the event of an Italian attack, we expected support from France by land, sea and air. Laval replied that the French Government had to make a reservation because of the presence in the Mediterranean of British naval forces much stronger than those usually stationed there. Italy, he said, could allege that this concentration went beyond the steps agreed to at Geneva for the execution of Article 16. This argument completely contradicted Laval's earlier attitude, for when told some weeks before of our naval reinforcements, he had expressed surprise that we had not despatched them earlier.

This incident made a grim impression on the Government at home, especially when joined to a refusal by the French Admiralty to discuss co-operation with the British Naval Attaché. It appeared from Sir George Clerk's account that the proposal for an Italian mandate over a large part of Abyssinia was again in favour with Laval. I telegraphed:

> It would seem that Laval has reverted to mandate proposal which he had himself abandoned when at Geneva. It can only be supposed that he has done this under Italian pressure since his return to Paris. Sir G. Clerk is of course perfectly correct in assuming that such a proposal would be quite unacceptable here, as has been many times explained to M. Laval while at Geneva.
>
> We can only assume M. Laval, being as determined as ever to negotiate and to avoid facing his responsibilities, has suddenly thought of using this qualification of his Covenant obligation to assist us in the event of an attack, as a means of obtaining something which he could offer Signor Mussolini as an inducement to negotiate. This view is supported by the fact that it is hard to believe that M. Laval's colleagues in the Cabinet would endorse this huckstering.

The effect of Laval's sophistry, as he may have intended, was to strengthen the hands of those in England who thought that we had been pressing too hard for sanctions. Hoare sent me a message, after a discussion with his colleagues the next day, that their meeting had been held in an atmosphere of great perturbation. Even though he had pointed out that other countries besides Great Britain had been firm about sanctions, the feeling persisted that I had recently been too much in the lead. It showed itself, Hoare explained, in a unanimous desire that I should go as slowly as possible and take the initiative as little as possible until Laval had withdrawn his reservation. The answer to this was, of course, that if a leading power does not lead it is not likely to see its policies succeed.

Another result of this meeting was that Sir George Clerk was told by His Majesty's Government to ask immediately for an unqualified assurance of French support. At the same time he was empowered to offer the conditional withdrawal from Gibraltar of the two battle-cruisers, as part of a suggestion to reduce tension in the Mediterranean, if the French would declare their willingness to fulfil their responsibilities and give us the use of French bases. Laval, Sir George reported, gave no assurance of support, saying that he would have to consult his Ministers, but 'derived immense comfort' from our conditional offer about the ships.

As it happened, the warning to me to go slow was a little late, for that day, in a statement to the Committee of Eighteen, I had spoken favourably of a refusal to take Italy's exports, which had been our policy from the first. Moreover, I had already invited the Committee of Eighteen to endorse the principle of mutual support. All undertook to resist any special measures which Mussolini might aim at one country. I now telephoned to Hoare that at the League we must soon reach a decision. I thought that we must press for an immediate answer from Laval and suggested that we should threaten to reveal at the League that his attitude was the reason for delay, if a satisfactory reply were not forthcoming. Sir George Clerk had in fact already spoken sternly and, as so often before, Laval came reluctantly to heel. The French reply of October 18th gave a promise of the military support for which we had asked.

The Committee had by now agreed to invite governments to apply financial sanctions, refusing loans or credits to Mussolini. In this examination, notice was taken of an outflow of gold from Rome to Paris which was christened '*Le Matin, L'Après-midi et Le Soir*', in reference to the payments some French newspapers were known to be receiving. On October 19th we passed resolutions, for submission to our governments, prohibiting the import of Italian goods and the export of a number of raw materials to Italy. We agreed to meet again on November 1st to fix a date when these sanctions should come into force. Some delay was inescapable to allow the fifty governments to endorse our proposals and make ready the action needed.

At this stage it appeared that economic sanctions, if honestly applied by all members of the League, would seriously affect Mussolini's ability to carry on his war. The attitude of the United States, which took 12 per cent. of Italy's exports, was also encouraging. The American Secretary of State, Mr. Cordell Hull, contacted Hoare and told him that the President proposed to issue a proclamation of neutrality at once and to warn persons trading with the belligerents that they would do so at their own risk. But he wished to know first whether this would embarrass our position with the League. Hoare thanked Hull and said that it would be useful if Roosevelt acted at once. Only war materials had been included in the American embargo, but the President hinted that he might consider a wider definition of munitions of war, if and when the League did so. A further American suggestion was that Roosevelt might mobilize the signatories of the Kellogg Pact.

I welcomed these signs of American interest and telegraphed to the Foreign Office that I hoped we should encourage them.

* * * * *

Now that the League of Nations had taken its decisions and referred them to the governments for endorsement, I was able to return to London to take part in a debate in the House of Commons, due to begin on October 22nd. Hoare had already hinted to me that the general election might take place shortly and Baldwin in fact announced during the debate that polling day would be November 14th. In view of this, the speeches became declarations by the parties to the electorate, the most important of which was the Foreign Secretary's. Hoare, having outlined the rapid onrush of events since the House last met, declared:

> Our policy has remained unchanged.... If the League does fail, the world at large, and Europe in particular, will be faced with a period of almost unrelieved danger and gloom.

After this accurate prediction, the Foreign Secretary went on to rebut the charge that I was constantly going beyond my instructions. But of military sanctions he said:

> The pre-condition for the enforcement of such sanctions, namely collective agreement at Geneva, has never existed.... We are not prepared, and we do not intend, to act alone.... The League, let us remember, is a great instrument of peace. Let the critics remember this fact when they say that we ought to block up the Suez Canal and cut the Italian communications.

This speech was regarded in Addis Ababa as showing a weakening of our attitude. Hoare was followed by Attlee, who expressed his support for economic sanctions, but his opposition to any programme of increased armaments. I countered this on the following day by saying:

> It is surely the height of folly to say that you must play your part, and a full part, in collective action in a fully armed world and yet not have the means to do it. The right hon. Gentleman is the worst example of this doctrine that I know.

Most of the Government's energies would soon be taken up with electioneering, but we had still to come to a decision about a date for the beginning of sanctions. Delaying tactics were freely employed. On

October 16th Mussolini saw Chambrun. After remarking that sanctions seemed bound to lead to war, the Duce outlined his conditions for peace with Abyssinia, which appeared still to include an Italian mandate over the non-Amharic areas, but to exclude the cession of a port. This offer was transmitted to Laval, who displayed eagerness to take it up.

While Hoare did not appear to wish to delay the imposition of sanctions, he was prepared to enter into conversations with Mussolini. The first stage of these was to centre round a partial withdrawal of British and Italian forces from the Mediterranean. News reached the Foreign Office on October 23rd that the Duce was about to remove one division from Libya. The British Government, assessing this move, considered that if they could definitely secure from France the use of the ports of Toulon and Bizerta in the event of Italian attack, they might withdraw the two battle-cruisers. But any settlement of the whole dispute must, the Government insisted, come within the framework of the League. Ministers were asked to lay stress in their speeches upon this pre-condition of agreement.

It was decided that the head of the Abyssinian Department, Mr. Maurice Peterson, should go to Paris to assist Sir George Clerk in discovering French intentions towards the Italian overtures and to explain our own views once more. But this visit was not in any way to delay the enforcement of sanctions. Peterson and his opposite number at the Quai d'Orsay, the Comte de St. Quentin, examined Mussolini's proposals. Naturally enough, they decided that the League could hardly agree to an Italian mandate over a great part of Abyssinia. They suggested that Italian advisers should have an important share in the administration of the non-Amharic areas, but only under the ægis of the advisers at Addis Ababa, who would be appointed by the League. An international, rather than an Italian, military force was proposed.

The Peterson–St. Quentin draft was carefully considered in the Foreign Office at the end of October. Any hopes of a more accommodating attitude in Rome were shattered by Mussolini, who complained bitterly to Drummond that I had gone beyond my duties in persuading countries like those of the Little Entente to follow our lead at Geneva. The truth was that they needed no persuading. They had a clearer understanding than Mussolini of what a failure by the League must mean to their future security. The Duce told the Ambassador he would not now consider any piecemeal adjustments in the Mediterranean, but only a general demobilization on land and sea. In his opinion we were heading for war, since he felt that we were bound to adopt military sanctions in the end. If Italy were faced with the choice of being forced to yield or of going to war, she would, Mussolini said, definitely choose war, even if it meant that the whole of Europe went up in a blaze.

* * * * *

Pausing only to deny to his constituents that he was less go-ahead than myself, Hoare flew to Geneva. While the Foreign Secretary was speaking in Chelsea, the Duce was opening new buildings at Rome University. Drummond telegraphed portentously to us at Geneva that when Mussolini alluded to the League and sanctions, his whole attitude altered. Wheareas he had hitherto been calm and even jocular, he then became demoniac in appearance and spat out his words. Our information from Addis Ababa was more serious; Barton said he believed that if League action proved ineffective, Abyssinia had no chance whatever of successful resistance. While he reported Abyssinian morale to be high, he thought that only economic pressure could prevent Italy from wearing down the Emperor's primitive armies. Even if peace terms were advanced which the Emperor might consider, Barton saw little prospect that the chiefs could be induced to concede anything which Mussolini was likely to accept. Any kind of compromise appeared to me increasingly difficult to reach; it looked like an all-out win for one side or the other.

On the morning of November 1st, the Foreign Secretary and I had a conversation at Geneva with Laval. Hoare began by stating that he would prefer proposals based on an exchange of territory, rather than an Italian mandate for large parts of Abyssinia. Laval was clearly anxious to be accommodating to Mussolini. It did not appear to occur to him, either then or later, that anyone other than Mussolini had also to be content. He drew attention again to the Peterson–St. Quentin draft's proposal for a special scheme of administration in the southern provinces. He thought that a similar scheme would have to be devised for Tigré, where Fascist forces were now making headway. There was a distinction, I retorted, between an exchange of territory promoted by our two countries and an invitation to the League to co-operate in granting a mandate as a reward for the aggressor. None of us disputed that the date for the entry into force of sanctions should be fixed at once. November 14th or 15th was suggested.

Titulescu, whom Hoare saw that afternoon, took great credit to himself for having converted Laval to full support of the League. He had certainly deserved a share of it. Sanctions admittedly pressed harder on some countries than others. Roumania, with her valuable oil exports to Italy, was a victim, which caused M. Titulescu to call shrilly, if reasonably, for help. Our Committee of Eighteen had, however, decided that it was not possible to determine compensation for hard cases. Despite this explanation, the Roumanian Foreign Minister begged to be allowed to make his plea to our Treasury officials, whom he eagerly invited to dinner. When I joined them later in the evening, I found that Titulescu had made no headway but was crying despairingly to the hurrying waiters: '*Encore du cognac pour les anglais, encore du cognac.*' His was very good brandy, which travelled with him, as did the caviar, but the Treasury men were Scots.

At Laval's request, Baron Aloisi had been sent to Geneva. Hoare saw him on November 2nd and a long discussion resulted. Aloisi insisted that Italy could not hand back Tigré to the Emperor, since its inhabitants had willingly submitted to the Italian army. Hoare did not point out that the Abyssinians' lack of arms and ammunition could have influenced their conduct. It appeared from this conversation that Mussolini might still be willing to consider withdrawing a division from Libya, if our battle-cruisers returned home. However, this project advanced no further, since Aloisi had apparently overstepped his instructions. Even when Hoare later offered to remove the ships at once, if Mussolini would promise to evacuate his troops in a few weeks' time, the Duce was not tempted.

The meetings of the Committee of Eighteen were business-like and reached their conclusions without delay. The refusal of Italian imports having been decided upon, we began to discuss the denial of essential raw materials. Our ordinary practice was to examine informally in the Committee the sources of supply in each instance and how these might be restricted. In one session, several raw materials might be proposed for examination, and no particular significance attached to the individual delegate who might suggest their consideration. We worked as a team. So it befell that one day the proposal to include oil products in the list for embargo was made by Dr. Riddell, the representative of Canada. Though supplies of oil were regarded as important, they were not then considered so outstanding or decisive as they later became. Dr. Riddell had in truth no more real responsibility than the rest of us for the proposal and the censure of his action, which he afterwards received from his Prime Minister, was unjust.

Meanwhile reports were coming in to us from the aggressor and his victim. The Commercial Counsellor at our Embassy in Rome described finance as Mussolini's chief weakness. There was a point beyond which manipulation of the currency could not go, and he thought that directly internal confidence in the regime declined, the financial structure of Italy would be in danger. This seemed likely enough to me, also that the confidence would be influenced by the effectiveness of League action. So far as could be judged in London, Italian military progress was slow. Sir Sidney Barton, however, believed that the Emperor must lose the war if we merely continued to apply what he called negative sanctions. He telegraphed in the middle of November that while there was no sign of any collapse of the Abyssinian defence, the real danger lay in the lack of arms and the eventual lack of food. Only positive assistance, such as the loan already asked for and refused at Geneva, could save Abyssinian independence.

* * * * *

In the sorry pass to which all of us, but especially the Abyssinians, were now being reduced, His Majesty's Government had a mordant responsibility for the refusal to supply arms to Abyssinia. The Treaty of 1930, signed by Great Britain, France, Italy and Abyssinia enabled the Emperor 'to obtain all the arms and munitions necessary for the defence of his territories from external aggression and for the preservation of internal order therein.' The signatory powers also bound themselves not to permit the transit of arms across their adjacent territories, if the attitude or condition of Abyssinia constituted a threat to peace or public order.

As early as May 1935, Messrs. Vickers had approached the Foreign Office to ask whether a licence to supply arms to Abyssinia would be granted. I had then recorded my view that it was impossible to refuse. However, my opinion did not prevail. In June, a Foreign Office minute had demonstrated that since Mussolini's arsenals were quite capable of supplying his requirements, an embargo penalized only Abyssinia. Sir Robert Vansittart held strongly the opinion that we should move in step with the French, who had already prohibited exports of arms to both countries. On my return from the visit to Mussolini, more applications for licences came in and I attempted again to get a favourable decision, Vansittart taking the opposite view. I minuted:

I find it very difficult to continue to refuse export licences to Abyssinia for the following reasons:

(i) We are pledged by treaty in the contrary sense. Our refusal is a clean breach of treaty obligation, assumed to meet precisely such an occasion as this.

(ii) We have already supplied arms to Italy.

(iii) It is surely difficult to justify—even were there no treaty—the refusal of arms to the victim of an aggression.

But the decision did not lie with me. It was not taken, on the grounds that negotiations with Mussolini were in a critical phase and he might break them off if we allowed the despatch of arms to Abyssinia. In July the problem was brought to a head by a request from the Abyssinian Government that His Majesty's Government should not oppose the supply of arms to them. Barton, in giving this message, submitted that the Abyssinian plea was justified, both legally and morally. I agreed. I minuted that the decision must be taken by the Cabinet that week. Hoare accepted this, adding that unless there were some material change in the situation, we should have to remove the embargo. Unfortunately he did not maintain that opinion. By now, newspapers in England were becoming restive. The News Department of the Foreign Office advised that a refusal to export arms to Abyssinia would cause very strong press criticism. Nevertheless, the Cabinet decided to apply an embargo to both Italy and Abyssinia; one minor concession being that the transit of arms destined for Abyssinia across British territory would be allowed.

Looking back on this faulty reasoning, it is inescapable that, if by negotiating without commitment, the Duce intended to prevent us giving effective help to Abyssinia until it was too late, he succeeded admirably. Every suggestion for raising the embargo on arms was always countered by the argument that we must not, by such action, prejudice the chances of a settlement.

The Emperor had received the bad news with dignity on July 29th, although he pointed out succinctly that Abyssinia was being deprived of the means of self-defence. Barton followed this up with a telegram a few days later, predicting that Mussolini would give no undertaking not to resort to force, but would complete his preparations and invade.

Despite a swelling tide of public protest, the Cabinet declined to change its policy, particularly in view of Laval's refusal to supply arms to either country. Threats in the Italian press about the violent action that would follow if the embargo were raised had their effect. Not until Mussolini had invaded did British policy change and even then the Government seemed to me to move with unnecessary caution. By the end of November only three export licences for arms had been granted to Abyssinia. These were for small numbers of military and ceremonial swords and for two million rounds of ammunition. The Emperor Haile Selassie was trying to buy surplus War Office stocks of rifles and some aeroplanes. Against this the War Office argued that Abyssinia must not be allowed any arms which bore marks showing them to have been Government property. On November 29th I minuted:

> I confess that the Abyssinians seem to me to have had a consistently raw deal from us in the matter of arms. For many months we maintained an arms embargo which had no justification in equity, but seriously handicapped the Abyssinians and has, according to the War Office, made it almost impossible for Abyssinia to win a victory. In addition to this, we are now refusing to allow them to buy from Soley Arms [an armaments company], though I believe that anyone else in the world, except Italy, can do so. Finally, we are to tell the Abyssinians that they cannot buy six aeroplanes from surplus Government stocks.

I concluded with a request that we should facilitate, and quickly, the purchase by the Abyssinians of the six aeroplanes they could afford from private firms in the country. The Air Ministry could do this, I argued, without interfering with the Government expansion programme. It would be gross injustice to refuse the sale of surplus war stores to these unfortunate people and then tell them that they could not buy anything that was new, because the factories were fully occupied with Government orders.

But it was now late in the day. The Emperor's Treasury was depleted and the Italian armies well entrenched. I cannot doubt that our failure to supply the Abyssinians with arms was not only inequitable, but a cardinal error of policy. If we had raised the embargo when I advocated this action in the early summer, or even in August, when Lloyd George advised us to 'drop a hint to Vickers', Abyssinian resistance would have been immeasurably stiffened. As it was, our policy was determined by an optimistic belief that Mussolini might still come to terms, by reluctance to do anything which might goad the Duce into some rash act, and by an insufficiently clear view of whose side we were on. In fact, wishful thinking and a desire to appease were already doing their insidious work, with the usual disastrous consequences.

XVI

HOARE-LAVAL

November – December 1935

M. Laval's proposals unacceptable – General Garibaldi sees Sir Samuel Hoare – Britain hesitates to apply oil sanction – The Foreign Secretary's 'double line' – My warning against M. Laval – Sir Samuel Hoare leaves for Paris – The Hoare–Laval Agreement – The Cabinet's dilemma – Public opinion is hostile – Reproaches from the League of Nations – Unfavourable reactions from the Dominions – The Government renounce the Agreement – The Foreign Secretary resigns – Conclusions on the Hoare–Laval Agreement

The election over, His Majesty's Government were free to continue the discussions with the Quai d'Orsay and it was decided that Mr. Maurice Peterson should go to Paris again. With the Foreign Secretary's consent, I held a meeting in his room, at which Mr. Peterson was present, to draft instructions. Basing ourselves on the Committee of Five's report, we agreed to consider putting Adowa and Adigrat into the scale for Italy, with a corresponding reduction in what had been proposed for her in the south. As a further counterweight, Abyssinia would receive both Assab and Zeila. We decided to offer the Italians a proportionate share, but no more, in any plan of assistance the League might propose for Abyssinia.

When Peterson opened the discussions in Paris, he soon found that Laval had very different ideas about the minimum which Mussolini should be offered. The whole of Tigré was to be converted into an autonomous principality under Italian suzerainty and a special zone created in southern Abyssinia, bounded on the north by the 8th parallel and on the west by the 37th meridian. This area, more than a third of the country, while nominally remaining under Abyssinian sovereignty, would in practice be reserved for economic development by an Italian chartered company. Laval offered no Italian concession in return. Peterson said immediately that he could not believe such proposals would be considered in London. He telegraphed that Laval was putting Italian demands higher than Mussolini did himself; in his opinion we must adhere to the terms decided before he went to Paris. On November 26th I minuted that I agreed,

> . . . subject of course to the proviso we have always made and must always maintain that a settlement must be acceptable to the three parties, Italy, Abyssinia and the League. How large the area might be for the Italian chartered company would have to be a matter of bargaining. The Emperor could never agree to a third of his territory, or more, being so dealt with, and such a proposal would certainly have to be combined with non-Italian League control. . . .

Peterson was accordingly told that Laval's proposals were unacceptable, and returned to the charge on the basis of his own suggestions, which did not differ in any important particular from his earlier instructions.

Meanwhile, we had modestly encouraging news from two countries outside the League. On November 9th, the German Government imposed restrictions on the export to Italy of many materials, including mineral oil, pig iron, aluminium, zinc, tin, nickel and non-ferrous alloys. This may have been due to a prudent doubt of Mussolini's fate. A few days later, Mr. Cordell Hull said at a press conference:

> The American people are entitled to know that there are certain commodities such as oil, copper, trucks, tractors, scrap iron and scrap steel, which are essential war materials, although not actually arms, ammunition or implements of war, and that according to recent Government and trade reports a considerably increased amount of these is being exported for war purposes. This class of trade is directly contrary to the policy of this Government . . . as it is also contrary to the general spirit of the Neutrality Act. . . .

This gave me some hopes that if we moved more firmly, the United States might follow, even though a lap or two behind.

Senhor Vasconcellos, as chairman of the Committee of Eighteen, was most anxious for a meeting as early as possible to consider the new sanctions, including oil. After much telephoning between Geneva and the Foreign Office, it was agreed that the Committee should be convened on November 29th. By the end of that month, the Governments of India, Iraq, the Netherlands, Roumania and Russia had agreed to apply the oil sanction against Italy, on condition that other producing and supplying countries did the same. Italy imported nearly all her oil. During the first six months of 1935, Roumania had provided 40·6 per cent. of Italy's oil supplies and Russia 16 per cent. A firm lead from Britain and France would no doubt succeed in cutting off the greater part of Italy's supply. At the very least, here was a weapon which might induce Mussolini to make reasonable terms. But it was not to be used in that way.

The handling of the oil sanction was timid and uncertain, while Laval's ingenuity proved more than a match for the British Government's tentative methods. As Mussolini saw the danger of an oil sanction approaching, he used every device of propaganda to scare the League and His Majesty's Government. His authority in Italy and his ability to use menacing bluster were immensely strengthened by the complete control of the press which his dictatorship gave him. There was no possibility of an impartial assessment by Italian opinion and it is a tribute to Italian perspicacity that there should have been critics, even silent ones, in such conditions. As our Consul in Palermo wrote, a week with a free press would have changed all this, but there was no such possibility.

General Garibaldi, grandson of the liberator of Italy, and a colleague of Hoare from the period when the latter had been on the Staff in Italy in the first world war, came to see the Foreign Secretary to tell him his fears of Mussolini's reaction to the oil sanction. Threats, dire forebodings and warnings of the consequences of such a deed, dark hints that the Duce would turn upon Britain were insinuated through every available channel. These unfortunately had their effect, so that His Majesty's Government began almost to welcome delay, which Laval was quick enough to exploit with a ministerial crisis. While the French Prime Minister manœuvred, the Emperor Haile Selassie was fighting for his nation's independence, which he could not hope to secure, unarmed and alone. If Mussolini had staked all on the conquest of Abyssinia, the Emperor had done the same on the efficacy of the Covenant.

The Prime Minister of France kept up his resistance to action. On November 29th Clerk telegraphed that Laval greatly feared an oil sanction would drive the Duce to open war. A day later he was telling Clerk of a statement by the Duce that an embargo on oil would mean disaster to the Italian forces in Abyssinia and would be an act of war against which he would react. Drummond, on the other hand, said that he could hardly believe that at this stage Mussolini would risk a

European conflict. I agreed with Drummond. Through all this time, Vasconcellos was becoming increasingly perturbed, fearing the effect of the delay in meeting on the United States and on members of the League, eleven of whom had now replied affirmatively to the proposed new sanctions. I shared his anxiety and asked that we should meet on December 6th. Had that date been accepted, much later trouble would have been averted. But Laval once again pretexted a ministerial crisis and won another week of delay, the 12th being finally fixed. These tactics were exasperating but difficult to counter, France's endorsement of any major decision being indispensable. The effect upon those who knew of them, which included my colleagues and the Chiefs of Staff and, in due course, the press, was deplorable, encouraging the faint-hearted and giving pause even to the resolute.

The hesitation corroding the British attitude was illustrated by a message which Hoare sent at the end of November to our Ambassador in Washington, which I did not see before despatch. In this the Foreign secretary expressed his fear that a delay in imposing the oil sanction would distress American opinion which, though acting independently of the League, had shown some signs of co-operation. He recounted how he had received a personal message from Laval saying that, because of a vital debate in the Chamber in the next week, it was impossible for him to go to Geneva until the week after. Hoare protested that he had therefore no choice but to acquiesce in the postponement of the meeting until December 12th. He then referred to reports, which he appeared to credit, that the oil sanction might drive Mussolini to a desperate act; lest this should happen, he wanted to use the interval to improve our arrangements with France and Yugoslavia. Hoare reported an accumulation of evidence, to which he also gave some authority, that Mussolini was beginning to realize the difficulties of his position and the advisability of making terms. He went on to argue that the imposition of an oil sanction would make the Duce more, rather than less, intransigent, with the result that the Foreign Secretary could not say for certain whether it would be wise to impose the embargo on December 12th.

Much of this showed a sad misreading of the working of a dictator's mind. Worst of all, the message contained not one reference to the position of Abyssinia or to that country's capacity to resist. There was no sign that the cries of the victim were being heard, the rescuer was too busy feeling the temperature of the water with his toes. Peterson having held firmly to his instructions, Laval began to put pressure on

Hoare for an early Anglo-French meeting, no doubt as another means at least to delay the endorsement of the oil sanction.

Only the long drawn-out Abyssinian agony had prevented Hoare from taking a holiday during the summer. His health was by now alarmingly bad. Working with him, I realized how tired he was. At this time he was also subject to what he described as 'black-outs'. One of these took place when we were at a cinema with a small party, which included Sir Samuel and Lady Maud Hoare with Philip Sassoon as host. Hoare got up to go out, but collapsed in the gangway. Fortunately there were few people in the gallery where we were sitting. Sassoon fetched me to where the Foreign Secretary was lying apparently unconscious. Lady Maud reassured us and with the attendant's help we got him out into the lobby where he soon recovered. Clearly all was not well with the Foreign Secretary, and the Christmas recess gave him the opportunity to take a skating holiday in Switzerland. In deference to Laval's request, he arranged to break his journey in Paris on the way. This was to be their first meeting together without me, and Hoare's first international negotiation of any importance, though we did not guess at its significance.

In preparation for a special meeting of our colleagues arranged for December 2nd, Hoare and I again went over the whole situation together. Although Italy's oil reserves would probably last two or three months, there could be no doubt that the banning of further exports to her would be a more effective sanction than any yet applied. Herriot told Sir Austen Chamberlain that the firmer our stand the stronger would be our support from French public opinion. Hoare, on the other hand, believed that, as the Duce's agents everywhere had said, Mussolini would become more intransigent if we fixed a date for the oil sanction. Therefore, while approving the principle of an oil embargo, he was ready to delay its enforcement, hoping that the threat of it would influence Mussolini to serious negotiation.

The oil sanction was the crucial question. I have no doubt now that in their handling of this the British Government made a most serious mistake of judgement. By early December, most member states of the League had said they would support the embargo if others did likewise, and President Roosevelt was trying to put pressure on the American oil companies not to increase their exports to Italy. Some Ministers feared that imposition of the oil sanction would drive the Duce to war with us.

I set out my views in a minute, after reading a technical paper on the oil sanction which was being submitted to the Cabinet and with which I was not content:

> It seems to me that so far as the efficient application of sanctions is concerned the decision upon oil will probably prove decisive. If the League decides to apply the oil sanction, then other nations who are not themselves concerned will be thereby encouraged to persist in the application of the sanctions already agreed upon, while the United States will also be stimulated to persist in the co-operation which she is affording us at present.
>
> If on the other hand, for whatever reason, we now hang back and discourage the imposition of the embargo upon oil, then certainly the United States will take the first opportunity of saying that in view of the League's attitude it is useless for her to continue to seek to play in so far as she can. There are already indications of this in the American press. Moreover, the other smaller countries, some of whom are suffering a considerable financial loss as the result of the sanctions already applied, will lose heart in the first instance because they will conclude that we are not prepared to impose sanctions which will definitely shorten the war and because they fear that a long period of attrition therefore stretches ahead of them.
>
> Against all this has to be set the military risk involved, i.e. that Signor Mussolini in despair will launch an attack upon us. I confess that this danger has always seemed to me very remote and I am quite unimpressed by the threats of such persons as the Marchese Theodoli, who has clearly been instructed to frighten us as much as possible. The manœuvre is so obvious as scarcely to require comment. In calculating the likelihood of a mad-dog act the isolation of the Italian forces in East Africa should not be overlooked.
>
> Moreover Signor Mussolini has never struck me as the kind of person who would commit suicide. He has been ill-informed about our attitude in this dispute and while he may well be exasperated there is a considerable gap between that condition and insanity.

I continued in my minute that one had to admit the possibility, though remote, of a mad-dog act, but I argued that despite this we should not modify our attitude towards sanctions. I pointed out that we had already secured from members of the League a reaffirmation of paragraph 3 of Article 16, which was the only obligation they had to help us under the Covenant. It was difficult to believe that if we were attacked we should be left altogether alone. To show nervousness in advance, I wrote, was not the way to determine the assistance of others.

My own belief was, and remains, that a firm policy would have compelled Mussolini to negotiate for terms which the Emperor could have accepted, such as those proposed by the Committee of Five at

Geneva. This would have immeasurably increased the League's authority, and have been a salutary warning to Hitler. I was sure that the only way to beat Laval's tactics was to make him face up to his commitments.

Hitler's interpreter, Dr. Schmidt, wrote after the second world war:

> In 1938, on the eve of the Munich Conference, Mussolini admitted that the League of Nations had very nearly succeeded in countering aggression by means of collective security. 'If the League of Nations had followed Eden's advice in the Abyssinian dispute,' he said to Hitler, 'and had extended economic sanctions to oil, I would have had to withdraw from Abyssinia within a week. That would have been an incalculable disaster for me!'*

The Government did not yet feel disposed to run the risks which they believed that the oil sanction entailed, and the Foreign Secretary preferred not to fix a date until he had seen Laval in Paris. I was, however, able to secure that if no progress was recorded towards a settlement, we must go ahead with the new sanctions proposed at Geneva, of which oil was the most important. Hoare still felt that French assurances of military support were inadequate. We all agreed that he should try to clear this matter up with Laval when they met on December 7th; in particular the Admiralty was rightly concerned to have the use of Bizerta, should the need arise. We did not, however, discuss any possible terms of peace, either at Cabinet or, so far as I know, between Ministers, because the meeting with Laval was not expected to reach conclusions about them. Lord Halifax later said of Sir Samuel Hoare's visit to Paris: 'As he was not going for the purpose of discussing peace terms with M. Laval, he went with no instructions as to possible terms of conciliation from his colleagues in His Majesty's Government.'† We had no reason to suppose that an acceptable settlement was within our immediate grasp, nor was there any cause for us to make peace at any price. Such reports as Barton was able to glean showed that Italian military progress was slow.

Hoare himself told the Dominion High Commissioners in London on December 5th that the possibility of a mad-dog act by Mussolini must not deter members of the League from proceeding with sanctions. I was present at this informal meeting, where the mood was certainly that, having taken our decision to act with the League, we must see the business through. Hoare appeared fully to accept this. Although the Italians were now talking of peace terms, three visits to the Foreign

* Dr. Paul Schmidt: *Hitler's Interpreter*, ed. R. H. C. Steed; Heinemann, 1951.

† House of Lords; December 19th, 1935.

Office by Grandi in the early days of December gave no indication that the Duce's appetite was moderating or that we could satisfy it.

When the Commons debated the Abyssinian question again on December 5th, Hoare explained that we had steadily followed a 'double line' of collective sanctions combined with efforts at conciliation. The Foreign Secretary recalled that when he and I had last been at Geneva the members of the League had given a particular blessing to Franco-British efforts to find the basis of a settlement. This was certainly true and might prove a disagreeable responsibility. Hoare, however, gave no indication, publicly or privately, that he was intending to embark on a serious negotiation with Laval. It was during this debate that he had a talk with Baldwin in his room at the House of Commons, and came to join me on the Government bench after it. The Foreign Secretary gave me no detailed account of the talk, nor did I press for one, but I certainly did not get the impression that any decision of importance had been taken. Rather the contrary, for Hoare was evidently depressed and I assumed that it was like so many interviews on foreign affairs with the Prime Minister, Baldwin being a passive listener rather than an active contributor.

I knew from experience how wily and persuasive Laval was. A short time before Hoare's departure, he and I stood talking at the top of the Foreign Office staircase. I warned him against Laval and added more lightly, remembering our August negotiations: 'Don't forget that in Paris, Van can be more French than the French.' 'Don't worry,' came the confident reply. 'I shall not commit you to anything. It wouldn't be fair on my way through to my holiday.' Many years later, Baldwin told me that he had no idea Hoare would sign anything. 'When he went off,' Baldwin said, 'I had only one idea, it was relief to see him going. I knew he was very tired and thought his skating holiday would do him good. I could not tell that he was going to fall on his nose.'

The Foreign Secretary arrived in Paris on the afternoon of Saturday, December 7th, and went immediately to the Quai d'Orsay. Laval employed his familiar tactics. The French Government, he said, knew through their Ambassador in Rome and Mussolini's in Paris that the Duce would regard the imposition of an oil sanction as a military act. Laval therefore deplored the fixing of even a remote date for the imposition of this sanction, although in reply to a question from Hoare, he affirmed that France would stand by Britain and give military assistance if necessary. He felt that Italian pretensions and British reservations were alike excessive. Mussolini must certainly have some of the conquered territory. For example, part of Tigré must be ceded and Italy must also have some areas south of the 8th parallel in which to settle her colonists, although Laval was prepared for Abyssinia to be given access to the sea.

For his part, Hoare felt that it was essential not to give the appearance of rewarding aggression. But he agreed that Italy must retain Adowa and Adigrat and that there should be an economic monopoly for Italy in the south-west. The two men decided to resume their talks at 10.30 the following morning. This meant that Hoare had to delay for a day his departure for Switzerland. That evening a short communiqué was issued:

> The two Ministers confirmed the existence of complete agreement between the two Governments for the continuation of a policy of close collaboration. They began an exchange of views which will be continued tomorrow in order to determine the bases which might be proposed for the friendly settlement of the Italo-Ethiopian dispute.

The text of this communiqué and the record of the conversation arrived at the Foreign Office during the morning of Sunday, December 8th. I was spending the weekend at my house in London and, after reading the documents, felt uneasy in spite of a telegram from Hoare, who considered that the conversation was satisfactory from the British point of view and showed a real attempt on the part of the French to come into line. I wondered how many cooks were stirring the broth in Paris. My qualms were not quieted when a further message arrived from the Foreign Secretary during the afternoon, asking that a Cabinet should be summoned for the next day. There was no explanation as to the reason for this. The Prime Minister was at No. 10 that evening so I decided to go to see him and give him the little information I had. Baldwin appeared as much in the dark as I about why a Cabinet should be summoned. He agreed that we ought to try to obtain more news. I went back to the Foreign Office, telephoned the Embassy in Paris and asked for Hoare. A secretary replied that the Foreign Secretary was resting and that Vansittart was at the Ritz Hotel, where he preferred to stay when in Paris, and was therefore not available. I asked for some indication of what had been going on. The secretary returned a minute or two later with the message: 'The Secretary of State and Sir Robert Vansittart are well satisfied with the day's work.' I was told that Hoare was about to leave for Switzerland and that Mr. Peterson was travelling overnight to London with a full record of the conversations. I reported this to Baldwin from the Foreign Office and we agreed that we could only await Peterson's arrival the next morning. I drew comfort from the fact that Hoare was continuing his journey to Switzerland for his holiday, which hardly seemed to indicate any exceptional event.

Meanwhile, the following communiqué was issued by Hoare and Laval in Paris:

> Animated by the same spirit of conciliation and inspired by close Franco-British friendship, we have in the course of our long conversations today and yesterday sought the formulae which might serve as a basis for a friendly settlement of the Italo-Ethiopian dispute.
>
> There could be no question at present of publishing these formulae. The British Government has not yet been informed of them and once its agreement has been received it will be necessary to submit them to the consideration of the interested governments and to discussion by the League of Nations.
>
> We have worked together with the same anxiety to reach as rapidly as possible a peaceful and honourable solution.
>
> We are both satisfied with the result which we have reached.

* * * * *

Mr. Peterson arrived at my house in London at breakfast time on Monday morning. First, he handed me a short letter from Hoare saying that it was essential that the Cabinet should come to a decision at once, as every moment counted. I would see, Hoare declared, that the proposals came well within the framework of the Committee of Five and were on the basis we had agreed in London. I then turned to a four-page document in French, evidently typed in a French government office, which bore signs of hasty drafting. It was initialled S.H., P.L. This set out the terms agreed by the two Ministers the previous evening. I was surprised that Hoare, who was competent rather than remarkable in his knowledge of the French language, had not insisted on a translation. But this mild reflection rapidly turned to astonishment as I read the 'peace plan'. It did not seem to me to be possible to reconcile these proposals with those of the Committee of Five, nor with the instructions given to Peterson. I knew of no other basis agreed upon in London.

It was now suggested that Mussolini should keep most of Tigré in the north, as well as receiving Abyssinian territory in the east and south-east, which we had previously decided might be ceded in exchange for access to the sea. In addition a large zone was to be allotted exclusively for Italian economic development. In fact, the Emperor was to surrender about one half of his territory. In return, Abyssinia would receive a port, either Assab or Zeila, together with a corridor connecting it to her own territory. Telephone exchanges with Paris confirmed that, if Abyssinia chose Zeila as the port, an Anglo-French corridor would be ceded, Mussolini would then make no comparable concession and there would be no territorial exchange. It later emerged that Abyssinia would not be allowed to construct a railway from this port through the corridor. As a result of firm messages to Paris this reservation was ultimately struck out. It had in the meanwhile led to a *Times* leader entitled 'A Corridor for Camels', and added fuel for public indignation. This basis of a settlement was to be referred to the League for approval or rejection. Meanwhile, Mussolini was to be told of the terms at once and asked to approve them in principle. The Emperor, on the other hand, was to be informed by the British and French Ministers that those two Governments were 'seeking a solution by conciliation' based upon the proposals made in September by the Committee of Five and accepted by Abyssinia. The Emperor was further to be told that the Abyssinian representative would be heard by the Committee of Five when it set to work on December 12th.

I expressed my astonishment at these terms, which went beyond any which Peterson had earlier been authorized to accept when he left for Paris. I asked how Hoare had come to sign them. Peterson had expected my reaction: 'I did not suppose that you would like them,' he said. I gained the impression that Peterson had had no part in the later discussions. He also told me that he thought he could have obtained considerably better terms himself, if he had been given more latitude. I had no doubt that this was true. It was remarkable that Peterson brought with him no account of any kind, not a hint of what was said by Hoare or Laval at any time in a full day of talks, only one copy of these four pages typed in French, which Peterson could not illuminate because, as I understood, he had not been an active participant. Of the previous day's less important proceedings, which Peterson attended, we had a verbatim account.

That morning the Prime Minister had to come across to the Foreign Office to open a naval conference. When it was over he came to see me and I explained the proposals on a map. Baldwin asked me what I thought of them. I told him how troubled I was and said two things were clear; the Emperor would not accept these terms, nor would the

League. Baldwin grunted and looked unhappy, and commented: 'That lets us out, doesn't it?' but he agreed that the Cabinet must meet that evening and seemed as uncertain as myself why Hoare had suddenly done this thing. Hoare's letter to him had only emphasized the great urgency of the question and the importance of keeping in line with the French.

The events of these days cannot be understood unless the reputation of Hoare is recalled as it stood with his colleagues at the time. Like all politicians, the Foreign Secretary had his detractors, but there was one conclusion in which most critics would have acquiesced, that he was cautious and shrewd. This belief strongly influenced members of the Government, including myself, and it explains, if it does not excuse, our conduct. Without doubt, we reasoned, Hoare must have had some very strong motives for agreeing to such proposals before consulting us. We had confidence in him, and did not want to reject the first appeal he had made to us, couched in such strong terms. There was also deep mistrust of Laval and many suspected that some unpalatable discovery of his state of mind must have influenced Hoare. I myself thought that there must be factors other than those disclosed in the documents which had led Hoare to conclude this hurried negotiation. Our strongest cards did not seem to have been played at all. After all, Laval was pledged to give us military support and was committed to sanctions. There was no reason why we should give way at his behest, even if he did intend to default on his obligations, of which intention I was sceptical. Laval could have no certainty that his Cabinet or the French people would support him if he parted from us. He had to carry his principal ally with him, as we had to carry ours. As Voltaire wrote, the French admiral was at least as far from the English admiral as the English was from the French. I could not doubt that if Hoare had firmly recalled Laval to his duty, he would have come into line.

My own position was extremely difficult and embarrassing. My wish was to have nothing to do with these proposals and to resign. When Lord Stanhope, Under-Secretary at the Foreign Office, came into my room later that afternoon, I told him so. He understood, but begged me not to go, pointing out how much was still uncertain about Hoare's reasons and even about what was to happen to the agreement. This was true and I was also influenced by my position as Hoare's Siamese twin. Hoare was out of the country without me, for the first time since our dual responsibility was established. How could I go back on an agreement he had made, without even knowing in any detail his motives for making it. It was, I think, excusable not to want to play such a part. The Cabinet in some sort shared this dilemma, for the Hoare–Laval communiqué, with its open admission that the Cabinet did not know of the proposals, gave Hoare's colleagues the choice of accepting the terms or disowning the absent Foreign Secretary without giving him a hearing. As Lord Halifax wrote to me a fortnight later when I became Foreign Secretary: 'The more I think of it, the more clearly do I feel that Sam's communiqué was the *fons et origo* of all our troubles. And I think it's an amazing mistake for him to have made.'

I have now no doubt what action should have been taken by the Prime Minister with the authority of the Cabinet that evening. Baldwin ought to have summoned Hoare home to explain his proposals to the Cabinet, telling him that the decisions for which he asked were too far-reaching to be taken in his absence. This was not done for a political reason, unwillingness to question Hoare's judgement to this extent, and for a human one, Hoare was just arriving in Switzerland for a holiday which he much needed. I have no doubt that another element entered into the decision. There was a hope that the League, which was due to meet in three days, would amend the proposals and that I would be able to take an active share in this. By the wording of the published Hoare–Laval communiqué the terms were not to be made public until the League had considered them, so that this was a possibility strong enough to tempt anxious men. To adapt Balzac, it is in prison and in politics that one believes in what one hopes for. Someone had probably thought of that one too; in any event full and substantially correct accounts of the terms of Laval's agreement with Hoare soon began to appear in the French press. Whether by chance or design, the consequence of this leakage was to commit the Government in London to their Foreign Secretary or compel them to renege upon him publicly, while increasing the difficulty of obtaining any substantial changes.

When Baldwin and I talked over these events in later years, he blamed himself for not having summoned Hoare home. Though this would have been the correct course, it would be wrong to suppose that it could have redeemed the situation. Once the British Foreign Secretary had signed these proposals with Laval the real harm had been done. Laval could be trusted to use them to the uttermost. If the attitude of the League, the British Government and the Emperor himself made it impossible to proceed with them, Hoare's signature would still be useful to Laval, and those who thought like him, as an excuse to halt or hinder any further action against Mussolini, which was precisely what happened.

I also think that I was to blame, for I ought to have urged Hoare's recall upon my colleagues and not have limited my warning to forecasts of the rejection of the terms by the League and by the Emperor. In the climate of the time it is not likely that I would have prevailed, but that does not excuse me. I ought not to have been so sensitive about apparent disloyalty to a Foreign Secretary who had been recently preferred to me. Like others I was tempted by the possibility of amending the terms at Geneva and had not reckoned on the swift breach of faith or the accident which let the terms be known.

Meanwhile some immediate decisions had to be taken, even before the Cabinet met at 6 p.m. that evening, December 9th. I determined that I must ask my colleagues to insist that the Emperor should be told in full of the proposals at the same time as Mussolini. Further, I did not consider that France and Britain could put pressure on the Committee of Eighteen to postpone its meeting arranged for December 12th. Laval had asked that we should do this. I went to Baldwin and told him that I proposed to telephone Vansittart in Paris on these two points. The Prime Minister agreed and I did so at once, saying that we must insist on both of them. Matters were made worse when I received a message from Laval saying that at Geneva he would want to interpret the Anglo-French proposals as generously as possible for Mussolini. I did not at the time plumb the full depths of Laval's scheme. Later I learnt that he had several times consulted the Duce by telephone during the talks of the previous day. The consequence of giving Mussolini details of the plan at once, and only telling the Emperor that the proposals were in accordance with the principles of the Committee of Five and would be discussed at Geneva on the 12th, might be far-reaching. If the Duce were to accept and if the Emperor, when he got to know them at Geneva three days later, were to refuse, Laval would have a plausible pretext for calling off sanctions.

The Government decided that we and France must inform both Addis Ababa and Rome simultaneously. But Ministers felt that we could not abandon Sir Samuel Hoare, and however misplaced, there was genuine loyalty in the decision. I was therefore instructed to press the Emperor and the Duce to accept the Hoare–Laval proposals, but there was little conviction that the former would do so and some hope that the League would improve them at its early meeting, publication being then neither authorized nor expected in advance of it. I gave my opinion that since the proposals went beyond the Committee of Five's report, they were unlikely to be accepted by Haile Selassie or by some members of the League.

The Government having decided, with varying degrees of reluctance, that they must support their absent Foreign Secretary, we had now to make the best we could of a business which developed at a galloping pace and became more wretchedly complicated every hour. I went straight across to the Foreign Office and spoke to Vansittart in Paris. He did not think that the French would make any difficulties about informing the Emperor. It soon became clear that he had been too sanguine. No sooner had I returned to the Foreign Office after dinner, than Vansittart telephoned to say that the French Government were pressing hard for the Abyssinian Government to receive only a shorter account of the proposals. I replied: 'This is a Cabinet decision reached after careful consideration. A partial account will not do, for what is proposed goes beyond the Committee of Five's report.' Vansittart undertook to see Laval again. I settled down to a long vigil in the Foreign Office.

Shortly after midnight a message came from Sir Robert that if Laval consented to inform the Emperor immediately, he would expect us to agree that the oil sanction should not be voted at Geneva. I answered that I could not possibly give such an assurance without the Prime Minister's, and probably the Cabinet's, consent. Moreover, I could not see how such a plan could in any event work out in practice. The Italian reply might be equivocal and open to divergent interpretation by the French and ourselves. Once more Vansittart undertook to speak to Laval. I thought it well to take a few hours' rest.

Early on the Tuesday morning a further cypher telegram arrived. Vansittart had seen the French Prime Minister at 2 a.m. Laval said that he had not wished to inform Abyssinia because he had reason to believe that the Emperor was bound to refuse, in order to bring the oil sanction into play. Laval wanted a definite Anglo-French engagement that if the proposals were rejected by Abyssinia, the oil sanction would not be imposed. He said that in such circumstances he would find it quite impossible to persuade his colleagues, or France, to accept the new sanction. Vansittart thought Laval almost certainly right in this.

I did not consider that we could accept Laval's condition. Accordingly, during the morning I drafted a message which was approved by a special meeting of my colleagues summoned by the Prime Minister. I telegraphed to Paris that to submit terms for a settlement to the aggressor, and withhold them from the victim of aggression, seemed to us indefensible. Early and complete communication of the proposals to the Emperor must be an essential condition of their communication to Italy, or of their presentation to the Committee of the League with our support. We could not give the undertaking for which Laval asked about the oil sanction, this was a matter for the League.

From time to time messages came through from Paris with a commentary or gloss on some part of the terms. They made matters worse, with the result that my colleagues as well as I became increasingly perturbed. While I was walking back to the Foreign Office across the Park on one of the rare interludes during these days, I met Lord Tyrrell. He stopped me and, stroking the side of his nose with his forefinger in a favourite gesture of his, commented: 'It may be that something of this kind was inescapable; I do not know, but, my friend, what a way to do it.' I could only reply that the action was as unexpected to me as to him. By now the British newspapers had produced accounts of the Hoare–Laval meetings and of their supposed outcome. The reaction of public opinion was indignant and ashamed. It was said that we should have no part in rewarding aggressors. Many felt that the Government had won the election less than a month before on false pretences and Members of Parliament were swamped by a tide of indignant letters.

It happened that the House of Commons was due to debate the reply to the Address on the afternoon of December 10th. Opposition Members were not slow to point out that even if the newspaper reports were only partially true, they amounted to an abandonment of the basis on which the Government had fought the election. I made out the best case I could, recalling that the Committee of Eighteen had specifically approved Franco-British attempts to find a basis of settlement. But I could give no reassurance on the terms of the proposals. Criticism gathered force, while the Government grew more anxious. I had, however, to leave the next morning for Geneva to confront the more serious international consequences of the Paris agreement.

* * * * *

I knew that at the League of Nations I should meet with reproaches and criticism from many delegates who were perplexed by the British Government's association with the proposals. At a meeting in London on December 10th, the Dominion High Commissioners showed themselves most uneasy at the rewards which were apparently being given to aggression. This was hardly surprising, as it was only five days since Hoare had appeared among them, as resolute as they. At Geneva the delegates of friendly powers came one after the other to voice their dismay. I had not been there twenty-four hours before I was forced to telegraph on December 12th:

The impression which the Paris proposals have made upon opinion here is even worse than I had anticipated. M. Vasconcellos, chairman of the Committee of Eighteen, came to see me this morning. He is himself ardently pro-English and one of our best friends here. He did not, however, disguise from me the devastating effect which the news of the Paris proposals had had. Members of the Committee were angry and dismayed and the general comment was 'Why have our countries been asked to put on sanctions, to suffer loss of trade and other inconvenience, if the only result is that Italy should be offered by France and Great Britain more, probably, than she would ever have achieved by herself alone, even if sanctions had not been put on?' There is also great anxiety here, M. Vasconcellos added, as to the situation which will be created if Italy accepts the proposals, as is generally anticipated, and the Emperor rejects them.

M. Vasconcellos went on to speak of the proposals themselves as they affected his own country. He said that the proposals constituted a terrible precedent. Was it to be laid down by the League that if a country showed itself an aggressor it was to be given the right of settling another country's territory? If so, it was to be supposed that Germany would soon be asking for such privileges in Portuguese colonies. He had received no instructions from his Government but he was quite confident that they would never allow him to approve these proposals.

This uncomfortable interview was in no way exceptional. Señor de Madariaga, for instance, said that he had no intention of sponsoring the terms agreed in Paris. M. Politis, the Greek delegate, told me that the members of the Balkan Entente were confounded. M. Pouritch, the Yugoslav representative, remarked that the world would regard these proposals as a triumph for the dictator. Mussolini might next decide to attack Albania and look to Germany for friendship, both of which forecasts were proved true. In my speech to the Committee of Eighteen, I had to recognize the strength of hostile feeling:

The proposals now put forward are neither definitive nor sacrosanct. They are suggestions which, it is hoped, may make possible the beginning of negotiations. If the League does not agree with these suggestions, we shall make no complaint; indeed, we should cordially welcome any suggestions for their improvement. The policy of His Majesty's Government remains today what it has been since the dispute began. Any final settlement must be acceptable to the League as well as to the two other parties in conflict.

M. Komarnicki, the Polish delegate, then proposed that until the reactions of Italy and Abyssinia to the Hoare–Laval plan were known, the Committee should postpone further consideration of the oil sanction. Already Abyssinian declarations showed that the Emperor had no intention of accepting the terms.

I heard from London that the situation there now looked ominous. Sir Ronald Lindsay telegraphed from Washington that if the terms published in the press represented the final policy of His Majesty's Government, they would effectively nullify any efforts on the part of the United States Government to influence American opinion in favour of collective security. Even the loyal Government of New Zealand regretted that they were quite unable to associate themselves with the Hoare–Laval terms. The Foreign Secretary, meanwhile, had been overtaken by further misfortunes. On the day of our debate in the House of Commons, December 10th, he was stricken with another fainting fit, fell heavily on the Swiss ice and broke his nose.

I telephoned to the Foreign Secretary soon after my arrival at Geneva on the 12th, told him of the deteriorating political situation at home and encouraged him to return to London as early as possible. He did not appear to consider the need so urgent. In any event this unhappy accident had forced him to take to his bed in Switzerland for several days. I returned to London late on Saturday, December 14th, to find that opposition to the Hoare–Laval proposals was mounting steeply. Members of Parliament were under severe pressure from their constituents. It might even be that Hoare, who had by now decided to return, as a result of a firm summons from No. 10, would have to resign. I found that opinion in the Foreign Office was divided. Some were in the same frame of mind as Haile Selassie, who, as Barton reported, was bewildered at the British Government's connection with the proposals. Others, including Vansittart, thought that the risk of war if the oil sanction were applied and French reluctance justified the terms. On December 16th I minuted:

> The Italian representative at Geneva described the oil sanction as an 'unfriendly act'. So far as I am aware, Signor Mussolini has *never* said that he would regard the oil sanction as an act of war.

I remained unconvinced that he would go to war if it were imposed.

My colleagues met early on the morning of December 17th, so that I could leave that afternoon for Geneva. I read to them the draft of a statement which I had prepared on the previous day. It had already been shown to Hoare, who had by now arrived in London, although still confined to his room. The Foreign Secretary had approved its substance. The draft sounded the death knell of the peace plan and was scrupulously examined without being materially modified. No other course was possible and Sir John Simon wrote to me that day expressing his relief that the draft had gone through. He told me he was horrified at the idea that Hoare should defend us by saying, in effect, that the peace terms were necessary as an alternative to war. He did not believe it, and to say so would be to give Mussolini the biggest score of his life and make Italy intolerable in the future.

The Cabinet over, Baldwin, Neville Chamberlain and I went to see Hoare. My own visit had to be short as I was on my way to the station. We found the Foreign Secretary looking thoroughly miserable. 'How do you feel?' Baldwin asked. 'I wish I were dead,' he replied. In our brief talk, I thanked Hoare for having approved the statement. Baldwin and Chamberlain settled down for a discussion with him and as I left the Foreign Secretary said: 'Thank you so much for all your loyal help.'

* * * * *

Laval was much perturbed when I read to him at Geneva the text the Cabinet had decided that I should use. He tried by all manner of means to modify it, pointing out that we had no justification as yet for indicating that the terms would not be accepted. I replied that world opinion had already given them their quietus. At the end of a long discussion, Laval remarked despondently that he never seemed to have much luck in his negotiations with the English. I told him that I could not modify the main lines of my speech, which my colleagues had endorsed. Accordingly I said that afternoon:

> It must be emphasized that the Paris proposals which were put forward last week were not advanced as proposals to be insisted on in any event. They were advanced in order to ascertain what the views of the two parties and the League might be upon them and His Majesty's Government recommended them only for this purpose. If, therefore, it transpired that these proposals . . . do not satisfy the essential condition of agreement by the two parties and the League, His Majesty's Government could not continue to

recommend or support them. In their mind this particular attempt at conciliation would not then be regarded as having achieved its object, and His Majesty's Government for their part would not wish to pursue it further.

After Laval had spoken of the League's duty to pronounce on the plan, the Abyssinian representative said that his country desired a peace based on justice and goodwill and not on capitulation and spoliation. If his country had possessed modern weapons, the slight Italian advance, carried out with overwhelming forces, would never have been made. He asked whether the victim of aggression must lose all hope of assistance.

I telephoned to London in the evening that the attitude of members of the Council had been understanding, even though they still felt the Hoare–Laval terms to have been a mistake. Bearing in mind the morrow's debate in the House of Commons I concluded my message:

> I feel that I must emphasize that since the atmosphere appears to be definitely improving here, it will be the gravest error to attempt to place the responsibility upon the alleged shortcomings of Geneva. This would cause such sharp resentment here as not only to undo any good which may have resulted from today's proceedings, but would also make the position of the United Kingdom representative untenable.

The Foreign Secretary resigned on December 18th. To this day I am unable to understand how Hoare could think that the proposals he agreed with Laval were compatible with his own speech, so much a personal declaration of faith and action, made to the Assembly at Geneva only three months before. I was glad to be away from Whitehall when the debate took place on December 19th following his resignation. Hoare defended his peace terms, while the Prime Minister simply admitted that a mistake had been made: 'It is perfectly obvious now that the proposals are absolutely and completely dead. The Government is certainly going to make no attempt to resurrect them.' Lord Halifax's speech in the House of Lords gave a more effective account of the unexpected dilemma in which the Foreign Secretary's action had placed his colleagues.

On the same day the Committee of Thirteen met. It was evident that the members rejected the Paris terms, but it was no less clear that confidence in two of their leading powers was grievously shaken. Some patient nursing would be necessary before faith was restored and this troubled me, because I was not sure that we had time for it.

As a start, I stated that the British Government did not wish the failure of the Hoare–Laval plan to mean any alteration in the policy of sanctions. That evening Laval left for Paris and I for London, each to take account of the political scene at home.

Two conclusions were in my thoughts. The Hoare–Laval terms had asked the Emperor to surrender too much and even if they had been whole-heartedly endorsed by the British and French Governments, the League would never have approved them. Both Governments would have been wiser never to have undertaken their mediatory task alone, for it was one of the exasperating consequences of the Paris proposals that they made any later and better balanced compromise infinitely more difficult.

* * * * *

One evening in the summer of 1943 Mr. Churchill telephoned to me to announce that Mussolini had resigned. I wrote in my diary that night:

> Looking back the thought comes again. Should we not have shown more determination in pressing through with sanctions in 1935 and if we had could we not have called Musso's bluff and at least postponed this war? The answer, I am sure, is yes. We built Musso into a great power, the Greeks first debunked him.

BOOK TWO

Responsibility

I

FOREIGN SECRETARY

December 1935 – March 1936

Strange interview with the Prime Minister – I become Foreign Secretary – A disordered heritage – Conversation with King George V – Relations with my colleagues – Signor Mussolini pursues his war – My despatches on Nazi intentions – Meeting of the League – Death of King George V – I press for oil sanctions against Italy – M. Flandin protests

Travelling back from Geneva in bad weather by train, Stanley Bruce and I discussed the situation created by Hoare's resignation. It seemed that the Cabinet had demanded this and that Chamberlain had been sent to see the Foreign Secretary to enforce it. Hoare's lapse was to have been too infirm of purpose and thus tricked by Laval.

Meanwhile, what was to be done. The Prime Minister and the Government were severely shaken and, what mattered more, international authority had suffered with them. Bruce and I agreed that this was the moment for a respected statesman at the Foreign Office, whose reputation could restore direction to our policy. We had to admit that after the strength of Hoare's speech in September and the weakness of his agreement with Laval, the world had lost confidence in us. We canvassed the possible candidates and considered that Austen Chamberlain would be the best choice. He carried more weight in foreign affairs than any other figure in our country. He had been an outspoken critic of the Hoare–Laval proposals and his integrity was nowhere questioned. Chamberlain's age might make it difficult for him to hold the office for long, but in our dilemma the next year or two seemed to us what mattered most. I made it quite clear to Bruce that I did not want to be Foreign Secretary in these conditions. He understood and agreed with me.

At Calais, the British Consul met me with a message from the Prime

Minister. Would I please drive at once to 10 Downing Street, on arrival, without communicating with anybody until I had seen him. I did as I was bid and found Baldwin in the little library which he sometimes used overlooking Downing Street. He was in a highly nervous state, pacing up and down during most of our talk and snapping his fingers, as he had a habit of doing when much put out. He said that he did not know how he could have come to let matters reach their present pass. However, I understood the trouble we were in, the question now was what to do about it. He wanted me to discuss the future of the Foreign Office with him, trying for the moment to put my personal feelings on one side. Who was the best man to be appointed Foreign Secretary in this situation? I replied that I had a clear view, Austen Chamberlain. He had the authority and the experience; so far as I was concerned, I had served him before, and would be very happy to do so again in any capacity. Baldwin shook his head and said that would not do. He was too old for it. When I began to protest, Baldwin cut me short, adding: 'Anyway, I saw him yesterday and told him so.' Chamberlain's own version of this conversation, which he gave me the next day, was: 'He told me I was ga-ga.'

I was distressed by this information and remained silent. Baldwin asked me if I had any other names to suggest. I had none that I could put forward with the same confidence, but I suggested Halifax. Baldwin did not think that he would do either. Apart from controversy about Halifax's Indian policy, a Foreign Secretary in the Lords was not the answer just now. Another silence followed; I had no more names to suggest, nor apparently had Baldwin. Eventually he turned to me and said: 'It looks as if it will have to be you.' Feeling by this time somewhat hurt at this eliminative method of being appointed, I replied that six months before I would have been very grateful for the chance to be Foreign Secretary, but that now I felt quite differently about it. Baldwin nodded understanding at this, and so this strange interview ended with my words being taken as tacit acceptance.

I was certainly succeeding to a wretchedly disordered heritage. It was now infinitely more difficult to impose an acceptable Abyssinian settlement on Mussolini, even with stricter sanctions, if such were possible in the new climate, which was unlikely. We should do well if we could restore any semblance of unity to the confused ranks of League members. Equally serious was the state of Anglo-French relations; they had not been worse since before the Entente of thirty years before. There was almost nation-wide resentment in Britain at France's policy over the Abyssinian dispute, in which Laval was held to represent his country's feelings. If France were only prepared to uphold the League when it suited her own ends, she might find herself alone when that time came. This sentiment, variously felt and expressed, was strong enough in Britain at this time to be my chief concern on taking over the Foreign Office.

Public opinion was not prepared to accept that, to the French, our attitude in supporting the League against Mussolini over Abyssinia also seemed at least partly selfish. Exasperated as I was by Laval's tactics, I was convinced that close Anglo-French understanding and co-ordinated action, endorsed as nearly as we could contrive by the United States, was the only way to keep the peace. At the moment, we were apart and lowering at each other. We had to find a way to survive the tests which the next few months must bring, from Hitler more importantly than Mussolini; we had to hold on and then rebuild the alliance.

On a bitter cold day just before Christmas I travelled to Sandringham to kiss hands on my appointment. King George v was coughing painfully, but he was in good spirits and very kind to me. After the ceremony His Majesty granted me an audience during which he spoke understandingly of the difficulties I had inherited and told me how interested he was in foreign affairs and in the appointment of ambassadors. He asked me to keep him fully informed and declared he would give me any help he could. The King said that he had talked to Hoare when he surrendered the seals and had told him that the Hoare–Laval proposals had been a blunder. You cannot drive a train full steam ahead in one direction, he said, and then, without warning, suddenly reverse without somebody coming off the rails. I thought His Majesty's reaction significant, because he had at an earlier audience spoken to me with vehemence about the importance he attached to good relations with Italy. He added: 'I said to your predecessor: "You know what they're all saying, no more coals to Newcastle, no more Hoares to Paris." The fellow didn't even laugh.'

At Christmas I took stock of our battered fortunes. The prospect was fairly described by Mr. Ronald Campbell, then our Minister in Belgrade and later our Ambassador in Paris in the darkest days of 1940: 'It is no exaggeration to say that the Paris proposals caused British prestige in Yugoslavia to slump to zero.'

Although there was nothing to be gained by saying it in public, I felt that the League after Hoare–Laval was a very different proposition from the League which had voted so solidly in favour of sanctions. While there could be no going back on the policy of sanctions, I could not believe that Geneva would be, at least for some time to come, an adequate guardian of peace. The Abyssinian conflict had brought into prominence the working, scope and limitations of the League of Nations. From its earliest days there had been two views of the League's purpose. Some considered that its function was merely to provide opportunities for statesmen to meet and reconcile their differences by discussion as best they might. Others, including myself, believed that the League must also, if it were to be a force in the world's politics, take resolute action against law-breakers. The British Government had fluctuated between conciliation and firmness in their dealings with Mussolini in 1935. Now that it was clearly demonstrated that firmness was more likely to bring results, the League was so physically and morally sick that its strength would have to be rebuilt before it could be used, if ever it could be used at all.

In the next few years, some of my colleagues were to protest that our close relations with France prevented us from reaching an understanding with Germany. Yet it was only those relations which stood between the world and domination by the dictators. It was true that the United States did not wish to see Europe prostrate. Our interests in the last resort were hers, but this peace-loving country would not exercise her giant's strength outside the American continent. Here was the one unexploited reserve which must make itself felt if the world was to be saved.

Britain's military defences were miserably weak. Many members of the Government thought that the Foreign Office ought to be able to resolve our European difficulties and so render rearmament unnecessary. I, on the other hand, was convinced that we could only reach worthwhile agreements if we were strong in spirit as our rearmament made itself felt. The Labour and Liberal Oppositions, though detesting the dictators, failed in their duty by voting and speaking against all measures to provide their country with the armaments to which alone Nazis and Fascists would give heed.

My difficulties were not only international. I was aware that my appointment was not welcome to all my elders in the Cabinet, where there was already no lack of former Foreign Secretaries and other aspirants to the office. I knew that Baldwin's support would be fitful and lethargic. I had also seen the practice, common to most Cabinets in those days, of a multiplicity of Ministers taking a hand at drafting a despatch. On one of these occasions about a year later, I began to protest vigorously, when Baldwin passed me a note: 'Don't be too indignant. I once saw Curzon burst into tears when the Cabinet was amending his despatches.' After the meeting he told me I must remember that out of my twenty colleagues, there was probably not more than one who thought he should be Minister of Labour and nineteen who thought they should be Foreign Secretary.

There were those, however, who sympathized with the Foreign Secretary as the victim of too much tutelary zeal. My diary for May 20th, 1936, records:

> Cabinet in a.m. Germany fairly satisfactory, though Kingsley [Wood] rather tiresome.... Outburst from Duff [Cooper] that Cabinet were always interfering in foreign affairs, result compromise, my policy thwarted. Much better leave matters to me—not interfere so much.

* * * * *

The post of Minister for League of Nations Affairs was not filled, nor did anyone suggest that it should be. Lord Halifax, who had then no departmental duties, was Lord Privy Seal, as I had previously been, and stood in for me at the Foreign Office from time to time. He did not have a room, nor a Private Secretary, or any official position, but he eased some of my burden, especially on my brief spells of leave. We had long been friends and I was grateful for an arrangement which never caused me any anxiety, even when we did not agree about the decisions to be taken, as happened later.

A few weeks after I had taken over the Foreign Office, Sir Warren Fisher, then Head of the Treasury, asked to see me. He opened the conversation by asking whom I was going to appoint to certain embassies which were then vacant. I said that I had not yet made up my mind, but was considering a number of names and gave him one example. Fisher said: 'Well, you must let me have them when you have decided, because they must be submitted to the Prime Minister, of course, through me.' I expressed my astonishment and he replied that, as head of the Civil Service, he was responsible to the Prime Minister for all appointments. I said I could not accept that, nor could I submit the appointments to the Prime Minister through him. I submitted them to the King and I consulted the Prime Minister about the major appointments, but the responsibility was mine. Fisher said that this was not the true position.

After some rather heated exchanges, I said I would put the matter to the Prime Minister and he could do the same. Accordingly, the next day I spoke to Baldwin, telling him that I had had this extraordinary interview but that, of course, I did not intend to do as Fisher asked. I suggested that, as First Lord of the Treasury, perhaps the Prime Minister would tell Warren Fisher that he must give up making suggestions of this kind. Baldwin showed signs of acute discomfort, as he was apt to do if anybody mentioned anything unpleasant to him and, after long cogitation, said perhaps I would have a word with Neville Chamberlain about it, as he was Chancellor of the Exchequer. I remarked that it had no more to do with Neville than with Fisher. I would resign rather than give way on what I regarded as a matter of principle. Baldwin looked more uncomfortable, but still asked me to see Chamberlain: 'Neville will help, I have no doubt,' he said, 'and he is the Minister in charge of the Treasury.' I saw the Chancellor, who was understanding. I did not ask his view, but told him my position and asked him to explain it to Fisher, which he did. After a few more exchanges, it was finally accepted that the appointments were my own and I could show them to the Prime Minister if I wished, before submitting them to the King. Some time afterwards, when the appointments came out, Chamberlain stopped me as I was leaving the Cabinet room one day and said with an enigmatic smile: 'It may interest you to know, Anthony, that Fisher warmly approves of your appointments.'

* * * * *

I had to begin by restoring confidence overseas. As a first step, it seemed prudent for the powers imposing sanctions to make themselves as secure as possible in the Mediterranean and for us to take the lead in doing so. Hitherto we had done most of the asking and in December the Governments of Turkey, Greece and Yugoslavia had given us assurances of support should Mussolini attempt a 'mad-dog' act. This action led to shrill protest in the Fascist press. At the beginning of January, Prince Paul, the Regent of Yugoslavia, told Campbell that his General Staff were studying their dispositions against the possibility of war with Italy. I now wished to show the smaller members of the League that the British Government would give them help if need be. A few days later, the Turkish Ambassador gave me the opening by asking whether his Government could count on the co-operation of His Majesty's naval forces should Mussolini make an unprovoked attack upon their country. I replied that in the event of such an unprovoked attack by the aggressor in this dispute upon a nation fulfilling its obligation under the Covenant, for example Turkey, we would come to their aid. Messages in the same sense were sent to Athens and Belgrade.

Meanwhile, there was no lack of other activity. Grandi was a frequent visitor to the Foreign Office and I was sure that he was sincerely anxious for improved relations between our two countries. I considered, however, that if the Duce wanted a relaxation of tension, he must contribute something himself. As an opening move, it seemed useful to expound our true motives once more. Accordingly, when I saw the Ambassador on the morning of January 6th, I told him that there was no foundation whatever for the reports, which had appeared too often in certain quarters, that I was anti-Italian, or that anything I had done in the last few months was caused by such sentiment. Still less was it true that during my conversations with Signor Mussolini in Rome in the summer, there had been any sharp personal differences. It seemed a pity that such reports should be allowed to circulate uncorrected, for they must further hamper our difficult task.

The Ambassador replied that he was very glad to hear me speak in such terms, for he had already, on my appointment as Secretary of State, reported on his own account to his Government in this sense. Signor Grandi went on to speak of his own position. He was afraid, he said, that he had been of very little use in this dispute. So long as he had had anything to do with the direction of Italian foreign policy, it had always been his ambition that Italy should play the part of a good European, which meant full collaboration at Geneva and close and cordial relations between Great Britain and Italy. Three years ago, however, his policy had been, in effect, turned down and he himself had been sent to London, where he could play no further part in shaping it. The Ambassador was confident that a solution could be found to our present difficulties, if neither side wanted a complete success. He felt that his country must now realize that no such outcome of the conflict was within its reach and he hoped that others would not try to win it, on their side.

Reports from our Embassy in Italy spoke of a 'general depression settling over the country' and of 'a distinct atmosphere of uneasiness.' Mussolini himself admitted in a public speech that a pause would now be necessary in the military operations. Léger told Hugh Lloyd Thomas, our Minister in Paris, that he would lay long odds against Mussolini surviving the year in power. Nevertheless, no peacemaking move came out of Rome, and Grandi was sufficiently conscious of this to wish to place the onus upon others. On January 10th he asked whether the Duce might expect any initiative for conciliation from Laval or myself. I replied that the British Government had no individual move in mind at the present time, nor I felt sure had M. Laval. I thought, however, that I should place responsibilities where they properly lay. Therefore I added that I did not know what the Committee of Eighteen intended, but if either of the two parties took the initiative by making proposals, I felt sure that they would be listened to. In reply to a question, I declined to give any assurance as to intentions about an oil sanction. Though I did not say so, I could not tell until the League met a week later what the possibilities might now be.

At this time a new element was obtruding itself into the fighting in Abyssinia. We began to hear more and more about Fascist disregard for the rules of war. On December 30th the Emperor protested to the League that the Italians were using poison gas in their attacks. Early in the New Year, it became known that Fascist aircraft had attacked a Swedish Red Cross ambulance serving on the Ogaden front. On January 4th another Red Cross ambulance, manned by Egyptian and British staff, was deliberately bombed. This and other reports of attacks on hospitals, of the burning of churches and the use of mustard gas, caused indignation against those who ordered such deeds. Here was the first presage of that organized brutality which the dictators later achieved.

* * * * *

In a speech in my own constituency on January 17th, while Parliament was in recess, I warned that collective security was not to be won easily and gave a definition of our purpose. Aggression should not be allowed to succeed and the members of the League should be strong and united enough to bring home to any aggressor that peaceful negotiation was the only successful way to remove discontents. At the same time, Hitler's Minister of Propaganda, Dr. Goebbels, was making a different speech. He offered his conception of foreign policy:

> Some people say that there is a world conscience which is the League of Nations, whose part it is to preserve the peace of the world, but I prefer to rely on guns.

I thought it necessary that those in authority in the Government should have a chance of understanding the Hitler menace as it appeared to me. Early in January, I supplied a preface to a number of despatches, which the Foreign Office had selected for private circulation as an educative warning. A copy of this document was purloined and in due course shown by Ciano to Hitler, whose reception of it was not favourable. I wrote:

> The most striking feature of this series of reports is the clear evidence which it contains of the steady and undeviating development under Hitler's guidance of German policy along certain definite and pre-ordained lines. . . .
>
> Hitler's foreign policy may be summed up as the destruction of the peace settlement and re-establishment of Germany as the dominant Power in Europe. The means by which this policy is to be effected are two-fold: (a) Internally through the militarization of the whole nation in all its aspects; (b) externally by economic and territorial expansion so as to absorb as far as possible all those of German race who are at present citizens of neighbouring states, to acquire new markets for German industry and new fields for German emigration, and to obtain control of some of the sources of those raw materials at present lacking to Germany. The form and direction of this expansion is the one still doubtful factor in Germany's plans for the future.

I then drew two conclusions. The first, I said, had had unfortunately to be emphasized more than once recently, the vital need to hasten and complete our own rearmament; in view of what was so openly going forward in Germany, we must be ready for all eventualities. Secondly, while pursuing our rearmament we should consider whether it was still possible to come to some *modus vivendi*, to put it no higher, with Hitler's Germany, which would be both honourable and safe for this country. I concluded with a warning that in the present temper of the German Government and people, this solution of our problems would not easily be realized.

A few weeks later I wrote a foreword to a thorough study Vansittart had made of Nazi intentions, remarking:

> . . . The poverty of Nazi Germany, measured in that country's dwindling export trade and increase of unemployment, may be expected to have the same effect as in Italy, and to encourage a dictator to launch his people on some foreign venture as the only means that remain to him to distract their attention from the failure of his policy at home. Our purpose being to avoid war, it should follow that we should be wise to do everything in our power to assist Germany's economic recovery, thereby easing the strain upon the German rulers, and making an outbreak less likely. The circumstances of this

particular case are, however, exceptional, and who could be sure that if, in fact, we do make efforts to improve Germany's economic position, her rulers will not use the advantages they may gain thereby in further prosecuting their rearmament and preparing their nation for war?

. . . it is to be expected that any attempt upon our part to initiate negotiations with a view to coming to terms with Germany is likely to arouse suspicions, superficially at least, in France and more fundamentally in Soviet Russia. There is therefore a certain risk that our attempt, were it to fail, would leave us with a confused situation of general mistrust and irritation. On balance, however, I am in favour of making some attempt to come to terms with Germany, but upon one indispensable condition: that we offer no sops to Germany. There must be no concession merely to keep Germany quiet, for that process only stimulates the appetite it is intended to satisfy. We should be prepared to make concessions to Germany, and they will have to be concessions of value to her if they are to achieve their object, but these concessions must only be offered as part of a final settlement which includes some further arms limitation and Germany's return to the League.

I had by this time occasionally used the word 'appeasement' in a speech or minute for the Foreign Office in the sense of the first meaning given in the *Oxford English Dictionary*, 'to bring to peace, settle (strife, etc.)'. It was not until some years later, when the results of the foreign policy pursued by Mr. Chamberlain became apparent, that the word was more strongly associated with the last meaning given in the dictionary, 'to pacify, by satisfying demands'.

* * * * *

I arrived in Geneva on January 19th, disagreeably conscious of the legacy of trouble the Hoare–Laval terms had bequeathed to us. Negotiation was stultified. The League had expressed world opinion in denouncing the agreement, but Mussolini would only reduce his demands if hard pressed and Laval would not help us in his last days of power. I had a long final conversation with the French Prime Minister the next day, during which he told me that he would have to resign. He would prefer this to facing certain defeat in the Chamber. We decided to report to the Committee of Eighteen the action we had taken to ensure mutual assistance in the Mediterranean, and to suggest that the other powers concerned should be invited to do the same. We also agreed that experts should examine the efficacy of an oil sanction. I could not get Laval one inch beyond this preliminary exercise, with which I would have preferred to dispense. The Committee which dealt with sanctions, seeing no hope of conciliation, at once appointed the group of experts, known as the Petroleum Committee.

Our controversies were now temporarily overshadowed by the news that King George v was seriously ill. In the early morning of January 21st we learned of his death. The Secretary-General cancelled all the day's official engagements and summoned the Council for that afternoon. During the morning the heads of all the delegations called on me to express their sympathy. Mr. Stanley Bruce presided over the meeting of the Council when all members paid their tributes to the King's memory.

The next day I held a number of interviews, some of which showed more optimism than I could feel. Titulescu, for instance, considered that the oil sanction must now be put on without delay, but he seemed to have no doubt that Mussolini was going to fail in Abyssinia. He thought that he should be seen to do so as a result of the League's actions. The same evening, I forwarded to the Secretary-General a memorandum setting out the steps we had taken to secure mutual assistance in the Mediterranean, together with the assurances given by the French, Turkish, Greek and Yugoslav Governments.

I telegraphed to the Foreign Office:

> I am confident that the solidarity thus displayed will have a good effect here. . . . The Italian delegation are said to have been considerably impressed and the risk of a 'mad-dog' act, whatever it was, should now be more remote.

* * * *

When I returned to London, many foreign dignitaries who had come for the late King's funeral took the opportunity to visit me at the Foreign Office. Baron von Neurath, the German Foreign Minister, declared on January 27th that in his opinion, Mussolini's attitude had recently undergone a considerable change. The Duce was no longer confident and would perhaps even agree to terms which had not been possible a short while before. Von Neurath described the financial and economic position of Italy as 'undoubtedly grave'.

On the same day I saw M. Flandin, Foreign Minister in the Government of M. Albert Sarraut, who had just replaced Laval. We compared reports on events in Abyssinia and both considered, wrongly, that the Fascist position was deteriorating. Neither of us was prepared to make any move to restart negotiations between the parties.

For the moment, I had two main preoccupations. The first was to try to make an oil sanction effective. The Petroleum Committee at Geneva got to work with despatch, while I asked Sir Ronald Lindsay for details of American exports of oil and petrol to Italy. His reply was disturbing, for it showed that they continued to increase. My second concern was to refute Fascist charges that British firms had illegally supplied explosive or 'dum-dum' ammunition to the Abyssinians for military purposes. It was alleged that subsidiary companies of Imperial Chemical Industries were guilty of this offence, although the chairman of that company had publicly denied the charge. A thorough investigation was made, from which it emerged that the accusation was baseless. The information was then collated in a memorandum which I had circulated to all members of the League. The Fascist press, with an undistinguished unanimity, lightly dismissed our carefully documented reply.

Before the middle of February, the Petroleum Committee published its report. This was much as I had feared and showed the cost of having missed the moment of opportunity two months before. It advised that if an oil sanction were universally applied by members of the League, it would become effective in about three to three and a half months, and then only if the United States were to limit its exports to Italy to their pre-1935 level. The campaign against this sanction was again being intensified in Italy. My own information showed that an embargo would cause difficulty in the refuelling of Italian oil-burning ships bound for East Africa, and that the East African campaign was using up more petrol than had been expected. Even so, any hope of decisive action now depended upon the American attitude. I asked Lindsay whether there was any chance that steps might be taken by the United States Government to limit their oil exports to Italy. While I awaited the reply to this telegram, Dr. Martin, the Abyssinian Minister in London, asked to see me and spoke of the instant need for some assistance, to help his country hold its own against the invaders.

On February 22nd came Lindsay's answer and it brought no comfort. He telegraphed that the United States was most unlikely to take effective action to restrict oil exports to their normal level. The Ambassador said that Congress preferred a rigid neutrality. Further, the American election was now approaching and I learnt, without surprise, that the Hoare–Laval plan had supplied valuable and telling arguments to all who, for political or commercial reasons, advocated isolationism. Sir Ronald added:

If the League imposed embargo regardless of the United States' attitude, I expect there would be expressions of shame and heartburnings in some volume and perhaps even pressure, but it would be ineffective, even if it became apparent that the United States alone were furnishing supplies. Nevertheless, this course of action would do more than anything else to restore the League's prestige and to influence American opinion in favour of the collective peace system.

Two days later a foreign policy debate was held in the House of Commons. Mr. Lees-Smith, for the Labour Party, advocated that Great Britain should take the lead in proposing the oil sanction when the Committee of Eighteen met. He seemed to have the impression that, whereas Great Britain and other League countries were continuing to increase or maintain their sales of oil to Italy, the United States was supplying less than before. Making my first parliamentary speech as Foreign Secretary, I gave the facts:

Taking the figures from January to September 1935, the exports from Persia—which is where the only British company concerned operates—were 13 per cent. of Italy's total taking. From October to December they had fallen to 4·4 per cent., a very small percentage in Italy's total taking. On the other hand, whereas the United States' percentage from January to September last year was 6·3, that percentage had risen in the October to December quarter to 17·8.

Later I said:

His Majesty's Government have departed neither from their original decision of principle regarding the oil sanction, a decision which was taken last November, nor from their resolve to take their full part with others in such collective action as the League may decide upon.

I then referred to the Committee of Five's report as being the basis on which any further attempts at conciliation should be made. There would be no hesitation on the part of the League, I added, if Italy and Abyssinia would accept its good offices. But no sign came that Mussolini wished to arrive at a settlement and on February 26th the Cabinet agreed that Great Britain should impose the oil sanction, if other members of the League would do likewise. This I still consider was the right decision, despite the pessimism, by then understandably prevalent about the American attitude.

As soon as I arrived back at Geneva, I had a talk with Flandin and told him of the Cabinet's decision, which I said I proposed to communicate to the Committee of Eighteen. Flandin professed to be indignant. He made play with a categorical statement of the Duce's to the French Ambassador in Rome, to the effect that if there were any further extension of sanctions, Italy would leave the League. I replied that the acceptance of this declaration would result in the aggressor choosing which sanctions were to be applied. Flandin continued to argue the Fascist case with blatant confidence, maintaining that the embargo would not work. I said that if the oil sanction were not going to be effective, it was difficult to understand why Mussolini was making so much noise about it. If the Committee of Eighteen did not impose the embargo, what were they going to do. Were they merely to say that the oil sanction would not work, and then disperse.

I admitted that the decision was a difficult one to take; an embargo by League members alone would not stop the war, but it was a chance to influence opinion in the United States. So the argument dragged wearily on, Flandin insisting that Mussolini was not bluffing, while I held to my position and added that I must inform my League colleagues of the opinion of the Government I represented. Flandin suggested that the time had come for a new peace move in Rome. I replied that I still thought it a good idea to fix a date for the application of the oil sanction now. This would not prevent negotiations in the meantime. Flandin asked that before the Committee of the League took a decision, an appeal should be addressed to Rome, perhaps by France and Great Britain. I said we should not act alone. This was a decision for the League.

Flandin then produced his final argument. He said that a meeting of Ministers in Paris had decided, before he left, that France could not agree to impose the oil sanction in the face of the categorical statements made by Mussolini to the French Ambassador. Here already was the situation which was to confront me again and again in the next two years. Was it wise to put increasing pressure on the Duce or would he be more willing, as Drummond and Flandin thought, to negotiate when free from the threat of sanctions. Would he become more reasonable if timely concessions and appeals were made. I thought not. I considered that strength, economic or military, was the factor which carried most weight with Mussolini and I did not believe in making piecemeal concessions in the problematical hope of some future return.

Flandin's attitude was indistinguishable from Laval's, but was more skilfully and consistently presented. The heart of these two Ministers was not sufficiently engaged in the dispute to want to make the League's action effective. Though the French Government had joined in condemning Fascist aggression, they wished to use the League machinery only in a quarrel of their own choosing. The world could not fail to note this, nor the consequence be avoided, when France in her turn had to call upon others. M. Pouritch, the Yugoslav representative, told me that M. Flandin had remarked to him: 'One of the disadvantages if Italy left Geneva would be that Britain would be left in a position of excessive preponderance in the League in future.' The collapse of the League was a danger for France, its dominance by Britain, had it come about, would have presented none, as Flandin's successors in authority, Blum, Delbos, Mandel, Reynaud and others would at once have understood. Unhappily they arrived too late for the crucial decisions. Flandin now proposed to the Committee of Eighteen that before the oil embargo were discussed, yet another attempt at conciliation should be made. The French Government having refused to support the embargo, I could not gainsay this, but I held to our position, telling the Committee that His Majesty's Government were in favour of the early imposition of the oil sanction. Flandin was resentful at my action, for he knew that many in his country would agree with me.

On March 3rd Flandin presented me with a document asking the British Government for an undertaking that they would fulfil their engagements under the Locarno Treaty, if necessary alone. He made the additional point that he could not now agree to an oil sanction until this assurance was received. I told Flandin that I was as anxious as he that Italy should not leave Geneva, but I was also acutely conscious that if the League could not function effectively now, it would be difficult to place any reliance upon it in the future. I undertook to consult my colleagues and to give Flandin an early reply to his note. On the same day, the Committee of Eighteen agreed to meet again in a week's time to hear the results of the attempt at conciliation, no longer pause was to be allowed. We then adjourned and I returned to London, very doubtful whether the Duce, who was now gaining more victories in the field, would respond to the offer Flandin had inspired. Sir Sidney Barton telegraphed that Fascist aircraft had again deliberately bombed a British Red Cross unit in Abyssinia. Mussolini's actions in East Africa had placed the peace of Europe in jeopardy.

Now was Hitler's opportunity.

II

THE RHINELAND

December 1935 – March 1936

Herr Hitler and the Locarno Treaty – M. Flandin's fears – Dr. Goebbels speaks – The Labour Party is against armaments – The Franco-Soviet Pact – Herr Hitler occupies the demilitarized zone – And asks to rejoin the League of Nations – Rhineland fait accompli

During my first three months as Foreign Secretary, Hitler had lain quiescent while his armed strength grew. I had no doubt that he was watching the Abyssinian struggle through all its phases and that he had taken heart from our failure to bring Mussolini to book. The League's weakness and Italy's preoccupation with Africa might be the Führer's opportunity, at a time of Anglo-French disarray.

Articles 42, 43 and 44 of the Versailles Treaty had laid down that Germany should not have fortifications or military establishments on the left bank of the Rhine, nor in a zone covering the land fifty kilometres from its right bank. This area was to be free from German troops and the whole arrangement gave France an overwhelming military advantage, because her forces could at any time penetrate into her neighbour's vitals. But the existence of the zone had a more recent authority. Hitler was not entitled to regard it as just another inequitable part of a peace enforced by the victors. The demilitarized zone was specifically guaranteed by the Locarno Treaty, freely signed by Germany, in 1925. The Chancellor had frequently declared that he would scrupulously respect treaties voluntarily signed. He had personally given this assurance about Locarno to me in 1934. Here, then, was a test of his good faith.

The pretended new element, according to the Nazi thesis, was the Franco-Soviet Pact, signed by Laval in May 1935 but still unratified in January 1936. This temporizing did not help the Pact, but may have encouraged Hitler to use it as a pretext. The Nazis began to say that it violated the Locarno Treaty by bringing a formidable new power on to the European scene. But, since France had already been allied to Poland when Locarno was signed, the distinction lay only in the power of the new ally which was more remote from the territories guaranteed by Locarno. On December 13th, 1935, in the midst of the Hoare–Laval crisis, Sir Eric Phipps had an interview with the Führer and the German Foreign Minister. Von Neurath referred to the effect of the Franco-Soviet Pact on the air defence of Germany and on the future of the Rhineland. France and Britain, he complained, could keep their aircraft right on the frontier, while Germany's would have to be behind the zone. Hitler then complacently remarked that he could quite well have proceeded to occupy the demilitarized zone in the previous March, but had been content with Locarno and had therefore abstained. François-Poncet, the French Ambassador in Berlin, expected that if the Franco-Soviet Pact were ratified, the Germans would march into the Rhineland, in which event, he said to Phipps, the French would certainly mobilize, but no statement of intentions was given to us by the French Government.

There now came from the other side of the Atlantic an indication of the potential strength and actual limitations of American policy. On January 6th, President Roosevelt, in a public speech, roughly criticized the aims and methods of dictators. I heard from our Ambassador in Berlin that the Führer was surprised and upset by these remarks. Phipps added, however, that this aspect of the President's speech carried no weight with Hitler, in comparison with Roosevelt's renewed declaration that America would in future remain aloof and observe neutrality in European affairs. 'There has', Hitler said, according to Phipps' report, 'been no development during recent years more welcome than this.'

* * * * *

The Nazi press now mounted a campaign against Britain, which alleged that, in return for French assurances of support in the Mediterranean, we were preparing to occupy air bases on France's north-eastern border as a security against German attack. I told Herr von Hoesch, the German Ambassador in London, that there was no word of truth in these tales, but the Nazi press insisted that we were making arrangements with France which were hostile to Locarno. At the same time, criticism of the Franco-Soviet Pact was intensified, about which François-Poncet protested in Berlin on January 16th.

Suspicion of these Nazi tactics was much in my mind when I met foreign statesmen who had come for the King's funeral in the last week in January. On January 27th I questioned Baron von Neurath, who assured me smoothly that there was no dispute between Germany and France now that the Saar problem had been happily settled. The German Government, he said, fully intended to respect the Treaty of Locarno. All that they asked was that others should observe it in the spirit as well as in the letter. I replied that I was glad to hear the German Foreign Minister say this. He might be assured that His Majesty's Government would on no account do anything to injure or even to weaken Locarno. We regarded that agreement as being of the greatest value to the preservation of peace in Western Europe. Von Neurath agreed, adding that he too considered that it would be a great pity if ever the Treaty ceased to be.

All this was superficially satisfactory. Von Neurath then went on to develop the thesis that Soviet Russia was a potential menace. Her air force was rapidly expanding and her propaganda tireless. Communism still had many adherents in the Reich, where there was not yet the stability which he would like to see and, in the circumstances, it was natural that the German Government should be watchful of Russia. Certainly, he said, if the Franco-Soviet Pact were ratified, it would mean that, combined with the pact which existed between Czechoslovakia and Russia, Germany would be very vulnerable to joint action by those powers from the air. This would render the negotiation of an air pact more difficult. Von Neurath emphasized that he did not say 'impossible'. I replied it seemed to me most important that we should reach an agreement for air limitation. Baron von Neurath agreed.

Though the German Foreign Minister was not a man to be trusted, nor one who necessarily knew Hitler's mind, there was nothing in this interview to arouse any undue alarm. When I saw M. Flandin later the same day, however, he told me that his Government were considerably preoccupied by the continuous references in Germany to Locarno and particularly to the demilitarized zone. It certainly looked, he said, as though the German Government were preparing to take some action there. If this were likely, he asked what advice I could give him about the attitude the French Government should adopt. I told Flandin of the assurance given to me by von Neurath and we agreed that, whatever Hitler's ultimate intentions, it seemed improbable that he would take any precipitate action in the near future. Flandin was convinced that

Germany was not likely to rest content with the continued existence of the zone if she contemplated any aggressive action elsewhere. For example, if Germany intended to attack Czechoslovakia, the Rhineland zone would leave a gap in her defences which would make her very vulnerable. The same consideration applied to any German attack on Belgium. I replied that the French attitude to a violation of the Rhineland was clearly a matter for the judgement of the French Government in the first instance. How much importance, I asked, did they attach to the demilitarized zone? Did they wish, for their part, to maintain it at all costs, or would the French Government prefer to bargain with the German Government while the existence of the zone still had value in German eyes? Flandin replied that these were just the subjects which he thought our Governments should carefully consider and on which they should then consult. This was hardly the attitude or language of a man determined to fight for the Rhineland.

Flandin told me that he expected both the Chamber and the Senate to ratify the Franco-Soviet Pact before the general election, which would take place at the end of April or the beginning of May. He thought that the present situation, in which the Pact was signed but unratified, was most unsatisfactory. The French Foreign Minister then asked me whether I thought the Pact would have a bad effect on Germany. Again he wanted to know whether I had any advice to give him. I replied that M. Flandin would know as well as I that the German Government had always shown resentment of the Pact, but it was scarcely possible for His Majesty's Government to advise the French Government on ratification, which was essentially a question of French policy. Flandin appeared to think that since Germany not only knew of the Pact's signature, but also seemed to expect its ratification, the event would not create any undue stir.

On the following evening the Belgian Prime Minister, M. Paul Van Zeeland, for whose judgement I had considerable respect, dined with me. He spoke very frankly of the deteriorating internal situation of Germany, which, he said, might prompt her Government to profit by any opportunity of making trouble abroad. As a result, his Government were shortly going to take action to strengthen Belgium's military defences. He observed that not only was the Stresa front broken, but he regarded the Locarno Treaty itself as weakened. We then spoke of the demilitarized zone, when I asked whether the German danger would materialize in that connection. M. Van Zeeland thought that, since the Germans had already violated the zone in a number of definite but inconspicuous ways, it was unnecessary for them to do more until actual hostilities began. If these took place at all, they would probably begin through Belgium and Holland. He did not believe that Germany would proceed to a sudden and flagrant violation of the zone. I thought this opinion quite likely to be right, since the violations to which Van Zeeland had referred had been taking place at least since they were reported by the French at Stresa nine months before. I added, however, that one of the results of the Italo-Abyssinian question was that Germany had convinced herself that France would only fight if French soil were violated. Hitler might therefore think France could be ignored in respect of the Rhineland. Van Zeeland suggested that, once the League had imposed its solution in the Abyssinian problem, it should try to settle the questions raised by Germany. He agreed with me when I said that Hitler did not want colonies for the sake of raw materials or colonization, but for reasons of power and prestige.

I thought it desirable that the French Government, as the power directly concerned, should make up their mind about the Rhineland. If they wished to negotiate with Hitler, they should do so; if they intended to repel a German invasion of the zone, they should lay their military plans. Any forcible action would depend on France, whose large army was still, on paper and in fact, far superior to that of Germany in experience and equipment. From my talk with Flandin, I had the impression that, while not prepared to use force to defend the zone, he was equally reluctant to negotiate about it. He might be tempted, however, to put the blame for inaction on either count elsewhere. I therefore telegraphed to Sir George Clerk, who had himself raised the question privately with Flandin, and warned him against a discussion of hypothetical cases. My message continued:

> Moreover, as the zone was constituted primarily to give security to France and Belgium, it is for these two Governments, in the first instance, to make up their minds as to what value they attach to, and what price they are prepared to pay for, its maintenance. . . . In the event of M. Flandin returning to the subject you should make it clear to him that, in the first instance, we expect to be told the views and intentions of his own Government, and you should not give him any encouragement to hope that His Majesty's Government would be prepared to discuss the matter on the basis of a statement of the British attitude.

I had called for reports from the General Staff and the Air Staff on the value to Great Britain, France and Belgium of the demilitarized zone.

On the basis of these I wrote in a note for my colleagues on February 14th:

... the disappearance of the demilitarized zone will not merely change local military values but is likely to lead to far-reaching political repercussions of a kind which will further weaken France's influence in Eastern and Central Europe, leaving a gap which may eventually be filled either by Germany or by Russia.

I set down my conclusions in the conviction that it was improbable that France would fight for the Rhineland:

Taking one thing with another, it seems undesirable to adopt an attitude where we would either have to fight for the zone or abandon it in the face of German reoccupation. It would be preferable for Great Britain and France to enter betimes into negotiations with the German Government for the surrender on conditions of our rights in the zone while such surrender still has a bargaining value.

* * * * *

Meanwhile, the German press became increasingly hostile towards Great Britain in the early part of February. At my request, Lord Cranborne had an interview with the German Chargé d'Affaires, Prince von Bismarck, on February 15th. Bismarck said that it was quite true that opinion in Germany had been profoundly shocked by what appeared to be a definite anti-German bias in the British press. There was also a tendency, he added, to throw the whole blame for British rearmament upon German rearmament. Later in the interview Bismarck complained of the harm done by the previous year's White Paper on disarmament. Lord Cranborne gave him no comfort, remarking that the Chargé d'Affaires must expect that in any White Paper on this subject the question of German rearmament must inevitably be mentioned. He also pointed out that the British public linked the question of German rearmament to certain speeches which had been made in Germany during the last few months, which connected the question of German armed strength with the satisfaction of legitimate or illegitimate German demands. Bismarck said that nothing Herr Hitler had said gave any colour to this supposition. Lord Cranborne reminded him that there were other speakers besides the Chancellor.

Events supported Cranborne's analysis. Speaking of foreign affairs at Magdeburg on February 21st, the German Minister of Propaganda, Dr.

Goebbels, dealt with the grumblers who always wanted to be told beforehand what the Government proposed to do. Even a chess player concealed his coming moves, he said. It was here that the people must show their confidence and they could rightly have confidence in a Government which had had so much success in the past. There were, in the sphere of foreign affairs, no differences in Germany and, when the Führer spoke, the world knew that Germany was speaking. Germany was today a fortified island of peace.

I had little faith in Goebbels' peaceful island. It was clearly necessary to increase our armed strength. When supplementary estimates were submitted to Parliament to cover the extra expenditure incurred in respect of our armed forces during the Abyssinian crisis, the Labour Party put down amendments to reduce all votes. In my speech of February 24th I said:

> If this country is to play its full part in a system of collective security, two conditions are indispensable. First, that the system should be truly collective and so powerful as to deter any would-be aggressor . . .; and secondly, that this country should be strong and determined enough in policy and in arms to play its full part therein. . . . So long as there is no general disarmament there can be no question of Great Britain continuing to practise unilateral disarmament. When I view the future of foreign policy I can see several different lines along which events may develop, but whichever course events may take the one element which appears as essential for every course is that Great Britain must be strong.

Later in the debate, Mr. Attlee stated that the Socialists would not be party to piling up armaments and following a policy of imperialism and alliances, but only to a policy of collective security through the League. He did not tell the House how security was to be provided when Germany, Japan and the United States were outside the League, Mussolini was busy breaking the Covenant, Soviet Russia was unpredictable and Britain was weak in armaments. The truth was that the active leadership of law-abiding countries had now fallen, perforce, upon France and Great Britain alone among the great powers. Moreover, the effect of Laval's conduct of policy over Abyssinia had been to weaken those who wished to found British policy on an Anglo-French alliance and to swell the number who were isolationist or considered that we must come to terms with Hitler, even though the price were high. The only line of conduct I could see open to a British Foreign Secretary was to increase our strength, hold on to the French alliance and, through the increased power of both, enforce respect for treaties and for the rights of nations.

* * * * *

Three days later, the French Chamber of Deputies at last approved the Franco-Soviet Pact. In his speech, Flandin offered to submit the question of the compatibility of the Pact and Locarno to the Permanent Court of International Justice at the Hague. Before I left London for the League Council meeting, I thought it prudent to send for von Hoesch. It seemed to me, I said, that Germany was taking this development too tragically. In any event, I continued, our own position was quite clear; we were not ourselves parties to the Pact, but it did not conflict, in our judgement, with the Covenant or with Locarno. This was on February 27th; on the following day there appeared in the *Paris-Midi* the account of an interview given by Hitler to M. Bertrand de Jouvenel, a French journalist, in which the Führer was reported to have observed:

> Is it not plainly to the advantage of both of our countries to keep on good terms? Would it not be disastrous for them to meet again on the field of battle? . . . I wish to succeed in achieving a *détente* with France. . . . It is extraordinary that you should still consider German aggression possible.

François-Poncet was instructed to take up Hitler's friendly references. I, meanwhile, arrived in Geneva for the Council meeting to find Flandin apprehensive of a possible invasion of the demilitarized zone. He feared that Mussolini would disinterest himself in Locarno. If there were a flagrant breach of the Treaty by Germany, France, he said, would instantly inform the League Council and consult Great Britain, Belgium and Italy with a view to concerting common action. Pending receipt of their views, France reserved the right to take any preparatory measures, including military ones, in anticipation of collective action by the League and the guarantors of Locarno. There was nothing to take exception to in this as a statement of intent, but it was one which must clearly be examined in London at once. I returned on the afternoon of March 5th and reported to the Cabinet that evening.

We had now to confront a situation which our own and French uncertainties in policy had helped to bring upon us. The French Government under Laval, having been cool towards their obligations to the League over Abyssinia, their successors now wished to invoke its authority over the Rhineland. To the British people this was a much more doubtful cause. There was not one man in a thousand in the country at that time prepared to take physical action with France against a German reoccupation of the Rhineland. Many went further than this and thought it unreasonable that Germany should not be allowed to do as she wished in her own territory, nearly twenty years after the end of the war. These opinions were represented among my colleagues, but I knew that I must rebuild the Anglo-French alliance for the sake of both our countries and that the Locarno Treaty must be kept alive, as the most effective deterrent to Hitler in the future.

I had first to try to forestall the growing threat of occupation. No declaration warning the Nazis off was possible, neither the British Government nor people would have been willing to carry it through, and it would have been useless to threaten when we were not prepared to act. The best chance lay in getting discussion going on some topic between the Locarno powers, then other opportunities might unfold. I therefore suggested to my colleagues that we should take the initiative towards the Germans, making a start at once with the question of the Air Pact. If I proposed this now, as the French Ambassador had urged me to do, I judged that the matter of the demilitarized zone would certainly be raised early, the French could then be drawn into the talks and the whole matter might yet be peaceably settled. My colleagues approved this suggestion.

Accordingly, I saw the German Ambassador the next day, and asked that he should refer to the Chancellor the possibility of the opening of serious discussions on the Air Pact. I drew his attention to the value of such an arrangement and suggested that we should try, through diplomatic channels, to agree on its principles. Herr von Hoesch was receptive and replied that the Chancellor had no objection in principle to an air pact. As he left, the Ambassador remarked that he had received warning from Berlin that a special messenger was on his way to London with an important declaration for me from the Chancellor. He therefore asked for an interview in order to deliver the message on the following morning, Saturday, March 7th. I learnt that the Reichstag had been summoned for noon on the same day.

Von Hoesch called on me at 10 a.m. He first raised a few desultory points in connection with a further Anglo-German Naval Agreement. The Ambassador then said: 'I have a communication of very great importance to make. I am afraid that the first part of it will not be to your taste, but the later portions contain an offer of greater importance than has been made at any time in recent history.' He proceeded to read out a memorandum repeating at length the German view that the Franco-Soviet Treaty violated Locarno. The crucial sentences were these:

> The German Government have continually emphasized during the negotiations of the last years their readiness to observe and fulfil all the obligations arising from the Rhine Pact as long as the other contracting parties are ready on their side to maintain the pact. This obvious and essential condition can no longer be regarded as being fulfilled by France. France has replied to the repeated friendly offers and peaceful assurances made by Germany by infringing the Rhine Pact through a military alliance with the Soviet Union exclusively directed against Germany. In this manner, however, the Locarno Rhine Pact has lost its inner meaning and ceased in practice to exist. Consequently, Germany regards herself for her part as no longer bound by this dissolved treaty. . . . In accordance with the fundamental right of a nation to secure its frontiers and ensure its possibilities of defence, the German Government have today restored the full and unrestricted sovereignty of Germany in the demilitarized zone of the Rhineland.

The German Government, however, 'in order to avoid any misinterpretation of their intentions and to establish beyond doubt the purely defensive character of these measures, as well as to express their unchangeable longing for a real pacification of Europe between states which are equals in rights and equally respected', offered to conclude new agreements. The memorandum spoke of another demilitarized zone, to be contributed to by France, Belgium and Germany and to be negotiated between them; non-aggression pacts to last twenty-five years were to be signed between the same states and maybe with the Netherlands, while Great Britain and Italy would act as guarantor powers. The German Government would also be willing to join a Western Air Pact and to enter into pacts of non-aggression with the countries to the east, including Lithuania. The final paragraph of the document stated:

> Now that Germany's equality of rights and the restoration of her full sovereignty over the entire territory of the German Reich have finally been attained, the German Government consider the chief reason for their withdrawal from the League of Nations to be removed. They are therefore willing to re-enter the League of Nations. In this connection they express the expectation that in the course of a reasonable period the question of colonial equality of rights and that of the separation of the League Covenant from its Versailles setting may be clarified through friendly negotiations.

I told the Ambassador that there was one observation I must make at once. I deeply regretted the information which he had given me about the action which the German Government were taking in the demilitarized zone. The Ambassador would understand that this amounted to the unilateral repudiation of a treaty freely negotiated and freely signed. I had a distinct recollection, I said, of the statement which the Chancellor had made to me at our first meeting in Berlin on the subject of Locarno, when he had precisely distinguished between that Treaty and the Treaty of Versailles and had emphasized that Germany had freely signed the former. Von Hoesch repeated that the Franco-Russian Pact had, in his view, violated Locarno, but I answered that this view was not shared by the other signatories of that Treaty. The effect of this unilateral repudiation of a treaty upon His Majesty's Government must inevitably be deplorable.

As for the German offers contained in the latter part of the memorandum, I said I would give them careful consideration, adding that the declaration about Germany's attitude towards the League was most important. Von Hoesch stated that this part of the memorandum was due to the Chancellor's desire to meet the views frequently expressed by the Prime Minister and myself in our speeches. We had emphasized that British policy was based upon the League and upon collective security. Germany was willing to share in such a policy. He must make it clear that there were no conditions attached to Germany's return to the League; she wished to return now. As for the Rhineland zone, the Ambassador added casually, a few small German detachments were today moving into the zone.

* * * * *

This was, so far, the most carefully prepared example of Hitler's brazen but skilful methods. The illegal deed was abundantly wrapped up with assurances for the present and promises for the future. Hitler, having no further demands, would rejoin the League at once and be on the side of the angels hereafter. The appeal was nicely judged. Most members of the British public would certainly see very little harm in Hitler's action. It would merely appear that he was taking full possession of territory which was his by right. The timing was perfect, including the usual choice of a weekend. France had a new Foreign Minister and a Government more than usually provisional, for a general election was due to be held. Mussolini had estranged himself from his former allies and was certainly cool to his Locarno engagements. Even so Hitler aroused resentment by his deed and created watchful foes. What is surprising is that this man could repeat the exercise so often in later years and still find many to excuse him. The answer is probably to be found in any intelligent dictator's understanding that the democracies are passionately sincere in their love of peace, and in his consequent ability to exploit this sentiment for his own ends. I could not forget how Hitler had spoken to me of Locarno; if he was not to be believed in this, he could not be believed in anything.

While von Hoesch was at the Foreign Office, Hitler addressed the Reichstag. All through the morning German troops were cheered into the Rhineland towns. Infantry battalions, supported by detachments of artillery, moved into strategic positions, with support from the air force. In all, 30,000 or more troops, as well as a large contingent of Green Police, were speedily placed in position.

I summoned the French Ambassador as soon as von Hoesch had left and told him that I deeply regretted Germany's action. I considered the denunciation of a treaty which Herr Hitler had freely accepted to be deplorable and I had already said so to Herr von Hoesch. The German memorandum would, however, require to be carefully considered by the Cabinet. I would arrange for this on Monday morning, after which we should want frank and thorough discussion with the French Government and with other signatories of Locarno. I felt sure that until this had taken place, the French Government would not do anything to make the situation more difficult, although there would no doubt be a considerable reaction on the part of French public opinion. There must be a steady and calm examination by all those interested, including, as M. Flandin had himself suggested, the Council of the League. Corbin replied that the German Government had themselves created an extremely difficult situation, not merely by denouncing the Treaty, but by sending in troops. The other powers were not being asked to negotiate, but were being put up against a *fait accompli*. I agreed and said I had already drawn the German Ambassador's attention to this result of the German Government's action. None the less, we must not close our eyes to the fact that counter-proposals were offered and these would have a very considerable effect on public opinion. We could not leave them unconsidered.

Flandin's proposal that the Council of the League should be summoned might imply that the French Government were not treating the matter as one of 'flagrant' violation calling for immediate counter-action under the Treaty. The summoning of the League Council was prescribed by the Treaty to deal with breaches of its terms which were not of that character. The definition 'flagrant' had, some argued, been intended to apply when the entry of troops into the Rhineland was an immediate prelude to an attack on France or Belgium. Since this was evidently not Hitler's present intention, nor within his power, the French Government were probably correct in their interpretation of Locarno, when they decided to summon the League Council. Moreover the absence of any evidence of an imminent German attack on France or Belgium reduced in many minds the cause for alarm. The Germans were to make use of this interpretation of the Treaty.

I had now to see the Prime Minister as soon as possible and discuss the whole situation with him, as well as the advice I proposed to give my colleagues. After short interviews with the Belgian Chargé d'Affaires and the Italian Ambassador, to both of whom I spoke as I had done to Corbin, I telephoned to Baldwin and set off at once for Chequers.

III

LOCARNO AND STAFF TALKS

March 1936

I see Mr. Baldwin at Chequers – My memorandum on the Rhineland – Lord Halifax and I visit Paris – The Locarno powers meet – We discuss sanctions against Germany – I see the German Ambassador in London – M. Flandin's views – M. Van Zeeland's views – The League Council at St. James's Palace – The League condemns Germany – Staff talks suggested – Herr von Ribbentrop reacts – Conservative doubts – 'The boys won't have it' – My speech to Parliament – Reflections on Hitler's technique

During the drive to Chequers I thought further about Hitler's action, which, by flouting agreements, had so havocked our policy of negotiation. Certainly France and Belgium would wish to condemn Germany for a breach of the Versailles Treaty and Britain could do no less. It was even possible that France might mobilize and invade the Rhineland immediately, calling for our assistance under Locarno, but Flandin, in our conversations at Geneva, had given no sign that he was likely to do this. I thought it more probable that France would appeal to the Council of the League and ask for an early meeting of the Locarno powers.

I told the Prime Minister of my interviews, gave him this summing up and spoke of the danger that would now beset the unity of the former war-time allies. Italy would not help, it was essential that we and the French should stay together, but this would not be easy. Baldwin said little, as was his wont on foreign affairs. Though personally friendly to France, he was clear in his mind that there would be no support in Britain for any military action by the French. I could only agree. I told him of the earnestness with which Hitler had spoken to me of Locarno. I could not believe him any more. Baldwin did not dissent and accepted that we must now await the French reaction, calling the Cabinet for Monday morning.

On my return to the Foreign Office, several important telegrams awaited me. I judged from Sir Eric Phipps' report that Baron von Neurath had had the grace to seem embarrassed when announcing to him Hitler's decision to march into the Rhineland. The Foreign Minister declared that Germany would be ready to negotiate at once, under conditions of complete equality with France and Belgium, about a demilitarized zone on either side of the frontier. The Ambassador asked von Neurath what value could attach to such an agreement after this unilateral violation, made despite the declared opinion of the other four signatories that the Franco-Soviet pact did not infringe Locarno. Some arbitration proceedings should have been suggested. Phipps told the Foreign Minister that this abrogation of a treaty, freely signed and often recognized by the Chancellor, would make a lamentable impression upon His Majesty's Government. It was, he added, the gravest event that had occurred since he had become Ambassador in Berlin.

* * * * *

Sir George Clerk reported that French reactions were as I had anticipated. M. Flandin had told him that the French Government did not wish to take up an isolated position, but to concert with the other Locarno powers in order to bring the matter before the Council of the League. The signatories of Locarno should meet in Paris and the Council in Geneva. Flandin said that, although no definite decision had yet been taken, his Government were thinking of asking the Council to condemn Germany's action, in terms like those used the previous April to condemn her rearmament. France had asked Belgium to join in communicating formally to the League Council the fact of Germany's violation. The French Government, Flandin concluded, were not definitely opposed to negotiation with Germany, but they had little confidence in her word and could not negotiate under the threat of the denunciation of Locarno, the menace of a remilitarized zone and the loss of French security.

With this temperate report before me, I set down my views for my colleagues. The Germans, I wrote, had violated Locarno by themselves deciding a question upon which they were bound to arbitrate. I drew attention to telegrams from Phipps showing that Hitler had acted against military advice and under the pressure of Göring and Nazi extremists. He had probably wished to move before British rearmament brought renewed confidence to the French and increased vigour to the League. The reoccupation of the Rhineland had deprived us of a useful bargaining counter, we should enter any negotiations with Germany at a disadvantage.

I then examined the German Government's new proposals, pointing out that the suggestion of a zone demilitarized on both sides of the frontier was impracticable and made purely for propaganda purposes. France had spent at least £40 million on the fortification of her eastern frontier and Belgium had also spent large sums. These fortifications allowed no space for a zone on the French and Belgian side. It was impossible, I wrote, to suggest that these two countries could consider scrapping their fortifications in exchange for a German promise, in which no confidence could be placed. Towards the other offers made in Hitler's memorandum, I expressed reserve. The conclusions I drew were:

> The myth is now exploded that Herr Hitler only repudiates treaties imposed on Germany by force. We must be prepared for him to repudiate any treaty even if freely negotiated (a) when it becomes inconvenient, and (b) when Germany is sufficiently strong and the circumstances are otherwise favourable for doing so.
>
> On the other hand, owing to Germany's growing material strength and power of mischief in Europe, it is in our interest to conclude with her as far-reaching and enduring a settlement as possible whilst Herr Hitler is in the mood to do so. But on entering upon this policy we must bear in mind that, whatever time-limits may be laid down in such a settlement, Herr Hitler's signature can only be considered as valid under the conditions specified above.

I warned my colleagues that it would be dangerous to accept any agreements with Germany which involved mutual restrictions or concessions of a serious character. Hitler might later repudiate them and we should find ourselves in difficulties. The French certainly would feel this danger over discussion of arms limitation, a guarantee of Austria or the cession of colonies. There would be no such disadvantage in an air pact or in Germany's return to the League.

I mentioned possible solutions of the immediate dilemma. While military action by France against Germany should be discouraged, one policy which might have its advocates would be for the Locarno signatories to call upon Hitler to evacuate the zone. It was difficult to suppose that he could agree to such a demand and it should certainly not be made, I advised, unless the powers concerned were prepared to enforce it by military action. M. Flandin had said that France would not act alone, but would take the matter to the Council. We should, I thought, support this course. The French public might, however, if further irritated or frightened, get restless at such a slow and indecisive action and demand armed retaliation such as, for instance, the reoccupation of the Saar. We ought to avoid such a development if we could.

As to tactics, I thought we must agree to a formal condemnation of Germany's action by the League, but resist any attempt to apply financial and economic sanctions, which would be too slow to be effective in this instance. I proposed that, in order to steady the situation, I should make a statement in Parliament at once about our intention to fulfil our Locarno obligations, despite the German abrogation of the Treaty.

On Sunday, March 8th, I sent this note to Vansittart, who approved it enthusiastically, describing it as lucid, dispassionate and realistic. His only suggestion, and a wise one, was that I should alter the wording of the statement for Parliament to make it clear that our guarantee was to France and Belgium alone, so as to give no possible offence to France. I agreed to this and decided that I would travel to Paris in time for a meeting of the Locarno powers on Tuesday morning. The French Ambassador, M. Corbin, assured me that his Government would not attempt to secure agreement on a resolution at that stage, though they would no doubt advance some proposals. I also learnt from Corbin that France and Belgium had already despatched their appeal to the League. All army leave in France had been stopped and the eastern frontier garrisons were being brought up to strength.

British opinion, so far as it was shown in the press, was even less sympathetic to the French case than I had expected. The first leading article in *The Times* on Monday morning, entitled 'A Chance to Rebuild', attributed Hitler's action to fear of encirclement. It drew a distinction between 'the march of detachments of German troops, sent to occupy territory indisputably under German sovereignty, and an act which carries fire and sword into a neighbour's territory.' It was my habit when I could to walk part of the way from my house near Manchester Square to the Foreign Office. I did so this morning, March 9th, taking a taxi to complete the journey. On arrival I asked the driver what he thought of the news: 'I suppose Jerry can do what he likes in his own back garden, can't he?' This, I was sure, represented the majority opinion in Britain, when once convinced that no German attack on France or Belgium was immediately intended.

French opinion, even as reflected in the Cabinet, was timid and undecided. Flandin tells us* that only four Cabinet Ministers were in favour of military action. Amongst these he includes himself, though the evidence of others, including Paul-Boncour, who was friendly to him, is against him on this point. Flandin also admits that no military plan of any kind existed and that he could not therefore tell the British in advance what the French intended to do. A further indication of the unready temper of the French Government at this time is Gamelin's admission that he had previously been asked by the Foreign Ministry to consider what price the General Staff would want for a negotiated German reoccupation of the Rhineland. Gamelin prepared a document accordingly.†

* * * * *

The British Cabinet met at 11 a.m. and approved the policy I had set out. It was decided, at my request, that Lord Halifax should accompany me to Paris. In view of the evident importance of this meeting, I thought it essential to have a senior colleague with me. I gave to the House of Commons that afternoon an account of my interviews of March 6th and 7th with the German Ambassador. I said:

> The course taken by the German Government in unilaterally repudiating obligations into which they have freely entered, and in simultaneously acting as if they did not exist, both complicates and aggravates the international situation. The abrogation of the Locarno Treaty and the occupation of the demilitarized zone have profoundly shaken confidence in any engagement into which the Government of Germany may in future enter.

I continued that if there should be an actual attack on France or Belgium while the new situation was being considered, His Majesty's Government would regard themselves as in honour bound to come to the assistance of the country attacked. No comment of any significance was made from any part of the House either upon this statement or upon the critical situation to which it referred.

Halifax and I left London that evening. The following morning we met the representatives of France, Belgium and Italy at the Quai d'Orsay, assembling formally in the *Salon de l'Horloge*, where I was so often to attend meetings in later years. While there was in our meeting

* Pierre-Étienne Flandin: *Politique Française, 1919–40*; Editions Nouvelles, 1948.
† General Gamelin: *Servir*; Plon, 1946.

all the seriousness which stamps an occasion expected by those present to influence their own and their country's future, there was no tension, shrill demands, or sharp answers. The temperaments of the three principal delegates had something to do with this, especially Flandin's. It was characteristic of him to keep discussion on a low note, his methods being those more often popularly attributed to Anglo-Saxon representatives than to his own countrymen. Equable, when things went ill, he was more given to mourn than to reproach. Then he would mark his regret or refusal in a manner which I was to know well, letting his hand fall across his body to his side, with a gesture between exasperation and acceptance.

Flandin began by saying that his Government had no intention of asking for any resolution to be voted at the meeting. On the contrary, what was needed was a serious and searching talk between all the powers affected by the German violation of the Locarno Treaty, so that they could take the same position at the League Council. I replied that this procedure seemed practical and satisfactory. The Italian Ambassador reserved his Government's position, because Italy was being subjected to sanctions. No Minister had travelled from Rome.

Flandin said there could be no possible disagreement over the events themselves. Germany had effectively reoccupied the Rhineland, not by symbolic detachments but in considerable force. She probably intended to construct fortifications there. France would ask the Council of the League to declare that there had been a breach of Articles 42 and 43 of the Treaty of Versailles. Once this had been done, his Government would put at the Council's disposal all their moral and material resources, including military, naval and air forces, in order to repress what they regarded as an attempt upon international peace. They expected the other Locarno powers and the members of the League to act with them to exert pressure upon the author of this action. The French Government did not wish to indicate by this that they would refuse to negotiate with Germany; but they could only do so when international law had been re-established in its full value, either willingly or unwillingly. Van Zeeland took up a similar position, reminding us that the zone was of primary importance to Belgium, a relatively weak country, which depended more than great powers upon respect for treaty obligations.

I noticed in Flandin's statements an assumption, which I thought ill-founded, that the League Council would endorse whatever action the Locarno powers took to put pressure upon Germany. I replied, however, that I was glad to hear from Flandin that there was no intention to try to reach decisions at the present meeting. The occasion for these would be at the meeting of the Council, the present was a useful opportunity for a preliminary exchange of opinions. In reference to our obligations under Locarno, I said that the position of the British Government had been made clear in my statement in the House of Commons the day before, these remained in force towards France and Belgium.

I would, I said, like to put some questions arising out of the statements that had just been made. The first was whether the French Government meant that there would be no negotiation until the Rhineland had been evacuated and, if so, how was it suggested that this result should be arrived at. Secondly, as M. Flandin had stated that France would place all her resources at the disposal of the League, I asked whether the French Government had any particular course of action in mind for the Council to follow. Flandin replied that the evacuation of the Rhineland ought to be demanded and obtained, if necessary by a successive series of sanctions, economic, financial and military. I next asked whether he was suggesting that these measures should be taken by the Locarno powers alone or by the members of the League or at least by the Council. Flandin thought that if the Locarno powers agreed, the Council would follow and recommend accordingly to other members of the League.

I told Flandin that I was not sure that the position of other members of the League was so certain or so simple as he supposed. I asked him what obligation the other members of the League had to proceed to military action in the present instance. Flandin mentioned the resolution passed by the Council of the League the previous April, condemning the repudiation of agreements and recommending sanctions in certain conditions. I replied that the resolution referred only to economic and financial action, not to the use of force. I could not see what obligation lay upon the members of the League, other than the Locarno powers, to proceed to military action. I had it in mind that, if Flandin persisted in his confidence, serious public differences might result when the League Council met. Finally, I asked whether the French Government contemplated the Locarno powers taking military measures by themselves. Flandin replied yes.

This put a sterner complexion upon our discussions and it seemed to me that we ought to probe French and Belgian intentions in a more restricted company. I therefore suggested an adjournment and a private meeting followed, limited to the principal representatives of each country. I then asked Flandin what he thought Germany's attitude would be if these successive stages of sanctions were applied. Both the French and Belgian Foreign Ministers replied they were confident that Germany would yield. Now was the moment to accept the German challenge. There was, Flandin admitted, doubt about Italy, but this could be dealt with, he commented cynically, if we could agree that, irrespective of her negotiations with Abyssinia, sanctions would be raised. This offer was made in the presence of the Italian Ambassador. It amounted to rewarding the earlier aggressor, in the hope that he would later help to contain the more powerful one. I did not think this a promising basis for a European policy. In any event, it seemed to me that the proposal, if seriously intended, should first have been made to the Belgians and ourselves.

Halifax and I both said that in our opinion, economic and financial sanctions could never be effective. The French Ministers did not dissent, adding that it would be no use entering on this course unless we were ready to see it through to a successful end. When we expressed some surprise that French public opinion should be prepared to consider using force against Germany, they replied that even the most pacifist sections realized that everything was at stake. If this comment were intended to convey that French opinion was united and ready to take military action, I thought it an exaggeration. Flandin's own account shows that even his colleagues were not agreed. 'When the Cabinet', he wrote, 'met in Paris there was pitiful confusion. . . . The War Minister stated to my utter stupefaction that all that was envisaged "was to man the Maginot line" and to move two divisions from the Rhône valley to the eastern frontier.' Action in the Rhineland would require general mobilization. Such action 'six weeks before a general election, what folly! declared some of my colleagues.'*

Van Zeeland supported Flandin's sentiments, saying that there was one chance in ten of war, but he did not share the view of French Ministers that complete evacuation of the Rhineland by Germany was an essential preliminary to all negotiations. He was less clear as to what intermediate course was possible, though favouring one which would combine the maximum pressure on Germany with saving Hitler's face with his own people. Belgium, he said, would take any action if France and the United Kingdom joined in.

I then had a conversation alone with the Belgian Prime Minister, at

* op. cit.

his request. Van Zeeland and I were friends and had confidence in each other. I had always found him intelligent and helpful in our various dealings at Geneva. Also, we were of the same generation, we had, therefore, no difficulty in thinking out loud together, as he expressed it. In agreement about the seriousness of the situation, we had to find some basis for negotiation and this must reduce the consequence of Nazi action. Van Zeeland made a number of suggestions. The most important of these was that we should find some additional guarantees to replace the security lost by the disappearance of the demilitarized zone. I asked the Prime Minister to elaborate. He wished Britain to state that Locarno would stand regardless of Germany's repudiation. Van Zeeland also proposed that the British Government should make their own obligation under Locarno precise and present it in a manner which would have more appeal to the public opinion of the countries guaranteed. For instance, could it not be said categorically that the intrusion of German troops upon French or Belgian soil would automatically involve a counter-action by British forces.

I liked this idea, which accorded with my conviction that, Hitler having broken the Locarno guarantee, we should substitute something more binding and more effective in its place. Since we could not join with the French in military action, this suggestion seemed to me the only way by which we could show Hitler that the breach of his engagements had not done him any good. M. Van Zeeland argued that the key to the whole position lay in London. He thought that much would be gained if further Locarno talks, and the meeting of the Council, were held there. This was sensible and, after some discussion with Flandin, we agreed that it should be done. Decisions had to be taken and our colleagues should be at hand to share in them.

In one respect, at least, the French and Belgian Ministers saw lucidly and straight. If Hitler were not pulled up now, he would be more troublesome to deal with, every year that passed. This was true, even if he were only checked by the counter-action and not overthrown. Here was a lesson I learnt, and was determined to apply if I could, twenty years later. A militant dictator's capacity for aggrandisement is only limited by the physical checks imposed upon him. Hitler was not challenged until his power had been swollen by a succession of triumphs, and the price to be paid changed the history of our planet.

* * * * *

The gravity of Flandin's statements exceeded anything which had been said before. The reoccupation of the Rhineland had been foreseen and its dangers forecast at Stresa a year earlier. Laval had mentioned the position in the zone in the French Cabinet on January 14th that year and Herriot had commented upon it as sufficiently anxious,* but we knew of no French preparations to meet this event, nor had we been asked to take part in any. We now know that none had been made. However, Britain had to take at its face value French insistence, with Belgian support, that sanctions, including the use of force, must be accepted. We also could not exclude the possibility that the French Cabinet, while not in truth determined on firm action, wished to put the blame elsewhere for not taking it, rather as the man who declares to spectators his intention of throwing himself over the cliff, hopefully glances at his coat-tails meanwhile. This impression was later borne out by the judgement of France's most experienced Ambassador, André François-Poncet, from his vantage point in Berlin. He wrote after the war:

> The [French] government of that time has been charged with weakness. Many have reproached them with missing an opportunity to inflict on Nazism a lesson which might have brought about its downfall. Later, we learnt that the Government examined very carefully the possibility of a military action. A force, made up of several army corps, would have entered the Saar and taken Saarbrücken. The civilian ministers strongly favoured this course; but all three service ministers opposed it. General Gamelin expressed the opinion that a military adventure, even of limited scope, involved risks which could not be foreseen and could therefore only be undertaken if preceded by general mobilization.
>
> The Government recoiled before such a contingency. They were neither sure of themselves nor unanimous. They could not be certain of the enthusiastic backing of public opinion, although it was hostile to Hitler's regime. Equally, the government could not rely on the approval of the Chambers. At this time, the pacifist tide still ran strongly and the idea of war was repugnant to the main body of opinion....
>
> ...If French forces had marched into the Rhineland, the German Army would probably have withdrawn behind the Rhine, leaving small numbers of troops to defend the outskirts of the towns and to hold up the enemy's advance. On the other hand, it is far less certain that the Hitler regime would have fallen because of such a rebuff. Already it held the country in a firm grip. More probably, it would have made a hot-headed angry reply and war would have broken out. What is unknown is whether at this point the

* Edouard Herriot: *Jadis*; Flammarion, 1952.

conditions would have been more favourable for us than in September 1939, and whether England and our other allies would have supported us. Historians, who in these matters have so many advantages over contemporaries, will be able to debate the question for a long time.*

I agree with François-Poncet's judgement and consider that in the event of a French force entering the Rhineland, there was at least an even chance of war. Through all these days, France was entitled at any time to say 'We march' and call upon us to follow. In fact, when the event was more than three days old, her Ministers advocated sanctions by stages, including military ones, to be taken by the Locarno powers. They are not to be blamed for this, but in view of their knowledge of British opinion, French Ministers must have realized what our answer had to be. Britain was profoundly pacific, as indeed was France, but British opinion also thought that the Germans, in this instance, had a reasonable case. Many people at home, as I told Flandin, had been influenced by France's unwillingness to conclude an agreement two years earlier, at a price lower than we now had to pay. No one in Britain felt enthusiasm for sanctions after recent experience of France's attitude to the Duce's African aggression. Laval's tactics had sapped the strength of the League. Moreover, whereas economic sanctions might influence the course of a long military campaign, they would certainly not affect Germany's rapid reoccupation of her own territory, already an accomplished fact. As for military sanctions, even a one in ten chance of war was a very serious risk for us. Britain's armed forces were inadequate and unprepared and our support, except at sea, could only be token.

France's best hope of expelling the Germans without provoking a European war would have been to put into action a carefully organized plan to seize instantly the key points in the zone. Such a plan did not exist. A counter-occupation of the Saar could not have been decisive, and would have evoked sharp resentment from a population recently rejoined to Germany by an overwhelming vote. World opinion would have regarded it as scarcely less blameworthy than Hitler's action and France would have been told that two wrongs do not make a right. Over all this contention and hesitation loomed the gravest of all dangers, proclaimed Anglo-French differences. A military operation by France could have divided her from her British ally as deeply as the occupation of the Ruhr and more deeply if blood had flowed. It must have weakened the alliance, it might have reduced the need for it. That

* André François-Poncet: *Souvenirs d'une Ambassade à Berlin*; Flammarion, 1947.

was all veiled in the mists of uncertainty. What I now believe to be true is that the French and Belgian Governments did not at the time have sufficient support in their public opinions to allow them to use effective force and that, being democracies, they could not have acted without it, even if they had wished to do so.

* * * * *

As so often happened in those days, Halifax and I had to cancel our flight back to London, because the weather was bad, and travel instead by rail and sea. As we journeyed we discussed our impressions. Evidently, our idea of condemning Germany's action, and then attempting to develop a negotiated European policy, had no chance of acceptance and our colleagues must be told so. We decided that if a negotiation were later to take place, France and Belgium must, in addition, at least be assured of our support in any new treaty replacing Locarno. The Cabinet met on the evening of March 11th and agreed that we must act along these lines. I thought myself that we might have to go further and agree specifically how help was to be given to France and Belgium in the event of an attack upon them.

With my colleagues' approval, I sent for the German Ambassador that night. I told von Hoesch that since my return we had held a Cabinet meeting and I could scarcely exaggerate to him the gravity of the view which His Majesty's Government took of the situation which had arisen. The Ambassador, I said, knew very well what we thought of the method adopted by the German Government in its violation of the Locarno Treaty. The German Government must also be conscious of the position in which they had placed us, in view of our Locarno obligations. They were aware what those obligations were, and they no doubt also had in mind that this country had a reputation for keeping its word.

I then reproached the German Government, in particular, for their action in relation to Belgium, who had signed no pact with Russia and along whose frontier lay the greater part of the demilitarized zone. I therefore asked the German Chancellor that as a contribution, the German Government should issue a declaration to the following effect: 'We have said we want the negotiation of a new pact because we want to create a new basis of peace in Europe. We meant what we said. To prove that we meant it, we will withdraw all but a symbolic number of troops from the zone and will undertake not to fortify the zone, at least for the period necessary for the negotiation of the pacts and for the regularization of the international situation.' I added that the German Government should find this course all the easier, because he himself had told me in London, and the Ambassadors of the Locarno powers had been informed in Berlin, that only a few symbolic German detachments would occupy the zone.

Herr von Hoesch said that while he appreciated the gravity of the situation, the French were surely using exaggerated language. It was true that the Locarno Treaty spoke of mutual assistance, but clearly this was only intended if an attack upon one of the guaranteed powers were impending. Obviously, that was not the case if Germany had made an offer of peace for twenty-five years. I replied that I did not think that the Treaty could be read in that way. The language applied to the demilitarized zone was precisely the same as the language applied to an attack on France or Belgium. It was for this reason that we viewed the situation so gravely. Moreover, though it was true that Germany had offered pacts for twenty-five years, might not other nations reply that no confidence could be placed in an offer of that kind, when Germany had herself deliberately violated a treaty to which she had set her name.

The Ambassador said that he thought he understood the position. He knew the French very well. The French argued that since Britain had so whole-heartedly supported the Covenant in recent months, they could rely upon Britain to stand by the Covenant on this occasion. But there was nothing in the Covenant which would justify the application of Article 16 in this instance. I replied that we were not discussing the Covenant, nor, so far as I was aware, was it a question of the application of Article 16 that was at issue. We had to consider, and all the signatories of Locarno had to consider, what their obligations were under that Treaty. I asked the Ambassador to represent the matter urgently to Berlin, and for a reply to be given to us before the Locarno powers met in London late the next afternoon. When Hitler's answer came within the time prescribed, he merely undertook not to increase the number of troops already in the Rhineland, but made no mention of the fortifications. I sent for von Hoesch again and told him that this was not a sufficient contribution.

During the afternoon and evening of March 12th, the Foreign Ministers of the Locarno powers met informally. Flandin's opening statement came as a surprise. He asked that the Council should invite Germany to withdraw her troops for the period of the negotiations, and should give at the same time what he called a '*quasi* promise' that if Hitler would agree to this, negotiations could begin immediately. It was understood that the result of negotiations would be to recognize the re-establishment of German military sovereignty over the zone and the military occupation of the Rhineland. Flandin said he made the offer on the understanding that the guarantor powers would undertake clear and automatic obligations in a new Locarno. I had no doubt that he wanted none of the ambiguity that had attached to the obligation of the signatories towards the demilitarized zone. The Foreign Minister explained that the French Government would ask for conversations between our General Staffs, in order to make immediate action possible. This offer was all the more remarkable because Flandin pointed out that, previous to the violation, Germany had had a considerable number of unauthorized troops in the zone. These he put at 20,000. He did not expect Germany to withdraw them, what she would be asked to withdraw were the nineteen battalions, the artillery and mechanized troops brought in as a consequence of her violation. Flandin added that, while the French Government might be willing to agree to legalize the presence of German troops in the zone, they could not adopt a similar attitude towards its fortification.

I said this was a proposal which could lead us to agreement. At my suggestion, Van Zeeland undertook to produce a resolution and to outline a procedure which we could discuss. The purpose of the resolution was to condemn Hitler's action and, while not refusing further discussions, to state that one of its results would be closer co-operation, including Staff talks, between the Locarno powers. I told my French and Belgian colleagues of my attempt to get a withdrawal of all but token German forces. They seemed to think that the effort had been worth making, although they were glum about the response.

Meanwhile, the British Chiefs of Staff had been examining our state of unreadiness. They reported on the evening of March 12th that if our armed forces and home defences were to have any value at all, mobilization of all three Services was essential. If there were any risk of a war with Germany, we should have to withdraw our forces from the Mediterranean, where all our efficient war material was concentrated. This, they said, applied particularly to the battle-cruisers *Hood* and *Renown*, which were the only ships in European waters capable of dealing effectively with the German pocket battleships.

* * * * *

Van Zeeland produced his memorandum the next day. M. Paul-Boncour, at this time French Minister for League Affairs, had now arrived from Paris and did not seem pleased. He said he was staggered to find how far we had travelled from French public opinion. A complete German withdrawal was an essential preliminary to talks. We had to point out that the French Government themselves had suggested a negotiation for the withdrawal of German forces, which would later return in full sovereignty. It did not seem possible to sacrifice lives in order to bring this about. M. Flandin argued that economic and financial sanctions with a blockade of Germany might suffice. We could not believe this and said so. Flandin then remarked that if he could gain some guarantees of security, he would at least have something with which he could do battle with his public opinion, and volunteered to produce draft proposals. I thought we had an obligation to try to give them substance.

The following evening, after the League Council had met, the French Foreign Minister told us, at a meeting of Ministers of the four Locarno powers, that he had consulted his colleagues by telephone and he was sorry to have to report that the French Government could not accept Van Zeeland's memorandum, even as a basis for further discussion. He regretted this because there were valuable features in the Belgian Prime Minister's proposals. He would have been prepared to negotiate on that basis, but his Government took a different view and he must accept it. Flandin, who seemed more than usually depressed, eventually agreed to prepare a paper showing French requirements from us in respect of security. I had been in part prepared for this event by a conversation I had had with him an hour or two before, which can best be described in the terms of a confidential message I sent to Sir George Clerk in Paris that evening:

After the lunch given by Mr. Bruce to the Council yesterday, M. Flandin drew me on one side for a few minutes' conversation. He intimated that he was a good deal perturbed at the reports which were reaching him of the play of internal politics in France. (From other sources I learn that M. Laval is doing his best to weaken M. Flandin's position.) In all the circumstances, M. Flandin thought it essential to gain time. He would, therefore, propose to me some such programme as the following:

If the Council were to meet on Monday and Tuesday they could take on the latter day a vote on the '*constatation*' of the violation, and on the Wednesday M. Flandin might return to Paris for a consultation with his colleagues, returning for a further meeting of the Council on Thursday. In the meanwhile M. Flandin suggested that we might perhaps avoid having any further meetings between the Locarno powers. He was afraid that the communication he would have to make to me at the meeting of the Locarno powers this afternoon would be a very unwelcome one, but he asked me not to take it too tragically. If I would content myself with saying that I would take note of what he said and suggest the adjournment of our meeting, this would assist him, for, in the meanwhile, in addition to preparing an official project, which he feared would be unwelcome, he would prepare an unofficial project, which would be his own, and which he would hand to me personally. This personal document would go as far as he could to meet our views, and he would much like my personal impression on it before he returned to Paris. The tactics he proposed to follow in Paris were to make plain to the French Government that what they hoped for was unattainable, and he indicated that what he hoped was to obtain a measure of agreement for his own personal project.

I replied that I fully appreciated M. Flandin's difficulties. For my part I was quite prepared to follow the procedure he had suggested, and receive any document that he might care to communicate to me. At the same time he would, of course, understand that it would not be possible for me to give him any views, even personal ones, at very short notice on a document of this importance, and therefore I hoped that he would let me have his proposals as early as possible.

I think that Flandin's spirits were in part affected by his delegation's contacts with members of the League. There was not the same unanimity now as there had been over Abyssinia. The Scandinavian representatives had set their pattern of neutralism and decided among themselves that they were under no obligation to take financial and economic sanctions against Germany. Colonel Beck, also, did not conceal that he would find sanctions most unwelcome. The Locarno Treaties, he said, had never been popular in Poland. He produced the mistaken argument that they were there regarded as a method of strengthening security in the West at the expense of the East; whereas the existence of the demilitarized zone afforded France a physical entry into Germany, through which she could, if need be, carry out her obligation to go to Poland's help. In general, members of the Council had not been slow to realize that those who were not signatories of Locarno, though they ought to condemn Germany, had no obligation to act against her.

In this tangled situation, I thought it desirable to get ready a statement of our opinions and again spent a Sunday drafting a memorandum. I set down my view of the future structure of security in Western

Europe, as a result of the German deed. First, there should be non-aggression pacts between Germany, France, Belgium and perhaps Holland. We would guarantee these. Secondly, a superstructure should be built which would consist of arrangements for mutual assistance between ourselves, France and Belgium. This would be open to Germany as a formality, though Hitler had expressed hostility to any such proposal. We must expect that France and Belgium would wish this pact to approach as near as possible to the 'automatic functioning' of which the Belgian Prime Minister had spoken. In any event, it was certain that both these countries would ask that the pact of mutual assistance should include agreements for contact between the General Staffs of the signatories. I thought that we had to be ready to do this.

* * * * *

When the Council met in St. James's Palace, its first sessions were spent in discussing and arranging for the presence of a German representative. Meanwhile, British, French and Belgian Ministers, with the Italian Ambassador as a spectator, continued their meetings. MacDonald, Halifax and Chamberlain attended at various times, while I presided throughout. My official staff included Sir William Malkin, whose drafting abilities were invaluable. Towards the end of the negotiation, when we were all tired, I complained to him: 'Will, we don't seem able to get this down right.' To which he justly replied: 'If you would only tell me, Secretary of State, exactly what it is you wish to say, I think that I can find a way to say it.'

A difficulty of these negotiations was that Flandin was apt to show understanding of, and indeed agreement with, the British point of view when alone with one of our delegates, and then to take a contrary position when we met together in conference. For instance, he told the Chancellor of the Exchequer, in a long private talk on March 16th, that he realized the British nation could not agree to sanctions against Germany as it had agreed against Italy. Yet two days later he was asking for sanctions against Germany, arguing that if the League would not carry out its duty now, it was the end of the League. France, he said, could not continue sanctions against Italy if they were not imposed against Germany. We replied that there was no analogy, members of the League having no obligation to enforce sanctions in this instance. When asked how military sanctions could be applied without war, Flandin said that he did not visualize them. He had in mind a financial sanction, milder than that applied against Italy and, possibly, a refusal to allow German ships to come to the ports of the Locarno powers. Flandin's text went far beyond this, as was pointed out to him.

These exchanges, not surprisingly, confirmed my conviction that neither before nor during the dispute were French Ministers firmly agreed upon a settled course of action. Theirs was the agony of an essentially pacific, democratic country believing that, in this instance, pacifism was not enough and searching for stronger action that might be carried through with the support of their own people, but without the risk of war. There was no such course, nor could the demilitarization of the Rhineland have been indefinitely enforced. It was knowledge of this which caused France's principal ally, though at heart equally confused, to desire negotiation before these events were determined to Hitler's advantage.

The time at our disposal in these crowded days was limited and the meetings had to be carried on into the small hours of the morning. A number of my senior colleagues were convened at regular intervals to hear reports of our discussions. These encounters were generally helpful, but from the first I met with some difficulty over Staff talks. John Simon was one of those who opposed them. He made his disagreement so widely known that Neville Chamberlain and I had to ask the Prime Minister to speak to him. Chamberlain supported me not least by seeing and guiding the press, and showing much patience during the negotiations.

Ribbentrop finally appeared on March 19th, when he made a discursive speech to no effect. The Council, with the single exception of Chile, condemned Germany's violation. On the same day, the Ministers of the Locarno powers concluded their negotiation in my room at the Foreign Office and made the results known. We reaffirmed our obligations under the Treaty and instructed our General Staffs to hold discussions so that we might be in a position to fulfil them. Germany was invited to lay her claim, that the Franco-Soviet Treaty was incompatible with Locarno, before the Hague court, and asked not to fortify the zone or increase her forces in it. The German Government were also invited to accept that an international force be placed in a narrow strip of German territory running along the frontiers with France and Belgium. If they would co-operate in this way, Britain, France and Belgium would take part in negotiations to examine Hitler's offers, revise the status of the Rhineland and draw up mutual assistance pacts open to all the signatories of Locarno.

These results were received by all in Britain with relief and by many with satisfaction. In so far as there was criticism, this favoured a discussion of Hitler's proposals, but complained of Staff talks to give our allies comfort. There was nowhere a suggestion that we should have been sharper with Hitler, still less that we should have joined in military sanctions in the Rhineland or the Saar. Opinion in France was divided. Flandin, while admitting that he would have liked more, claimed in his speech that he brought to France the consolidation of peace. 'We have been able to achieve this result', he declared, 'without any departure from the principles . . . laid down at the outset of the present crisis.' Of interest, despite a previous record of defeatism, was the private judgement of M. Joseph Caillaux, expressed to a member of our Embassy, that, 'contrary to what was asserted in the *salons* of Paris, French public opinion was much more favourable to Great Britain than might perhaps be realized in England or in English circles in France.' In parliamentary circles and among the political parties whose representatives he happened to have seen, M. Caillaux said, it had been realized that our rather slow methods had staved off the adoption of measures which would have resulted in war, for in his opinion a French mobilization would certainly have brought about war. Sir George Clerk later confirmed that, during the London talks, the French Government had shown themselves far more rigid than their own public opinion, or even than the French press.

I now had to see what I could get out of Ribbentrop. During several interviews he discoursed endlessly about honour and sovereignty, but made no concession. On the other hand, he reacted violently against the project of Staff talks. On the afternoon of March 25th I told him that these were intended strictly for the purpose of providing against acts of unprovoked aggression. I had a fairly clear recollection, I said, that more than once the German Chancellor had told me that he would have no objection to such arrangements, since Germany did not contemplate aggression. I therefore asked whether the Chancellor would reaffirm this.

Ribbentrop did not like this request. He at once stated his personal conviction that his Government would not agree. Since Germany had only a few troops in a still unfortified zone, facing a French force of 200,000 men, what earthly purpose could Staff conversations serve? I replied that it was not a question of the military value of such conversations. What we were trying to do, as I had very many times explained to him, was to find some means of reassuring opinion in

France and Belgium, which was profoundly disturbed by the action of the German Government. Ribbentrop would not give way and indeed had the impudence to say that he much hoped I would make no reference to Staff conversations in my speech to Parliament the next day.

Dr. Schmidt, who interpreted at this conversation, wrote many years later:

> The phrase 'Staff talks' to Ribbentrop at that time was like a red rag to a bull. He felt instinctively that concrete military arrangements between England and France would be a very high price to pay for the militarization of the Rhineland. He protested against them to Eden and other Englishmen in much the same way as Stalin now protests against the military agreements within the framework of the Atlantic Pact.*

Ribbentrop was not so far out in his estimate. Hitler's reoccupation of the Rhineland could have divided France from Britain, as well as giving the German army control of the zone. The alliance, having survived that test, was able to go forward, not in strength, unhappily, for in weapons we continued to lag woefully, but on a treaty basis reinforced by Staff talks, and in fair confidence and intimacy as the dangers grew.

* * * * *

Before the debate on the ratification, I had a few words with the Prime Minister in his room in the House of Commons. Though he did his best to conceal it from me, I could see that he was anxious. He admitted that Kingsley Wood had been to see him to tell him, in characteristic phrase, that the Staff talks were unpopular on the Conservative back benches. 'The boys won't have it' was his verdict. I did not believe this judgement to be well-founded, but the report was useful, for it stimulated me to make a freer and more vigorous speech than I might otherwise have done. Speaking on foreign affairs as the Minister responsible for their conduct can be a frustrating business. Words have to be so carefully weighed that it is rash to depart from the typewritten script, and yet diplomatic jargon is as ugly to listen to as any other. I had, however, given so much thought to the argument I was to present in this debate, that I decided I could rely mainly on memory. The result was better than I had dared to hope; the House was understanding and the majority of Members was fervent in support.

I began by an expression of thanks to the nation for the restraint which had been shown and which was all the more remarkable in that

* Dr. Paul Schmidt: op. cit.

it was assumed and maintained on a purely voluntary basis. Perhaps, I said, if the same conditions of liberty of the press and speech, and the same distinction between liberty and licence, were today observed throughout Europe, we should not now be confronted with the problems which unfortunately beset us. If, in giving an account of our stewardship . . .

I should depart somewhat from the usual formal restraint in speeches on international affairs, I shall justify myself in so doing because what I have to say is in the main spoken, not to nations overseas, but to the people of my own country. It is imperative in the present international situation that this country should visualize its problems in a true perspective. We can only do that if I, as Foreign Secretary, speak frankly.

I then distinguished between what might be national sentiment and what were, for good or ill, our national obligations:

Likely enough, there may be many people in this country who say to themselves now: 'In our judgement the territories of France and Germany should be treated on exactly equal terms.' It may be that people feel that, but those are not the terms of the Treaty of Locarno. Those are not the terms of the treaty of which we are guarantors and which has formed a main element in the security of Western Europe for the last ten years.

I then gave an account of the demilitarized zone, recalling that after the war, the French aim had been to guarantee their country's security by the separation of the Rhineland provinces from the rest of Germany. The French Government were persuaded to abandon that position by means of an arrangement which comprised a fifteen years' occupation of the zone itself, its permanent demilitarization and, most important of all, a guarantee of security from ourselves and the United States. That guarantee was never forthcoming. The United States failed to ratify and, since our ratification was dependent upon theirs, the guarantee came to nothing. Then the demilitarized zone was embodied in the Treaty of Versailles. There were time limits to certain provisions of that Treaty, notably in respect of the occupation of the Rhineland, which came to an end before the time had expired. There was no time limit for this demilitarized zone. It was, under the Treaty, an enduring undertaking. I continued:

The House may imagine that this zone forms part of the Treaty of Locarno because from the outset France and Belgium clamantly demanded it. That is not the position at all. This demand for the demilitarized zone figured in the original demand put forward by Germany, who herself initiated the conversations which led to the signature of the Locarno Treaty. It figured from the start in the original German proposals, and I do not think it is very difficult, looking back, to see why that was. The Locarno Treaty was signed not very long after the Ruhr, and it would not be astonishing if the German Government of that day reflected that some guarantee from us in those conditions would be of service to her.

I recalled that successive governments in Germany and in France and Britain had reaffirmed Locarno. The present Chancellor of the German Reich had reaffirmed it. If Germany wished to modify any part of this Treaty, negotiations were open to her. That was the course which, under the Treaty, she should have pursued when claiming that the Franco-Soviet Pact was inconsistent with the Locarno Treaty. Germany could have gone to the Hague court, as the French Government were willing to do. Germany did not do so, but ignored Article 3 of the Treaty and decided for herself that the Franco-Soviet Pact was incompatible with Locarno. After referring to Belgium's special position, 'more than half this zone runs along the Belgian frontier', and paying tribute to the 'cool courage and constructive statesmanship of M. Van Zeeland', I summed up the earlier part of what I wished to say to the House:

> I believe it to be the judgement of this country that even those . . . who think that Germany has a strong case deprecate the fact that she has chosen to present it by force and not by reason. . . .
>
> There are some who may regard us as freely and fortunately placed at this anxious moment in European affairs, some who regard us as arbiters with a fortunate destiny. But we are not arbiters in this business; that is not so. We are guarantors of this treaty, and as guarantors, for good or ill . . . we have certain commitments and they are very definite.

I listed the articles of the Treaty which detailed our commitment and concluded:

> It cannot be said, in the light of them, that we are uncommitted and free arbiters. Our position is far different. . . . I am not prepared to be the first British Foreign Secretary to go back on a British signature; and yet our objective throughout this difficult period has been to seek a peaceful and an agreed solution. I consider that we are bound to do so by article 7 of the Locarno Treaty itself, which states:
>
> 'The present treaty, which . . . is in conformity with the Covenant of the League of Nations, shall not be interpreted as restricting the duty of the League to take whatever action may be deemed wise and effectual to safeguard the peace of the world.'

We had sought conciliation, I said, in the spirit of that article.

Having given the House an account of the negotiation in Paris and London, I dealt with the undertakings we had given for three different stages: those pending negotiation, those that could form part of the general settlement which we hoped to bring about and, finally, those we were prepared to give in the event of a breakdown of negotiations. In reference to the Staff talks, I said that the undertaking was deliberately designed 'to compensate for the loss of security suffered by France and Belgium at this time owing to the violation of the demilitarized zone.' It was strictly limited and clearly defined. In this respect, I argued, it differed from the Staff conversations of the years before 1914, when we had no political commitments. Our obligations in the present instance were clearly set out by treaty and the only question that could be at issue was whether or not we were prepared to make arrangements to meet these obligations, should the need arise. To those who wished that we should turn a blind eye to all that happened in Europe I replied:

> . . . that is to take no account at all of realities. We have never been able in all our history to dissociate ourselves from events in the Low Countries, neither in the time of Queen Elizabeth, nor in the time of Marlborough, nor in the time of Napoleon, and still less at the present day, when modern developments of science have brought striking force so much nearer to our shores. It is a vital interest of this country that the integrity of France and Belgium should be maintained and that no hostile force should cross their frontiers. The truth is, and I say it with apologies to my right hon. Friend the Member for West Birmingham [Sir Austen Chamberlain], there was nothing very new in Locarno.

With this Sir Austen agreed. I continued:

> It was a new label, but it was an old fact, and that fact has been the underlying purpose of British foreign policy throughout history. To affirm it again is a threat to no one, for its purpose is purely defensive, and in every single article where these conversations are mentioned it is clearly shown that they only apply in a case of unprovoked aggression. I hope that those conditions will never arise, but I am quite confident that they are much less likely to arise if we make quite clear our own position.

Our world-wide obligations were those of the Covenant of the League. We were not adding to them except in the area already covered by the Locarno Treaty. In that area there was to be no new commitment, only arrangements for the more effectual fulfilment of commitments which already existed. I concluded:

These issues far transcend the ordinary limitations of party politics. When the whole future of our civilization may be at stake, who cares about party labels? I would ask for the continuance of that support which has been so generously extended to me in the last few weeks, and I would ask it because I believe that the purpose for which I am working—with how many errors and through how many discussions—is one which is shared by the great majority of the men and women of this country. It is to maintain peace, to strengthen the League, to uphold the sanctity of treaties, and above all to seek, without respite, to fashion from the troubled present a future which may be freed from the haunting fears that shadow our own time.

The chief criticism came from Lloyd George and the chief support from Austen Chamberlain. The Labour Party complained of the Staff talks and of the idea of an international force stationed on German territory, but in the main their dislike was for a regional arrangement for security, which they considered a departure from pure League doctrine. This was not true, any more than it was true of the Treaty of Dunkirk, signed by Mr. Bevin eleven years later, since the arrangement was, as I said, 'not inconsistent with the Covenant but complementary to it and, in fact, the idea of these regional pacts has been blessed by Geneva.' The disagreeable reality was, however, becoming very sharply evident, that the League depended for its survival upon close Anglo-French co-operation. It was the chief justification of the arrangements I was presenting to Parliament that they had realized the unity of the two countries after ten hazardous days.

My speech, and the outcome of the debate, brought me a flood of kindly letters. Two gave me special pleasure, one from Baldwin and one which he sent me from that most warmhearted and unpredictable man, Josiah Wedgwood. I also learnt that the French liked the speech and that Ribbentrop did not.

Hitler's technique was to accompany each blow with an offer nicely calculated to tempt the victim. Even if the offer did not compensate for the blow, it made it all the more difficult to strike back. It is pardonable that this tactic should have enjoyed some success when it was first employed, but it is extraordinary that it should have continued to do so. Perhaps, however, this was because there was more eagerness to accept the offer than to return the blow, which was human but costly.

If, as Clemenceau tells us, politics is the art of the possible, Hitler's occupation of the Rhineland was an occasion when the British and French Governments should have attempted the impossible. Academically speaking, there is little dispute that Hitler should have been called to order, if need be forcibly, at his first breach of an accepted international engagement. But nobody was prepared to do it, in this country literally nobody. Even the most warlike proclaimed that the League Council must be called, which would not have endorsed the use of force. Military action was only possible by France immediately. Had it been taken, it would only have been successful if aimed at the Rhineland, where fighting would probably have resulted. I doubt if world opinion would have approved in 1936, and for a melancholy reason, the conviction that international order must be upheld was already fading. The growing tendency to find excuses had been fertilized by the Abyssinian failure.

All of which has its lesson for today. Once the obligation to uphold international engagements is evaded, pretext will follow pretext, until the structure of confidence is destroyed and respect for treaties hangs 'like a rusty mail in monumental mockery'. Asia and Africa have already furnished their examples in flouting engagements with impunity. The West must be on its guard, therefore, and be punctilious in fulfilling its word, to the newfound ally as to the old one, to West Germany as to France. For the issues that concern any of the free nations concern us all. The Soviets will not then be deceived into thinking that they can divide us, and there will be peace.

IV

FAILURE AND SOME RECOVERY

March – August 1936

I draw three conclusions – Staff talks begin in London – The questionnaire to Herr Hitler – He becomes more strident – Mr. Baldwin on foreign affairs – Bad news from Abyssinia – The Emperor in retreat – Bombing and gas warfare – The Fascists triumphant – My first meeting with M. Blum – Sir Samuel Hoare rejoins the Government – Mr. Chamberlain changes policy – The sanctions front crumbles – The Emperor attends the League Assembly – Danzig – Three-power talks – Signing of the Anglo-Egyptian Treaty

I had now to consider the impact of these events upon the balance of power in Europe. The League, as originally conceived, was to include all independent nations, who would act together against any of their number transgressing the Covenant. Now the gangster powers outside were approaching equality in strength with the decimated League. While I hoped that Germany would return to the League and that Italy would not leave, I had to take account of these shifts in power. They compelled me to three conclusions: to strengthen our alliances, hasten our rearmament and inform British opinion, beginning with my colleagues.

I circulated to them two despatches from Berlin, from our Military Attaché and the Ambassador, adding my own comments. Colonel Hotblack reported that the German General Staff preferred separate pacts with each country, against which remark I noted that it would obviously suit the Nazi book if conflict with a small state could be localized. Most German officers, Hotblack wrote, accepted as a matter of course that Germany would expand eastwards and many were eager to play their part. I thought that this showed there was no moderate party in Germany, any more than there then was in Japan. Rather, there were two sets of contenders who wished to arrive at the same end at a different pace. Sir Eric Phipps' despatch showed that German youth was being imbued with dreams of expansion eastwards and westwards. He contrasted the warlike tone of private Nazi publications with the reassuring terms of Hitler's public declarations.

Of these despatches I wrote:

> They present a gloomy view of the future for Europe. I fear that any rosier view would be illusory. They will not, of course, make any difference to our intention to probe and explore Herr Hitler's offers and to construct, if possible, something reliable out of them. But we should not be under any illusion as to the aims that underlie German policy. The Germany of today (and, I fear, of tomorrow, in view of the forces of miseducation which are perverting her youth) has no intention of respecting the integrity of her smaller neighbours, no matter what papers she may sign. There will always be the mental reservation that national interests override treaty obligations.
>
> We must, I submit, shape our policy and preparations according to facts, however hard and unpleasant, to which we cannot close our eyes, and at the same time endeavour to educate our own public to a realization of these facts.

I drew the conclusion:

> It seems to me more than ever necessary to do all we can to increase the *tempo* of our own re-equipment.

Ribbentrop did his best, on March 27th, to persuade me that Staff conversations between Britain, France and Belgium would prevent negotiations, desired by the people in his country and my own and in France, from proceeding in a calm atmosphere. These talks, he said, would stifle the voice of the people. In his opinion, Staff talks were Staff talks, and it would be quite impossible for the Germans to understand the necessity for a step of this kind. I reminded Ribbentrop that on March 7th Germany had acted by force, not by argument. He must not be surprised if fear had been created. The German Government had been asked to do three things and had not accepted any of them. I said that Staff talks would begin at once, being limited to considering the means by which we might resist aggression. I repeated several times that they were intended to give that sense of security without which negotiations could not begin. After this exchange, Herr von Ribbentrop flew back to Germany, where the plebiscite campaign to approve the Rhineland occupation was under way.

Hitler had just declared: 'If other peoples cling to the letter of the treaty, I cling to everlasting morality. If they confront us with texts, I confront them with the eternal rights and eternal duties of my people.' I thought that the process of unveiling Nazi intentions in more precise terms must be continued. Accordingly, I suggested to the French Ambassador that the British Government should draw up a number of questions which might be put to the German Chancellor. He seemed to like the idea and this was the origin of our questionnaire, which Hitler was to resent and some in Britain to criticize.

At the end of March, Ribbentrop returned to London bearing a memorandum from Hitler, who proposed a four-month standstill, during which Germany would agree not to reinforce her troops in the Rhineland, so long as the French and Belgians would act in like manner on the other side of the frontier. Negotiations would then begin for non-aggression pacts with Germany's western and eastern neighbours. I asked Ribbentrop whether the German Government would agree not to fortify the zone in this interim period, if the French would do the same on their side. Ribbentrop replied that they could give no pledge, although it would be impossible, for technical reasons, to construct fortifications in the next four months. This was not worth anything.

An interview which took place soon after Ribbentrop became German Ambassador on August 11th, is still in my mind. It was characteristic of him. He talked at length about his close friendship with the Führer and what an advantage it was going to be for us to have an Ambassador in London who knew him so closely and could give us his thought. He proceeded to do so. When he drew breath I thanked him, but said that there was another aspect of his mission I wanted to talk about. We were glad to hear the Führer's opinions from him and we had, of course, also an Ambassador in Berlin whose duty it was to report to us the opinions of the German Government. What we looked for particularly from Herr von Ribbentrop was that he should report to his Government the views of His Majesty's Government and the opinions of the British people, so that there might be no misunderstanding at any time on that account. This was received in sulky acquiescence.

* * * * *

I thought that the moment had now come to hand the French and Belgian Ambassadors the letter promising Staff conversations. This I did on April 2nd, despite further voluble protests from Ribbentrop. As I attached importance to these conversations, I was glad to learn that the Deputy Chief of the French General Staff, General Schweisguth, had told our Military Attaché in Paris that an agreed plan to meet immediate needs could quickly be evolved in broad outline. It would then be the task of the General Staffs to fill in the detail. Arrangements for the conversations were quickly made. Sir Eric Phipps telegraphed that these had intensified the feeling of pessimism in responsible German circles. Even in the Nazi Party itself, doubts were being entertained for the first time about the wisdom of Hitler's decision to enter the Rhineland.

French, Belgian and British officers of all three services met on April 15th in London, the visiting powers being represented by their Deputy Chiefs of Staff. Lieutenant-General Dill, later to be Chief of the Imperial General Staff and a most valued friend, represented the British army. In the course of two days' discussions, the Naval Staffs exchanged information about ports, communications, liaison officers and signalling codes. Our army representatives gave details of the British forces available in an emergency, which were slender enough, and asked for facts about facilities at the ports and transport to the assembly areas. It was agreed that these matters should be studied in the War Ministries, after which the results would be transmitted through the Military Attachés. Meanwhile, the airmen compared respective strengths and discussed the availability of aerodromes. The French and Belgian representatives all declared themselves satisfied with the talks, which laid the foundations for the closer military collaboration later enforced by Hitler's aggressions.

Several further meetings of the Locarno powers took place in the earlier part of April and my proposal to put a number of questions to Hitler was discussed. The French Government favoured this action and later told us which questions they wished to include. The Foreign Office drew up a memorandum covering the French questions and adding some more of our own. During a weekend which I spent with him in Dorset, Lord Cranborne and I combed this draft carefully. I showed it to Baldwin and later to Neville Chamberlain, with whom I had a luncheon alone on April 27th, our relations then being close and friendly. He made no objection.

* * * * *

It was some time before I secured final agreement from my colleagues to the questionnaire. Some members of the Government appeared unable to understand why we need ask any questions at all, ignoring the fact that we sought information only to expose Hitler's intentions. We based our inquiries on his own memoranda of March 24th and March 31st. The words 'provocative' and 'pinprick' figured largely at these meetings and reluctantly I had to agree to cut out or modify portions of my draft, depriving it, in my judgement, of some of its usefulness, part of the purpose having been to educate opinion outside Germany, whether Hitler replied or not. In particular, some questions I wished to ask were robbed of much of their point and punch.

I told the French Ambassador on May 4th that I thought it better for the questions to come from ourselves alone, as guarantors of the Locarno Treaty. In this Flandin acquiesced. It was one of his last decisions as Foreign Minister, for the French elections had resulted in a victory for the left. Sarraut and Flandin soon resigned, and were replaced by M. Léon Blum and M. Yvon Delbos. This was not to the taste of Hitler, who, as Phipps reported, had hoped to negotiate with M. Laval. But for me a new and much happier era of relations with France now opened up. From this moment until my resignation in February 1938, French Ministers and I worked together without even a momentary breach of an understanding which grew increasingly confident.

Though I learnt that Hitler had been irritated by newspaper forecasts of the terms of our questionnaire, this seemed no reason for not putting it. On May 6th I instructed Phipps to seek an interview with him to search out the ambiguities in the German memoranda. First, we had to know whether Germany now regarded herself as in a position to conclude 'genuine treaties'; this was Hitler's phrase. We then asked whether the German Government drew any distinction between the Reich and the German nation. I had in mind that Hitler might later regard himself as protector, or even ruler, of German communities in Austria, Danzig or Czechoslovakia. If Hitler still had claims to make, the world had better know them. Accordingly, our despatch inquired whether 'Germany now considers that a point has been reached at which she can signify that she recognizes and intends to respect the existing territorial and political status of Europe, except in so far as this might subsequently be modified by free negotiation and agreement.' While accepting Hitler's proposed non-aggression pacts, we asked for them to be extended to cover what seemed to us areas of danger, Soviet Russia, Latvia and Estonia.

Phipps delivered our questionnaire to von Neurath, but had to wait more than a week before the Chancellor would receive the document, which had in the meantime been published because of a leakage to the press. This had the unexpected result that other countries could tell me what they thought before Hitler spoke. On May 11th, when I was at Geneva, Beck expressed himself as very well pleased. Our note had had a good reception in Poland and his Government were particularly gratified by our question on Hitler's attitude to the political and territorial status of Europe. This, Beck said, was just what everybody wanted to know from Germany. His Ambassador in Berlin had reported that the Nazis disliked two features of the questionnaire in particular. First, the mention of Soviet Russia and, secondly, the form, which, they considered, seemed to show that doubt was conceivable about their good faith. The next day Litvinov, who never concealed his apprehension about Hitler's intentions, said he was generally satisfied with our note. He hoped that we should now leave the Germans to answer it. In Paris, M. Blum told our Ambassador that the policy of his Government would be stiffer towards Hitler than that of previous administrations. I believed this to be the correct line to follow, a conviction which was reinforced by Sir Eric Phipps' account of the long-awaited interview with Hitler on May 14th.

The Chancellor said at the outset that since the new French Government would not be in the saddle for several weeks, he would hold up his reply to our questions. There followed an outburst against bolshevism and the alarming progress it was making in Spain and France. Hitler refused to conclude any pact with Russia. Towards the end of the interview he indulged in a tirade about 'equality of rights'. The Führer declared that the Treaty of Versailles was divided into two parts. He had altered that which dealt with the limitation of German sovereignty, but accepted that the other, dealing with territorial clauses, could not be altered except by agreement. Hitler's conduct soon belied the assurance.

I was already receiving reliable reports that German fortification of the Rhineland was proceeding apace, while the tone of Hitler's speeches was becoming noticeably more strident and hectoring since his overwhelming success in the plebiscite six weeks earlier. On May 1st Phipps reported that the Chancellor had delivered a harangue, saying:

> Just because we have drawn up far-reaching plans, just because we have assumed enormous tasks, we want to keep the peace. This is what so many wretched little politicians in other countries are incapable of grasping. . . . Lies are being spread abroad that Germany will tomorrow or the next day fall upon Austria. [Laughter.] Who are these elements who will allow no

peace, no rest and no understanding, who intrigue incessantly and sow distrust? Who are these people? [Tumultuous applause and cries of 'the Jews!']

Disquieting despatches and telegrams from Germany were constantly circulated to my colleagues. I thought, however, that they should see this specimen and other evidence of what was being said and thought in Berlin. At my request, our Embassy there and the Central Department at the Foreign Office prepared a summary of Hitler's odious creed in a memorandum of eleven pages, liberally illustrated with revealing extracts from *Mein Kampf*. At least there should be no pretext that unpleasant realities were not exposed to those with whom responsibility lay.

* * * * *

Two extracts from my diary at this time are revealing about the Prime Minister's attitude to foreign affairs. The first is on May 20th:

> Talk with S.B. in evening. Did not get much out of it save that he wants better relations with Hitler than with Musso—we must get nearer to Germany. 'How?' I asked. 'I have no idea, that is your job.'

The second is a fortnight later:

> Saw S.B. Warned him that object of German foreign policy was to divide us from French. Hence Anglo-German Naval Agreement and Ribbentrop's repeated missions here. At the moment . . . we had asked Hitler a number of perfectly reasonable questions which in fact he could only fail to answer if his intentions were bad. It was therefore most important that he should be given no occasion to cloud the issue; above all that S.B. should not. I think S.B. saw the force and was rather alarmed.

* * * * *

The Rhineland crisis dimmed events in Africa but did not help the Abyssinians. In the first days of March, Flandin resisted the oil sanction by calling for another effort of conciliation. This came to nothing, as it was bound to do, for the Duce would not be satisfied with anything less than the complete subjugation of Abyssinia and the Emperor was resolved never to accept this. Mussolini made use of the Western European crisis to regroup his forces in Abyssinia and intensify gas attacks and bombing raids, which spared neither Red Cross units nor undefended towns. The effect of the gas was cruel and militarily severe, for the Ethiopian soldiers fought barefoot and suffered terrible burns. In the last half of March, the Fascist armies began to make swifter progress towards Addis Ababa from the north. Flandin himself told me that the French General Staff had thought it would take the Italians several years to conquer Abyssinia. François-Poncet reported that this was also the opinion of the German General Staff, and our War Office thought likewise. These forecasts proved false, although their authors could well plead that they had not foreseen the extent to which the arms embargo would leave Abyssinia defenceless, nor had they allowed for the use of poison gas.

On the afternoon of April 3rd an Abyssinian envoy, specially sent from Paris, called on me to deliver a message from his Foreign Minister in Addis Ababa. The military situation was very grave. The army was tired, he said, as a result of its continuous bombardment and subjection to gas. There was, he believed, imminent danger of a complete collapse, although the Emperor was still at the front. The envoy asked what advice I could give his Government. I could only say that we had already asked that the powers most concerned should be summoned at Geneva and suggest that he should support our action. The next morning Italian aircraft arrived over Addis Ababa itself, which was completely open to attack. The Italians had now broken the northern front at the battle of Ashangi on March 31st and the Emperor was in retreat.

In reply to an inquiry from me, Sir Sidney Barton telegraphed that the most urgent and tangible help that could be given to the Abyssinians would be the elimination of gas from the Italian armoury. 'The whole atmosphere here is poisoned, both literally and metaphorically.' He added:

> Quite apart from questions of international obligations, the continuous use of gas complicates enormously the problem of security for foreigners in this country, while even the French express great apprehension at its future reactions for colonial powers.

We had been pressing for the Committee of Thirteen to meet and on the morning of April 8th, it did so, under the chairmanship of Señor de Madariaga, who did everything in his power to give point and decision to its deliberations. At the first meeting reports on the use of gas were discussed. There was agreement that efforts must be made to collect the most reliable information available. M. Flandin's only contribution was to ask whether there was any record of inquiries into the Abyssinians' use of dum-dum bullets and into atrocities committed by them. I had to remind him that the prohibition in the 1925 Gas Protocol, which had been signed by both parties to the present dispute, was absolute. There was no provision that the use of gas might be permitted on account of the methods of warfare adopted by the other belligerent. Accordingly, the question must be examined at once if international conventions were to have any meaning in the future.

During an adjournment, a private Anglo-French meeting was held. It was sour and showed that no agreement was possible. I said that, in my view, the League of Nations had lost greatly in prestige in many countries during the last few weeks. A despairing message had now been received from the Abyssinian Government. I wanted to know if the Committee was to do no more than to suggest that its chairman should see the Italian representative and thus give the Italian Government an opportunity for further delay. The Committee of Eighteen, which bore political responsibility, should now, I considered, be handling matters. Sir Robert Vansittart put the same opinion at this time to the French Ambassador in London, saying that the continuance of the present state of affairs exposed the League to ridicule. I returned to the subject of poison gas, pointing out to Flandin that, apart from the horror in Abyssinia, this was a question which must cause great uneasiness to our two countries. The threat was not to Africa only. Dictator states might well use gas in Europe, while democratic countries were quite unprepared for such warfare.

Flandin said that he had no objection to an inquiry, provided that it related to all alleged violations of the laws of war. I replied that there was a distinction between the irresponsible atrocities of undisciplined military forces and the use of poison gas which could not be other than a governmental act. Flandin agreed, and said that the Italians were very stupid to use this form of warfare. But he doubted the wisdom of issuing a formal condemnation at a moment when an attempt was being made to bring hostilities to an end, for this might disturb the negotiations. He was also anxious to avoid any form or suspicion of an ultimatum, or any threat such as the fixing of a date for the Committee of Eighteen.

In such conditions there was little any committee could achieve, as my telegraphed account shows:

> Today's meetings of Committee of Thirteen were very difficult. M. Flandin argued the Italian case with confident cynicism and did what he could to obstruct any action by the Committee either against the use of gas by the Italians or in favour of pressure for cessation of hostilities. In urging an inquiry into the use of gas and an early result to the effort of conciliation I received encouragement only from the Australian and Danish representatives.

The following morning a group of Abyssinian representatives, headed by M. Wolde Mariam, the Abyssinian delegate at Geneva, called upon me. They said that even now their Government would not accept anything which went so far as the Hoare–Laval plan. The delegates had been expressly instructed from Addis Ababa to tell me that the Government regarded Great Britain as having done everything in her power for Abyssinia. They fully recognized that such help as they had received was entirely due to us. If the League had not achieved all they had hoped for, the Abyssinian Government appreciated that this was in no way the fault of His Majesty's Government, and wished to say so. I thought this as generous and brave as when, five years later, the Greek people showered flowers upon our troops in defeat as they had done in victory.

I had already asked Sir Eric Drummond and his colleagues in Rome to obtain renewed assurances from Suvich that Italian aircraft would not bomb undefended Addis Ababa. The French, German, Belgian, Greek, Turkish and Egyptian representatives all took this action. The United States Ambassador did not make a similar *démarche*, but contented himself with sending a letter giving a list of Abyssinian towns in which his country had interests in one form or another. Sir Ronald Lindsay's impression, that the United States had for some time past lost interest in Abyssinia, seemed sadly justified.

Profound pessimism prevailed at Geneva. I telegraphed:

> This was expressed to me today by M. Titulescu, amongst others, as being the consequence of M. Laval's behaviour last summer as exemplified by his continued refusal to co-operate whole-heartedly with the League, culminating in the Paris proposals of last December. '*Ce cochon de Laval,*' M. Titulescu graphically described him in his peroration to me. Most members of the Committee of Thirteen are now acutely conscious of their quandary created by the desperate condition of the Abyssinian army and the intransigence of Signor Mussolini.

Mussolini, in a speech to his Council of Ministers that morning, welcomed recent victories because they brought Italy

> . . . nearer to the realization of her first objective, to attain which she was compelled to have recourse to arms . . .; that is to say, the security of our colonies. This security will be reached in full with the total annihilation of the Abyssinian military formations, and this annihilation can neither fail to take place nor be delayed.

Even when the situation was as desperate as this, Flandin wasted much time in legalistic argument, contending that our committee was not competent to investigate the question of gas warfare. Madariaga answered admirably that common sense should prevail over legalistic interpretations of the Covenant. In his view, it was well within the mandate given to the Committee of Thirteen by the Council to inquire into the truth of statements which had been made to it. The sharpness of the divergence was sometimes expressed. I reminded Flandin that all the difficulties with which the Committee was faced flowed from a flagrant violation of the Covenant and the invasion of the territory of one member of the League by the armed forces of another.

Flandin had now reached the point of saying that the mediation of the League in this dispute would be deplorable. I replied that Abyssinia had said she would negotiate only through the League. Did he seriously suggest that the League should say to the victim of aggression 'We are not concerned in the solution of the dispute'. As Flandin held to his position, an adjournment was the only course remaining, while Madariaga was charged with the almost impossible task of trying to bring about Italo-Abyssinian talks. But for pressure from the British delegation, the adjournment would have been longer than six days. This was a miserable period of dissension and the price of Anglo-French discord.

Back in England, I motored to Trent Park to see the Prime Minister, to whom I gave an account of events at Geneva. He was more vehement against Mussolini than I had ever known him. 'The man is a savage,' he said, but Baldwin still hankered after some arrangement, if it could be reached. I told him that Abyssinia even now would not accept terms like those of the Hoare–Laval pact. At this stage I thought it of no avail to press for new sanctions, which would certainly not be agreed to by the French. The best we could do was to hold the sanctions front together, even though for the purpose of domestic politics it would be attractive to prove that we had tried to do more and had not been supported. The only remaining hope was that the Abyssinians could hold out until the rains, which I thought they still might do if they were not lured into another pitched battle, but I did not realize the deadly hurt done to Abyssinia's resistance by the repeated gas attacks. I repeated these opinions and an account of my talk with Baldwin in a letter to Halifax thanking him for his help.

No compromise was possible between the Italian and Abyssinian positions. That was true at the beginning and remained true to the end. Mussolini would only negotiate with Abyssinia direct, away from

Geneva, and would not call a truce meanwhile. When I returned to the League meetings, Madariaga told me that he was disturbed at the attitude which the Secretary-General had taken up. At luncheon on April 16th I found this well justified. Avenol surpassed the French Ministers in excuses for Mussolini's attitude. I asked whether it was the view of the Secretary-General of the League that the victim of aggression was not entitled to ask that negotiations to settle his fate should take place at Geneva in the presence of the League. To this I got no clear reply.

Senhor Vasconcellos, the stalwart chairman of the Committee of Eighteen, told me that it might have to consider whether sanctions should be extended, if other members so wished. He added that the Portuguese Government were not much in favour of the application of an oil sanction only, as this would not be likely to produce its effects within any useful time. He said that if it could have been applied last October or November, it would almost certainly have brought the war to an end within three months. But for M. Laval, he remarked, the present situation would never have arisen and the whole business would have been over before now.

The Council was summoned for April 20th, when I reaffirmed that the British Government would continue the existing sanctions and be willing to consider any further economic and financial ones. The Council, with the exception of Aloisi, agreed that conciliation was at an end and that we should continue the present sanctions, meeting again in the middle of May. French elections were imminent and no more vigorous action was possible, but I thought we should keep the front in being, though the chances for the Abyssinians were fading fast. Another consideration in my mind was that, as I telegraphed to London:

> An open Anglo-French rift upon this issue must have an unwelcome reaction upon the general European situation and the attitude of the two dictators. Moreover, there is no financial or economic sanction which could be serious, the effect of which would be immediate, and it is probable that the fate of Italy's Abyssinian campaign will depend upon the power of the Emperor to keep his weakened armies in being during the next few weeks.

* * * * *

One of the tragedies of the Abyssinian campaign was the suffering of the wounded. The Emperor, in an interview when his usual calm dignity seemed tinged with despair, told Sir Sidney Barton that his armies had been demoralized by the use of gas, while the civil population had been bombed. He had even been deprived, through the attacks on the Red Cross, of the medical aid organized by foreign sympathizers. After the heaviest fighting in the war, at Ashangi, no medical help at all had been available for large numbers of gassed and wounded.

On May 1st the Emperor assembled his Ministers and dignitaries and announced his departure from Abyssinia. I had already offered transport for the Empress and her family from Djibouti to Haifa, and now arranged that Haile Selassie should accompany them in a British warship. Shortly after his departure, looting began in the capital and the business quarter of Addis Ababa was laid in ruins. Over two thousand refugees were shepherded into the British Legation, from which parties constantly set forth to rescue Europeans in danger.

On May 5th I told the House of Commons that the greatest credit was due to the Legation staff and above all to Sir Sidney Barton, whose conduct of affairs throughout had been beyond praise. The next day, we had to withstand our first assault from Opposition critics. In my reply, I reminded the House that we had always known that sanctions would not be immediately effective. I complained that the Opposition voted against all the armaments estimates. 'The truth is', I said, 'that while hon. Gentlemen opposite protest to support the League with horse, foot and artillery, they really only mean to support it with threats, insults and perorations.'

By this time Marshal Badoglio had already entered Addis Ababa and, on May 9th, the King of Italy proclaimed himself Emperor of Ethiopia. Drummond reported a comment on the Abyssinian campaign made by King Victor Emmanuel to the Comte de Chambrun. His Majesty remarked that the Italian armies had had great good fortune. The offensive taken by the Emperor at the battle of Ashangi had been the decisive point. He had been very ill-advised to attack; if he had retired, the Italians would hardly have been able to follow quickly enough to bring him to action. As a result, their difficulties would have been very great and their subsequent victories unobtainable. If the Emperor's army had been intact when the rains began, the King doubted whether the campaign could have been carried, at any rate in such a short time, to a successful conclusion. The King was probably right and this was one of the conditionals of history, but the immediate consequences of the dictator's triumph were real enough.

* * * * *

On my return from an abortive meeting of the League, I stopped in Paris for my first informal conversations with M. Blum on May 15th. This I enjoyed, reflecting ruefully how much it must have advantaged our two countries if he had been our partner in the last two years of missed opportunities. The French Prime Minister was very cordial in his welcome and, I considered, sincere in the emphasis he laid upon Anglo-French co-operation. In this respect, and in his antipathy to dictatorships wherever they might be, we were at one. I rejoiced at the improvement he would be on his predecessors.

M. Blum was anxious to secure international disarmament, without which collective security could not work effectively. I had to reply that while I shared his conception of the ideal to be aimed at, it seemed to me hardly attainable at present, in a world in which dictatorships played so large a part. Blum somewhat reluctantly assented. He then began to talk about his relations with the Labour Party in England. He wanted no possibility of misunderstanding on this point, he said. He was a Socialist, and naturally had friendly relations with the Labour Party. But in no circumstances would he work with that Party in order to embarrass His Majesty's Government. This pledge he fulfilled with complete loyalty.

As I grew to know Blum better, I several times met him in his own beautiful house on the Ile St. Louis in Paris, where he had a rare library in which it was a delight to browse. Many of his books had been presented to him by their authors. I was in those days, and still am, an admirer of the writings of Anatole France. On one occasion, Blum gave me a copy of *La Rôtisserie de la Reine Pédauque*, inscribed to him by the author and re-inscribed to me. On another, I gave Blum an early edition of one of Fielding's novels. These were the pleasant by-paths of politics. I respected Blum's intelligence, integrity and courage and our friendship was never marred by a serious difference or even a misunderstanding. After my resignation, we did not meet again until the war was over and his long ordeal of imprisonment behind him. He came to see me in London, frail but with all the natural dignity I had remembered, which no harsh treatment could impair.

At our first talk, we had to discuss Mussolini's campaign in Abyssinia and its consequences. Blum asked me for the views of the British Government, since he was most anxious to conform to them if possible. I replied that I had not yet had an opportunity to consult my colleagues, after the Geneva meeting from which I was returning, and I would like a little leisure to turn the matter over in my mind. I had noticed that the representatives of many countries at Geneva thought the League would be faced with two alternatives in June. The first was that we should say we had in no way changed our original attitude to the dispute. We were not prepared to modify our verdict about aggression or to recognize its fruits, and we were determined to maintain, and if necessary increase, existing sanctions, until Mussolini was willing to negotiate a peace upon terms within the framework of the League and in the spirit of the Covenant. There were formidable difficulties in this course. If it could be successfully prosecuted it would almost certainly lead to war and, in view of the collapse of Abyssinia and the Emperor's flight, the task of restoring anything like the *status quo ante* in Abyssinia would be prodigious. The second alternative was to admit that sanctions had failed to attain their object, but to refuse to recognize Italy's conquest or to revoke the League's previous verdict upon her actions, and to consider what could be done to organize a more secure order of things in the Mediterranean. Blum did not appear to be much attracted to either of these courses.

We then considered the possibility of negotiating a Mediterranean Pact while sanctions were still in force. We both liked that idea, if it could be realized. In any event, I was convinced that we must take some decision to give confidence and support to those powers in the Mediterranean which had taken part in sanctions against Mussolini. Towards the end of our talk the Prime Minister commented on the difference of outlook between public opinion in our two countries. Apparently, some people in Great Britain were criticizing His Majesty's Government for their failure to lead in the Italo-Abyssinian dispute. In France, however, M. Blum declared, 'you are regarded as a sanctionist power *par excellence*. Clearly, therefore, I cannot take a lead in advance of what you would be prepared to do. My public would never understand that at all.'

In a reference to the relations of Signor Mussolini and Herr Hitler, Blum expressed his conviction that it would not be possible to keep these two dictators apart. Sooner or later their policies would converge. He was afraid that British public opinion was at the moment making the same mistake about Hitler as French public opinion had made about Italy; the latter had attempted to secure Mussolini's support against Hitler, and now it looked as though we were attempting to secure Hitler's support against Mussolini. I assured Blum that no such intention was in our mind.

* * * * *

Back in England, I was soon involved in discussions on the future of sanctions. Pressure to remove them mounted rapidly at many meetings held with colleagues. The arguments were economic as well as naval and political. Unemployment was high, especially in South Wales, an area hard hit by the loss of our coal trade with Italy. Our exports and re-exports to Italy had been valued in 1934 at £11 million, a trade which had now dwindled to nothing. While sanctions continued, our non-sanctionist competitors, especially Germany, would certainly entrench themselves in the Italian market. In addition, the Admiralty and Chiefs of Staff were anxious to bring the Home Fleet back to its own waters and relax some of our stringent precautions in the Mediterranean. For eight months our fleet had been held in readiness for war. No leave had been granted and the problem of manning the ships was becoming acute. I was warned that we should shortly have to call up reservists, unless the position could be eased.

These were hard arguments, much urged by my colleagues in these weeks. Some of them advanced the theory that to raise sanctions at once would prevent Mussolini from moving towards Hitler. I was not so hopeful, nor did I think it acceptable for Great Britain to reduce her strength in the eastern Mediterranean. Our position in Egypt, the Persian Gulf, the Mediterranean and Red Sea basins, and the Middle East, had been assured by British sea power. Events had now placed in doubt our ability and determination to maintain that predominance and I refused to agree to any weakening of our position.

Towards the end of May Baldwin told me that he had asked Hoare to rejoin the Government as First Lord of the Admiralty. He went on to assure me that I need not be worried that Hoare would interfere with foreign affairs. The importance of this, according to Baldwin, had been explained and accepted. I felt no enthusiasm for this appointment in itself and some disquiet at its possible consequences. I explained that there would now be three former Foreign Secretaries in the Cabinet and that although I was sure MacDonald would always be as helpful as he could, this was not a particularly happy state of affairs for me. Baldwin spoke comfortably, repeating his assurances. Lord Halifax, however, was much more outspoken when we met the next day. He criticized Baldwin sharply for yielding to Hoare's importunity. A few weeks earlier, Sir Samuel had made a speech in Parliament about Baldwin so adulatory as to be embarrassing to all who heard it.

* * * * *

I saw Grandi on May 28th, when he indicated that the Duce sincerely wanted an improvement in Anglo-Italian relations. He did not conceal that sanctions had had some effect. The Ambassador then spoke of the fact that both ends of the Mediterranean were in British hands and I surmised that Mussolini had ambitions about the eastern end of that sea. At this stage, my preference was that the League should take no decision until the Assembly met in September. I hoped that if we continued to apply sanctions, we might trade their withdrawal against a declaration by the Italian Government not to raise an army in Abyssinia, to maintain the 'open door' in trade, and to respect her obligations in future. With this Neville Chamberlain agreed, though most of my colleagues did not. I thought that Mussolini might truly want a *détente* but, as I said at the time, I had no confidence in its duration once it had ceased to suit him, nor did I wish to enter upon private negotiations with Mussolini, whose dispute was with the whole League.

In the early days of June, as it became clear that no Abyssinian Government remained at all, I grew less confident that any good purpose was being served by continuing sanctions, a point of view strongly held by Sir Austen Chamberlain, who had been in the lead against the Hoare–Laval proposals. Some supporters of the League in Britain, and one or two of the smaller Mediterranean powers, were ready for us to close the Suez Canal, but there was never any hope of collective agreement about this. On the contrary, the sanctions front was now weakening and, according to French information as early as the middle of May, thirteen countries were already in serious breach of their undertakings. While, therefore, I had to accept that the negotiable value of sanctions was a wasting asset, I was still of the opinion that they ought to be taken off, as they had been imposed, collectively. The Italians hoped that the sanctions front would crumble away gradually, not only for political reasons. The Under-Secretary for Trade and Exchange was reported to have declared in a private conversation that he did not believe it would be in Italy's best interests for all the powers to raise sanctions together. This would mean a demand for a large immediate payment which Italy could hardly afford. But if one country after another defected, a settlement could more advantageously be reached with each one separately.

In the disintegrating atmosphere, Neville Chamberlain's speech on June 10th was to me unexpected, not least because his support of my arguments for maintaining sanctions had been so consistent and firm.

The Chancellor of the Exchequer, addressing a Conservative political club that evening, put forward some 'provisional conclusions' which might be drawn from our failure to stop Mussolini. He referred to the idea that if we continued with sanctions, or intensified them, the independence of Abyssinia could be preserved. Chamberlain went on:

> That seems to me the very midsummer of madness.... Is it not apparent that the policy of sanctions involves, I do not say war, but a risk of war?... Is it not also apparent from what has happened that, in the presence of such a risk, nations cannot be relied upon to proceed to the last extremity until their vital interests are threatened?

Whatever the merit of this argument, its timing was explosive. I had known nothing of Chamberlain's intention to express these sentiments, which aroused a storm in the House of Commons. Baldwin dissociated the Government from them and Chamberlain wrote to me, saying that he felt he owed a word of explanation, and perhaps of apology, for not having consulted me before making the speech. He had been so full of work that he had had to put off consideration of what he should say until the last moment. He was on the Treasury Bench until 7.30 p.m. and had not had time to put his thoughts into a form which he could show me. He was sorry that I had been embarrassed by his speech. Chamberlain having been such a steadfast colleague, it did not occur to me that the lapse could be other than accidental and I had no wish to make anything of it. But the Chancellor of the Exchequer's diary for June 17th, as quoted by his biographer, gives another emphasis:

> I did it deliberately because I felt that the party and the country needed a lead, and an indication that the Government was not wavering and drifting without a policy.... I did not consult Anthony Eden, because he would have been bound to beg me not to say what I proposed.... He himself has been as nice as possible about it, though it is of course true that to some extent he has had to suffer in the public interest.*

Despite Baldwin's truthful denial of Government responsibility, the sanctions front was now out of joint. There was no dispute that sanctions would have to be called off soon, the question was where and when. I concluded that while it would be easy, as I said in the debate which followed, to leave the lead to someone else, this was not the right attitude for Great Britain to take. As early as May 20th, in the

* Keith Feiling: *Life of Neville Chamberlain*; Macmillan, 1946.

transitional period between the Sarraut and Blum Governments, Léger told our Ambassador in Paris that, in his opinion, the new French Government would insist at the forthcoming Council meeting on the immediate raising of sanctions. On legal grounds, he said, there was nothing in the Covenant which justified their maintenance once fighting had stopped. On practical grounds, he had come to the conclusion that the maintenance of sanctions would be of no avail. M. Delbos told Sir George Clerk that the French Government were not prepared to take the initiative in removing sanctions, but that he desired to keep in step with us. This seemed only natural in a newly elected government of the left, but placed more responsibility upon us. The French Ambassador, while admittedly without specific instructions on the point, on June 17th, said that he was confident his Government could not disagree with a declaration by us that the continuance of sanctions would serve no useful purpose.

On the next day I told the House of Commons that this was our opinion, although we would wait for the League as a whole to pronounce. I said that so far as we were aware, no Abyssinian government survived in any part of the Emperor's territory. This was a situation which nothing but military action from outside the country could possibly reverse. I added this indisputable truth:

> If the League means to enforce in Abyssinia a peace which the League can rightly approve, then the League must take action of a kind which must inevitably lead to war in the Mediterranean.

None the less, I now consider that it would have been to the advantage of the League powers to hold together and act together when the League met. Chamberlain's judgement of the national interest was hasty and mistaken. Nothing was gained by our earlier declaration and some feathers lost.

There remained the problem of our allies in the Mediterranean. To maintain the alliance built up during the sanctions period, I announced that the assurances we had given to some Mediterranean powers in the previous December would continue during the period of uncertainty which would follow the raising of sanctions. I added that Britain would now maintain permanently in the Mediterranean a defensive position stronger than that which existed before the Abyssinian dispute.

The debate which followed was vehement and accusing, with Mr. Lloyd George at the height of his debating powers. He marred his argument, however, by one passage near the end of his speech. Having dubbed us cowards for abandoning sanctions, Lloyd George declared that, whatever government was in power, the British people would never go to war again for an Austrian quarrel. I urged Baldwin, who was to follow him, to seize the opportunity to show that this speech contradicted itself, but he would not. Sir John Simon was not the man to miss such an opening. A few days later he dealt ruthlessly with this distinction of taste between the causes for which the British should fight. Simon asked:

> How is that consistent with the view that any and every violation of the Covenant calls for forcible action on our part and that if we do not take that forcible action we are cowards? What is the difference from the League point of view between the violation of Austrian integrity and the violation of Abyssinian integrity?

No doubt His Majesty's Government had a share of the blame to bear for events in Abyssinia, but they neither committed the crime nor favoured it. They would even have liked to halt it without accepting the consequence, that its perpetrator could not be brigand in one continent and custodian of the law in another. There was a failure to see in advance that any effective sanctions, even economic ones, must carry with them the risk of war. This was also a general fault, most conspicuous in the Opposition, which called for sanctions while voting against armaments and saw no nonsense in it. The British Government's failure was one of will. They had not a strong enough conviction to see the business through and there was a constant tug of war between those who wanted the Stresa front and those who wanted the League. Once Mussolini had determined on the conquest of Abyssinia, they could not have both, though many among them wanted to and some tried to, with damaging consequences. It needed a firm faith to counter and corner Laval and to hold him to his part in enforcing the law, but our persuading hand faltered, perhaps from weakness, though more probably from uncertainty which way it should point.

A few days earlier Mr. Menzies, then Attorney-General of Australia, dined with me and gave a vigorous report of the backing which was being given to me in the Dominions. He begged me not to worry unduly, but to go ahead confident that I should get fair support for a decided line. Such reflections did not prevent these days from being very unhappy ones for me. I did not feel called upon to resign, for I had not had control of policy, either in the earlier stages of the dispute, or during the critical first period in the imposition of sanctions, when my own decisions would have been more persistent and far-reaching than those which were taken. Nor would the Abyssinians have remained unarmed if I had had my way.

I went to Geneva a few days later in a depressed state of mind, to witness the final stages, for the time being, of the Abyssinian conflict. The Emperor attended the Assembly. His behaviour was, as always, brave, calm and dignified. In that great audience, his was probably the only mind at rest. He had done all he could, and gazed in quiet contempt at the hysterical Fascist journalists, hurling vulgar abuse, who had to be removed from the gallery. Titulescu, enraged at their conduct, rose in his seat, crying '*A la porte les sauvages!*'

Of all the public figures then in a position of power and playing a major part in world affairs, only one still rules as I write,* his authority undiminished, the Emperor Haile Selassie. Our next meeting was to be in a house in Khartoum four years later, when, with General Wavell, I went to discuss what could be done to enable the Negus to campaign for the liberation of his land.

* * * * *

These were wretched days at Geneva. In a week two incidents expressed the darkening scene. One morning during an Assembly session about Abyssinia, with M. Van Zeeland in the Chair and the hall little more than half full, I suddenly heard a report and saw a figure fall on the benches at my right hand. Until the police ran up to him, I did not understand what had happened. A Czech spectator had shot himself dead after a cry of warning, apparently about the fate of small countries. His death was a message sealed to his countrymen with his life.

That same evening the League Council had to discuss Danzig. I was for the moment its President and still rapporteur. The session was public and at times sharp, the League's High Commissioner, Mr. Lester, and Herr Greiser, the representative of the Senate, were present. Greiser was even more truculent than usual, his Prussian manner being scarcely veneered even when speaking to the President. Colonel Beck, the Polish Foreign Minister, a few places off on my left, stirred uneasily. Eventually Greiser accepted the Council's recommendation, but with

* November 1961.

so many reservations and in a manner so threatening, that I thought we could not send our High Commissioner back to Danzig without taking some precautions. I declared the item concluded, formally thanked the High Commissioner and the Danzig representatives, and turned to the Secretary-General beside me to ask him to obtain Beck's agreement for a secret meeting of the Council as soon as our business was finished. At this moment a clamour broke out from the stands where the press sat in rising tiers on the side of the room facing my seat. Many of the pressmen were on their feet and most were shouting. Above the noise, Mr. Dell, doyen of the British journalists, was to be seen gesticulating to me frantically and exclaiming, for some reason in voluble but almost incoherent French: '*Monsieur le Président, la Presse du monde insultée.*' Not having seen the incident, I was able, in the manner of Mr. Speaker, in the House of Commons, to say with truth that I had not noticed anything and that we had better get on with the next business. I was soon informed that on his way out of the Council Chamber, Herr Greiser had turned derisively to the ranks of the press, some of whom may have been baiting him, and cocked a snook at them.

The meeting over, we adjourned for our closed session. After consultation with Beck, I said that we could not send our High Commissioner back to Danzig in these conditions, without some specific undertaking for his safety. I asked the Polish Foreign Minister to inform us whether Polish forces would be prepared to go to the assistance of Mr. Lester, should he call for them and should they be needed. Colonel Beck replied quietly that they would and that the necessary instructions would be sent that night to the Polish armed forces to be in readiness. I asked the Council to take note and endorse this decision. They did so unanimously.

* * * * *

As the summer passed, Hitler showed no sign of returning an answer to our questionnaire, which was hardly surprising if, as I concluded, he did not want to make his intentions known. Not unnaturally, however, the French and Belgian Governments were impatient to hold a preparatory meeting of the other Locarno powers, even if the Germans would not attend. I agreed, but insisted that Italy was to be invited. Mussolini soon solved that problem by saying he would not come while sanctions were still in force. The British Government then asked the French and Belgian representatives to London, and

Blum and Delbos, Van Zeeland and Spaak foregathered with Baldwin and myself on July 23rd. I found our allies ready to make a reasonable agreement with Germany and Italy, if there were any like desire on the part of Hitler and Mussolini. With the authority of the British Government, I took the opportunity of this meeting to reaffirm that our country would stand by her engagements, in the event of unprovoked aggression upon the territory of France and Belgium.

At the conclusion of our discussions, we agreed on a statement inviting the German and Italian Governments to attend a five-power meeting, which would negotiate a new settlement in place of Locarno. Both Governments accepted before the end of July. Von Neurath, however, told Vansittart in Berlin that Germany, while agreeing in principle to this plan, could not be ready for the meeting until the middle of October. This temporizing, even if not entirely unexpected, did not augur well for Europe, and whatever faint hopes were raised by the acceptance of Hitler and Mussolini in July, dwindled as they exploited the Spanish turmoil.

★ ★ ★ ★ ★

The only event which had given me any satisfaction during these dismal months was the signature of a treaty with Egypt. Many British governments since the beginning of the century had tried to regularize our position in Egypt, but never with durable results. In 1922, Britain recognized Egypt as a sovereign state, subject to four reserved points. These related to the defence of Egypt against aggression, imperial communications, especially through the Suez Canal, the protection of foreign interests and minorities, and the Sudan. Attempts had been made in 1928 and 1930 to put relations on a more permanent footing, but these had always run into difficulties about our military needs. Meanwhile we faced all the problems common to powers who have military bases on unfriendly soil.

Mussolini's Abyssinian adventure and his concentration of troops in Libya wrought a change. They made the Egyptians uneasy and fearful of Italian encroachment on two fronts. As a consequence, they began to frown less on British armed strength. The prospects for negotiation improved, but the Egyptians also knew that Britain desired their friendship all the more now that Fascist ambitions threatened, so their price was high. Though Egyptian armed forces were admittedly incapable of defending the country, the presence of British troops still raised sensitive questions of pride and sovereignty. It was evidently in the interests of both countries that concessions should be made, but there was plenty of scope for argument as to who should cede what. I thought that if once the military clauses could be agreed, the rest of the treaty would not present difficulties. So it proved. For several months discussions revolved around these defence points. The talks took place in Cairo, where the British delegation was ably led by Sir Miles Lampson, our High Commissioner in Egypt, who showed much skill in keeping the wheels of negotiation oiled and always moving, while inevitably referring constantly to me in London.

At the end of 1935, a United Front government was formed in Egypt, partly for the purpose of negotiating with us. I had been familiar with the papers and the points at issue before I took over the Foreign Office and, on January 3rd, I telegraphed to Lampson that I wished him to examine the proposals previously made by Mr. Henderson in 1930, to see whether:

> (i) any such suggestions . . . would prove acceptable to the Egyptians and whether
>
> (ii) they would constitute a fair offer, having regard to legitimate Egyptian aspirations and to vital Imperial interests, an offer which could be successfully defended before both British and world opinion and one which sensible Egyptians would in their hearts know to be fair. It is most desirable that the final terms shall, if possible, fulfil both conditions, but if the Egyptians prove unreasonable, His Majesty's Government will be compelled to abandon the first and rely on the fairness of their offer to justify the consequences.

On January 16th, I instructed Lampson to tell the Egyptians that we were prepared to negotiate a treaty forthwith between the two governments as future allies, and that the military clauses must be settled first. Next came the question of personalities. If any treaty were to be worth the paper it was written on, it had to be negotiated by Nahas Pasha, leader of the largest party, the Wafd. By the end of January, King Fuad provided himself with a government under Ali Maher, with Nahas as leader of the negotiating commission, four members of which had also been involved in the 1930 talks.

I had expected that the War Office, whom I had asked to state their needs, would put forward stiff demands, but I was myself ready to forgo some paper safeguards for the sake of a helpful and friendly Egypt. During February, we pared the military demands to fair proportions and decided to try for the right to keep our forces on the

Suez Canal, at or near Alexandria and at Helouan, some sixteen miles from Cairo. We did not, of course, open the talks on this basis. Lampson was asked to offer, first, a pooling of British and Egyptian forces, with no limitation on numbers or dispositions. If this proved unobtainable, he was to offer withdrawal from the centre of Cairo to the outskirts of the city. Only when this failed, was he to offer withdrawal to Helouan.

From the start, Sir Miles told us that we must place some time limit on the presence of all our forces in Egypt. Our first proposals were stonily received and Lampson was compelled to announce at once that we would move our troops out of the centre of Cairo. Nahas was not prepared to allow our forces to be in Alexandria. On the other hand, he offered us an increased number of troops in the Canal zone, important improvements in road and rail communications, facilities for the Royal Air Force and a large training ground south of Ismailia. This was a fair response and I thought that steady pressure might encourage Nahas further.

The Egyptian negotiators urged that a formal consultation with their Government should take place before we moved increased forces into the Canal zone. We insisted that the safeguarding of our imperial communications could not be dependent upon any outside authority. Nahas finally agreed that we should have the right to reinforce without limit 'in the case of an apprehended emergency and before a state of acute crisis is reached.' He was also prepared for a British peacetime garrison in the zone of up to 10,000 land troops, with a contingent of four hundred pilots and the necessary ground forces.

In these circumstances and not without wrangling, I persuaded my colleagues that we should do without a base in or near Cairo. But Ministers insisted that if after twenty years the treaty were revised, it should be understood now that our right to defend the Canal would be provided for in the revision. On more than one occasion, I had difficulty in persuading my colleagues of the importance to us of a treaty with Egypt, which by now had a triumphant Fascist neighbour. Members of our delegation in Cairo held the same opinion. Lampson telegraphed:

> Broadly, we all feel that a special opportunity is offered which should be grasped in a bold and constructive spirit. Whereas in previous negotiations the Egyptian side were thinking only in terms of nationalism and were willing to *accept alliance* as the price insisted on by us, they now themselves sincerely (at least so we believe) desire alliance, and at present, at any rate,

really seem to intend to work it whole-heartedly, provided always it *is* an alliance and not camouflage perpetuating existing regime.

The Egyptian negotiators did not show any willingness to meet our modified requirements and I called Lampson home for consultation at the beginning of June. While the High Commissioner was in London, Nahas put a new complexion on the whole matter by telling Mr. Kelly, the Counsellor at our Embassy, that even after Britain had withdrawn her troops from Cairo and Alexandria, we could send them back without limit at any time. This in effect provided us with a continuing military alliance, on the basis of which we were able to agree that either country could refer the question of the Canal and its defence to the League after twenty years if, at that time, we were at odds upon the subject.

I had wanted to keep the negotiations in Cairo, for there was always the danger that any Minister who came to London, and signed, would be overthrown on his return, so compelling was our power of seduction thought to be. For the same reason, we insisted that all Egyptian political parties should be represented in the delegation which came to London to sign, a demand that the Opposition at home stigmatized as undemocratic, protesting that we ought to deal with the Egyptian Government of the day. I did not accept this, being convinced that all known Egyptian public figures should have their part in the Treaty and therefore be without pretext to go back upon it in a critical hour.

After Lampson's return to Cairo, the Treaty was quickly put into shape. The Egyptians agreed that the defence of Sudanese territory should be in the hands of Sudan forces, with the aid of both British and Egyptians. We also undertook to use our influence with other powers, who had special rights in Egypt, to persuade them to remove all restrictions on the application of Egyptian legislation to foreigners.

A large Egyptian delegation visited London in August, when Nahas told me of his desire for real Anglo-Egyptian collaboration. He was as good as his word. The signature took place on August 26th in the Locarno room at the Foreign Office with ceremony, Mr. Ramsay MacDonald, Sir John Simon and Lord Halifax attending with me, and thirteen Egyptian representatives putting their names to the deed. In later years on visits which I made to Cairo, Sir Miles Lampson, who became Lord Killearn about that time, once or twice arranged parties for the signatories, which merged happily into occasions for mutual congratulation. Certainly the Treaty stood the test of experience in war and its authors never attempted to renege upon it. Even in the darkest hour of our joint fortunes, Nahas and I exchanged messages of confidence which brought against me foolish and much applauded charges of complacency in Parliament. It was necessary to maintain faith and to uphold an unusual but invaluable arrangement by which an Egypt, nominally neutral, afforded us every facility to meet our wartime needs. This Treaty was one of the very few worthwhile settlements negotiated in that time of international lawlessness.

V

THE SPANISH CIVIL WAR

February – December 1936

Nature of the Spanish Republic – General Franco sent to the Canaries – The Civil War begins – It becomes an international battlefield – A conversation with Senhor Monteiro – France and Britain decide not to intervene – Mr. Baldwin's absence through illness – I announce an arms embargo – Reports of Spanish atrocities – London meeting of the Non-Intervention Committee – Geneva interlude – The Prime Minister returns to London – 'Have you had any letters about the King?' – Difficulties of non-intervention – General Franco's blockade – Foreign volunteers – I consider naval action

After the abdication of King Alfonso XIII in April 1931, the Spanish Republic pursued its buffeted course, amid growing dangers for the Spanish people. Its opening was auspicious, subsequently almost everything went wrong. Some of the Republic's troubles were its own fault, others were inherited, such as the regional struggles for autonomy, or just plain misfortune. At the start it moved cautiously, yet the choice of men, though well-intentioned, was seldom happy. The centre parties probably had the majority of the country behind them, but they failed to establish their authority. The centripetal forces never seemed quite strong enough, the centrifugal ones had their way. Perhaps they had to. What should have been a solid centre was fragmented. The multiplicity of parties, there were nineteen of them at one general election, added to the weakness, while bitter rivalries divided the socialists. The creed of anarchy had its true devotees and suited the individualistic temperament of the Spaniards, but hardly made for unity.

Personalities made matters worse. The Radical Party, under Don Alejandro Lerroux, ought to have been allied to Señor Manuel Azaña

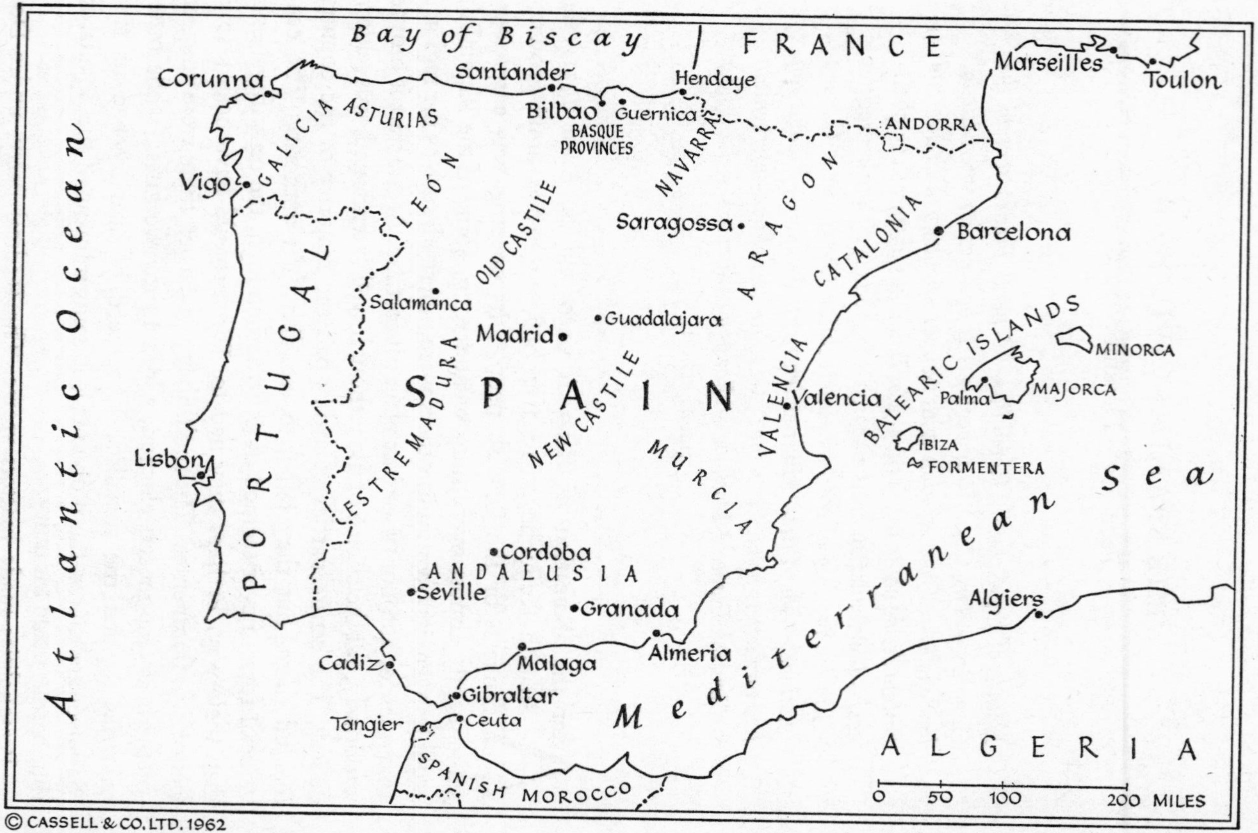

Bay of Biscay
FRANCE
Marseilles
Toulon
Corunna
Santander
Hendaye
Bilbao
Guernica
BASQUE PROVINCES
ANDORRA
GALICIA
ASTURIAS
NAVARRA
LEÓN
OLD CASTILE
ARAGON
CATALONIA
Vigo
Saragossa
Barcelona
PORTUGAL
Salamanca
Guadalajara
Madrid
BALEARIC ISLANDS
MINORCA
MAJORCA
Palma
SPAIN
VALENCIA
Valencia
ESTREMADURA
NEW CASTILE
MURCIA
IBIZA
FORMENTERA
Lisbon
Atlantic Ocean
Mediterranean Sea
Cordoba
ANDALUSIA
Seville
Granada
Algiers
Cadiz
Malaga
Almeria
Gibraltar
Tangier
Ceuta
SPANISH MOROCCO
ALGERIA
0 50 100 200 MILES

and his party of Republican Action, but it did not work out that way, the two men being in complete antipathy. The result was three periods with short spasms of government, first left, then right, then left again and civil war. Spain and Russia, the two European countries which suffered bloody revolutions in this century, were the two most backward, where extremes of poverty and wealth existed, with little stabilizing force to weigh down extremism on either side.

The Spanish Republic, in its early days and first enthusiasm, made two capital errors. Its actions provoked sympathy for the church and alerted the army. Soon comparable resistance on the left, led by Señor Largo Caballero, pointed to civil war, the origins of which came from within Spain. The rebellion of the right in 1936 had been preceded by a rebellion of the left in 1934, hardly more excusable. The powers without sought to profit from the struggle as it developed. They did not and could not promote it, nor was the rebellion when it came just another Fascist plot. Its origins were much deeper, in Spanish politics and character.

The figures for the election in February 1936 have been much disputed, though the results showed a complete victory for the left. Yet they did not bring confidence, for it was the extreme left which had gained most and the right which had suffered under the electoral law, with the result that the right had one deputy to 25,000 votes, the Popular Front one to 16,300, the centre one to 11,000. In any reckoning of the Spanish nation's verdict that fatal year, much depends upon the interpretation of the centre votes. If these were added to the right, admittedly an arbitrary exercise, then the Popular Front was in a minority. All that can be said with certainty about such calculations is that support for the left centre was not overwhelming and, against the background of the previous four years of lawlessness and murder, the new Government could only bring peace if they showed firmness towards the unbridled elements among their supporters. This they failed to do, while from the moment of declared victory, hostile factions on the right contended that the voting had been rigged and that the Government had no true mandate.

Rioting and arson soon broke out again, as extreme members of the Popular Front wreaked their will unchecked. The Government made frequent appeals for democratic discipline, but these fell upon unheeding ears. By midsummer, anarchy threatened. The outstanding figure among opponents of the regime was Señor Calvo Sotelo. No monarchist or other right wing leader reached to his shoulder. He spoke out boldly, perhaps dangerously, after Señor Robles had read to the Cortes details of the outrages committed by left wing supporters of the Government.

The army occupied a special position of authority in Spain and some high offices were solely reserved for generals. As the threat of civil war grew nearer, the Government deemed it prudent to take precautions, and the two most popular commanders, General Goded and General Franco, were sent away for better security, the former to the Balearic Islands and the latter to the Canaries, while the army was being purged of officers whose loyalty was thought doubtful. On June 23rd General Franco addressed a remonstrance to the Government, containing, we were told, the ominous phrase that the army had almost had enough.

On the night of July 12th–13th, Lieutenant Castillo, a communist military police officer, was murdered in Madrid. The following night, a party of uniformed guards killed Sotelo, fulfilling the sinister prophecy of La Pasionaria, a communist woman member of the Cortes. After Sotelo's most recent intervention in debate, she had exclaimed: 'That is your last speech!' Within four days most of Spain was aflame and the Republican Government were fighting for their lives against a rebellion led by General Franco. The revolt was ill-planned and exploded prematurely, first in Spanish Morocco and then in the principal garrisons. There were no organized forces to meet it, though some of the airmen and most of the sailors remained loyal to the Government, who were able to capture large stocks of arms and distribute them to their civilian supporters. General Goded's attempted rising in Barcelona failed and he was shot.

General Franco, having overcome local resistance in the Canary Islands, flew to Morocco, where the insurgents were soon in control. By the end of July our reports showed that they commanded most of northern Spain, except the coastline, as well as Majorca. Cadiz, Seville and Cordoba had been quickly taken, but the greater part of the south remained loyal to the Government. As the campaign developed, General Franco and his supporters tried to strike northwards to the Basque country and southwards towards Madrid, but their progress was slow and the campaign bitterly fought.

Neither side in this struggle was coherent or closely knit, but simple terms were used to describe them. General Franco and his men dubbed the Government and their supporters Communists, who retorted by calling their opponents Fascists. Substance was soon given to this reading of the situation by reports of foreign aid, though it was some months before outside intervention had any serious influence on the fighting. At the beginning of August, both Hitler and Mussolini began to give active help to Franco, while Soviet Russia sent money and materials to the Government, but in its early phase, until November, this was essentially a Spanish civil war. Later it was to fire the imagination of the younger generation in many countries, enlisting the devotion unto death of thousands of true volunteers.

As the internal struggle became an ideological and international battlefield, fought over by both sides with the utmost cruelty, the great powers who intervened did not do so only to establish a government of their colour. The conflict became part of a contest for the balance of power in Europe. The Soviets hoped that a left wing Spanish government would cause no anxiety to Blum's *Front Populaire*, which would continue to direct its eyes eastwards to the Nazi menace. Hitler and Mussolini, on the other hand, believed that if Franco were once established in power, France could no longer feel sure of her southern flank and would be correspondingly weakened in the east. Mussolini would also be soothed to feel that the western end of the Mediterranean was in the hands of a government indebted to him, and from whom he could hope to obtain raw materials for his rearmament. History should, however, have taught him that his political reward was not likely to be rich.

Each contending party had strongly entrenched positions even before the fighting broke out. The insurgents could call upon the support of monarchists, landowners, the hierarchy of the church, a number of professional men and most army officers. Many liberals, with socialists and communists, remained loyal to the Government, as did nationalists in the Basque region, with its strongly Catholic and separatist tendencies. The resources of the rich industrial area round Bilbao were thus available to the Government, while Basque shipowners and iron and steel manufacturers found themselves backing a cause supported by the communists.

As soon as news reached London that civil war had begun, I asked that British warships be ordered to the more important Spanish ports to protect our subjects. The Royal Navy carried out its duties with despatch and I learnt a few days later from our Consul-General, Mr. Norman King, that the prompt arrival of our ships at Barcelona relieved the anxieties not only of the British colony there but of all foreigners, particularly the Americans. The death of General Goded was followed by wholesale executions over a long period, which far exceeded anything warranted by the abortive revolt. All through August our Consul-General attempted to enlist the help of his colleagues to make remonstrance, but with one accord they excused themselves. After paying a visit to the morgue himself, he sent me a description which rivalled the most harrowing of Goya's drawings.

Meanwhile, the Spanish Ambassador in London, Señor Olivan, a friend for many years, came to see me on July 24th in a mood of depression and concern. From the way he spoke, I thought that Olivan regarded a communist government as the most likely outcome of the civil war, in which event, he said, not only he, but several other members of the Spanish Embassy staff, would resign. It was a commentary on the tragedy engulfing Spain that he would have to take the same action, he told me, if the rebels won. Small wonder that he found the general position inconceivably wretched for anyone who loved Spain.

The question of the supply of munitions of war became immediately acute. A few days later, Olivan spoke to me about reports that four British aircraft had been sold to Spain. I replied that these were apparently civil machines, over the sale of which we had no control. The Ambassador asked me if I could tell him that His Majesty's Government would not obstruct the provision of supplies for the Spanish Government. I replied that they would not. Olivan then inquired whether the same policy would apply to the delivery of arms and munitions. I answered that these would require a licence and if the Spanish Government made an application, it would certainly be considered. Finally, he asked whether the League could do anything in this conflict. He admitted the difficulties created by the League's loss of membership and authority, but even so, perhaps it could achieve something. He feared that the struggle, if left to itself, would continue for many months, until one side or the other was virtually annihilated. In this Olivan was a true prophet.

On July 30th, the Portuguese Foreign Minister, Senhor Monteiro, came to see me at the Foreign Office, fearful of an invasion of his country if the left should triumph in Spain. I told him that I found such a forecast hardly credible, but he was not reassured. At the same time, he said, Portugal would not feel comfortable if a Spanish government were established which had strong ties with Germany and Italy. The Foreign Minister had been spending some weeks in France and had come away very apprehensive of the spirit which he found there. He would be much relieved if France got through the next few months without some serious internal conflict. Monteiro was one of the first to think that France might be shattered, because the hatreds within the country were greater than the hatred of some Frenchmen for the foreign enemy. The *Comité des Forges*, for instance, was so anti-Blum that it had scarcely time to be anti-German. Monteiro and I saw this with regret, Hitler with satisfaction.

I told the Foreign Minister that, as he would know, we were not willing to mix ourselves up in the internal affairs of Spain. In the course of this long discussion, the Foreign Minister gave me some grisly details of the horrors in Spain. The civil war was bringing out the worst facets of the Spanish character. Monteiro begged me several times not to neglect the situation in Spain, he was certain that the repercussions would be very ominous for Europe. I had to agree. When, the next day, I left London for a fortnight in Yorkshire, I arranged that all important papers should be sent to me and I remained in close touch with London by telephone. Lord Halifax took charge of day-to-day events at the Foreign Office.

* * * * *

The French Government were even more intimately concerned than ourselves with the Spanish upheaval. Although Blum was under pressure to support the Government in Madrid, he announced on July 26th that France was in no way able to intervene. He and Delbos knew only too well that any other course of action would sharply divide France, while open intervention by the great powers could lead to a European war. We agreed with this French decision of policy. There were forceful reasons why Britain must favour non-intervention. First, because if the fighting in Spain were once internationalized, its consequences would be uncontrollable. Our authority was the strongest in Europe in favour of localizing the conflict and must be used for that purpose, if the immediate danger of a European war was to be averted. Secondly, the British Government had no wish to be involved in a Spanish civil war, nor were they convinced that, whatever its outcome, the Spaniards would feel any gratitude to those who had intervened. This lesson had been learnt in the Peninsular War more than a century before, when British soldiers and statesmen found their allies brave, but proud, unpunctual and xenophobe. The question now was whether a non-intervention policy could be made effective; it had to be tried.

Events in Spain fulfilled Blum's prophecy to me. They brought Hitler and Mussolini into more intimate company, both openly expressing support for Franco and detestation of the 'reds'. The French Government now took a bold initiative. On August 2nd, they proposed that France, Italy and Britain, as the three powers most interested in Spanish events, should formally agree not to intervene in Spain. This agreement, which they suggested should later be extended to other countries, would prohibit all exports of arms to any Spanish destination. I replied that we were as concerned as the French Government lest other powers should intervene. My note continued:

> His Majesty's Government would in present circumstances welcome an early agreement between all powers who may be in a position to supply arms and munitions, to refrain from doing so and to prevent the supply of arms and munitions from their territories, on the principle of non-interference in Spanish affairs.

I gave it as my opinion, however, that the agreement should be accepted by the governments of Germany and Portugal as well as France, Italy and ourselves. I hoped that in time it would be subscribed to by all other powers concerned with events in Spain and I undertook to apply the principle of non-intervention at once, if France and Italy would do the same. On August 6th Great Britain supported the French Government in submitting a draft agreement to all the European powers, but the initiative was French and the Quai d'Orsay determined the capitals in which we should each have our say, choosing Moscow for themselves and allotting Lisbon to us.

Action was certainly timely. Lord Chilston reported from Moscow that up to August 2nd, fifteen days after the opening of the civil war, not a word had been said in Russia about any 'popular' demonstration in favour of the Spanish Government. The Soviet Government then decided to act. On August 3rd indignation meetings and 'popular' demonstrations took place by the thousand all over Russia. Workers showed their solidarity with Spanish comrades by contributing a proportion of their wages. Within a few days, half a million pounds were made over in this way to the Spanish Government.

The French Government acted most loyally by us and the Chargé d'Affaires at their London Embassy, M. Roger Cambon, called at the Foreign Office frequently to report and to concert policy. On August 12th Cambon put forward a suggestion from his Government that, once we had arrived at some arrangement for non-intervention, a committee of control should be set up to supervise the Agreement and consider further action. This was the origin of the Non-Intervention

Committee. On the same day Delbos appealed to His Majesty's Government, through Sir George Clerk, to secure a quick agreement. Speed, Delbos said, was necessary on account of the internal situation in France. He thought that the French Government could claim to have acted with a certain courage, but it was growing daily, almost hourly, more difficult to withstand the pressure of their supporters.

On reading through all these documents while in Yorkshire, I felt as apprehensive as the French. The newspapers seemed to indicate that we had taken up an acquiescent attitude, rather than one of firm support of Blum's proposals. On the morning of August 14th I telephoned to the Foreign Office, asking if we were really doing everything possible. I was assured that we were and accordingly asked that a statement should be put out explaining both the purpose of our policy and what action we were taking. This was done. The next day, the British and French Governments publicly exchanged notes, undertaking to prohibit the export of arms to Spain and to enforce this ban as soon as Italy, Germany, Russia and Portugal agreed.

* * * * *

I returned to the Foreign Office on the 16th. But the Prime Minister, whose health had been poor all the summer, had now been ordered three months' complete rest and was convalescing in South Wales. I was therefore responsible for directing our policy without frequent reference to him. On August 19th I decided to announce that Britain would apply an arms embargo to Spain without waiting for other powers. I wrote to Mr. Baldwin:

> I have been back here since Tuesday in the throes of the situation created by this Spanish horror. You will have seen the action which we took yesterday to prevent arms or aeroplanes going from this country to Spain. I felt it necessary to do this even before we achieved international agreement in order that we might, by setting an example, do our best to induce others, more particularly Germany and Italy, to follow suit.

I had not yet learnt that it is dangerous to offer such gestures to dictators, who are more likely to misinterpret than to follow them. For the moment, these moves appeared to produce the effects we desired. On August 21st the Italian Government formally accepted the French proposal, though I noticed that Ciano's note drew a distinction between direct and indirect interference. The Italian Government, he said, understood the latter to concern the sending of subscriptions and the enrolment of volunteers, and made their reservations on the subject.

Three evenings later the French Ambassador came to see me, when he said that he had originally asked for the interview to tell me how anxious the French Government were at the delay in securing agreement on non-intervention. M. Blum and M. Delbos had, indeed, been near the end of their tether. Happily, however, within the last hour he had received a message from Paris which radically changed the whole situation. The German Government had accepted the French invitation and the Ambassador handed me the text of the terms of the acceptance.

M. Corbin went on to say that he had a request to make to me from the French Government. If non-intervention was to work, then, in the view of his Government, it was essential that a committee should be set up to deal with the many technical details which would inevitably arise. The question was, where was that committee to be situated? The French Government felt very strongly that London was the best place, and they much hoped that His Majesty's Government would agree. M. Corbin said later that they felt our capital was more neutral than that of any other great power in this difficult business. After some discussion of the committee's composition, I told the Ambassador that we were willing to lend our aid by agreeing that the committee should meet in London.

We then discussed the possibility of an Anglo-French intervention on purely humanitarian grounds, especially on behalf of prisoners, a proposal I had recently put to the French Government. We determined to pursue this further. Finally I asked the Ambassador to congratulate his Government from the British Government on the success of the policy they had pursued in this dispute. M. Blum had, we felt, shown great courage in taking the initiative, and nobody was happier than we were to find that courage rewarded.

The Cabinet did not meet from the end of July until the beginning of September and British policy was in fact decided in the Foreign Office. Baldwin was not well enough to attend the signing of the Egyptian Treaty, nor was he dealing with any but the most essential business. According to the press, he and I were working in close conjunction. I wrote in my diary on August 24th:

> The communiqué in the press this morning announcing that S.B. is not coming up to London is a little 'tall', since his 'constant touch' with me has consisted in one letter and one telephone call this month, and these about my spending a weekend with him in South Wales.

The Labour Party, as the official Opposition, had every right to full information about the reasons which lay behind our Spanish policy. Mr. Arthur Greenwood and Sir Walter Citrine, with other Labour supporters, asked to see me on August 19th, when I explained confidentially to them the action we had taken, remarking that the initiative for non-intervention had come from the French Government. At this point, a member of the deputation interjected that I was perhaps aware of the rumour that the initiative had been taken by the French, but under pressure from the British Government. I replied that there was no truth whatever in this suggestion and my statement was at once accepted. A week later, the same deputation came to the Foreign Office again and, after discussion of other aspects of the war in Spain, asked once more about the origins of the proposed Non-Intervention Agreement, which, according to information they had received from Paris, had emanated from London, probably at the time of the three-power discussions between France, Belgium and ourselves. I denied this statement, adding that I should have been glad to be able to say that non-intervention was my proposal, as I considered it the best which could have been devised in the circumstances.

On August 20th the Spanish Ambassador spoke in gloomy tones of the situation in his country. He agreed with the view Señor de Madariaga had recently expressed to me, and which I quoted to him, that, apart from foreign intervention, the sides were so evenly balanced that neither could win. He also shared Madariaga's opinion that this was not a war of liberty and democracy against tyranny, for neither side could be said to represent democracy and liberty. Olivan thought it was probably wrong to suppose that a government of the right would necessarily be very close in foreign policy to Germany and Italy, since such a regime would not be stable and the traditional foreign policy of Spain would always make itself strongly felt. Señor Olivan remarked that he did not, for instance, believe the rumours current that General Franco had entered into some agreement with Signor Mussolini about Ceuta or one of the Balearic Islands. If General Franco were to do anything of the kind, he would at once be overthrown by his own supporters, who, being of the right, were more nationalist, and, if anything, more determined not to surrender Spanish territory, than those of the left. Olivan's judgement proved near the mark on all these points.

On August 28th I again saw the French Ambassador. M. Corbin told me that it would be some time before the French Government would receive replies to enable us to go ahead with calling the Non-Intervention Committee together in London. The Ambassador then asked me whether I had any information about the attitude of our own Labour Party on the question of Spain. He rather had the impression that they were not very much interested. I replied that I did not think that this was so, though I had been somewhat intrigued at the story which one of them had brought back from Paris that the suggestion of non-intervention was not originally French but British. I had said that there was, of course, no truth in this, though I had always thought M. Blum's initiative a wise one. The Ambassador remarked that, so far as he could recollect, there had been no discussion of the Spanish problem during our three-power meeting. That is also my own recollection and the evidence of the records in London. The reason was, no doubt, that Blum's visit was for a few hours only and concerned with the effort we were then making to summon a five-power conference on Europe's future.

* * * * *

During August, the reports of our Consul-General at Barcelona showed that the shooting of victims suspected of political affiliations with the right continued unabated. On one day, he stated, seventy-two people were taken from the prison-ship at Tarragona. Some were thrown overboard with weights attached to their feet, others taken into the country and shot. 'Even local opinion was shocked', the Consul-General wrote, 'by the murder of Señor Planas, a promising young journalist of the extreme left, whose only crime seems to have been that he deprecated the use of too much violence in an article he wrote some weeks ago.'

At the same time I received from Mr. Ogilvie-Forbes, who was in charge of our Embassy in Madrid, an account of his return by railway from Barcelona to the capital. During the journey, the conductor on the train drew Ogilvie-Forbes aside and, bursting into tears, begged him, as the representative of Great Britain, to do something to try to stop the wave of murder which was spreading over the land and which was by no means restricted to the rich. The conductor said he was in daily terror of his life and, such was the system of private vendetta, that no man knew when his brother would strike him down.

I discussed with Olivan the possibility of some humanitarian campaign and during the coming weeks we continued to search for ways of reducing the toll of suffering, particularly to prisoners and hostages.

Eventually, these efforts, to which our Ambassador and Consuls throughout Spain devoted eagerness and ingenuity, saved many lives. But the danger to Europe now began to threaten less from the Spaniards than from the foreigners who showed signs of fighting their battles for them. In these conditions, I was encouraged to hear from Sir George Clerk that Blum had delivered a well-argued speech in defence of his policy. After stating that the Spanish Government were faced with a military rebellion, he added that while the legal government of Spain alone had the right to obtain shipments of arms from abroad, the possibility existed that foreign governments might recognize the rebel junta as a *de facto* government. There might be argument about the interpretation of international law, but, to ensure its strict observance, Blum asked what method was open except the use of force with all its possible consequences. He explained that to avoid this, and the equal recognition of the two forces in Spain, the French Government had concluded the Non-Intervention Agreement.

Negotiations, in which the French took the lead, to get the Non-Intervention Committee started, resulted at last in a first meeting in London on September 9th. Twenty-six European countries came, including all those with a direct interest in Spanish affairs, with the exception of Portugal, which joined a fortnight later. The chief contenders, Russia, Germany, Italy and France, chose their Ambassadors to represent them. They were skilful protagonists. Italy and France were well matched in Grandi and Corbin; the former was perhaps dialectically more effective, but Corbin's diplomacy was tenacious beneath a bland surface. The Russian Ambassador, Mr. Ivan Maisky, never missed a trick that could by any argument be his and was unsubdued by even the sternest rebuffs. Ribbentrop was clumsier in his methods, but he learnt as the discussions went along. The thankless task of presiding over this adroit company fell to Great Britain, represented at the outset by Mr. W. S. Morrison and thereafter by Lord Plymouth, then Parliamentary Under-Secretary at the Foreign Office. The first few meetings passed off amiably enough. It was settled that when breaches of the Agreement were alleged, the complaint must be laid by a government which was a party to the Agreement.

While these matters of procedure were being thrashed out at the end of September, I went to Geneva, where the Spanish Foreign Minister, Señor del Vayo, spoke to me about the civil war. Del Vayo had been appointed a few weeks before, when the Government had taken a shift to the left under the premiership of Señor Caballero. The Foreign Minister's communist sympathies were in tune with this move. He assured me of his Government's desire to protect British interests. I replied that I thought a large section of British opinion was concerned not so much for British interests, as at the savagery with which the civil war was now being waged. Del Vayo directed the rest of his plea to showing that a policy of non-intervention militated against the Spanish Government. I gave him no encouragement to think that we would modify our policy. The Foreign Minister left with me documents and photographs to prove the extent to which Hitler and Mussolini were violating the agreement.

I found Delbos also preoccupied with Italian activities. He asked whether we were watching the situation in the Balearics, which we were doing. Delbos remarked that the generals in Spain seemed uncommonly like Fascist governments elsewhere. They gave explicit assurances that they would not consider policies which they were in fact actively pursuing. For instance, while the generals had spoken of their determination to preserve Spanish integrity, it was impossible to ignore either German activity in connection with the Canaries or Italian activities in the Balearics. Events were to prove, though, that however malevolent the intentions of Hitler or Mussolini towards these two groups of islands may have been, Spanish character was to be true to itself and not yield an acre.

The League Assembly decided, on September 23rd, to admit the Abyssinian representatives from the rightful but fugitive Government, which caused loud Fascist indignation. It seemed possible that Mussolini might withdraw from the League, at least temporarily. The French Ministers suggested that in view of this and of the Spanish situation, fresh consideration should be given to a Mediterranean Pact. If, they argued, the British and French Governments were prepared to propose such a pact jointly to the Mediterranean powers, it would have a useful, steadying effect in the present disturbed state of Spain and also help by perpetuating the balance of power in the area. I liked this idea and we decided to pursue it.

When the Assembly adjourned, I spent a few days in the South of France. On my way home I stopped in Paris, where Blum and I had luncheon together on October 9th. The Non-Intervention Committee had that morning experienced its stormiest meeting to date, when it had considered evidence of breaches of the Agreement by Germany, Italy and Portugal. This evidence had been sent to London by the

Spanish Government and we had placed it before the Committee. Grandi instantly objected to this procedure, while Maisky, without any proof, took up the charges and pressed for full investigation. He alleged that Portugal was guilty of further breaches, also without producing evidence.

I gave Blum an account of these proceedings, saying that I thought the method followed by the Soviet Government had been unfortunate. To make charges of bad faith before even pretending to sift the evidence, was contrary to the practice which the Committee had agreed to follow and had unnecessarily complicated matters. I did not know what effect this might have upon the future of the Committee. Blum fully shared my preoccupations. The pressure upon him in France was mounting steadily and he agreed ruefully that the Soviet move was untimely.

In reply to a question from me, the French Prime Minister said categorically that he continued to think non-intervention was the correct policy. We must do all in our power to make it effective. Blum added that he was himself convinced that, had there been no Non-Intervention Agreement, the Spanish Government would have suffered more than the rebels. I agreed with this reasoning, because the dictator powers could supply arms much more readily to the insurgents than the democracies could to the Spanish Government. The manufacture of arms in the dictatorships was multiplying rapidly, whilst both France and ourselves were still woefully short, even of necessities. This unpleasant reality was not understood by opinion in Britain and France at the time, nor could it be publicly proclaimed, but it influenced both Governments.

Speaking at the Cutlers' Feast in Sheffield a few days later, I continued to defend our action:

> I am well aware of the criticisms which are being directed against the agreement. It is even being suggested that the time has now come to give up this effort. His Majesty's Government do not share that view. The impatience revealed in some quarters at the slowness of the committee's method and work has not been balanced by the production of any practical alternative proposals for dealing with the situation....

Later, I referred to the British programme of rearmament which was now belatedly under way:

> We should have preferred an arms agreement; but in the world as it is today the strengthening of our defences becomes not only a desirable objective but an imperative national duty. This strengthening of our forces

will not be used to accompany our diplomatic proposals with threats. Such are not our methods. Its usefulness will lie in this: that Europe may be convinced that we are strong enough to play our part to keep the peace and that violent courses can be met with firm resistance.

* * * * *

In the third week of October, Baldwin returned to London and I had my first talk with him for three months. Naturally I was impatient to deploy the course of events and to take counsel with him, particularly about the Spanish civil war, which had become so international a menace since our last talk together. Baldwin listened for a while, but his mind was evidently not on the subject. I thought this unconcern exasperating. At a pause in my dissertation Baldwin astonished me by saying: 'Have you had any letters about the King?' 'No, not as far as I know,' I said, 'why should I have?' 'Well,' Baldwin went on, 'I wish you would inquire. I expect that you have had some. I fear we may have difficulties there.' He added: 'I hope that you will try not to trouble me too much with foreign affairs just now.' After three months without a comment from the Prime Minister, I found this an astonishing doctrine and suspected at the time that it was another example of Baldwin's reluctance to face the unpleasant realities which were our daily fare at the Foreign Office. But I was wrong. When I got back to my room I found that there had been letters from overseas, where there was no press restraint, such as our own newspapers had voluntarily assumed, and where both foreign and British subjects were at liberty to express their opinions and anxieties. These wrote of the King and Mrs. Simpson and her impending divorce suit and they were critical.

Baldwin had at once sensed the dangers for the country and Empire of any action by the Crown which might divide its peoples. All through the sad crisis he understood the instinctive reactions of the British people at every stage of a very human problem. From first to last he never had any doubt as to what they would think. I do not pretend to have had any such infallible instinct, as events unrolled which made many of us very unhappy. There can, however, be no question that the decision taken was inescapable. It was arrived at as a result of independent advice by each one of the Dominions, in reply to telegrams worded with a scrupulous impartiality, which would have defied the reader to guess the judgement of the Government at home in Britain. That was how it had to be.

* * * * *

The charges now being bandied about in the Non-Intervention Committee found echoes without. The British Labour Party passed a resolution at their annual conference that the Fascist powers had broken their pledges not to intervene. They demanded immediate investigation and, if definite violations were proved or the Agreement were found ineffective, that Britain and France should restore the freedom of the Spanish Government to buy arms. But this was only part of the story. In Soviet Russia the system of imposing a levy on trade unions to help the Spanish Government was being extended to all co-operative farms. The Russians were openly sending supplies to Spain and the evidence we had at this time was more specific against them than against the dictators in Rome and Berlin.

A meeting of the Non-Intervention Committee was due to take place on October 23rd. The Germans had already answered the charges against them, but neither the Italian nor the Portuguese Governments had done so. I pressed their representatives to hurry, for it was by now evident that unless some urgency could be injected into its proceedings, the survival of the Committee would be in jeopardy. I was not therefore surprised when Corbin asked to see me on the morning of October 23rd. The Ambassador spoke of his anxiety about the Committee's future, saying that he had been considering what line it should now take. He had come to the conclusion that the Committee might consider a proposal to supervise its work on the spot. If this supervision were to be effective, it would require the approval of both belligerents in Spain and Corbin doubted whether the Spanish Government would give theirs. Nevertheless we agreed that a sub-committee should examine this and other proposals to make the Non-Intervention Agreement function. The work was put in hand and had consequences.

The insurgents' military campaign was now making headway and at the end of this interview I remarked to Corbin that I should be inclined to recognize the insurgents as belligerents, if and when they took Madrid. I asked the Ambassador to inquire whether his Government agreed. He promised to do so, but his own impression was that his Government might see difficulty in recognizing the insurgents as belligerents, because of the rights which they must in consequence enjoy. I afterwards came to share this view. Five days later, Maisky developed the suggestion for supervision which Corbin and I had discussed. He proposed that the Committee should examine the control of Portuguese ports and Spanish ports and frontiers. Grandi and Corbin both agreed to consider this. Thus ended non-intervention's first phase. After little more than a month, the nations had to accept that non-intervention without supervision would not work. The Committee had now to devise a control scheme to restrain its own members.

* * * * *

I knew the Committee's limitations and thought about alternatives to its continued life, but found none that was feasible or acceptable. The discussions between members on reported infractions of the Agreement had a certain curbing effect upon the scale of foreign intervention, at least in the earlier stages, while the existence of the Committee gave Blum and his friends sufficient cause not to take a hand in Spain. Any other policy, by weakening France's power and unity, as intervention must have done, could only have played into Hitler's hands. Britain's neutrality also gave her a special authority, which she could and did use to arrange exchanges of hostages in danger of being butchered. This was not a small thing. A generation which had not plumbed the depths of Hitler's bestiality was appalled at the hatred and violence now unleashed in Spain.

I was looking at the matter from a purely pragmatic point of view, as I explained to the House of Commons on October 29th:

> The chief complainant among the nations against the working of the Non-Intervention agreement is Soviet Russia. Almost the whole burden of the criticisms of Soviet Russia, is addressed against one country, and that the smallest of the three Powers, Portugal. . . . Nor have we any information whatever to support the Soviet charges. . . . No single government has withdrawn from this agreement. They are still on the committee, even Soviet Russia. . . . There is no alternative policy except to allow the free export of arms to either side—not by us, but one set of governments supporting the one side and the other the other. . . . In that way lies confusion, international recrimination, and, maybe, war. . . . It [non-intervention] is a device, admittedly a device, by means of which we hope to limit the risks of war. It is an improvised safety curtain.

Tattered and full of holes no doubt, but better than total war in Spain and a European war out of that.

As General Franco's forces drew nearer to Madrid, governments favourable to him upheld his cause more openly. Before the end of October the Portuguese had suspended recognition of the Spanish Government, despite a British appeal not to do so. As the insurgents' power grew, we had to decide whether we should, as a matter of convenience, grant belligerent rights. France did not wish to recognize

Franco in this way and proposed to withdraw her Chargé d'Affaires from Madrid, when the Spanish Government removed to Valencia on November 8th. A few days later, Hitler and Mussolini recognized Franco's administration as the legal Government of Spain.

General Franco announced on November 17th his intention to stop the traffic in arms which was being carried on through Barcelona. To do this he would, if necessary, destroy the port. He warned all foreigners and foreign ships to leave. We interpreted this announcement as implying a blockade, but Franco could not make this effective without exercising belligerent rights and we should certainly help him if we granted them. On the other hand, four or five British ships were known to be gun-running, mainly for the Spanish Government. British shipowners had been asked not to allow this, but it was a lucrative business and the carrying of arms from foreign ports to Spain was perfectly legal. Furthermore, we had reports of intensified Italian naval activity at both ends of the Mediterranean. It looked as though the Italians might be intending to intercept Russian ships on their way to Spain.

Before this quickening of events, our instructions to the Royal Navy had been to protect British ships outside the three-mile limit of Spanish territorial waters. Now, in view of the increasing likelihood of incidents, new orders were drawn up by the Admiralty under which our ships would not be protected. I did not like these instructions. The First Lord of the Admiralty wished to follow them by granting belligerent rights to Franco, but I did not want to take this short cut. I preferred to find a policy which would protect our interests and minimize the risk of an encounter, without helping the insurgents. I thought that we should achieve our purpose if we forbade British ships to carry arms to Spain, at the same time giving notice that our vessels would be protected on all legitimate trade. On Saturday, November 21st, I wrote in my diary:

A heavy and difficult day at the office. Admiralty have got out some interim regulations for Mediterranean which will not do for more than a few hours. After speaking to Sam [Hoare] and S.B. [Baldwin], I arranged a meeting of some Ministers for tomorrow afternoon. My own feeling is at present against granting of belligerent rights to Franco for international rather than Spanish reasons. I do not want even to appear to follow Hitler and Mussolini at the moment, but would prefer to 'show a tooth' in the Mediterranean; still less do I want to facilitate an attempt at a blockade that is maybe intended to starve Madrid.

A long tussle duly took place on the following afternoon. I drew attention to Franco's statement that he would stop all ships on the high seas. To grant belligerent rights would isolate us among non-dictator powers, for neither France nor the United States was thinking of such action. Moreover, its effect would be to give *de facto* recognition to Franco, although the military situation had not changed significantly in his favour. I preferred that we should show ourselves strong in the Mediterranean by protecting all our ships engaged in legitimate trade, while forbidding them to carry arms. Eventually, Ministers agreed that my policy should be carried out and I despatched telegrams that night to the Spanish Government and to the insurgents.

* * * * *

On the morning of the 23rd, the French Ambassador told me that I was at liberty to say in the House that the French Government had not asked us to reconsider our attitude to non-intervention; on the contrary, they were definitely of the opinion that non-intervention should continue. Because close consultation between ourselves and the French now prevailed, I gave Corbin an account of the statement on Spain that I was to make to Parliament that afternoon. He agreed with its terms, saying that he was particularly glad we were not granting belligerent rights at present. This would have given the impression that we were going to facilitate General Franco's blockade, which in turn would have encouraged Mussolini to assist Franco to make his blockade effective, which he certainly could not do alone. By our statement, the Ambassador added, we would check, if we did not actually stop, any Italian tendencies in this direction, which was most important. I thought this an accurate reading of the situation and a realistic appraisal of the Duce's ambitions. I wished that the same foresight had prevailed in Paris twelve months earlier.

Later in the morning, the Spanish Ambassador told me he was sure that my statement would be welcomed by his Government. I announced in the House that afternoon:

> The policy of His Majesty's Government is to take no part in the Spanish war and to give no assistance to either side in the struggle. In pursuance of this policy His Majesty's Government have been considering further the importation of arms into Spain by sea and the problems arising therefrom. His Majesty's Government have not so far accorded belligerent rights at sea to either side in the Spanish struggle, and they have no present intention of

according such rights. As a consequence, His Majesty's ships will, should it prove necessary, protect British merchant ships on the high seas against interference by the ships of either party engaged in the conflict in Spain outside the three-mile limit.

At the same time it is not the intention of His Majesty's Government that British shipping should carry war material from any foreign port to any port in Spain. In order to make this as effective as possible in the circumstances the Government intend to introduce legislation immediately rendering the carriage of arms to Spain illegal, and I take this opportunity of warning all British shipping accordingly.

Anglo-French relations were now most cordial. At the end of November I received a letter from the French Ambassador, saying that his Foreign Minister had just telephoned to him. M. Delbos had spoken to the Foreign Affairs Commission of the Chamber of Deputies and asked Corbin to give me the substance of his speech. He had insisted on the close and trusting friendship between France and Britain and had affirmed the full reciprocity of their convictions and interests. These declarations, Corbin wrote, received the unanimous support of the Commission and Delbos proposed to repeat them to the Chamber itself. He would at the same time indicate that France was going to take up the same attitude as Britain, in face of the threats to blockade Spanish ports. While the French could not, on account of parliamentary difficulties, pass a law forbidding French ships to carry war materials, Corbin assured me that the Minister of Marine would in practice take steps to prevent it.

The Non-Intervention Committee's lengthy meetings continued throughout November. Accusations were met with flat denials and the results of both were sterile. In these conditions, we decided in the Foreign Office to elaborate into a plan of our own the suggestion made earlier by Corbin to me and by Maisky to the Committee. We proposed to supervise the entry of all war material into Spain, an ambitious project which would require a large number of observers to be stationed at ports and along the land frontiers. The plan had some disadvantages. It would cost about £1 million a year to operate, which was a lot of money, but cheaper than European war. It would also depend upon the approval of both parties in Spain. But so many breaches of the Agreement were now being alleged and tempers were mounting so sharply in discussing them, that a new scheme was imperative. A breakdown of the Committee would have baleful consequences, perhaps even on the Anglo-French alliance, which

I regarded as indispensable to our joint survival and that of freedom in Europe. To those who criticized non-intervention I gave the answer in a public speech:

> Because some who should be firemen take a hand now and again at feeding the flames, that is no reason why the whole fire brigade should leave their posts and join in fanning Europe into a furnace.

Our supervision scheme was eventually accepted by the Committee, subject to endorsement by governments. We quickly sent in British approval. Corbin and I had already spoken about following this up with another effort to stop the fighting. The French idea was that we should jointly approach Germany, Italy, Soviet Russia and Portugal. I suggested that we should also inform the United States Government and ask for their sympathy and approval. The French Government thought that, as Franco was not doing too well militarily, the dictator powers might welcome an opportunity to rid themselves of an embarrassing commitment. Accordingly, we made our joint appeal on December 4th, asking the four powers to abstain from any intervention in Spain. But the replies were slow in arriving and lukewarm when they did.

The truth was that the dictator powers were now engaging themselves more heavily. Five thousand Germans, formed into battalions, had recently arrived in the south and regular units were pouring in from Italy. The British Government asked the Non-Intervention Committee to consider this situation at once, while on December 8th I called in Ribbentrop and Grandi and told them that at the present rate of progress the nations of Europe would soon be fighting each other on the battlefields of Spain. I spoke of the perilous consequences of this for all our countries. Somewhat to my surprise, the members of the Non-Intervention Committee asked their Governments, some presumably as a manœuvre, to extend the agreement to cover volunteers and other forms of 'indirect intervention', a euphemistic phrase which was admitted to cover the regular foreign troops in Spain. I thought that we had to press for early replies and meanwhile search for other methods of control against the possibility that they would be dilatory or unfavourable.

Early in December, the Spanish Government decided to make an appeal to the League Council and their Ambassador, now Señor Azcarate, who had been until recently a Deputy Secretary-General on the League Secretariat, came to talk to me about it. I knew, he said, that his Government had not liked the policy of non-intervention, but, if the policy were to be combined with a scheme of supervision, that is, if it were to be made really effective, he thought they might support it at Geneva. I asked the Ambassador whether his Government's support would go so far as to endorse efforts to prevent the flow of so-called volunteers into Spain. The present position was, in our opinion, extremely serious. It could not be in the interest of Spain herself that thousands of foreigners should pour into the country and make Spain their battleground. Some day the present tragic chapter of Spanish history would have to be brought to a close. The presence of these foreigners fighting on both sides might then present a stubborn problem. It was therefore in Spain's interest as well as in ours to put a stop to the influx. The Ambassador agreed and, while inclined at first to argue that there was a difference between individual volunteers arriving on the Government side and actual military units from Germany serving with the insurgents, promised he would think over what his Government could do in this way.

The Non-Intervention Committee's mounting controversy restricted its decisions to the realm of words. Neither party in Spain was making any haste to give an opinion on the projected scheme of supervision, nor was there any check to the arrival of the well-drilled 'volunteers'. In an interview with me on December 18th, Ribbentrop alleged that Soviet Russia had already sent 50,000 men to Spain, while three days later Maisky told me that Germany was planning to send 60,000. When I told the Soviet Ambassador of the reports that Russia had 50,000 men in Spain, he immediately denied that the number of his countrymen approached this figure. In any event, he added, they had not sent regiments of soldiers, but only a small number of technical experts. I interjected 'and aviators.' The Ambassador did not specifically deny this, but affirmed that his Government were prepared to join in any international action to stop the flow of volunteers.

Later the same day, Corbin spoke to me about conversations he had recently had with Delbos and Blum. The latter's position was once again becoming very difficult and there was immediate need for some system of control of arms into Spain. I replied that it seemed to me even more important that we should try to stop foreign nationals from going to fight there. The Ambassador answered, with truth, that after recent experience, promises would scarcely be believed unless their sincerity could be checked. I gave him some account of my interview with Maisky, and Corbin remarked that if Germany were to send

50,000 or more men to Spain, he really did not know how French opinion could be restrained.

It was now hardly disputable that Hitler, Mussolini and Stalin would break any engagement, if it suited their purposes in Spain. I thought I should point to the consequences of such action. In a speech at Bradford I first gave a general warning about the consequences of neglect of solemn undertakings, which is even more closely applicable today:

> There must be a limit to unilateral denunciations or we shall reach a point where force and force alone is to be the sole arbiter of international relations and where no treaty will be worth the paper on which it is written. Tearing up a scrap of paper led to the war of 1914. If Europe is to be littered with scraps of paper in 1936 and thereafter, nobody can look ahead with any confidence. I repeat, therefore, that international relations are guided not by forms of government but by the manner in which governments observe their undertakings....
>
> If we, the nations of Europe, cannot collaborate to deal with the Spanish problem, then we shall be moving into deeper and more dangerous waters. ... There is a spirit of violence abroad in Europe today which bodes ill for the future unless all the restraining and responsible influences in humanity are brought to bear to check it.

I now saw no prospect of the Non-Intervention Committee grappling with the situation effectively, though it would no doubt be necessary to go on trying for results. As a consequence, I began to think about more forceful methods to show we intended that the engagements given to the Committee would be fulfilled. For this purpose naval action by Britain was the appropriate answer. The conviction of our neutrality had its diplomatic value, maybe I could cash in upon it, to the point of securing general acceptance of supervision at sea by Britain alone. It would be a bold bid, but, I thought, worth making.

VI

THE GENTLEMAN'S AGREEMENT

July 1936 – April 1937

The Montreux Conference – Signor Mussolini's character – Conversations with Count Grandi – He asks for a British gesture – My speech to the House of Commons – The Mediterranean a main artery – Mussolini suggests a Gentleman's Agreement – French reactions – Count Ciano evasive about propaganda – The Agreement is signed – It fails over Spain – I propose an international naval patrol – The First Lord of the Admiralty objects – I make a prediction – Volunteers fighting in Spain – Fascist reverse at Guadalajara

In the summer of 1935 the Turkish Government told us that they wanted to modify the Lausanne Treaty of 1923, which had forbidden the fortification of the European and Asiatic shores of the Bosphorus and Dardanelles. Throughout my political life I have believed in the importance of close friendship between Great Britain and Turkey. When I became Foreign Secretary, I read through all the documents relating to the revision of the Lausanne Treaty and decided that we must help the Turkish Government if they wished to modify the Treaty. I was encouraged in this by the opinion of the Admiralty, which considered that the disadvantages of fortification were outweighed by the value to Great Britain of Turkish co-operation.

The Turkish Government were anxious for our backing in putting their arguments for revision before the other signatories of Lausanne, but I preferred that we should not appear to be doing a private deal with Turkey in return for that country's firm support in the Abyssinian dispute. I therefore suggested to the Foreign Minister, M. Aras, that he should approach all the signatories of the Lausanne Treaty. This he did in a note of April 11th, 1936.

Events in the Mediterranean now made me sure that this action was right. Mussolini's recent fortification of the Dodecanese and his avowed intention to upset the Mediterranean balance of power increased Turkey's significance. Moreover, despite Litvinov's assurances, Soviet Russia's propaganda and influence were also at work against Great Britain and I thought it would be no bad thing if Anglo-Turkish friendship were seen by the Kremlin to be firm. I had also noticed that Hitler was offering long-term credits in Turkey and the Balkans and I did not want Germany to become the predominant power in Turkey, as she had been before the first world war. I had one other important motive. Here was an opportunity to encourage the revision of treaties by discussion.

The British Government, therefore, quickly agreed to the Turkish request and it was decided that a conference should be convened at Montreux in June 1936. Early in that month I wrote in a memorandum for my colleagues that the British delegation

> . . . should be authorized to agree at once to the abrogation of those Articles of the existing Straits Convention which provide for the demilitarization of the Straits zone. I may explain that if the Turks had decided to follow the example of Germany and repudiate the Straits Convention unilaterally, we should not have been able to prevent them from doing so. The fact that they have acted in so proper and correct a manner in trying to secure the revision of this treaty instrument by negotiation and agreement gives them a very strong claim to favourable treatment. It is most important on general grounds that it should be made clear that treaty revision by agreement can pay as well as, or better than, unilateral repudiation. Moreover, we have the strongest interest, from the political point of view, in developing and strengthening the friendly relations at present existing between Turkey and ourselves, and in responding to her recent advances in this direction. I therefore consider that from every point of view it is most important that this concession . . . should be made as generously and completely as possible from the outset.

The Turks had given notice that they wished also to revise the clauses of the Convention dealing with the passage of warships through the Straits. When I was at Geneva towards the end of June, the stream of telegrams from Montreux showed that Russia was asking for large concessions in this connection. I learnt privately that M. Aras was disturbed, but unwilling to take a firm stand against the Soviet demands. Accordingly, when Litvinov came to see me on June 27th, I said that so far as I could understand the situation, his Government were asking too much. It did not seem to me a reasonable proposition that the Soviet Government should maintain their right to send a fleet into the

Mediterranean, while virtually closing the Black Sea to all the powers whose territories did not border that sea. It was at present proposed that the limitation on global naval tonnage which might enter the Black Sea should be 30,000 tons. I therefore suggested that this tonnage be raised on a sliding scale, if the Soviet Government were to increase the size of their fleet in the Black Sea.

Litvinov undertook to submit this to his Government and a slightly modified version was agreed a few days later. But this was not the only obstacle. The French, Russian and Roumanian delegations wanted to be sure that in time of war Turkey would not prohibit the passage even of warships, if they were acting by virtue of any pact concluded under the League of Nations. The Turkish Government did not want to accept this obligation and I understood the difficulties which it might present. At my suggestion it was eventually agreed that this undertaking would only operate in respect of pacts to which Turkey was herself a party.

Mussolini was a notable absentee from the Montreux Conference, though Italy had been a signatory of the Straits Convention. While arguing that he would not attend until sanctions had been lifted, the Duce apparently believed that no settlement could be reached without him. The Conference, however, went quietly on with its business and reached its conclusion without Fascist help. We were well represented in these discussions by Lord Stanley, then a Minister at the Admiralty. Turkey fortified the Straits, while our relations grew steadily closer. These events had their influence upon the course of the second world war, when Turkey's neutrality in the earlier years was of undoubted benefit to us.

* * * * *

The League's withdrawal of sanctions brought hope to many that good relations between Italy and Britain could now be restored. The argument often put to me was that, if we would only make a concession to the Duce, he would reciprocate and our relations would soon mend. I had little confidence that this would be so, for the reasoning appeared to be founded on a misreading of Mussolini's character. To me, he was a tough and clever opportunist, who would rate concessions as weakness and who cared nothing for the principles of the League or for the Stresa front. He would incline to whichever side seemed to offer him the greater advantages. We could not, for moral and practical reasons, enter such a competition or offer him the plunder he sought;

therefore Hitler and Mussolini would inevitably be drawn closer together. The Duce had made his choice between African adventure and European stability. He abandoned Austria when he marched against Abyssinia. Despite rumours, Mussolini and I had no personal quarrel and our relations were not a factor in the unfolding of policy on either side.

I thought that our attitude towards Rome should therefore be one of cautious advances. We should give evidence of goodwill, but surrender no vital interest, nor count upon Fascism to keep its promises when they became inconvenient. Certainly I tried to remove causes of grievance, and at the end of July I announced in the House of Commons that we now considered the period of Mediterranean tension at an end. I was able to do this with confidence in the firmer relations we had established with Turkey, through the success of the conference at Montreux. As a result, the reciprocal assurances given by Greece, Turkey, Yugoslavia and Great Britain were nullified. Any good effect this declaration might have had in Italy was submerged by the Spanish war. Moreover, Fascist intrigue and propaganda against Britain were ceaseless, an intensive campaign being conducted in most of the Mediterranean countries and as far east as Iran and India. In these conditions, I attached continuing importance to a friendly Turkey; together we could protect our joint position in the eastern Mediterranean. I was also considering other plans for the same purpose and when I returned to the Foreign Office in the middle of August I minuted:

> We should proceed with the development of Cyprus as a new naval and air base without delay. We shall need it whatever the future orientation of our policy, or that of others, in the Eastern Mediterranean.

Events in Spain raised new dangers. If Mussolini were to occupy the Balearic Islands, he would gain a base for naval and military operations 250 miles nearer Gibraltar. In spite of this, my own belief was that no Spanish government, whether of the right or the left, would willingly grant to a foreigner facilities of such importance as to threaten our sea communications, if only for reasons of national pride. But there could be no certainty. We had, until this time, counted upon a friendly or neutral Spain. If a Communist or Fascist government were established there, we could no longer assume the safety of our communications through the Mediterranean or by way of the Atlantic. This was a powerful reason for the enforcement of non-intervention. It was important to us that the winning side should not grant territorial prizes or negotiate closer military relations with other powers. Even so, we could not tell whether Mussolini would extract some concessions from a victorious Franco. I minuted:

I fear that whichever side wins, the outlook for us must be anxious and we must have the ultimate position of Gibraltar constantly in mind.

* * * * *

On September 18th, Grandi and I discussed Anglo-Italian relations at length. He told me that he had found in Rome a deep-seated conviction that British policy was now directed against Italy in the Mediterranean. There had, he said, even been reports that we were contemplating the creation of a new base in the Adriatic. I told the Ambassador that this was quite untrue and, incidentally, impossible, since we had no territory in the Adriatic. I now think that these rumours may have been circulated as preliminary pretexts for the Fascist invasion of Albania. Grandi said he was confident that Mussolini himself really desired a return to the previous relations between our two countries. I said that this was also the wish of His Majesty's Government; the state of Europe was much too serious for anything else.

Sir Eric Drummond happened to be on leave at this time and we discussed the possibility of improving the climate between London and Rome. I told him that I had no wish to perpetuate the deep feelings aroused by Italian action in Abyssinia, but I could not accept to limit our rearmament. Drummond repeated this to the Italian Foreign Minister on October 7th, when he also complained of anti-British propaganda being inspired from Italian sources. He warned Ciano that if this became known, there would be a strong public reaction in England. Count Ciano professed ignorance of any such propaganda.

A few days after this, I heard again from Grandi how anxious the Duce was to co-operate with us as he had done before 1935. The Ambassador asked me whether there was not some small gesture of goodwill which we could make, which would have a psychological effect on Italian opinion quite out of proportion to its real importance. He instanced the withdrawal of our Consul from Gore in Abyssinia as having produced a very good effect in Rome. I replied that there was in this action a lesson in our mutual relations for us both. Mr. Erskine's withdrawal from Gore was not carried out in order to give satisfaction to Italy, but because the main purpose for which the Consul had been at Gore, the protection of British lives and property, had been fulfilled, the British subjects having been evacuated. Mr. Erskine's duties, I said, were not political, but no doubt because the Italian Government suspected that they might be, their relief was the greater at his departure. All the same, the Ambassador thought that another gesture of this kind would have a good effect. I told him that he was not setting me an easy task.

Towards the end of this conversation, Grandi came to what appeared to be the main reason for his visit. He referred to reports that British troops in Egypt had been reinforced by two battalions, which were being stationed at Mersa Matruh. I told him that I thought the reports inaccurate, I noticed that 3,000 men was mentioned as the total and no two British battalions could reach so large a figure. Later I checked up and sent word to the Ambassador that there was no truth in the report.

This conversation did, however, encourage me to make a further attempt to bring down the temperature between our two countries and I asked Drummond for his suggestions. As I expected, he replied that the real crux of the problem lay in the Mediterranean. Italy would like to discuss the subject directly with us. I replied that I was perfectly willing to hold such conversations but had looked in vain, so far, for any worthwhile evidence of Fascist reciprocity.

On October 24th Mussolini made a speech at Bologna which hardly helped matters. The Duce, having, in the words of Drummond's telegram, expatiated on the glorious and speedy conquest of Abyssinia and referred in scathing terms to League opposition, stated that he wished to launch a message beyond the mountains and seas:

> At the close of the year 14 [of the Fascist era] I raise a large olive branch. This olive branch rises from an immense forest; it is a forest of eight million bayonets well sharpened and wielded by young intrepid hearts.

Both Drummond and Vansittart urged that I should say something publicly or privately in appreciation of Mussolini's latest declaration. I did not feel I could go as far as this and minuted: 'The world would laugh too loudly. If the Italians really want better relations with us they must do better than this.' It happened that we were about to remove the guard from our Legation in Addis Ababa. So I added: 'Perhaps this move may give them occasion to find an olive branch elsewhere than on a bayonet.'

To Drummond I telegraphed:

> I do not see how I can possibly express appreciation of Signor Mussolini's olive branch declaration, accompanied as it is by his reference to a forest of

eight million bayonets. Viewed from here it is difficult to see the branch for the forest.

A well-publicized visit by Count Ciano to Berlin gave point to the arguments of those who maintained that only prompt concessions by Great Britain could restore the Stresa front. Then, as now, we were too often being urged to make gestures of goodwill to countries, only to find that their rulers interpreted them as weakness on our part. While I was always open to any approach from Rome, we had no cause to crave negotiation with Fascist Italy, our navy and air force were far more powerful than hers. Furthermore, we could at any time of emergency prevent Mussolini's ships from passing the Straits of Gibraltar, or cut off the route to Abyssinia by closing the Suez Canal.

The next move came from the Duce. At Milan on November 1st he made an offer of friendship in less strident terms:

> Italy is an island in the Mediterranean. This sea is for Great Britain a road, one of many roads indeed, a short cut by which the British Empire reaches its outlying territories more quickly. If for the others the Mediterranean is a road, for us it is life. We have said a thousand times and we repeat before this great assembly that we have no intention of threatening it or interrupting it; but, on the other hand, we demand that our rights and vital interests be respected. There are no alternatives.... There is one solution only, an understanding sincere, swift and complete on the basis of respect for our mutual rights.

I thought that these were sentiments to which we could respond, even though we could not admit Mussolini's claim that the Mediterranean was for us a 'short cut'. Four days afterwards, when the House debated foreign affairs, I first recalled that the deterioration in our relations with Italy was due to the fulfilment of our obligations under the Covenant; there had never been an Anglo-Italian quarrel so far as our country was concerned. I continued:

> The implication that freedom to come and go in the Mediterranean is for this country a convenience rather than a vital interest is one which does not fully describe our interests. For us the Mediterranean is not a short cut but a main arterial road. We do not challenge Signor Mussolini's words that for Italy 'the Mediterranean is her very life', but we affirm that freedom of communication in these waters is also a vital interest, in a full sense of the word, to the British Commonwealth of Nations. In years gone by, the interests of the two countries in the Mediterranean have been complementary

rather than divergent. On the part of His Majesty's Government there is every desire that those relations should be preserved in future.

Consequently we take note of, and welcome, the assurance that Signor Mussolini gives that Italy does not mean to threaten this route nor propose to interrupt it. Nor do we. Our position is the same. I repeat the assurance that we have no desire to threaten, or intention to attack, any Italian interest in the Mediterranean. In these conditions it should, in our view, be possible for each country to continue to maintain its vital interests in the Mediterranean not only without conflict with each other, but even with mutual advantage.

When Grandi saw me the next morning, he told me that though he had received no instructions, he was sure that his Government had hoped for something more. The Ambassador pleaded for recognition of the Italian conquest of Abyssinia. He feared that it would seem to Mussolini that Italy had made an advance and received a rebuff. I replied that I could not accept the Ambassador's description. If a man from Mars were to compare the texts of our two speeches, I was convinced that he would not decide that Signor Mussolini's was the more forthcoming. I asked Grandi to accept that my statement, which had been carefully considered by the Government, was definitely intended as an attempt to bring about improved relations between our countries. But I refused to make any move over Abyssinia.

* * * * *

British Ministers had varying views about the situation which was developing. Some considered we were tied up too much with France, which prevented us from getting on terms with the dictators; others, that our public opinion would like a five-power agreement. Most members of the Government, as well as the Chiefs of Staff, thought that we must remove Italy from the list of countries with whom we might have to reckon. I had to say that I saw no chance of any agreement which would allow us to slow down our defensive preparations in the Mediterranean. I minuted on November 7th that if Anglo-Italian relations improved, it would be because it suited Mussolini and that

. . . no amount of promises or understandings or renewed professions of friendship or even humble crawlings on our part will affect Mussolini's course. On the other hand, a little plain speaking may. We must be on our guard against increasing the dictators' prestige by our own excessive submissiveness.

I had said my say in the House of Commons and was determined that there should be no more approaches to Mussolini, official or unofficial, until we knew, and had studied, the Duce's response to my speech. I instructed the Foreign Office accordingly. The reaction in Rome was favourable and on November 8th most organs of the Fascist-controlled press recognized that British communications in the Mediterranean were of vital interest to us. We received the first hints, from more than one quarter, that Mussolini would like what he described in an interview as a 'Gentleman's Agreement' between the two countries. Its purpose would be to ensure reciprocal protection of British and Italian interests in the Mediterranean.

While ready to follow this up, I was determined to do so in step with the French, who had lately been showing growing concern at Italy's attitude to European problems. Corbin told me on November 11th that while the French Government sincerely desired better Anglo-Italian relations, they felt some anxiety about the effect upon the League. It was to France's advantage, he continued, as well as to everybody else's in the Mediterranean, that there should be some betterment of Anglo-Italian relations. He only wished me to have in mind the influence this might have upon smaller powers in the League. I reassured him that we would never take any action to the detriment of a third party and that we would keep his Government informed.

Grandi was due to leave London on November 14th for a meeting of the Fascist Grand Council and I asked him to come to see me on the previous evening. In order to smooth the way, I thanked him for some courtesies that Marshal Graziani had shown to our Chargé d'Affaires at Addis Ababa on the departure of our Legation guard. Grandi heard this with pleasure and commented that our relations were improving at a greater speed than he would have dared to hope. He added that my observation that the Mediterranean was not a short cut but a main arterial road, had been fully understood in Rome.

We then had some discussion as to how the better atmosphere was to be used. I said I understood that Signor Mussolini was anxious to carry matters a stage further. We were quite ready to do this, but I did not know what the Duce had in mind when he referred to a Gentleman's Agreement. I thought it probable that he did not intend anything in the nature of a pact. Personally, I hoped this was his opinion for a variety of reasons. Grandi at once replied that he felt confident Signor Mussolini had not a pact in mind. We agreed that an exchange of assurances was the best way to handle the business, but I said that it seemed to me much better to treat the Abyssinian problem separately. The Ambassador left in good spirits.

On the same day I set out in a memorandum for the Foreign Office my opinion about relations with Mussolini, stating that what swayed Nazi Germany towards Fascist Italy was

... not so much her defiance of the Covenant; it was her success. While sanctions were still in operation, there was little sign of any *rapprochement* between the two dictators. It was only when sanctions were raised and the League Powers acknowledged their failure that the German people, who only respect force, found something in Italy worth cultivating. Any appearance now of over-keenness by us to ingratiate ourselves with Italy would only accentuate her charms in the eyes of Herr Hitler. Nor is it only Herr Hitler who would be impressed. All the smaller Mediterranean powers, who till now have pinned their faith to us, would begin to think of making their peace with the Mammon of unrighteousness. It may also be borne in mind that it is exceedingly doubtful how far any gesture of friendliness by us would induce Fascist Italy fundamentally to alter or modify her policy in the Mediterranean. What is her main aim, constantly reaffirmed? The re-constitution of the Roman Empire. That aim may seem far off, may seem to us utterly fantastic and unreal; but so long as she is moving along these lines, she can hardly enter into sincere collaboration with England, the one great obstacle in her path....

Despite this reservation, I was quite ready for tactical reasons to see what could be done, even to reduce the temperature for a while:

To sum up: unless some further reply be made to Signor Mussolini's advances, he will undoubtedly recur to the suspicions and animosities of the last eighteen months and employ with increased energy the numerous methods open to him by which the nuisance value of Italy's policy can be directed to our detriment. Among these will be an increasing collaboration and understanding with Germany, which will be worked not only to our detriment but to our eventual danger. An early, careful and not ungenerous response on the other hand might help to produce a *détente* in the Mediterranean while British rearmament proceeds.

... it is of the first importance that we should show ourselves strong. We must continue all our preparations in the Mediterranean on a scale with which Italy cannot easily compete. That will impress not only the Mediterranean powers, but Germany, and make Italy less attractive in German eyes. Subject to this consideration, the balance of arguments would seem to be in favour of making a friendly approach. The unreliability of Italy is a reason for circumspection rather than inaction. Also it may be assumed that as our rearmament proceeds and our military and naval strength grows more marked, it will become increasingly worth while for Italy to continue to maintain and to foster with Great Britain relations of friendship and co-operation, once these have been re-established on a proper footing.

On November 14th I telegraphed to Drummond that I was relieved to learn that Mussolini had declarations of policy, rather than a treaty, in mind. They should follow the lines of my speech of November 5th. I repeated that we were not prepared to take any course liable to arouse the fears and suspicions of other Mediterranean countries, nor would we limit the size and location of our military and naval forces in the Mediterranean or Red Sea. I refused for the present to recognize the Italian conquest of Abyssinia. We wished the Italian Government to accept without qualification the territorial *status quo* in the Mediterranean and to renounce anti-British propaganda in the Near East. I asked Drummond whether, within these limitations, he thought there was a prospect of further improving relations through direct conversations in Rome. Drummond replied that there was, while I received through the Italian Embassy a message from Mussolini to say how pleased he had been with the report of my meeting with Grandi.

I was careful to reassure our Mediterranean friends. Prince Paul, Regent of Yugoslavia, happened to be on a visit to England at this time. I told him that we had no intention of coming to any arrangements which would affect our good relations with a third party and I spoke in a similar sense to the Turkish Ambassador. The French Government, however, were still very apprehensive. Corbin told me on November 23rd that they felt the need for the greatest caution in order to ensure, whatever our intentions, that an Anglo-Italian arrangement was not interpreted in certain quarters as being directed against France. There might be several motives in the Italian wish for *rapprochement*. It could be, Corbin said, a genuine desire to ease the tension between the two countries, or possibly it was an attempt, not ill-regarded from Berlin, to show that France might be left out of important negotiations. I told the French Ambassador that France's fears seemed to me exaggerated and again promised to keep him fully informed of all developments.

These were not slow in coming. On the evening of November 25th, Grandi, having returned from Rome, again called on me. I learnt from him that Mussolini and Ciano fully understood that we could not bargain over Abyssinia. Mussolini had asked the Ambassador to say that there would be no difficulty on the Italian side about the form which the Gentleman's Agreement was to take. He suggested that this document might embody some reference to the complementary nature of our interests in the Mediterranean and agreed with me that it would be wiser to have no pact.

The course now seemed to be set fair and at the beginning of December I authorized Drummond to open conversations. I said that in any declaration it was important to find a form of words which would not offend the susceptibilities of the French, whose interests in the Mediterranean were as vital as those of Great Britain and Italy. I proposed to make no concessions to Mussolini and stipulated that we should need some guarantee that Fascist intrigue against us would cease. When our Ambassador gave Ciano a formula, based on my speech of November 5th, it was well received. Ciano had prepared a draft which accorded with our own and Drummond anticipated little difficulty in arriving at a satisfactory form of words.

When, early in the negotiations, Drummond mentioned the possibility of France being associated in some form with our exchange of assurances, Ciano was perturbed. I did not wish to insist on this and, to keep the wheels oiled while we considered important questions still to be resolved, telegraphed to Rome a tempering reply. Ciano, according to Drummond, was 'obviously pleased and considerably relieved' and foresaw no further difficulties. All the same, I was most anxious to remain in step with the French Government. The more so because Delbos had shown us many acts of friendship recently, not least in using his influence, during the Abdication crisis, to restrain his country's press. I therefore asked Sir George Clerk to give the Foreign Minister a full account of the negotiations. This he did on December 12th. Delbos replied without equivocation that he had no qualms whatever about the subjects or the issue of our discussions with the Italian Government. He had the fullest confidence in our loyalty and in the friendship between our two countries, which he felt had never been firmer and franker than it was now. He entirely agreed with my view that an improvement in Anglo-Italian relations was as much in the interests of France as of Great Britain.

Meanwhile, reports had come in of renewed Italian activities in the Balearic Isles. I instructed Drummond to speak about this to Ciano, who tried to dispose of the whole matter in a light-hearted fashion, which did not reassure me. I therefore proposed that, in the declaration, the two countries should 'disclaim any desire to modify, or, so far as they are concerned, to see modified, the national status of the territories in the Mediterranean area, particularly the territories of Spain.' In the same telegram, on December 18th, I insisted that Ciano should give attention to the propaganda question.

As I had expected, the detailed negotiations with Ciano became difficult over the topic of Spain. I attached importance to getting from the Fascist Government a declaration that they would in all circumstances respect the territorial integrity of Spain. I desired this, because there could be no certainty about the outcome of the civil war and I did not want Mussolini to have any pretext for staying in any part of Spanish territories, especially the Balearic Islands. Ciano at first resisted, on the grounds that he could not include in the Mediterranean Agreement a statement that might imply that General Franco would consider ceding any Spanish territory.

I argued back that if this were the only difficulty, it could be met by a separate exchange of notes on the subject of Spain. Ciano eventually yielded with indifferent grace, to the accompaniment of a diatribe about the injustice of asking such questions of Italy alone. The exchange of notes referred to an earlier statement of mine in Parliament, in which I had quoted Ciano's assurance that no negotiations would be held with General Franco which would change the *status quo* in the Mediterranean. We now asked for formal confirmation. Ciano replied: 'So far as Italy is concerned, the integrity of the present territories of Spain shall in all circumstances remain intact and unmodified.'

In discussion with Drummond, Ciano was evasive about anti-British propaganda. When pressed, he promised to take note of our complaints but, as events showed, made no effort to meet them. The question of propaganda was to play a part in my attitude when, a year later, Britain was again discussing the possibility of negotiations with Mussolini. For the moment, we had forced a public statement of good intent, for what that might be worth.

Thus the Gentleman's Agreement was reached, Ciano accepting our request for a forty-eight hour delay so that we might inform the French of its terms. The text of the Agreement read as follows:

His Majesty's Government in the United Kingdom and the Italian Government:

Animated by the desire to contribute increasingly, in the interests of the general cause of peace and security, to the betterment of relations between them and between all the Mediterranean Powers, and resolved to respect the rights and interests of those Powers;

Recognize that the freedom of entry into, exit from, and transit through, the Mediterranean is a vital interest both to the different parts of the British Empire and to Italy, and that these interests are in no way inconsistent with each other;

Disclaim any desire to modify or, so far as they are concerned, to see modified the *status quo* as regards national sovereignty of territories in the Mediterranean area;

Undertake to respect each other's rights and interests in the said area;

Agree to use their best endeavours to discourage any activities liable to impair the good relations which it is the object of the present declaration to consolidate.

This declaration is designed to further the ends of peace and is not directed against any other Power.

* * * * *

On January 4th I returned from Yorkshire to the Foreign Office, to learn that further large consignments of Italian volunteers had just arrived in Spain. Since the Agreement had been signed two days before, it seemed only too likely that Mussolini had used our negotiations as a cover plan for his further intervention. To make matters worse, the Nazi press was now mischief-making, seeking to interpret our Agreement as an encouragement to Franco. Happily, as I wrote in my diary, 'the French Government have behaved very well, and I have been repaid for keeping Delbos informed and making the Italians wait for forty-eight hours before the publication of the Exchange of Assurances by an excellent message of goodwill which Delbos gave the French press.' I added:

> It is fortunate that I insisted on an exchange of letters about Majorca and the integrity of Spanish territory. . . . At least we have given nothing away to Italy. It remains to be seen whether what we have gained will prove of any material value. Time alone will show and nothing would be more foolish than openly to attempt to woo Mussolini away from Hitler.

The next day the Spanish Ambassador called at the Foreign Office and said that Spain had at first had hopes of the Gentleman's Agreement. His Government had welcomed it because of its references to Spanish territorial integrity. This good effect had now been destroyed by the landing of further large numbers of Italian volunteers. The impression was all the worse because a suggestion had been made that His Majesty's Government were now disinteresting themselves from the question of volunteers. I told Azcarate that this was not true and gave him an account of our activities. All the same I had no doubt in my mind that the increased Fascist intervention in Spain was a violation of the spirit of the Agreement. Mussolini knew perfectly well that this action must 'impair the good relations which it is the object of the present declaration to consolidate'. But he did not care enough to modify his plans or projects.

* * * * *

The failure of the so-called Gentleman's Agreement taught me a lesson, that there was no value in negotiating with Mussolini again, unless he first carried out the engagements he had already entered into. This was true even though we had yielded nothing to get this Agreement. On the other hand its existence, in spite of being smirched, would strengthen the British position if we put forward a plan of our own for effective control of the Non-Intervention Agreement. All the interested governments had publicly committed themselves, with varying degrees of sincerity, to this policy. I thought that a firm and definite proposal would have an astringent effect on their attitudes and would at least bring the issue to a fine point.

I set out in a memorandum, on January 7th, the wider implications of the conflict:

> The Spanish civil war has ceased to be an internal Spanish issue and has become an international battle-ground. The character of the future government of Spain has now become less important to the peace of Europe than that the dictators should not be victorious in that country. The extent and character of the intervention now practised by Germany and Italy have made it clear to the world that the object of these powers is to secure General Franco's victory whether or not it represents the will of the Spanish people....
>
> The position in Italy is difficult to estimate. If we are to judge from Count Ciano's interviews with Sir Eric Drummond the Italian Government does not wish to proceed to extreme lengths in Spain and would be willing to accept a practical solution of the problem of volunteers.

I pointed out that the arrival of Italian volunteers, 4,000 of them according to our latest reports, had damaged the good effect of the Agreement. Despite appearances, however, it might still, I contended, be productive of good results. It was necessary to put forward proposals which Italy could accept and which would enable her to put pressure on Germany to do the same. My use of these arguments, even after Mussolini's overt breach of the Agreement, showed that I was, if anything, too complaisant towards the Fascist dictator.

It was above all important, I wrote, to see the Spanish problem in relation to Germany. We had received many indications that the more cautious elements in that country, of which the army and the Foreign Office had the most authority, were opposed to the Spanish adventure. The same influences had opposed the march into the Rhineland. They were overruled and, since that *coup* was successful, ignoring them was held in German eyes to have been justified. If no attempt were made to check the Nazi adventure in Spain, we might be certain that on a subsequent occasion, when the Nazi Party urged extreme courses, the more cautious influences would have no opportunity to make themselves felt in Europe's other danger points, Memel, Danzig and Czechoslovakia. My paper continued:

It is therefore my conviction that unless we cry a halt in Spain, we shall have trouble this year in one or other of the danger points I have referred to. It follows that to be firm in Spain is to gain time, and to gain time is what we want. We cannot in this instance gain time by marking it. It is to be remembered that in the language of the Nazi Party any adventure is a minor adventure. They spoke thus of the Rhineland last year, they are speaking thus of Spain today, they will speak thus of Memel, Danzig or Czechoslovakia tomorrow. It is only by showing them that these dangerous distinctions are false that we can hope to avert a greater calamity.

My memorandum declared it imperative that we should spare no effort to put a stop to intervention in Spain, the abuse was becoming a menace to the peace of the world. I then summarized the Portuguese, Italian, German and Russian replies to our representations about volunteers. Despite mutual suspicion of good faith, these four Governments professed to be willing to prohibit the enlistment or recruitment of volunteers. This was on condition that others did the same.

I thought we must take these countries at their word and devise a plan which would hold them publicly to their declarations and, because we were known to be truly neutral, we could take the heaviest share of responsibility. I proposed that we should offer the services of the Royal Navy to supervise at sea all approaches to ports and harbours, both round the Spanish coast and in Spanish overseas possessions, to prevent either volunteers or war material entering these territories. The other nations would be asked to agree that our ships should be entitled to visit and search merchant vessels or send them into a convenient port, if inspection could not be completed at sea. To bear witness to our impartiality, I proposed that each British ship employed in this task would carry a naval officer of one of the countries which had signed the Non-Intervention Agreement.

In making this offer, Great Britain would call upon the Soviet, German, Italian, Portuguese and French Governments to carry out their pledges to stop the flow of volunteers, and upon the last two Governments to close their frontiers with Spain. We would discuss with the French the advisability of inviting neutral officers to co-operate in the frontier control. His Majesty's Government, for their part, would state publicly that the Foreign Enlistment Act would be strictly enforced, to prevent the enrolment of any British volunteers.

I went to see Baldwin and explained to him the substance and purpose of this memorandum. He approved the policy and I felt confident I should get his support. At my request, the Prime Minister collected some of the principal Ministers for an informal meeting on January 8th. Just before the meeting, Halifax said to me: 'I've read your plan and I like it very much.' However, the discussion went badly. I explained that the object of my proposals was to avoid a European war. If we did not stand up to the dictator powers now, war would be brought nearer and we should lose the support of our friends in Europe if war came. The danger to Europe, I told my colleagues, did not arise from what might happen at sea. If Germany and Italy were not checked in their Spanish ambitions, we might arrive at a situation in which those countries would, in effect, conquer Spain. I had in mind the immediate danger of this, even though Spain would never in the long term accept any rule based on foreign power.

Sir Samuel Hoare, the First Lord of the Admiralty, did not like the plan. He thought that we were getting to a point when, as a nation, we were trying to stop General Franco from winning. But there were others, he said, who were very anxious that the Soviets should not win in Spain. Hoare produced every kind of technical argument to invalidate my plan: the Spanish coast was very long, with many ports; a large number of ships would be required to examine the many neutral vessels; it would involve mobilizing the Home and Mediterranean Fleets exclusively for the purpose and calling up the naval reserve; it was very difficult to carry out a blockade on the high seas, no blockade was ever watertight; and further chatter of this kind.

I explained that I was not proposing to carry out a blockade, but a watch on non-intervention, there were already British ships in most of the main Spanish harbours. I accepted that everything depended on the goodwill of the powers and on what lay behind their answers. Baldwin said nothing on behalf of my plan and I was unable to convince my colleagues, several of whom talked of the dangers of an incident with Italy or Russia. We were far stronger at sea than either power and I did not believe this risk to be serious. In any event, I believed it to be the lesser evil. The essential was to pin the other powers to action which their own words would make it difficult for them to refuse. I was urged to ask governments not to send any more volunteers. As we had done this before, I thought it useless to repeat the request and I spoke seriously of the dangers which would arise if the situation were allowed to drift. Hoare wanted to have ships inspected at the ports where men and materials might be embarking, but I pointed out that the German and Italian Governments had already refused inspection in their own countries, where it would, in any event, have been more difficult to carry out. The most to which Ministers would agree was that we should welcome the recent replies of the other powers and fasten on the general desire to exclude foreign volunteers from Spain. We should, instead of my proposal to use the Royal Navy, work for a more effective version of the Non-Intervention Committee's existing control scheme.

I was bitterly disappointed. I felt that the withdrawal of sanctions six months before had been the nadir of the Government's fortunes. But, by the end of 1936, our growing power and intimacy with France had given me hope that our foreign policy was regaining its strength and direction. An arresting British action might have drained the Spanish ulcer of its poison. It could certainly not have weakened Britain's authority and the dictators would have had either to recant or agree. It is my belief that they would have had to accept our offer, or something like it. At the time, I more than suspected that the naval arguments advanced by Hoare were not sound, but I could not prove it. The First Lord's technical objections impressed my colleagues, most of whom had no experience with which to counter them.

Our truncated proposals were sent off on January 10th, after approval by the French Government. On the following day I announced that it was an offence for any Briton to engage in the conflict or influence another to do so. The Portuguese Government quickly replied to our note that they were willing to prevent the enlistment of volunteers or their transit through Portuguese territory, if other powers would legislate in the same way. On January 14th I told Grandi that I hoped his Government's reply would be in a similar strain. The Ambassador then made a reference to the volunteers crossing into Spain from France. I replied that, though this might be happening, there was a definite difference between the positions of the two countries: the French Government had now undertaken to stop volunteers crossing the frontier. Was it not possible for the Italian Government to take up a similar position? Grandi said he understood the force of this and would do his best with his Government. A few days ago, the Ambassador added, he had been instructed to explain to me that the Italian Government must have as many volunteers in Spain as the Germans. He had not, however, made this communication at the time. I rejoined that my information now was that Italy had three times as many volunteers in Spain as Germany. If this were so, they could well call a halt if others would do the same.

* * * * *

In my speech in the House of Commons on January 19th I referred to the desire of the peoples of the world for peace, which was so overpowering that, were all barriers to freedom of intercourse and speech broken down, threats to peace would largely be allayed. There was unfortunately no prospect that the peoples would be free to express their will, any more than there is today. Nevertheless, I thought that history showed the Spaniards to be sinewy and independent. A little later in my speech I made a prediction:

> If any hon. Member believes that as the outcome of the civil war in Spain any single foreign power, or pair of foreign powers, is going to dominate Spain for a generation, to rule its life, to direct its foreign policies, then I am convinced he is mistaken in his judgement, and I would reply to him that of all the possible outcomes of this civil war, that is the most unlikely. I will tell the House why.
>
> We should be strongly opposed to any such happening, and I have no doubt that we should not be alone in our opposition.... Almost the only thing that can unite Spain, profoundly, bitterly divided as she is, would be a common hatred of the foreigner. That strong partisans on one side or the other will feel gratitude to those who have helped them in the civil strife is likely enough, but, unless the whole past history of Spain is belied in this conflict, the great mass of the proud Spanish people will feel the least ill-will to those nations which have intervened the least.... The form of government in Spain should be a matter for the Spanish people, and no one else....
>
> There is no word, no line, no comma, in the Anglo-Italian declaration which could give any foreign power a right to intervene in Spain, whatever the complexion of the government in any part of that country.

I spoke of Britain's economic purpose:

Our objective in this country must be the prosperity of all, by which I mean the raising of the standard of life in the countries in which it is today low as well as its further improvement where it is today comparatively high. We are willing to help towards a further advance along the line of increased economic opportunity, but this should be . . . on one condition. Economic collaboration and political appeasement must go hand in hand.'

and concluded with a comment which is apposite today:

If economic and financial accommodation merely result in more armaments and more political disturbance, the cause of peace will be hindered rather than helped. . . . We do not accept that the alternative for Europe lies between dictatorship of the right and the left. We do not accept . . . that democracies are the breeding ground of communism. We regard them rather as its antidote.

The House and the country endorsed these arguments, as they would, I felt confident, have endorsed firmer action to enforce non-intervention.

In the latter half of January we received replies from the Governments principally implicated in the question of volunteers. The Germans and Italians declared that they were ready to stop volunteers leaving for Spain if other nations would do the same. Accordingly we tried once more to make the Non-Intervention Committee less of a charade and asked that the Agreement should now be extended to cover the recruitment of volunteers. On February 20th the Governments represented on the Committee took this action, at least on paper, and there was a lull for a while.

As no prohibition was likely to be respected without supervision, the British Government persisted with an emasculated edition of the scheme I had put to my colleagues at the beginning of the year. This came before the Committee early in March and proposed that supervision in Portugal should be carried out by British observers, while international staffs would be established at suitable points on the other Spanish frontiers. All merchant vessels belonging to countries which had signed the Non-Intervention Agreement were to embark an observer, who would watch the unloading of the cargo at Spanish ports and be given all facilities to carry out investigations. The plan provided for observation at sea.

The navies of Great Britain, Italy, France and Germany were to take part, each being responsible for a portion of the Spanish coast, but they could do no more than look out for ships not reported as having submitted to observation, board them and warn them. If a ship refused to take notice of the warning, this was to be regarded as *prima facie* evidence of a breach of the Non-Intervention Agreement. The scheme could have been made to work if there had been the will to do so, but, as there was not, holes were soon found in it. British observation under my proposals would have stopped these, thereby giving confidence. Many irritating delays followed before even this scheme could be enforced. Under its provisions the Royal Navy patrolled a large part of the Spanish coast with only two flotillas of destroyers. There was no need to mobilize a man. Here was the answer to the First Lord's principal objection.

Mr. Maisky then intruded another complication. He refused to discuss any matter affecting the external assets of the Spanish Government, thus intensifying the suspicion that Spanish gold had found its way to Russia. His attitude blocked all progress on another form of intervention, the question of financial assistance to either party in Spain, and was used by Hitler and Mussolini as a pretext for stalling on the withdrawal of volunteers already in Spain. Despite decrees and promises, Fascist intervention continued. I heard from Corbin that the French Ambassador in Rome had faced Count Ciano with facts and figures. Ciano denied them, but would not allow his denial to be published. British and French intelligence from the battlefront left no doubt that Fascist forces in Spain were now very large.

* * * * *

In the latter part of March, Sir Henry Chilton telegraphed from Hendaye that Reuters' correspondent had just given him, from German sources, an account of a recent Fascist defeat before Guadalajara. According to this, the Italians engaged numbered about 38,000, and were well equipped. After advancing confidently for two days with strong air and artillery support, they were held up by atrocious weather which disrupted their supply columns and grounded their aircraft. The opposing air force, however, had the use of concrete runways and inflicted fearful damage, as did their infantry, before whom many of the Fascists fled. Others resisted stoutly and Italian losses were heavy, some estimating up to 3,000 killed. Reuters' correspondent wrote:

> Many Spaniards are offended at the outwardly arrogant way in which Italian assistance has been given and many, though distressed at the military consequences of the Guadalajara fiasco, cannot refrain from a malicious chuckle.

The Spanish Republican forces took many prisoners in this battle and the Government at once instructed Azcarate to inform me of the situation. According to the document he gave me, statements made by prisoners showed that numerous Italian regular troops with equipment, arms and supplies, had landed at Cadiz early in February. I thought it more likely that the Italians had been drilled and made into military formations while in Spain. But the fact that these Fascist troops had now come into action must increase indignation in all countries and sharpen tension generally. I wrote in my diary on March 15th: 'I am still convinced that the course we have taken is the only possible one. The only alternative to "non-intervention" is "intervention".'

I noticed from the newspapers that Mr. Ernest Bevin, then Chairman of the General Council of the Trades Union Congress, seemed to have put the Government's case extremely well at an International Socialist Conference in London, which was attended by Spanish delegates. His conclusion was that intervention would lead to a European war and neither France nor Great Britain was prepared to incur that risk. Bevin suggested a combined effort to secure the withdrawal of all foreign combatants. The *Daily Worker* attacked him strongly.

The reverse at Guadalajara, which was publicized all over the world, had its unhappy consequence. The Duce now felt that his personal fortunes were more than ever bound up with General Franco's victory, while Grandi refused to discuss the question of volunteers at the Non-Intervention Committee, which had to be adjourned on March 24th. This event inevitably perturbed the French Ambassador, who told me that he thought his Government would ask him to press for a renewal of the Committee's sessions without delay. If this were not practicable, they might have to reconsider their own position under the Agreement. For the first time in nine months even the steadier elements in French opinion showed critical restiveness. Corbin and I agreed that any further despatch of Italian volunteers to Spain would put our whole Agreement in jeopardy and that I must make this clear to Grandi. I duly did so, and in a day or two the Committee resumed its labours.

International dangers were growing and I took the occasion of a speech at Liverpool to state the realities as I saw them. I welcomed the fact that the supervision scheme was shortly to come into effect, which would put an end to the prolonged period of rumour, charge and counter-charge. I doubted whether there would be any speedy victory for either side and continued:

The Spanish people will after this civil war, as for centuries before it, continue to display that proud independence, that almost arrogant individualism which is a distinctive characteristic of the race. There are 24 million reasons why Spain will never for long be dominated by the forces, or controlled by the advice, of any foreign power, and they are the 24 million Spaniards that today inhabit war-ridden Spain. Six months ago I told the House of Commons of my conviction that intervention in Spain was both bad humanity and bad politics. Nothing that has happened since that date has caused me to modify that judgement, some events have caused me to confirm it.

This judgement was borne out by events in the second world war.

At the outbreak of the Spanish civil war, I had no political sympathy with either side, but only wished that the Spaniards should determine their own future. As the war progressed, however, I became more concerned lest the insurgents should win, because the foreign powers backing them were themselves a menace to peace. From the early months of 1937, if I had had to choose, I would have preferred a Government victory.

VII

CHAMBERLAIN TAKES OVER

April – August 1937

The Opposition on belligerent rights – The bombing of Guernica – The Imperial Conference – Mr. Baldwin and the dictators – Good relations with Mr. Chamberlain – Sir Horace Wilson's tea-party – I define our Mediterranean interests – A good reaction from Rome – Mr. Chamberlain's friendly letter – I am not consulted – Over-optimism of the press – A British tanker is attacked in the Mediterranean – Submarine warfare begins

The insurgent forces in Spain were bearing down through the Basque country on Bilbao, while General Franco's vessels tried to blockade the besieged port and prevent food and supplies from entering. Our shipping had not been allowed to sail unmolested and early in April a nationalist cruiser tried to prevent a British merchant vessel from entering Bilbao harbour. Three destroyers of the Royal Navy had to interpose themselves between the two ships before the merchantman could steam into port. We had now to decide whether our shipping should be protected, not only on the high seas but also within Spanish territorial waters. To do this would be construed by some governments as breaking the Non-Intervention Agreement. Naturally, the Royal Navy did not wish to escort British ships up to territorial waters, only to see them captured within sight. The Admiralty wanted us to avoid all incidents by not forcing our ships into Bilbao; this would have meant acquiescing in Franco's blockade.

I thought that we must be stiffer. On April 11th we telegraphed to Franco through Sir Henry Chilton that, although we would advise our ships not to sail to Bilbao, we could not tolerate interference with any that did. The Prime Minister announced this in Parliament on the following day. He added that the war was now getting very close to Bilbao. The approaches to the harbour had been mined by both sides and there was danger of bombing. This decision raised what I still think was an unjustified storm. On April 14th Mr. Attlee deplored 'the failure of His Majesty's Government to give protection to British merchant ships on their lawful occasions.' The debate became very heated and the Government were accused of betraying democracy.

At this point Mr. Churchill came trenchantly to our defence, and hoped that the Government would not be provoked by charges of 'hoisting the white flag' into abandoning the policy of non-intervention. Churchill said that he proposed to give me his vote, because in the last six or seven months I had so guided our affairs 'as to avoid a number of frightful pitfalls'. Replying to the debate, I explained that if we had granted belligerent rights to both sides, they would have been entitled to stop our shipping, on the high seas as well as in territorial waters. We could never intervene in territorial waters, but if British vessels ignored our warning and pressed forward to Bilbao, they would still be protected on the high seas against interference by either side, up to the three-mile limit. The Opposition were not satisfied and repeatedly taunted the Government with favouritism to Fascism and tyranny. The Labour Party has always had its share of vicarious warriors.

By the end of April Franco's blockade was effective, except when the Royal Navy took a hand. The fleet had virtually forced six British ships through to the three-mile limit, after which they had met no resistance in entering the harbour. Under the Non-Intervention Agreement, we were now preventing arms and volunteers from reaching Spain, while escorting food ships into Bilbao. Only our action broke Franco's blockade, though we had been abused in Parliament for pandering to him. Political controversy can give strange twists to truth.

Events at Bilbao now became a prelude to organized barbarity, as I had foretold in the House of Commons six years before. On April 26th, Guernica was destroyed by bombardment from the air with heavy loss of life. This was the first blitz of the second world war, carried out, according to our reports, by German aircraft. The deed was brought before the Non-Intervention Committee, despite Ribbentrop's call for delay, and was discussed on May 4th. Ribbentrop afterwards complained to me that inaccurate reports of his attitude had been leaked to the press. He accused the Soviet Ambassador of responsibility and said that, if this went on, he would have to advise Berlin to withdraw from the Committee. He claimed that a French agency had announced that 'the reds' were responsible for bombing Guernica. I replied that our evidence conflicted with this report and that I could not agree with him. I then suggested an inquiry to establish the facts, which seemed to take the Ambassador aback, to the extent of leaving him without an opinion.

During these weeks we tried hard to help the unhappy Spaniards in Bilbao, whatever their political opinions. The Basque Government told us that they wanted to evacuate women, children and the sick, and asked us to give naval protection for the operation. We informed General Franco that we were going to do this, on the understanding that complete political impartiality was exercised in selecting those to be evacuated. Despite his protests, the British and French navies both gave protection to this humanitarian operation. Our Ambassador's comment, that by removing useless mouths from Bilbao, the British Government had prolonged the city's resistance, had also some truth in it. By the middle of May, however, the attention of the British people was temporarily distracted from Spain to happier events at home.

* * * * *

The Coronation of King George VI and Queen Elizabeth was marked by affectionate demonstrations and relief that the position of the Crown had not been shaken by the events of the previous December. In accordance with custom, an Imperial Conference was summoned.

As so often in later years, I found my first experience of a meeting with all the Dominion Prime Ministers stimulating. I consulted with Stanley Bruce, the Australian High Commissioner, and he wisely advised me to do the best I could to elicit the views of the Dominion statesmen. With this in mind, I prepared, with the help of the Foreign Office, a number of papers on such besetting problems as the Spanish civil war, the position in central and southern Europe, Germany's colonial claims and our commitments in imperial defence. All these subjects were thoroughly and helpfully discussed. I explained our strategy of holding existing political positions while building up the necessary military strength behind them. Unhappily, I said, the second part was moving slowly, even allowing for the inevitable delays in the early stages of rearmament.

At the end of the meeting on May 23rd, when I was sitting on Baldwin's left, he remarked to me: 'I don't often say anything on foreign affairs. Do you mind if I do so now?' 'Of course not,' I replied, 'please do.' For a few minutes he gave a pessimistic account of the dangers in Europe, which he attributed to Hitler and Mussolini.

Baldwin concluded: 'We have two madmen loose in Europe. Anything may befall.' I thought that this was in the nature of a political testament, for, as had been expected, Baldwin retired after the Coronation, Neville Chamberlain succeeding him.

Before Chamberlain became Prime Minister, I would think it true that he and I were closer to each other than to any other member of the Government, exchanging opinions on many Cabinet matters without any disagreement. I would sometimes on a Sunday evening, if we were both in London, call in at No. 11 Downing Street, for a quiet talk. A Foreign Secretary and a Chancellor of the Exchequer, the Prime Minister's two principal colleagues, are apt to be thrown together, particularly if the Prime Minister is holding the reins very loosely, as Baldwin was during his last months in office. One May morning, when I was about to leave for Geneva and we were talking in Chamberlain's beautiful room at the Treasury, I was not at all surprised when he mentioned that he was soon to take over from Baldwin and added the hope that I would continue with my work at the Foreign Office. Nor was I dismayed when he said with a smile: 'I know you won't mind if I take more interest in foreign policy than S.B.' We both knew that no one could have taken less. Neville Chamberlain became Prime Minister on May 28th, at the age of sixty-eight.

Some months before this event, Chamberlain had asked me to dinner at No. 11 Downing Street to meet his half-brother on his return from a visit to Czechoslovakia and Austria. This was one of the last occasions on which I saw Sir Austen before his death. Neville was a delightful host and food and drink were always excellent at his table. I enjoyed my evening and Austen told us about his visits to Beneš and what he thought of the dangers in Austria, while Neville and I listened, Neville in particular taking very little part in the conversation. However, towards the end of the evening he did venture to make certain comments on the situation as he saw it, whereupon Austen said, 'Neville, you must remember you don't know anything about foreign affairs.' Neville smiled wryly and remarked that this was rather hard on a man at his own dinner table. Austen made one of his sweeping, deprecatory gestures, half apologetic, and went on his way.

While I was always grateful for Baldwin's personal kindness to me, I looked forward to working with a Prime Minister who would give his Foreign Secretary energetic backing. When in later years Baldwin came to be blamed for our unreadiness for war, he was made a scapegoat for all that went wrong between his retirement and the early phase of the war. He put no drive behind the rearmament programme, which was probably antipathetic to him anyway, and for this he must bear responsibility. But, as far as I know, he never had any illusions about the dictators. Baldwin and I continued to meet and correspond intermittently until his death. On one such occasion, after we had dined together in the autumn of 1941, I wrote:

> I felt very sorry for S.B. He has grand things about him. He attempts no self-justification. I believe that history will treat him more kindly than his contemporaries now do. He did much to kill class hatred and to unite the country. He did not understand the storms that raged without, nor did he make Neville's mistake of believing that he did.

At his own request, Hoare moved from the Admiralty to the Home Office, the senior Secretaryship of State. On this I heard two comments, that of Stanley Baldwin: 'You do not become Prime Minister by putting your hat on the chair' and that of Winston Churchill: 'The first man I've ever known to prefer Jack Ketch to Jack Tar.'

* * * * *

Once the supervision of non-intervention had been accepted, the withdrawal of foreign forces already fighting in Spain became our next objective. While the German and Italian Governments had already agreed to this early in 1937, they prevaricated skilfully to avoid action upon it. Even attempts to prevent the despatch of more volunteers to Spain brought no good results. On March 31st the Italian Government gave me an assurance through Grandi that no more 'volunteers' would leave for Spain. Within a few weeks we had evidence that this promise was being broken.

On May 29th, the League Council met and once again endorsed the policy of non-intervention, while deploring the bombing of open towns, a ruthless feature of the war. While the Council was in session, Spanish Government aircraft attacked the German battleship *Deutschland*, killing thirty seamen and wounding many others. This was apparently a desperate act of indiscipline. Hitler, in retaliation, ordered the bombardment of the undefended port of Almeria on the morning of May 31st. He and Mussolini then took their warships out of the naval control scheme. After a fortnight's argument, principally between Ribbentrop and myself in several interviews, both countries were back again, for a spell. On June 18th the Germans alleged that the cruiser *Leipzig* had been attacked by a submarine and asked that the four powers engaged in the patrol, France, Germany, Italy and ourselves, should meet at once. At the meeting Ribbentrop demanded a joint naval demonstration and the despatch of a stern note to the Spanish Government. This neither we nor the French Government would accept without investigation, with the result that Germany withdrew from the patrol scheme, Italy again following suit. The full patrol was never resumed.

In our attempts to bring the Fascist and Nazi Governments to some observance of their engagement, we and the French Government had one bargaining weapon, the granting of belligerent rights. After discussion with Corbin, I decided to use this by proposing, on July 14th, that belligerent rights might be granted when 'substantial progress' had been made with the withdrawal of foreign forces. The now incomplete naval patrol would then be abandoned in favour of observers at the Spanish ports. No government liked this compromise, but the Non-Intervention Committee unanimously accepted it for discussion. When they saw that the rights would not be granted while their forces were in Spain, the German and Italian Governments concluded that General Franco must do without them, as the lesser evil from their point of view. Belligerent rights were, in consequence, withheld.

* * * * *

In May 1937, Mr. J. P. L. Thomas became my Parliamentary Private Secretary, in succession to Roger Lumley, who had been appointed Governor of Bombay. I had not known Thomas at all well previously and it was the Government Chief Whip, Mr. David Margesson, who recommended his name, a deed which gave me a friend and many years' most loyal service. Thomas has left a record of this period, in which he writes of an incident which occurred only a fortnight after he took up his work with me:

> Sir Horace Wilson, who incidentally was Industrial Adviser to the Prime Minister, told me that Sir Warren Fisher, the head of the Civil Service, wanted to meet me and that he, Sir Horace, would take me to tea with him.
>
> I had no idea what this was about but it was soon made clear that both Fisher and Wilson were thoroughly dissatisfied with the Foreign Office and especially with Vansittart. They told me that Vansittart was an alarmist, that he hampered all attempts of the Government to make friendly contact with the dictator states and that his influence over Anthony Eden was very great. For this reason they had strongly backed the idea that I, whom

Horace Wilson knew well, should become P.P.S. at the Foreign Office because I would be in a position to help them to build a bridge between 10 Downing Street and the Foreign Office, and to create a better understanding between the two Departments. This might lessen the damage which had been done by the Foreign Office in general and by Vansittart in particular.

I replied that they had placed me in an intolerable position for, although I did not even know Vansittart and therefore held no brief for him, it seemed to me that they expected me to work behind the back of my own chief. If I had any complaints about the Foreign Office I should certainly make them to Eden and to nobody else; whereupon Sir Horace Wilson hastily left the room. . . .

The next day Sir Horace spoke to me again and said that Sir Warren was rather impulsive and that he did not think that I had obtained a clear view of what was wanted of me. I replied that the view was only too clear.

* * * * *

Throughout the summer of 1937, Mussolini's ambitions were directed with greater force and less subterfuge to the Mediterranean and Near East. He seemed to have no wish to play an effective part in support of Austrian independence and his controlled press and radio frothed endlessly about re-creating the glories of the Roman Empire. Anti-British propaganda was continuous and virulent, while Bari Radio exploited our difficulties as a mandatory power in Palestine. Fascist newspapers carried on brisk polemics with the British press and Italian school text-books wrote of British decadence.

Our position in Egypt and the Near East guarded our communications with India and Australasia. It was, therefore, essential to us that Mussolini should not win control of the Mediterranean, or appear to be doing so, which would be almost as menacing for the smaller Mediterranean powers. These had to be encouraged at a time when Mussolini was inviting each of them to separate negotiations with him, in accordance with the now evident practice of dictators. Even if our naval action at Bilbao could be interpreted as inconsistent with non-intervention, a reminder of British naval strength could only be salutary.

As the months passed, Italian demands for *de jure* recognition of the Abyssinian conquest became more vocal. Our Ambassador in Rome believed that our relations with Mussolini would not improve until this claim were met and Count Grandi showed skill in developing an argument which I was often to hear until I resigned. It was contended that if we would only do this distasteful thing, a better atmosphere would result and other quarrels might be composed. The disequilibrium in this bargain was that we should be giving at once, and only receiving in an uncertain future. There was also the danger that such a gesture would merely be taken for feebleness. I heard from Drummond that Ciano had threatened 'something more than a press campaign' if Mussolini's alleged grievances were not met. Sir Miles Lampson telegraphed from Cairo of Fascist intrigue all over the Moslem world.

Early in July, Sir Eric Drummond wrote to Vansittart, to say that Mussolini was putting out a string of articles with a strong anti-British bias. The Ambassador did not know whether the Duce was working up his public opinion for an eventual war with Britain. If this were his intention, Drummond observed, he would hardly go about it otherwise. The technique was unpleasantly reminiscent, in the Ambassador's opinion, of that used in the early months of 1935 to bring Italian public opinion up to pitch for the Abyssinian adventure. Drummond repeated an Italian statement that Mussolini was now a paranoiac, adding that he certainly showed less of the calmly balanced outlook for which, so the Ambassador wrote, he had formerly been remarkable.

Reports of the imminent despatch of two more divisions to Libya and of the holding of naval manœuvres around Sicily lent substance to Drummond's warning. In the middle of July, I consulted Sir Ronald Graham, a former Ambassador in Rome who had known Mussolini well. Like me, he regarded Ciano as then completely hypnotized by Germany. Graham believed that Drummond's apprehensions might be well-founded, so did our Commander-in-Chief in the Mediterranean, Admiral Sir Dudley Pound. Sir Ronald also thought it probable that the argument of the Fascists, that we were rearming to deal with them and therefore they had better deal with us first, carried some conviction. This at least could be dealt with publicly and, in the next speech I made in Parliament, on July 19th, having repeated our intention of defending our own interests in the Mediterranean, I said that we had no intention of challenging those of others:

> That is why we made with Italy the Mediterranean Agreement of last January. We stand by that Agreement. If the Mediterranean is for us a main arterial road, and it is, yet there is plenty of room for all on such a road. If we intend to maintain our place on it, and we do, we have no intention of seeking to turn anybody else off it. Least of all do we wish to interfere with those who geographically dwell upon it. There is ample room for all. Free traffic through and out of the Mediterranean is the common interest of Great Britain and of all the Mediterranean powers.

In the light of certain reports which have reached me there is one further categorical assurance I should like to give. This country has no intention of pursuing towards any other country a policy either of aggression or of revenge. Such a possibility has never even occurred to the British people. The word 'vendetta' has no English equivalent. . . . What I have said about the Mediterranean applies equally to the Red Sea. It has always been, and it is today, a major British interest that no great power should establish itself on the eastern shore of the Red Sea. I need hardly add that this applies to ourselves no less than to others.

On July 21st Count Grandi told me that my speech had had an excellent press in Italy. The situation seemed to be so much easier that he was encouraged to give to me a message for the Prime Minister, which Signor Mussolini had authorized him to make use of some time ago. The Ambassador, who had been given discretion in the matter, had thought it wiser to hold up delivery of the message until the moment was more propitious. He hoped that the moment had now come. In any event, he would tell me what Signor Mussolini had said. The Duce had emphasized his desire for permanent friendship with this country. He regarded the agreement of last January as the frame, but the picture had yet to be filled in. He hoped that this would be done by further understandings, defining closer relations between our two countries. Signor Mussolini had instructed him to repeat what had been said many times, that the Italian Government had no political ambitions whatever in Spain, still less, of course, any territorial ambitions. Mussolini was always ready to discuss any proposals to further the interests of our two countries. Grandi then added that, as he was returning to Italy at the end of the month, it would help him if I could arrange an interview with the Prime Minister before then. This I did, and it was agreed that the Ambassador should call on Neville Chamberlain on July 27th.

On the day after his interview with me, Count Grandi went to see the Secretary of State for War, Mr. Hore-Belisha, and said that Mussolini thought Britain was getting ready to make war on Italy and that this could only result in more intense Italian preparations. I noted: 'Italy has made hers.' The Duce, Grandi went on to tell Hore-Belisha, suggested that we should establish confidential relations between our respective military staffs and disclose to one another the nature of our defences. A curious deduction from the premise, but it was welcomed by the War Office.

On July 24th I endorsed an opinion expressed by Sir Robert

Vansittart in a minute, that it was a great mistake to believe that Italy was arming only because she was afraid we might attack her. There were, Sir Robert argued, very strong and notorious expansionist tendencies in Fascist Italy. They might not be intended for any early application, but their presence was incontestable. I wrote:

Mussolini has the mentality of a gangster, and if he were contemplating an act of aggression against us the procedure he is at present following is clearly the right one for him. He proclaims that he is frightened of being attacked and can thus both work up his own people and produce some kind of excuse before the world, if need be. That is why I view with some suspicion Signor Grandi's approaches to Mr. Hore-Belisha. If necessary they will one day proclaim: 'We did our best to reach an understanding, the British would not meet us. We had to act when we did as the last moment when we had a chance of defending ourselves.'

All these suspicions of mine may be unfounded, they probably are, but they should not be ruled out entirely. Therefore while reciprocating any advances we should be watchful in the extreme.

As Mr. Chamberlain's interview with Grandi was due in the next few days, I asked Vansittart to prepare a brief which would serve as a basis for their talk. Sir Robert suggested that the Prime Minister might begin by repeating my declaration of July 19th which had been so well received in Italy. Progress towards better relations would be difficult, so long as complete sincerity was not recognized and when wholly groundless suspicions were being worked up into alarms. Vansittart gave as an example of this latter tendency the accusation made by Grandi at the outset of his conversation with Hore-Belisha, that Britain was incessantly strengthening her defences in the Mediterranean and preparing for war. Inquiry would show that this was the opposite of the truth. It was known that since the lifting of sanctions, Britain had reverted to her normal Mediterranean strength, and had been encouraged in this policy by the Agreement of January 2nd. Unfortunately, the memorandum went on, the Italian Government was doing the opposite by now proposing to increase the Libyan garrison to the abnormal strength which it had previously reached during the imposition of sanctions. It was therefore suggested that the Prime Minister should ask Grandi for an explanation and add that we hoped to hear it was the Fascist Government's intention to maintain the garrison in Libya only at its normal strength.

Two days later the Secretary of the Cabinet, Sir Maurice Hankey, remarked to Vansittart that he had a suspicious mind in this matter. Thus provoked, Sir Robert wrote a further note, which I also sent to the Prime Minister. Vansittart explained the position about the Libyan garrison, which would, by August, consist of 60,000 men, including 40,000 motorized white troops. This would be the most powerful striking force that had ever existed in North Africa. Sir Robert argued that if the Italian Government were unwilling to reduce this figure substantially, we would be unwise to attach any solid worth to Grandi's conversation with Hore-Belisha. This is still my judgement. It seemed to Vansittart, and I entirely shared his view, that Mussolini, having brought his own preparations to as high a pitch as possible, might now be seeking to deter us from any return to our own former readiness. The note asked whether Chamberlain could suggest to Grandi that a reduction of Italian forces would speak louder than words. It was within Mussolini's power to take an action, at no cost to himself, which would have an instant effect in this country.

I awaited with interest the results of Count Grandi's meeting with the Prime Minister, who sent across to the Foreign Office his account of it on the afternoon of July 27th. This recorded that the Ambassador had not left a copy of Mussolini's letter, which Chamberlain described as being of four pages, but had read to him a translation so much broken by comments that the Prime Minister had difficulty in distinguishing what was Grandi and what was Mussolini. It emerged that Mussolini wanted *de jure* recognition of his conquest of Abyssinia, which Grandi had not mentioned to me six days before. The reinforcement of the Libya garrison by two divisions was explained by the fact that the Italians had been 'frightened out of their wits' by our expenditure on defences in the Mediterranean and by the visit paid to that sea by Sir Samuel Hoare in the previous autumn.

Chamberlain dealt suitably with these alarming portents and expressed a readiness for conversations. He then asked whether a personal note to the Duce would be appreciated and, on being assured that it would, wrote there and then a letter very friendly in tone. I should have had no objection in principle to a message of greeting, though I would have imposed some conditions to the opening of discussions if I had seen the letter before it was sent, and I would have made some suggestions to guard the sender from appearing too gullible to the recipient. I made no difficulty about the incident at the time, thinking that there was no deliberate intent to by-pass me as Foreign Secretary, but that it was merely a slip by a Prime Minister new to international affairs.

In this judgement I was apparently wrong, for some months later Chamberlain wrote of this episode:

> I did not show my letter to the Foreign Secretary, for I had the feeling that he would object to it.*

This behaviour was in strong contrast to my experience with Mr. Churchill, during the four and a half years we were together in the war in the same two offices. Even in the times of highest pressure, he never sent a message with international implications without either showing it to me himself or sending it across to the Foreign Office for my approval before despatch. As Prime Minister, he was meticulous in such matters, without any request or complaint having ever been made by me. Complete confidence and candour between Prime Minister and Foreign Secretary are indispensable conditions for the conduct of a successful foreign policy under our parliamentary system. Evidently they were already fading from Mr. Chamberlain's mind, though I did not know it and he only recorded the fact subsequently.

On July 29th I had a conversation with Grandi, which was the result of a talk between Chamberlain and myself. I told Grandi that the Prime Minister had been thinking over the interview of two days before and there was one point he had asked me to bring to the Ambassador's notice. There had been no response in Italy to my assurances of July 19th, that Great Britain would never pursue a policy of either aggression or revenge and that we wished to live in peace and friendship with our neighbours in the Mediterranean. The Prime Minister agreed with me that it would be helpful if Signor Mussolini himself, or Count Ciano, could reciprocate these sentiments.

The Ambassador seemed fully to understand the point. Count Ciano himself did not make speeches, he said, but there was always the possibility of an article by Signor Mussolini. Grandi would be frank with me and say that he himself was a little apprehensive of this method, for whatever Signor Mussolini's intentions, the expressions he might employ in such an article might not always produce the result desired. In any event, he would be grateful if I would leave it to him to deal with this matter as seemed best.

I thanked the Ambassador, adding that I was glad he had mentioned Signor Mussolini's articles, since the last one had ended with this phrase: 'One day these stately houses will be upset by the reality that has in all

* Keith Feiling: op. cit.

times gone by one single serious irreplaceable name.' I asked the Count what this name could be. He professed to be unable to supply it, but most vehemently denied that the missing word could be war.

* * * * *

I now left London and went to a house I had taken at Fawley, on Southampton Water, for the summer holidays of my two sons. I learnt from the newspapers that Mussolini had despatched a prompt reply, delivered by Grandi, to Chamberlain's letter. The Foreign Office sent me the Prime Minister's record of this second conversation. The Ambassador had said that Ciano and Mussolini would both make friendly references to Great Britain in the near future. It would be quite possible for the Italian Government to enter into discussions with Drummond during August, though Grandi feared that if the subject of *de jure* recognition of the conquest of Abyssinia were not raised at Geneva in September, nothing further could be done for another year. To this, Chamberlain very properly replied that these were matters for the Foreign Secretary. Count Ciano had publicly welcomed the 'very important exchange of letters'. I felt that the Italian Government had skilfully committed us to conversations before we had decided what was to be their content and how much we wanted them. Within a fortnight of these protestations of goodwill, Mussolini's submarines were sinking British merchantmen on their lawful occasions in the Mediterranean Sea.

Meanwhile, in view of the opinions expressed in a number of British newspapers, which were astonishingly optimistic about the results of Anglo-Italian talks, I telephoned to Vansittart, asking him to do what he could to put a brake on the press. He reported to me on August 4th that a hint had been dropped to him that leakages from the Cabinet were responsible for some of the press statements. Sir Robert thought and so did I, that the Italian Embassy was not backward in making the most of the situation. I wrote to him on the same day:

I am presuming that there will be no further correspondence between No. 10 and Rome without my seeing it. I naturally attach importance to this.

Meanwhile I think that the French are taking a more realistic view of this Italian move than some of our press. No doubt Mussolini wants recognition of Abyssinia, but so do we want the Italians out of Majorca, mechanized divisions out of Libya, explanation of fortified islands in the Mediterranean and Red Sea, etc. It would be the height of folly to concede in fact what the Italians want, in return for mere promises. . . . I think it important that our

> press should emphasize the connection in our mind between Italians in Spain and better Anglo-Italian relations. . . . We must not be backward in setting out our *desiderata* vis-à-vis Italy and there must be an end of giving and of not getting. . . . By all means let us show ourselves ready to talk, but in no scrambling hurry to offer incense on a dictator's altar. . . . We have to remember in all our dealings with Italy that Mussolini's object is to show himself courted, not his only object but an important one. He likes also to point to us as the waning weakling. We must give him no pretext for that, or we shall damage ourselves in the Near and Middle East at a time when our authority is important to us for Palestine, etc. . . .
>
> Personally I feel that we have a chance now of bettering conditions in Europe, but this depends on two things:
>
> (1) our own firmness
>
> (2) maintenance of friendship with France, which alone has maintained peace these last difficult eighteen months.

I insisted that the negotiations should not take place until I had returned to duty and was able to handle them personally. There was no problem about this, for, while I was still away from the Foreign Office, Ciano spoke to Drummond of starting the conversations at 'the end of August or the beginning of September.'

During the first fortnight in August, many letters were exchanged between Southampton and the Foreign Office. Sir Eric Drummond came home for a few weeks' leave and attended discussions at the Foreign Office, where Lord Halifax was temporarily in charge. These showed that the *de jure* recognition of Mussolini's conquest of Abyssinia was becoming the centre of debate. On this subject I had minuted earlier in the summer:

> I have so often been promised that such and such action on our part would improve Anglo-Italian relations, and so often been disappointed, that I do not share these optimistic views of *de jure* recognition. We proposed the withdrawal of sanctions, closed our Legation, withdrew our guard at Addis Ababa, none of these things had more than an ephemeral effect. I fear that the cause is that Italy is determined to revive the Roman Empire and we are in the way.

I added agreement with Sir Robert Vansittart's minute that only strength would impress Mussolini.

It seemed that the Prime Minister intended to lose no time. In a letter to Halifax of August 7th, a copy of which was sent on to me, Chamberlain expressed a surprising opinion of the men we had to deal with. It was very necessary to remember, he wrote, that the dictators were men of moods. If we caught them in the right mood they would give us anything we asked for. But if the mood changed they might shut up 'like an oyster'. The moral of this was, in the Prime Minister's opinion, that we must make Mussolini feel that things were moving all the time. I was to hear the same sanguine but ill-founded judgements six months later.

Meanwhile, I had been considering how the Fascist authorities in Abyssinia were faring. Their forces had not so far been able to pacify parts of the country. A few months earlier, an attempt had been made on the life of Marshal Graziani in Addis Ababa. Savage reprisals had followed. I wrote to Halifax on August 11th:

> We shall be delighted to see you any time that you like. 18th would suit us very well and we would send to meet you at Southampton by any train that suits you. Come as early as you can and we can walk through the pine trees by the sea shore, or play tennis, or what you will, within the sphere of our slender resources.
>
> I am very reluctant to recognize *de jure* conquest of Abyssinia and really do not think I could bring myself to any kind of approval of what Italy has done, though I share your desire to be a realist. If it be true that she cannot 'make a job' of Abyssinia without *de jure* recognition from us, I find it all the more difficult to give it.
>
> Have you thought of the possibility of a Mediterranean pact instead of an Anglo-Italian arrangement? It has many advantages:
>
> (a) Includes our friends
>
> (b) Consistent with our policy of regional agreements (bi-lateral is what dictators always want)
>
> (c) Would really contribute to pacify a region. An arrangement between us and Italy alone could never do that, for we are not alone concerned.
>
> I know that there are technical difficulties, but I believe that a great effort should be made to overcome them.
>
> As to Spain, Franco's manners seem poor, and he appears not even to answer our notes. The time has almost come for us to seize a cargo or two of his and hold them till he behaves! You will see how strong I am feeling after my ten days of sea breezes.

Lord Halifax hardly met my point by replying that you do not condone or approve murder by recognizing that some unfortunate has been murdered. My mood at this time was well expressed in an article which Halifax sent me by Mr. W. N. Ewer, the well-known diplomatic correspondent of the *Daily Herald*, who was a personal friend of mine.

It recalled that Mussolini was an admirer of Machiavelli and suggested that the same tactics of lure which had been used to obtain the Gentleman's Agreement were now being employed to gain *de jure* recognition. I had no intention of repeating our performance of the previous autumn and, in thanking Lord Halifax for the article, I told him that it represented my views more closely than did some of the Foreign Office discussions over which he had been presiding. Halifax, as always, took this in good part.

* * * * *

My stay on the Solent did not remain undisturbed for long. Serious events arose in the Mediterranean which were soon to wreck all immediate prospects of conversations with Mussolini and to endanger much else besides. Aeroplanes attacked the tanker *British Corporal* off the Spanish coast on August 10th. Vansittart gave the Italian Chargé d'Affaires, Signor Crolla, a private warning two days later. He said that we knew for a fact that these aeroplanes were based on Palma, where the Italians were prominent. Crolla replied that his Government were convinced that 'red' aircraft were responsible. In the following days, submarine attacks were made upon the ships of other countries. On August 17th I decided to ask for a meeting of Ministers, since the Admiralty held reliable information that Italian submarines had orders to attack oil tankers of any nationality sailing to ports controlled by the Spanish Government. The meeting was unanimous that our shipping should be protected by the Royal Navy, and issued the following statement to the press:

> His Majesty's Government have been seriously perturbed at the increasing number of attacks upon shipping which have occurred of late in Mediterranean waters and at the extension of the area in which these incidents are now taking place.
>
> His Majesty's Government have issued instructions through the Admiralty that if any British merchant ship is attacked by a submarine without warning, His Majesty's ships are authorized to counter attack the submarine.

The following afternoon, August 18th, Lord Halifax visited me at Southampton, when I told him we would soon find that our relations with Mussolini were as bad as ever, if we gave him what he most wanted, without settling the dominant question of Fascist intervention in Spain. A week later, General Franco's forces took Santander, upon which Mussolini sent him this message:

> I am particularly glad that during ten days of hard fighting the Italian legionary troops have made a valiant contribution to the splendid victory of Santander. . . . This comradeship of arms, now so close, is a guarantee of the final victory which will liberate Spain and the Mediterranean from all threats to the civilization we share.

Two vessels of the Spanish Government were torpedoed off the Turkish coast, one on August 17th and one on the 19th. On my instructions, Mr. Maurice Ingram, our Chargé d'Affaires in Rome, interviewed the Foreign Minister about this increased naval activity in the Mediterranean, at distances remote from Spanish ports. Count Ciano was told that masters of British vessels had been commenting freely on the extent to which Italian ships were watching their movements. He smoothly brushed aside the possibility that Fascist aeroplanes could have attacked merchantmen. The comments of British sea-captains were to be explained, he said, by the fact that many Italian ships were cruising about in Sicilian waters during manœuvres.

I concluded from this pert reply that Count Ciano did not put the success of talks with us very high on his list of priorities. We now know that he recorded in his diary a few days later:

> Decided, in principle, to send 5,000 men to Spain—we can't maintain the formations we already have there without them. I fear reactions in Europe may be violent. There is also a serious risk of wrecking the negotiations with London.*

This expressed the Fascist Government's policy as I understood it. They were quite ready to hold conversations with the British Government, provided that these did not deflect Fascist policies in any degree. But unless the talks did have such a consequence, they were of no value to His Majesty's Government. Hence their repeated postponement or failure.

* *Ciano's Diary, 1937-8*; Methuen, 1952.

VIII

NYON

August – December 1937

M. Delbos proposes a meeting – British ships torpedoed – Preparing for the Conference of Mediterranean powers – The Nyon Agreement on naval patrols – Pirate submarines return to port – Signor Mussolini visits Berlin – Conflict over Llandudno meeting – My speech there – A possibility of talks with Italy – They come to nothing

Towards the end of August I took charge at the Foreign Office again. The attacks on merchant ships were increasing in number and caused mounting anger in London and Paris. On August 26th, M. Cambon, the French Chargé d'Affaires, told me that his Government had also taken steps to protect their shipping. Paris had suggested that our two countries should hold conversations with Rome, before the League meeting in September, to try to reduce tension in the Mediterranean. I doubted whether this procedure would produce anything but the usual flat denials of guilt, and replied that I was not quite clear what the objectives of these conversations would be. Cambon said he would find out. He also left me with the firm impression that the French Government would take no initiative over the recognition of the Fascist conquest of Abyssinia that year.

Two days later, Cambon left a long note with me. In this, M. Delbos suggested that the British and French Governments should arrange a meeting of the Mediterranean powers, France, Great Britain, Yugoslavia, Greece, Turkey and Egypt, at Geneva. Together they would examine the best means of assuring the protection of navigation and of air lines in the Mediterranean. The French note said it would be advisable to consider whether Russia, Bulgaria and Roumania, as Black Sea powers, should also attend. This was the germ of the Nyon Conference. Delbos proposed that our two countries should once again look into the possibility of a Mediterranean pact; he also wished to refer Mussolini's Santander message to the Non-Intervention Committee. I arranged for the French note to be sent at once to the Prime Minister, who was on holiday in Scotland.

I favoured the suggestion for conversations between the Mediterranean powers at Geneva and a meeting of British Ministers was arranged for September 2nd. I telephoned to Neville Chamberlain to tell him that I thought it desirable to hold a Cabinet before I left. The Prime Minister said that he would come south himself for the occasion. He shared my opinion that we must be ready to discuss the Mediterranean situation at Geneva if the other Mediterranean powers wished it, and agreed with my suggestion that we should reinforce our destroyer strength in the western Mediterranean.

That same day H.M.S. *Havock*, a destroyer, was unsuccessfully attacked by a submarine sixty miles south of Valencia. *Havock* retaliated with depth charges and a search for the submarine was organized. Count Ciano records in his diary for September 2nd:

> The navy is very active—three torpedoings and one prize. But international opinion is getting worked up. Particularly in England, as a result of the attack on the destroyer *Havock*, fortunately not hit. It was the *Iride*. The row has already started.
>
> The Duce pretends to have a bone to pick with Egypt about her armaments. When I proved to him that they only exist on paper, he replied that he meant to provide himself with a subject of dispute for the right moment. 'Egypt will serve my purpose. We must begin now to say that it is Egypt who is troubling the waters.'*

Here was the perfect pattern of a dictator's technique; first select your victim, then declare him provocative.

Just before the meeting of Ministers on September 2nd, news was received that s.s. *Woodford*, a British tanker, had been torpedoed and sunk off the south-east coast of Spain with the loss of one killed and six injured. Even if every submarine possessed by the two sides in Spain had been seaworthy, which they certainly were not, we realized that they could not by themselves account for all this activity. There was little doubt that about fifteen Italian submarines were attacking ships in the Mediterranean. A submarine which had sunk ships off Tenedos flew the flag of General Franco and carried the marking C3, but it had

* op. cit.

been noticed that this vessel carried two guns, while the Spanish C3 carried only one. Evidently, General Franco's allies were determined to prevent munitions, oil and foodstuffs from reaching Valencia and Barcelona and seemed prepared to run any risks to achieve this.

* * * * *

In Britain, the national reaction to these events was one of growing indignation, yet there was also a strange mood of masochism. I remember that when advocating to my colleagues that we should increase our destroyer strength in the western Mediterranean, I was warned that this could only be accomplished by taking a flotilla from home waters. If we did this, and the attacks continued, public opinion would be even more critical. The artless argument was put forward that no mistake had been made and that the Italians had intended to attack British ships, in which event we should merely be giving them more targets by sending these destroyers. However, the fact that I had already enlisted the Prime Minister's support enabled us to announce on the evening of September 2nd that more destroyers would be sent at once.

Immediately after the meeting, I told M. Cambon that we thought the discussions at Geneva had better be limited at the outset to the Mediterranean powers. I added that we had already spoken to the Italians about submarine activity in the Mediterranean and suggested that his Government might make representations in the same way about Mussolini's Santander message. I was reluctant, I said to Cambon, to give up non-intervention, unless I was quite clear about the alternative policy and unless our two Governments were agreed about how to pursue it.

On the following day, I explained to Cambon the line of policy I had in mind. At Geneva we ought to try to get agreement upon a joint request to both parties in Spain that their submarines should not operate outside territorial waters, on pain of being sunk. The other Mediterranean powers would undertake that their submarines would not be submerged outside clearly defined limits; any submarine, therefore, detected in the open sea, would be liable to be attacked and destroyed. These proposals allowed for the co-operation of Mussolini, which we then thought might be forthcoming, not from choice but of necessity. Signor Crolla, the Italian Chargé d'Affaires, told Vansittart that he thought the meeting should take place and that his country ought to be represented, although the choice of Geneva as a meeting place might give rise to difficulty.

Our preparations now moved forward rapidly. On Saturday, September 4th, a reply was received from Paris, from which it appeared that Delbos still wished to exclude Italy, but to invite Russia. During the afternoon I twice spoke to the Foreign Minister by telephone, insisting that Italy should be invited. Delbos accepted this with reluctance, but refused to exclude Russia. If we did, he said, he would have to resign and we should be responsible for a ministerial crisis in France. I certainly did not want this, nor did I plan to exclude Russia as long as the two other Black Sea powers were invited, and Germany too, in order to give all the principal powers an opportunity to attend. On this understanding, the British and French Governments on September 5th addressed invitations to a meeting to be held five days later in the small town of Nyon.

Ciano's first reaction was favourable, but at this moment Litvinov sent a strong note of protest to Rome, blaming the Fascist Government for the torpedoing of two Russian ships. I thought that Rome might use this as a pretext to temporize on our invitation, but I still did my best to secure Italy's attendance, telling Crolla on September 7th that we attached great importance to the Nyon Conference, not only because we must deal with piracy, but because I could think of no better prelude for the Anglo-Italian conversations than its successful outcome. If the Soviet note were an attempt to sabotage the Conference, as Count Ciano had argued, I could imagine no more effective retort than for Italy to show, by attending herself, that it had failed.

Despite these exchanges, I had now to amend my policy to take account of a probable Italian, and therefore German, refusal to attend. The Admiralty and Foreign Office worked out a plan by which the Mediterranean was to be divided into zones. Britain and France would play the major part in policing the western basin, while Russia and some eastern Mediterranean countries might be asked to watch the Aegean.

In a memorandum I suggested that Britain should try to secure agreement at the Conference on the following proposals:

(i) That in view of the piratical acts carried out by submarines in the Mediterranean against the shipping of various countries, the powers concerned shall give instructions to their naval forces to take the action indicated in (ii) and (iii) below with a view to the protection of all shipping.

(ii) That any submarine attacking a merchant ship in a manner contrary to the rules as to the action of submarines with regard to merchant ships contained in the Procès-Verbal signed in London on the 6th November 1936, is to be counter-attacked and, if possible, destroyed.

(iii) This instruction extends to any submarine in the vicinity of a position in which a merchant ship has recently been attacked or sunk.

(iv) The above instruction shall remain in force for one month at the end of which the position will be reviewed.

The rules referred to in paragraph (ii) were already being flouted by the Fascist Government.

I discussed the position informally with several colleagues. Rather to my surprise, those who were in favour of placating Mussolini regarded their policies as realistic. There was also evidently some disappointment that I was not prepared to take any present initiative over *de jure* recognition of the conquest of Abyssinia. On September 3rd Count Ciano wrote in his diary:

I have received authorization for the reinforcements to be sent to Spain after the decision in Geneva about the recognition of the Empire: Either they refuse to recognize us, and we are free to act. Or they recognize us, and we are equally free, because of the Fascist rule that once a thing is done it's done. *

There could be no more revealing commentary on the whole course of negotiations with the Fascist Government up to the outbreak of the second world war.

On September 8th the Cabinet endorsed the policy laid down in my memorandum. Mr. Churchill, with whom my relations were now close, wrote to say that he had discussed the situation with Mr. Lloyd George, and they agreed that if it were hoped to have good relations with Italy in the future, matters should be brought to a head now. Both statesmen assured me of their support in Parliament and outside, if I felt able to act firmly at Nyon.

On September 9th we heard that the Italian Government would not go to Nyon, but wished to refer the matter of piracy to the Non-Intervention Committee in London. I learnt later that the Prime Minister, while anticipating that the proposal would be rejected as not being *bona fide*, had asked for the views of the Foreign Office, as he thought there was something to be said for it. Although at the time, perhaps, the Prime Minister did not know it, he was trying to reconcile

* op. cit.

two incompatibles: the theory of being on good terms with dictators, and the practice of dealing with their behaviour as exemplified in the Abyssinian war, the Spanish war and Mediterranean piracy.

However, we had concluded our agreement at Nyon before Mr. Chamberlain's request reached the Foreign Office. Even at the moment when it was written, our decisions had already been taken and I was about to leave for Geneva. Plans were ready for co-operation between the British, French and other navies and there could be no question of halting them. I expressed in a letter to King George VI the hope that the Conference would achieve its main task within forty-eight hours of meeting. So it proved.

I thought that the Service Ministers were sometimes apt to exaggerate not so much our own weakness, as its relation to the still limited power of the dictators, especially at sea. Accordingly, I had written to the Prime Minister just before leaving for Nyon, where I hoped to make use of the overwhelming Anglo-French sea power in the Mediterranean:

> From time to time remarks have been made in our discussions, naturally enough in the main by Service Ministers, which emphasize that our foreign policy must be dictated by the state of our defences and it is sometimes added that our position in this respect, in particular at sea, is worse than in 1914. While it may be true that our navy today is not as strong as it was in 1914, that is not, I think, the proper basis of comparison. Our navy in Europe is today relatively much stronger than in 1914; the German navy of today bears no comparison to that of pre-war days, the French navy is stronger than that of 1914, and relative to the German navy, very much stronger. It is quite true that Italy remains an uncertain factor, but she was that in 1914, in fact she was officially tied by treaty to Germany in those days. Therefore in Europe surely our position is much better than it was in 1914. So far as the world situation is concerned, the naval strength of the United States is on a level with our own, but our relations with that country are better than they were in 1914.

I went on to relate that Lindsay, when he had come to see me a few days before, had described the relations of the two countries as being at present remarkably good. My letter continued:

> We can surely therefore rule out the possibility of our being involved in a war with the United States. We could not do that in 1914.... There remains, of course, Japan, which is the one great naval power with whom our relations are far from satisfactory.

I have not attempted in this letter to deal with the other arms, and I have no doubt that there are dark sides to the picture. None the less I wanted to put this other aspect down on paper, because I think it is at least worth considering.

* * * * *

On the afternoon of September 9th, Lord Cranborne, Lord Chatfield, the First Sea Lord, and I flew to Paris, where Vansittart joined us. At the dinner which Delbos gave for us that evening, I said I thought that our meetings at Nyon should be brief and mainly technical in character, avoiding international polemics. I was glad to learn from our Minister in Paris, Hugh Lloyd Thomas, that public opinion in France was steadfast in support of British and French determination. Earlier that day the French Government had announced that four more destroyers would be sent to the Mediterranean to strengthen their patrol.

When we arrived at Geneva, Delbos and I concerted a telegram for despatch to Rome and Berlin, saying that the question of the illegal attacks in the Mediterranean was one of special urgency and importance, which we did not think it feasible to refer to the Non-Intervention Committee. The Conference was therefore beginning its labours and we would inform the German and Italian Governments of its progress.

That same morning, September 10th, Delbos and I agreed that the aim of the Nyon Conference should be to organize the naval forces available in the Mediterranean, so that unlawful attacks on shipping would be dealt with promptly. In practice this meant that we should go ahead with or without Italy's co-operation. We also decided that in the interest of speed, the Conference should deal first with submarine warfare only. Attacks by surface vessels and aircraft would be examined later, during the course of the League Assembly.

That afternoon we moved to Nyon, fifteen miles from Geneva on the shores of the lake. After the Mayor had welcomed the representatives of the nine powers attending, I proposed that M. Delbos, as first delegate of the power which proposed the Conference, should preside. This he did, admirably. In his opening speech, which he had shown to me in advance, Delbos said:

> The present state of insecurity which exists in the Mediterranean cannot be allowed to continue without grave risk. It is not possible that shipping should remain at the mercy of piratical undertakings which do not respect

any flag and which torpedo merchant ships without warning and without consideration either of cargo or of destination, according to methods which we might have thought had been abolished, and which are directly contrary to the Protocol of 1936 on the humanization of submarine warfare.

Litvinov weighed in with a more entertaining, if less judicious, speech, publicly blaming 'the government of a European state' for organized piracy. All Mediterranean powers must wish to participate in the Conference, he said, except those who considered themselves guaranteed against piracy, either because they organized it themselves, or because of their extreme intimacy with the pirates. After this, I merely added that the Conference would no doubt wish to keep Germany and Italy fully informed. We then went into private session.

The delegates were given details of the Anglo-French plan, by which the Mediterranean would be patrolled in zones. One of these we proposed should be offered to Italy. It seemed impossible to cover the entire Mediterranean, so we decided to concentrate on those areas where attacks had been most frequent. Great Britain and France would police the western Mediterranean basin, while the Aegean would be patrolled by Russia and Turkey in the north, and Greece and Yugoslavia in the south. We knew, of course, that the smaller powers would need help from Great Britain and France in carrying out their duties. However, we soon realized that the eastern Mediterranean countries were most unwilling to have any co-operation at all from the Russians. I was surprised at the strength of this feeling, which was shared by all, including the Turks, who at that time had friendly relations with the Soviets. At a private meeting that night, these sentiments led to an altercation with the Russians and for an hour no progress was made. I reported at the end of the first day that it seemed as though this difficulty would wreck the hope of agreement. The Conference would then have to admit failure, with most unhappy consequences.

The following morning, however, we devised a solution more satisfactory than our original plan. This was in part the result of the vigorous attitude of the French, who offered more destroyers, so that we and they could join in patrolling the Aegean, to the comfort of those who feared the Russians. Lord Chatfield and our naval experts had expected that most of the patrolling would fall to British warships. In the light of Laval's meagre efforts during the Abyssinian crisis, this was natural. However, Chatfield was surprised, and so was I, at the splendid contribution the French were prepared to make, which gave a fresh impetus to our plans. We now canvassed the idea that, rather than divide up the Mediterranean into zones, Britain and France would take over the brunt of the work in the western basin and in the Aegean as well. This was popular and during the morning of September 11th all agreed that instead of helping the smaller powers to patrol the Aegean, we should ask them to help us. The arrangement gave the French and British Admiralties control, and they reserved the right to call upon the Russians for help in the area. Thus all faces were saved, while, in practice, our plan would keep the Russians out of the Aegean. To my surprise, Litvinov accepted this situation. Possibly he was taken aback by Russia's unpopularity among the small states, which did not hold a lofty view of Soviet intentions, and was wise enough not to want to give publicity to that condition of affairs.

Before midnight on September 11th, little more than twenty-four hours after our first meeting, we reached full agreement. Great Britain and France would together patrol the main Mediterranean trade routes from Suez to Gibraltar, from the Dardanelles to Gibraltar, and from the North African ports to Marseilles. For this purpose, the two countries would provide at least sixty destroyers. The eastern Mediterranean powers would police their own territorial waters and would assist us, on request, to patrol the main routes. It had not been foreseen by the Cabinet that Britain and France would assume so heavy a responsibility, but I had no doubt that we must accept it, to make sure of success. Our Agreement specifically excluded some areas, particularly the Tyrrhenian Sea, from the patrol scheme, because they might 'form the subject of special arrangements'. This was done in order to offer a large area, as befitted Fascist dignity, to Mussolini, who could then send his warships to hunt his own submarines where it mattered least. We did not expect that Italy would accept this offer outright, but it could form the basis of a bargain, and our position was strong.

We published immediately the instructions which the nine powers had decided to give to the patrols. They were to fire to sink any submarine attacking a non-Spanish ship. This would apply not only to submarines seen in the act of attacking, but also to any seen near an attacked ship in circumstances which gave 'valid ground for the belief that the submarine was guilty of the attack in question'. The Nyon powers agreed that none of their submarines would put to sea in the Mediterranean, unless accompanied by a surface vessel. We announced that Britain would supply thirty-five destroyers, and the French offered to provide twenty-eight, taking some out of the reserve for the purpose.

We sent full details of the Agreement to Rome on September 12th. Ingram and his French colleague, Blondel, presented them jointly on the next day to Ciano, who went through all the movements of surprise, doubt and indignation. He said that he must consult Mussolini, but his personal reaction was that it would be impossible for Italy to accept the excessively small share allotted to her in the control scheme. Ciano apparently did not know which way to turn, for he was put out by the speed of our decision and its consequences for Fascist plans. We had heard nothing from him by September 14th, when all the Nyon powers had signified their approval of the Agreement. Our representatives in Rome were then told to explain that we could wait no longer. Accordingly, we signed the Agreement that day, without Mussolini's concurrence.

* * * * *

The effect of the Nyon Agreement on the influence and authority of Britain and France was excellent. On September 14th I wrote to Mr. Churchill:

I hope you will agree that the results of the Conference are satisfactory. They seem so as viewed from here. The really important political fact is that we have emphasized that co-operation between Britain and France can be effective, and that the two Western democracies can still play a decisive part in European affairs. . . .

I agree that what we have done here only deals with one aspect of the Spanish problem. But it has much increased our authority among the nations at a time when we needed such an increase badly. The attitude of the smaller powers of the Mediterranean was no less satisfactory. They played up well under the almost effusively friendly lead of Turkey. Chatfield has been a great success with everyone and I feel that the Nyon Conference, by its brevity and success, has done something to put us on the map again. I hope that this may be your feeling too.

After the Conference dispersed, the British and French Naval Staffs continued their consultations. They agreed that, as long as the Nyon Agreement lasted, the forces of both countries could visit each other's ports and fly over and land on each other's territory, without previous notice and without the usual diplomatic sanction. We had indeed travelled a long way since the autumn of 1935. The Nyon decisions were put into effect at once. The British battleship *Barham*, flagship of the Mediterranean Fleet, sailed from Malta to begin patrol duty off

French North Africa. Two squadrons of flying-boats were sent out from England to Malta.

We could not have obtained the Agreement without the invaluable help of the Admiralty representatives. A cruise by the Mediterranean Fleet to Turkish waters had evidently made a remarkable impression. I wrote to Chamberlain on September 14th:

> Rüștü Aras [the Turkish Foreign Minister] indeed delighted Chatfield this morning by asking him for an estimate of the cost and time needed for the construction of two cruisers and three destroyers in British yards exactly similar to those which had recently visited Constantinople. This visit seems to have been such a success that Ataturk is apparently determined to have ships like ours, after which, Aras explained privately, he would be able to look after the Aegean by himself. . . .
>
> Chatfield has been of the greatest help possible to us throughout this business. . . . All the foreigners have been delighted with him. Indeed he is something of a hero of the ideal British naval type. No doubt he is all the more welcome just now when he brings with him the ideal British ships.
>
> It is possible no doubt that the Rome reaction will be violent. All the more so perhaps because for the first twenty-four hours they did not know what to say. But if this is so I am sure that there is no alternative for us but to stand firmly and quietly by our decision. This is an issue upon which we have, I am convinced, support of all public opinion and the Dominions. This was very clear at a Dominions meeting we had here last night. Whatever political decision Hitler may take, German opinion will feel no enthusiasm for a Mediterranean controversy. So far as Mussolini himself is concerned, though he may be very angry for a while, he is likely to respect us all the more in the end. Be that as it may, we could not I am convinced have allowed this conference to end in failure. It was more than time that the democracies should make themselves felt in Europe.

After the signing of the Agreement, I met a number of press representatives as I came out. W. N. Ewer was among them and he asked me if Nyon would mean the end of submarine piracy. 'If there's another attack, I'll eat my hat,' I replied. Happily, I had little cause to regret this hostage to fortune. In a broadcast from Nyon I said:

> Submarines of unknown nationality have repeatedly and indiscriminately attacked and sunk merchant ships. Each of the parties in Spain has disclaimed responsibility for the acts of these pirate submarines. The problem, therefore, confronting the conference was that of the masked highwayman who does not stop short of manslaughter or even murder.
>
> A conference was necessary to mark clearly the horror which surely must be felt by all civilized peoples at the barbarous method employed in these

submarine attacks. Moreover, the size of the Mediterranean and the consequent extent of the problem made collective deliberation leading to swift collective action imperative. . . .

We took as the kernel of the arrangement the rules laid down in the London Naval Treaty of 1930, which were reaffirmed in November of last year. Recent submarine sinkings have shown an utter disregard for these rules and constituted a kind of gangster terrorism of the seas.

We believe we have put a stop to submarine piracy in the Mediterranean. We have set up in that sea a police force. If any submarines attempt again to embark on evil courses they will, I hope and believe, receive the punishment they deserve.

* * * * *

The outcome of the Nyon Conference was welcomed in the United States, whereas in Italy the reaction was confused and resentful. The Fascist Government returned a reply to the effect that the share allotted to them in the Nyon Agreement appeared unacceptable. Italy's vital interests in the Mediterranean made it necessary that she 'should have conditions of absolute equality with any other power in any zone of the Mediterranean'. After further exchanges, Mussolini decided that the lesser evil was to take part. Accordingly, Signor Bova-Scoppa, the Italian representative to the League, soon gave hints to the French delegation that the Fascist Government might have comments to make on the Nyon Agreement. Delbos replied firmly, saying that we had done everything possible to bring Italy into the Conference. The French Government were quite ready to listen to any observations from Rome, but they were not asking for anything. The Agreement would come into force on September 20th and there was no question of its signatories running after the Italian Government to get them to change their mind. I was told of this reply, which exactly represented my own view. Vansittart and I decided that in any event there should be no further discussions with the Italians at Geneva for the moment, with which conclusion the French agreed.

The meetings of the League Assembly at Geneva made it obvious that there was no sympathy for *de jure* recognition of the Abyssinian conquest. Even the Austrian Foreign Minister, who had been urged by the Duce to take the initiative on this, felt compelled to reply that he could not attempt so hopeless a task. On September 16th I telegraphed to London:

It is no doubt possible that Signor Mussolini will endeavour to obtain support in Berlin for some vigorous and face-saving reaction such as more active intervention in Spain, with the double objective of recovering any prestige he may have thought he had lost by reason of Nyon and of bringing the Spanish war to an end this winter, thus saving himself continuance of the heavy strain of that campaign. . . .

The truth is that the atmosphere here cannot become friendly to Italy while Signor Mussolini continues to tear up treaties before the ink is dry. The fate of the submarine protocol signed only last autumn is regarded as the most recent example of this. So long as Signor Mussolini continues to intervene actively in Spanish affairs, there is the virtual certainty that he will continue to take steps in connection with that campaign which will maintain international suspicion of him.

Perhaps the Nazi Government were surprised at the speed and expedition of Nyon. For a few days the German press did not know what to say, for there was nobody present in Berlin competent to give it instructions. Not until September 16th did our Chargé d'Affaires, Mr. Ivone Kirkpatrick, report that the newspapers had described Italy's attitude as fully justified. They insisted that if the Anglo-Italian conversations were not to be nipped in the bud, the Nyon Agreement must be altered to meet the Duce's requirements. It was not.

The French and British Governments had always said that they were willing to give Italy a share in the work of the patrols. The Nyon Agreement provided for revision at the end of the first month and, when that time came, Mussolini was allotted his part and accepted it. However, the moment was not favourable for conversations with Italy and we so informed the Duce. I dictated a note on these events for the Foreign Office when the Conference was over:

There are those who say that at all costs we must avoid being brought into opposition with Germany, Japan and Italy. This is certainly true, but it is not true that the best way to avoid such a state of affairs is continually to retreat before all three of them. To do so is to invite their converging upon us. In any retreat there must on occasion be counter-attack, and the correct method of counter-attack is to do so against the weakest member of the three in overwhelming force. That is the justification of Nyon.

* * * * *

I returned to London on September 22nd and went to see the Prime Minister, who had sent me a congratulatory letter on the outcome of the Nyon Conference. At the end of a brief general talk on the international situation, Chamberlain said that he hoped I would now take a really good holiday. I answered that I wanted to go away for a week, before speaking at a mass meeting which the Conservative

Central Office had arranged for me at Llandudno on October 15th. Jim Thomas, my Parliamentary Private Secretary and himself a Welshman, and Miss Maxse at the Central Office had a hand in these arrangements. The Prime Minister said at once that I ought to cancel this engagement, I must have rest. Anyhow, he would not have his Foreign Secretary used as a party hack. Nor was it a suitable time for a big speech to be made in the country on foreign policy. I said that I did not think that I could cancel the meeting, at least not until I had had a talk to Central Office, because I imagined that the arrangements had now all been made and I would not want to let the local people down. The Prime Minister said that he would see the Chairman of the Party, Sir Douglas Hacking, that afternoon and speak very strongly to him about cancelling the meeting.

When I got back to the Foreign Office, I told Thomas what had happened. He said that it was quite impossible to cancel the meeting, for which there had already been twenty-two thousand applications for seats. To do so would create a most unfavourable impression in the country. He then telephoned to Miss Maxse, who was so much put out by the idea that she warned Hacking of the line the Prime Minister would take in the interview that afternoon. The result was that the Chairman remained firm and the Prime Minister did not persist in his request.

At the Llandudno meeting on October 15th, I spoke of the Spanish situation, recalling that the Duke of Wellington, who had surely some experience of Spanish conflicts, had written more than a hundred years ago: 'There is no country in Europe in the affairs of which foreigners can interfere with so little advantage as Spain.' I continued:

> Looking back over the past year I am convinced that the policy of non-intervention, pursued by His Majesty's Government and endorsed by the British people as a whole, was the right one. We have observed that policy in the spirit and in the letter and I for one am thankful that no British aircraft have been operating in Spain and that no British aeroplane has crashed on Spanish lines.
>
> But in saying this I want to make a clear distinction between non-intervention and indifference. We are not indifferent to the maintenance of the territorial integrity of Spain. We are not indifferent to the foreign policy of any future Spanish government. We are not indifferent to the complications which may arise in the Mediterranean as the result of the intervention of others in Spain. We are not indifferent to vital British interests in the Mediterranean. A clear distinction must be made between non-intervention in

what is purely a Spanish affair and non-intervention where British interests are at stake.

Piracy in the Mediterranean was an example of the latter. The freedom of commerce in the Mediterranean had become menaced, merchant ships were being attacked and even sunk without notice when engaged upon their lawful occasions. Such conditions in the Mediterranean were intolerable and so the Nyon Conference was held and its decisions were taken, and rapidly taken. The measures there agreed upon have proved effective. Piracy upon the high seas has ceased. We shall continue to be watchful to see that those interests of ours in the Mediterranean, and in the maintenance of our line of communications with the Near East and India, are not endangered.

I welcomed President Roosevelt's speech at Chicago, adding:

> . . . it is well for us that the President of the most powerful republic in the world should remind us in these forceful words that it is not so long since we all pledged ourselves to refrain from resort to force as an instrument of international policy.

I next referred to the nine-power conference soon to open at Brussels; we would go there to work in the spirit of the President's declaration, which was our spirit also. I spoke of 'one satisfactory feature which has emerged prominently during the past year', the strengthening of our relations with France, a very welcome change, compared with 1935.

I expressed our faith in a free democracy: 'It is so much a part of our life that we do not proclaim our allegiance to it either by mass parades or by clothing', and ended by condemning the double-dealing of the times:

> Obligations are ignored, engagements cynically torn up, confidence has been shaken, methods of making war without declaring war are being adopted, while all the time each nation declares that its one desire is for peace.

In face of these dangers I thought party polemics merely obscured the truths and I called for national unity against them.

In this speech I was expressing a theme to which I tried persistently to rally national opinion at this time: it was with the democracies that our natural affinities lay. While we and France were in the forefront of the danger in Europe, there was an almost equal peril in the Far East, and every occasion should be taken to effect a closer unity with the United States. The Llandudno meeting was a stimulating experience and I was more than glad to have fulfilled the engagement, though I did not then know that this was to be almost the last public meeting I was to address as Foreign Secretary in the years before the war.

* * * * *

I was convinced that any general conversations with Italy must be linked with Spain. On September 22nd, the Italian Government gave M. Delbos an assurance, later repeated to us, that no more volunteers would be sent there. A few days afterwards, M. Delbos and I discussed this situation at Geneva and agreed that we should approach Rome and suggest three-power conversations, our purpose being to hold the Fascist Government to their renewed promise. On October 1st, therefore, I instructed Lord Perth, as Sir Eric Drummond had now become on the death of his brother, to speak to Ciano about Spain and suggest Anglo-Italian conversations of a limited scope, which would deal with areas where our activities clashed, such as the Red Sea and the eastern Mediterranean. Ciano made no response.

For a brief moment in October, perseverance with non-intervention appeared to be likely to meet some reward. Count Grandi told the Non-Intervention Committee that he was authorized to accept our proposals for the withdrawal of foreign forces. A few days later, presumably under pressure from Rome, he retracted, to my indignation.

To try to open up the negotiation again, I suggested that Count Ciano might come to the Brussels Conference and that he and I might have general discussions there. He was apparently tempted, but Mussolini vetoed the idea. Even if Ciano had come I do not now believe that we could have achieved anything, for Fascist policy, especially in the eastern Mediterranean, was now too active against us and Mussolini would not have changed his ways. We estimated Italian troops in Libya to number 60,000. Meanwhile, confirmation that Mussolini was already violating his latest promise to Delbos and to me, little more than a month old, by despatching troops to Spain, showed how worthless the results of any discussion with the Fascist Government were likely to be.

When, therefore, MM. Chautemps and Delbos visited London for talks with Mr. Chamberlain and myself at the end of November, 1937, we agreed that conversations with Italy would be worth pursuing only if Italian propaganda against our two countries ceased. We also agreed that we could not give *de jure* recognition except after a decision by the League. As Chamberlain himself said during the talks, Italy had made it impossible for anything to be done at Geneva. On December 2nd I told Grandi of our conclusion. As usual, the Ambassador spoke of *de jure* recognition as the one result which his Government hoped to get out of the conversations. I replied that we realized the importance which this had now come to assume in Italian eyes. The request was very different from what had been said to us when his Government asked us to give *de facto* recognition, through the withdrawal of our Legation at Addis Ababa. Then, I reflected, the significance of *de jure* recognition had been played down.

Nevertheless, on December 7th I was still persevering with the intention of conversations, even though we could not give this recognition. I wrote in a minute for the Foreign Office:

> I should like to improve our relations with Italy.... Propaganda is certainly a live issue. I would not start this subject menacingly, but simply say: 'we have noted Italian propaganda activities against us and that they are on the increase. If this process continues it is clear that our relations must deteriorate. We have already taken steps to broadcast in Arabic, not propaganda but straight news. We shall inevitably have to consider further steps if this propaganda against us continues. Would it not be much better at the outset of our conversations to make an effort to better this state of things.' Then our conversations could take place in a steadily improving atmosphere. In such conditions far-reaching results, which are alone worthwhile, might be attained.

The Foreign Office was painstaking, as was its duty, in examining possible contributions on our part to smooth discussions with Italy. About one of these, which suggested that we should on our own account offer Mussolini a declaration of non-aggression, I had to write:

> This really is not conceivable. It is not we who are vomiting fire twice a week. The British public would never stand for it, and rightly.

Shortly before Christmas, 1937, Signor Crolla, the Italian Chargé d'Affaires, handed me a document in reply to my conversation with Grandi of December 2nd. This stated that the question of *de jure* recognition, although a 'purely moral' one, was fundamental for Italian public opinion and could not be left out. The Italian Government reminded me of the Prime Minister's promise of the preceding July, in his letter to Signor Mussolini, that we should be 'ready at any time to enter upon conversations' and declared that they were ready to do so.

I remarked to Crolla that his document did less than justice to the point of view of His Majesty's Government; the question of propaganda was not dealt with at all. Signor Crolla then complained that we had not recognized *de jure*, and many in Italy, including members of the Government, believed that we were animated by motives of hostility towards their country. His Government were beginning to wonder whether a permanent state of bad relations between the two countries must be regarded as normal.

I replied that the answer rested with the Italian Government themselves. They had shown no desire to meet us. I pointed out that the despatch of Italian troops to Spain, the reinforcement of the garrison in Libya and the sinking of neutral merchant ships in the Mediterranean by submarines of unknown nationality, were none of them attributable to His Majesty's Government. Finally, I reiterated that we desired improved relations with the Italian Government, but that these could only be realized on a basis of reciprocity. That reciprocity was never forthcoming then, or later, until Mussolini brought his reluctant nation into the second world war.

In the last week of September, Mussolini had visited Hitler in Berlin. It was on this visit that the two dictators agreed, according to the German records, that 'quite generally, Italy will not be impeded by Germany in the Mediterranean whereas on the other hand, the special German interests in Austria will not be impaired by Italy.'* No hint, of course, was publicly given of any such agreement at the time, though from the behaviour of both Governments I began, during the autumn months, increasingly to suspect something of the kind. This conviction was to influence my own attitude towards conversations with either dictator.

* *Documents on German Foreign Policy 1918–1945*; Series D, Vol. I; H.M.S.O., 1949.

IX

DELAYS IN REARMAMENT

November 1936 – February 1938

My definition of our rearmament – Progress is slow – I advocate anti-aircraft defence – General Milch's manœuvre – The three Services in arrears – I ask for more Staff talks with France and Belgium – The British Chiefs of Staff demur – Their fear of disturbing relations with Germany – The Government decide against them

I thought it important to define to the country the purpose for which our rearmament was destined. I did this in a speech to my constituents at Leamington on November 20th. The definition provoked much discussion but was, on the whole, widely approved. Having affirmed our own attachment to parliamentary government, I said:

It would be wrong and foolish to pretend that nations can only co-operate in international affairs if their systems of government are similar. That is not true, nor is it desirable. There are at Geneva today states co-operating in the organization of peace who have every variety and form of government. . . . It would be a tragedy if the League of Nations were to become the home of any ideology, except the ideology of peace. All that we in this country require and expect is that the rule of law should govern international relations, and not the rule of war.

Describing the principles which inspired the work of the League of Nations I continued:

The defections from the League which have taken place in recent days have not changed our view that the principles of the League are the best yet devised for the conduct of international relations. These principles are entirely in accord with British ideas, and it would not be our nature to abandon them merely because in some parts of the world they have fallen on rocky ground, and we shall certainly not do so.

I declared that in a rearming world we must have strength if our ideals were to prevail:

> Our first task is to equip ourselves as a nation so thoroughly and so strongly that the whole world may see that we mean what we say, and that our conceptions of international order have behind them adequate force. There can be no doubt that attempts to uphold international law have not benefited from the comparative decline of British strength in arms which has existed in recent years. The equilibrium is now being restored—nobody but a would-be aggressor will complain.

Finally, I spoke of the purpose of our rearmament:

> These arms will never be used in a war of aggression. They will never be used for a purpose inconsistent with the Covenant of the League or the Pact of Paris. They may, and if the occasion arose they would, be used in our own defence and in defence of the territories of the British Commonwealth of Nations. They may, and if the occasion arose they would, be used in the defence of France and Belgium against unprovoked aggression in accordance with our existing obligations. They may, and, if a new Western European settlement can be reached, they would, be used in defence of Germany were she the victim of unprovoked aggression by any of the other signatories of such a settlement. Those, together with our treaty of alliance with Iraq and our projected treaty with Egypt, are our definite obligations. In addition our armaments *may* be used in bringing help to a victim of aggression in any case where, in our judgement, it would be proper under the provisions of the Covenant to do so. I use the word 'may' deliberately, since in such an instance there is no automatic obligation to take military action. It is, moreover, right that this should be so, for nations cannot be expected to incur automatic military obligations save for areas where their vital interests are concerned.

This doctrine admittedly had its limitations. There was no universal commitment, but the possibility of action was not excluded anywhere. This, I believe, was in accordance with the mood of the nation at the time and probably still is so. N.A.T.O. and our grouped engagements in the Middle East and South-East Asia are in harmony with the principles I tabled twenty-five years ago.

* * * * *

I had realized that it must be some time before our rearmament programme could show tangible results. In March 1936, the Ministry for the Co-ordination of Defence was created, but it did not speed rearmament as much as it could and should have done, in part because the choice of Minister was an unhappy one. Sir Thomas Inskip was a likeable man, friendly and patient, but too much inclined to take a cosy view. He was not the man to make trouble, which must have been welcome to Baldwin, who did not like facing it. Though Inskip had some gifts of co-ordination, he was not an administrator of drive or energy, nor had he any first-hand knowledge of the work he had to do, which might have made up for these deficiencies. If the business was to be serious, he deserved a larger staff than one private secretary and two typists, of which exiguous assistance I once heard him complain.

During the later months of 1936 the shortcomings in our government organization began to trouble me. Baldwin was now in failing health and more reluctant than ever to grasp the problems of defence. Under his chairmanship, discussions on this subject at the Cabinet and at the Committee of Imperial Defence were too often inconclusive. The situation was not much better on the Defence Requirements Committee under Inskip's placid leadership. I was among its dozen members and the slow progress became intensely irksome, even allowing for the difficulties inherent at the start of any rearmament programme. There was also a Defence Plans Committee, upon which the leading members of the Cabinet served, whose purpose was to give political guidance on which the Defence Requirements Committee could do its work.

Our machinery was cumbersome. Sub-committees flourished, but they lacked the impulse of a central driving force. Most senior members of the Government had little or no first-hand experience of war. The lack of personal knowledge of the problems we were discussing inevitably handicapped them in their approach. Nor were all the members of the Government, and of the Service departments, wholly convinced that we must rearm with all speed. In many memoranda and meetings, the Foreign Office insisted that 1938 and 1939 would be most perilous years. The Spanish civil war brought the danger nearer. Our defence plans were at this time based on the supposition that we might have to fight Germany or Japan, or both. Italy was still not listed as a probable enemy and it was quite properly urged upon me that our foreign policy must be so directed that she would not become one. However, the extent to which a man like Mussolini could be impressed depended upon our armaments and our spirit. The two dictators, both ex-servicemen and younger in years, had little respect for elderly non-combatants, as they regarded those who led us. Both

Hitler and Mussolini, as I many times explained, were much more likely to heed us if they found a determination in Britain to rearm and a stalwart national temper.

Towards the end of 1936, being oppressed with the dangers of our position, I asked that Sir Thomas Inskip should prepare a comprehensive report on our readiness for war, in comparison with other powers, as on May 1st, 1937. I was promised that this paper would be ready in February. Meanwhile, in order to impress my opinions upon my colleagues, I determined to make a short report on the international outlook at the first Cabinet of 1937, indicating that the main danger came from Germany. For this I made these notes:

> This is likely to be a critical year in foreign affairs. Many reports reaching the Foreign Office indicate that Germany's internal condition is poor. It looks, therefore, as though this year will determine Germany in following a policy alternatively of co-operation or foreign adventure.
>
> There are two schools of thought in Germany, the first and more cautious of which includes the army, the Foreign Office and, among others, Dr. Schacht. The second and more aggressive school of thought is the Nazi Party. Our object must be to try to restrain the latter.
>
> There is one means by which assistance can be given to the Foreign Office in our difficult task. Anything that shows that we are determined to press on with our rearmament and that it is proceeding vigorously will have a steadying effect. For example, if, before Hitler speaks to the Reichstag on January 30th, Sir Thomas Inskip can make an encouraging statement on the execution of our programmes, it may tell in our favour.

When international affairs were discussed on January 13th, 1937, some of my colleagues appeared to imagine that our difficulties with the Nazi Government sprang from minor causes. Lord Halifax considered it unwholesome that our contacts with Germany were tenuous while they were very good with France. Our efforts in the Spanish conflict, he thought, were affected by this. In reply, I accepted that we should try to improve contacts with Germany, but pointed out that one difference between France and Germany was that France had always been ready to stop volunteers from crossing into Spain, if others would do the same. Baldwin added soothingly that he knew that I wanted to improve contacts with Germany, but it was very difficult. It certainly was, so was the character of this dictatorship, which so many were reluctant to perceive.

The army was being treated as the Cinderella of the three Services, and this had to be accepted, up to a point. Even so, decisions were unnecessarily slow in coming. Sir Thomas Inskip had been ill early in the New Year, so that I could not raise this aspect of rearmament with my colleagues then, as I had intended to do. In the circumstances, I telephoned to Sir Maurice Hankey, the Secretary to the Cabinet, asking in particular whether Inskip could announce our intention to make a start at once with the rearmament of the Territorial army, which had been discussed between us. Hankey promised to pass this message on, together with my plea for an encouraging statement on the progress of our rearmament in general. A few days later came the depressing reply. Inskip did not feel that he could truthfully make a statement which would be sufficiently striking to produce any effect. No decision had been reached about the territorials, nor was there any prospect of arriving at one before the end of the month.

At sea, Germany's navy, even if combined with that of Italy, was no match for Anglo-French power, but the situation in the Far East created acute anxiety. There could only be hope, but unhappily no certainty, that in a conflict in those seas we and the United States would be acting together.

It was with the British rate of rearmament in the air and upon land that I was chiefly concerned. I argued repeatedly that our own plans to combat Hitler's were not going forward swiftly enough. As early as the autumn of 1935, when I was still Minister for League of Nations Affairs, I had urged upon the Government the necessity for providing adequate anti-aircraft defences for Great Britain. In October 1936, the Committee of Imperial Defence had, largely as a result of persistent Foreign Office pressure, accepted the urgency of inquiring about the purchase of anti-aircraft material abroad. In agreement with the War Office, inquiries were made in Washington about the possibility of buying equipment on the American pattern. The United States War Department refused, on grounds of secrecy, to release details of their own designs, so that American firms could manufacture for us. It did suggest, however, that certain specified firms might be interested in supplying equipment from our designs. The War Department seemed to me anxious to help and its refusal appeared to be reluctantly given.

As a result of discussion on our Committee, I telegraphed on December 15th to Sir Ronald Lindsay, asking him to take up this question with President Roosevelt. I suggested that he should try to persuade the President to make an exception to normal practice in view of the importance to the United States of British preparedness. Lindsay thought it wiser to hold a secret meeting with the Secretary for War, Mr. H. H. Woodring, who now proved more forthcoming. He told the Ambassador that his Department would be prepared to release to their civil industry in America the designs of the 3-inch mobile, and 4·15-inch fixed, anti-aircraft guns in which we were interested. This would be on condition that we placed a sufficiently large order, in which event first deliveries might be expected after eight months, with an increasing flow of guns thereafter. As an alternative he suggested that we might prefer to arrange for manufacture in the United States of guns from our own patterns. Sir Ronald considered that the War Department would prefer the second course and would be prepared to help us to preserve secrecy.

I thought that this opening should be seized, but the War Office was not enthusiastic, holding that the technical difficulties were considerable. They argued that their 'technical experts' did not think it likely that they could save time in production by this method. There was in those days too much readiness to defer to technical objections, with which Mr. Churchill's genius during the second world war was often impatient. He may not always have been right in such encounters, but his refusal to accept these contentions at their face value was a principal contribution to victory.

I suggested in a minute, on January 19th, 1937, that at our next meeting we should consider proceeding further with the idea of having guns manufactured to our own patterns in the United States. I wanted to do this not only to get the guns, but because I believed that once a contact of this kind had been established with the United States, we might obtain other armaments, which we badly needed, from that country. At this juncture, however, some suggestions were made from Canada about manufacturing guns for us. These, though admirable in their intention, unhappily led the Committee to decline my proposal. A costly delay ensued.

On February 25th I wrote to Sir Thomas Inskip:

> . . . It seems to me that our chief dangers in Europe this year are two-fold: first Central Europe, and more particularly Czechoslovakia, and second the chances of some sudden attack by Germany on this country or on this country and France. With the former I don't want to deal now. The risk of the latter we may hope to be remote. None the less it is so essential that we should spare no effort to make it more remote, that I want to put to you certain reflections that have occurred to me since yesterday's Cabinet.

Having accepted the account given us that everything possible was being done to build long-range bombers, my letter continued:

> Any further indication which we could give within the next few weeks, before any possible campaigning season opens, that we are setting our house in order now, will be very valuable.
>
> There is another aspect of the deterrent to a German attack on this country, namely, the anti-aircraft defence of London. We know that the Germans have paid great attention to their own anti-aircraft defence. Their A.A. guns are reported to be very successful in Spain and the Germans are no doubt watching very closely to see how we are dealing with this subject. Here again we cannot presumably accelerate our manufacture, but I have been wondering whether we could not announce some steps, the taking of which would impress Germany.
>
> For instance am I right in thinking that the anti-aircraft defence of London is at present entirely in the hands of territorials? Would it be possible without disheartening the latter to strengthen them by units from the regular army? All this may be quite impracticable from the technical point of view, but it does seem to me that nothing could help us more effectively to get through this year, without major trouble arising directly between us and Germany, than that the latter should know that we were going ahead with our Air Force expansion and were taking the anti-aircraft defence of London very seriously.

My persistence in this matter of anti-aircraft defence was due to psychological as well as to military causes. I had not forgotten the warning in my maiden speech, that we were the most vulnerable country to air attack in Europe. How effective anti-aircraft guns would prove was arguable, but it was not in dispute that to suffer air bombardment without the accompaniment of any reply was unendurable. It was essential to hear something going off.

* * * * *

It was, however, the progress of the Royal Air Force which we watched most closely at the Foreign Office throughout these months. Vansittart and others were constantly bringing to me disturbing accounts of difficulties and delays. Even at this time, January 1937, we knew that by April 1939 Germany would have at least 2,500 first-line aircraft with a striking force of more than 1,700 bombers. Against this formidable force our own programme was already in arrears. If it were completed on time, we should have only 1,750 machines by that date, rather more than 1,000 of which would be bombers. It was, the

Air Ministry told us, impossible to do more without a complete dislocation of industry. Moreover, we were given reassuring reports about the quality of our aeroplanes as compared with those of Germany, Italy and Russia, now being freely used in Spain. The Russian fighters, although good, were said to be inferior in performance to our own Gauntlet and Fury types. The new German fighters were apparently only just coming forward. Unhappily, ours were not. Although the prototypes of the eight-gun metal monoplanes, the Hurricane and Spitfire, had flown in November 1935 and March 1936 respectively, neither type came into large-scale production until the autumn of 1938, which was later than we had been told to expect. In the meantime, our squadrons were equipped with obsolescent biplanes.

The Air Ministry advanced the argument, on January 27th, that our superior quality should be taken into account when considering whether Baldwin's pledge was being fulfilled. Nevertheless, the Government were told that both numerically and in actual strength we should be equal to Germany's air power until the middle of 1938. This had to be reconciled with an admission later in the same discussion that we were somewhat behind on a 'purely numerical calculation.' I was shown the minutes of this meeting on my return from Geneva, and endorsed the view of the Foreign Office that this falling behind in our strength could not be ignored, even though I shared to the full the Air Ministry's conviction of the importance of quality. Further surprising developments followed.

In the summer of 1936, Lord Swinton, who had succeeded Londonderry at the Air Ministry, had discussed British and German air strengths with General Milch, then Under-Secretary for Air. Swinton had remarked that it was a pity that Germany could not give the world some particulars of her progress in the air. In the autumn, Milch sent a message to say that, provided complete secrecy could be guaranteed, the German Government would give us information. The Committee of Imperial Defence decided, quite reasonably, to accept this offer, and received figures in October corresponding closely with our own estimates of German strength.

In January 1937, a mission of Air Staff officers visited Germany. Milch invited one of them, Air Vice-Marshal Courtney, to come to the German Air Ministry, where he would be shown the Nazi Government's plans. It was stipulated that no other Staff officer or representative of the British Embassy should be present. General Milch received the British officer and produced volumes containing the German air programme. He offered to give the fullest information. This showed that Germany would, by the autumn of 1938, have a total of 1,755 first-line aircraft, while Britain, if she continued her present scheme of expansion, would have 1,736. General Milch also gave a breakdown of the figures by categories.

This information was passed on to us by the Secretary of State for Air, who assured us that it tallied with the Air Ministry's own intelligence. Milch had added the proviso that political considerations might lead to new programmes, but kindly offered to supply us with details in advance if this should happen. The First Lord of the Admiralty, Sir Samuel Hoare, weighed in with the news that his department too had been given accurate information by the Germans. The purpose of this joint German action was clearly to soothe, and there were early indications that Milch's tactics might have a soporific influence on the British Government. Vansittart reported to me that at his level, Air Ministry representatives had even indicated that there might be a slowing down of our programme. I made my own inquiries and satisfied myself that this would not happen, but the Foreign Office remained rightly suspicious of Milch's manœuvre. We thought that he was lying and, as I was going away for a few days, Vansittart wrote, with my knowledge, to Sir Maurice Hankey, setting out our opinion and our reasons for it. It seemed all the more necessary to do this, since the Air Staff admitted that Germany had greater present manufacturing capacity than Britain.

The Cabinet had now agreed on a much larger rearmament programme, to cost £1,500 million over a five-year period. It was decided that while most of the cost would be met out of taxation, a loan of £400 million must be raised. This proposal was debated by the House of Commons on February 17th and 18th. Members of the Opposition, in conformity with their consistent record on rearmament, opposed the loan. Mr. Attlee complained:

> Throughout this document and throughout the speeches we have heard, there runs the cry: 'The time is short, get ready now.' . . . Armaments are piling up.

So they were, most of all in Hitler's Germany, where the Government were now spending about £1,000 million a year upon them, or more than three times our own proposed expenditure.

Apart from the unhappy occasions when some large international issue becomes a cause of controversy between the parties, a Foreign

Secretary should always want to do what he can to gain national support for the policies he is pursuing. This sometimes makes parliamentary debate difficult for him and I remember that Chamberlain once complained to me on this count. I was not sharp enough with the Opposition. 'Why don't you go for them more, Noel-Baker, for instance,' he said, 'their position is utterly illogical. They oppose any increase in our armaments but they want us to interfere all over the world.' I said that I agreed with this criticism, but I thought that Foreign Secretaries ought to be as far as possible above the battle; I always had it in mind that one day I might have to go down to the House of Commons and tell the nation that it was at war.

On February 23rd I arrived at the Foreign Office to find upon my desk Inskip's report for which I had asked a few weeks before, dealing with our readiness for war as compared with that of other powers on May 1st, 1937. It was revealing and disturbing. The Chiefs of Staff thought that Germany would at that date be able to put thirty-nine divisions into the field, though their state of readiness and equipment would not encourage Hitler to risk a war. But by 1939, we were told, Germany would have marked superiority over France on land. The naval position was more comforting, although only two of our twelve capital ships were of post-war design. But the sternest reading was this latest account of what we must expect in the air. By May 1st, 1937, Germany would have 800 long-range bombers against our 48. Only by means of this arm could Germany and Italy launch an immediate offensive against us with a real chance of success. I did not think it likely that they would do so yet, but we were clearly very far in arrears. I raised the matter with my colleagues the next day, only to be told that we must not assume that the air force programme was not being carried out. The assurance was only partly justified. True, we had 200 per cent. reserves behind our meagre air front line and our output was expanding, but nothing could conceal the fact that we were already at a grievous disadvantage, the effect of which would fall upon our diplomacy in negotiation with men whose criterion was military power.

* * * * *

As Foreign Secretary, I was naturally conscious of the effects abroad of our rearmament programme. Not only would a more powerful Britain be a guarantee of peace, but our ability to intervene swiftly in Europe might make all the difference, if war came. Although we might still hope to prevent the division of Europe into Fascist and anti-Fascist camps, our real affinities and interests, strategic as well as political, lay with France, a fact which some of my colleagues were most reluctant to recognize. Indeed, a few of them felt that if only we were less close to France, we should soon be on better terms with Hitler and Mussolini. An incident after the Cabinet had broken up one day was typical. Kingsley Wood was standing by the fireplace at 10 Downing Street, within earshot of the Prime Minister and also of myself, as I moved away on the other side of the table. He said, in tones clearly intended to be heard by me, as well as by the Prime Minister: 'It's time that the Foreign Office thought less about France and tried to get on terms with Germany.' I made no comment then.

I was convinced that in dealing with nations who thought so much in terms of armies, we must be prepared to make our contribution on land, while building large numbers of long-range bombers to give us the maximum striking power in the air. When I was dining at Geneva with Delbos and Pierre Viénot, then Under-Secretary at the Quai d'Orsay, towards the end of January 1937, conversation turned to military matters. The Foreign Minister assured me that, although the French air force had had its ups and downs, it was now in good shape and growing. Furthermore, the army was in excellent heart and a high state of efficiency. Unfortunately, these views only coincided in part with other information. Our Air Attaché in Paris, while reporting that M. Pierre Cot's plans for reorganization of the French air force would do good, had added the rider that they were bound to cause some confusion at first. The Foreign Office believed that the first-line strength of the French air force, and its rate of production, were less reassuring than Delbos thought.

In the same month I learnt that the French had made approaches in London and Paris, asking that we should make ready a British striking force of two armoured divisions for use in the event of war with Germany. In the circumstances, theirs was a slender request. Our own General Staff, however, doubted whether this policy would suit us, armoured divisions were far more costly to equip than infantry divisions. These two could only be formed at the expense of our infantry and would thus produce an ill-balanced force, unsuitable for our world-wide commitments. Moreover, armoured divisions presupposed a large supply of medium tanks, which we did not possess. Nor did it seem that we should have any before 1939. I was not at all convinced that this was the right answer. Much might depend upon our ability to despatch an effective fighting force to France and Belgium, if they were attacked, and this should, I thought, include at least one armoured division. As the French were bearing almost the whole burden on land it was only fair that we should make a contribution in armour, even if it were expensive.

When, in the spring of 1937, the Government considered the role of the British army, I accepted that it was not possible, owing to air and other demands, to organize an army on the scale of 1914–18. But I thought that Mr. Duff Cooper, then Secretary of State for War, was right to ask for a minimum expeditionary force of five divisions, to be supported by four territorial divisions within four months of the outbreak of war. An alternative suggestion was that a smaller number of regular divisions, and a larger number of territorial divisions, should be equipped to go to the Continent at short notice. After some talk, Sir Thomas Inskip agreed with Mr. Chamberlain's proposal that the role of the British army be investigated. At this, the Secretary of State for War was justifiably provoked. Indignantly he recalled that this decision had already been under investigation for the better part of two years.

I strongly favoured Duff Cooper's plan and suggested to the Cabinet that we should support these five divisions by bringing home regular army battalions from India when war broke out and replacing them by territorials. The plan was not accepted, though it was executed by me with Mr. Churchill's vigorous endorsement, when I was at the War Office in 1940. The Government did, however, decide, in May 1937, that the whole regular army and the two anti-aircraft territorial divisions should be provided with the most efficient and complete equipment. But we still had not the tanks available or further forward than the drawing-board. I suggested, therefore, that we should place an order for the French *Char* '*B*'. This, however, was not accepted.

Neville Chamberlain and the majority of Ministers shared what was certainly the popular view at the time, that we could support our allies effectively on a basis of limited liability. This was probably never true, for psychological as well as military reasons. It was only rational if our contribution in the air could be dominant over Germany's, of which there was by this time no hope in any war within the next few years.

* * * * *

The Nazi and Fascist press left us in no doubt that even our pace of rearmament was extremely unwelcome to the dictators, who expended much energy in spreading stories that we lacked the will and means to carry through our programme. At the beginning of April, the Hungarian Minister told Vansittart it was being widely said in Germany that because of this failure we should soon have to restore all the German colonies. I minuted: 'It is for consideration whether we can do anything to help our Embassies abroad to counter this kind of nonsense.'

With the help of Sir Thomas Inskip, the Foreign Office collated information about our plans and progress. I sent this with a covering despatch to all our Embassies and Legations in July, introducing the information with this paragraph:

> My attention has been drawn in recent weeks to the allegation that is frequently to be heard in many countries abroad that this country is incapable of carrying out the rearmament programme. There seems to be a tendency, particularly in certain totalitarian states, to underrate the will and power of democracies in general and of the United Kingdom in particular to fulfil the tasks which they have set themselves. It would be a great mistake to misapprehend either the spirit or the resources of this country. His Majesty's Government are fully determined to go through with their rearmament programme in any circumstances and to show no signs of slackening in its prosecution until the position of the United Kingdom throughout the world is all that they desire that it should be. That the people of the country are behind the Government in this resolve is evident from the spirit in which both Parliament and the press have received the proposals for rearmament and the very heavy expenditure which they involve. The execution of the programme is gaining in momentum every month; and although the British public would in normal times have thought such large expenditure on armaments to be wasteful and unwise, there is no doubt that the United Kingdom will be able to stand the strain longer than other countries.

We were now midway through the second year of our large-scale rearmament and I still hoped that, by the beginning of 1938, our foreign policy would have more power behind it. If we were obliged through military impotence to yield concessions to Hitler and Mussolini, we should merely whet their appetite for plunder. The outcome must be a European war.

At a meeting held just before the summer recess I learned that our naval programme was in arrears. Production on new ships and modernization of the old were delayed, partly because guns, gun mountings and fire control instruments were not forthcoming. As against this, one

Italian battleship was to be completed that year and another in 1938. I decided to write to Inskip about the position now being revealed:

> When I first took over this Office at the end of '35 I realized that for two years at least we should be in a very precarious position on account of the state of our defences, and that we must do everything in our power to gain time. I did think, however, that by the third year, i.e. 1938, our growing strength would begin to make itself felt and our diplomacy have a correspondingly better chance.

Sir Thomas reassured me that generally speaking we were growing stronger every day, but admitted that until 1940 we should have only twelve capital ships, seven of which would not be fully modernized. Although I returned to this charge later, I felt sufficient confidence to exploit our naval supremacy, when the opportunity came, at the Nyon Conference. Normally, however, we were forced to tread very warily. The British Empire had responsibilities all over the world which the Foreign Secretary was expected to meet. It was impossible to do this without the help of the French in Europe and the United States in the Far East, until we were stronger. I knew that we could not indefinitely play for time. How long we had was to become a serious cause of difference between the Prime Minister and myself.

As the autumn drew on, constant reading of Foreign Office telegrams revealed to me the harmful effects produced on the smaller European nations by what they regarded as our leisurely rearmament. The stream of reports from secret sources left no room for doubt that Germany's expenditure on armaments in 1937 was mounting fast and would exceed that of the preceding year; a high level which many had thought could scarcely be held. Our intelligence services estimated that each year Hitler was spending on armaments alone a sum almost as great as the total British budget. The conclusion from this disagreeable study was plain; unless we could make a more vehement effort, we would soon be receiving marching orders from Berlin. Mussolini was now deeply committed to a policy of Mediterranean adventure, compelling us to be watchful about our strategic position in that sea. Simultaneously, Japan was running amok in China and might soon menace our position in the Far East. Each of these countries would heed British armed strength and ignore professions of good intent. I could not accept the argument that the nation was not prepared to make the sacrifices to sustain the necessary effort. Without a successful foreign policy, Great Britain could not have a domestic policy; without faster progress in rearmament, no foreign policy stood a chance in that militant world.

Although I had minuted earlier in the summer that I thought the Nazis impressed by our rearmament, I noticed in the German press frequent references to our weakness in comparison with their strength. In particular, Nazi commentators were constantly pointing out that we were experiencing difficulties in recruiting and in building up the Royal Air Force. This situation was contrasted with Germany's thorough preparation, for instance in the matter of anti-aircraft defence. Despite Foreign Office warnings nearly twelve months before, warnings which were admittedly easier to give than to act upon, Great Britain in November 1937 had scarcely any defence for her great cities against air attack. Our supposed strongholds all over the world were in the same condition, and I was receiving many telegrams from Egypt pleading for modern equipment.

* * * * *

On the evening of November 1st, I had to go straight from the House of Commons to catch my train for the Brussels Conference and therefore had no opportunity to speak to Chamberlain, who had been unable through illness to take part in the debate on the King's Speech. Accordingly, as soon as I reached Brussels, I wrote him a letter, explaining my reasons for using firm language towards the dictators in a speech I had made in his absence. I went on to express my thoughts on the state of our defences:

> I must confess to you that I am profoundly worried about the state of our rearmament in relation to the present international situation. You will have seen the telegrams that are raining upon us from Egypt, and I am conscious in this Conference of an atmosphere of doubt as to our determination to put through a big rearmament programme. No doubt Germany and Italy will take every opportunity to disseminate reports that we are decadent and that our rearmament is not serious. None of this would matter so much if it were not for the danger of its effect upon our friends. In the Near East at present there are a number of nations who are for all practical purposes our allies, and if they be once convinced that we shall not prove in the long run to be the winning horse, they will leave us. I appreciate, of course, the force of the argument that our industry is already fully occupied and that we cannot hasten the pace at which anti-aircraft guns and such like are now being turned out, but I am convinced that the next year is going to be so critical that we simply cannot afford to rest content with such comfort as we

can derive from the fact that two years from now our strength will begin to show itself. This brings me to the question of purchase; could we not seek to buy anti-aircraft guns for Egypt—if need be for London? I am convinced that the efficacy for peace of a hundred anti-aircraft guns in Egypt to-day would be infinitely greater than the prospect of two hundred three years hence.

I do not know whether immediate purchase is possible but it could at least be tried, either in the United States or in France. The former is now on such friendly terms with us that they might be willing to allow us to have some guns without waiting. Of course, I admit at once that I am very ignorant of the financial aspect of all this question. None the less I do feel that our strength in armaments within the next twelve months may be decisive for peace and, therefore, the financial consideration appears to be secondary. If I judge the temper of our people aright, they are ready to make sacrifices and appreciate, perhaps more clearly than some of our colleagues, that we have got to meet the challenges of the dictators and that to do so we have to be strong in armaments, even at some cost in other spheres.

My chief anxiety was still for the Royal Air Force. During the summer we had learnt from our secret sources that, shortly after his interview with Air Vice-Marshal Courtney, General Milch had ordered a substantial expansion of Germany's air programme. In October 1937, a memorandum by the Air Staff exposed the weakness of our position. It showed that by the end of 1939 Germany would have 3,240 first-line aircraft, with a striking force of nearly 1,500 bombers. Under our existing scheme, we should have, on the most favourable estimate, 1,736 first-line aircraft, with about 1,000 bombers. The general tenor of this document, in contrast with previous Air Ministry forecasts, was that we were two years behind Germany. Our position in regard to anti-aircraft artillery and searchlights was even worse. The Air Staff urged a greater programme of expansion, which might involve abandoning the principle of not interfering with normal trade. They quoted from a speech made by Sir Edward Grey in 1912:

> In the first place, you must not rely upon your foreign policy to protect the United Kingdom. That is to say, if you let your margin of naval strength in Home waters fall below that which may be brought to bear against you rapidly, you are setting foreign policy a task which you ought not to set it. The risk of an attack on the United Kingdom, stronger in force than we could meet with the ships we keep in Home waters, is one not to be settled by diplomacy.

I came back to London a few days later and decided to have a talk with the Prime Minister personally about the pace of our rearmament. My diary for Monday, November 8th, records:

Had a talk with N.C. in the morning about rearmament based on new Air Force paper. Told him of my conviction that rearmament must go faster, and that we should buy from abroad if necessary. I knew that some of my colleagues thought we at Foreign Office were insufficiently insistent in our efforts to improve relations with dictator powers. This, however, was not the true position. Unless it were known that we were rearming effectively, our efforts in international sphere today were useless. In this connection I emphasized the Grey quotation which appeared in the Air Force paper. N.C. did not, I think, share my view and clearly had the financial situation much in mind. I maintained that good financial position would be small consolation to us if London were laid flat because our Air Force had been insufficient. N.C. thought this was today too alarmist a view. Despite darkening international outlook, which he admitted, he did not think anybody was going to attack us for the next two years. It was necessary to follow a very cautious foreign policy.

N.C. undertook, however, to have a Committee for discussion of the whole situation on my return from Brussels.

Our exchanges did result in a meeting of five Ministers that evening to discuss a particular point which I had raised with Inskip, the provision of anti-aircraft guns. A month before I had circulated a paper from our Chargé d'Affaires at Berlin, giving a remarkable picture of the effectiveness of German anti-aircraft defence. I did not see how we could hope to match this without the purchase of guns from abroad, and specifically from the United States and Sweden. I had suggested a direct approach from the Prime Minister to the President about the guns. We had a good discussion, which resulted in a speeding of the existing programme. Approaches to the United States were to be prepared and we agreed to purchase Bofors guns from Sweden, a project for which I had been pressing for some time. It was the Swedish Minister who first said to me, 'Why do you not buy some of our Bofors guns? They are first-class.' They were. After I had resigned, further efforts were made to accelerate the anti-aircraft programme by buying from the United States. More of the Bofors guns and their ammunition would have helped our expeditionary force, two and a half years later.

On my final return from Brussels a week afterwards, I found no comfort in what the Foreign Office told me about the Whitehall attitude to defence. I decided to speak to the Prime Minister again on the subject. The opportunity soon arose, when I went to see him to discuss Lord Halifax's visit to Berchtesgaden.* I was left once again with the conviction that Chamberlain did not share my judgement about the urgency called for in our effort.

Soon after this meeting I circulated a document commenting on the Air Staff's memorandum of a few weeks before. I wrote that the picture there revealed was one which filled me with grave apprehension, not only for the future of our influence in the world but for our national security itself. I confined myself chiefly to the question of German air strength and the problem of home defence. I wrote:

> It is alarming to find, with every new report that we receive, that the day of security never comes any nearer, but is successively postponed to a still more distant future. It is now apparently about four years ahead, and so far as active ground defence is concerned, even more than that.

I drew attention to Sir Edward Grey's remark about 'setting foreign policy a task which you ought not to set to it', commenting:

> For some years now our foreign policy has been set this kind of task; and it is now clear that the burden must be borne by our diplomacy for several years more, in conditions not of diminishing but of increasing danger. . . . If our own safety has been ensured so far, this is due to Germany's present unreadiness and the close Anglo-French connection. But if we are too obviously outstripped in the race for material strength, the forces of diplomacy, however prudently and resourcefully used, cannot be relied on to guarantee our safety, except at the cost of deep national humiliation. This is all the more true now that the three great expansionist powers have succeeded, under cover of the anti-Comintern Pact, in setting up a system of mutual co-operation and support which can, if and when needed, be equally well directed against British interests. The original Germano-Japanese Agreement may in its origin have been directed solely against Soviet Russia, but it can hardly be doubted that its recent extension so as to include Italy in the present triangular pact is the result of the common desire of Germany and Italy to place themselves in a position to bring pressure jointly to bear on Great Britain when occasion should require it. If so, it is essential that we should take this new combination into account when planning for our future defence. Moreover, the existence of this combination will in large measure counter-balance the assets enumerated in this paragraph on which we have been counting up till now.

I therefore urged that the revised programme asked for by the Air Ministry should be completed as nearly as possible to keep pace with the German programme:

* Described in Chapter X.

. . . Although it may be admitted that Germany is neither fully prepared for war nor desirous of provoking it at present, yet the military preparations which Germany has undertaken in every department of her national life bear witness to an expectation of war so confident that it is not easily distinguishable from a will to make war.

If it is established that we cannot hope to provide ourselves with what the Air Staff consider to be our minimum requirements in the matter of air armaments and air defence before the summer of 1941, without some modification of our present industrial policy and even of our system of voluntary recruitment, I would urge that the possibility of making some such modification should be earnestly studied, or failing this, that our material requirements should be met by purchases from abroad. The situation is one which calls for a special endeavour to mobilize our abundant national energies. It is becoming more and more doubtful whether we shall be able by diplomatic means to continue to meet the potential challenge to our security and our international position by ambitious nations organized for immediate and total war and prepared to act in conjunction with each other, unless we make some more deliberate and conscious national effort than that upon which we are at present engaged.

In spite of which, finance prevailed in our discussions and the Air Ministry had to accept what was in effect a delay in their new scheme of expansion.

* * * * *

On the morning of December 17th, the French Ambassador remarked to me that there were certain aspects of the world situation which caused him considerable anxiety. The Rome–Berlin Axis, he said, was certainly not founded on a very sincere friendship, yet it did work very well in the technical sphere. Indeed, in that respect the German and Italian collaboration was much closer than that between England and France, though the real community of interests between our two countries was much greater. This seemed to him not altogether satisfactory. M. Corbin explained that he was only speaking personally, but, on my encouraging him to continue, he gave an example: in the Far East today we were faced by a menacing position; he imagined that it would be dangerous for His Majesty's Government to attempt to take any action there alone when the European situation was so strained. Yet he presumed it was a possible development that in the future we might wish to make dispositions in our fleet, different from those which then existed. So far as he was aware, however, there had been no kind of Staff conversations between our two Admiralties. With the world as it was at that time, any change in the political situation in any part of it was apt to result in the need for fleet movements. Between us our naval strength was very great, yet we had, it appeared, made no dispositions for any of the eventualities which might arise. He thought this was a state of affairs which should be remedied.

I told the French Ambassador that I had much sympathy with what he said. He would remember that the Prime Minister, during the recent meetings with the French Ministers, had made it quite clear that we were ready to exchange information with the French Government. If events in the Far East necessitated any change in our naval dispositions, the first thing we should wish to do would be to consult with the French Government. The question was whether there should not be exchanges of view now, so that we might each to some extent be prepared for the worst that might happen.

As an example of close technical co-operation between Hitler and Mussolini, Corbin cited the fact that the area around Gibraltar seemed to be used by Germany, and not by Italy, for Mediterranean training. A short while before, the French Government had even had cause to complain that the German Government had more ships in Tangier harbour than were allowed them by treaty. These ships were being continually changed and the Ambassador was quite confident that the procedure was designed to give the whole German fleet, by stages, experience of Mediterranean conditions. M. Corbin then stated that his Government now had a considerable part of their fleet in the Atlantic and, in certain eventualities, they would no doubt be able to move these ships to the Mediterranean. This was surely a step which might be discussed between us. We agreed that I would refer this subject to my colleagues, while Corbin would inform his Government of his suggestion.

I spoke at once to Neville Chamberlain about the Ambassador's proposal and then wrote to Duff Cooper:

I enclose herewith the record of a conversation which I had this morning with the French Ambassador. I feel myself that there is much to be gained and nothing to be lost by an exchange of views between our Admiralty and the French naval authorities on the naval situation in its relation to the international outlook as a whole. I have had a word on the matter with the Prime Minister and, subject, of course, to what you may feel, he is, I think, in general agreement with what I suggest. I remember that you remarked during our recent conversation on the Far Eastern situation that a first step in any redistribution of our naval forces in order to increase our strength in the Far East would be to consult the French. It seems to me, therefore, that there is much to be gained by entering into discussions with the French so that, should such an eventuality arise, we and they should both know what arrangements we wish to make in Europe.

The Far Eastern turmoil revealed, in December 1937, the close interdependence of foreign policy and armed strength. The sinking of British and American ships in the Yangtse, and our subsequent efforts to induce Roosevelt to act with us in the Pacific, were a sharp argument for increasing our naval strength. In particular, I thought it would be valuable if our reconditioned capital ships could be made available sooner. I wrote about this in the second part of my letter to Duff Cooper, asking whether it would be possible to speed the reconditioning of our first-line ships, so as to increase our naval strength in the late summer of 1939, a period which I considered likely to prove a very critical one.

Duff Cooper's first reply gave me some hopes that the modernization could be accelerated by the working of night and day shifts. When, however, I wrote on January 17th, welcoming the possibility of this better result, which would give us an extra capital ship in December 1938, another in February 1939, and another in the autumn of that year, I received a very depressing reply. The earlier dates were now only considered by the Admiralty to be possible if they were working under war conditions, and there had been further delays, in part owing to the action we had taken to prepare the fleet for the Far East before Christmas. The dates for completion had fallen behind even those originally promised. Delays of some kind are inevitable in any rearmament programme, but this disappointing forecast made the Staff conversations with the French even more important.

* * * * *

In December 1937, the position of those of us who believed we must have an expeditionary force, even though for the present this must rank in priority after essential air and naval needs, had not been helped by some recent assurances of a soothing character from French Ministers as to what our contribution should be. Even M. Delbos had said that France only expected us to make available two mechanized divisions, and M. Daladier was reported by the Secretary of State for War as saying something of the same kind.

I was perturbed to learn, however, during one meeting before Christmas, that even these two mechanized divisions were not now to be provided. For I did not believe that France could sustain the effort on land by herself. In speaking of my anxieties to my colleagues, I told them that if war were to take place in western Europe, an attack on France by Germany was the form which the operation would most probably take. While I did not underrate the value of the Maginot Line, I doubted if it would hold out more than a few weeks and I was sure that we must inevitably be called upon to help. There was some substance in this warning.

I admitted the statements made by Delbos and Daladier, but pointed out that these did not take account of Belgium, and were made on the assumption that Belgium could look after herself. If, however, there was an invasion of Belgium or Holland, this would be the chosen method to break through into France, as the Chiefs of Staff had repeatedly shown. I did not ask for a change in the order of priority, but I thought that when a decision had been taken, the French Government should be told, so that the Governments might consider together how their countries were to be defended.

A difficulty which confronted the British Government at this period was that a high priority, too high as is now evident, was placed on the maintenance of our economic stability. This argument found particular favour with the Prime Minister and was constantly used by the Treasury, but it certainly made difficulties for the Service departments, whose political chiefs and staffs had to spend many hours trying to curb their demands within Treasury figures which had no particular significance in terms of defence. While economic stability was important, it would not have been seriously affected by larger expenditure than was approved a few days before Christmas 1937, at a time when we had nearly a million and a half unemployed.

Sir Thomas Inskip was inclined to lend much weight to the Treasury argument. The Chancellor's frequent contentions, that the sums for which he was being asked were stupendous, and his assertion that to borrow even a first instalment of £400 million had produced a tremendous effect, were out of scale with the effort which the nation had to make within two years. As we were even then competing with countries which had no comparable inhibitions about defence expenditure, our Service Ministers were at a disadvantage.

The criticisms I felt obliged to make did not mean that I was indifferent to the difficulties facing the Service Ministries. The long period during which the ten-year rule operated had reduced capacity to increase our defences rapidly. That decision of 1919 declared that 'the

British Empire will not be engaged in any great war during the next ten years and that no expeditionary force will be required.' It continued to prevail in the spirit and the letter until 1932. When, at last, the signal was given, the Air Staff in particular, despite some early errors, deserved the credit for ordering Hurricanes and Spitfires and, in 1936, for the foresight which resulted in the Lancaster bomber. The Air Ministry also showed wisdom in preparing shadow factories. Most important of all, it provided the funds for the secret development of radar and gave authority to test its possibilities in practice. This won for Britain a decisive advantage in its use in war.

* * * * *

It was inevitable that, in the opinions and correspondence which Ministers exchanged at this period, the prospect of three great powers arrayed against us should daunt the bravest. The Foreign Secretary was in consequence increasingly under pressure to contrive some reduction in their number. My replies could not be accommodating. I pointed out that Germany, Italy and Japan each had ambitions and we were in the way of their fulfilment. Hitler stood by what he had written in *Mein Kampf*, though he had since added colonies to his demands. Mussolini was ambitious to restore the Roman Empire, while Japan had plans to increase her conquests in the Far East. The difficulties in reducing the number of our enemies were therefore based on realities. This did not mean that there was nothing we could do. I suggested that we should court our friends and find out in detail how best we could give each other help.

In this connection the Foreign Office, on my instructions, prepared a paper in which they asked that consideration should be given to the revival and, within certain limits, to the extension of Staff conversations with France and Belgium. It was explained that these had at first been limited in scope, because we still hoped in 1936 that a treaty of mutual guarantee might be negotiated between the five Locarno powers, on the model of the old Treaty. Since Germany objected to these Staff conversations, negotiations for a new treaty would have been prejudiced, if we had then extended their scope too widely. This consideration hardly applied any longer, because the prospect of concluding a new western pact had become very remote.

Therefore, I argued, we ought to consider what we could do to hold mutually profitable discussions with Belgium and France. M. Spaak, during the visit of the King of the Belgians in November, had shown that his Government were ready to continue to give us any information in their power about their defences and their plans. If there was a point on which we wished to approach them, they were prepared to hear whatever we had to say. This was an offer which should, in my opinion, be taken up.

I considered that the British Government were justified in examining the Anglo-French and Anglo-Belgian military problems, which would arise if Britain were called upon to fulfil her obligations to France and Belgium under the Locarno Treaty. If it should be necessary for a substantial proportion of our air force to operate from French or Belgian soil, in order to be used effectively against Germany, the argument for such a study was all the stronger. The speed with which we could bring our forces into play would be of very great importance. I therefore argued that, on grounds of national security, we must reduce to a minimum the delay in making our military effort in support of France or Belgium.

Co-operation with the French and Belgian Staffs would also give us greater authority to seek information and to offer observations on branches of French and Belgian arms about which we were anxious. This would apply, for instance, to the equipment of the French air force.

My paper recalled an incident when French Ministers had been in London a fortnight earlier. The Prime Minister learnt that, until Sir Thomas Inskip had furnished some figures the evening before, the French Ministers had not known the extent of our aircraft production. Mr. Chamberlain had expressed surprise, and had said that if at any time the French Government wished for such information they had only to ask and it would be given. There had been an immediate response from the French Government, who had suggested methods by which the desired information might be made available to them. Most of these were related to contacts between the French and British General Staffs. My paper concluded that I felt the moment had come for a further development and a wider scope in the exchanges between British, French and Belgian Staffs.

On February 4th, 1938, the Chiefs of Staff circulated a reply which showed an extraordinary and misplaced reluctance to work with the French and Belgian Chiefs of Staff. It was admitted that, from the purely military point of view, collaboration would be desirable, as, for instance, over aerodrome arrangements, supplies of fuel and transport facilities. The Chiefs of Staff did not, however, advocate that such discussion should be authorized. They felt certain that the opportunity of turning these conversations to their own political advantage would be seized upon by the French with avidity. The temptation to arrange a leakage of the information that such a collaboration was taking place, would, in their opinion, prove irresistible to them, in order to flaunt the Anglo-French accord in the face of Germany. In our present effort to reach a *détente* with Germany, the Chiefs of Staff argued that it was most important, from the military standpoint, that we should not appear to have both feet in the French camp. They therefore considered that the military plans for closer collaboration with the French upon concerted measures against Germany, however logical they might appear, would be outweighed by the grave risk of precipitating the very situation we wished to avoid, namely, the irreconcilable suspicion and hostility of Germany.

The Chiefs of Staff did, however, think that there were certain contacts we could make with the French without disturbing our relations with Germany. General Milch and other German air force officers having recently visited this country, it would seem natural, they suggested, to invite, in their turn, officers of the French air force.

The general tone of this paper not only showed no bias towards France and Belgium, but was, if anything, slanted the other way. I was indignant. The arguments used for not undertaking these conversations were almost wholly political and I thought erroneous. In my judgement, the closer the contacts, both political and military, we could establish with France and Belgium, the more effective the deterrent to war. Neither Hitler nor Mussolini would be sobered by the knowledge that we were holding back from defence arrangements with countries which might be victims of their aggressive acts, for fear of offending their susceptibilities. On the other hand, knowledge that the democracies were preparing their defensive plans together would be salutary. I asked to see the Prime Minister and the Minister of Co-ordination of Defence, told them my sentiments and asked that this paper should be withdrawn and that the issue should be considered at the Cabinet. This was done, when the Government decided that the action I had asked for should be set on foot. Mr. Chamberlain and Sir John Simon supported my stand, but both Lord Halifax and Sir Kingsley Wood, especially the latter, were critical, fearing its detrimental effect upon the Germans. Even after his own experience, Halifax continued to look for results from contacts with Nazi leaders.

X

DICTATION FROM NONE

October 1936 – December 1937

Our policy towards Germany's southern neighbours – I appoint Sir Nevile Henderson Ambassador to Berlin – Light interlude with Herr von Ribbentrop – My speech on European dangers – 'Co-operation to all, dictation from none' – Lord Halifax is invited to Berlin and lured to Berchtesgaden – An aimless encounter – Conversations with French Ministers – The Czech-Sudeten problem – My views on Russian policy – Sir Robert Vansittart becomes Chief Diplomatic Adviser

In October 1936, Dr. Hjalmar Schacht, Reich Minister for Economic Affairs, visited Paris for discussions with M. Blum and raised the topic of Germany's former colonies, pleading his country's need for access to raw materials. Blum had been a little unwary in his reaction, saying that he must consult us before he could give an answer. I thought that this would enable Schacht to protest, when he was back in Berlin, that some response should be expected. So I warned Blum, when I saw him personally in Paris on October 2nd, that in my opinion Schacht was clever, if not cunning. The real attitude of Germany might be that she genuinely desired a European settlement. If this were so, she certainly would not be put off in her attempts by our attitude over mandates. Alternatively, Germany might wish to induce us to express a willingness to discuss mandates, while her hands remained entirely free. We had to guard ourselves against this. Blum acquiesced good-naturedly, and did not pursue his exchanges with Schacht.

During the autumn of 1936 we heard the first rumblings of the Sudeten Germans' grievances against the Czechoslovaks. We had known of the problem before, but at this time it began to be active, prompted no doubt by Berlin. Having called for a report from our Minister in Prague, Sir Joseph Addison, I commented upon his reply that I did not believe that he realized the European dangers of the problem. Sir Joseph had been critical of the Czechoslovak state and I wrote:

> Whatever the faults of the Czechs, they are tough and they have a good fighting record. What is to be the position of France if this problem leads to conflict between Germany and Czechoslovakia, and our position? These matters should be further considered by the department.

As a result of this examination by the Foreign Office, I reached the conclusion that the Sudeten problem was not one in which we could properly arbitrate, or give more than general advice to Czechs and Germans. My principal reason was that I did not believe this to be just a minority problem. If it were, there was no sufficient motive for intervention or arbitration, because the Czechs treated their minorities better than most countries which had minority obligations under the Peace Treaties. There was a danger that pressure upon the Czechs if carried beyond a general admonition, would play Hitler's game, if he were trying to use a minority problem to weaken the Czechoslovak state. Therefore I told Mr. Basil Newton, when he took up his appointment as Minister at Prague in March 1937, that His Majesty's Government were 'not prepared to take the responsibility for counselling Dr. Beneš to negotiate a settlement of whose terms they are quite unaware, and which might, indeed, entail dangerous or humiliating concessions.'

I thought that our attitude on policy towards Austria should be prudent, but not disinterested. This was what the Austrians wanted. Dr. Guido Schmidt, the Austrian Foreign Minister, when he called at the Foreign Office in May 1937, told me that Britain could best render service to Austria by showing a general interest in Central European affairs, rather than by referring to Austria specifically by name. I took his advice and Vienna approved the result. While our military strength was still limited it was the best that we could do.

* * * * *

I attached much importance to the selection of a new British Ambassador to Germany, when Phipps moved in the spring of 1937 to Paris, which was his spiritual home. Eventually I selected Sir Nevile Henderson. The responsibility for this decision was, of course, entirely mine, but the recommendation in his favour was strong and no one foresaw the opinions he was to hold. Henderson was then serving in the Argentine and I did not know him personally, but his previous experience had lain in Yugoslavia, where he was thought to have done well in his relations with King Alexander. Strangely enough, Vansittart was a convinced supporter of this appointment. The most fancied alternatives were Sir Miles Lampson and Sir Percy Loraine, and I deeply regret that I did not choose either of them in preference to the diplomat who was recommended to me.

It was an international misfortune that we should have been represented in Berlin at this time by a man who, so far from warning the Nazis, was constantly making excuses for them, often in their company. Henderson kept his hostility for the Czechs. He grew to see himself as the man predestined to make peace with the Nazis. Sincerely believing this to be possible, he came to regard me, and others at the Foreign Office who shared my opinions, as obstacles to his purpose. More than once in the next nine months, I had to warn him against the recurring habit of interpreting my instructions in a fashion too friendly to the Nazis. Lord Halifax was to suffer the same experience later more intensely than I could have tolerated. Henderson's confidence in Nazi good intentions and his support of their claims in Austria and Czechoslovakia accelerated events which it was his duty to retard. Despite all this, Hitler felt an increasing antipathy towards him.*

When I resigned in February 1938, Henderson was unable to conceal his delight. 'Now we shall be able to get on terms with the Germans,' he exclaimed to a British visitor in the Berlin Embassy. Three days later Henderson talked to Mastný, the Czechoslovak Minister in Berlin:

> 'I said,' writes Mastný, 'that I knew I could congratulate him who never hid his dislike of Eden's policy. . . .' Later on, Henderson remarked: 'If there is another change and Eden returns, you will have Eden but also war. . . .'†

* * * * *

At the end of October, 1937, I recorded this account of a visit from Herr von Ribbentrop:

> The German Ambassador said that on his return from his conversation with Herr Hitler in Germany he was anxious to review with me the general international situation. In effect, however, Herr von Ribbentrop's conversation was almost exclusively concerned with the activities of the Communist Party in various parts of the world, which seem now to obsess him to the

* Paul Schmidt: op. cit.

† Sir Lewis Namier: *Europe in Decay*; Macmillan, 1950, in footnote quoting *Der Hochverrätsprozess gegen Dr. Guido Schmidt*, 1947.

exclusion of all other considerations. He expressed himself concerned by the reports that Dimitroff was now in Paris and by the rumours of increased Communist activity in Brussels and in Holland, and asked me anxiously what was the state of affairs in England. I replied that we had virtually no communists in this country, except those whom Sir Oswald Mosley was creating. This comment seemed to puzzle his Excellency, who asked me to elucidate my meaning and to explain how it was conceivable that fascism could create communism. After some minutes spent in unfruitful attempts to explain to the German Ambassador to the United Kingdom something of the political outlook of the people whose views it is his duty to report to the German Government, I then turned the conversation to the situation in the Far East. . . .*

His Excellency said that he believed that there had been various reasons given for his visit to Rome. This, however, was entirely concerned with his anti-communist activities. It was this point of view and not major political decisions which had resulted in Rome and Berlin being drawn closer together. Both their political religions were founded on antagonism to communism. I would understand that he was the Führer's first adviser on foreign policy and, therefore, he had often to make these journeys in pursuance of the Führer's instructions. He regretted that the British press should criticize this practice. I replied that, if I might speak frankly, such criticism was inevitable. We here regarded his Excellency as Ambassador to the Court of St. James's. In such conditions it was an unusual experience for us, and by no means a popular one, to see an Ambassador accredited here spending time in capitals other than our own and his own. While we understood that the Ambassador might wish to consult his own Government personally at intervals, we certainly did not understand that he should find it necessary to proceed to other capitals. I feared that, if this practice were persisted in, criticism in this country would continue, and it would not be possible for us to say that it had no justification. His Excellency would perhaps not be offended at the knowledge that we much desired that he would spend the greatest possible measure of time in his work with us in London. Herr von Ribbentrop appeared gratified at this aspect of the matter, which had not previously occurred to him, and left assuring me once again of his satisfaction at the better relations between England and Germany. I refrained from telling his Excellency my view of the contribution which he had made to this alleged improvement.

* * * * *

During the late summer and autumn of 1937 the Sudeten pressure was increasing. I took an opportunity to discuss the situation with M. Delbos on November 6th, and we agreed that it was important

* See Chapter XI, page 535.

enough to be a main topic in the Anglo-French discussions which were to be held at the end of that month. Meanwhile, we each sent Beneš general counsel about the demands of the Sudetens. Our purpose in doing this was to strengthen our hands to enable us to be the firmer with Hitler in any remonstrance we made to him. This was clearly stated at the London talks which Mr. Chamberlain held with M. Chautemps, who succeeded M. Blum as Prime Minister of France.

At the time of the debate on the King's Speech after the opening of Parliament in 1937, Chamberlain having been laid low with an attack of gout and being unable to take part himself, it fell to me to make the main speech on the international situation and I decided to do so with a freedom I seldom used. As this speech fully explains my political thought at this time, I am quoting from it extensively. I referred at the outset to the support which Mussolini had recently given to Hitler's colonial claim:

> The House will no doubt have observed that during recent days a country that had itself, as the outcome of the Great War, gained very considerable accessions of territory in Europe, and also received certain territorial concessions in Africa from countries which were her Allies in the Great War, has now championed the claim of Germany to African possessions. I do not desire to add anything at this moment about this claim so far as it concerns Germany and ourselves. But I must now declare plainly that we do not admit the right of any government to call upon us for a contribution when there is no evidence to show that that government are prepared to make any contribution on their own account.

I then dealt with some criticism by Mr. Attlee:

> . . . in his reference to the Nyon Agreement [Attlee] contrasted the promptitude with which, he said, we had acted there, with the delays of the Non-Intervention Committee, arguing that we were active for Imperialist interests, but less active in what concerns international law. I do not accept the right hon. Gentleman's censure. He drew this distinction and I wish to point out to the House that it has no existence whatever in fact. It is difficult to imagine an arrangement which is less exclusively concerned with our own interests. The Agreement was reached among all the powers there, to protect the freedom of commerce in the Mediterranean. It is true that action falls almost exclusively on our Navy and the French Navy, but we are not acting and have not been acting, all these weeks, on our own behalf alone. The ships of all nations were being sunk—Danish, Dutch, even Russian—and all those nations are now having their commerce protected as well as our own. We reported what we had done to the Council of the League, who certainly did

not feel that we had been either selfish or Imperialist and, indeed, expressed their approval of what we had done.

I then replied to Mr. Philip Noel-Baker, who I thought 'must have pride of place in unreality'. He had complained that the League did not handle the Spanish dispute. I continued:

He knows, of course, that on two occasions the League itself by unanimous resolution blessed the work of the Non-Intervention Committee. I know the hon. Gentleman thinks that that action was solely due to my Machiavellian influence. He has been good enough to say so in his speeches in the country. He seems to blame me; he seems to think that the League would have loved to seize this prickly and difficult problem, but that I would not let them do what they wanted to do.

Let me assure him that the League never showed any enthusiasm to handle the Spanish problem, for the very simple reason that the League knew how sharp were the divergences of view within that organization about Spain. Twice they approved the reference of the matter to the Non-Intervention Committee. The third time that it had to deal with the question was in the Assembly this year. I think the [League] Committee wrestled for days, and I am not sure that they did not wrestle by night, trying to secure agreement on a resolution which they could put before the whole Assembly. At length they thought they had got it. They brought it before the Assembly and, as the House knows, two voted against it. There were fourteen abstentions, and the House can see for itself what the position would have been if an attempt had been made to induce the League to do what the hon. Gentleman wants and to impose sanctions in the Spanish dispute.

Whatever the merits or otherwise of trying to impose sanctions in the Spanish dispute, there was never the remotest chance of the League doing anything of the kind, and, frankly, I do not think it right to come to this House even to discuss the possibility of these things, when we know how utterly unreal it all is. The truth is, and it must be faced, that the whole world does not look upon the Spanish dispute exactly in the same way as hon. Gentlemen opposite. There are, discreditable though hon. Gentlemen opposite no doubt think it, a great many nations, members of the League, who want General Franco to win.

After replies to criticism of the working of the Non-Intervention Committee, I summed up our foreign policy in these words:

While we are determined, should the necessity arise, to defend our own vital interests and fulfil our international obligations, we will embark on no action which would be contrary to the text or the spirit of the Covenant, or contrary to the Pact of Paris which we have signed. We believe in the principle of the settlement of disputes by peaceful means and we will do our utmost to secure a general acceptance and observance of that principle.

While we recognize that the League is at present seriously handicapped by incomplete membership, we believe it still provides the best means for obtaining that result. We shall not be deaf to proposals for League reform, provided they are really calculated to strengthen international confidence and to make the League more capable of fulfilling the aims I have outlined. Such being our object, it follows that we will join no anti-communist and no anti-fascist *bloc*. It is nations' foreign policies, not their internal policies, with which we are concerned. We will work wholeheartedly with other nations who are like-minded with us, and there are many such. We offer co-operation to all, but we will accept dictation from none.

The speech seemed to have an impact on Parliament. Unfortunately, the Prime Minister did not like it and Lord Dunglass, his Parliamentary Private Secretary, commented to Jim Thomas that he feared the Prime Minister would be upset, as this speech would undo much of his own conciliatory work, especially with Mussolini. Thomas recorded this at the time.

Nevertheless, I was sure that the speech had to be made, for reasons which I explained to Chamberlain from Brussels:

You will see that I dealt somewhat bluntly with Mussolini's championship of Germany's colonial claim in the debate, but I felt that the time had come to speak out on the subject. Unhappily this *Times* correspondence on the colonial question has without doubt encouraged the Germans to think that we are in a condition to be bullied on that issue. This is the worst possible frame of mind to allow the Germans to be in. I asked Dawson some time ago to stop this correspondence, but without success. My speech was an attempt to stop some form of ultimatum about the colonies, such as may be, I fear, impending. I do not flatter myself that it will have succeeded, but it was anyhow worth trying and may cause more caution in the presentation of the demands.

* * * * *

There had been Nazi suggestions earlier in 1937 that Lord Halifax might pay a visit to Germany. Neither Chamberlain nor I had then thought it was wise for him to accept, but the issue became pointed when Halifax received from the German Hunting Association an invitation to attend the International Sporting Exhibition in Berlin, which was under Göring's sponsorship. It may be thought odd that the Germans did not ask me to go to Berlin, if they wished for a visit from a British Minister. I was not surprised. Apart from the German press attacks, which were already intermittently active, I more than suspected by this time that Hitler did not like me.* Lord Halifax told

* Paul Schmidt (op. cit.) seems to confirm this as of an even earlier date.

me of this invitation, in Mr. Churchill's presence, after a dinner which I had been giving for M. Stoyadinovitch, Prime Minister of Yugoslavia, on October 14th. Mr. Churchill's account runs:

> Lord Halifax came up and said in a genial way that Göring had invited him to Germany on a sports visit, and the hope was held out that he would certainly be able to see Hitler. He said that he had spoken about it to the Prime Minister, who thought it would be a very good thing, and therefore he had accepted. I had the impression that Eden was surprised and did not like it; but everything passed off pleasantly.*

My own recollection is that, when I first heard of this proposal I was not eager, but saw no sufficient reason to oppose it. I did not suppose that it would have any influence on our relations with Hitler, but I was sure that Lord Halifax wanted to go and thought it probable that the Prime Minister would have the same sentiments. This seemed an instance where I could reasonably meet them and it would be best to do so with a good grace. I thought it quite likely that Hitler's attitude, which I had no doubt would be unforthcoming, would have its effect upon Halifax. Therefore, at the start 'everything passed off pleasantly'.

I was due to go to Brussels on November 1st and I had heard from our Embassy in Berlin that von Neurath might attend the Conference there for the express purpose of meeting me. If Halifax went to Berlin very shortly afterwards, it would certainly appear that his purpose was to follow up our conversation. I was quite aware of this possibility and that care must be taken not to exaggerate the scope of the Lord President's visit. Accordingly, I held a meeting at the end of October with Halifax and our Ambassador from Berlin, who was in London on a few days' leave. After this conversation I minuted:

> I have spoken to Lord Halifax and Sir Nevile Henderson together. The former will listen and confine himself to warning comment on Austria and Czechoslovakia. I have impressed on Sir N. Henderson the need for doing all we can to discourage German intervention in these two states. We must keep Germany guessing as to our attitude. It is all we can do until we are strong enough to talk to Germany.

I arrived back in London on the evening of November 6th to find the Prime Minister and Halifax pressing eagerly ahead with arrangements for the visit. The original intention had been that Halifax should see Hitler in Berlin during the Sports Exhibition, and it was on this understanding that I had agreed he should go. A series of telegrams from Henderson now told us that Hitler would not be in Berlin at the

* Winston S. Churchill: *The Gathering Storm*; Cassell, 1948.

material time and that he showed no inclination to meet Halifax there. Moreover, it was found impossible to prolong the Exhibition. If Halifax wished to meet the Chancellor, he would have to go to his eyrie at Berchtesgaden. It even appeared that the Germans wanted to pretend that the whole idea emanated from us. Here was the precise sequence of events I had wished to avoid. By the time all this information had come through, I had been forced to return to Brussels. I did not think it good, either for Hitler or for us, that we should appear to be running after him, particularly when the tripartite pact between Germany, Italy and Japan had just been announced on November 6th. So I telegraphed to London:

. . . from point of view of our position in Europe and public opinion at home it is essential to avoid giving the impression of our being in pursuit of German Chancellor.

At the same time I explained my views by telephone to Lord Cranborne and asked him to speak to Chamberlain. Cranborne did so that afternoon, saying that it would be most undesirable that we should appear in the role of suppliant. He retailed my opinion that, if it became necessary for Halifax to wait for Hitler in Berlin, or propose himself to Berchtesgaden without encouragement, undue expectations might be aroused. Under such circumstances, I thought that the visit would hardly be justified. The Prime Minister, however, clearly had great expectations of the visit and said he was most anxious that it should take place. I think he had the idea that the Foreign Office was unduly hostile to Hitler's Germany and that its methods were too slow for modern times. He hoped for better results from personal contacts. It was, however, as unlikely then, as it is today, that a summit meeting on specific subjects would achieve worthwhile results, unless diplomatic exchanges had revealed signs of a possible agreement. Hard facts normally prove stronger than good intentions. So it happened on this occasion. In Brussels I discussed the matter with Malcolm MacDonald, Cadogan and Harvey. Reluctantly I agreed that the visit must now take place, but I wanted at least to have time to discuss with Chamberlain and Halifax the exact nature of the statements to be made to the Führer, and this was arranged.

Unfortunately, news of the visit leaked out in the press in London while I was still in Brussels, and before we had time to complete the arrangements. The Government therefore announced officially in the House of Commons that Lord Halifax was going to Berlin. I had not yet told the French of all this and on the evening of November 13th, M. Delbos spoke to me with some anxiety of the reports which were reaching Paris of Halifax's impending visit. It was unfortunate, he said, that the French Government had not known of it beforehand. I lamely explained that though the visit was purely private and unofficial, we had of course intended to inform the French Government well in advance of any final decision. Delbos replied that he fully understood the position and, for his own part, was not opposed to the journey, though he anticipated that Lord Halifax would be asked some awkward questions. It was, however, imperative to do nothing at this time to weaken the good relations between our two countries. His Majesty's Government must surely be aware that this was the continuing purpose of both Rome and Berlin; nothing could give either of these capitals more satisfaction than an indication that our solidarity was being undermined.

Later we spoke of the expected subject matter of the interview. Delbos begged that we should be very careful to give no encouragement to anything in the nature of a Nazi adventure in Czechoslovakia. In these days, he said, it was not enough to warn against war and invasion; there was a new technique. This was the reason why, in a recent speech, he had referred to France's guarantee to Czechoslovakia as being operative in general terms, and had not limited it only to invasion. He had wished specifically to make it plain that intervention in the internal affairs of Czechoslovakia, in order to facilitate aggression, would be as serious as a direct attack. He hoped to speak to Beneš in the near future about all this.

When I arrived back in London from Brussels on November 14th, I asked Mr. Rex Leeper of the Foreign Office News Department to prepare a note for the press, referring to the informal character of the Halifax visit and emphasizing that it implied no change of policy. At this juncture I fell victim to a mild attack of influenza and was ordered to spend a few days at home. To my annoyance, I found that some newspapers on November 16th carried most exaggerated accounts of the scope of the visit, while Leeper's note did not appear at all. I suspected official inspiration. Chamberlain in several speeches had referred to the importance of making new approaches to Germany and Italy.

I decided to go down to the Foreign Office, where I found that Halifax, too, was troubled by these press accounts. After talking with him I crossed over to see the Prime Minister. The interview went badly from the start. Chamberlain did, it is true, undertake to see the press himself and damp down its enthusiasm, but he insisted on the value of Halifax's visit. He went on to express his annoyance at the Brussels Conference, which he seemed to think had been a complete waste of time, though I had many times explained that this exercise was being carried through by me for the benefit of Anglo-American relations. In turn, I complained of the slowness, lack of imagination and drive shown by my colleagues in the matter of rearmament. Finally, at the end of some exchanges which became rather sharp, the Prime Minister adjured me to go home and take an aspirin. This scarcely seemed an adequate remedy for the national deficiencies, so I returned to the Foreign Office and wrote to Chamberlain:

Since you are going to see the press this afternoon it may be some help to you if I give you the note which I had hoped to get into the press of today and which, I am sure myself, is the line we must take in connection with the Halifax visit: 'Not to exaggerate the significance of the visit. It is an occasion for an unofficial and informal contact and not for negotiations. That being so, it is even more ridiculous to suggest that a visit of this character is indicative of any change in the fundamentals of British foreign policy. Just as there can, of course, be no question of seeking to weaken the Berlin–Rome Axis, so there is no question of there being any change in the cordial relations between Great Britain and France.' I should also hope that it might be explained in the press tomorrow that when in Brussels I informed Delbos not only that Halifax was going to Berlin but also of the limited scope and purpose of his visit.

When I spoke to Edward [Lord Halifax] this morning, I found him equally anxious to reduce the significance of the visit in the press as much as possible. I am sure that this is indeed imperative if we are not to run risks of a serious setback owing to exaggerated expectations. While I have always thought that there were advantages in informal contact such as this, the risks inevitably become greater when the visit does not take place in Berlin and when there is no very definite invitation to Berchtesgaden. If on top of these risks the press magnifies the affair to the proportions of anything in the nature of a negotiation, we run grave danger of doing more harm than good.

I am sorry if you thought me 'feverish' on the subject of rearmament this morning, but I do feel that we are passing through a most critical period when our own rearmament may prove the decisive factor. Papers like that submitted by the Air Ministry recently are, therefore, of profound significance for they show that, despite comforting speeches, we are not in truth getting stronger *vis-à-vis* Germany at least. Therefore I feel personally that we should in present conditions buy material from everywhere we can get it, because it is the situation during the next eighteen months that may decide the future of Europe. Moreover, the knowledge of the fact that we are taking steps to make ourselves strong by purchase abroad as well as by manufacture would in itself, I am sure, have an excellent tonic effect and do much to meet such anxieties as are expressed by Miles Lampson in his recent telegram.

The Prime Minister replied in a soothing way, which bore no relation to the main issue which we had been discussing. He attributed my concern about rearmament to my illness and hoped that I would shortly be able to take a holiday.

Though I had already spoken to Halifax about his conversations in Berlin, I did not want him to be in any doubt about my policy towards Central Europe. I heard that Sir Nevile Henderson had asked Lord Halifax to read a memorandum he had prepared about our policy towards Germany, which was much too loose and yielding a document. Therefore I also sent to Halifax a carefully prepared paper by Mr. Strang, analysing and correcting Henderson's opinions. Strang rightly laid emphasis on the importance of being circumspect and avoiding any statement which the Nazis could use as evidence of acquiescence in their ambitions in Central Europe. Lord Halifax left for Berlin on November 17th. At the same time Jim Thomas, on his own initiative, spoke frankly to Sir Horace Wilson about relations between the Prime Minister and myself. Wilson avowed that no question of personal jealousy arose, but that Chamberlain did think his own policy of 'getting together' with the dictators was the right one. He was determined to go on with it and genuinely thought that he was 'saving me from myself'.

* * * * *

The Lord President, Lord Halifax, returned to London on the afternoon of November 22nd and immediately came to the Foreign Office. Together we went over to see Chamberlain. Halifax's main impressions had been that Hitler was very sincere and that he felt no necessity to ask favours of us, since time was on his side. It appeared that the conversations had not made an auspicious beginning. According to his own account, Halifax had at first not recognized the Führer, who had been in a sulky mood throughout the day. Nevertheless, the account of the meeting was revealing. The German Foreign Office obligingly provided the notes made by the official interpreter, Dr. Schmidt. These were more detailed than Lord Halifax's record and enabled me to savour the full force of the Führer's philosophy. One part of his discourse had run:

> There were two possibilities in the shaping of relations between the peoples. The interplay of free forces, which was often synonymous with great and grave encroachments upon the life of the peoples and which could bring in its train a serious convulsion which would shake the civilization we had built up with so much trouble. The second possibility lay in setting up, in the place of the play of free forces, the rules of a 'higher reason'; in this case, however, one must clearly realize that this higher reason must lead to approximately similar results to those which had followed from the working of free forces. He (the Chancellor) had often asked himself during recent years whether humanity today was intelligent enough to replace the play of free forces by the method of higher reason.

In other words, would we be good enough to give what otherwise he would be compelled to take.

Hitler then launched off into a subdued tirade about the difficulty of doing business with democratic countries. All his offers, disarmament and political, had been wrecked on this rock. To this Halifax had replied that if they were to wait for any advance until Great Britain ceased to maintain a democratic system, he had clearly wasted his time in coming to Berchtesgaden, for he hoped that Great Britain would never be likely to change her method of government. He added that the German offers on disarmament had in fact failed because other nations did not feel satisfied about the security they afforded. Later, Hitler remarked irritably that he could not understand why we should attach so much importance to Germany's being in the League, when we did not mind the United States being outside it. Certainly Germany would not join the League, constituted and functioning as it then was. The Führer made no pretence of being interested in disarmament. Experience suggested, he said, that the respect paid to nations varied with the weight of their armaments.

All this was menacing, but it was the later part of the conversation which interested me most of all. Hitler had referred to the colonial question as the only real matter at issue between the two countries, but not one in which Germany could state her wishes. There were two possibilities. First, the free play of forces. What Germany would take in the way of colonies in that event, he would not say. The second possibility was a reasonable solution which must have a legal basis. Germany had a claim to her former property. Lord Halifax, as had been agreed in London, insisted that no British Government could touch the colonial question, except in the context of a general settlement, which would give our people a prospect of real understanding and of relief from the prevailing tension.

I noticed, too, that Lord Halifax, in the words of Schmidt's record, had spoken of

> possible alterations in the European order which might be destined to come about with the passage of time. Amongst these questions were Danzig, Austria and Czechoslovakia. England was interested to see that any alterations should come through the course of peaceful evolution and that methods should be avoided which might cause far-reaching disturbances, which neither the Chancellor nor other countries desired.

Hitler had replied that a settlement with Austria and Czechoslovakia could be reached, given a reasonable attitude. He hoped that the recent agreement with Austria* would lead to the removal of all difficulties. Czechoslovakia was herself in a position to clear away existing difficulties. She only needed to treat the Germans living within her borders well, and they would be entirely happy. Germany set great store by good relations with all her neighbours, he announced. We now know that a fortnight before this interview, Hitler had secretly announced to his Foreign Minister, War Minister and Chiefs of Staff his plans for subjugating Austria and Czechoslovakia, as a first step towards conquering more territory for Germany in Europe.

I wished that Halifax had warned Hitler more strongly against intervention in Central Europe. 'Alterations through the course of peaceful evolution' meant one thing to Halifax and probably something quite different to the Führer. Hitler was capable of taking this as giving him freedom to increase subversive Nazi activity in Austria, or to stir up the grievances of the Sudeten Germans.

Towards the end of this rather aimless and therefore hazardous discussion, Halifax expressed the hope that it might be followed up by direct Anglo-German negotiations. Hitler did not respond, replying that talks or conferences always needed careful preparation. He did not believe in a conference every three months that achieved nothing and therefore thought it wiser that we should apply ourselves to preparation through the diplomatic channel. He hoped, too, that we might get away from the atmosphere of 'imminent catastrophe', which was the work of an excitable and malevolent press. Of course, remarked the Führer in tones of reproof, if you believed the newspapers, you would

* Signed on July 11th, 1936, by which Austria remained independent while recognizing herself as a Germanic state.

expect to wake up one day to see German armed forces in Vienna or Prague. This last sally prudently did not figure in the German record.

The conversation was carefully studied in the Foreign Office, where it was noticed that Hitler had now adopted the theme that a general settlement was not practical politics, that immediate negotiations between Great Britain and Germany were unnecessary, but that if Britain really wanted to improve relations, she could do so by satisfying German colonial claims. It was noticeable that Hitler had offered no guarantees about his policy in Central Europe. Once more we were going to be asked to make all the concessions without any return. I minuted: 'If we do not get, we shall not give.'

Lord Halifax told me that at luncheon Hitler had said he was unable to understand why we put up with unrest in India. 'All you have to do,' he remarked briskly, 'is to shoot Gandhi. If necessary, shoot more leaders of Congress. You will be surprised how quickly the trouble will die down.' This conception of trusteeship did not inspire me to make any haste in granting Hitler colonial territories. It seemed, however, a sensible precaution for the Foreign Office and Colonial Office to examine the problem together.

As I had feared, Lord Halifax's visit was without positive results. My loyal collaborators at the Foreign Office were proved right in the uneasiness which they had expressed about it from the start. One of its effects was to weaken my own position and I was mistaken in ever tolerating it.

★ ★ ★ ★ ★

The meeting with French Ministers took place on November 29th and 30th, when Lord Halifax reported to them on his discussions with Hitler. M. Delbos was shortly to make a journey to Czechoslovakia and the discussions turned on the tactics to be pursued. Chamberlain soon spoke of British public opinion. There was a strong feeling, he said, that we ought not to be entangled in a war on account of Czechoslovakia, which was a long way off and with which we had not a great deal in common. He did not think that it would be possible to mobilize opinion in England in support of forcible intervention against Germany on behalf of Czechoslovakia, but there would be support for any attempt to bring about a reasonable and peaceful settlement between Germany and Czechoslovakia. People here, Mr. Chamberlain stated, were of the opinion that the Sudeten Germans were not getting fair treatment from the Czechoslovaks. He likened the position, rather unfortunately, to that in the Transvaal before the Boer War, when the British Government made strong representations to President Kruger on behalf of the Uitlanders. Conditions in the Transvaal were, of course, worse than in Czechoslovakia, he admitted, but there was a certain similarity.

M. Delbos replied firmly that allied efforts should be directed to both sides. He feared that what Germany really wanted was to absorb the Sudeten territory, and not that the Sudeten Germans should receive better treatment. The absorption of Austria and part of Czechoslovakia by Germany would not be without consequence for the structure of Europe. It would mean German hegemony, and a new appetite on the part of Germany for further conquest. It was also necessary, Delbos continued, that treaties should be respected, for this was the basis of the law of nations. France had a treaty with Czechoslovakia and could not set a bad example by abandoning that treaty.

I said that there was no question of our asking France to reconsider her obligations, or of our asking her not to carry them out, nor, indeed, of our failing to fulfil our own. But there was a feeling here that the Sudeten Germans had certain grievances, which ought to be dealt with. The French pointed out the difficulty of pressing the Czechs beyond a certain point. To ask them to accept autonomy would be going too far, it would also encourage the Germans to make still further claims. This was at once agreed to by the British Ministers, Chamberlain saying he did not believe that the Germans would go so far in their demands as to ask for autonomy for the Sudeten Germans.

In the second discussion, Chautemps rightly drew attention to the treaty which bound Germany to use arbitration in any differences which she had with Czechoslovakia. But in general there was no serious divergence between our two countries, and all wished Delbos well in the visit he was about to pay.

The remainder of the Anglo-French discussion was in the main notable for an admirable definition by Delbos of his country's attitude to the Spanish civil war. The French Government, he said, would prefer that the Spanish Government should win. But they did not think that their interests would necessarily be menaced if Franco won. It was only through Germany and Italy that menace would arise. M. Chautemps, in his turn, showed some anxiety lest, in the development of conversations with Mussolini, France should be excluded from the discussion of matters which concerned his country in common with Great Britain. Spain and Abyssinia were examples. It was desirable, he said, to avoid a bilateral Anglo-Italian agreement on matters of concern to France. This seemed to me a fair request and to our own interest also.

The next day I had a conversation with Ribbentrop, who came to see me about the outcome of the Anglo-French discussions. He accepted the significance of the fact that the question of colonies was, for the first time, mentioned in an international communiqué. I asked the Ambassador to understand that it was not possible for the British Government to deal with this question in isolation. On that subject the communiqué was clear. Ribbentrop asked me what were the other subjects which we contemplated as part of a general settlement. I would know that the German Government considered that they had a right to colonies, and he would regret it if this question became embedded in a number of other political questions which had been impossible to settle in the past.

I replied that the Ambassador must also understand that the British Government had been asked to consider the cession of colonial territory. This was a formidable request to put to the British public. I was clear in my own mind, and his Excellency would no doubt share my view from his knowledge of British opinion, that it would be quite impossible for His Majesty's Government to contemplate the cession of colonial territory unless they received some counterpart. What was that counterpart? I was not in a position to tell him in detail at present, but it could be summed up in the sentence: 'An increased sense of international security and enhanced prospects for the preservation of peace.' An indispensable element in such a counterpart would be an arms agreement. The Ambassador said that an arms agreement would be difficult, to which I replied that there were also great difficulties in contemplating the cession of colonial territory. In the meanwhile it would be helpful if the German Government would not engage upon colonial propaganda of the kind which consisted in saying with increasing force: 'Germany must have colonies. Germany has a right to colonies. Germany shall have colonies.' The Ambassador knew British character well enough to be aware that language of that kind was not calculated to bring about a settlement. Ribbentrop said that he understood the force of that reasoning, but he reiterated his apprehension at the prolonged negotation which must result.

I had by now become extremely sceptical about the chances of a comprehensive settlement of European problems, or the possibility of negotiating a Five-Power Pact. As a consequence, I was determined that, in considering the German demands for colonies, we should not budge from the decision that nothing could be yielded, except in return for a general settlement. I thought it unlikely that Hitler would agree to such a settlement, but it seemed to me a good position to hold that we were not prepared to contemplate any decisions as fundamental as the cession of colonies, unless Germany were to make the kind of peaceful contribution which would transform the international outlook. Disarmament must form a part of this.

I became troubled, therefore, when in some of the discussions amongst Ministers, the Prime Minister was apt to talk at considerable length without mentioning the relation of the question of colonies to a general settlement with Germany. When I demurred at this, Chamberlain accepted my correction, but I was again alarmed when he spoke of treating the subject in vague and general terms. I said that, in the circumstances, we should be very careful indeed in what we said to Germany, and give her no possible excuse for insinuating that we were trying to effect a colonial settlement at the expense of other powers interested in tropical Africa.

Samuel Hoare agreed with my concern and spoke up against the Prime Minister's ideas. It was natural enough that there was a reluctance to decide which colony, if any, was to be the subject of negotiation with Germany. The Prime Minister did not want to be so definite, but I thought it dangerous to speak about colonies to the Germans and give them an opening to say that they were ready to discuss the Prime Minister's ideas, but wished to know in advance precisely which territories they were going to receive.

When consulted, Henderson's forecast of the Nazi reaction was the same as mine. This did not, however, check the Prime Minister and, while I was in Geneva towards the end of January, he summoned Henderson back to London for consultation on this subject. He was impatient to make progress and was not to be put off later by Germany's behaviour towards Austria, despite my opposition to any negotiation with Hitler about colonies, after his treatment of Dr. von Schuschnigg.

* * * * *

During these two years as Foreign Secretary, I often considered our relations with Russia and the possibility that her power might be put into the scales in resistance to the demands of Germany, Italy and Japan. This was also a topic of discussion from time to time with Delbos, a man prudently sensible in his judgements. Throughout the period, it seemed to me that the Soviets were pursuing a dual policy. Mr. Litvinov's speeches and conversations abounded in spacious assurances of Russia's good intentions and of a refusal to countenance aggression. Yet reports constantly arrived on my desk about the Comintern's world-wide activities against the British Empire. It was not possible to work in confidence with a power which pursued such methods.

Admittedly the Soviets had problems at home, intensified to outside observers by Stalin's purges. These events may have influenced Soviet policy, which showed no sign of taking any effective action against Germany while continuing to supply raw materials essential to Hitler's rearmament programme. Relations with Japan were more tense, with occasional frontier scrapping. Yet against this background I felt sure that Stalin would act with characteristic caution and not allow his country to be involved in even a risk of war, unless its vital interests were directly threatened. It was improbable that the Soviet Government would intervene against Hitler, unless the states on their western frontier, particularly Poland and Roumania, were attacked by Germany. Even so, Russia would only act if the Western Powers were involved, or if no twist or turn in manœuvre remained. Then a Russian intervention might have decisive value if it were practicable, for Poland would resist to the utmost any attempt to use her territory as a battlefield between Hitler and Stalin. Britain and France had, I considered, no choice but to build up their armed strength together, doing what they could to maintain equable relations with Russia, but not counting on any help from her. If it came, it would be an unexpected benefice.

There was another hazard, which was the most perilous of all. Against this I warned my principal colleagues and the Chiefs of Staff, in December 1937:

> The outstanding feature of the present political situation is its extreme fluidity. It is impossible to foretell what the international alignment will be in a year's time. Who, for example, can say what Stalin's re-orientation of Russian policy will be? If it should result in a Moscow–Berlin Axis, will not this be a more formidable combination than the existing Rome–Berlin Axis. In these circumstances it is clear that we should make every possible effort to come to terms with each or all of our potential enemies, but not by conduct which would lose us our friends, both actual and potential.

★ ★ ★ ★ ★

During the last months of 1937 I again considered the position of Sir Robert Vansittart, who had now been Permanent Under-Secretary for nearly seven years. About a year earlier Baldwin and I had agreed that Vansittart should be offered the Embassy in Paris, as high a position as any in the foreign service. His spell at the Foreign Office had already been longer than average and it had been the practice for those who held that office to conclude their careers in an important embassy. Both Lord Tyrrell and Sir Ronald Lindsay had done this in my own time. I felt that a change could be advantageous from several points of view. Vansittart would be welcome in Paris and could exercise an exceptional influence there. It was also true that a new figure as Permanent Under-Secretary would now make more impact on Whitehall.

Baldwin, whose Private Secretary Vansittart had been, offered to talk to him on the topic, to reinforce my own opinion. Vansittart, however, refused the appointment, partly on account of his health and partly for the thoughtful reason that he believed he would be able to help me more at home in the coming months, if he remained at the Foreign Office.

In the autumn of 1937, however, I felt that the time had come for a change which would strengthen my staff at the Foreign Office. Mr. Chamberlain, now Prime Minister, was insistent, but this of itself would not have been enough if I had not felt that there were other advantages. I decided to appoint Sir Alexander Cadogan, whom I had made a deputy Under-Secretary the previous year, to be Permanent Under-Secretary and, in agreement with Chamberlain, to create the new office of Chief Diplomatic Adviser to His Majesty's Government, a post parallel to that of Sir Horace Wilson, who was Chief Industrial Adviser. The appointment of Sir Robert Vansittart to this post was well received when it was announced in the New Year, 1938. I have no doubt that my team was fortified by the new arrangement, which worked reasonably well, in my experience, at a time of stress, largely because the two men had a will to make it do so.

An attempt was made by Sir Warren Fisher to persuade me to accept the transfer of the head of another department to be Under-Secretary at the Foreign Office. This was Sir Findlater Stewart, then at the India Office. Despite my respect for him, however, I was firmly convinced that it made no sense to bring someone who was inexperienced in international diplomacy into the most responsible advisory position in the Foreign Office.

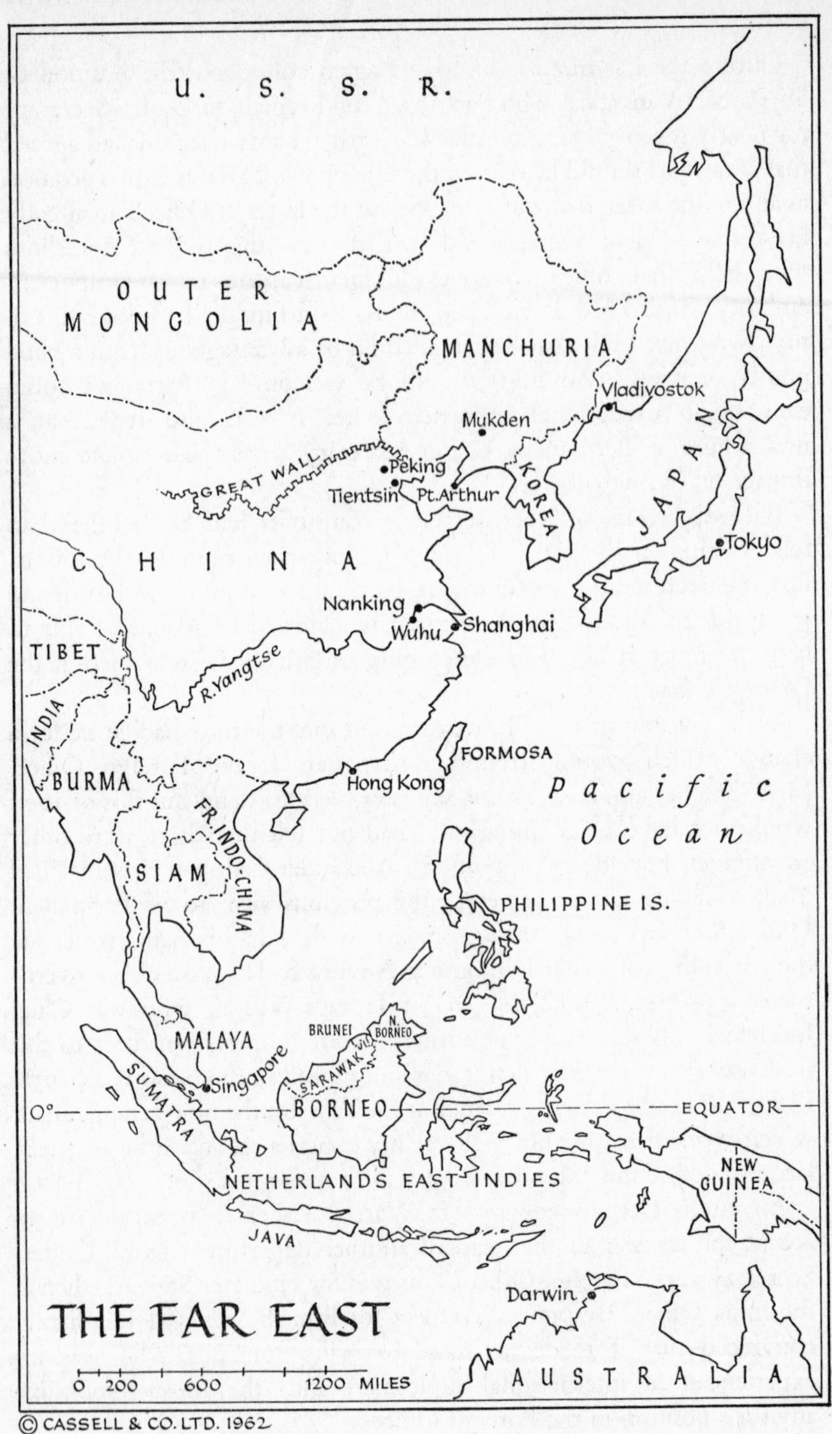
U. S. S. R.
OUTER MONGOLIA
MANCHURIA
Vladivostok
Mukden
GREAT WALL
Peking
Tientsin
Pt. Arthur
KOREA
JAPAN
Tokyo
C H I N A
Nanking
Wuhu
Shanghai
TIBET
R. Yangtse
INDIA
FORMOSA
BURMA
Hong Kong
Pacific Ocean
FR. INDO-CHINA
SIAM
PHILIPPINE IS.
BRUNEI
N. BORNEO
MALAYA
SARAWAK
Singapore
SUMATRA
BORNEO
0°
EQUATOR
NEW GUINEA
NETHERLANDS EAST INDIES
JAVA
Darwin
THE FAR EAST
0 200 600 1200 MILES
AUSTRALIA

XI

THE FAR EASTERN WAR

November 1936 – January 1938

Japan on the war-path – President Roosevelt wants a world conference – Sir Ronald Lindsay's wise message – Our Ambassador in Nanking fired on by Japanese aircraft – The Brussels Conference on the Far East – British and United States ships attacked in the Yangtse river – I again plead for joint action – President Roosevelt sends Captain Ingersoll to Britain

The conquest of Manchuria had not sated Japan's appetite for plunder. Between 1932 and 1937, militarism was increasing in Tokyo and further slices of China's territory disappeared into the Japanese maw. This process could only have been halted if the United States and Great Britain had been prepared to act together, for the British Government, with their European preoccupations, could not afford to send the greater part of the fleet to Far Eastern waters. We could have made a naval contribution, by no means a negligible one, in the Far East, but it would not have been of the necessary size to be effective, unless the United States took at least an equal share.

American opinion, though resistant to the idea of alliance with Great Britain or any other country, was favourably disposed and concerned by the world-wide growth of lawlessness and ill-faith. I did not regard Europe and the Far East as separate problems; but if, as I had to accept, there was to be no effective American participation in Europe for the present, it seemed reasonable to hope that we could mount and prosecute a joint policy in the Far East. Progress was slow. There was unfortunately a heritage of suspicion, many Americans believing that Japanese expansion would have been curbed in 1932, had Sir John Simon accepted an alleged proposal for economic sanctions made by Mr. Stimson, the American Secretary of State. Stimson had himself propagated this theory, and I took an opportunity during

1936 to read carefully through the relevant papers in the Foreign Office. These have since been published. They seemed to me to show that the American proposal had been nebulous, and I was satisfied that Simon had not been seriously at fault. Nevertheless, the episode left behind a mood of recrimination, which I had now to try to dissipate.

Certainly Japan was profiting by Anglo-American failure to agree. The year 1933 had seen the Chinese Government, weakened by a long internal feud between communists and nationalists, and without any effective foreign help, able only to temporize. They set up a buffer state under the Peking Political Council, which made a truce with the invaders and agreed to withdraw to the north of the Great Wall. This truce caused a further weakening. A demilitarized area was left to the south, where Japanese military agents showed much ingenuity in discovering powerful movements for local autonomy, a method later perfected by Hitler in Central Europe. As the Chinese sadly commented, Japan was trying to eat up North China 'leaf by leaf like an artichoke'.

Meanwhile, we did what we could to strengthen the Chinese economy. Credits for the railways and for exports were granted in 1934, to the accompaniment of shrill protests from Tokyo, and the next year, in response to the requests of Sir Alexander Cadogan, then our Ambassador in Peking, Sir Frederick Leith-Ross travelled out to reform the Chinese currency. He did an excellent piece of work, which did not prevent Japan making the most of Britain's preoccupation and America's neutrality. In 1934 she denounced the Washington Treaty of 1922, which had laid down naval ratios, and later withdrew from the London Naval Conference. Though Japan could scarcely expect to win a naval race with the United States, she no doubt hoped to use her temporary advantage to detach further provinces from China.

In our political discussions at home, predictions were frequently made that Japan's economic position was perilous and that this would at the least check her expansive mood. I remember the Chancellor of the Exchequer, Mr. Chamberlain, reporting in 1936 that this was the Treasury's opinion. I was sceptical that lack of funds would bring Japan back to the paths of peace, any more than I believed similar forecasts about Germany and Italy.

* * * * *

Franklin Roosevelt was re-elected President of the United States in the autumn of 1936. Rumours soon began to circulate that he was disturbed by the dangers of the world situation and considering plans to meet them. On November 7th, 1936, I received from Sir Eric Phipps an account of a conversation with the United States Ambassador in Berlin, Mr. William Dodd. The latter said that he had received from Mr. Cordell Hull a cable attributing the President's overwhelming victory partly to his foreign policy, which consisted in giving no kind of encouragement to Fascist states and concluding no fresh commercial treaties with them, so long as they persisted in their existing gangster methods. Nor were credits or commercial advantages to be given to Italy or Germany, unless they mended their blustering and truculent ways. Mr. Dodd reported that the President bore a special grudge against Herr Hitler, who had long before given him a personal written promise that there would be no more Nazi propaganda in the United States. This promise was violated from the start, so that when Hitler sent a telegram congratulating Roosevelt on his recent birthday, the President had not even acknowledged it.

The Ambassador further told Phipps that Roosevelt was all in favour of 'keeping Germany lean'. It appeared that the President had no intention of recognizing Italy's Abyssinian empire or General Franco's dictatorship. Finally, Mr. Dodd added that the President had in mind the summoning of a world peace conference in the following spring. If the 'gangster powers' declined to attend, or to give satisfactory undertakings at the conference, the peace-loving states should come to a close agreement amongst themselves.

Naturally, some of my advisers were sceptical about the prospects of this project for peace. I was, however, in favour of supporting it and wrote in a Foreign Office minute:

> Maybe it will not succeed, but if the attempt were made, and failure the fault of the dictator powers, the process of education on world opinion (and particularly U.S. opinion) should be salutary.
>
> In any event it would be clearly a great error for us to discourage the President in his idea, if it is his idea.

At my request, Sir Robert Vansittart told our Ambassador in Washington of the importance we attached to thorough preparation for a world conference. Sir Ronald Lindsay was asked to try to arrange that invitations should not be sent out until there had been time for confidential discussion between our two countries. If the United States Government had decided to summon a conference, Sir Robert added, they should be left in no doubt that we would give every assistance in our power to make it a success.

Lindsay replied early in December that he had so far failed to find out anything definite at the State Department about the President's plans. He assured us that we had the Administration's goodwill, adding:

> I feel that if the President is seriously contemplating a conference he may very likely have it in the back of his mind to pillory Hitler.

Our Ambassador drew attention to the difficulty of securing adequate consultation between the two Governments in advance of the proposed conference. On this document I minuted:

> I am sure that the all-important thing is not to discourage Roosevelt. If the conference can be prepared so much the better, but it is vital that we should say and do nothing to put the Americans off from taking any action they want to take, even in their own way.

To Sir Ronald Lindsay I wrote in this sense, adding as a final paragraph:

> I share your conviction that the attitude of the United States towards Europe may prove of vital importance to us and that we have a most valuable asset in the present frame of mind of the Administration.

On February 11th, 1937, the United States Secretary to the Treasury, Mr. Henry Morgenthau, summoned our Commercial Attaché, Mr. Bewley, and asked him to take a message to the Chancellor of the Exchequer. This was to the effect that Morgenthau felt very pessimistic about the international financial outlook. He thought expenditure on armaments was at the bottom of the trouble and wanted to know whether the Chancellor had any suggestion to make to him about this. We were told that Roosevelt had specially authorized Morgenthau to send the message, which was accompanied by some dramatic frills, a destroyer even being offered to take Bewley home.

At a second meeting, the Secretary to the Treasury said he had been discussing the European situation with the President. He thought that it might be saved by a bold initiative from the United States and Great Britain, and wondered whether we could suggest something. No one else, except the President, knew of this move and the Commercial Attaché had little doubt that the message came directly from Roosevelt.

Neville Chamberlain sent these documents to the Foreign Office early in March and I prepared a reply, which insisted that our rearmament must go ahead, because Britain's material strength had suffered a relative decline since the re-emergence of Germany as one of the dominant military powers in Europe. We wished to keep in close touch with the American Government, I wrote, both to ensure that no opportunity was missed to reopen the question of arms limitation and also to avoid the risks of premature action. Meanwhile, we would like to negotiate a commercial agreement with the United States. I suggested that one of the greatest contributions the United States could make to world peace would be to amend the existing neutrality legislation:

> Under this legislation an embargo would be imposed on the export from the United States of arms and munitions, irrespective of whether a country is an aggressor or the victim of an aggression. It is obvious that the existing neutrality law and, *a fortiori*, any extension of it so as to include raw materials, suits the requirements of a country contemplating an aggression, which can and would lay up large stores of war materials with the knowledge that its intended victim will, when the time comes, be precluded from obtaining supplies in one of the greatest world markets. The legislation in its present form constitutes an indirect but potent encouragement to aggression.

I discussed this draft with Chamberlain, who immediately accepted most of it, adding, to my satisfaction, a passage which placed the onus for European unrest squarely upon Germany.

I thought that this exchange should be followed up. On March 10th I telegraphed to Sir Ronald Lindsay, telling him of the crucial importance I attached to retaining the goodwill of the United States Government and public opinion, in the event of a major crisis in Europe. While I knew the Ambassador's general views, I told Lindsay that it would help me to have a full report suggesting the lines of policy the British Government should follow to secure this object. I asked that his message should cover as wide a field as possible.

Sir Ronald Lindsay's reply arrived three weeks later in the shape of a despatch to which I often turned to fortify myself in the coming months. The Ambassador thought that we should abstain for the moment from taking any initiative with the United States on a major political issue, but added:

> It would be most unwise of His Majesty's Government to refuse any offer of co-operation that may be tendered to them by the United States Government. Obviously, if you want to please a party, you should do your best to fall in with his wishes and always stretch a point in his favour. But there is a good psychological reason for the axiom which I am laying down.

America is still extraordinarily youthful and sensitive. And such is the prestige today of Great Britain that co-operation with His Majesty's Government would be regarded as a compliment by the public opinion of even so powerful a state as America. But there is an even more important converse to this principle, namely, that refusal of co-operation will be regarded as a snub.

I had cause to remember this message nine months later.

Meanwhile, Mr. Robert Bingham, the United States Ambassador in London, asked me to luncheon alone with him on March 20th. I had always found Mr. Bingham thoughtful and helpful and, as with many subsequent American Ambassadors, our relations were those of complete confidence. Here is my record of this important conversation:

Mr. Bingham gave me at some length an appreciation of the United States attitude to the present European situation. He emphasized that there was a close parallel between President Roosevelt's position today and that of President Wilson before the war. The latter had planned a considerable programme of domestic reform. These plans had been overset by the outbreak of the war. President Roosevelt was determined to do all in his power to avoid a similar experience. We could therefore count upon his whole-hearted collaboration for the preservation of peace.

The Ambassador said it was quite true that President Roosevelt had been contemplating some initiative to attempt to better the present international situation. He was, however, determined to take no initiative except in close consultation with us. What, therefore, the Ambassador wished me to know was that President Roosevelt was not only ready but eager to help, that he would be ready to take an initiative if and when we thought the moment right, and that he would take none unless we were in accord as to its appropriateness. This message, the Ambassador said, he had been specifically instructed by the President to deliver personally to me. The Ambassador continued that it was his own impression that the time for any initiative by President Roosevelt was not yet. He had given the United States Government a full record of our last conversation, and made it clear that this was my view also. He had further explained the apprehension I felt lest any premature move might create an impression that our armaments programme was bluff. At the same time, if he understood our position aright, we thought careful watch should be kept so that the appropriate moment was not missed. I replied that His Excellency had correctly defined our position.

This being so, the Ambassador continued, he had a further request to make. It was inevitable that our information about the international situation, and more particularly about Europe, should be more complete and accurate than that of the United States Government. If, therefore, at any time we thought that the moment had come to invite President Roosevelt to take an initiative, he begged that we should not hesitate to do so. At the same time, Mr. Bingham added in response to a question, the United States Government would not hesitate to approach us if for any reason they thought the moment opportune.

Throughout the conversation the Ambassador was extremely cordial and emphasized more than once his conviction that the close co-operation between our two countries would constitute the best means of averting war. I took the opportunity to speak once again of the neutrality legislation in the United States, when the Ambassador replied that he had already reported my remarks some time ago to President Roosevelt, both in writing and verbally, more particularly the argument that to refuse supplies in time of war to everyone was to the advantage of a potential aggressor. He was sure that President Roosevelt was himself fully alive to the force of these arguments and anxious to obtain some discretionary powers for the President. We would know, however, that the matter was a difficult one of internal politics, and President Roosevelt might not be able to obtain all the powers that he wished. He would, however, the Ambassador felt sure, be able to improve to some extent on the present position.

It was not until the following January that the President made his move and then without the preparation which Mr. Bingham and I had forecast, and which, but for the Ambassador's lamented death later in 1937, he would have been careful to arrange.

* * * * *

In this same month of March, the Far Eastern scene lightened for a brief spell. The Hayashi Government in Tokyo showed a more pacific temper, while Chinese resistance stiffened. Thus encouraged, our Ambassador, Sir Hughe Knatchbull-Hugessen, sent me a long despatch from Nanking advocating a three-power agreement between Russia, Japan and China as a means of resolving existing differences. I did not expect, however, that Japanese aggression could be so easily halted; nor was I sure how much peace would benefit if Russia and Japan were only to compose their present quarrels and feel free for more distant mischief. I minuted:

> A Sino-Japanese *détente* could presumably be accompanied by better relations between Japan and this country and this is what we should work for. I had rather detach Tokyo from Berlin as a result of improved Anglo-Japanese relations than seek to improve Russo-Japanese relations which might not in the end result in separating Tokyo from Berlin, but in freeing Tokyo

to work with Berlin against us in a new sphere. The triangle for us to work in is ourselves, Japan and China, with U.S.A. constantly in touch. Russia can be left for the moment where she is, a not unhealthy cause of anxiety in Tokyo.

* * * * *

When Sir Ronald Lindsay had been in London on leave in the autumn of 1936, we had discussed together the possibility that I might visit the United States. The Ambassador said that it was important for me to have a definite invitation from America, otherwise I might be thought to be entangling a reluctant United States in European squabbles. I remembered this advice when Mr. Norman Davis visited me early in May 1937, saying that Roosevelt would be glad if Chamberlain or I would go to the United States. Bingham and Lindsay both urged me to accept, but, as occasionally happened where Davis was concerned, his good intentions outran his discretion and misunderstandings arose. Davis had apparently taken the Prime Minister's general expressions of goodwill to imply a definite willingness to visit Roosevelt in the autumn.

Chamberlain and I discussed the position with the American Ambassador, who was much irritated by Davis' capacity for creating confusion. It transpired that the invitation had only been addressed to the Prime Minister. We agreed that neither of us should go unless there were a prospect of worthwhile results, and that I might then make the journey. The signing of a commercial agreement could have provided such an opportunity, but progress towards this was slow. Although I think that no other decision was possible at the time, I regret that I was not able to visit the United States in 1937, for if the meeting had met with some success, its steadying effect upon the dictators could have been important. In the event, I was not to meet Roosevelt and his principal lieutenants until December 1938, when I was out of office.

* * * * *

At the end of May, the Hayashi Government fell in Japan, to be replaced by a Cabinet under Prince Konoye. In the weeks that followed, chauvinism once more possessed the Japanese, while their press worked up a campaign against the supposedly aggressive intentions of China.

By the Boxer Protocol of 1901, Japan was entitled to maintain in the Tientsin area sufficient military forces to provide a legation guard at

Peking and protect communications between there and the sea. The most had been made of this concession. Tanks, artillery and infantry were openly paraded, and Japanese aircraft flew over the capital. The military carried out extensive manœuvres, which gave rise to an incident which was to plunge all Asia into a decade of war and suffering. Its origin was, as usual, disputed. The Japanese claimed that their troops were fired on without provocation, while the Chinese asserted, with more probability, that they were forced to resist because Japanese forces launched a full-scale assault with artillery adjacent to the Marco Polo bridge. It was certain that the incident offered, as it was intended to do, a good opportunity for the Japanese military to strengthen their position in north China.

We made representations in Tokyo and I saw the Japanese Ambassador, Mr. Yoshida, in London, but counsels of moderation were hardly likely to be heeded, especially when not concerted between Britain and Washington. Therefore, on July 20th, I telegraphed to Lindsay, offering a joint approach with the United States to the Japanese and Chinese Governments, asking them to agree to issue instructions that all further movement of troops be suspended, and to accept that the United States Government and ourselves should put forward proposals in an attempt to end the existing deadlock.

The same afternoon I saw the United States Ambassador. I told Mr. Bingham that the situation seemed to me to be growing ever graver. As he knew, we were willing to co-operate with the United States Government in any step they might wish to take, but we were not anxious to make any further move alone. We had been asked by the Chinese Government to take action together with other governments. As a result of our representations, the British Embassy in Tokyo telegraphed that we had created the impression of being more interested than the United States Government. I felt sure Mr. Bingham would realize this was undesirable. I therefore attached importance to joint action in any further step we might decide to take.

The Ambassador replied that he fully understood our point of view and added that the collaboration of the United States Government would be easier to obtain in the Far East than in Europe. I was not sure that in practice we should find this distinction so encouraging. Meanwhile an interim reply came from Lindsay which gave very little hope that the Secretary of State, Mr. Cordell Hull, would agree to joint action. The head of the Far Eastern Department in Washington had told Lindsay that military elements had taken charge of the

Government in Japan and that nothing would stop them. He seemed convinced that joint action would merely exacerbate an already desperate situation.

Before this reply was received, Bingham asked to see me, and spoke on his own account:

> Could we not consider the possibility of approaching the United States Government to ask them to join with us in an embargo on Japanese trade? I asked the Ambassador whether he meant an embargo on Japanese imports into our respective countries, or an embargo on our exports to Japan. The Ambassador replied that he meant both. There should be a cessation of all trade. In his view the present situation was extremely serious, and if some attempt were not made to call a halt to Japanese aggression there would soon be an end not only to the trade of both our countries with China, but also a total loss of the large investments both our countries possessed in the Far East.
>
> I asked the Ambassador whether the United States neutrality legislation would allow the United States Government to put into force the policy to which the Ambassador referred. Mr. Bingham replied that he thought so, but on my expressing my doubt undertook to look into the matter further.
>
> I then told His Excellency that while I was grateful to him for putting to me his personal view which I fully understood was exclusively his own, I wished to inform him of the telegram which I had sent Sir Ronald Lindsay the evening before. It seemed to me that before considering the Ambassador's proposal it was desirable to see what the response of the United States Government would be to the line of action we had already proposed. The Ambassador agreed and added that if the United States Government were not prepared to co-operate to the extent we had already suggested, it was hardly possible to expect them to agree to the more drastic action which the Ambassador himself had in mind. Meanwhile Mr. Bingham begged that I would keep his suggestion to myself. He agreed, however, that I should tell the Prime Minister.

Immediately after this interview, I had to go to a meeting at 10 Downing Street. I wrote the substance of Bingham's proposal on a sheet of notepaper and passed it to Chamberlain. He read it through and replied that he rather hoped Bingham's proposal would not go any further. It smacked very much of sanctions; it would certainly antagonize Japan and might so damage our relations with her that it would cost us millions in defensive measures in the Far East. Our proposal was not open to these objections. This was true enough, but Bingham's suggestion contained possibilities for Anglo-American joint action which at that time could not have been withstood.

Unfortunately, it was soon demonstrated from Washington that no joint action was feasible for the moment. This bad news was conveyed in a wandering memorandum from the State Department, which began:

> Government of United States share grave preoccupation of British Government as a result of developments in the Far East. It fully concurs in feelings expressed by British Government that every practicable effort should be made to avert hostilities which undoubtedly might have far-reaching consequences. It desires to co-operate with British Government in urging upon both parties that hostilities are not warranted and should be avoided. It further believes that co-operation between the two Governments in urging a peaceful solution of the controversy which has arisen is eminently desirable.

The document went on to suggest that,

> in continuation of a common effort to avert hostilities, both Governments should again, each in its own way, urge upon the Japanese and Chinese Governments the importance of maintaining peace.

At this time, Mr. Cordell Hull informed us that he had seen the Japanese and Chinese Ambassadors at Washington, to tell them that his Government hoped that both their countries would exercise effective self-restraint. Hull had volunteered the United States' good offices and instructed the American Ambassadors to Japan and China to speak in the same sense. The Secretary of State asked whether similar action by us might not be helpful. I did as Mr. Hull suggested, for the moment no other move was open to me, but events made it plainer every day that polite diplomatic appeals were being smoothly disregarded. Japanese reinforcements began to move into North China, while Chiang Kai-Shek, who had now made peace with the communists in order to fight the common enemy, prepared to resist.

The war began to be waged without regard for the rules generally accepted in less barbaric times. Towards the end of August, Sir Hughe Knatchbull-Hugessen was travelling towards Shanghai. He and his party were in two civilian cars flying the Union Jack, when both were attacked by Japanese aircraft and the Ambassador was seriously wounded. The Japanese Ambassador in London at once expressed his Government's and his own regret and he was much distressed. I told him that his words could not be accepted as an official apology, since they did not admit any responsibility. The Chinese Ambassador also called the same afternoon, August 27th. He said that what had happened was characteristic of the anarchy now prevailing in the Far East. These young Japanese airmen would stop at nothing in their hostility to the Western powers and in pursuit of their slogan, 'The East for the Asiatics.'

On the following day, I sent to our Embassy in Tokyo a note rejecting the plea that the attack might have been an accident. I requested a formal apology, the punishment of those responsible for the attack and action by the Japanese authorities to prevent the recurrence of such incidents.

In a further exchange of messages, our Chargé d'Affaires in Tokyo explained that the Japanese navy were principally responsible for refusing our requests. I replied that, however that might be, we could not weaken in our demands. At length, on September 21st, after further pressure from London, the Japanese Government conveyed a formal and public expression of their deep regret and a less satisfactory assurance about the punishment of those responsible. The incident was closed, but it had illustrated the fitful control of the Japanese Government over their military forces, whose methods were to become a by-word for brutality in the second world war.

* * * * *

By the end of September I decided to make another attempt at joint Anglo-American intervention in the Far East. Accordingly, I drafted a telegram to Washington saying that there was a strong feeling, not only in Great Britain, that effective international action should be taken. At present this pressure seemed to be for a lead by the United Kingdom and United States in some form of economic boycott. I recognized that we could not ask the Americans about their attitude without informing them of our own. Therefore my telegram stated that we should be ready to consider any action likely to shorten the war, if we were convinced of its effectiveness.

Since I had to leave the Foreign Office that evening, I asked Vansittart to take this message to Chamberlain for his approval. The Prime Minister redrafted the last sentence to the effect that we were not convinced that economic action would be effective, but we should be quite prepared to examine it further if the United States Government considered it worth pursuing. I was not consulted before the despatch of this message, the effect of which could only be discouraging. It was therefore no surprise when on October 5th the State Department sent a reply replete with emollient phrases.

In advocating that we should consider any action to stop the war, I was aware that economic sanctions entailed the risk of conflict, as I pointed out in a further telegram to Washington a few days later. But to discourage economic action, as Chamberlain's amendment appeared to do, only encouraged a further American psychological withdrawal.

* * * * *

Although I told the Japanese Ambassador on October 8th that his country ought to be represented at the Nine-Power Conference in Brussels, I knew that the prospect of its doing so was remote. In a broadcast address on October 12th, the President of the United States indicated that the purpose of any conference on the Far East must be mediation, of which there seemed to me little possibility. To our direct inquiries, the State Department said that the question of sanctions did not arise.

We could find out nothing more than this, since Norman Davis, leader of the American delegation, whom I had invited to London, telegraphed to explain that a visit by him would be misconstrued in political circles in the United States. He was, however, willing to meet me in Paris or Brussels before the start of the Conference. Meanwhile, the Americans, who had originally suggested Brussels as the site of the Conference, were becoming worried at the delay in fixing a time and meeting place. At last, the Belgian Government gave its consent and formal invitations were sent out for signatories of the China Treaty to meet in Brussels on November 3rd.

Japan declined the invitation and when the Belgian Government invited the Soviet Union and Germany, neither power being a signatory of the Treaty, but both possessing Far Eastern interests, Germany also declined, on the grounds that she had not been a party to the original Treaty. A vague hint of German mediation was thrown out, but when I spoke to Ribbentrop on October 27th, he paid no attention to my warning that a continuation of the war must have serious consequences for all those countries which had a large trade in the Far East, amongst them Germany. I soon found that the Ambassador saw Far Eastern affairs through the same anti-communist spectacles which he then focused on other international problems. He was convinced that Japan must be victorious. He added that he had nothing against the Chinese people, but since Japan was the enemy of Russia and Russia was the fount of all evil, it was desirable that Japan should be strengthened against Russia.

The prospect of an effective Anglo-American policy in the Far East appeared to have dimmed appreciably since Roosevelt's quarantine speech. The President had spoken on international co-operation at Chicago on October 5th: 'World lawlessness is spreading. When an epidemic of physical disease starts to spread, the community . . . joins in a quarantine of the patients in order to protect the health of the community.' This passage in the speech aroused a storm of criticism across the country, especially among isolationists, because in their minds the exercise of quarantine implied some action by the United States. The strength of the protest hobbled American activity at the Conference. On the eve of its opening, I dealt in the House of Commons with a criticism by Mr. Philip Noel-Baker that the Conference was being held at Brussels and not at Geneva:

> At Geneva the United States representative was only an observer, taking no part in the proceedings and having no responsibility for the decision. We all know that any action, whatever the character of that action, that can be taken in this Far Eastern dispute does essentially depend upon the co-operation of the United States, and I say without hesitation, unlike the hon. Gentleman, that in order to get the full co-operation on an equal basis of the United States Government in an international conference, I would travel, not only from Geneva to Brussels, but from Melbourne to Alaska, more particularly in the present state of the international situation.

At the end of my speech I referred to a helpful comment by Mr. Herbert Morrison:

> He used certain words which were to this effect: 'Would we in this dangerous and difficult Far Eastern situation go as far as the United States, in full accord with them, not rushing in front but not being left behind.' I wholly accept that definition as our guide.

The Conference was an exercise from which I expected no good, except to show the Americans that what they would do, we would do, and to build confidence between us by a repetition of this maxim.

* * * * *

On arrival in Brussels the following morning, November 2nd, I went with Malcolm MacDonald and Alexander Cadogan for a preliminary conversation with Norman Davis and his advisers. Davis began by saying that he supposed we had had enough of sanctions. This was a trifle disingenuous, since we had so far shown ourselves more ready for action than the United States Government. I replied that while the present business of the Conference was mediation, he must not assume that we were unwilling to take part in any international action. I told him and repeated in private conversation afterwards, that His Majesty's Government were ready for the fullest co-operation with the United States Government. It was, however, useless to ignore the European situation and we could take no action in the Far East while the present conditions persisted in Europe, except in full co-operation with the United States.

From further discussion it emerged that the United States delegation hoped that a small committee would probe the possibility of mediation. If this exercise failed, the fact and its causes would have to be made known to the world. This procedure was, the Americans indicated, intended to ensure that if the Conference broke down, world opinion and particularly United States opinion, would be educated in the process.

After this meeting, Norman Davis and I talked alone. I telegraphed to London:

> Mr. Davis made it plain that the President is deeply concerned at world outlook and sincerely anxious to co-operate in an attempt to stop the rot. Mr. Davis explained that the President had put it to him that the Conference would either succeed or, having failed, would confront the world with a futile situation in which further action by the United States could not be excluded. All liberty depends in the President's view upon the course of the Conference and state of American public opinion at the end of it. Mr. Davis also intimated that the President was deeply perturbed at the prospects in the Far East. He thought that Great Britain might be compelled to withdraw from her position there and that as a consequence the United States might some day have to deal, maybe alone, with a greatly strengthened Japanese power across the Pacific Ocean. It was this formidable prospect that was making the President wish, if he could, to do something to check the tendency now.

In the course of a luncheon the same day, Mr. Hornbeck, Political Adviser to the Far Eastern Section of the State Department, said he thought we were overestimating the power of Japan. He was convinced that she was not sufficiently formidable to attempt to attack either Great Britain or the United States in the Far East. In a message to the Foreign Office I summed up our conclusion, that the Americans attached importance to the Conference as an influence for educating their public. They did not know what step they might be able to take next, but they hoped the Conference would gain more energetic public support for them. Evidently it was all to be a slow business, but Britain had no choice.

Davis' speech at the opening of the Conference on November 3rd did not tell us anything and he was only a little more forthcoming in conversation that afternoon. He hoped that I should not hurry away after the early meetings of the Conference and be seen no more. I assured him that I would be willing to stay in Brussels indefinitely for the sake of achieving co-operation with his Government.

On November 5th Mr. Davis and I had a conversation on our way back from a meeting about what action we should take if the present policy towards Japan failed. The United States Ambassador-at-large lowered his voice confidentially and said: 'I'll tell you, we won't put on any of these sanctions, we will just refuse to buy Japanese goods, that's what we'll do. We won't refuse to allow our ships to take their goods, or our goods to go to them—we will just refuse to buy.'

I had to explain that this particular measure had formed the most serious of the sanctions imposed upon Italy and had not been conspicuously successful. The Ambassador maintained, however, that since we and the United States took 75 per cent. of Japan's goods, sanctions must be effective. This was the same proportion of the Italian export trade, I reflected, as was taken by the League in 1935.

During the course of a subsequent conversation, Mr. Davis mentioned that he was most anxious not to repeat the experience of 1932. He knew that we blamed them and they blamed us for that misunderstanding. I replied that I cordially shared his view and, in order to make the position absolutely clear, I wished to explain to him how the sanctions problem appeared to us. There were two kinds of sanctions, effective and ineffective. To apply the latter was provocative and useless. If we were to apply the former, we ran the risk of war, and it would be dangerous to shut our eyes to the fact. As we had previously explained to the United States Government, we were perfectly willing to examine this question with them and discuss what steps, if any, could be taken, but it must be with our eyes open and with a willingness to share the risks, whatever they might be, right through to the end. Davis appeared fully to understand the force of this and did not demur at my analysis. He thought, however, that it was easy to exaggerate the action which Japan could take in reply to the sanctions which might be imposed upon her.

* * * * *

I flew back to London for a few days, while a further invitation to attend the Conference was being sent to Japan. At the Foreign Office I found a telegram from Sir Robert Craigie, who stressed that Japan saw Britain, and not the United States, as her chief enemy. I thought that our Ambassador's fears were exaggerated, although, with Japanese opinion so inflamed against us, it was always possible that some incident might spark off trouble. I declined to endorse the sedative he prescribed, to stop all arms traffic through Hong Kong. This would have been a genuflectory concession to Japan, by closing one of China's few remaining channels of supply. Until the Conference was over and we knew more of the United States' intentions, I thought that we should wait upon events. Accordingly I noted:

> I found many at the Brussels Conference who thought that Japan was going to her '1812' in China. This may not be so, but we should do what we can cautiously to make it possible.

Before returning to Brussels, I discussed the Conference with Neville Chamberlain. I repeated my view, held throughout the summer, that we should go as far as America would go. The Prime Minister also had not changed the opinion which he had first expressed when Bingham proposed an economic boycott and had later confirmed by altering my telegram at the end of September. Chamberlain now exclaimed: 'On no account will I impose a sanction!' 'Do you want me to say that to Norman Davis?' I asked. Chamberlain agreed that he did not.

I returned to Brussels on November 9th to find that the United States showed no more sign than before of taking any firm action, though Davis did go so far as to suggest that our Governments might both supply arms to China, or decline to recognize Japan's conquests and withhold loans. On November 10th Delbos and I both promised co-operation in collective action. However, there was still no sign of an American undertaking, without which neither ourselves nor the Dominions, with whom we were in daily contact, could act.

After Japan had again refused to attend the Conference, Davis told me that he was now hopeful that his Government might refuse credits and the recognition of Japanese conquests. He asked whether I could assure him of British co-operation in these steps and I at once asked my colleagues for the necessary authority. At last there seemed a chance of joint action. But again we were disappointed. When Lindsay saw the Under-Secretary of State on November 12th, Sumner Welles said that Davis had been going too far and indicated that America now wanted the Conference simply to appoint a standing committee, which would examine future possibilities. This retreat considerably depressed Davis, and I telegraphed to Lindsay that the Conference would probably produce an 'indictment of Japan, with an implied confession of impotence . . . which, from the broader aspect of maintaining the sanctity of treaties and world peace, is discouraging, to say the least.'

I submitted a report to King George VI:

> The main object which Your Majesty's delegation has had constantly before it during the Brussels Conference has been to ensure the closest possible co-operation with the Government of the United States. Even though such co-operation may not emerge in definite joint action in the present crisis, the future of world peace depends to so great an extent upon Anglo-American co-operation that Mr. Eden feels that no effort should be spared to consolidate it. That is why he has spent so much of his time in Brussels during the last ten days.

I added that there had been some reward. Mr. Davis was now working closely with me and the suspicion which had rankled since the Manchurian events of 1932 was eliminated.

As the days passed, Washington seemed less than ever inclined to any action. Norman Davis told Malcolm MacDonald on November 23rd that a telegram had arrived from Cordell Hull, deploring Roosevelt's use of the word 'quarantine' and explaining that the President had not wished to use any words which 'might seem to indicate that hostile action was a possibility.' The Conference ended on November 24th with a report of its work and an anodyne resolution deprecating the use of force. The contrast with Nyon could scarcely have been more marked, for preponderant power was at the disposal of the Conference.

* * * * *

While the Brussels Conference was floundering, we once again considered whether Great Britain could act alone in the Far East. Large parts of the British and French fleets were patrolling the Mediterranean, as agreed at Nyon. Lord Chatfield felt that the despatch of two capital ships to the Far East would merely weaken us at home, without giving overwhelming strength against Japan. I agreed with this opinion which was accepted by my colleagues. I had hopes, however, that our firmness in the Mediterranean might soon enable Britain to present a stronger front to Japan.

Although no official state of war existed, the Japanese and Chinese forces were now in full-scale combat. The wounding of our Ambassador had been the first of a series of attacks upon British nationals and property. We complained and protested and the Japanese Government usually apologized with an ill grace. The seizure of all the customs vessels in Tientsin and Shanghai in the last week of November decided me to approach Washington with an offer to send warships, if the United States would do the same. Accordingly, I told Lindsay to propose naval Staff conversations to the American Government. Sumner Welles promised to consult the President, but hinted that the European situation must surely prevent us from being able to send many ships to the Far East.

Thinking that no harm would be done by repeating our views in London, I told the American Chargé d'Affaires on December 3rd that the present situation would continue and, perhaps, grow worse, unless and until it was possible for the foreign powers interested to take effective action. The Japanese Government were not slow to supply proof for this judgement. Two days later, a number of British ships lying off Wuhu were attacked by Japanese aircraft. The Japanese Government promptly informed Craigie that they were prepared to consider paying compensation, which meant that the Government would disgorge the indispensable minimum in atonement for the behaviour of the military, who were their real masters.

I spent the following weekend in Oxfordshire and while waiting for my train at Bicester on the morning of Monday, December 13th, saw on a newspaper placard 'Warships Attacked in Yangtse'. From the scanty press reports I assumed that these were ours and spent a miserable journey. When I finally reached the Foreign Office and sank into my chair before the familiar table, Oliver Harvey, my patient and invaluable Private Secretary, appeared and inquired whether he should send for the United States' Chargé d'Affaires. I asked him why. He replied, 'Because an American gunboat has been sunk in the Yangtse.'

Harvey handed me the first telegrams. From these it appeared that, early on the previous day, British merchantmen and warships had been bombed between Nanking and Wuhu. A field-gun battery attacked H.M.S. *Ladybird* at Wuhu itself, killing one sailor and injuring several others. Immediate protests to the senior Japanese military officer in the district, Colonel Hashimoto, merely produced the answer that although firing on the warships was a mistake, he had orders to fire at every ship on the river. At the same time, the United States naval gunboat

Panay was attacked and sunk by bombing from Japanese aircraft. A small boat carrying the wounded ashore was then machine-gunned. H.M.S. *Ladybird* and *Bee* helped to rescue the survivors under fire, for which service they were thanked by the American Government.

When the American Chargé d'Affaires, Mr. Herschel Johnson, arrived, I told him that I had been deeply grieved to hear of the attacks which had been made upon the ships of our two countries in the Yangtse. This was just the kind of incident which I had feared might happen, if no restraint were imposed upon the Japanese Government by evidence of joint Anglo-American determination to resist the increasingly overbearing attitude of the Japanese military. I did not, of course, know what action the United States Government were now contemplating, but I emphasized to the Chargé d'Affaires our desire that the United States Government should consult with us before coming to any decision, since it was extremely desirable that any action which we now took should be joint action. We were sure that this would be much more likely to produce results than anything we could either of us do separately. I had telegraphed to Sir Ronald Lindsay in greater detail, but I would ask Mr. Johnson to tell his Government at once that instructions were on their way to our Ambassador and to ask them to see him before they took any final decision.

My telegram to Sir Ronald Lindsay said:

You will have seen that the Japanese have not only fired on and hit a British warship but have also actually sunk an United States warship. They have also made a bombing attack on another British warship. These acts appear to have been deliberate on the part of those firing, and the sustained fire can indeed hardly have been anything else, though those in higher authority will presumably go through all the procedure of diplomatic apology. I mention this to emphasize the aggressive state of mind of those who indulge in these provocative acts. It seems clear that some action will have to be taken by both the United States Government and His Majesty's Government to curb this dangerous spirit before it goes to still more intolerable lengths. There is no doubt that this action should be taken jointly otherwise it will fail to achieve an end which will in any case be difficult to attain. But before considering this action in any detail I would like to have urgently the views of the United States Government.

No doubt United States Government will be contemplating the presentation of a series of stiffly worded demands and if we could have information as to what they are we should be prepared to send similar intimation. More important is the question whether the United States Government will be taking simultaneous action of a more menacing character such as the mobilization of their fleet, or a part of it, pending the receipt of the Japanese reply. If anything of the kind were contemplated we should wish to know as soon as possible, as in that case we should probably desire to take similar action, although of course our ships could not reach eastern waters as soon as United States ships.

Even in these conditions, the United States Government preferred to act independently. Their protest to Japan was sent off at once on the evening of December 13th, ostensibly in order to forestall the Japanese apology. We had no option but to send a separate note through Sir Robert Craigie, while I took the Japanese Ambassador to task when he called to apologize.

It was disappointing that we were not able to secure effective joint action, but there were reasons of internal United States policy for this. Suspicion was rife that British diplomacy had as its aim to entangle the United States in problems which were not properly its concern, and that we were trying to get that country to pull our chestnuts out of the fire. There was a strong isolationist lobby, which the United States Government had to take into account, even though they did not share its views. The dilemma was expressed by Mr. Hull, himself certainly circumspect:

> While advocating international co-operation at all times, we were faced with the extremely delicate task of being careful not to present and urge measures in such numbers as to alarm the people and precipitate isolation as an acute political issue in the nation.*

All this was a pity, but had to be accepted.

A week before these events, I had telegraphed to Sir Ronald Lindsay telling him that we were considering how to make our power felt in the Far East. The problem would be very different if the United States would act with us. Having suggested Staff conversations to determine what could be done to show that we were both in earnest, I indicated Britain's readiness to make a substantial contribution to any general naval display, and mentioned a figure of eight or nine capital ships and other vessels, if the United States would make at least an equivalent effort. Such a fleet might be ready to sail in three or four weeks.

I gave Lindsay latitude as to whether to make these proposals or not. If the Americans would not go so far, I asked them to consider a less drastic step, such as getting the fleet into a state of greater readiness,

* *The Memoirs of Cordell Hull,* Vol. I; Macmillan, 1948.

which for us would involve calling up naval reservists, together with Staff conversations. I said that I was receiving evidence of the loss of prestige in the Far East, affecting not only the United Kingdom but also all democracies. I thought that some action should be taken to restore the situation. I understood the difficulties the United States Government experienced with their public opinion, but I hoped that they might be willing to consider mobilization as a first step.

Sir Ronald Lindsay had a conversation with Mr. Hull on December 14th, as a result of which an interview with the President was arranged in all secrecy for the night of December 16th. As soon as he knew of this, Lindsay telegraphed for instructions.

Meanwhile, at the Ambassador's request, I had sent him a further telegram authorizing him to use at the meeting any of the suggestions which I had telegraphed to him. I explained that I had thought it useful to give him a definite idea of what we were prepared to do, because I felt that our attitude of being ready to do whatever the United States Government would do, had become embarrassing to them. It might be easier for them to be told privately what our ideas were and what contribution we could make. I added that firmness would have its effect, not only in the Far East but also in Europe, and would give notice to the dictators that the democratic governments were as zealous for their authority as the dictators were, and as willing and able to maintain it. I repeated that I knew how difficult it was for the United States Government. They could count on us to do everything in our power to facilitate Anglo-American collaboration. 'More than ever do we believe that only thus can the peace of the world be assured without a shot being fired.'

When Lindsay saw the President, Roosevelt plunged at once into the question of Staff conversations. He wanted an arrangement like the one which had existed in 1916–17, when an exchange of secret information had been established between the Admiralty and the Navy Department. This had been most fruitful. The President said that the officers concerned must be fully familiar with the latest Staff plans and thoughts of their respective navies, and seemed to consider that secrecy would be more easily secured in London than in Washington. He would have no difficulty in finding a suitable person to send to London at short notice.

The President spoke of a blockade, coming into operation upon further outrages by the Japanese. Its purpose would be to cut Japan off from raw materials and it might take eighteen months to produce results. The blockade would be carried out by cruisers, with battleships in reserve. The President was against a demonstration by our navies, because, though it might have an effect upon a Japanese Government under civil control, it would have none on the military authorities who were now in power. He did speak later of advancing the date of naval manœuvres, due to begin at Hawaii in three months' time, and of a visit of American cruisers to Singapore, which idea Lindsay encouraged as much as he could.

The Ambassador gave the President information about the number of ships we could make available. The President thought such an offer inadvisable and that it was more important for the British Government to keep their battleships to look after the situation in Europe. A reinforcement of destroyers, cruisers and long-range submarines would be sufficient, though he also mentioned, 'in passing', one or two battleships.

The President told Lindsay that he thought opinion in the United States was moving favourably. His correspondence was eighty per cent. in favour of vigorous action, but he admitted that reports to him were still rather preliminary. Mr. Hull, in his only contribution to the conversation, spoke of the inadvisability of any talk in London about joint action with the United States. The President endorsed this strongly.

I told Lindsay, in reply to his telegram, that His Majesty's Government would prefer that action should not be delayed until other outrages occurred, and hoped that preparatory measures by the two Governments might be taken, because that knowledge might restrain Japan from further bad deeds. Meanwhile, we should be delighted to receive the officer the President might select, and we hoped that he would come with the least possible delay. It had been my intention to leave for a short holiday immediately after Christmas but I decided to postpone this when I learnt that the officer chosen by the President, Captain Ingersoll, was to arrive on New Year's day.

After welcoming Captain Ingersoll and assuring him that he could count on our full co-operation, I asked him if he could give me a little more information about what was in the mind of the United States Government. Ingersoll replied that the plans of the Navy Department for naval action in the Pacific were based on certain assumptions made in Washington about the dispositions we might be able to make. He imagined that the same was true of our plans. The time had now come, in the opinion of the President and Admiral Leahy, to carry matters a stage further by exchanging information in order to co-ordinate our plans more closely. He could tell us of the dispositions of the United States Navy in certain eventualities and would be glad to know what our corresponding dispositions would be. There were also several purely technical arrangements which would have to be made if our two fleets were to co-operate in the Pacific, such as the codes to be used between them. All these preparations could be made in advance.

I asked Ingersoll whether he could tell me if his Government considered that some joint action should be taken now, or whether the discussions which were to be held between himself and the Admiralty would be limited to future incidents against which joint action might later be taken. Ingersoll replied that, in the view of the Navy Department, no move could be made at all in the Pacific, unless full preparation had been made for every eventuality, including war. He thought that we should proceed with a technical examination first. When we knew the outcome of that, it would be easier to consider any political decisions which might have to be taken. He visualized a week or ten days for conversations between himself and the Admiralty as a first step. I then told Ingersoll about the date of the opening of the new dock at Singapore and said how much we would welcome a visit from some United States' ships.

On January 10th Lindsay telegraphed to me that the President had decided to announce at once that three cruisers would proceed on a visit to Singapore. He also proposed to announce a few days later that the date for the manœuvres in the Pacific would be advanced by two or three weeks, so as to start in the middle of February.

All this, though not decisive, was helpful and encouraging to me in my pursuit of closer Anglo-American co-operation as the only effective deterrent to Japan in the Pacific. Japan's partners in Europe, Hitler and Mussolini might also note that the power of the democracies was being aligned.

XII

ROOSEVELT MAKES A MOVE

January 1938

A luncheon with Mr. Churchill and Mr. Lloyd George on the Riviera – I am called home by the Foreign Office – President Roosevelt's offer – Mr. Chamberlain's hasty reply – He asks the President to hold his hand – I telegraph to our Ambassador in Washington – A resentful interview at Chequers – I contend for the President's plan – My colleagues divided – Despatch of four telegrams to Washington – The breach widens between the Prime Minister and myself

At last I was able to take a few days' holiday in the South of France. I felt that, for the moment, the Prime Minister and I were in closer agreement about foreign affairs, and early in the New Year we exchanged friendly letters. Winston Churchill was also on the Riviera and asked me to have luncheon with him, telling me that the other guest would be Lloyd George. When I arrived at *La Bonne Auberge*, Lloyd George was already there. After exchanging greetings I said: 'Where's our host?' Lloyd George laughed: 'Have you ever known Winston in time for a meal yet?' Churchill soon arrived. There had been no important divergence between us since I had become Foreign Secretary and he had recently given me strong support on one or two occasions in the House of Commons. We discussed the state of Europe and the threats of the two dictators. Both Lloyd George and Churchill expressed warm approval of the Nyon Conference and equal opposition to any *de jure* recognition of the Italian conquest of Abyssinia. They did not believe that Mussolini would hold to any bond he gave. We spoke of the United States. I gave an account of the efforts I had been making to encourage American co-operation and was gratified to find them apparently impressed with the progress we had made. None of us guessed that within a few days there would arise a greater opportunity to work with the United States than any so far.

I played tennis and the days rolled uneventfully by, until the morning of Friday, January 14th, when I was called to the telephone to speak to Sir Alexander Cadogan. He told me that there were developments which could not be described over the open line, but which demanded my instant return. I gathered that a Foreign Office bag, containing the relevant telegrams, was already on its way to our Consul-General at Marseilles. With Harold Caccia, then my junior Private Secretary, I set off for home from Cannes that night by train, arranging to fly from Paris to London. But all the careful plans went awry. The train was divided into two parts at Marseilles and the telegrams did not reach me; when I arrived in Paris the weather was so tempestuous that the air service had been cancelled. I continued the journey on a very rough sea. Then the boat ran into the pier at Folkestone, doing itself £3,000 worth of damage, and we were late in docking.

It was not until five o'clock that I shook hands with Cadogan and Harvey, who had come to meet me at the quay. They had troubled faces and a large file of papers. At last I could learn the reason for my dislocated journey and I settled down in the train to read the telegrams. It appeared that on the evening of January 11th the American Under-Secretary of State, Mr. Sumner Welles, had called upon our Ambassador at Washington, Sir Ronald Lindsay, by direction of the President. His purpose was to convey a message, which was a most secret communication from Roosevelt to Neville Chamberlain. Welles had explained that the President was deeply impressed by the deterioration of the world situation. He particularly noticed how the smaller states of Europe were falling away from the ideals and loyalties to which they would have preferred to adhere, in order to gravitate into the orbit of the dictators. In his opinion, this tendency was due to the loss of influence of the democratic states, which must be restored at the earliest possible moment.

Roosevelt, Welles continued, was more than ever impressed by the danger of war, unless some exceptional efforts were made immediately. He accordingly wished to take action along the only lines open to him, given the state of American public opinion. This initiative, the Under-Secretary had said, was designed to work parallel to the effort which the British Government were making with the Central European powers. The President believed that it would have the effect of lending that effort good support. Roosevelt would keep us in close touch with all that happened in Washington and wanted to have full information about the talks in Europe.

The President proposed to call the whole Diplomatic Corps of Washington to the White House on January 22nd. He would speak of the decline of international standards, the world's frantic rearmament and the barbarities of modern warfare, and then lay before all governments the suggestion that they should agree on the essential principles to be observed in the conduct of international relations. These were the reduction of armaments, equal access to raw materials, and the laws of warfare. If the response were favourable, Welles said, the United States Government would be prepared to ask a small number of governments among the lesser powers to join them immediately to work out tentative proposals, which could then be submitted to the other nations.

The President's draft speech recognized that agreement on these principles might not alone secure peace. In an apparent reference to the Treaty of Versailles, he added that it was possible some inequities of the post-war settlements might have to be removed. The United States Government could not depart from their 'traditional policy of freedom from political involvement', but it seemed to the President that adjustments might more readily be made if all countries agreed about how to govern their relations.

Sumner Welles impressed on our Ambassador that the President was communicating his scheme to His Majesty's Government alone, with the stipulation that no other power should be informed of its nature or even of its existence. Roosevelt would only proceed with it if he received an assurance from Chamberlain, no later than January 17th, that it met with the 'cordial approval and whole-hearted support of His Majesty's Government.' He would then warn the Governments of France, Germany and Italy confidentially of the general lines of the plan, informing them that he was making a similar communication to us.

As Mr. Sumner Welles later revealed,* it seemed to the President and himself that as the bandit nations drew together, their respective policies became more and more clearly synchronized. Though the American people were not yet alive to the danger or willing to support any forthright policy by their Government, the President was convinced that he must try by every possible constitutional method to

* Sumner Welles: *The Time for Decision*; Harper & Row, New York, and Hamish Hamilton, London, 1944. The full text of the relevant pages of this book is printed as Appendix A.

check the progress of the dictators in their aim of world domination. This exhaustive analysis of events expressed my own thought.

The telegrams from our Ambassador had arrived at the Foreign Office during the morning of January 12th and, having been decyphered, reached Cadogan in the late afternoon. The Prime Minister was at Chequers and Sir Alexander immediately sent him all the papers accompanied by a minute pointing out the pitfalls in Roosevelt's initiative, but recommending that we should welcome it. Early the next morning, January 13th, two more telegrams had arrived from Sir Ronald Lindsay, who had formerly been Permanent Under-Secretary at the Foreign Office, the post now occupied by Cadogan, as well as Ambassador at Berlin. He was much respected by all who knew his work, for his character and ability, as well as for his quite exceptional experience of diplomacy.

Lindsay had described the President's plan as 'a genuine effort to relax the tension of the world, to stop the prevalent deterioration and to restore the influence of the democracies.' He agreed with the President's belief that the combination of disarmament with the relaxation of economic pressure would align American opinion behind the scheme. 'I have long held', he continued, 'that the best chance of averting disaster is to range not only the United States Administration but also United States public opinion behind the objectives of the democratic governments. We definitely have no anxiety as to the Administration and this present scheme must have a profound effect on the public also.' Lindsay had warned that if the scheme should break down because of the reluctance of some powers to support it, those powers would be blamed by the American Government and people. Equally, His Majesty's Government would be blamed by the United States Government if they killed the scheme before it was propounded, by withholding their support. This would annul all the progress we had made in the last two years. Lindsay had concluded:

> Destructive criticisms, reservations or attempts to define the issues more clearly can only accomplish very little in favour of anything you may wish to put forward while they will create a disproportionate bad impression in the thoughts of the Administration. I therefore urge respectfully but very earnestly that His Majesty's Government give their reply to this invaluable initiative with a very quick and cordial acceptance.

The advice was authoritative and should have been compelling.

Meanwhile, the Prime Minister had telephoned to Cadogan, asking him to discuss the situation with the Government's Chief Industrial Adviser, Sir Horace Wilson, who did not welcome Roosevelt's move. As a result of seeing Wilson, Cadogan prepared a draft reply to Washington, pointing out that Roosevelt's plan seemed to cut across the discussions we were shortly to open with Germany and Italy. In these circumstances, the President might wish to defer his initiative until the result of our talks became known. But, if he still preferred to go ahead immediately, we could only assure him of our whole-hearted support. Cadogan's intention was that this draft should be sent out to the South of France for my approval before despatch.

These last two suggestions, however, had not met with the approval of the Prime Minister, who returned to London in the early evening. As Cadogan wrote to me, Chamberlain evidently viewed the President's initiative 'with the gravest concern'. He refused to make any offer of support towards it and determined to send his reply without consulting me or any other member of the Cabinet. Lindsay's telegram of endorsement had been laid before Chamberlain, but ignored. So was Cadogan's advice. Chamberlain's answer, sent that night, recognized that the President was impelled to make his proposal by consideration of what he had described as the progressive deterioration of international relations and the consequent danger of general conflagration. Chamberlain commented:

> No one who has followed closely recent developments can fail to be impressed with the great dangers that beset us. On the other hand, it may be permissible to look forward to some improvement in the immediate future.

As soon as I read this forecast, I put a large question mark in the margin of the telegram, which went on:

> In the case of Italy, His Majesty's Government would be prepared, for their part, if possible with the authority of the League of Nations, to recognize *de jure* the Italian conquest of Abyssinia (by which Signor Mussolini sets great store) and to take certain other action if they found that the Italian Government, on their side, were ready to give evidence of their desire to contribute to the restoration of confidence and friendly relations.

Chamberlain trusted that before long we might be able to begin conversations with Germany. He wondered, in the terms of the earlier draft, whether the President's proposal might cut across these efforts, and felt that the dictators might refuse negotiations with us on concrete issues, on the ground that these were all merged in the President's wider proposal:

My fear is that, if the President's suggestions are put forward at the present time, Germany and Italy may feel constrained to take advantage of them, both to delay the consideration of specific points which must be settled if appeasement is to be achieved and to put forward demands over and above what they would put forward to us if we were in direct negotiation with them.

The Prime Minister finally asked the President to consider whether it would not be wiser to hold his hand for a short while. Sumner Welles wrote that this reply was 'in the nature of a douche of cold water'.*

Mr. Welles later deplored the outcome of the President's attempt to get British support in advance. It was his conviction that, if the President had not taken these preliminary soundings but had carried out his original idea of a world-wide appeal, neither the British Government nor the Axis powers could have refused at least apparent co-operation. Mr. Welles' judgement was probably correct, but the Prime Minister's rebuff had another and most unhappy consequence. The growing tendency for confidential Anglo-American discussions on a deteriorating world scene, which I had been doing my best to encourage, was clumsily nipped.

* * * * *

The telegrams and my two advisers put me in the picture as we sped to London. I was outraged and uneasy at the way in which this opportunity had been handled and agreed with Lindsay that, if we were not careful, we would lose all that we had gained in the last two years in our relations with the United States, to which he and I had devoted so much effort. My immediate reaction was that we must accept Roosevelt's offer outright, while suggesting some amendments to the wording of his draft statement. I had no doubt that the purpose of this move, which was a combination of the President's instinct and Sumner Welles' knowledge, was to put obstacles in the way of Hitler and Mussolini by the only method open to Roosevelt. Both the dictators would dislike the whole exercise and want to resist being tangled in negotiations of this kind. This was no reason for deprecating them. At the worst, Roosevelt's offer would gain us time and bring the United States a little nearer to a divided Europe. I thought Lindsay's advice absolutely correct and regarded the Prime Minister's telegram as much too chilling and unjustifiably optimistic about the prospects of

* op. cit.

our own efforts. I also felt that I should have been summoned to London or consulted by telegraph, before any reply was sent. Roosevelt had asked for an answer by January 17th. It was now only the 15th.

Cadogan gave me dinner that night at his home, where Lord Cranborne was waiting. He had already seen the telegrams and his judgement exactly accorded with mine. It was now getting late and I decided not to go to Chequers until the next morning. Soon after dinner a short message arrived from Lindsay:

Under-Secretary of State has telephoned to say that the President will send the Prime Minister a written reply on Monday. He will indicate his willingness to postpone his scheme 'for a while' but Welles says he feels a little disappointed.

Determined to modify this calamitous sequence of events if I could, I replied at once that I had returned to consult with the Prime Minister on the President's initiative and had just seen the Ambassador's message. My telegram continued:

I am sure the Prime Minister will be very grateful for the President's message and for his willingness to postpone his scheme for a while.

Mention of a written reply makes me fear that the President may be registering disappointment at finding what he considers to be a negative attitude on our part. That, I am convinced, was not the impression which it was intended to convey.

I hope therefore that we need not regard the President's written reply, whatever it may contain, as assuming any such attitude on our part. I shall be in consultation with the Prime Minister tomorrow, Sunday, and hope to be able to give you further guidance. The President will surely understand that we were in some difficulty owing to the very short time given us for the consideration of his very far-reaching proposals, more particularly in view of the impossibility of consultation between the Prime Minister and myself.

I then telephoned to Lindsay, who confirmed that Roosevelt was undoubtedly disappointed at our reply. The Ambassador advised that we should wait for the written American answer on Monday.

* * * * *

On Sunday morning I motored to Chequers, where I found Neville Chamberlain apparently in excellent spirits. He seemed unaffected by the widening rift between us, or the gloom of the house so splendidly set in the Chilterns. Years afterwards, I found at Chequers a charming and erudite monograph which he had written about the trees in the park. Our meeting was stiff and we continued our discussion on a walk together. For the first time our relations were seriously at odds. The Prime Minister showed that he resented my action in telegraphing to Lindsay the previous evening and refused to send a further telegram endorsing mine. I told him that I resented his action in sending a reply to Roosevelt without consultation, when he knew I could be home in twenty-four hours. Chamberlain apparently believed with increasing conviction that our approaches to the dictators were likely to lead very soon to genuine settlements. I expostulated with him, but only received the reply that the Foreign Office was not sincere in its efforts.

After luncheon we went on with the discussion. I told the Prime Minister that we had been working for a long time in the hope that the United States would take just such an initiative. Chamberlain said it was vague and would fail. I replied that the President was just as well able to assess that as we were. He knew his own public opinion and this was probably as far as he felt able to go at the present time. Even if the initiative did fail, we should have gained immeasurably from this first American intervention in Europe and another might follow. I said that I agreed with Roosevelt's appreciation of the European situation and that I did not feel optimistic about our discussions with the dictators, though we should have a better chance if Roosevelt were also dealing with them. My view was that we should work on parallel lines, doing our best to improve Anglo-American relations while preparing for discussion with Germany and Italy. All my instincts were against according *de jure* recognition of Mussolini's conquest of Abyssinia at the present time.

I reminded the Prime Minister that, within a week of signing the 'Gentleman's Agreement', Mussolini had sent 4,000 men to Spain. I feared that I had no more confidence in his promises. This argument did not commend itself to Chamberlain. He told me that the situation was different now and we had a wonderful chance of coming to terms with Italy about the future of the Mediterranean. This did not convince me and I said that recognition of Mussolini's Abyssinian empire would increase his authority and therefore make him more attractive to Hitler. Still, I promised to discuss this matter with the French and to put Chamberlain's point of view to them as fairly as I could. Meanwhile, I said the questions raised by Roosevelt's message were so important that I thought we should have the opinion of our colleagues about them and I asked that Ministers should meet for this purpose. Chamberlain agreed without enthusiasm and said that he would issue the necessary instructions. On this note, a profoundly unsatisfactory conversation closed.

We were now head-on and this brought out in the Prime Minister's character a streak of ruthlessness reminiscent of his father, Joseph Chamberlain. He was evidently determined to see the whole American business only in the context of his impending talks with the dictators. In this sense, Roosevelt, our French allies and I were all in the same boat. We were all held to be obstructing these negotiations, in which Chamberlain had dogmatic faith.

As soon as I returned from Chequers, I went again through the file of telegrams relating to Roosevelt's plan. A careful re-reading confirmed the impression formed in the train coming from Folkestone. I would have liked to modify one or two phrases in Roosevelt's message, notably those dealing with the 'inequities' of Versailles and with 'political involvement'. There was also a risk of some confusion from the method which the President wished to employ and from the fact that his Government, if only for reasons of geography, lacked our intimate knowledge of European affairs. All this I wrote to the Prime Minister on the morning of the 17th and continued:

> But these things seem to be of minor importance against the significant fact that President Roosevelt, with all the authority of his position which is unique in the world, wishes to help to avert a general war. Of his good intentions there can be no question; on this, you and I are, I believe, completely in agreement. I am no less confident that the United States initiative, based on collaboration with us even though that collaboration be not publicly revealed, must be of the greatest service in steadying the situation generally.
>
> I really do not feel that this initiative of the President need necessarily injure the attempts which we are making to improve relations with Germany, nor even have any repercussions on the conversations which I know you are so anxious to start with Italy. It may be that you think that I exaggerate, but I truly believe that with the world as it is now, it is almost impossible to overestimate the effect which an indication of United States interest in European affairs may be calculated to produce. I know that you fear that the dictators would resent the tone of his communication and that there would be, in consequence, a blast and counterblast between democracies and dictatorships. I do not myself think this would be the result, though I agree that neither of the dictators would like Roosevelt's initiative; they would probably, however, be constrained to conceal their dislike and might even become more negotiable as a result of their knowledge of President Roosevelt's attitude.

I then explained that, for domestic reasons, Roosevelt could not make his initiative jointly with us and had to employ other methods. I again told Chamberlain that I was convinced that we should have committed the greatest mistake if, as a result of any action of ours, President Roosevelt were deterred from launching his appeal. I still hoped privately that we might retrieve the situation and concluded my letter:

> I am afraid that our first telegram has been a disappointment to Roosevelt but it is difficult to see what further action we can now take pending the communication Lindsay tells us he is expecting from the President today. I do, however, feel most strongly that we should make the fullest use of any opening that communication may give us in order to convince the President that we are ready to give support in the fullest measure possible to his proposed initiative.

There seemed no more that I could do.

* * * * *

I had just sent off this letter when Sir Horace Wilson was announced. He explained that the Prime Minister had left for Chequers, but that my letter would be sent on to him. He then asked if I would mind if he spoke to me about foreign affairs. I said no, and he delivered himself of what was, in the main, an appeal for a more understanding attitude on my part towards the dictators. He told me that the Prime Minister was much disturbed about our difference of opinion, more especially over *de jure* recognition of the conquest of Abyssinia, which he regarded as more important than the American proposal. I argued against this obvious fallacy but with little effect, so eventually I told Sir Horace that if ever it fell to my lot to have to cross the road to Downing Street, and I had there to deal with an industrial problem, I would send for him and almost certainly take his advice, for I knew that he understood industrial affairs, but I asked him to believe me that he did not understand foreign affairs. The meeting did not end well and I doubt whether mine was a wise comment. Harvey and I then had a gloomy luncheon at the Savoy. I greatly disliked the position into which we had been led and felt that I could not endorse a refusal by the Prime Minister to welcome Roosevelt's initiative.

I had another preoccupation. It was difficult to escape the conclusion that the Prime Minister had deliberately withheld the information from me, sensing that I would disagree. Only a few weeks before, we had had an argument about Anglo-American relations and he knew well the importance which I attached to them. To Chamberlain, Roosevelt's initiative seemed naïve and woolly. To me also it might be both these things, but this did not weigh a feather in the scale beside the significance of an American intervention in Europe at this moment.

I decided to telephone to Lindsay again in the hope of providing him with a little more ammunition. I told him that I entirely agreed with the advice he had submitted in the first place and would do everything possible to support that point of view in London. I hoped that no one in Washington would be persuaded to chuck their hand in, because if they returned to the charge, I was sure we should be able to help. I added that if I had been in London when the original telegrams had been received, our answer might have been different. Sir Ronald replied that this message was most helpful and would be a valuable guide in a visit he was about to pay to the State Department.

We could now only await Roosevelt's reply. It arrived on the morning of Tuesday the 18th, agreeing to a short postponement, but speaking strongly of the dangers of according *de jure* recognition to the Italian conquest at a time when respect for treaty obligations was of such vital importance. Lindsay inferred that Roosevelt's disappointment had been keenly felt. Sumner Welles' commentary was even stronger than the text of the message, and Mr. Cordell Hull's yet more so, Lindsay reported. In particular, the Secretary of State, speaking of *de jure* recognition, declared that 'the desperado nations would capitalize it as a virtual ratification of their policy of outright treaty wrecking and the seizure of land by force of arms.' Welles, on the President's instructions, told Lindsay that Roosevelt thought opinion in the United States was crystallizing favourably in the direction he desired. He was confident that *de jure* recognition, given in the wrong conditions, would turn it right back. The question touched both the material interests of the United States in the Far East, which were not different from those of His Majesty's Government, and the moral sentiments of the people. Welles added:

> It would rouse a feeling of disgust; would revive and multiply all fear of pulling the chestnuts out of the fire; and it would be represented as a corrupt bargain completed in Europe at the expense of interests in the Far East in which the United States are intimately concerned.

Lindsay said our immediate practical difficulty was that as soon as the talks with Italy began, we should be confronted with something like an ultimatum, requiring immediate *de jure* recognition if the conversations were not to be broken off. Welles replied that this would be pure blackmail. If Britain yielded, it would very soon be echoed by unconscionable demands from Germany, later re-echoed by further similar demands from Italy. Not surprisingly, the Ambassador was impressed with the strength of American feeling against any recognition of Mussolini's Abyssinian conquests.

I agreed with every word of Hull's and Sumner Welles' commentaries and indeed, as one of my staff said, I might have drafted the President's reply myself. These reactions showed that the United States Government felt much more strongly against *de jure* recognition than the Prime Minister, or even I, had anticipated. I considered that we must now drop any idea of early *de jure* recognition and back Roosevelt to the hilt. Both the United States and ourselves had every reason to be anxious about the Far Eastern situation and the prospects of further Japanese aggression. Indeed, one of the strongest arguments of my critics was that we could not face Germany, Italy and Japan together. Here was an opportunity to improve our co-operation with the United States, the country best placed to offer stern opposition to Japanese intentions. It must on no account be missed. I therefore drafted a statement to lay before the Prime Minister. It included these sentences:

> I am afraid that it is clear from the President's message that he has been disappointed at what he considers to be the negative nature of the reply sent to him. It is true that he offers none the less to defer making the proposal he had intended to make 'for a short while'. It might, therefore, be argued that we could . . . ask the President to hold his hand for some months and do our best in the interval to go ahead in our negotiations with Germany and Italy. I am convinced, however, that to pursue this course would be to commit a grave error. This message shows that the President and Mr. Hull feel more strongly against *de jure* recognition than Sir R. Lindsay had anticipated. . . . Even if our negotiations with Italy were ultimately successful . . . we must anticipate that the outcome would not only be received without enthusiasm in this country but be actively condemned by opinion in the United States. A still graver danger is that the President, disappointed by our failure to support his initiative and being himself critical of the character of our negotiations, would withdraw more and more into isolation. . . . Such an event I should regard as the greatest possible disaster to the peace of the world.
>
> The decision we have to take seems to me to depend upon the significance which we attach to Anglo-American co-operation. What we have to choose

between is Anglo-American co-operation in an attempt to ensure world peace and a piecemeal settlement approached by way of problematical agreement with Mussolini. . . . I do not take the view that this initiative need injure the prospects of our negotiations with Germany. . . . In fact, the closer the sympathy and co-operation between the United States and ourselves, the stronger will be our position in dealing with Germany.

The paper concluded by asking that we should strongly support President Roosevelt's initiative.*

I took it across to 10 Downing Street, at 5 p.m. on January 18th. Chamberlain began by saying that he regarded Roosevelt's communication as not too bad, from which it afterwards emerged that his idea was to persist in asking Roosevelt to withhold his initiative, but to go on with our negotiations, excluding *de jure* recognition. He also wished to argue with Roosevelt about this, despite the reasoning in my memorandum. The Prime Minister had been greatly influenced by a letter received from his sister-in-law, Lady Chamberlain, widow of Sir Austen, apparently in reply to one of his own. Later I asked the Prime Minister for details about this letter to his sister-in-law. He explained to me that he had written to Lady Chamberlain in his own hand on Downing Street notepaper and sent it through the open post. She had now been received by Ciano, and had shown him the Prime Minister's letter. Ciano had told her that this was a 'psychological' moment and that Mussolini was ready for a settlement. The Prime Minister was indignant when I suggested it was likely that, in a Fascist state, Ciano would be aware of the contents of the letter even before Lady Chamberlain showed it to him, and would therefore be ready with his answer. Chamberlain was sceptical of the extent of United States co-operation and thought that, in appraising a difficult situation, we must at all costs come to terms with Italy. Germany, he said, could wait. I again deployed my arguments, but to no effect. After two hours' wrangling, Chamberlain admitted that there was a deep difference between us. I began to think that we would not be able to work together much longer. We agreed that the matter should be further ventilated when the Foreign Affairs Committee of the Cabinet met on the following afternoon.

That night I noted in my diary:

I fear that fundamentally the difficulty is that Neville believes that he is a man with a mission to come to terms with the dictators. Indeed, one of his

* The full text of this paper is printed as Appendix B.

chief objections to Roosevelt's initiative was that with its strong reference to International Law it would greatly irritate the dictator powers.

The more I turned over these events in my mind, the more convinced I became that everything must give way before the paramount importance of good Anglo-American relations. I might previously have swallowed *de jure* recognition in return for full British support for Roosevelt's move. But the President's feelings on this subject, as we now knew them, had changed all that. I determined that if the Cabinet Committee would not support Roosevelt's scheme, I must resign.

* * * * *

On the morning of January 19th, I received a letter from the Italian Ambassador. Count Grandi's sense of timing was acute. He hoped that I had had a good holiday and asked for an informal talk with the Prime Minister and myself. I thought that Grandi might have something to say which would be relevant to our discussions. At my request, he came to the Foreign Office that afternoon, when he stressed Italy's anxiety for conversations and insisted that *de jure* recognition must be included if they were to lead anywhere.

The Foreign Affairs Committee met for two and a half hours that evening. Sir Thomas Inskip used to sit on my left in Cabinet, while I was opposite the Prime Minister. Before the meeting began, I saw the top note in his bundle of papers in his own writing: 'Eden's policy to line up the U.S.A., Great Britain and France, result war.' I understood Inskip's reasoning, because he was a fervent believer in the danger of a Fascist and anti-Fascist confrontation and held it possible to detach one of the dictator powers. I told him I could not help seeing his note and added: 'I swear to you, Tom, that if we can really get this line-up of the United States, Great Britain and France there will be no question of war. You will then see the dictators behave themselves for the first time.' He shook his head sadly.

The truth was that some of my seniors in the Cabinet, like Inskip, could not believe that Mussolini and Hitler were as untrustworthy as I painted them. After all, had not Mussolini defeated the reds and made the trains in Italy run on time. Moreover, as old-fashioned Conservatives, they felt little sympathy with Roosevelt whom they instinctively regarded as something of a demagogue. Nevertheless, I thought it necessary to repeat to my colleagues the conviction I had just expressed to Inskip.

Chamberlain, Halifax, Simon and Inskip were all very strong against Roosevelt's plan, on the grounds that America would do nothing practical to help, while we now had a real chance to reach agreement with the dictators. The Prime Minister quoted long extracts from one of Lady Chamberlain's letters, more notable for its good intentions than judgement. He then produced a draft telegram, in which I thought I detected the touch of Sir Horace Wilson, re-explaining to the President his hopes of *de jure* recognition and asking him to use his influence with Italy to help us reach agreement. I told my colleagues that the question of recognizing Mussolini's Abyssinian conquest was not one for us alone and could not be settled at once. On the other hand, I said, our relations with the United States since the Brussels Conference had been excellent, and I cited as examples the despatch of American cruisers to Singapore, and the sending of a Staff officer to London to discuss naval co-operation. The Prime Minister, in his turn, conceded that I had not the same confidence as he himself had that Mussolini would enter upon conversations with the serious intention of carrying out any agreement reached. He then announced that he had first written privately to Lady Chamberlain saying that he expected conversations to begin. Without his permission she had shown the letter to Count Ciano. This might well make the Italians think we were serious, in which case they would be furious if told that *de jure* recognition must wait for Roosevelt's proposals. I again pointed out that, in fact, recognition must wait, at least for the agreement of the League.

Towards the end of a frustrating discussion, I said that my opinion had not altered. From what had happened at Brussels, I was sure that we could not hope to move either Roosevelt or Hull over *de jure* recognition. If my colleagues doubted this, they should inquire what Lindsay thought. I personally was convinced that the more we argued, the worse relations with the United States would become. If it were known that our Italian negotiations had held up the American proposals, this would be regarded not as a world settlement, but as a 'deal'. In a further effort to meet my colleagues' views, I suggested that perhaps we might say, after Roosevelt's announcement had been made, that we were not prepared to discuss recognition apart from it. This they would not accept. Finally I said that this was a subject on which I felt strongly. I would therefore like to consider the draft further and to discuss the question again with the Prime Minister. We then dispersed wearily.

Later that evening, when I got back to the Foreign Office, I looked through my notes on the Prime Minister's objections and considered the comment which he had made that the President's message would be greeted with shouts of laughter in Nazi Germany. I read again the passage which Chamberlain had quoted from Roosevelt's draft speech:

> New generations have reached adult age since that time and find themselves in a world surcharged with anxiety, where governments are frantically rearming, where the whole people live in constant fear and where physical and economic security for the individual are lacking.

The Prime Minister had said that they did not believe that in Nazi Germany. Maybe, I reflected, they did not, but this seemed to be no reason why we should not state it. He had also criticized the four points on which the President wanted the governments of the world to agree, the first of them being: 'Essential and fundamental principles which should be observed in international relations.' Was it likely, Chamberlain had asked, that the same principles would appeal to the Germans as would appeal to the democratic nations? Perhaps not, I thought, but that should not prevent us from stating our principles publicly, and from supporting the United States when they were doing so.

After dinner, Cadogan, Cranborne, Thomas and Harvey met at my house. Malcolm MacDonald joined us later. Cranborne and I agreed that if we followed the policy of questioning the President further, we ran a grave risk of annoying him, for nothing worthwhile. It was better for us to refuse any more concessions, and resign if necessary. My position was now very difficult, for in a few days' time I was to meet Delbos at Geneva. How could I ask him to agree to recognition, while withholding the information about Roosevelt's initiative and his attitude to such recognition. MacDonald was in a similar predicament. He could scarcely urge the Dominions to accept *de jure* recognition, while keeping them in the dark about American policy. Cadogan was concerned at the possible consequences, if I resigned upon an issue like Anglo-American co-operation. Roosevelt's plan had to remain secret and I should have been unable to defend myself with a full explanation of my resignation. For this and other reasons he wanted to prevent a definite breach between Neville Chamberlain and myself. He said he would draft another telegram, which I agreed to consider, though I had no hopes from it.

During the morning of January 20th, Jim Thomas again saw Sir Horace Wilson, who dismissed the Roosevelt initiative as 'woolly rubbish' and made it perfectly plain that he was using all his powers to persuade the Prime Minister to pour cold water on the American effort, while going ahead with his own plans to appease the dictators. For the first time, Wilson admitted that there was a fundamental difference between Chamberlain and myself in our outlook on foreign policy. Thomas replied that I might have to consider resignation, although that would be difficult because of the need for secrecy about the President's scheme. Thomas's record continues:

> The interview was stormy. I said that if A.E. did resign it might well be that the whole of this American business might leak out from the American end and that the country would then know that the P.M. preferred to turn down the help of a democracy in order that he might pursue his flirtations with the dictators untrammelled. H.W., who was in a towering rage—the first time I have ever seen him in this state—warned me that if America produced the facts he would use the full power of the Government machine in an attack upon A.E's past record with regard to the dictators and the shameful obstruction by the F.O. of the P.M's attempts to save the peace of the world.

Thomas, who drew the conclusion that Wilson had been working up the Prime Minister in no mean fashion, added:

> However, this particular storm passed, although Harvey and Cranborne and I myself felt that the evil was only postponed and almost wished that the break had already come. The atmosphere was becoming intolerable.

When I saw the Prime Minister soon after noon, I had the impression that he was less sure of himself, but he was nothing if not stubborn and still argued tenaciously. He had now, apparently, reached the position of agreeing to parallel action; Roosevelt would go ahead with his plan while we pursued the Duce. In view of the President's declared stand on *de jure* recognition, this seemed an unreal attitude, and I said so to my colleagues when the Foreign Affairs Committee met that afternoon. I reminded them that Sir Ronald Lindsay, after receiving the President's answer to Chamberlain's message, had telegraphed:

> I am impressed at receiving this third warning in regard to *de jure* recognition and Welles' commentary, delivered by the President's instructions, was even more emphatic than the actual message.

I now found a number of Ministers noticeably less stiff. Perhaps the Prime Minister had been shaken by the support given to me by some members of the Committee. MacDonald and Stanley spoke up on my side, while Halifax and Inskip appeared no longer so easy in their minds. Chamberlain, nevertheless, thought that the dictators would regard the Roosevelt plan as being directed specifically at themselves. This seemed to me no valid argument against it. I repeated that I could not approach France or the Dominions about recognition of the conquest of Abyssinia until the American attitude was clarified. In the end, it was agreed that I should produce three draft telegrams. The first would be to the President, asking him to defer his initiative no longer, the second would explain to the President why we had been considering *de jure* recognition, but saying that we now intended to defer this negotiation, and the third would ask Lindsay to obtain certain modifications in the wording of Roosevelt's appeal, if he thought it possible. This amounted, on the face of it, to a reversal of the Prime Minister's attitude. But I had no feeling of triumph. Rather, I wondered whether I could get my colleagues to endorse telegrams couched in terms sufficiently enthusiastic to overcome the President's initial disappointment. I was conscious also that much time had elapsed, it now being more than a week since we had received Lindsay's original telegrams.

* * * * *

On the following morning, January 21st, I produced my draft telegrams at a further meeting of the Committee. The discussion went badly from the first. Some liked my drafts, but more did not. This latter category included the Prime Minister. He remarked ironically that although I had doubtless not intended it, the effect of my telegrams was to put the Italian negotiations out of court. The Committee had in fact agreed, by the instructions given to me the previous day, that they should be subordinated to Roosevelt's new ideas. After much argument, the telegrams were again redrafted, this time by Stanley and MacDonald. I told the Committee that it would save time if I were to state my attitude. I asked whether they had made up their minds to go ahead with the Italian conversations on the basis of *de jure* recognition. As Roosevelt's plan had been intended to improve Anglo-American relations, I did not think we could do something which he had told us would injure them. The Committee accepted that we were not committed to Italian conversations until we could assess the reception given to President Roosevelt's plan.

Four telegrams were finally despatched. Though they were an improvement on the Prime Minister's first reactions, they were a compromise and not what I would have wished to send. The first was a short message from Chamberlain to Roosevelt, concluding:

> I warmly welcome the President's initiative and I will do my best to contribute to the success of his scheme whenever he decides to launch it.

This was less than the assurance which had been originally asked for. A further message to the President set out at length our reasons for contemplating *de jure* recognition and for desiring an appeasement in the Mediterranean situation. The Prime Minister expressed the belief that there might now be a chance to bring Italy and Germany to a frame of mind in which they would co-operate in settling political problems. I did not share this conviction.

The other two telegrams were addressed to Lindsay. One explained that His Majesty's Government were in fact walking a tightrope:

> We are anxious to avoid the position in which the world regards us as sharing with the President the responsibility for his proposals. Lest these proposals receive, shortly after they are launched, a bad reception, we are at the same time anxious that the President should not be able then to turn round and say that we had given him no warning but had given him unqualified encouragement.

Lindsay was told to conduct his conversation with the President so that this balance was kept. He was further instructed to bear in mind several considerations, amongst which were these:

> While the dictators and Japan may decide it to be impolitic to reject the scheme out of hand, they are almost sure, in their hearts, to dislike it. Much of the President's draft circular will cause them intense irritation and will dispose them to use every device to obstruct him at every stage.
>
> In general, the President's scheme is very ambitious. His two main points are the limitation of armaments and equal access to raw materials. We know what difficulties these questions have presented in the past and if the President's scheme runs headlong into these obstructions it may prove very difficult to pull it through.

The other message to Lindsay emphasized the urgency of coming to terms with Italy, but added that we should not in any event embark on conversations for a further week. This was inserted because I feared that Roosevelt might think we were intending to start negotiations with Italy immediately after his appeal had been launched. Fortunately, Lindsay was given discretion to use the telegrams as he saw fit and could be relied upon to lighten their burden and fortify what support we offered.

I felt unhappy at these messages. If the whole business had not been secret, I should have resigned there and then. As it was, I had to content myself with telegraphing personally to Lindsay:

> These telegrams represent a compromise arrived at after long and arduous discussions. If they are not all that I could wish they are the best I could

achieve, and will I trust help you. What seems to me most important in all this is that we should take no step here that might jeopardize growing Anglo-American confidence. It must now rest with the President, Mr. Hull and yourself to tell us frankly whether any course envisaged here, as indicated in those telegrams, could have that effect.

When Lindsay delivered the Prime Minister's messages, Sumner Welles expressed a decided opinion that the President would be pleased. But it was an inconclusive conversation, from which it emerged that Roosevelt was not now likely to launch his plan for a week or more. It seemed that the President would probably wish to ask us further questions. As I expected, Welles registered relief at the assurance that His Majesty's Government would only grant *de jure* recognition in the context of a general settlement with Italy. He said that the President regarded recognition as an unpleasant pill which we should both have to swallow and he wished that we should both swallow it together. His Majesty's Government, he added, wished to swallow it in a general settlement with Italy and the President in a general settlement involving world appeasement.

A strange feature of these discussions before the Foreign Affairs Committee of the Cabinet was that they resulted in four meetings, held over many hours, with much coming and going in Downing Street, without attracting any public attention. The Committee consisted of half the members of the Cabinet including almost all the senior ones, which makes it the more surprising that our deliberations passed unnoticed. Since there have been authoritative statements that the Cabinet, like the public, were not aware of the events I have here described, I must reply that, on January 24th, I gave it a full account of the negotiations and arguments of the previous days. On the morning of the 25th, we received a message to the effect that the President had been 'deeply gratified by the contents of the Prime Minister's two messages'. Further conversations between Lindsay and Welles were promised. I wrote the same day to express my fears privately to our Ambassador:

You will perhaps have guessed from the telegrams that we have been through a very difficult week here. I must confess that when I returned to find the Prime Minister had not accepted the advice you had given him in your telegram I was deeply disappointed. I am sure that we should have been wiser to give the President's scheme full backing from the start while, of course, commenting upon any points which seemed to us to call for it. I am now apprehensive lest the working of recent months should be prejudiced.

To me nothing matters so much in the world today as the steady growth of Anglo-American understanding. It is for this reason that since I have been back I have done my best to induce the Prime Minister to modify the attitude taken up in his earlier telegram. Personally I now hope that Roosevelt will now go ahead. This will probably be known long before you get my letter.

Next time I hope the President will not choose one of my rare leaves in order to take initiatives with the Prime Minister.

* * * * *

On January 25th, I left for the League of Nations Council, having obtained my colleagues' permission to discourage the discussion of *de jure* recognition. Several days passed without further news of the American plan and on January 28th, in my absence at Geneva, the Prime Minister telegraphed to Lindsay saying that it was very difficult to proceed with our policy towards Germany, Italy or Japan until we knew more of Roosevelt's intentions. No very clear statement came from Washington, but it seemed that the United States Administration had no objection to the British Government going ahead with negotiations in Europe, it being understood that *de jure* recognition would only be accorded as part of a general settlement. A few days after this, we learnt that in view of the increased grasp of power by the Nazis in Germany, the President had decided to postpone his plan, at least until after Hitler had spoken on February 20th. I was not mollified to learn from Lindsay's reply to my letter of January 25th that he thought we should have committed a capital error if we had turned the plan down, which was in fact what we had done. The Roosevelt initiative was never made.

This was the most clear-cut division which had so far arisen between Neville Chamberlain and myself. Nothing could have exposed more sharply our differences of approach. In the early days of this episode, no representations from without influenced our judgement. Chamberlain's first reaction on reading Roosevelt's message was the exact opposite of mine. He believed the dictators to be anxious for genuine agreements and himself to be the only man who could negotiate them. His attitude was only excusable on these grounds. I strongly doubted whether either Hitler or Mussolini was in any way interested in coming to worthwhile terms with us and I wanted to strengthen our hand by every means, amongst which, closer Anglo-American relations had a first place. The Prime Minister, and most of his Cabinet, did not look beyond the Roosevelt plan itself, which admittedly might have failed, to the beneficent consequences which might have flowed from it, even in failure. This was exactly the situation which Chamberlain's mind, accustomed to judging plans on the short view, was unable to master.

* * * * *

Many years later, when I was out of office after the war, I was in Washington to attend the unveiling by President Truman of the memorial to my friend Field-Marshal Sir John Dill in Arlington Cemetery, an honour never before or since accorded to a British soldier. During my brief stay, Sumner Welles asked me to visit him at his lovely home in Maryland. I have known no man in the United States who had a clearer perception than he of the course of international diplomacy in the last years before the second world war. We agreed that a comparable opportunity had never occurred, nor been created, after this date to avert that catastrophe.

XIII

PEACE IN YOUR TIME

January – February 1938

A question of Italy and Spain – I require conversations on our terms – Further divergence over President Roosevelt's plan – Mr. Chamberlain hardens his attitude – 'Peace in your time' – The Italian Ambassador declines an interview – Lady Chamberlain's letter – The Foreign Affairs Committee of back-benchers – The Prime Minister, Count Grandi and myself – The incident of the taxi-cab – Sir John Simon's advice – A telephone conversation with Mr. Churchill

On my way to Geneva on January 25th, I stopped off in Paris, as I had so often done before. The atmosphere was now very different from the equivocal days of Flandin and Laval. I dined with the French Prime Minister, M. Chautemps, and the Foreign Minister, M. Delbos. We discussed possible conversations with Italy and I told them that His Majesty's Government had not yet taken any final decision, but that they had in mind the opening of talks with the Italian Government. Great Britain, I said, could only grant *de jure* recognition of the conquest of Abyssinia as part of a general settlement, which would include propaganda, Spain, the Italian garrison in Libya, the Red Sea and possibly some demilitarization in the Mediterranean itself. The French Ministers shared this opinion, attaching importance to the inclusion of the Spanish question among the essential subjects of agreement. I told them that His Majesty's Government wished to act in this matter only with the full support of the French Government and asked them to let me know what their requirements would be.

Three days later, Cranborne and I saw Delbos again, this time at Geneva. He feared that the Italian Government might despatch further men and materials to Spain. It would be impossible, he said, to hold conversations which must depend for their success on confidence in Mussolini's undertakings, if he were all the time violating his promises. When I returned to London on January 30th, I minuted to the Foreign Office about our projected talks with the Duce:

Do we really believe that we can reach an agreement with Italy of any real value if the Spanish question is not dealt with? A year ago we attempted this: we signed an agreement which ignored the Spanish situation and a fortnight afterwards Italy began sending men in large quantities to Spain. Any repetition of such an event—and it can surely not be ruled out as a possibility—would finally destroy our new agreement as it began to destroy our old agreement a year ago. If we are to ask the League to approve our agreement with Italy and to authorize us to grant *de jure* recognition on account of that agreement, there must be some contribution in it to European appeasement. Spain is clearly the largest contribution of this kind that can be made.

Moreover, is it so certain that Signor Mussolini would dislike to discuss the Spanish situation with us in our conversations? After all, he has clearly some anxious decisions to take in the next few months.

In any event it is surely true that so long as the Spanish situation continues with recurrent bombings of the civilian population by Italian aeroplanes and other manifestations of Italian intervention in one form or another, there cannot be an improvement in relations between this country and Italy. Signor Grandi well realizes this, indeed, he often refers to the Spanish shadow. As soon as we have received President Roosevelt's reaction, I would therefore favour opening conversations with the Italians, making it clear that *de jure* was among the topics to be discussed and Spain also. Our objective in respect of Spain would be no more than the fulfilment of the British plan which the Italian Government accepted several months ago. Once that was carried through, *de jure* could be given. A Red Sea agreement in addition would be useful, also agreements about Libya and propaganda; but if an agreement could be reached about Spain this would be the most important. In other words, I should, subject again to what President Roosevelt has to say, be prepared to barter *de jure* against the liquidation of foreign intervention in Spain, on the basis of our own plan.

That evening I went to see Neville Chamberlain. He was reading *The House that Hitler Built*, a book written by Stephen Roberts, an Australian, which contained a realistic account of the Nazi regime, its practices and purposes. I too had read it and thought it good, but it said no more than the Foreign Office had been saying for months. Yet it had deeply impressed the Prime Minister. As we talked of it, Chamberlain even went so far as to suggest that if we could not reach agreement, we might have to aim at the encirclement of Germany and a possible alliance with Russia. I was encouraged by this realism though I did not understand its cause. The mood did not last. There were always those ready to persuade Chamberlain that a fresh initiative towards the dictators would yield lasting results and that he was the man in all the world to make it. On this score he was the subject of incessant flattery. This is a form of adulation to which Prime Ministers must expect to be subject, it is gratifying to indulge and hard to resist.

We next discussed Italian problems and I told Chamberlain that I had reached some definite conclusions on the subject. I was convinced that Spain must be covered in any agreement with Mussolini. Apart from the merits of doing this, we could not carry the French with us otherwise. If we were able to secure the withdrawal of foreign volunteers from the civil war, it would be a contribution to peace and would be so regarded by the rest of the world. On the other hand, an individual settlement with Italy would merely look like a rather shady bargain and would certainly not be acceptable either to Roosevelt or to the League of Nations. Moreover, if, as I feared was likely, the Italian troops were only withdrawn from Libya to be sent to Spain, or if the bombing of Barcelona by Fascist aeroplanes continued, any good result from an Anglo-Italian *détente* would be destroyed. The Prime Minister appeared to agree.

* * * * *

There was no improvement in, or off, Spain. At the beginning of February, two of our ships had been sunk, one by submarine and the other by air attack. We retaliated by resuming the full Nyon patrol, which had recently been relaxed, and public opinion supported us in ascribing the sudden intensification of the war to Mussolini's action. I saw the French and Italian Ambassadors and told them we intended to sink any submerged submarine encountered in our area. The Admiralty feared that this would impair the relations which they had established with General Franco's Admiral Moreno, who was informing us confidentially where his submarines were working. Despite the slightly Gilbertian flavour of all this, I would not agree to call off the patrol, and the French Government took similar action in their area.

These events brought with them, as firmness towards Mussolini so often did, an improvement in our relations with Rome. On February 4th Count Grandi delivered a note, in which the Italian Government agreed to resume its part in the Nyon patrols. He spoke of Spain as the great stumbling block in the way of improving relations between our two countries, and said he wished we could work together to ease the civil war. He agreed with two points which I then put to him; that a stalemate had been reached in Spain and that there was now far less danger of either Bolshevism or of Fascism. I told him that if we could together clear up the position in Spain, immediate difficulties in the way of Anglo-Italian conversations would be removed.

This talk left me wondering how much it was safe to deduce from the Ambassador's remarks. If Grandi really represented Mussolini, it might be that he was putting out a feeler with the object of disentangling Italy from Spain, though this was hard to credit. At this stage we still did not know when President Roosevelt might launch his plan. Meanwhile I wanted to go ahead methodically with my conversations with Grandi, for to show ourselves too eager would not help agreement. We now had a strong moral position which, coupled with our rearmament, was bringing us increasing authority in the world, while Mussolini's position was weakening.

I was confirmed in my views as to how to treat the negotiation with the Duce by a memorandum written by Lord Cranborne, who had returned from Geneva on February 3rd. He reported that he had heard many tributes to the increasingly tough British attitude as a stabilizing factor in the international situation. Cranborne's opinion, with which I entirely agreed, was that we had no need to run after Mussolini, whose economic position was precarious and whose policy was almost certainly to seek friendship with both Germany and Great Britain, playing off the one against the other.

On Friday, February 4th, I received a message from Chamberlain asking me to summon Grandi to meet us on the following Tuesday. I reminded him that the Cabinet had decided that the question of opening conversations with Italy was to be reconsidered by them after Roosevelt's reactions had become known. But I did see Grandi on February 5th and indicated to him that the question of anti-British propaganda was among the difficulties which persisted between us and that I had told the House of Commons we would not open conversations until the position had improved. The Ambassador, reasonably enough, suggested that I might give him a dossier of our complaints. I agreed to discuss them with him and suggested that neither of us would look upon such an exchange as an opening of conversations, but rather as paving the way for them. Later, Grandi said that in many respects he would prefer that the conversations themselves should take place in Rome, where Count Ciano could speak with full authority, but, after all, four of us were concerned with Anglo-Italian relations, he and I in London and Count Ciano and Lord Perth in Rome. I suggested that if he and I could make some preliminary progress with the really difficult subjects, which were Spain and propaganda, then other matters, like the Red Sea, and even Libya, would be easier of solution. Grandi assented and agreed that the main difficulty for his Government, as he saw it, was to reconcile our requirements in respect of Spain with their obligations to General Franco, whom they could not abandon completely.

Returning to the Foreign Office after the weekend, I was much annoyed to find telegrams from Lord Perth showing that Lady Chamberlain had been visiting Mussolini and Ciano and reading to them another letter from the Prime Minister.

The Duce had taken the opportunity to dictate a reply which included four points which the agreement should cover. These were propaganda, the Mediterranean, colonies and economics. This was the first time we had heard of colonies or of economics as issues between us. There was no mention of Spain. Mussolini was good enough also to explain that it would be useful for the Conservative Party to make such an agreement, because he thought that the Labour Party, if they won the next election, would make one, as Mr. Ramsay MacDonald had done in 1924. I did not know whether this referred to the agreement with Soviet Russia in that year, or to the cession of Jubaland to Mussolini, probably the latter. In any event, this was no way to conduct diplomacy. Lady Chamberlain's activities were creating confusion and the news that she had elected to stay a further month in Rome did not raise my spirits. I wrote to the Prime Minister on February 8th complaining that this kind of unofficial diplomacy placed me in a most difficult position:

> It recreates in Mussolini's mind the impression that he can divide us and he will be the less ready to pay attention to what I have to say to Grandi. Indeed, I can see that whatever Ciano reports from Grandi, Mussolini will say: 'I know that the Prime Minister is determined to open conversations in February, so do not pay any attention to any conditions Eden may be trying to impose.' Mussolini has clearly and, as he would, very skilfully, taken every advantage of the opening which Lady Chamberlain afforded him and will no doubt gain the impression from that interview that we are most eager for conversations. Already Rome is giving out the impression from that interview that we are courting her, with the purpose, no doubt, of showing Berlin how worth courting she is. This is exactly the hand which Mussolini

always likes to play and plays with so much skill when he gets a chance. I do not think we should let him.

I then tried to impress on the Prime Minister the real facts:

As I see it, the position is now this. Mussolini is in an extremely uncomfortable position. He has commitments in Abyssinia and Spain, neither of which is turning out well. He now sees a government in power in Berlin which, it is quite true, is comparatively enthusiastic for the Rome–Berlin Axis, but which is also apparently determined to pursue a more active foreign policy in Central Europe with Austria as the first item on its list of intended victims. In such a position we have nothing to gain by showing ourselves over-eager. If Mussolini is really anxious to reach a settlement with us, then the opportunity we are affording him of liquidating his commitments in Spain gives him an excellent chance of proving his sincerity. He will now, moreover, have heard from Grandi how ready we are to take up this question without delay.

I held to this opinion throughout the next fortnight. At this stage it appeared that the Prime Minister agreed. After saying blandly that he did not think Lady Chamberlain's unorthodox procedure had done any harm, he added that he quite appreciated our strong position in relation to Italy, which we could use when bargaining. But the Prime Minister thought that we should avoid giving the impression of not wanting conversations at all.

I did not dissent from this, for I was in favour of continuing my own talks with Grandi. If the hostile broadcasts diminished as a result, we might advance step by step to other subjects. This course would be preferable to the inauguration of formal conversations between Perth and Ciano in Rome, with all the publicity involved. I feared that unless Spain were brought at once into the discussions, some new incident, such as the despatch of fresh Italian reinforcements to that country, would halt further progress. These considerations were placed before the Cabinet, which endorsed them.

I hoped at this time that we were on the point of bringing off a mass exchange of prisoners and hostages in Spain, under British auspices. If Mussolini had now decided that his Spanish commitment was embarrassing, here was an opportunity for him and others to disengage. With Grandi in his present mood, there was a fair chance that I would be able to make progress in my conversations with him, since Britain was negotiating from strength. But at this juncture a press campaign began in Britain, bearing all the marks of authoritative inspiration and speaking of the prospects of early and complete agreement with the Duce. I thought this most unwise. The Foreign Office News Department told me that the source of this silly campaign was No. 10 Downing Street. I taxed the Prime Minister with it, but he denied all knowledge. However, there could be no doubt that these ideas emanated from outside the Foreign Office and I heard that the story had been given out by Sir Joseph Ball, head of the Research Department of the Conservative Central Office. It seemed just the way to arouse exaggerated hopes and to make Mussolini more intransigent, for he must certainly think that we would pay a high price for an agreement if this were our temper. I gathered that even the Italian Ambassador was alarmed.

On February 10th, I had another talk with Grandi lasting more than an hour. He reported that the Italian Government were ready to open conversations at any time, on as wide a basis as possible, to include *de jure* recognition, but not excluding Spain. He stated that the number of Italian volunteers there had been reduced. I put to him the difficulty of the British Government over *de jure* recognition, in that they must act as loyal members of the League of Nations, and observed that if our two Governments could make a real contribution to better European relations, world opinion would approve. Hence the importance of dealing with Spain. I gave him details of the scheme for withdrawing volunteers and establishing the criterion of 'substantial progress' which I intended to put to the two parties in Spain. I also took the opportunity to hand the Italian Ambassador a summary of recent Bari broadcasts with their incessantly hostile references to Britain. I finished this interview with a faint feeling of confidence that Mussolini might possibly want talks between us to succeed.

* * * * *

Our exchanges with Washington had by this time shown that we could not expect the President to make a move for another fortnight. Now we learnt from our Embassy that Cordell Hull, though not the President, thought the British Government only lukewarm towards the Roosevelt plan. I gave the Prime Minister a draft reply in which we assured Roosevelt that we most certainly did welcome his initiative. Once again, Chamberlain wished to weaken the text and in the end a telegram only fairly satisfactory from my point of view was despatched. It became clearer every day that we had discouraged Roosevelt's scheme to death.

It was on February 7th that Vansittart came to see me to report a conversation in which a member of the Cabinet had said that Sir Robert had been 'kicked upstairs'. This colleague had gone on to say that, from now on, foreign affairs would be run by the Prime Minister, with the help of a small committee, of which the spokesman naturally would be a member, and that if I myself did not fall in with their wishes, I should follow Vansittart pretty soon. One of Sir Robert's friends who was present had written the conversation down and brought it to him. I thought the Prime Minister should know of this, so I told him. He greeted the story with astonishment. I was not reassured. Nevertheless, in the mood of candour, almost of co-operation which this conversation induced, I determined to ask for the Prime Minister's help about Staff conversations with the French. This he undertook to give me.

On the evening of Saturday, February 12th, I spoke to the Junior Imperial League of the Western Midlands area at Birmingham. This was an intelligently organized and fervent meeting in a packed Town Hall, with the young Unionist Member of Parliament, Ronald Cartland, in the chair. Cartland was a brilliant speaker and he shared my beliefs with passionate conviction. By a coincidence, the last big political meeting which I addressed as Foreign Secretary in 1938 and the last which I addressed as Prime Minister in 1956, were both of young Conservatives. In 1938 I was near them in age and in 1956 I was too far their senior, but on each occasion they provided me with a most cherished memory of my public life. I was sure the country's mood was anti-dictator and anti-defeatist and I spoke as I felt, in terms which secured enthusiastic agreement:

> If I say that the life of a Foreign Secretary is a busy and anxious one, do not think that I am complaining; but in the present state of the world the difficulties are bound at times to seem overwhelming, and they would indeed be overwhelming without the sympathy and understanding of the younger generation. I say especially the 'younger generation' because the Government today must strive in its foreign policy not only for peace in our time but for peace in yours. And if we are to have peace in your time it means that in any agreements we make today there must be no sacrifice of principles and no shirking of responsibilities merely to obtain quick results that may not be permanent. . . . We offer friendship to all, but on equal terms. For it is not by seeking to buy temporary goodwill that peace is made, but on a basis of frank reciprocity with mutual respect. . . .
>
> In a very changing world there is one thing which does not change—the qualities which have created for the British nation the position it holds in the

world today. Those who take a pessimistic view of our future would do well to study again the records of our past, they would do well to note the constant re-assertion of that same British character which, in spite of failures and defects, has made our history. So long as that remains, true and unimpaired, I see no cause for pessimism, or for that particular form of political pessimism which goes by the name of defeatism. An ugly name for an ugly thing.

* * * * *

Although we did not know it until a few days later, while I was speaking in Birmingham, the Austrian Chancellor, Dr. Kurt von Schuschnigg, was being browbeaten at Berchtesgaden. As always in dictatorships, the crux of the matter was control of the police. Hitler insisted that the Austrian Nazi, Artur von Seyss-Inquart, should become Minister of the Interior. I thought that the Austrian President, Wilhelm Miklas, might refuse to accept this surrender, but it was only a faint hope. From these events, we in the Foreign Office drew a conclusion, which our secret information confirmed. Mussolini had given Hitler at least a nod of acquiescence in his Austrian enterprise, probably in return for a pledge of support in Spain. If it had been possible to save Austria by a discussion in Rome, I would have been ready to do so, but it was not. Mussolini had no power to hold Addis Ababa and Cadiz as well as Austria.

Ciano had written in his diary a few weeks earlier:

> Mussolini is annoyed. He said this morning that when the Spanish question is liquidated, he will invite Göring to Nazify Austria.*

Argumentative exchanges were still continuing between the Prime Minister and myself about a meeting with Grandi. On February 16th I wrote to Chamberlain, suggesting that it would be unwise to court the publicity involved in a visit to No. 10:

> I might ask Grandi to come and see me tomorrow—after all, his Spanish answer is long overdue—and in the course of conversation, which would include Austria, propose a meeting with you for a few days hence. Perhaps the best form of all would be to ask him and you both to lunch at my house. This would give an opportunity for the talk without the dramatic effect which a meeting between us at No. 10 at this juncture must have in Europe.

But later that day the Prime Minister told me that the Italian Ambassador has asked to see him. Whether intermediaries between the

* op. cit.

Italian Embassy and No. 10 played any part in these arrangements, I do not know. From Lord Templewood's account it appears that they did.* If so, they certainly served Mussolini well.

I told the Prime Minister that I preferred to continue with the conversations on which I was already engaged and to ask Grandi for Mussolini's reply about the Spanish withdrawal scheme. We could then arrange a joint meeting with the Prime Minister for the following week. Chamberlain first of all agreed, but when I summoned Grandi, the Ambassador excused himself from coming to the Foreign Office on purely frivolous grounds, he wanted to play golf. I was quite sure he would not have sent such a reply unless he had been encouraged to do so, as I then imagined, from Rome. When I met Chamberlain at a luncheon on the next day, I said that I still thought it right I should see Grandi alone in the first instance. This failed to convince the Prime Minister, who was frostily determined to see Grandi himself. Reluctantly I accepted that we should foregather on the following day. I was sorry about this, for I believed that my method of doing business with Grandi was more likely to lead to results than the over-eager intervention of No. 10.

There was no information from Rome to show that any real progress was in sight, so I wrote to Chamberlain again:

> I have just seen the telegrams from Perth. These would seem to indicate that Grandi will at our interview tomorrow make an earnest appeal for the immediate opening of conversations in Rome. It does not appear that he will bring us much in the way of a contribution about Spain, but that of course remains to be seen. My own strong feeling is that we must be very careful not to commit ourselves either way in response to Grandi's prayer—if a prayer it be—until we have had time to go carefully into all the implications. It may be that the decisions we shall have to take will entail momentous consequences. Such information as we have here tends to strengthen the view that there is some kind of arrangement between Rome and Berlin and that Mussolini has, or thinks he has, some kind of *quid pro quo* from Berlin in in return for his acquiescence in Austrian events. That, at least, is my belief, though I should be the first to admit the extreme difficulty of assessing anything accurately in this situation.
>
> My petition, therefore, is that whatever Grandi says to us tomorrow we should content ourselves with saying that we will carefully consider it and send for him again.
>
> Vansittart, who as you know has always been a strong partisan for Anglo-Italian conversations, has just come into my room. He agrees with this, and

* Viscount Templewood: *Nine Troubled Years*; Collins, 1954.

is now very doubtful whether Mussolini is sincere, or whether he may not be 'playing us along'.

I feel sure you will agree we should not commit ourselves tomorrow.

In the next day or two I became increasingly convinced, especially from our secret sources, that Hitler intended to seize Austria and that Mussolini had acquiesced. I was therefore more and more reluctant to open conversations in Rome at this moment. It would be humiliating for us to be talking there when Hitler marched into Vienna, and while Mussolini was reinforcing his troops in Spain and asking for recognition of his Abyssinian empire.

That evening a message arrived from Lady Chamberlain for the Prime Minister:

Count Ciano lunched with me today and asked me whether I had any further message from you. I said 'no'. He then begged me to let you know time is everything. Today an agreement will be easy but things are happening in Europe which will make it impossible tomorrow.

This message greatly impressed Chamberlain, but to me it was familiar language. We had been told before that we must make yet another concession or Mussolini would agree with Hitler. The same argument had been used to justify the raising of sanctions and the Gentleman's Agreement. Neither had had encouraging results. I did not like the note of threat. As almost always with dictators, the appetite grows with what it feeds upon, so that this time the language was more vehement than before. Ciano summed it all up admirably in his diary: 'Mussolini, when he has obtained something, always asks for more.'*

On the morning of February 18th, I read the record of a meeting held the previous evening by the Foreign Affairs Committee, which was composed of Members of Parliament supporting the National Government. They had shown themselves robust. Mr. Harold Nicolson had said that any nervous advances to Germany or Italy would suggest fear and this was not a moment to show the slightest move in the direction of *de jure* recognition of Italy's conquest of Abyssinia. This last remark was cheered by the Committee, which appeared to be unanimous against attempting to buy Italian friendship on this condition. Mr. Winston Churchill spoke of me in generous terms and asked the Committee to rally behind me at this difficult time. He remarked that if we were weak now, the risk of war would inevitably

* op. cit., May 7th, 1939.

be greater in the future; his private information service was, as always, excellent.

The officers of the Committee included Mr. Paul Emrys-Evans as chairman, Mr. Nicolson as vice-chairman and Mr. John McEwen as secretary. They had all been in the Diplomatic Service and were then friendly to me and my opinions. The purpose of the meeting had clearly been to strengthen my hand in what they rightly sensed to be a time for decision. Their enterprise caused disquiet in the Whips' office, where the Chief Whip, Captain David Margesson, sought to persuade Mr. Emrys-Evans to tone down the firm terms of his communiqué. The milder version which he offered in compromise aroused an indignant commentary from Mr. Churchill. At the time, I knew nothing of all this save the barest outlines.

On the morning of February 18th, I walked across to 10 Downing Street to join the Prime Minister. Together we received the Italian Ambassador. I print as Appendix C the British record of this meeting. I made this record and it was afterwards approved as correct by the Prime Minister and given to the Cabinet. Count Grandi's record* was not known to us until the Italian archives were opened after the war.

The Prime Minister began by remarking upon the anxious international situation, with Austria as its most recent development. Grandi regretted what had happened in that country, but assured the Prime Minister that there was no truth in what people were saying, that there was some agreement between Germany and Italy in the matter. He admitted, however, that Italy had been expecting this to happen. Grandi thought Mussolini had done very well to 'preserve the integrity of events in Austria' during the past three years. When Chamberlain suggested that all was not yet lost in Austria, the Ambassador replied that possibly we were only at the end of the third act of four. In the view of Italy, however, Germany was now at the Brenner. Italy could not be left alone with two great potential enemies, Germany and Great Britain.

There followed a remarkable account of Anglo-Italian relations since Stresa, from which it appeared that all the faults lay on our side. The post-sanctions period, Grandi said, had been worse than the sanctions period itself. Disappointments had further poisoned the atmosphere. The hopes of the Gentleman's Agreement had not been fulfilled. The Ambassador did not mention the reason why they were dashed, which was the despatch of Fascist forces to Spain. He complained that

* *Ciano's Diplomatic Papers*; Odhams Press, 1948. See also Appendix D.

'the happy fortnight', after the Prime Minister's letter to Mussolini, had been 'marred by events in the Mediterranean'. There was no mention that these events were the sinking of British and other merchant ships by Italian submarines.

Chamberlain drew Grandi's attention to Ciano's remark that an early start should be made with our conversations, in view of the possibility of certain future happenings, and mentioned the message to the same effect which he had received from his sister-in-law. The Prime Minister asked Count Grandi to throw light on what should have been apparent as characteristic Fascist blackmail. Grandi obliged most skilfully by explaining that there was very little time left before Italy drew still closer to Germany.

The agenda for the conversations was then discussed, Grandi explaining that, in the view of his Government, the talks should include everything and we could both raise any subject that we desired. Chamberlain having said that he had hoped to hold the talks in London, Grandi explained that he thought Ciano would wish to take part from the beginning. He therefore did not think it possible for conversations to be held with the best chance of success anywhere but in Rome. There seemed to me no reason why Ciano should be immobile. I had not so far said a word, but before we were committed to Canossa I decided to intervene. I asked Grandi what effect the opening of conversations might have on the Italian attitude towards Austria. Count Grandi replied that it was difficult for him to answer that, except to say that it would give his people more courage.

I then inquired whether the Italian Government could now exchange views with the other Stresa signatories on the subject of Austria. In reply, the Ambassador made it clear that his Government would not be able to do that; indeed, he said he had no instructions at all to mention Austria. This was an honest answer, which left me in no doubt that there was nothing to be gained, on Austria's behalf, by the immediate exchange of talks in Rome. I glanced across at the Prime Minister to see if he had seized the point, but he only looked impatient to get on.

The conversation concluded with a discussion of the Spanish problem. I asked Grandi whether he was yet in a position to give the Italian reply about my formula for the withdrawal of volunteers from Spain, which had been proposed to him ten days before. The Ambassador's answer showed that Mussolini was not yet prepared to accept this. On the Spanish question generally, Grandi maintained that it would be a mistake to hold up progress in Anglo-Italian conversations over a matter which involved others. Chamberlain asked the Italian Ambassador to return at 3 p.m., explaining that he wished to talk over the situation with me.

* * * * *

These are the notes which I wrote some fifteen years ago about this meeting:

This was a most extraordinary interview. Chamberlain did not want me to be present, but I insisted, Grandi having ducked me for some days.

N.C. asked Grandi to speak to us of Anglo-Italian relations and Grandi, who was a very skilful diplomat, did his stuff admirably. Whenever he paused, N.C. encouraged him. He sat there nodding his head approvingly, while Grandi detailed one grievance after another. The more N.C. nodded the more outrageous became Grandi's account until in the end it would almost seem that we had invaded Abyssinia. If N.C. had kept his head still we should have been spared two-thirds of this. But it was after Grandi's departure that N.C. was most amazing.

I recorded in my diary at the time:

After the conversation with Grandi, which had been adjourned, N.C. made it clear that he knew exactly what he wanted to do. He wanted to tell Grandi at 3 o'clock that we would open conversations at once, send for Perth and announce that he was coming home in order to prepare for opening conversations in Rome.

I demurred, pointing out that we had still made very little progress with the Spanish affair and that I was frankly suspicious of the 'now or never' attitude, or 'last chance' atmosphere of the telegram [reporting Count Ciano's remarks to Lady Chamberlain]. We had been told that so often before.

Upon this, N.C. became very vehement, more vehement than I have ever seen him, and strode up and down the room saying with great emphasis, 'Anthony, you have missed chance after chance. You simply cannot go on like this.'

I said, 'Your methods are right if you have faith in the man you are negotiating with.' N.C. replied, 'I have.'

We then discussed what we should do next. I said that I could not agree to the course he proposed and asked that we should take the advice of our colleagues before any decision was reached.

I then lunched in the Foreign Office with Cranborne and Alec Cadogan. We were all agreed that it was quite impossible to announce conversations now and that this question must come before the Cabinet, to whom I would state my views. We could not be rushed into a published decision of this importance without even getting agreement with the French. *De jure* recognition concerned not only the League, but also the small powers. They would not thank us for giving the doctrine of non-recognition a mortal blow, thereby creating a precedent which might affect any one of them. Moreover, one of the main provisions of the Gentleman's Agreement concerned anti-British propaganda, which had not ceased, but had indeed been intensified. An object of the agreement now suggested was to induce Mussolini to do what he had already pledged himself to do, while we made substantial concessions. I was not prepared to accept this. I told Cranborne and Cadogan that if the Cabinet disagreed with me, as I feared they would, I should resign.

I saw Chamberlain again at 2.30 p.m. After an argument, he agreed to hold a Cabinet on the following day, Saturday, and to press the Ambassador for some expression of the Italian Government's attitude to our formula for the withdrawal of volunteers from Spain. This much decided, we sat gloomily side by side waiting for Grandi, who called at 3 p.m. The Prime Minister told him that he proposed to consult his colleagues and would give the considered view of His Majesty's Government on Monday. When asked about the formula, Grandi retreated from the modest advance he had previously made, to the extent of describing it as a trap, in its present form. It would not be possible for the Italian Government to accept the formula, which would have the appearance of letting down General Franco. I explained to Grandi that the whole purpose of the formula was to avoid that. The Ambassador eventually said that he would consult his Government further on this question.

Count Grandi's account of events loses nothing in the telling. He had, however, correctly gauged Chamberlain's eagerness to begin conversations and his consequent willingness to accept Italian wishes as to time and place and to make no conditions. There was a sting in the tail of the despatch, which was to cause charges and counter-charges ten years later. This was a reference by Grandi to alleged contacts between himself and a confidential agent of the Prime Minister, which included an appointment in a taxi-cab after our meeting in Downing Street.

During these weeks, I had neither knowledge nor suspicion of any contact between the Prime Minister and the Italian Embassy. The full story will probably never be known, but the existing accounts are published as Appendix D to this book.

* * * * *

The pressure from Mussolini and Ciano for these talks to begin at once might seem difficult to explain, since even when they got their way after my departure from office, they made no haste to conclude them. I did not think so. The explanation is that Mussolini knew that the occupation of Austria was not far off and that the further help he must give General Franco with volunteers from Italy would be unpopular at home. He badly needed a prestige success. The opening of conversations which were to include, as the Duce could be trusted to let it be known, the *de jure* recognition of his Abyssinian conquest by the great power which had principally opposed it, would be a feather in his cap worth flaunting against the winds which must blow from the Brenner. As Sir Lewis Namier was to write some years later:

> A friendly Mussolini was, in the schemes of the appeasers, to restrain Hitler and his encroachments: seldom has a more inappropriate part been assigned to a jackal.*

* * * * *

A little later in the afternoon of February 18th, Neville Chamberlain rang me up to say that he had just seen Simon on another matter and had told him of our differences. He added: 'Though I don't suppose it will influence you, I can tell you that he agreed with me.' I replied: 'That will certainly not influence me.' The Prime Minister then said: 'I felt I ought to tell you this. I have no objection if you wish to mention the matter to one of our colleagues.' I did so to Walter Elliot, who was perturbed.

Soon afterwards I received a message from John Simon that he would like to see me urgently. I tried to avoid this meeting, since I had to leave in a few minutes for an appointment in my constituency that evening. But Simon was very insistent and, short of being rude, I was obliged to agree. To my surprise, when he came over to the Foreign Office he walked up and down my room, speaking of several matters, but did not even mention my differences with the Prime Minister. After a time, I said I was sorry to have to hurry him, but I really must leave to catch my train. He was perfectly amiable, turned on his heel and said: 'Take care of yourself, Anthony. You look rather tired. Are you certain that you're all right?' I assured him that I was in perfect health. Simon had perhaps forgotten how he had told me that the last question in a cross-examination is the one that counts.

* Sir Lewis Namier: *Europe in Decay*; Macmillan, 1950.

This interview had a sequel of which the following is Jim Thomas' account:

On Simon's return to the Treasury he telephoned to me and asked to see me. I offered to go over to him but he said (presumably to flatter me) that he would come to me at the Foreign Office. As I had no room of my own this extraordinary interview took place in the passage. He opened by saying that he was as fond of Anthony as if he had been his own son, that he was becoming more and more depressed in watching A.E. at Cabinet Meetings and in realizing that he was both physically and mentally ill. Nothing but six months' holiday could restore him and that it was very important that I should go away with him. During this period he and his Cabinet colleagues would keep his seat warm for him and look after foreign affairs.

I replied that Anthony had just returned from a good holiday in the South of France and that his health had indeed never been better. Simon then told me that resignation would be 'fatal to the Government, the country, nay the peace of the whole world'; that all this lay in my hands, and he begged me to be sensible and take Anthony away. On my direct negative he popped his hat on his head, walked down the stairs and did not speak to me again until he had become Lord Chancellor in May 1940.

* * * * *

One night in the winter of 1948, I arrived back at my house in London to find a message from Mr. Winston Churchill, asking me to telephone him in the country, however late I got in. I rang up Chartwell, to find him in high spirits. 'Have you read the Grandi despatch?' he asked. I had to admit that I had not. 'You must. It is most important. It will make you purr like six kittens.' 'I've been told that it shows Neville was foolish in trusting to Grandi's assurances.' 'Foolish! It shows that he was determined to do you in. After this the Municheers can never hold up their heads again.'

Mr. Churchill then sent for his spectacles and read me out long extracts. Finally, he reached the point where I was described as being an inveterate enemy of Fascism: 'You ought to put that in your next election address.'

XIV

RESIGNATION

February 1938

Conversations with Italy still debated – The first crucial Cabinet meeting – The Prime Minister speaks – I deploy my arguments – Reactions in the Cabinet – A Sunday talk with the Prime Minister – The second Cabinet meeting – Pressures behind the scenes – The final meeting – I tender my resignation – Reflections on my relations with Mr. Chamberlain – I explain my position to the House of Commons – Letters from two Ambassadors and others – My speech to my constituents – Their unanimous support

I was back in London on Saturday, February 19th, about an hour before the Cabinet was due to meet, and began to prepare my brief. I set down my opinion, already known to the Prime Minister, that it was imprudent to open formal conversations at once in Rome, and that there must be some indication of Mussolini's good faith before we did so. We were not, after all, asking that Mussolini should make new commitments in advance; we were only asking him to honour promises already made and broken at his will. I was ready to continue my conversations with Grandi at the Foreign Office and I thought that we could make useful preliminary progress this way and get some earlier promises honoured, once Mussolini understood that he could not have his *de jure* recognition of the conquest of Abyssina in any other way.

At the Foreign Office I discussed the prospects with Sir Alexander Cadogan, who suggested that I might agree to open conversations in Rome, provided that they were linked with a Spanish settlement. Another view was that I should agree, so long as it was stressed that Mussolini had asked for conversations and that it was made clear beyond all doubt that nothing would be signed until all Italians had left Spain. I did not like these compromises and considered that to open conversations in Rome now, when the diplomatic floor was littered with Mussolini's earlier broken promises, was too humiliating. Even a halt to hostile Italian broadcasts would be some progress. As it was, we were simply debasing international good faith. I had had enough of that. I resolved to resign if the Cabinet disagreed with me.

A Minister should never threaten resignation lightly, nor should he imagine that under our system of government he can always have his own way. He is responsible for the running of his department, not only to his colleagues and to Parliament, but also to the nation and to himself, and there may come a time when he has to insist that a proposed step is injurious to the country's best interests. He must then resign rather than carry it out. The relationship between a Foreign Secretary and a Prime Minister is particularly delicate. They must be in sympathy or they cannot achieve anything. Chamberlain admitted that our readings of the dictators and their intentions were in conflict. As Lord Halifax was to write many years later: 'the parting was inevitable.'* I felt that I had reached the point when I must declare this and accept the consequences.

The early part of the afternoon brought two visitors, Malcolm MacDonald, who declared roundly that No. 10 had treated me abominably, and John Simon, who failed to see that any question of principle arose. According to him, it was only a question of timing.

The rumours of disagreements in the Cabinet had caused a large crowd to gather in Downing Street. They gave me a friendly cheer as I walked across to the crucial meeting. The Prime Minister explained his desire to improve relations with Germany and Italy. He complained of the heavy financial burden imposed by rearmament, which we could not escape unless we could make some arrangement which would include a reduction of armaments within a reasonable time. He had therefore thought it necessary to consider whether to make yet another attempt to ease the situation, either by some concessions to Germany or by some adjustment with Italy. He considered that Italy was like a hysterical woman. She felt that we had thwarted her in her assault on Abyssinia and deeply resented it. However, he went on, the Italians had recently become rather more amenable. When we had given drastic instructions to our warships as to submarine attacks, Mussolini had volunteered to do the same. The Prime Minister admitted this might have little practical effect, but argued that it was a valuable gesture. He

* Earl of Halifax: *Fulness of Days*; Collins, 1957.

had no doubt it was due to Fascist belief that there was some prospect of conversations. I thought that the more probable reason was that Mussolini had no choice but to join us or be ignored, as after Nyon.

Chamberlain believed that events in Austria must be unpalatable to Mussolini and mentioned a report that the Duce had tried on the telephone to persuade Hitler to adopt an attitude of moderation, without success. This information had not reached me at the time and has not been confirmed since by Italian or captured German documents. On the other hand, Count Ciano had noted in his diary a few days earlier:

> The meeting between the Führer and Schuschnigg will take place at Berchtesgaden tomorrow. It is an event of great interest.... Nothing has leaked out yet. But it proves that the Führer's intentions towards Austria have not altered for the worse recently. Mussolini on the other hand has become more radical. He told me this morning that he is in favour of the Nazification of Austria. Anything that is not thoroughgoing is not safe....*

The Prime Minister then gave my record of our conversation with Grandi. He told the Cabinet that the Ambassador had assured us that there was no agreement with Germany over Austria. Chamberlain added that I was not prepared to accept this as the whole truth, but he felt that if there were an agreement, it was difficult to see why Signor Mussolini should be so anxious for conversations with us. Chamberlain's opinion was that this was one of those opportunities which came at rare intervals and did not recur. He assured the Cabinet that he had watched the Ambassador carefully at very close quarters and felt satisfied that he was speaking the truth. He therefore wished to tell the Ambassador on Monday that Great Britain was prepared to start conversations in Rome. This terminated Chamberlain's dissertation. The Cabinet had listened sombrely to his account, from which at least those who were members of the Foreign Affairs Committee must have glimpsed the confrontation that was coming. It was now my turn to deploy my arguments.

I said that much depended on our appreciation of Mussolini's motives. It was possible to take the view that the Italians had been terrified by the German action in Austria and were anxious to come over into our camp, at the same time closing the Abyssinian chapter and returning to their attitude prior to that episode. If we believed this, it would be worthwhile risking these conversations and the conditions attached

* op. cit.

to them. Without some proof, however, I could not take the view that Signor Mussolini had changed his attitude. It was not true that the Foreign Office had never given him a fair chance. I had recommended the raising of sanctions, a particularly difficult decision for me, the main purpose of which had been to improve Anglo-Italian relations. I had negotiated the Gentleman's Agreement for the same reason, but the Italians began to send troops to Spain almost at the same moment. Nor had they fulfilled their obligations under the submarine agreement of November 1936. I could see no evidence of a change of heart at this time.

I went on to suggest that an explanation of the Italian Government's silence over Austria was that they had given Hitler a free hand there, in return for some assurance about their own plans for the Mediterranean. The Prime Minister had asked why Mussolini wished to open conversations with us at this time. The reason was that the Duce wanted to repair some of the damage which developments in Austria had done to his reputation. To open conversations with us now in Rome, including *de jure* recognition of the conquest, would recover his prestige. Mussolini and Ciano wanted the announcement of conversations now and the arrangements for them later. It would be better, I continued, to follow the normal practice and prepare the ground and settle the details first. Instead of carefully preparing for the discussions, Mussolini and Ciano wanted to make an immediate announcement that they were to be held. They might then try to let matters drag on until the main question at issue, Spain, was settled, after which the onus of breaking off negotiations would be put on us. From every point of view this was the wrong time to announce discussions with Italy. We should be regarded as running after the Italian Government, and this would increase Mussolini's value in Hitler's eyes. Mussolini could easily give evidence of goodwill if he really wanted to restore his former relations with us; but he would not even have negotiations in London, they had to be in Rome. All this would be regarded as another surrender to the dictators.

An indication of Italian good faith might be sought in the Spanish question. If Mussolini would agree to our formula and co-operate to the point where withdrawal of his volunteers had actually begun, the moment would then be appropriate to begin conversations. It would be a further help if by then his anti-British propaganda were toned down. Meanwhile we could tell Grandi that we were ready to continue informal talks in London, such as had recently been taking place; but I did not feel justified in taking the grave risks which I believed to be involved in any other course.

The Cabinet then gave their views. While most of my colleagues wanted to open conversations immediately, very few seemed to know what benefits they could bring, nor was there any attempt to refute my judgement that Mussolini was undependable. Some imagined that any positive step, however fruitless, was worthwhile, which reminded me of Lord Melbourne's dictum that when a colleague said 'we must do something', he always knew that he wanted to do something damned silly. One member remarked that he was doubtful whether we should insist upon evidence of Italian goodwill, as this might not exist. A senior colleague said that the last twelve years had shown that we were always too late; he thought that the alternative to the immediate opening of conversations was the division of Europe into two camps. It was evident that the majority of the Cabinet, particularly among the older members, agreed with the Prime Minister. A notable exception, however, was Lord Zetland, who was robust in facing the dictators and with whom I had in the past frequently found myself in agreement.

Some of my younger colleagues also had their doubts. One of them urged careful preparation before formal conversations, on the ground that we must be certain that there were reasonable chances of progress. At least we should ensure that we did not look ridiculous. He would have liked an undertaking for the withdrawal from Spain of the Fascist 'volunteers' before any announcement of talks was made. If Mussolini really wanted the conversations, he could hardly object. Later in the discussion, it was pointed out that much difficulty would arise in the House of Commons if we did not stand firm over Spain. We were contemplating negotiations through fear, a fact of which smaller nations were perfectly aware. In effect, we should be entering upon conversations which we had undertaken to bring to a successful conclusion. This remark aroused protests.

After three hours' discussion, the Prime Minister summed up. He said firmly that he proposed to go ahead. On the previous day, Grandi had promised to consult his Government regarding the withdrawal formula. But even if there were no satisfactory answer, we should open conversations. I now felt bound to tell my colleagues that I could not recommend to the House of Commons a course with which I did not agree. If the Cabinet were against my view, I hoped that they would find someone else to carry through their decision. In reply to a request for an explanation, I repeated that I could not recommend a course in which I did not believe. There was a long silence. Then several Ministers expressed concern and dismay, but the Prime Minister did not budge from his position. He remarked drily that this was a distressing situation, the more so because he held the opposite view so strongly that he could not accept any other decision.

When the Cabinet adjourned, I returned to the Foreign Office, where Cranborne and Cadogan were waiting. I told them of the position I had taken with my colleagues.

* * * * *

Towards the end of the Cabinet meeting, Lord Halifax had put forward a compromise solution. We should announce the conversations at once, he said, but with the reservation that nothing was to be delivered until the Spanish situation was cleared up. I now discussed this suggestion with my advisers. Cadogan, from the official point of view, thought that it might be feasible, but I think none of us liked the idea. In any event I doubted whether Mussolini would accept these terms, and then I would be pressed to yield more. I felt that the gulf between myself and the majority of my colleagues was so wide that they would do better without me. This was not the first instance of disagreement between us and if I stayed in office I could not hope that it would be the last. Ever since the discussions on Roosevelt's offer, I had realized how deep was the difference in outlook and opinion between the Prime Minister and myself.

These considerations were strongly present to my mind when Malcolm MacDonald and I discussed the future that night at his house in Hampstead. He thought that Chamberlain wanted me to go. He knew that the Prime Minister and I held different points of view and remembered being with me at Brussels while arguments were bandied with London about Halifax's visit to Hitler. The only alternative, he said, was that I should stay on for a short while and then resign on grounds of ill-health. We both agreed, however, that nobody would really believe this story and that I should only be acting against my own convictions for nothing. MacDonald was troubled about whether he should resign too, and believed that the reactions in the country to my resignation would be very bad. He had no doubt that I should resign. On this note we parted.

The following morning I read in the Sunday papers long accounts of the Cabinet crisis. Most commentators expected my resignation. MacDonald telephoned to say that he had been summoned by the Prime Minister. If I did not object, he intended to tell Chamberlain that there was a real divergence of view and that we had better put an end to the situation in the national interest. Later, MacDonald telephoned again to say that he had found the Prime Minister of the same opinion.

About 12.30 p.m., my diary records, the Prime Minister sent for me and asked whether I had qualified my view of the night before. I replied that I had not. In the conversation which followed, Chamberlain said that, with infinite reluctance, he had come to the conclusion that it was in the national interest for us to part; we were at present making the worst of both worlds. I answered that I was greatly relieved to hear that this was his view, since it confirmed my own decision. Chamberlain remarked: 'You will have a lot of persuasion from some of the colleagues, though, when we meet this afternoon.' To which I replied: 'No doubt that will be so, but they will not alter my decision. I hope that the meeting will not be too long, for it will only prolong the agony.'

After we had reached this conclusion, the Prime Minister mentioned it was only fair I should know that the Italians had now accepted my formula for the withdrawal of volunteers from Spain. I retorted: 'Have they, Neville? I have heard nothing of it. No word has reached the Foreign Office and I am still Foreign Secretary.' Chamberlain was visibly embarrassed. He continued: 'I cannot tell you how I heard it, but you can take it from me that it is true.' I felt some astonishment, but did not press the matter further at the time, merely replying, 'This will make no difference to my decision. Anyway, my head on a charger ought to be worth more to you than a formula.' The Prime Minister smiled wryly, but made no comment.

Downing Street was even more crowded than on the previous day when I walked across to the Cabinet at three o'clock. This was a strenuous but ineffectual meeting. I announced at the outset that on the merits of the position I had nothing to add. All the facts were before the Cabinet and I could not recommend to Parliament a policy with which I was not in agreement. I could not disguise, also, that there was a difference of outlook on foreign affairs generally between myself and some of my colleagues, including the Prime Minister. As an example, I mentioned the answer sent to President Roosevelt at the beginning of the year. I felt that some of my colleagues thought that opportunities for improving relations with Italy and Germany had been missed. There were very difficult decisions before the Cabinet in the field of foreign affairs, especially in Central Europe, about which again we might not see eye to eye. I thought, for example, that Germany's behaviour in Austria should stiffen our attitude against any offer of colonies. I finished by thanking my colleagues for the years of close co-operation.

The Prime Minister in his turn told the Cabinet that he and I had been discussing the matter that morning, and we had found that the course I proposed was the right one. Chamberlain said his opinion arose out of a conclusion to which he had only recently come, namely that the difficulties were not merely of time and method, but of a deeper outlook. It was no use asking him to pretend that there were no real differences. He could not say how much he hated losing a colleague to whom he was devoted, but he feared it was inevitable.

Several members of the Cabinet said that these statements came as a complete shock to them. The argument which followed was largely about whether they had known of our differences or not. The Chancellor of the Exchequer, Sir John Simon, was particularly zealous in advocating our disagreements away, while Lord Zetland, Mr. MacDonald and others did not attempt to conceal that there was a divergence and that they knew of it. Many suggestions were made with the object of keeping me in the Foreign Office. Some expressed the opinion that my departure would seriously weaken the Government, since Chamberlain and I were the two members of the Cabinet best known to the public. In particular, the Colonial Secretary, Mr. Ormsby Gore, generously offered to abandon his own office in an attempt to provide me with a post in the Government which I could accept. I thanked the Colonial Secretary for his thought and told him that I could not possibly entertain his offer. I could see also that the Prime Minister did not much like the idea.

The pressure to reach some accommodation was very strong and was continued for three and a half hours with only brief adjournments. During one of them, Kingsley Wood drew me on one side and begged me to reconsider my decision. He said: 'I know Neville well. He has had his lesson and this will not happen again.' But I was sceptical. I was aware that some members of the Government thought that I was too suspicious of the dictators and that Kingsley Wood was one of the critics. Recalling the incident of a few months before,* I looked at him and said 'I don't see why you should be worried. After all, you'll be able to improve your relations with Hitler now.'

Towards the end of the meeting, as the pressure grew, I passed a note across the table to the Prime Minister:

> This is very painful, but it really does not help. It is what you expected.

He glanced at it and wrote underneath that it was what he expected and he could not contest the weight of the representations made. The difference between us, he thought, was not of ultimate aims or principles but of outlook and method. Even now, if any way out could be suggested by which the distressing decision could be avoided, without reversing the view expressed by the majority the day before, he would welcome it most heartily. That offered me nothing and I shook my head.

Eventually, more as a last hope than with any real confidence in a result, a small sub-committee of the Cabinet was formed to try to reconcile the Prime Minister's opinions and mine. It was suggested that I should accept the formal opening of conversations, provided that Italy accepted the formula for withdrawing volunteers. Though the agreement would be signed without conditions, no *de jure* recognition would be given until the Spanish problem was settled. This attempt failed, as it was bound to do, for it was the formal opening to which I objected, as an imprudent concession to Mussolini and one likely to divide us from the French Government, which had not as yet even been consulted.

During an adjournment, I went over to the Foreign Office where Cranborne, Thomas, Cadogan, Leeper and Harvey were waiting. Malcolm MacDonald came across and urged me to accept this compromise. He remarked that my friends in the Cabinet all thought I ought to agree; they had moved far to meet me, and I was putting personal considerations before the National Government. MacDonald admitted that there was sure to be another row with the Prime Minister in ten days, and said I could go then. I replied that I really could not agree to a policy which, I was absolutely convinced, was wrong and would lead nowhere. I should have to defend it in the House of Commons the very next day. I was sure that the compromise would not work and it represented in fact no advance towards my original position, which was no publicized conversations in Rome until there

* See page 487.

had been performance and not only promises. There were, I said, only two alternatives. Either we must follow the Prime Minister's policy of immediate formal conversations with no conditions, or mine of informal talks while the Spanish situation was being cleared up. A middle course would be the worst of both worlds and not acceptable, even to Mussolini.

I more than suspected that Mussolini wanted to dominate the Mediterranean. If he did, a British Government should not give way to him. If he did not, normal diplomatic exchanges would clarify the issues. All the public gestures of direct approaches to the Duce and Grandi's visits to Downing Street were better avoided, for if the attempts were to fail, the publicity would ensure that our relations were worse than ever. Anyway, I did not feel that we could afford, as Sir Orme Sargent said two years later in a like context, to take a season ticket to Canossa.

Sir Lewis Namier summed up the argument admirably:

> The more *empressement* the British Government showed to gain Mussolini's friendship, the more he was convinced of their timorous weakness and the more he despised them. A firm attitude and a strictly correct approach, such as are of the tradition of British diplomacy might have disconcerted Mussolini: courting him swelled his self-important conceit.*

Meanwhile Jim Thomas had walked across to the private secretaries' office at No. 10 Downing Street, where he had once worked. He records in his narrative:

> There was now no sign of Sir Horace Wilson, but he had telephoned to me that morning to say that he presumed that all was up and that Anthony would resign for reasons of health. I asked why, when Anthony was so thoroughly fit. 'Because it would be better for him', was the reply, 'and what is more, it would be better for you if you persuaded him to do so.' I put the telephone receiver down and did not see Sir Horace again until he spoke to me at Mr. Chamberlain's funeral.

* * * * *

As arranged I saw my principal colleagues once more at 7.30 that evening in the Cabinet room. After only a brief discussion I told them that I could not change my attitude, and said to the Prime Minister that I would write to him to offer my resignation. Walking back across the street, I thought ironically of the last incident. As I had risen from the

* op. cit.

Cabinet table, there had been a suggestion that in order to keep me as Foreign Secretary, I should be allowed to conduct the Italian negotiations as I wished. The Prime Minister had ignored this and merely repeated, 'Then you will send me your letter.'

Back in the Foreign Office for what I thought was the last time, I wrote to the Prime Minister:

> The events of the last few days have made plain a difference between us on a decision of great importance in itself and far-reaching in its consequences. I cannot recommend to Parliament a policy with which I am not in agreement. Apart from this, I have become increasingly conscious, as I know you have also, of a difference of outlook between us in respect to the international problems of the day and also as to the methods by which we should seek to resolve them. It cannot be in the country's interest that those who are called upon to direct its affairs should work in an uneasy partnership, fully conscious of differences in outlook yet hoping that they will not recur. This applies with a special force to the relationship between the Prime Minister and the Foreign Secretary. It is for these reasons that with very deep regret I have decided that I must leave you and your colleagues with whom I have been associated during years of great difficulty and stress.
>
> May I end on a personal note? I can never forget the help and counsel that you have always so readily given me, both before and since you became Prime Minister. Our differences, whatever they may be, cannot efface that memory nor influence our friendship.

This letter was sent across immediately. Cranborne and Thomas resigned at the same time. That evening Cranborne and I dined together at my house. I think that we both felt a sense of utter relief that the tension and arguments of these last days were over. We then began to prepare our statements for the House of Commons on the following day. At midnight I received a reply from the Prime Minister:

> It is with the most profound regret, shared by all our colleagues, that I have received your intimation of your decision to resign the great office which you have administered with such distinction ever since you occupied it.
>
> The regret is all the greater because such differences as have arisen between us in no way concern our ultimate aims or the fundamentals of our policy. The decision which you find yourself unable to accept is whether the present moment is appropriate for the commencement of Anglo-Italian conversations. We had hoped that you would not feel this of sufficient importance to necessitate a parting which is painful to all of us.
>
> There has been so large a measure of agreement between us not only on fundamental policy but on many practical applications of it that I had hoped until a very short time ago that any difference of outlook to which you allude

would not be found incompatible with our further collaboration. Since, however, your letter shows that unhappily this is not the case, I have no alternative but to accept your decision. I will accordingly submit your resignation to His Majesty the King for his approval.

I should like to thank you very warmly for your loyal and helpful comradeship during all the time we have worked together and to assure you that nothing which has happened has impaired my admiration of your gifts and my affection for yourself.

This hardly reflected the divergences which the Prime Minister and I, at our last interview alone, earlier that same day, had agreed existed between us. Chamberlain had himself spoken of these to the Cabinet at the opening of Sunday's meeting, and knew that our differences were not merely those of timing.

It was neither timing nor temperament nor the gap in years, nor any other of the minor influences which have from time to time been attributed, which made it impossible for me to continue as Chamberlain's Foreign Secretary. The differences which divided us were about matters which are decisive to the successful conduct of foreign affairs at any time. They include the proposition that a leading democracy, in negotiating with a militant dictatorship, must not go cap in hand in search of fresh negotiations to cover long-standing differences, until there is evidence that the dictator is going to carry out the engagements he has already undertaken to the democracy. If, either from weakness or impatience, the democracy ignores this rule, other countries will take their cue from this action. As a consequence, potential friends will be in disarray, the public in the democracy will be bewildered and the dictators will underestimate the toughness of the democracy at the hour of decision.

On reflection, I think that there is also another lesson to be drawn from my difference with Chamberlain. The more critical the negotiating position of a democracy, the more important it is to hold to the tested forms of diplomacy, to proceed step by step, to make sure of agreement on the preliminaries before embarking on the detailed negotiation. To enter upon publicized discussion in order to cover broken engagements, without any evidence that a better fate will befall the new engagements than the old, is to run the most reckless of hazards. Reading over the papers concerning my resignation, it is my conviction that if the Foreign Secretary had been allowed to continue to handle the negotiations with Count Grandi, in his own time and by his own methods, which were those of normal diplomacy, he would have secured, with less risk, as much progress in Anglo-Italian relations as the mood of the dictator in Rome made possible. Maybe he would also have gained for his country something of the respect which the gangster feels for one whom he knows to be unafraid of him.

* * * * *

The public support for my action was much greater than I had expected. Although many of the newspapers claimed that the Prime Minister's attitude was realistic, which seemed to me odd, because his assessment of the dictators was optimistic and unreal, the British people did not necessarily share this opinion. Within the next few days I received many thousands of messages. A manuscript letter which reached me before the debate in the House of Commons asked that I should not allow personal feelings of friendship for my late colleagues to hamper me in doing full justice to my case. This was from Mr. Winston Churchill, who wrote:

> Above all you should not say anything that fetters your action in the future. You owe this not only to yourself—which you no doubt feel the least part of the event—but to your cause, which is also the cause of England.

Underneath his signature he had added: '*Alle zoll recht kommen.*'

As we now know, Count Ciano was writing in his diary:

> In London the crisis is on. The Duce has been telephoning from Terminillo for information every half hour. . . . The crisis is perhaps one of the most important which has ever taken place. It may mean peace or war. I have authorized Grandi to take any step which may add an arrow to Chamberlain's quiver. An Eden Cabinet would have as its aim the fight against the dictatorships—Mussolini's first. . . .*

On the following morning the Italian Foreign Minister wrote again:

> It was at a party at the Colonnas' that I learnt of Eden's fall last night. There was a general cheer at the news. The Prince and Princess of Piedmont were there and the Prince insisted on drinking several toasts with me. From the Colonnas' I gave instructions for the press not to be too triumphant—we don't want to turn Eden into a victim of Fascism. In fact the papers today present what has happened as a normal development of an internal British Cabinet crisis. Perth, who is taking it well, telephoned this morning to suggest that I should do just what I had already done.†

In spite of the intentions of Ciano and the Ambassador, many Italian newspapers correctly hailed my resignation as a victory for Il Duce,

* op. cit. † op. cit.

who had been proclaiming in his press that there would be no progress in negotiations while I was at the Foreign Office.

Meanwhile, as I completed my statement for the afternoon's debate on February 21st, large crowds gathered outside my house. When I left after luncheon they cheered enthusiastically. Lord Cranborne and I took our seats on the back bench traditionally associated with Ministers who have resigned. In the course of my speech I said:

The immediate issue is as to whether official conversations should be opened in Rome now. It is my conviction that the attitude of the Italian Government to international problems in general, and to this country in particular, is not yet such as to justify this course. The ground has been in no respect prepared. Propaganda against this country by the Italian Government is rife throughout the world. I am myself pledged to this House not to open conversations until this hostile propaganda ceases....

I recounted the history of the attempts to improve our relations with Mussolini and gave instances of Fascist bad faith, particularly with regard to Spain. Then I went on:

I think it likely that the House may wonder why I at this hour place so much emphasis on performance as opposed to promise, and even why I speak so much of the Spanish problem. It is only because it happens to be in this instance an example. We cannot consider this problem except in relation to the international situation as a whole.... Recent months, recent weeks, recent days have seen the successive violation of international agreements and attempts to secure political decisions by forcible means. We are in the presence of the progressive deterioration of respect for international obligations. It is quite impossible to judge these things in a vacuum. In the light—my judgement may well be wrong—of the present international situation, this is a moment for this country to stand firm, not to plunge into negotiations unprepared, with the full knowledge that the chief obstacle to their success has not been resolved.

The programme which I have outlined seems to me a not unreasonable programme. Indeed, if the desire of the two parties be to reach agreement on all subjects outstanding between them, including Spain, I am quite confident that it is the best method to pursue. It is the traditional method of diplomacy to prepare for coversations before they are formally opened. It is seldom right to depart from that traditional method, which has been tested by time and experience. It is certainly never right to do so because one party to the negotiations intimates that it is 'now or never'. Agreements that are worthwhile are never made on the basis of a threat. Nor in the past has this country been willing to negotiate in such conditions. I repeat that if our objective is to promote a Mediterranean agreement, to promote lasting appeasement, then the method which I have described is not only the best, but the only one possible, and the only one consonant with our position in the world....

A little later I mentioned, in veiled terms, the Roosevelt initiative, and towards the close of my speech set out my view of the realities of the situation:

I have spoken to the House of the immediate difference that has divided me from my colleagues, but I should not be frank with the House if I were to pretend that is an isolated issue as between my right hon. Friend the Prime Minister and myself. It is not. Within the last few weeks upon one most important decision of foreign policy which did not concern Italy at all, the difference was fundamental. My right hon. Friend is, I know, conscious of this. Moreover, it has recently become clear to me, and I think to him, that there is between us a real difference of outlook and method. It may be argued, perhaps I shall be told, that this is not a difference of fundamental principles. Well, in the sense that the object of all foreign policy is the maintenance of peace, that is of course perfectly true. But in international affairs can anyone define where outlook and methods end and principles begin? If the Government of this country is to speak with undivided voice in international affairs, it is essential that the Prime Minister and the Foreign Secretary should have a similar outlook and wish to pursue similar methods. ... Of late the conviction has steadily grown upon me that there has been too keen a desire on our part to make terms with others, rather than that others should make terms with us. This never was the attitude of this country in the past. It should not, in the interests of peace, be our attitude today. The events of the last few days, which have dealt with one particular issue, have merely brought to a head other and more far-reaching differences, not, if you will, in objectives, but in outlook and approach. I do not believe that we can make progress in European appeasement, more particularly in the light of the events of the past few days and those events must surely be present in all our minds—if we allow the impression to gain currency abroad that we yield to constant pressure. I am certain in my own mind that progress depends above all on the temper of the nation, and that temper must find expression in a firm spirit. That spirit, I am confident, is there. Not to give voice to it is, I believe, fair neither to this country nor to the world.

Lord Cranborne made a characteristic speech, with some sentences which visibly stung the Government front bench. Chamberlain replied, but I felt that he left the House bewildered as to the real differences between us. This was because he had now again accepted the argument of Simon and others, who tried to minimize the real divide which existed.

On the morning of February 22nd, after taking leave of my faithful helpers at the Foreign Office, I delivered up my seals of Office to King George VI, who received me for what proved to be the friendliest audience I had ever had with him. His Majesty said that he had sympathy with my point of view and that he did not think it would be long before he saw me again. Before the audience I had an unexpected and most welcome experience. In accordance with custom, I first went in to the Private Secretary's room. Though I had known Sir Alexander Hardinge well before this occasion, we had had no recent discussion of international affairs and I did not know what his opinion might be. His father had been permanent head of the Foreign Office, as well as Viceroy of India and Ambassador in St. Petersburg and Paris. Hardinge himself had been brought up in the atmosphere of diplomacy and was familiar with international problems. After we had shaken hands, he said to me, 'As part of my duty I have read every telegram and all the minutes in connection with this difference between you and the Prime Minister and I should like to tell you that in my judgement you are right at all points.' I was astonished and gratified.

Rumours were rife that my decision could be attributed to ill-health and I had read in *The Times* that Simon was continuing with his *canard*, and had told National Liberal Members of Parliament that I had felt the strain of recent events and was far from well. He later wrote to me, denying that he had said my resignation was influenced by health reasons. Partly in order to show that I was well, I attended the House that afternoon, when the Opposition moved a vote of censure on the Government. Lloyd George, in the course of his attack upon the Prime Minister, brought up the question of the Italian message accepting our formula. He tried to prove that Chamberlain had concealed it from me. This was not true, since the Prime Minister had told me about it at luncheon time on Sunday. I therefore intervened in the exchange to say that no Italian message or document had reached the Foreign Office while I was there, but that in any case it would not have affected my decision. Oddly enough, no one then observed the strange fact that a Prime Minister had accepted a message from an Ambassador, through an unofficial channel, on an issue of sufficient importance to involve the resignation of a Foreign Secretary.

In this debate, the Prime Minister spoke of the League of Nations as something to be laid aside for better times. This seemed to me an intimation to the dictators that we would stand by and watch, while they swallowed the smaller countries of Europe. I felt that even if the

Italian issue had not arisen, I should have been forced to resign after this speech. In the division after the debate about fifty Government supporters abstained.

That evening I had a talk with some of my friends. I told them that I must now determine my future attitude towards Chamberlain's administration. I had therefore decided to meet my constituents soon and set out my faith again, then to await reactions. I thought that facts and events must be given their opportunity to show whether the Government's policy or mine was right.

* * * * *

Some of the letters which I received on my resignation are of more than ephemeral interest. Among the many experienced members of the Foreign Office who agreed with my judgement, there were two whose opinion I valued most highly, Sir Ronald Campbell, the British Minister in Belgrade, who was always a close friend, and Sir Horace Rumbold, many years my senior and the greatest of our Ambassadors in my experience. Campbell wrote:

> I have never been so unhappy or so indignant! I hate the idea of having another Secretary of State but you and feel that there can never—until you return—be the same interest again in one's work.
>
> As for the merits of the case I am simply in despair. I don't think that anybody disputes that what Musso really wants is the control of the Mediterranean. Are we or are we not going to let him have it? If we were quite impotent we should have no alternative but to make the best of a bad job and resign ourselves to sinking to the position of a second-rate power. But I am quite certain that Musso—and with reason—is more afraid of us than we need be of him. . . . To choose this of all moments to go blindfold into a negotiation, without any preliminary guarantee, and while he still has some hope of bluffing us into giving more than we can afford to give, or need give! . . . On almost every possible subject of negotiation it is he who stands to gain and we who stand to lose. I cannot see what we can hope to get beyond a promise, which will be broken almost before it is given, to cease from working against us by propaganda and other methods. . . .

Rumbold wrote from Egypt:

> You must be snowed under with letters and it would appear almost tactless of me to add to their number, but I have been such a wholehearted adherent of yours since you took office and have so warmly admired the way in which you have handled almost impossible situations, that I could not resist telling you how deeply I regret the necessity under which you have resigned the Foreign Office. . . .

The unreliability of the Italians is historical and is increased in the present day by their being in the grip of a man responsible only to himself and subject to rushes of blood to the head. If he wants to stand well with us he should give us proof of his good intentions by liquidating his Spanish adventure which, I hear, is anyhow increasingly unpopular in his own country. To enter into conversations with him first in the hope that he will then be a good boy seems to me to be putting the cart before the horse. According to the telegrams we have received here the effect in America of the crisis at home has been bad and the P.M. is accused of being ready to sacrifice fundamentals.

As I see the situation, there is a race between the gangster or aggressive states and the big democracies in the sense that the former are trying and will try to get away with as much as they can before the democracies are strong enough to call a halt. A diplomatist is also an observer of his own country and if I read British public opinion rightly it is very hostile to Italy at the present moment—far more so, in fact, than towards Germany. Both countries have developed a nuisance value which has to be taken into account.

Sir Horace added as a postscript:

The Government would do well to bear the Delcassé case in mind.

I received from Norman Davis confirmation that Rumbold's assessment of American reactions was near the mark:

The democracies are unquestionably at a disadvantage in dealing with ruthless dictators or militarists, as in the case of Germany, Italy and Japan. So far as the situation in this country is concerned, the American people have been so eager for peace and so determined to avoid war that they are still embracing the fallacy that their detachment and freedom from commitments will enable them, through a policy of isolation and storm-cellar neutrality, to escape the consequences of a breakdown of law and order in the rest of the world. Fortunately this fallacy is waning. There seems to be a growing realization that we cannot get peace and escape trouble by running to cover, and that the only way we can do it is to take a firm and courageous stand in the defense of principles and the respect for treaties. . . .

And from my friend Robert Menzies, then Attorney-General of the Commonwealth of Australia, came this firm support:

This is just a hurried note to tell you how profoundly I sympathize with you in the difficulties which have led to your resignation. While the press out here is disposed to take what it believes to be the 'realistic' point of view, there is a very widespread public feeling in your favour. Personally I share that feeling. But whoever turns out to have been right, everybody here agrees about the magnificent work that you have done for all of us. We are all confident that your absence from the Government will be quite temporary and that your greatest work for the British world has still to be done. Permit an obscure Dominions Minister to say that the peace of Europe has owed a great deal to your own knowledge and patience and loftiness of outlook.

* * * * *

My constituency meeting at Leamington took place on the evening of Friday, February 25th. I had decided to hold it in the largest hall available in the town, which was the public baths, covered over during the winter. The place was packed and there were crowds standing outside. I had no idea what view my constituents, or even the officers of my Association, would take. My President, Mr. Spenser Flower, was in the South of France and I had telegraphed asking him to return, though I did not know until ten minutes before the meeting what his opinion was. Fortunately, he agreed with me and made a brilliantly effective introductory speech. An unexpected visitor who appeared upon the platform was my sister's aunt by marriage, Lady Algernon Gordon-Lennox, who had spent part of her life in Italy and owned a lovely villa at Anacapri. She had come straight back from Italy for the meeting because, as she informed us, I knew how to deal with Mussolini and the Government evidently did not. Before the meeting opened, my agent asked me somewhat anxiously whether I wanted a vote taken in such a large assembly. I said, 'Certainly. I must know where I stand with my constituents.' Neither of us could tell how it might go.

I began my speech by thanking the audience for the support which they had given in the past and for the many messages they had sent to me in the last few days. Then I took the opportunity to pay this tribute to Lord Cranborne:

During the last two years as Under-Secretary, and for much longer than that in a less official capacity, Lord Cranborne has given me invaluable help at the Foreign Office. It is no exaggeration to say that without his co-operation the burden of work would have been intolerable.

I can never adequately express what his counsel, his patience, his courage, his unswerving sense of duty have meant to me. Whatever the future may hold for some of us there can be no doubt that Lord Cranborne is destined to play a much larger part in national affairs in the years that lie ahead.

I dealt with the charge that my judgement had been impaired by ill-health:

You can judge for yourselves whether I look like a sick man. You shall be my witnesses that there is no shred of truth in that suggestion.

I said of my resignation:

Tonight, nearly a week afterwards, I can say to you with absolute sincerity that, looking back upon that decision, I am more than ever convinced that it was right. I should be despising myself this evening had I taken any other course.

I insisted that

progress should first have been made with the fulfilment of engagements already entered into before seeking to negotiate other agreements covering the same issues. If we must not be obsessed by the past, we should not entirely ignore it.

The course the Government have chosen is an indication of the sincerity of their desire to reach an agreement, it is not necessarily an indication of wise judgement in international affairs. I cannot help feeling that it was perfectly possible to stand firm and obtain the same results, if they are there to be obtained, without the risks attendant on the present course.

This deep anxiety is present to my mind tonight and I must give it expression. Is it to be agreement when you can get it negotiated on a solid basis, or is it to be agreement if you can get it regardless of the basis?

I said in conclusion:

It is with the great democracies of Europe and America that our natural affinities must lie. We must stand by our conception of international order, without which there can be no lasting peace. Nor must we for one instant weaken in our own faith in parliamentary government and individual liberty. These are the things that count. They are the fundamental articles of our faith and our contribution to what survives of civilization today. However anxious the future, the need for unity and forbearance becomes not less but greater.

In that spirit let us approach the future. It is in that spirit that I ask tonight for your continued loyalty and support.

My constituents found my argument more convincing than my colleagues had done and gave me an enthusiastic vote of confidence, without a single dissentient hand or voice. This was the most splendid tribute I have received in my public life.

★ ★ ★ ★ ★

This ended the period of my direct responsibility for the control of foreign affairs in the nineteen thirties. More than eighteen months followed to the outbreak of war on September 3rd, 1939.

During that period the Western powers made repeated concessions to the Axis powers, without being able to assuage the appetites of the dictators. Having failed to defend Czechoslovakia, they gave hurried guarantees to more distant Poland and Roumania. None of this availed, nor did the dictatorships believe in the will of the democracies to act as they had pledged.

These events, and my return to office at the outbreak of war, together with the conduct of the Allied campaign as I witnessed it at the War Office and the Foreign Office and as a member of the War Cabinet, will be the subject of my next volume.

APPENDICES

APPENDIX A

Extract from *The Time for Decision* by Mr. Sumner Welles*:

The President was only too fully aware that the peace was daily being more gravely imperilled by the German and Italian Governments. Their course had its Japanese parallel in the Far East, and as the bandit nations drew together, their respective policies became more and more clearly synchronized. Even though public opinion here [in the United States] was not yet alive to the danger, and even though the American people were not yet willing to support any forthright and preventive policy on the part of their Government, the President was convinced that, because of his responsibility to defend the national interests, he should nevertheless try by every possible constitutional method to check the progress of the totalitarian powers in their aim of world domination.

In October, 1937, he considered one step of this kind which he could take at once. On the coming Armistice Day at a White House meeting of all the Diplomatic Corps, he would deliver a message to the other governments of the world. He would state that he had reached the final conclusion that, unless the nations of the earth speedily resumed their observance of those fundamental rules of conduct which the judgement of nineteen centuries and the experience of recent years had demonstrated as being necessary in relations between states, world peace could not much longer be maintained. He would continue by saying that doubtless some would predict that, because many efforts to better the chances of preserving world peace had failed, this new effort would also fail. He was unwilling to accept any such prediction as an excuse for a failure on his part to make one more fervent appeal. He would state that he was making this appeal in the knowledge held by every man and woman in every nation that if new wars broke out, and no binding accord existed covering rules and measures to mitigate their horrors, especially the horrors involving civilian populations, no man could say that such a war would not destroy all that which was salvaged from the first world war. . . .

The President planned to conclude this message by urging that all the governments strive to reach at the earliest date unanimous agreement upon the following matters: first, the essential principles of international conduct;

* Harper & Row, New York, and Hamish Hamilton, London, 1944.

second, the most effective methods for achieving a general limitation and reduction of armaments; third, effective ways of promoting the economic security, stability, and welfare of all nations through equality of treatment and opportunity; and, finally, effective measures for ensuring that in the event of war maximum respect would be given to humanitarian considerations.

The President intended to end his appeal with the assurance that, should the governments of the world be favourably disposed to his major proposals, the Government of the United States would, if they wished, request a number of other governments to join it in drawing up tentative proposals which would be submitted to all nations as a basis for universal agreement. He would make it clear that he was not proposing any general international conference.

At the time that the President was considering this plan, the Nine-Power Conference was about to inaugurate its sessions in Brussels in order to make a final attempt to prevent Japan from continuing her policy of armed expansion in eastern Asia. If the President's world-wide appeal had been made, its impact upon Japan would have strengthened the hands of the powers at Brussels.

Were his proposals to be accepted, the President was considering the creation of a working committee of ten nations, representative of all regions of the world, to elaborate a clear-cut agenda on the basis of which a world agreement might later be obtained. To this executive committee the President would have invited representatives of the European powers not already directly involved in acute major controversies, together with representatives of the American republics and of nations of the Near East. Simultaneously he would have advised the governments of the other powers that they would be kept completely informed of all developments taking place in the executive committee in order that their suggestions and views might be given full consideration. It was hoped that the proposal in itself would lend impetus to the efforts of Great Britain and France to prevent any further deterioration in European affairs.

The President believed that, even if the major powers of Europe, including the Soviet Union, did not succeed in making any progress toward understanding, the United States would at least have obtained the support of all governments, except the Berlin–Rome Axis, for her efforts to maintain world peace. He felt that the rousing of public opinion on a world scale would in itself be productive of practical good and would have instant repercussions on the German and Italian peoples. It would have a tonic effect upon the smaller countries of Europe which had felt increasingly during the preceding three years that the great democracies had surrendered all initiative and all semblance of leadership.

Finally, if the policies of Germany and Italy were halted through an understanding with Great Britain and France, the support which the former two powers were giving Japan would be weakened at least sufficiently to oblige

Japan to make peace with China upon terms consistent with the Nine-Power Treaty.

The project which the President had under consideration was almost hysterically opposed by certain of his closest advisers. They insisted that it involved great dangers to the prestige of the United States. They argued that any such dramatic appeal to the nations of the world on Armistice Day would be highly unwise unless the President had earlier received, at least confidentially, the assurance that the British or the French Government would not regard it as running counter to negotiations which they already had in hand or to policies upon which they had previously determined.

Consequently, the President for a short while reluctantly postponed action. On January 12, 1938, he secretly sounded out the views of the British Prime Minister as a preliminary step. Unfortunately, the Chamberlain Cabinet was not the Churchill Cabinet. The reply made by Neville Chamberlain was in the nature of a douche of cold water. While courteously expressing appreciation of the President's purposes, he voiced the fear that were the President to put forward his proposals at that time, Germany as well as Italy would take advantage of them to delay consideration of specific points which must be settled between Great Britain, France, Germany, and Italy 'if appeasement were to be achieved', and to make demands over and above those which they would make if no other negotiations existed. The Prime Minister further said that he would keep the President informed of the steps already taken and under contemplation by the British Government. In the same message, he gave the President the startling information that under certain circumstances the British Government was prepared, if possible with the authority of the League of Nations, to recognize the Italian conquest of Ethiopia as *de jure*.

By sounding the British Government in this manner the President was now confronted with a positive warning that British support for his proposals would not be forthcoming. It has always been my conviction that had the President not been advised to make these preliminary confidential soundings, and had he carried out his original idea of a world-wide appeal on Armistice Day of 1937, neither the British Government nor the Axis powers could then have refused, under the pressure of circumstances and public opinion, to lend at least apparent co-operation.

However, in view of the situation created by Mr. Chamberlain's reply, the President felt he had no alternative but to defer 'for a short while' the proposal he had hoped to make. But in his reply to Mr. Chamberlain he took occasion to state clearly that he was deeply concerned by the indication that the British Government might give official recognition to the Italian conquest of Ethiopia. He warned Mr. Chamberlain that a surrender by the British Government of the principle of non-recognition of territories seized by aggression would at that time inevitably have a serious effect upon public opinion in the United States. The American people, he said emphatically, would not support their Government in measures of specific co-operation with other nations unless those measures were destined to re-establish and maintain principles of international law and morality.

It happened that at the time the President's confidential inquiry was received in London, Mr. Eden, then Secretary of State for Foreign Affairs, was absent in the south of Europe. As soon as he was advised of the proposal and of Mr. Chamberlain's reply, he at once returned to London. It is generally understood that it was due to his direct intervention that, at the end of the same month of January, Mr. Chamberlain sent a new and different message to the President. In this message the Prime Minister stated that, as a result of a few days' reconsideration, he had reached the conclusion that he should welcome the President's initiative and that the British Government would do its utmost to contribute to the success of the scheme whenever the President decided to launch it. He insisted, however, that since *de jure* recognition had already been given by a great many other governments to the conquest of Ethiopia, the Italian Government would regard the continued failure of Great Britain to recognize the conquest as positive proof that she desired no general understanding with Italy governing the Mediterranean and the Red Sea. The present tension would thereby not only be continued but aggravated to an extreme degree. Mr. Chamberlain expressed the opinion that no economic concessions would be sufficient in themselves to satisfy the Axis powers. He felt certain, nevertheless, that if they could be brought to a co-operative frame of mind in the settlement of political problems they would also desire co-operative assistance on the economic side. He said he believed that there was a chance to bring them to that point of view.

By this time, of course, many invaluable weeks had passed. The situation within Germany was reaching a boiling point. In an interview which the British Ambassador in Berlin had with Hitler on March 3, Hitler dismissed as unimportant the question of colonial adjustments and insisted upon the need for an immediate solution, in a manner satisfactory to him, of the problems of Austria and Czechoslovakia. Hitler stated that, in so far as the limitation of armaments was concerned, Germany would refuse to deal with Great Britain (against whom, he alleged, Germany was not arming) unless Great Britain had previously begun satisfactory discussions with the Soviet Union. It was already apparent, therefore, that the German Government was about to seize Austria and the Sudetenland as its first step toward the creation of a greater Germany. The time for such constructive and preventive remedies as those embodied in the President's proposals had passed.

This chapter in the President's efforts to avert the impending world crisis must always remain a subject for speculation. In November, 1937, the European situation was still fluid. While Hitler had undoubtedly already fully formulated his plans in co-operation with the German General Staff, the policies of Italy were far from crystallized. The full participation by the United States in such a world-wide effort to keep the peace as that envisaged by the President might have given Italy pause. It might have resulted in a radical modification of Japanese policy. Under those conditions Hitler would have been forced to think far more carefully before embarking on his last moves towards world war. In November, 1937, an appeal by the President, and the constructive programme he had in mind, might well have rallied a still vocal public opinion in Europe sufficiently to have changed the course of the events of the next two years.

APPENDIX B

The following is the text of Mr. Eden's paper for Mr. Chamberlain, dated January 18th, 1938:

I am afraid that it is clear from the President's message that he has been disappointed at what he considers to be the negative nature of the reply sent to him in telegram No. —. It is true that he offers none the less to defer making the proposal he had intended to make 'for a short while'. It might, therefore, be argued that we could maintain the position set out in telegram No. —, ask the President to hold his hand for some months and do our best in the interval to go ahead in our negotiations with Germany and Italy. I am convinced, however, that to pursue this course would be to commit a grave error. This message shows that the President and Mr. Hull feel more strongly against *de jure* recognition than Sir R. Lindsay had anticipated. If, having asked the President to refrain from an initiative he is anxious to take, we should then find ourselves engaged in a protracted negotiation on a basis which is repugnant to him, such a process must be injurious to Anglo-American relations, might produce constant friction and would make collaboration between the United States and ourselves in the Far East more difficult. Even if our negotiations with Italy were ultimately successful and the difficulties are great—I mention only the French attitude, that of the League and that of some of our own Dominions, quite apart from Mussolini's expected reluctance to grant anything which our public would regard as worthwhile in exchange—we must anticipate that the outcome would not only be received without enthusiasm in this country but be actively condemned by opinion in the United States. Therefore at best we should have succeeded in improving relations with Mussolini at the cost of imperilling them with President Roosevelt. A still graver danger is that the President, disappointed by our failure to support his initiative and being himself critical of the character of our negotiations, would withdraw more and more into isolation. The result of our patient efforts over the last six months to build up Anglo-American co-operation would then be completely destroyed. Such an event I should regard as the greatest possible disaster to the peace of the world.

The decision we have to take seems to me to depend upon the significance which we attach to Anglo-American co-operation. What we have to choose between is Anglo-American co-operation in an attempt to ensure world peace and a piecemeal settlement approached by way of problematical agreement with Mussolini. If, as is clear to me, we must choose the former alternative, then it seems that we should reconsider our attitude and strongly support President Roosevelt's initiative. As you know, I do not take the view that this initiative need injure the prospects of our negotiations with Germany, which I regard as the more important of the two sets of negotiations we were considering. In fact, the closer the sympathy and co-operation between the United States and ourselves, the stronger will be our position in dealing with Germany.

Moreover, if we now decide to support the President's initiative, we should be fully justified in asking him to make certain modifications in his text. Those I have in mind would deal particularly with the points which I mentioned to you in my last letter, the reference to 'inequities' of the peace treaty and the term 'involvement'.

APPENDIX C

Mr. Eden's account, approved by Mr. Chamberlain as correct, of the meeting with Count Grandi on February 18th, 1938:

MR. EDEN TO THE EARL OF PERTH (ROME)

The Prime Minister asked Count Grandi to come and call at No. 10 Downing Street today, when a conversation took place on the European situation in general and Anglo-Italian conversations in particular. The Prime Minister began by remarking upon the anxious international situation with which we were faced. Austria was the most recent development. Count Grandi indicated that he regretted what had happened in that country. The Prime Minister continued that he wished to be absolutely frank; that many people were saying that there was some agreement between Germany and Italy in the matter. The Ambassador assured the Prime Minister that there was none. Italy had, indeed, been expecting this to happen, it had not in that sense come as a surprise to them; but it was not the result of an agreement. Count Grandi thought it remarkable that, during the past three years since Stresa, Signor Mussolini had been able to preserve the integrity of events in Austria, despite the divergence of views on other matters between this country and France on the one hand, and his country on the other. Now, when the event had occurred, there was nothing to be done owing to the state of relations between the Stresa powers.

On the Prime Minister suggesting that all was not yet lost in Austria, Count Grandi said that possibly we were only at the end of the third act of four. In the view of Italy, however, Germany was now at the Brenner. It was impossible for Italy to be left alone in the world with two great potential enemies—Germany and Great Britain.

Count Grandi gave a detailed account of Anglo-Italian relations since Stresa, and emphasized particularly that the post-sanctions period had been worse than the sanctions period itself. Disappointments had further poisoned the atmosphere. After the gentlemen's agreement of a year ago, the hopes then maintained were not fulfilled. After the July exchange of letters between Signor Mussolini and Mr. Chamberlain, there had been a happy fortnight, which had again been marred by events in the Mediterranean. Now the Italian Government were asking themselves whether His Majesty's Government really meant to open conversations.

The Prime Minister then drew Count Grandi's attention to a phrase used by Count Ciano and reported by your Lordship in your telegram No. —, to the effect that an early start should be made with Anglo-Italian conversations, in view of the possibility of certain future happenings. The Prime Minister also mentioned that he had received a message from Lady Chamberlain reporting a conversation in which Count Ciano had used very similar language to her. He had urged the earliest opening of conversations, adding 'things are happening in Europe which will make it impossible tomorrow.' The Prime Minister asked Count Grandi whether he could throw any light on these phrases. Count Grandi replied that he had explained that Italy could not in present conditions visualize the possibility of both Germany and Great Britain being hostile to her. If it was impossible to improve relations with Great Britain, then it would be necessary for Italy to draw still closer to Germany. The decision would then be final. It was not final yet, but there was very little time left.

In reply to further questions, Count Grandi explained that in the view of the Italian Government the conversations should include everything and we could both raise any subject that we desired. He also explained that the Italian Government desired that the conversations should take place in Rome because it had originally been the intention that they should take place in that capital last September. The Prime Minister explained that he did not think any final decision in that sense had been taken and explained that in his mind he thought it would be possible for progress to be made between Count Grandi and myself in London and that at the final stage Count Ciano might have been brought in by a visit to London. Count Grandi explained that these were very delicate matters, but that he thought that Count Ciano would wish to be in the conversations from the beginning, as had originally been intended. He therefore did not think it would be possible for conversations to be held with the best chance of success anywhere but in Rome.

Count Grandi was then asked what effect the opening of conversations might have on the Italian attitude towards Austria. Count Grandi replied that it was difficult for him to answer that except to say that it would give his people more courage. On being asked whether the Italian Government could now exchange views with the other Stresa signatories on the subject of Austria, the Ambassador made it clear that his Government would not be able to do that—indeed, he said he had no instructions at all to mention Austria.

The conversation then turned to the Spanish problem. Count Grandi was asked whether he was yet in a position to give the reply of his Government on the subject of the formula for the withdrawal of volunteers from Spain which had been proposed to him ten days ago. The Ambassador replied that he was afraid that he had perhaps been a little optimistic in his conversation with me about the formula proposed. His Government had now instructed him to ask for certain clarifications. Perhaps he could explain these to me or

Lord Plymouth in the near future. The Ambassador appeared to indicate, however, that if conversations could be opened these difficulties would not be serious.

As to the Spanish question generally, Count Grandi maintained that it would be a mistake to hold up progress in Anglo-Italian conversations on account of a question in which others were involved besides ourselves. It would be hardly possible to maintain that the development of Anglo-Italian relations must depend on other nations agreeing with us about the withdrawal of volunteers.

At the conclusion of the conversation, the Prime Minister asked Count Grandi to return at 3 o'clock, explaining that he wished in the interval to have an opportunity to talk over the situation with me.

When he called again at 3 p.m. Count Grandi was informed by the Prime Minister that he proposed to consult his colleagues on the outcome of the conversations which had taken place between us, and that he would see Count Grandi again on February 21st to give him the considered view of His Majesty's Government.

Meanwhile the Prime Minister and I had agreed that it would be desirable if we could at the second interview obtain some clarification of the Italian Government's attitude towards our proposed formula for the withdrawal of volunteers. At the second interview the Prime Minister therefore told Count Grandi that he had understood from the conversation of the morning that the Italian Government would be in a position to accept our proposals in respect of the withdrawal of volunteers if conversations were opened at once. Count Grandi explained that he did not think that he had made himself quite clear. The formula I had proposed to him was a very difficult one for the Italian Government to accept. Indeed, in its present form it seemed to be a trap. He had, as he had told us in the morning, been over-optimistic perhaps in his conversation with me. None the less, the Italian Government wished to make progress, and he was wondering whether the best course would not be to leave the question of what constituted a substantial withdrawal to be settled by the commissions in Spain in conjunction with the two parties. It would not be possible for the Italian Government to accept a formula which would have the appearance of letting down General Franco. It was explained to Count Grandi that the whole purpose of the formula was to avoid that. Since it was maintained by the partisans of each side in Spain that the number of volunteers was larger on their opponent's side, it was difficult to see how such an impression could be created. Count Grandi eventually said that he would consult his Government further on this question.

APPENDIX D

(i) Extracts from the Despatch of Count Grandi to the Italian Foreign Minister, February 19th, 1938*:

. . . I have also informed Your Excellency that after my having refused, on the pretext mentioned above, to present myself at the Foreign Office, there came to see me on Thursday afternoon the confidential agent of Chamberlain, who, since the month of October last year, has been functioning as a direct and 'secret' link between myself and Chamberlain. This agent, with whom one may say I have been in almost daily contact since the 15th January, told me he was instructed by Chamberlain to draw my attention to the fact that it would be opportune not to avoid the conversation requested by Eden, since 'it was very probable' (these are the exact words used) 'that the Prime Minister, Mr. Chamberlain, would himself take part in the conversation.' I sketched the reasons why I, for my part, considered I must avoid a meeting with Eden at the present time. I simply could not lend myself, I said, to anything which might possibly be exploited, in England or abroad, as a manœuvre against the Rome–Berlin Axis, and against the solidarity of relations between Fascist Italy and Nazi Germany. If the Prime Minister thought fit to have personal contact with me, I was ready to present myself at Downing Street at any minute. The agent immediately consulted Chamberlain, and later in the evening, at 8 o'clock, there reached the Embassy direct from the offices at 10 Downing Street, Chamberlain's telephoned invitation to present myself at 11.30 the following day for a conversation with the Prime Minister.

. . . Chamberlain, in fact, in addressing his questions directly to me, expected from me—this was obvious—nothing more nor less than those details and definite answers which were useful to him as ammunition against Eden. This I at once realized and naturally tried to supply Chamberlain with all the ammunition which I considered might be useful to him to this end. There is no doubt that in this connection the contacts previously established between myself and Chamberlain through his confidential agent proved to be very valuable. Purely as a matter of historical interest, I inform Your Excellency that yesterday evening after the Downing Street meeting, Chamberlain secretly sent his agent to me (we made an appointment in an ordinary public

* *Ciano's Diplomatic Papers*; Odhams Press, 1948.

taxi) to say that he 'sent me cordial greetings, that he had appreciated my statements, which had been very useful to him, and that he was confident that everything would go very well next day.'

In the Italian edition of Ciano's Diplomatic Papers, L'Europa Verso La Catastrofe (Mondadori, 1948), *the name of the agent is given as Sir Joseph Ball.*

(ii) Extract from *Nine Troubled Years* by Lord Templewood*:

Eden wished to discover Mussolini's reactions to Hitler's Austrian *coup*, and to postpone the start of negotiations until the position was clarified. Chamberlain, on the other hand, felt that any delay would destroy the goodwill between the two countries that he had created since he became Prime Minister and that, once lost, might be very difficult to recover. Grandi was even more anxious than Chamberlain to avoid the Austrian issue and restrict any discussion to the question of Anglo-Italian relations. When, therefore, Eden asked him to come to the Foreign Office, the Ambassador made the excuse of a golf engagement for not accepting the invitation. Chamberlain, at the same time, urgently wished to see Grandi about the Italian negotiations, and Grandi, guessing what was in Chamberlain's mind, was ready to go to Downing Street, as he rightly assumed that the talk would not be about Hitler's Austrian *coup*, but about Mussolini's relations with Great Britain. Whilst this was the position in London, Ciano in Rome was pressing for direct talks between the Prime Minister and Grandi. It was to break the deadlock between the Foreign Office and Italian Embassy that Chamberlain stepped outside the channel of regular communication, and used as a go-between an official in the Conservative Party Office, who had worked with him for many years, to propose to Grandi a meeting in Downing Street. The background of this unconventional approach was found in a long-standing contact between Chamberlain's messenger and a subordinate member of the Italian Embassy. Whilst the Foreign Office knew of the association and attached little importance to it, it had occasionally provided Chamberlain with scraps of information that had helped him to assess Mussolini's attitude towards the negotiations and in particular towards the question of the withdrawal of Italian troops from Spain. When, therefore, an *impasse* had been reached between the Foreign Office and the Italian Embassy, he turned to his old confidant, and authorised him to make it known to the Ambassador, through the intermediary, that he would welcome a visit to Downing Street.

There followed the long discussion between Grandi, Chamberlain and Eden in Downing Street on February 12.† Grandi, delighted with the importance that the interview gave him, and the chance of painting the kind of picture that Mussolini wished to see, immediately described in a lengthy dispatch to Ciano his version of the story. The picture that he produced could not have been more vivid and dramatic. Chamberlain's secret intrigues to circumvent the Foreign Office, the meetings with the intermediary, the

* Collins, 1954.

† Lord Templewood was in error. The date of this discussion was February 18th.

battle between Chamberlain and Eden before Grandi's eyes—what a subject for an Ambassador with Grandi's lively imagination! Certainly the Ambassador made the most of his subject, and produced as good a story as was ever put into a diplomatic dispatch. Indeed, it was one of those pictures that had every quality except a resemblance to the original. Grandi's claim that he had 'almost daily contacts' with Chamberlain's messsenger greatly exaggerated what had actually happened. In point of fact, he himself seldom saw the messenger, and the later story that has been circulated, that they met in a taxi, is entirely untrue. The two intermediaries exchanged information on a much lower level.

(iii) Extract from *Neville Chamberlain* by Mr. Iain Macleod*:

Grandi did very occasionally use his personal acquaintance with [Sir Joseph] Ball to air views he expected would reach Chamberlain. Scraps of information were also conveyed to Ball through a British subject called Dingli who was acting as a legal adviser to the Italian Embassy. The Prime Minister himself was unaware of the man's existence, but Ball had thought it wise in the summer of 1937 to inform the Foreign Office of his contact and had received a reply from Eden's P.P.S., J. P. L. Thomas, minimizing its importance but asking him to pass on to the Foreign Office any genuine information derived from it. This letter is still in existence. It was Dingli who got Ball up from the country on February 20th to acquaint him with the Italian response on the withdrawal of troops from Spain. The two men met at Waterloo Station and drove in a taxi to the offices of the Research Department in Old Queen Street. There the information was given to Ball who immediately passed it on to the Prime Minister's private office—hoping, he wrote at the time, that Chamberlain 'might be able to use it in such a way as to prevent Eden resigning'. This account squares with Ball's reputation as a man of honour and distinction.

In connection with this last account, I must state that I never at any time had even a remote suspicion that Sir Joseph Ball might be an intermediary between the Italian Embassy and 10 Downing Street. Nor, I am confident, was this in Thomas' mind when he wrote to Ball agreeing that he should continue his personal contact.

AVON

* Muller, 1961.

(iv) Extract from Count Ciano's diary,* April 5th, 1940:

I received an impression of weakness on the part of the Allies this morning in my conversation with Dingli, legal adviser to the Embassy in London and a friend of Chamberlain. Grandi had a great deal of respect for this man, who impresses me as being of rather secondary importance. He brought a useless and very general message from the Prime Minister, one of those messages of good-will destined from the start to remain unanswered. But more important than this was the manifest lack of faith in victory. If this really represented British morale, the fate of Europe would be tragically sealed. But I do not believe that it does.

* *Ciano's Diary, 1939–43*; Heinemann, 1947.

(v) Extract from *Au Feu des Evénements* by Paul-Louis Bret.* The author states that he knew well 'W.P.' [Wladimir Poliakoff], who was of the opinion that Mussolini could be bought off and used against Hitler:

This point of view was thought judicious in Downing Street, while . . . the Foreign Office judged it to be fatal to the League. It gave my friend, for some time, great authority with the Prime Minister's entourage but made his relations with the diplomats difficult. Up to the declaration of war in 1940, he served as an official intermediary between Downing Street, the Italian Embassy and even the Duce, to whom he had access.

Extract from Count Ciano's Diary,† September 4th, 1937:

Poliakoff—I got the impression that in London they have no clear idea of the question of the recognition of the Empire. Without recognition there is no possibility of agreement. Poliakoff took note of this and will mention it to Chamberlain.

* Plon, 1959.
† op. cit.

(c) Extract from *Au feu des événements* by Paul-Louis Bret*. The author states that he knew well "W.P." [Wladimir Poliakoff], who was of the opinion that Mussolini could be bought off and used against Hitler.

This point of view was thought judicious in Downing Street, while the Foreign Office judged it to be fatal to the League. It gave my friend, for some time, great authority with the Prime Minister's entourage but made his relations with the diplomats difficult. Up to the declaration of war in 1939, he served as an official intermediary between Downing Street, the Italian Embassy, and even the Duce, to whom W.P. had access.

Extract from Count Ciano's Diary,† September 14th, 1937:

Poliakoff—I got the impression that in London they have no clear idea of the question of the recognition of the Empire. Without recognition there is no possibility of agreement. Poliakoff took note of this and will mention it to Chamberlain.

INDEX

INDEX